The
Program
Development
Process

The Program Development Process

Part II
THE PROGRAMMING TEAM

J. D. ARON
IBM Corporation

ADDISON-WESLEY PUBLISHING COMPANY
Reading, Massachusetts • Menlo Park, California
London • Amsterdam • Don Mills, Ontario • Sydney

This book is in the
Addison-Wesley Systems Programming Series

Consulting editors: IBM Editorial Board

Library of Congress Cataloging in Publication Data (Revised)

Aron, J. D. (Joel D.)
  The program development process.

  (Addison-Wesley systems programming series)
  Includes bibliographical references and index.
  Contents: pt. 1. The individual programmer—
pt. 2. The programming team.
    1. Electronic digital computers—Programming.
I. Title. II. Series.
QA76.6.A75   001.64′2   74-2847
ISBN 0-201-14451-4   AACR2
ISBN 0-201-14463-8 (pt. 2)

ISBN 0-201-14463-8
ABCDEFGHIJ-HA-89876543

THE SYSTEMS PROGRAMMING SERIES

* The Program Development Process
  Part I—The Individual Programmer   Joel D. Aron
* The Program Development Process
  Part II—The Programming Team   Joel D. Aron
* Mathematical Foundations of
  Programming   Frank Beckman
* An Introduction to Operating Systems   Harvey M. Deitel
* Structured Programming: Theory   Richard C. Linger
  and Practice   Harlan D. Mills
      Bernard I. Witt

* Coded Character Sets: History and
  Development   Charles E. Mackenzie
* The Structure and Design of Program-
  ming Languages   John E. Nicholls
* The Environment for Systems Programs   Frederic G. Withington
* Communications Architecture for
  Distributed Systems   R. J. Cypser
* An Introduction to Database Systems,
  Third Edition   C. J. Date
* An Introduction to Database Systems:
  Vol. II   C. J. Date
* Database Security and Integrity   Eduardo B. Fernandez
      R. C. Summers
      C. Wood
* Fundamentals of Interactive   James Foley
  Computer Graphics   Andries Van Dam
* Compiler Design Theory   Philip M. Lewis II
      Daniel J. Rosenkrantz
      Richard E. Stearns
* Sorting and Sort Systems   Harold Lorin
* Operating Systems   Harold Lorin
      Harvey M. Deitel

* Recursive Programming Techniques   William Burge
* Modeling and Analysis: An Introduc-
  tion to System Performance Evaluation
  Methodology   Hisashi Kobayashi
* Conceptual Structures: Information
  Processing in Mind and Machines   John F. Sowa

* Published

Foreword

The field of systems programming primarily grew out of the efforts of many programmers and managers whose creative energy went into producing practical, utilitarian systems programs needed by the rapidly growing computer industry. Programming was practiced as an art where each programmer invented unique solutions to problems with little guidance beyond that provided by immediate associates. In 1968, the late Ascher Opler, then at IBM, recognized that it was necessary to bring programming knowledge together in a form that would be accessible to all systems programmers. Surveying the state of the art, he decided that enough useful material existed to justify a significant codification effort. On his recommendation, IBM decided to sponsor The Systems Programming Series as a long-term project to collect, organize, and publish those principles and techniques that would have lasting value throughout the industry.

The Series consists of an open-ended collection of text-reference books. The contents of each book represent the individual author's view of the subject area and do not necessarily reflect the views of the IBM Corporation. Each is organized for course use but is detailed enough for reference. Further, the Series is organized in three levels: broad introductory material in the foundation volumes, more specialized material in the software volumes, and very specialized theory in the computer science volumes. As such, the Series meets the needs of the novice, the experienced programmer, and the computer scientist.

Taken together, the Series is a record of the state of the art in systems programming that can form the technological base for the systems programming discipline.

The Editorial Board

Preface

In Part I of *The Program Development Process,* guidelines are given that help an individual programmer be an effective member of a programming team. Part II deals with programming teams and their effective use in building program systems. As programming workload grows, the project team encounters more and more problems that can only be resolved by better management and control—as opposed to better programming. Therefore, much of Part II is about management in a programming environment.

Program system development is a sequential process that starts with a requirement and ends with a product meeting the requirement. Part II is organized in the same sequence. First, the term "system" as it is used in the text is defined, with programming examples. Next, the factors that affect system behavior are introduced. These factors recur in the later chapters; they usually show up as constraints that force a project manager to operate under less than ideal conditions. The sequential development process is quantified in the "system development life cycle." The life cycle model is used to show how project resources are managed. Many management decisions can be conveniently illustrated by showing their effect on a given life cycle. Subsequent chapters follow the life cycle from the system analysis stage to completion of the test stage, at which time the program system is released for use. Related topics such as maintenance of the released product and organization of the development teams are discussed at appropriate points in the life cycle.

The dominant characteristic of large systems is complexity. An attempt to talk about complexity in a terse way ends up simplistic. In the past, simplistic descriptions of complex systems have made project teams overconfident to the point they neglected important controls. I have chosen to use complex examples and expose their complexity in plain language. This requires more effort on the part of the reader, but it is intended to show why the extensive controls recommended for large projects are justified. The examples are realistic situations chosen from fields familiar to the reader. Their purpose is to show, "It can happen to you."

To avoid endless discussions of alternative ways of doing things, I frequently state one way which my experience indicates is effective. This should not be taken as a reason to ignore alternatives. When at times the text says "the manager *must* do so-and-so," read, "Under many circumstances, the advisable course of action is to do so-and-so." "All programmers are responsive to management direction" means, "Normally, in business data processing and program system development organizations (as opposed perhaps to research or university environments), programmers work as part of a team, following instructions received from their manager." As the result of such shorthand, I am free to take a position or state a guideline without excessive ifs, ands, or buts.

Exercises and discussion questions are included in this book, but no answers are provided. As the text makes clear, there are seldom cut and tried answers to any of the problems that arise in program system development. There can be several valid answers to the exercises in most cases. All of the answers, however, will fall within a class of response which follows directly from the text.

It has taken a number of years to write Part II of *The Program Development Process*. An unexpected side effect of the long preparation time has been that the state-of-the-art of program development has improved substantially during the period. The advances are reflected in the text.

Throughout the entire period that this text has been in process, I have benefitted from excellent assistance provided by the late Mrs. Peg Brittion. The text has been improved by the excellent suggestions of Dr. Kyu Y. Lee of Seattle University, Professor Sid Huff of the University of Western Ontario, Mr. Robert H. Glaser of IBM, and the Editorial Board of the Systems Programming Series, among others. I wish to thank them for their valuable support.

J. D. A.

Contents

CHAPTER 5
PROJECT MANAGEMENT AND ORGANIZATION

1
Characteristics
of Systems

The program development process has earned a reputation as one of the most challenging technical activities of modern times. Increasingly large projects have been undertaken over the years with considerable benefit to the users of the end products. Yet, many of these projects were late and cost more than expected. The purpose of this book is to identify the sources of such problems and offer guidelines for managing projects to a successful conclusion.

The answer does not lie solely in managing the programming efforts of the individuals in a project team. Success depends far more on the effectiveness of system management. Within a team project there are many interrelationships. Some are well-documented, but others are not. Furthermore, the relationships change with time. System management consists of managing the known relationships and coping with the unknowns while doing the productive work called for by the project requirements. *System* is an all-purpose word. Even in information processing jargon, the word has many meanings. In this chapter, "system" is described rather than defined for the purpose of showing where the complexities arise that make it difficult to manage team projects. Prominent historical examples are used to highlight specific system characteristics. Some methods of reducing complexity are introduced here and elaborated in later chapters.

A *system* is a structured aggregate of elements that satisfies a set of functional and performance objectives. Many aggregates fit this definition, but, to be practical, the structure and its elements must be significantly complex before one bothers to identify the aggregate as a system. Complexity is relative. It depends both on the conceptual ability of the observer and the level of abstraction used to describe the elements.

1

The combined hardware/software/people system known as the Apollo project [1] was obviously a system. It was easy to recognize the characteristics of a system in Apollo: The primary *objective* of landing a man on the moon was clear; the large *number of elements* involved was the basis for many reports in the news media; and the intricate *structural relationship* needed among the elements in order to make a successful moon shot was evident to anyone with the slightest knowledge of technology. At the other extreme, some things called systems by their builders look like simple devices to other people. For instance, a physicist working on the fabrication of a semiconductor chip that behaves like a microprocessor may consider the combination of this chip with memory and input/output chips to be a "microcomputer system." To the designer of a "large-scale computer system" this microcomputer may be simply a device, say a keyboard interface unit, ordered out of a parts catalog. No simple characterization of things that are systems versus things that are not systems will achieve general agreement; however, experience in the data-processing industry establishes some norms that apply to "systems" in the context of this book.

Programs built in projects involving only one or two programmers are not generally called systems, regardless of their logical structure. Programs built in projects involving more than two programmers; i.e., teams, are systems when there is a distinguishable set of project objectives requiring coordination of the team members. In some cases the program is conceived as a unit but implemented as several components that reside in separate machines to improve cost or performance. The decision to break the project up into smaller communicating components creates a need for a set of interface definitions and system controls to maintain order. The communication requirements within a system are a major source of system problems. In fact, the complexity of a system can be measured in a subjective way by examining its communications requirements, as will be shown later.

Programmers involved with single-program units can concentrate on the problem itself; teams involved with systems must, in addition, concentrate on the development process which coordinates their joint activities. Indeed, an important aspect of system management is making the individual programmers aware of their interdependence. This is easier for a first-level manager to do than for higher-level managers. The first-level manager directly supervises the programmers and others in the department. Person-to-person contact is good. Lines of authority are simple. Everyone is motivated to accomplish the team objectives. Higher-level managers supervise managers whose individual department goals often conflict with the system objectives of the higher-level manager. Such management problems are another manifestation of system complexity, and can often be predicted. In fact, after participating in several hundred project reviews, the author drew the following conclusions about project size and system complexity.

- Projects that can be performed by a team of less than ten people working under a first-level manager are usually *successful.* That is, they are completed *on schedule, within the budget,* and the *user is happy* with the result.

- Projects that require two levels of management, such as a thirty-programmer information handling system with four first-level managers and one second-level manager, succeed when the management team is effective. (Auditors learned that in unsuccessful second-level projects the management team did not provide effective plans or controls at various identifiable points in the project.)

- Larger projects generally do not meet one or more of the criteria for success: schedule, budget, or customer satisfaction. Furthermore, a post-mortem of the large project will not pinpoint the explicit causes of failure.

Large projects are so complex that the managers cannot estimate the size and must constantly replan their approach, usually forcing up the cost and stretching the schedule. One major exception to the large system syndrome was the Apollo Mission Support project consisting of a real-time operating system and associated application programs for ground support of moon explorations. It had about 300 programmers at its peak and successfully supported every moon shot. Audits, however, explained the source of this success when they revealed that Apollo was managed as a series of 20 to 50 programmer projects, one for each moon shot. In this way, it fell back into the category of projects which depended on the ability of the management team. Because of this, Apollo stands out as probably the most successful example of large program system development since the pioneering SAGE system. (SAGE stands for *Semi*Automated *G*round *E*nvironment. In the late 1950s, it was built to provide surveillance and control for the U.S. Air Defense complex. Using radar data, weather reports, aircraft flight plans, and weapons status reports, SAGE could track aircraft and direct weapons against those identified as hostile. SAGE was a major success, but no one thought to document the reasons why; therefore, at least ten years passed before the techniques for managing such projects were rediscovered.)

Based on history, one can expect a project that follows appropriate guidelines for project management and programming methodology to have a high probability of success if it is *small* enough to be run by a first-level manager. Even a weak manager can often run a small job successfully. Because errors of omission that occurred in the past can be avoided in the future, hopefully, all *medium*-sized projects will succeed if the guidelines are followed. Medium projects are harder than small projects; success depends on the ability of the management team.

Projects that require three or more levels of management verge on being unmanageable; therefore, success cannot be assured. Such *large* projects, if they cannot be subdivided into meaningful stand-alone subsystems, will run into problems that can only be addressed effectively when the criteria for success are flexible. That is, the user will have to settle for the system as built rather than as requested. It may do less or run slower or cost more. It is unrealistic to believe that a programming project involving hundreds of people can be so perfectly defined at the start that a firm, unvarying schedule and budget can be established. On the other hand, it is realistic to try to subdivide almost any project into smaller systems the way Apollo was handled. To do this, it is necessary to understand what makes a system complex. This chapter discusses complexity and shows why, as systems grow, they change in character. It also introduces some guidelines for subdividing a complex system.

Note the warning in these introductory paragraphs: Methods that were successful on small projects are not sufficient for large projects. Many people do not believe this message. Incredulity is particularly strong among executives and project development people who are about to embark on their first large system. Up to this point, they have built several small systems and many independent programs with no trouble. With such a good track record they feel confident about their ability to tackle a large system. They are unwilling to accept the concept that large systems are different *in kind* from small systems. Furthermore, costly project management techniques are distasteful. Any number of managers who solicit advice on building their first large system reject the advice when they find it doubles the estimated (or budgeted) cost of their project. The same managers then proceed on a plan that is a direct extension of their last successful small project—and they fail. Only on their second attempt do they provide all the controls and supporting structures they neglected the first time around. Such sad experiences are too expensive. It is the author's sincere hope that the readers will accept the lessons of history and protect themselves with adequate plans when they undertake a large system.

1.1 WHAT IS A SYSTEM?

To repeat, a *system* is a structured aggregate of elements that satisfies a set of functional and performance objectives. The elements can be anything including smaller systems; however, this book is primarily concerned with program systems and the system environment in which programs are developed. Specific terms used include:

- *Program system*: a system whose deliverable elements are computer programs and their related documentation.

- *Computer system*: a system whose deliverable elements are various hardware devices, interconnected to provide means for input/output, storage, arithmetic, and control.

- *System program*: a program or a program system that is designed to make a computer system more productive or easier to use.

- *Application program*: a program or a program system that solves a user's problem.

- *System of procedures*: a collection of related directives, usually documented in a procedures manual. The system of procedures makes the independent activities of many individuals manageable as an ensemble. An activity is *systematic* when it follows a system of procedures.

- *Subsystem*: a logical part of a system that is itself a system.

- *Data-processing system*: a system whose subsystems include a computer system and appropriate system and application programs.

It is one thing to define a system; it is another matter to recognize one. Several examples of systems can help illustrate the essential attributes of any system.

1.1.1 OS/360—System Structure and Interactions

OS/360 is a system program that manages the allocation and use of the resources of a computer system compatible with the IBM System/360 computer architecture. OS/360 starts user programs when the appropriate I/O devices and memory space are available. It interrupts user programs when necessary to run higher-priority tasks or to keep the central processor busy when the user is waiting for I/O. Later, OS/360 restarts the interrupted task where it left off, having kept a record of machine status at the time of the interruption. Among the objectives of OS/360 are:

- Maximizing the use of critical resources

- Maximizing system throughput; i.e., user work done per hour or per day

- Minimizing response time; i.e., time user waits for results

OS/360 was developed to support the IBM S/360 line of computers. Over 1,000 people were involved in its initial release and up to 900 were continuously required to maintain and improve it. Its basic concepts and facilities were sound enough to be carried forward to the generation of IBM S/370 computers. The complexity of OS/360 was unanticipated; nothing like it had been done before. The process of mastering the huge system took a year longer than scheduled [2]. The vendor's costs outran the budget but, more significantly, the user community suffered delays in getting new applications installed and found their in-house costs for migrating to OS/360 were exceeding budget. This experience had sufficient economic impact on the data-processing industry to cause all vendors to ask themselves how to avoid repetitions of the OS/360 story. Out of their studies came new procedures and training programs, all of which emphasized the system aspects of development that had largely been ignored earlier. (OS/360 is one of many operating systems available. In later chapters, *OS* alone refers to operating systems in general.)

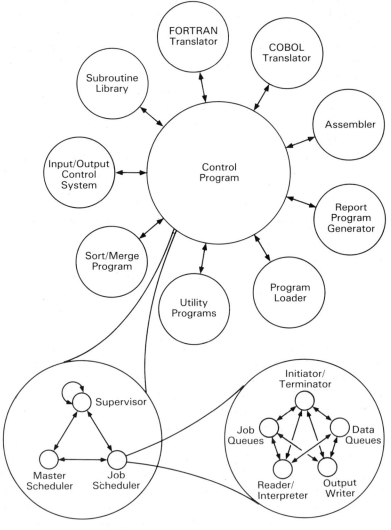

Fig. 1.1 A system is a system is a system.

The elements of OS/360 are programs that supervise and schedule all events [3]. The control program itself is a system (indicated in Fig. 1.1), as are the program units within the control program. What makes OS/360 a system is the fact that it contains elements—the program units—that interact. The interactions that are permitted are complex. Each unit may interact with more than one other unit. The interfaces between units depend on which specific units are present, their sequential relationships, and their physical structure. As indicated in Fig. 1.1, the OS/360 hierarchy is deep. (The *program unit,* which is the smallest defined module of a program system, is the work of one person; it is a *unit of work.* All higher levels represent assemblies of units. Different levels of the hierarchy are sometimes given different names, as indicated in Fig. 1.2. It is not uncommon for the higher levels to represent the work assigned to organizational entities. A subpackage may consist of the programs assigned to one department; it may belong to the package managed by the next higher level manager.)

When received from the manufacturer, the operating system consists of a large number of independent program units stored in a library file. Accompanying the library shipment is a starter package with which the user can tailor OS to local requirements. This system generation process selects the appropriate units from the library, initializes them, and links them together so they can be used. (Note that while the programs in the library are designed as a system, they do not constitute an operational system until the system generator establishes the interfaces that permit them to interact.) The OS undergoes a dynamic reconfiguration every time it is used. Each user program calls on some combination of the programs available in the tailored system. The sequence in which the OS units are called can vary, as can the space available in memory; hence, a unit may take several different

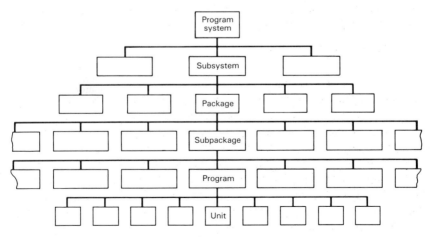

Fig. 1.2 Program system terminology.

forms at different times. Under all of these conditions, the OS must continue to operate and the program units must perform according to their specifications.

The concept of complex interfaces is not essential in a system but it is characteristic of large systems. Figure 1.3a shows independent programs; e.g., the OS library prior to system generation. It contains six elements. In Fig. 1.3b, the elements are connected sequentially to form a very simple system with simple interactions. In this example, the output of one element is the input to the next. Such a string of elements can easily be replaced by a single element consisting of the concatenation of the six programs into one larger program; however, small modules tend to be easier to build and maintain with a high level of quality. Sequential strings are common in practice. One such string might occur in payroll preparation where the first step is to prepare an up-to-date list of employees and their rates of pay. The second step is to calculate the current week's earnings from time card inputs. The third step is to calculate the payroll, including deductions, taxes, contributions, overtime, bonuses, etc. The next step is to prepare checks. The fifth step is to update the master payroll records for the year-to-date. The last step is to prepare summary reports for tax purposes, for accounting analysis, etc. The process is broken into parts for convenience. Some of the events occur on different days, some are separated by manual audits, and some are simply broken down to fit the computer better. The resulting string has elements and interactions, but, since the interactions are all uniquely defined by the path through the system, it is very easy to manage the program development project.

The most complex system, as seen in Fig. 1.3c, permits each element to interact with every other element, including itself. A change in the status of any one element may cause a change in all others. The effects of a change are further magnified by echoes and ripples; i.e., a change in element 1 interacts with elements 2 through 6, causing changes in them which, in turn, affect element 1 and so on. The system is a dynamic organism which is hopefully stable so that the effects of a single stimulus eventually die out. You would not intentionally design a system of maximum complexity, but many systems are initially defined to permit a large number of interactions and are consequently complex.

System management attempts to reduce the complexity of a system through restructuring. In OS/360 this is done during the design of the programs by blocking interactions between certain program units and forcing them to communicate using the control program as an intermediary. This rule creates a focal point in the control program and organizes the system structure into a less complex form, as in Fig. 1.3d. Note that the design affects the *static* interactions shown, say, in the flow chart of a program system. A good design also reduces the number of *dynamic* interactions that occur when a program is executed.

a. Independent units

b. A sequential string system

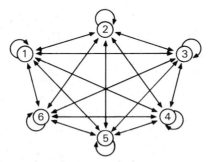

c. A system of maximum complexity

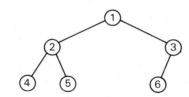

d. A structured system

Fig. 1.3 System structures.

The specific structure shown in Fig. 1.3d is a *rooted tree* in which there is a hierarchical relationship among the program units. There is only one path for information and commands flowing between the root node and any other node. Because there are no cross-connections, nodes at the same level can only communicate with the assistance of a higher-level node; consequently, the tree structure has a well-defined chain of command. Trees are basic structures used in organizations of people, database organizations, sort and search decision algorithms, syntax analysis algorithms, and other situations involving well-defined hierarchical precedence relationships [4]. Although it is not always possible or desirable to structure a program system or a programming project into a perfect hierarchy, it is usually a good idea to strive for a tree structure. The closer the actual project is to a hierarchy, the more likely it is to be manageable.

Nonsystem projects are collections of independent tasks. No thought goes into tying the independent tasks together, and, in fact, any attempt to integrate the results of the separate tasks will fail due to their incompatibilities. Obviously, if the goal of a project is to produce a system, appropriate management and design techniques must be used from the start.

OS/360 illustrates the fact that a system is a *structured assembly of elements that interact*. The term *structure* implies here that the system has, by design, less than maximal complexity.

1.1.2 SAGE—Functional and Performance Objectives

The elements in OS/360 are all programs, yet there are systems that contain other kinds of elements. For example, an air defense system is a structured assembly of elements that interact to detect threats and take defensive action. The SAGE system has elements ranging from programs to machines to services and especially to people [5]. It is the heterogeneity of most large systems that challenges the ingenuity of managers. They must have great technical breadth to understand the diverse elements of the system, and they must develop comprehensive yet consistent rules for system management that apply equally well to all the elements. They must structure the system to create clean, recognizable, simple interfaces between elements, yet they must be prepared to react to interactions that are not delineated in the system structure plan [6].

Each element of the system plays a part in meeting the objectives of the system. If it fails, the system fails.

An actual problem of this general type was reported on February 21, 1971. One aspect of air defense is to notify the civilian population that an emergency exists. This notification is issued by the military operations staff in the form of a preprinted message distributed via the news services to all commercial broadcasting stations who are to pass it on to their audience before going off the air. Periodically the system is tested using a separate preprinted message that clearly indicates that a test is in progress. According to an article in the *Washington Post,* however, it never occurred to anyone that the test and the actual emergency tapes could be confused [7]. As a result, there was no verification procedure to ensure that the correct tape was used. On the day in question, an operator made the "simple human error" of putting the wrong tape into the transmitter. He sent a message, containing the code word for the day, "hatefulness," that told the stations it was the real thing, which could have led to mobilization, evacuation, or panic. But few of the stations paid attention and nothing happened. The operators had heard the test message so often, they treated it as a routine announcement to be ignored.

This single human error unexpectedly was a good system test case because it demonstrated the inadequacy of the entire air defense alert system design. Not only did the false alarm get transmitted, but everything else went wrong too. Some stations went off the air without broadcasting the alert. Some did not check their teletype until two hours after the false alarm, which by then had been canceled. Other locations never received the false alarm because of data transmission problems. Some stations ignored the alert. Only a very few attempted to verify it. It is hard to believe that so many errors could occur, yet that is not unusual in a large system. There are too many potential interactions for anyone to be aware of, much less control.[1]

The air defense system example illustrates heterogeneity, responsiveness, and hidden interactions, and it stresses utility: The system has certain functional capabilities and a purpose. Combining these thoughts: *A system is a structured assembly of heterogeneous elements that interact cooperatively to satisfy a set of functional and performance objectives* [8].

Typically, a system should also have such attributes as:

- Reliability
- Expandability
- Modifiability
- Maintainability
- Ease of use
- Adaptability
- Stability
- Predictability
- Manageability
- Completeness
- Self-checking

The air defense system possesses these attributes in varying degrees. It may be impossible to measure how well it performs since a true test would require a full-scale attack, which is obviously impractical. Other systems in constant use are easier to evaluate.

---

1. A complicated new procedure was installed to prevent a recurrence. The new system failed March 6, 1972. In this case, the error was a mechanical breakdown in the communications system. Subsequently, no errors have been reported. However, according to the *Washington Star* and *Science* magazine, a computer-generated crisis nearly occurred November 9, 1979. On this date, a war game was loaded at the air defense command. Somehow the game was routed to an active computer, generating a real nuclear attack alert. During the six minutes it took to recognize the mistake, interceptors took off, missiles were alerted, and commercial aircraft were notified. Similar reports of failure continue to appear from time to time in the press.

1.1.3   The Telephone System—Growth Capability

Today's telephone system is an immense man-made system. The earliest telephone entrepreneurs did not approach the communications business systematically. Each one set up a central office and strung wire to subscribers. There were no interconnections between the competitive companies. This shortly led to an inefficient quagmire of telephone lines with expensive, unsatisfactory service to the subscribers. Soon the government stepped in to bring order to the young business. It permitted the creation of a telephone monopoly to absorb all of the competitors and restructure them into a single integrated system. The remaining independent companies learned how to interact with the monopoly. The results were extraordinarily successful. The system design was so straightforward that the system has grown without interruption ever since. It has adapted to technological changes which substituted electro-mechanical switches for manual connections, introduced automatic rotary dialing, added electronic switching centers, converted some transmission links to microwave and satellite links, added pushbutton dialing, and provided data and image transmission as well as voice communication.[2] Furthermore, all these modes of operation coexist in the same system [9]. A hierarchical structure with only five levels permits a telephone subscriber to place a call to anyone in the network. The hierarchy balances the cost of facilities against the requirement for connectivity. Individual telephones are connected to local offices (level #5). Local offices are grouped to feed toll offices (level #4) on up through district and regional offices. Each call follows the shortest path through the tree structure. By providing redundant elements, the system performs reliably even when some elements are out of action. The individual elements are practically service-free and can easily be replaced if they fail. The addressing scheme has survived all the changes and has accommodated world-wide direct dialing without requiring the user to learn anything except a longer phone number. In fact, the use of the telephone is so easy everyone over the age of six is expected to be able to make a call without instruction.

A feature of the telephone system that facilitates its growth, its flexibility, and its modifiability is modularity. A *module* is an element that has a clearly defined set of inputs and outputs, internally controlled procedures

---

2. At the end of 1980, the Bell System in the United States had 142 million telephones in service. They handled 206 billion messages that year, according to the company's annual report. Some 17.5 billion long distance calls in 1980 represented a 7.8-percent increase over 1979. During 1980, some $17.3 billion was invested in construction, adding 4 million telephones, new coaxial cables and microwave facilities, satellite earth stations, additional electronic switching systems, etc. New system functions included a digital data transmission network to service the data-processing community. In addition, the Bell System interconnects to a nationwide network serving about 180 million telephones via 1.4 billion carrier circuit miles of radio, cable, and wire, plus 12,000 satellite circuits.

or producing the outputs from the inputs, and no other explicit or implicit interactions. It can be treated as a black box that transforms the inputs into the outputs. Its internal processes are irrelevant as far as the rest of the system is concerned. Therefore a module can be removed and replaced by a black box with equivalent I/O without changing the system in any way. In hardware systems such modules are often called *pluggable units.* If a unit fails it is replaced by plugging in a similar module. The old module is either discarded or repaired and returned to inventory.

1.1.4 Movie-Making — Modularity

The black box characteristic of modules is indispensable in one system-oriented industry: movie-making. Film producers want to minimize costs and maximize profits. They minimize costs by carefully planning the logistics of a movie to use only what is needed and arranging to use each resource in a specific place for the minimum length of time. For instance, a historical epic with two superstars and a cast of thousands may take twenty-four months to complete. The substantial cost of star salary and perquisites can be reduced by compressing all of the scenes requiring the stars into a six-month period. Similarly, the crowd scenes might best be planned by hiring the total adult population of several towns for one month, selecting the month with the best weather and scenic conditions for that geographic area. The stars may have to spend four months in a Hollywood studio and two months on location, with some overlap between the schedule for the stars and the schedule for the crowds. Similar plans will be set up for the remaining scenes that employ only the supporting cast. Finally, the whole schedule will be optimized, say with mathematical techniques, to minimize total cost of production, including cast and crew salaries, sets, transportation, editing and rework, etc., within the constraints of weather, cash flow union contracts, and so on.

With the objective of minimizing cost handled in this way, the producers will try to maximize profit by selecting a good story, hiring popular stars, and assigning a director who knows how to tell a story so that audiences will pay to see it. The director has seemingly insurmountable obstacles. With the logistics plan all chopped up for economic reasons how can a coherent story be told? The answer is to abandon continuity and break the story into modules or scenes. The director visualizes the story as a sequence of scenes, each of which consists of an initial situation, a set of actions, and an ending situation. Once the story is broken into scenes, there is no need to film the scenes in sequence. The director can film them in whatever order best fits the logistics plan. At worst, the cast may have to be called back for retakes, but even this can be avoided by shooting several variations of each scene, which the director can compare in the editing room to select the best one.

Alfred Hitchcock, the master of suspense movies, has told interviewers that his success was based on carefully conceiving every scene and determining every camera angle before he ever reached the sound stage [10]. A single scene in his movie *Psycho* that lasted only forty-five seconds on the screen consisted of 118 shots all neatly described on numbered file cards. One result of his method is that even the actors were surprised at what came out on the screen. Hitchcock was a skillful top-down designer whose conceptual ability enveloped a whole story; yet he implemented from the bottom up. He filmed all the modules before integrating them to make the movie that he envisioned from the start.

1.2 SYSTEM STRUCTURE

In each of the illustrated systems, a great deal of work has gone into finding the appropriate system structure. Examples of typical commercial computer applications stress this fact by displaying the system as a tree-structured chart [11, 12]. Without a structure, the elements in the system are all free to interact with one another, creating an unmanageable complex mess. The term *bowl of spaghetti* aptly describes the resulting system. Several authors have used this term to describe the kind of program system that is large and complex, hard to use, and expensive to maintain. System design imposes an orderly structure on the elements and their interactions. Structured programming preserves the order in the code itself. The result of this process is a network in which the allowable interactions are under control. The benefit of manageability obtained in this way is sometimes purchased at the expense of flexibility and responsiveness, but at least a workable system can be built. (There is an argument that says a system constrained by its system design to be less than optimally efficient is not worth building. This is an extreme position. In general, the users of the system need some definable level of performance, which should be expressed in the system objectives. That is the target to be met by the design. When the target is unattainable, the users may be willing to relax their requirements further in order to obtain other benefits of the system. Optimization is not always of prime importance.)

1.2.1 Logical Interactions

The dual role of system design is to define the system elements and to structure the interactions among the elements.[3] Starting with the most complex

---

3. In later chapters, a distinction is made between two aspects of system design: *architecture* which defines interfaces and allocates functions to each side of an interface, and *design* which defines the elements that provide the functions. The architect describes the external appearance of the system—how it looks to the user. The designer describes the internal workings. The distinction is useful in large commercial systems where long-term, multivendor compatibility among many types of elements is desired.

system, the structuring steps remove unnecessary interactions and block undesirable interactions, leaving a reduced network consisting only of the logically essential interactions. In addition, structuring arranges the logical interactions in such a way that the system meets its objectives economically, reliably, and effectively. This is accomplished by arranging elements so that there are strong relations *within* subsystems and weak relations *between* subsystems; i.e., maximize binding, minimize coupling [13, 14].

Binding refers to the internal cohesiveness of subelements within each element of the system. A tightly bound unit contains all the resources, services, and supervisory control needed to carry out its single function. A loosely bound unit collects various functions for convenience or to save space or time. Tightly bound modules are distinguished by two main characteristics:

1. All parts of the module contribute to the accomplishment of the single function of the module; no superfluous parts are included.
2. There is a relatively large amount of information common to the module (i.e., information/data that would have to be passed or shared if the module were split apart).

The effect of tight binding is readily observed in a system of people. (It should be clear by now that organizations of people satisfy all the definitions of a system.) The most cohesive organization is a project team reporting to a first-level manager. Less cohesive is a committee drawn from various groups. (This point is arguable. A committee is also tightly bound; however, a project team is like eight oarsmen pulling together in a regatta, while a committee is like eight runners each trying to accumulate the high score for their side in the weekend marathon.) The least cohesive is a holding organization which is formed to provide administrative coordination of unrelated people who happen to be on lengthy assignments remote from their home base. A project team is effective because it has one manager and all the people and equipment needed to do its job. It acts like a pluggable unit which can do its job in any environment. Thus, infantry squads, oil well fire-fighting teams, football teams, and small program development groups are effective because they are tightly bound for a single purpose. By contrast, a committee is not thought of as an entity. It is pictured as a collection of individuals—and it acts that way—even though it has a single purpose. In the holding organization each individual has a separate purpose unrelated to the others and takes direction from a remote manager rather than the manager of the holding organization.

Coupling refers to interactions between elements. Interactions represent information transfers and can be measured by the number of external interfaces an element has. Simple initial and terminal elements have only one interface. Simple intermediate elements have two interfaces, one in and one out. Elements with more than one input and/or output are more strongly coupled. Since the existence of an interaction implies that two elements are connected in such a way that a change in one can affect the other, multiply coupled elements are more likely to have side effects. A change in an element that is connected to two others on its output side may be fully consistent with one of the successors, but it may cause trouble in the other. As the amount of coupling increases, it becomes increasingly, even exponentially, more difficult to anticipate all possible side effects.

Excessive coupling is avoided by properly designing modules to minimize interactions among elements or subsystems. Some interactions can be eliminated because they are unnecessary or illogical. Others are expendable; i.e., they can be eliminated without seriously affecting system functions or performance. Beyond this, it is possible to reduce coupling by adding *coordinating elements*. Cross-connections among a number of elements are cut. In their place, connections are made to a new element which controls interelement communication. Control programs and department managers are common examples of coordinating elements. They are also examples of hierarchical design in which a control level has been created. Note that coordinating elements are often loosely bound and could be the source of system errors.

Coupling is accomplished in either of two ways. The most common method of coupling elements in a tree-structured system is by *user/server relationships*. One element uses services provided by the other. For instance, a programming team uses the services of a computer facility, or an application program uses the services of a database access program. In either case, the user must find out what procedures have been established by the server in order to take advantage of the services. Where necessary, the user has to adapt to the requirements of the server or forego the service. Thus a computer facility may insist on receiving an authorized billing account number before it will process a request for service. It is up to the user to obtain the authorization and submit it in the proper form. Likewise, an application program that wants to use a database access method must format the database index information properly—even if that means additional program steps in the application. The server specifies the services it can provide and the protocols that it will recognize as requests for service. It will also specify the nature of the responses it will return to the user when the service is complete or when errors occur. The user provides his or her own *adapter* to fit the *request/response interface* protocols, as shown in Fig. 1.4 where A is a user of B. Although in many user/server relationships the server is at a lower hierarchical level than the user, this is not necessarily the case—any element can be either a user or a server if the design permits. A programmer who uses the computer facility can also provide a service for the computer facility, say, by writing a customer billing program on request. Role reversal is not uncommon; relationships can change, contributing to system dynamics.

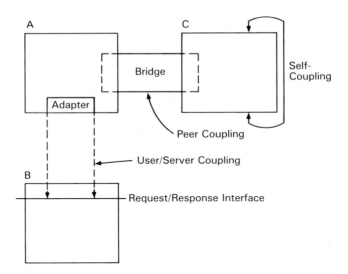

Fig. 1.4. Element-to-element coupling.

The second coupling method is also shown in Fig. 1.4. It is *peer coupling* represented by a *bridge* between A and C. The bridge is developed jointly by the two equal partners. In this way, a bridge differs from an adapter; the latter is the sole responsibility of a user in a user/server relationship. Peer coupling is found in decentralized systems where information flow between the two elements is infrequent. An example would be a distributed data base in which the files are set up in geographic regions. Most inquiries go directly to the regional file that contains the answer. A few inquiries arrive in the wrong region, as might happen when someone on a trip cashes a check in a branch bank far from home. The branch that cashes the check will arrange to hand the check over to the traveler's home branch. One way to do it is to pick up the telephone and call the home branch,

"Say, I've got an item that belongs to you. How should I handle it?"

"Well, if it is less than $1000.00, give me the amount, account number, and name over the phone so I can get it into tonight's account balancing run. On the other hand, if it is a large check we have to verify the signature, so put it in the mail and we will pay you in a couple of days."

"It is a large item, but rather than wait for the mail can we use facsimile transmission? We have a fax machine made by X Company."

"That's a good idea. We have a similar machine. I'll have my secretary ready to take the transmission in five minutes."

The bridge is established by this conversational exchange. Some parts of the procedure may be fixed, such as the rule that the telephone be used to make initial contact. Other parts of the procedure depend on the state of the peer elements at the time coupling is required; i.e., the use of facsimile transmission would only apply if both peers have compatible equipment in working order. The exchange of procedural and status information is often called "handshaking." In data communications network architectures, the principle of peer coupling is formalized. The International Standards Organization (ISO) Open System Architecture, for example, specifies seven layers of communication, ranging from the electrical signals on a transmission link to the handshaking between application programs. In order for two applications to communicate there must be coupling at all lower levels between peer functions at each end of the link. (An example of a network architecture is given in Chapter 6.)

As a special case of either user/server coupling or peer coupling, a single module may be *self-coupled*. It may generate an output which is immediately returned as the next input in a recursive procedure, for example. A simulator may have a module that represents the behavior of a communications transit node; if there are several such nodes in sequence, there will be one instance of the module for each node and control will flow from one to the next. In an accounting program, one module may prepare summary totals; weekdays it is invoked once for daily totals; monthly it is run for daily totals then again for monthly totals; quarterly and yearly totals cause the module to cycle further. Self-coupling may be set up as a user/server relationship to take advantage of code and procedures that are already in place. Peer self-coupling would be more common, involving relatively little code since no external handshaking is required.

As implied in the example, peer coupling involves handshaking for every connection and generally takes a lot of communication in both directions. User/server relationships can usually be set up once and left alone so that each exchange of information is relatively efficient. In both the hierarchical and peer relationships two types of information flow between system elements. *Data* is the information consumed, stored, or produced by the system. *Control information* affects the behavior of the system by initiating, modifying, and terminating system functions.

Binding and coupling have an effect on concepts of module ownership, program unit documentation, and even program product marketing practices. The effects are seen in the external specifications for a program unit (or a corresponding hardware unit). Only the information needed for coupling is contained in the external specifications. It must be there in order for the user to know how to communicate with the module specified. Further, it must be stable so the units coupled to the specified module are protected when new releases of the module are installed. This is particularly true of general purpose vendor programs that have wide usage and multiple releases. Vendors, therefore, create *externally defined interfaces* which they try to maintain unchanged over the life of the program. On the other hand, vendors may withhold information on the *internally defined interfaces* of

bound modules. By treating the internal interfaces as proprietary information, the vendor satisfies several objectives.

- The user is protected against malfunctions caused by his or her own
  tampering with intricate code.
- The user is encouraged to operate at a high-level interface and is
  relieved of learning the details of implementation within a module. The
  vendor expects the user to be more productive as a result.
- Published documentation costs may be reduced (for widely used system
  programs, mainly).
- The vendor can gain freedom of action without impacting the users.
- The vendor can add features which give a module a competitive advantage. By exercising proprietary control over the unique techniques
  employed in implementing the features, the vendor can extend the economic life of the module.

For these reasons, design decisions regarding logical interfaces are really
business decisions.

1.2.2   Data Interfaces

The simplest interaction is a data interface. Each system element accepts
input data, operates on it, and generates output data. A few elements generate their own data so they need no data input. Others accept an input and
interpret it in order to pass control information to another element, but they
pass no data forward. These special cases are primarily of interest in the
housekeeping and termination portions of a system. In general, it is appropriate to treat every element as a black box with at least two data interfaces,
one input and one output. Thus each element can be both a *source* of data
and a *sink*. It depends on how one looks at it. All elements that supply data
to a given element are sources to the given element which, in turn, is their
sink. The given element is also a source for its successors.

   In order to compare different designs, it is useful to quantify the main
features of each design. There are many ways to do this. None are precise,
but if the designer realizes only gross comparisons can be made, fairly
simple methods can be useful. To illustrate this in the following sections, a
set of quantification rules will be used that is reasonable for sequential application programs.[4] Figure 1.5 illustrates three types of data interfaces.
Each element has two data interfaces: one in and one out. In special cases it
could have one, as mentioned earlier. It could also have multiple input or

---

4. Database access methods and parallel process monitors can be much more complicated because they involve implicit functions such as index search routines or
interrupt handlers that are not shown in the example.

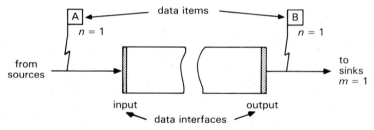

a. Simple Data Interface, single data item, single sink

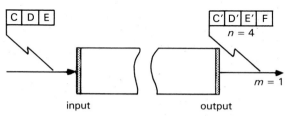

b. Average Data Interface, multiple data items, single sink

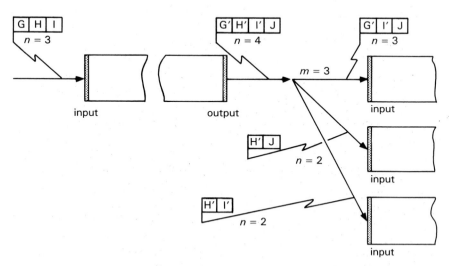

c. Complex Output Data Interface, multiple data items, multiple sinks

Fig. 1.5 Data interfaces.

output data interfaces; e.g., a transmission program could support binary synchronous link controls (BSC) separate from synchronous data link controls (SDLC), or a security monitor could have physically distinct input interfaces for each user. In a poorly structured program, a program unit could have multiple input data interfaces if separate sources are permitted to enter it at different points. These cases are not shown in Fig. 1.5. The illustration assumes all inputs arrive at one interface and all outputs depart from one interface, although the outputs may be directed to multiple sinks. Activity within the sink, such as making a copy of inputs for recovery purposes or modifying a control block, affects the relation between the sources and the sink. The effects of such activity are accounted for in the total complexity of the data interfaces at an element. The number of input data items can differ from the number of output data items at an element. Likewise, the number of sources (fan-in) feeding an element can differ from the number of sinks (fan-out) it feeds. An objective of good design is to keep the sum total of the data interface complexity as small as possible.

For program units, the three types of interface differ in the degree of complexity they represent. Consequently, they differ in the degree of difficulty they present to implementers or maintenance programmers.

- A *simple data interface* (Figure 1.5a) is either an input interface that receives a single named data item or an output interface that sends a single data item to a single addressee. A data item is a record or a field or even a file. The volume of data is not relevant as long as all instances of a data item are of the same type, having a common format, the same number of data fields with the same interpretation, the same editing rules, and the same error indications.

- An *average data interface* (Figure 1.5b) is either an input interface that receives more than one data item or an output interface that sends more than one data item to a single addressee.

- A *complex data interface* (Figure 1.5c) is an output interface that sends multiple data items to multiple sinks.

The degrees of complexity distinguish between single sinks and multiple sinks but are unconcerned about the number of sources. The assumption behind this approach is that all data arriving at an input interface is uniquely defined as to form, meaning, and source. This is a fair assumption for well-designed program units. It takes care of the case where two data items have the same name. For instance, program units A and B both process a data item NAME. Within A, NAME designates employee names in full, last name first, followed by first name, initials, and "Jr." or other appendage; the length of the field is variable up to forty characters, and names that do not fit within forty characters have the last name truncated. B has a local data item NAME which designates employee names also but contains only a short form of the name used for indexing records. B's NAME is a fixed field of seventeen characters consisting of the first seven letters of the last name (padded with blanks where necessary), two initials, month and last two digits of year of birth, and a five-digit pointer to the full NAME provided by A. When A and B provide NAME data to C, NAME becomes a global data item that will lead to errors because C will have only one set of procedures for NAME regardless of source. A well-designed system will distinguish ANAME from BNAME. In fact, most organizations employ data control specialists to define terms and prevent duplication [15].

Program designers should avoid complex data structures when they can because multisource, multisink structures frequently weaken system integrity by permitting too much freedom of action. A free access structure allows common data to be modified by one element without other elements knowing about it. As a result, program unit A may try to recover a value it placed in the common store only to obtain a different value put there by program unit B. When this occurs in a test session, it is almost impossible to figure out what happened. Coordinating elements can help to restore system integrity.

In Fig. 1.5, the number of data items at an interface is labelled n; the number of sinks for an output data interface is m. The degree of complexity, hence the degree of difficulty of a data interface, is arbitrarily defined as a function of n and m. The function can be developed from the conventional wisdom of programmers. Ask a programmer whether the number of data items in a program unit affects one's work and the answer will be "yes." How much more difficult than one data item is two? How much more difficult than two is three?

"Well," the programmer will say, "you are trying to be more precise than I can be. What I know is this: As the number of input data items increases I have to do more work. One type of work grows linearly with the number of data items; namely, the effort that goes into editing, interpreting, and possibly converting the data according to the rules for that data item. Let's not count that as a complexity factor since it only affects my estimate of workload, not my understanding of the job. The second type of work definitely does complicate my task. If there are multiple input data items, I have to add code to analyze each message in order to determine to which data item it belongs. When the number of items is large, I also consider efficiency. This may lead me to set up a transfer vector so the shortest switching time is associated with the item that occurs most often. I will also look for common processing functions used by several data items, which can be handled by a shared subroutine. Finally, I will look for common error messages or other constant data appearing in several data item routines and try to share the storage. Each of these steps to consolidate the program adds control functions to the program and adds to my documentation load.

"But, as I think about the design decisions I would make when I have multiple data items, I have to admit that they do not increase my work linearly. The biggest increase comes from the fact that I must allow for more than one item. Every item added beyond two has some effect, but I would guess that the complexity of the job never doubles regardless of the number of data items."

In other words, the contribution to complexity due to the number of data items ranges from 1 to 2. One literal representation of what the programmer said leads to the following function:

$$f(n) = 2 \sum_{k=1}^{n} \frac{1}{k(k+1)}.$$

When there is only one data item $f(n) = 1$. Two data items would sum

$$2 \left[\frac{1}{1(2)} + \frac{1}{2(3)} \right] = 1\ 1/3.$$

This result gives heavy weight to the second data item. The contribution of successive data items gets smaller and smaller. While this function is a reasonable outcome of a discussion between knowledgeable programmers, you should remember that it is not supported by reliable data. It is an arbitrary but useful expression of experience and might well be wrong in your environment. (In general, all you want is a relative estimate of implementation difficulty. Therefore, while the examples in this chapter will include detailed complexity formulas to illustrate the factors contributing to complexity, simpler guidelines will be offered for estimating difficulty. Difficulty will be taken as the upper bound of complexity.)

Output data interfaces are further complicated by the number of sinks. Another discussion with a programmer will show how.

"The preparation of data to be sent to another program unit entails getting the data properly formatted, attaching appropriate header and trailer information to identify the data item and mark the boundaries of the message, segmenting the message to fit the buffers in the sink and adding sequence numbers to the message segments, adding the sink's address and other communication controls to the segments, and building queues to hold the segments until they have been transmitted and an acknowledgment has been received. Of course, I can dispense with a lot of this effort if there is only one sink. I could probably get rid of the queues and segmenting routines by reaching agreement with the sink to exchange only whole messages on a request/response basis. But if there are two or more sinks, I not only have to provide all the functions, but I have to be prepared for conflicting demands from the sinks. I may have to have different size buffers and queue lengths for each sink and I may have to supply unique communication controls for each link. As a result, I find in general that serving two sinks is twice as hard as serving one; three sinks three times as hard as one; etc."

In other words, the degree of complexity of one output data interface with n data items and m sinks could be modeled as:

$$mf(n) = 2m \sum_{k=1}^{n} \frac{1}{k(k+1)}$$

which ranges from m to $2m$. If there are several output data interfaces on one unit, the total degree of complexity is the sum of the individual values. For instance, a unit sending four items of data to three sinks, three different items to a fourth sink, and one of the previous items to two additional sinks, has an aggregate degree of complexity of:

$$2 \cdot 3 \sum_{1}^{4} \frac{1}{k(k+1)} + 2 \sum_{1}^{3} \frac{1}{k(k+1)} + 2 \cdot 2 \sum_{1}^{1} \frac{1}{k(k+1)} = 8.3.$$

Alternatively, everything can be lumped to give a more conservative value

$$2 \cdot 6 \sum_{1}^{7} \frac{1}{k(k+1)} = 10.5.$$

Using the functions to assess the implementation *difficulty* of data interfaces leads to the following conclusions.

- A simple data interface ($n = 1$, $m = 1$) has a value of 1.
- An average data interface ($n > 1$, $m = 1$) has a complexity value of $f(n)$ which is less than or equal to 2. Difficulty in this case is 2.
- A complex output data interface ($n > 1$, $m > 1$) has a complexity value of $mf(n)$ which is less than $2m$. Difficulty is $2m$.
- The difficulty of a single program unit due to data interfaces is the sum of the values of all the data interfaces in the unit. Normally there are two data interfaces per unit, one input and one output.
- The difficulty of a program system due to data interfaces is the sum of the values of all the program units.

Simple data interfaces occur in sequential processing where single values are passed through several programs to produce one output. Average data interfaces correspond to normal record processing where various transactions are processed by one program to update a master file. Complex data interfaces occur in file processing where a program accesses several databases or in communications processing where a central router directs data to many destination programs. They also occur in various operating systems which must overlay one program on another. If both programs use the same data it can be segregated and retained in a pool that always remains in memory. Data pooling reduces the number of data interfaces that must be managed. General purpose database management systems have been developed precisely for this reason. To see why, consider the requirements of personnel/payroll processing in a medium-sized firm [16].

The firm has about 10,000 employees. Data about them is recorded in about fifty personnel and financial forms such as employment applications, payroll change requests, organization charts, appraisal reports, awards, skill inventory, time cards, address lists, personal histories, job records, etc. Some one hundred reports are produced for ten using departments, including multiple versions of the same data. For example, payroll calculations result in checks and check stubs, disbursing journals, new master files, bank transfers, tax reports, inputs to job accounting processes, and more. Some fifty program units do all the processing. When first written, the programs were independent, occasionally sharing files. A great deal of data flowed among the units, however. Only about fifteen of the units dealt with a single item of data input. Only five of the fifteen had a simple output data interface. Another twenty had only one sink. The rest served an average of four other units. The total difficulty of all fifty program units was 330.

	Input	*Output*	
Simple	15	5	
Average	35×2	20×2	
Complex	_____	$25 \times 2 \times 4$	
Total =	85	+ 245	= 330

When the personnel/payroll system was revamped, an integrated database was established and a general purpose database management system (DBMS) was installed. Using a common data dictionary, the database manager accepted all inputs, edited them, and stored them. Any program unit could access the database to obtain elementary data items (a simple interface) or, using the query facilities of the DBMS, could obtain various data items. Likewise, it could place its results in the database and signal a general purpose report writer to develop the formatted outputs to be delivered to ten users. The new system had forty program units, including the two general purpose subsystems. The difficulty was quite different because the application program units were all simple or average; only the subsystems were complex.[5]

---

5. Application programs: 10 simple input, 28 average input, 5 simple output, 33 average output.

    Subsystems: DBMS/average input, complex output to 39 other program units, Report Writer/average input, complex output to 10 users.

    Because the weights used here are completely arbitrary, they are only good for illustrating the nature of data interfaces. They are not useful for making quantitative statements about the efficiency of actual program systems. At most, they give a qualitative indication of complex interfaces that may cause trouble in the system. They are most useful in *comparative* analysis as opposed to *absolute* analysis.

	Input	*Output*
Simple	10	5
Average	30×2	33×2
Complex		$(1 \times 2 \times 39) + (1 \times 2 \times 10)$
	70	169 = 239

Management of the database itself is a significant activity, but it at least has an upper bound. No matter how many sources are connected to it, the input side of the DBMS has an interface of average difficulty. The output side of the DBMS is complex, but this single complex interface replaces many complex interfaces that existed before pooling. Furthermore, total system difficulty is more resistant to design changes when a DBMS is used. Adding one program unit to the old personnel/payroll system and allowing it to receive data from the twenty-five complex units adds fifty points to system difficulty. Adding a similar unit to the DBMS system costs only two points since the twenty-five units supplying the data are unaffected; only the DBMS must cope with the change. In practice, most commercial DBMS products anticipate design changes. They contain built-in capabilities for adding data items, adding application program units, and changing relations in the database [17]. The concept of simplifying a program system by reducing the number of complex data interfaces is well supported by DBMS products when you initially design a system and, later, when you must modify it.

Referring again to the analogy between program systems and people organizations, a data interface corresponds to communication between managers and employees. When a manager tells one employee one thing, the information generally sinks in. When the message contains too much data, the employee will have trouble remembering it all. Worse, when the manager hands out a lot of data at a department meeting, different employees will remember different parts of the message. It is much harder to control the information transfer in the last case.

1.2.3 Control Interfaces

Data interfaces are static; they do not directly control the flow of activity in a system. Control interfaces do affect flow and, therefore, represent the dynamic structure of the system.

The distinction between data and control interfaces is not always clear. In many program systems, each unit refers to a table to determine how to proceed. References to the table are control interfaces as well as data interfaces. More evident control interfaces are: (1) the direct transfer of control from one element to another, and (2) the indirect control of an element by setting the value of its control parameters. In each case, the distinguishing characteristic of a control interface is that an event in one element dynamically affects the behavior of another element.

A program control interface is more complex than a data interface because it involves activity outside the scope of an element. When a data item is passed, the using element can analyze it and edit it. In this way, the using element protects itself against faulty inputs. When control is passed, an affected module is often physically modified before it starts to execute; that is, key instructions have had new values assigned to them since the last execution of the module. It has no knowledge of its own condition and must behave the way it has been controlled to behave.[6] Thus greater attention must be paid to the design of control interfaces to ensure that they cannot lead to incorrect system activity.

In the simplest *direct control interaction,* one element passes control directly to a single successor (Fig. 1.6a). As the first element, A, completes its activity, it leaves the system in a particular state (A). In a program system, the system state is recorded in various tables, machine registers, displays, files, and indicators. The final state of the first element is the starting state of the next element, B. A direct control interaction passes control from the last executed instruction of element one to the first instruction of element two. Assuming state (A) is a valid initial state for B (as it would be in a well-designed system), B will execute transforming the system state to (B).

More difficult is a *parameterized control interaction* in which element A, regarding B as data in memory, places control data in parameter fields of element B. A program unit which calculates a value "CTRL" has a parameterized control interaction when CTRL appears in another program unit, say, as part of a conditional expression:

```
IF CTRL = 1 THEN CALL ABLE;
ELSE CALL BETA;
```

or a DO loop:

```
DO WHILE (K<CTRL);
```

As shown in Fig. 1.6b, the parameter need not be set in the next program in the sequence of execution. As an extreme example, a compiler A may set a parameter in the object code of a program B which will not be executed for days. When the object code is finally called, it may be modified by the calling program K. Consequently, the value of the parameter must be valid for all initial states of B, such as (K). It may have no meaning with respect to the terminal state of A. This is obviously a potential source of problems since the programmer building A may have insufficient knowledge of B's status to test the control interface. When the parameter affects many other elements, the interaction is more complex, and when many elements are controlled by many others, the system approaches maximum complexity (Fig. 1.6c).

---

6. In people organizations, discipline is imposed to encourage people to follow instructions without question; however, few people organizations have the blind obedience that is characteristic of hardware and software systems.

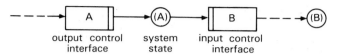

output control   system   input control
interface   state   interface

a. Direct Control Interface

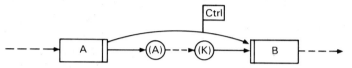

b. Parameterized Control Interface

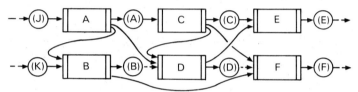

c. Multi-Way Parameterized Control Interfaces

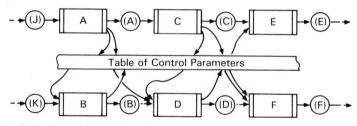

d. Table-Driven Control Interfaces

Fig. 1.6 Control interfaces.

The dynamics of flow control in an executing program similar to Fig. 1.6c are such that unit A is no longer available when unit B is running. Consequently, if a problem arises in the execution of B, a search must be made back through all the intervening states to determine whether A caused B to behave in this manner. In table-driven systems a static record of control decisions is maintained in a parameter table (Fig. 1.6d). Now, instead of modifying B, A stores the appropriate control parameters in the table. When B is called, it refers to the table to find out how to set its control parameters. If a problem develops, the supervisor can refer to the control data which is still sitting in the table and see that it should notify A to initiate a recovery procedure. The use of a table requires A to calculate "CTRL" as before and then store it as "APARAM" in a table whose entries have been globally defined to all program units that access it. B now adds an assignment of the form

```
BCTRL = APARAM;
```

before executing its conditional expression or DO loop.

Data interfaces are concerned only with information transfer. Both information transfer and the consequences of control actions must be analyzed when designing a direct or parametric control interface. A higher weight is therefore assigned to a control interface and a slightly more complicated set of definitions is required for control interfaces than for data interfaces. The choice of guidelines is based on the assumptions that (1) direct control is easier to handle than parametric control, (2) direct and parametric controls can occur in the same output interface, and (3) the minimum difficulty of a control interface is equivalent to one direct control interface.

- A *simple control interface* is either an input interface directly controlled by one other element or an output interface directly controlling one other element.

- An *average control interface* is either an input interface directly controlled by multiple elements or an output interface directly controlling multiple elements.

- A *complex control interface* is an output interface that parametrically controls one or more elements and also directly controls one or more additional elements.

The fact that a program unit can loop on itself could increase the degree of difficulty of an otherwise simple control interface; however, if you assume that all program units are built according to the rules of structured programming with a single entry and single exit point, looping is easy to manage. For this reason, explicit looping is ignored when classifying control interfaces. Serially reusable program units and reentrant program units have average input control interfaces, but they involve more work than nonreusable units. Locks must be set and released for each use of the serially reusable unit. Extra design review is needed to verify that a reentrant unit is indeed not modified during execution. Thus these designs affect workload without necessarily affecting complexity as defined here.

The restriction of complex interfaces to the output of an element implies a design philosophy that each element is responsible for its actions but not for its initial state. Furthermore, the actions of an element are reversible if something goes wrong. Hence, the element that sets a parameter must protect the system against the effects. An element receiving control, direct or parametric, is only responsible for keeping the lines of communication open. In an organization of people this approach amounts to manager follow-up. After giving instructions, the manager checks to see that they are properly followed. Some employees may check the orders carefully; others may not. The manager is responsible for the outcome in any case, so a follow-up procedure is always part of the manager's job, whereas checking instructions need not be part of an employee's job description. The obvious exception to this rule occurs when the manager's directives are not reversible. In situations where the activity is destructive and nonrecoverable, the employee should be required to ask, "Would you repeat the order so I am sure I have it right? You realize that if I execute this order the following things will happen. Do you want me to proceed?"

The difficulty of a control interface is due less to the amount of control data involved than to the relationships between the two units interacting at the interface. The mere fact that the programmer of unit A has to work with the programmer of unit B to define the system states involved in their interaction makes control interfaces harder than data interfaces. Once the system state has been agreed to, the programmer of the controlling unit, A, must verify that the design of A produces that system state only when it is supposed to. The programmer of the controlled unit, B, must make sure there is only one possible interpretation of the system state in B. To represent this design analysis, the difficulty of a simple control interface is set at 2, compared to 1 for a simple data interface.

If program unit A has direct control interfaces with B, C, D, and E, the effect is similar to having a data interface handling four data types. Thus an average control interface with q partners has a degree of complexity of

$$2 \times 2 \sum_{k=1}^{q} \frac{1}{k(k+1)}$$

which ranges from 2 to 4.

A complex control interface has at least one parametrically controlled partner. Each parametric relationship has a weight of 2 and, unlike direct controls, no saving is realized when there are multiple parametric relationships. Thus a complex control interface with p parametric and q direct relationships has a degree of complexity of

$$2p + 4 \sum_{k=1}^{q} \frac{1}{k(k+1)}.$$

To establish the minimum value of a parameterized control interface at $2p + 2$, i.e., greater than a simple control interface, q is taken to be at least 1, as it would be if A sets parameters in B but passes control to C.

1.2.4   Measures of Complexity

The degrees of complexity proposed in the last two sections can be generalized by redefining the factors m, n, p, and q to be fan-in/fan-out numbers
having values on input as well as output. The definitions of n and q are not
affected by this decision. Since, by convention, all input data arrives at a
single point, the fan-in is one, $m = 1$. Control parameters, however, are not
set by an input control interface; therefore, $p = 0$ at the input. Now, the following expressions cover all cases:

$$\text{Degree of Complexity of a Data Interface} = 2m \sum_{k=1}^{n} \frac{1}{k(k+1)}$$

$$\text{Degree of Complexity of a Control Interface} = 2p + 4 \sum_{k=1}^{q} \frac{1}{k(k+1)}$$

Table 1.1 summarizes the values of these expressions for the various cases
shown earlier. As noted earlier, since these expressions give a false picture
of precision and since they are unnecessarily hard to calculate, it is recommended that the maximum values in Table 1.1 be used to estimate implementation difficulty.

The special case of a table-driven control interface is handled by treating it as a direct control interface. The rationale is that the true control
interaction is between the program that sets the parameters and the table;
however, the parameters are known only as data, not as controls by the
table manager; therefore, parameter passing is a data interaction accompanied by direct transfer of control to an unmodified successor via a simple
control interface.

Given a method for weighing the degree of *complexity* at an interface,
the weights can be used to compare alternate designs of a single function or
unit to compare the relative complexity of various elements in a system.
Larger subsystems can be adequately compared by examining their relative
difficulty. Used this way, the measures of complexity can help designers
simplify a design. They can also help managers identify difficult implementation areas that should be assigned to the most capable people and tracked
with the most care.

As in Fig. 1.5, each element must be evaluated by itself, looking at the
input side separately from the output side. This method of isolating the
inputs or outputs at a single node treats the node as a *free body*. A free-
body analysis remains valid even if the surrounding environment changes,
as long as none of the changes interact directly with the free body. This
makes it possible in a programming system to assign a total weight to each
system element which will remain constant until some interaction at that
node changes.

TABLE 1.1. INTERFACE COMPLEXITY/DIFFICULTY

Type of Interface	Factors		Complexity Value	Difficulty (max. complexity)
Data Interface	*m* Sinks	*n* Data Items		
Simple	1	1	1	1
Average	1	>1	$2\sum\limits_{k=1}^{n}\dfrac{1}{k(k+1)}$	2
Complex (output)	>1	≥ 1	$2m\sum\limits_{k=1}^{n}\dfrac{1}{k(k+1)}$	$2m$
Control Interface	*p* Parameterized	*q* Direct		
Simple	0	1	2	2
Average	0	>1	$4\sum\limits_{k=1}^{q}\dfrac{1}{k(k+1)}$	4
Complex (output) minimum $= 2p + 2$	>0	≥ 1	$2p + 4\sum\limits_{k=1}^{q}\dfrac{1}{k(k+1)}$	$2p + 4$

Data Interface values for

$m = 1$										
$n =$	1	2	3	4	5	6	7	8	9	10
Value	1.00	1.33	1.50	1.60	1.67	1.71	1.75	1.80	1.82	1.84

for $m > 1$, multiply table entry by m

Control Interface values for

$p = 0$										
$q = 0$	1	2	3	4	5	6	7	8	9	10
Value	0	2.00	2.67	3.00	3.20	3.33	3.43	3.50	3.60	3.64	3.68

for $p > 0$, add $2p$ to table entry

The total weight at an element is the sum of the data interaction weights and the control interaction weights at both the input and output—plus a size factor. The size factor allows for the fact that small program modules are less complex to write and maintain than large ones. The size factor used here is 1/50 the number of higher-level language statements in a unit (or 1/200 the number of assembly language statements). The choice is somewhat arbitrary but is based on two factors. One factor is the structured programming guideline that program segments be limited to one page. Programs that do not fit on one page are structured in a hierarchical form that permits references from one page to any number of others to create a long chain of program steps. By restricting the structured programs in this way, the programmer maintains better control of design and tends to produce more readable code that is easier to maintain and modify. A page of high-level source language has less than fifty statements.

The second factor is based on the experience of independent test teams who invariably note that the number of errors found in component and system tests is at least proportional to the size of the program being tested. Many testers believe the number of errors grows as the square of program size. In any case, the rate of errors found during test is considered tolerable for program units on the order of 200 object lines in length. Thus, a 100 statement PL/1 program with an average input data interface, receiving control directly from a single predecessor and passing data and control to any of four routines by setting parameters in those routines, has a total difficulty of:

Data In	Data Out	Control In	Control Out	Size	Total Difficulty
2	8	2	12	2	26

The result is the sum of the components. The decision to add them together is based on the belief that data and control interfaces are properly scaled with respect to each other. Size is added to yield a simple, consistent procedure for estimating implementation difficulty, one that can support design comparisons in practice.

1.3   SYSTEM STRUCTURE EXAMPLE — INFORMATION RETRIEVAL

Assume that a novice was given the job of building a general-purpose information retrieval system. Thirteen elements represent the functions identified as basic to the system. The individual got this far by study, by analysis and design, and by discussion with more experienced programmers. So far the novice has done a good job; however, she has interpreted "general-purpose" as meaning that any system element can talk to any other, so she has explicitly allowed for such communication, maximizing the system interactions.

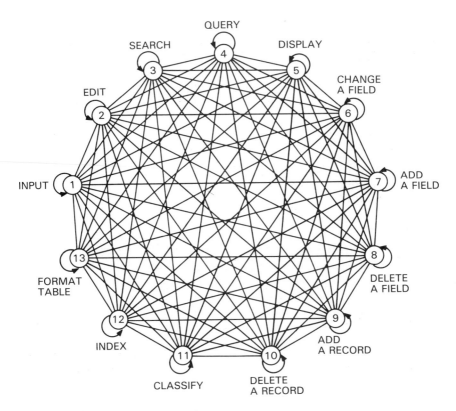

Fig. 1.7 Information retrieval — Maximal subsystem.

An oversimplified picture of the information retrieval subsystem consisting of an aggregate of thirteen functional elements is shown in Fig. 1.7. Only the activities related to processing transactions against a database are included; all of the operating system services that support the information retrieval activities are omitted. Within the subsystem, all possible interactions are shown:[7] There are 91 lines in the drawing, representing a maximal system with 169 interactions.

A simple graphic representation of a system such as Fig. 1.7 uses circles (or dots) to represent elements; lines represent interactions. The elements can be labeled if space permits. Each interaction line represents two interactions unless arrowheads are added to show that the interactions are di-

---

7. Under certain conditions, each data item or each parameter of control could be shown separately, yielding a denser graph. Since these features will be treated by complexity weights, they are omitted from the figure.

rected in only one direction. Since a program unit can iterate using its output as the next input, it is permissible and, indeed, normal to have loops in a system diagram. The total number of interactions in a maximal system of n elements (taking element-element connections as two interactions and element-self as one) is n^2. The minimum number is $(n - 1)$ for a loop-free sequential system.

Matrices can be used to summarize relations in a form that may be easier to use than a graph.[8] A *connection matrix* is an array of 1's and 0's where each 1 indicates a relation between the column element and the row element (Table 1.2); namely, that there is a connection *from* the row element *to* the column element. In Table 1.2, element 2 is connected to (sets or uses or calls) elements 3 and 5; it can also loop on itself.

The total number of 1's equals the number of directed interaction lines in a system graph. The connection matrix of Fig. 1.7 would be all 1's since there are paths from each element to every element [19].

The absence of a line in the system graph, corresponding to a zero (or blank) in a connection matrix, is a strong condition meaning that all possible interactions at that point have been blocked by control mechanisms in the design. In order for such a strong condition to apply, an orderly procedure should be followed in the top-down design process:

Assume that each element in the system can interact with all others and make explicit design decisions to eliminate undesirable interactions.

This rule ensures that missing interactions are the result of analysis and not simple oversights. All element builders should know when they start what other elements they can communicate with.

TABLE 1.2.   CONNECTION MATRIX

i \ j	1	2	3	4	5	6	Sum
1	1	1					2
2		1	1		1		3
3	1		1			1	3
4		1	1		1		3
5				1			1
6	1	1	1				3
Sum	3	4	4	1	2	1	15

8. Readers familiar with graph theory will recognize that system structures are graphs; therefore, the mathematical techniques for operating on graphs can be used for simplifying or tracking paths through systems [18].

1.3.1   The Information Retrieval Elements

The thirteen elements of Fig. 1.7 are programs and tables involving some 800 high-level source statements.[9] Briefly, they do the following:

1. INPUT: receives file update data from a number of input devices, including display consoles. The data contains a transaction code defining the update as a field operation (add, change, or delete a field) or a record operation (add or delete a record) in an existing file. The data also contains FILENAME, RECNAME, and the data to be added or changed. The actual data may range from one character to the full text of a lengthy article. (In the latter case, the transaction may be ADD A RECORD with the intent of creating a record describing the new article and placing the index record in the appropriate files covering the subject(s) of the article. FILENAME is empty for this transaction; the file-handling portion of the system is expected to classify the article into one or more subject areas by analyzing the words in the text.) Long messages may be made of several input segments. INPUT will process these up to the end-of-message mark. INPUT converts the data from device code to system code and arranges the input messages in a standard format called SYSIN. INPUT sets a parameter in EDIT to identify the type of input and transfers control to EDIT.

2. EDIT: receives SYSIN messages regardless of length one at a time from INPUT. Within EDIT the pointer DEVICE (set by INPUT) identifies the source of the message and consequently the type of editing required. EDIT examines the transaction code to determine which of the device editing routines to apply to SYSIN. Edited routines are stored in a queue, FILEIN. Control then passes to SEARCH. If errors are detected during editing, EDIT sets a device parameter and an error flag in INPUT which can request retransmission from the device. In case of error, nothing is added to the FILEIN queue; control is returned to INPUT. As an option, SEARCH can acknowledge completion (or failure) of an update by returning ACK to EDIT which relays it to INPUT.

3. SEARCH: processes the input queues, FILEIN and QUERYIN, giving priority to FILEIN. SEARCH looks for a FILENAM in the input message. If one is present for updates, SEARCH will call the appropriate update program and pass it to the FILEIN data. For queries, SEARCH will consult INDEX and FORMAT TABLE to obtain the requested records and pass them to QUERY. QUERYIN is returned along with the response to assist QUERY in matching out-of-sequence responses with queries. If no FILENAM is provided, SEARCH will pass the input message to CLASSI-

---

9. The example is illustrative only. This design might be quite inadequate for real information retrieval. In addition, enough details have been omitted that there are built-in inconsistencies. These do not affect the discussion of the example.

FY to obtain a list of files that may be applicable; i.e., CLASSIFY returns one or more FILENAM values. As implied, one record may appear in several subject files. When no FILENAM is specified, field and record operations are applied to all occurrences of the named record. SEARCH sets no parameters in other programs.

4. QUERY: receives retrieval requests (REQ) from DISPLAY, edits them, labels them as queries, and queues them in QUERYIN. Control is passed to SEARCH. Responses (RESP) are returned to QUERY by SEARCH which will organize each response into the report format (RPT) requested by the inquirer (as part of REQ) and pass control with the report as data to DISPLAY. The device on which the report is to be displayed is indicated by a parameter in DISPLAY set by QUERY. QUERY does not check for data errors.

5. DISPLAY: accepts queries from several types of display terminals assigned to interactive users and displays responses. DISPLAY sets a parameter in QUERY to identify the input device originating a request and passes control to QUERY. Interactive users are not permitted to update records or files; however, the same devices may be used at times for DISPLAY and at other times for INPUT.

6. CHANGE A FIELD: modifies the contents of a single field. Given FILEIN, CHANGE A FIELD consults INDEX and FORMAT TABLE to fetch the record, makes the change, restores the record, and prepares an UPDATE to be used by SEARCH for recovery purposes. CHANGE A FIELD cannot modify the length of a field. If the transaction calls for this, CHANGE A FIELD creates a DELETE A FIELD followed by an ADD A FIELD.

7. ADD A FIELD: adds a field to the format of all records in a file. If the transaction contains data to be placed in the new field for the record (RECNAM), ADD A FIELD calls CHANGE A FIELD. ADD A FIELD modifies FORMAT TABLE to reflect the change in the record structure. An UPDATE is prepared for SEARCH. The UPDATE goes only to SEARCH but the format change is available to any successor program. This permits one record to be modified several times before the next record is fetched. If RECNAM is specified, but there is no such record in the INDEX, ADD A FIELD will pass control to ADD A RECORD which will create one new record containing data in only one field.

8. DELETE A FIELD: deletes a field from all records in a file. Modifies the FORMAT TABLE and creates an UPDATE as above.

9. ADD A RECORD: adds one entire record to a file, placing blanks in all required fields (as specified in the FORMAT TABLE) for which no data is given by FILEIN. ADD A RECORD updates the record count in the FORMAT TABLE and adds the record location (RECLOC) to the INDEX.

10. DELETE A RECORD: deletes one or more entire records and updates FORMAT TABLE record count and INDEX record location.

11. CLASSIFY: on request from SEARCH, CLASSIFY reads the FILE-IN data text, analyzes the word frequency distribution, and produces a number characteristic of the probable subject of the input. Each file is described by a similar number. CLASSIFY matches the input value against each file value to determine which file is most likely to contain a response or which is the best candidate to receive a new record. Multiple answers are possible. The FILENAMs of selected files are passed as data and control is returned to SEARCH.

12. INDEX: on request, INDEX provides record location (LOC) by searching a table of FILENAM/RECNAM vs. physical storage locations. The table must be modified whenever a record is moved, added, or deleted.

13. FORMAT TABLE: on request, FORMAT TABLE provides information about fields by using a data description table containing the record format of each file. A current count of the number of records in each file is maintained in the data description table. FORMAT TABLE modifies the data descriptions whenever a field is added or deleted and modifies the count when a record is added or deleted.

1.3.2   System Simplification

The maximal system of Fig. 1.7 is unnecessarily complex. Given the preceding definitions, it is possible to simplify the system structure as shown in Fig. 1.8 and Table 1.3. The result is an improved design that takes advantage of the fact that, in this information retrieval system, terminal users may not modify the files. All file updates are defined as coming from FILE-IN via INPUT and EDIT. Only queries arrive via the interactive DISPLAY and QUERY modules. Although both FILEIN and QUERYIN are inputs to SEARCH, there need be no communication links between INPUT, EDIT, FILEIN on one hand, and DISPLAY, QUERY, QUERYIN on the other. Similarly, all connections can be broken to CLASSIFY except for the SEARCH-CLASSIFY link since only SEARCH uses this function. There is no need for ADD A RECORD to CHANGE or DELETE A FIELD nor for DELETE A RECORD to tie to the three field-handling functions. Each processing program fetches and restores the record it uses.

The next step in design is to rearrange the interactions so as to simplify the figure without disrupting the logic. A rearrangement suggested by Fig. 1.8 focuses on SEARCH. All I/O is handed to SEARCH, which could find the records to be processed by the record and field handling routines. Why not make SEARCH *the* focal point—the coordinator of all other activities? Doing this would mean that SEARCH would decide what processing was required by each transaction and then call the appropriate routines one at a

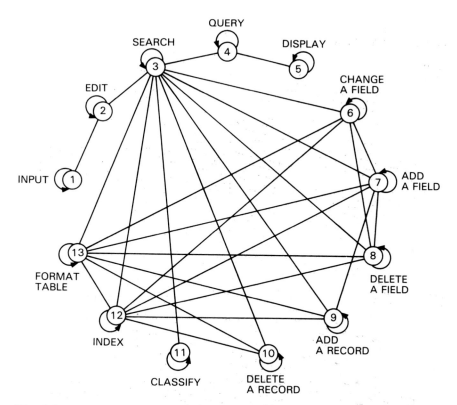

Fig. 1.8 Information retrieval—Logical subsystem.

TABLE 1.3.   INFORMATION RETRIEVAL—LOGICAL SUBSYSTEM

Module	1	2	3	4	5	6	7	8	9	10	11	12	13	Sum
1	1	1												2
2	1	1	1											3
3		1	1	1		1	1	1	1	1	1	1	1	11
4			1	1	1									3
5				1	1									2
6			1			1	1	1				1	1	6
7			1			1	1	1	1			1	1	7
8			1			1	1	1				1	1	6
9			1				1		1			1	1	5
10			1							1		1	1	4
11			1								1			2
12			1			1	1	1	1	1		1	1	8
13			1			1	1	1	1	1		1	1	8
Sum	2	3	11	3	2	6	7	6	5	4	2	8	8	67

time, recovering control after each routine completes its assignment. This decision breaks many of the interaction paths and leads to Fig. 1.9 and Table 1.4. The original maximal system had 169 interactions. The logic of the information retrieval system reduced this to 67 interactions. Structuring the design around SEARCH as a coordinating element eliminated 36 more interactions, leaving only 31.

By simply asking what steps must be performed by the system, the information retrieval system designer has substantially simplified the system. There are now several natural subsystems with the bulk of the system control focused on a one-element subsystem, the SEARCH routine. All interactions in the design are now directed connections. In other words, EDIT can call SEARCH, but SEARCH cannot call EDIT. (This may be a poor design in that the success of updates is not acknowledged except in the audit trail; nevertheless, it is an explicit specification that can be built and tested.) Most of the routines are iterative (they can process multiple fields, etc.); however, the record-handling and classification functions are not permitted to repeat. They execute only once and return control to SEARCH. Thus many "self-loops" have been eliminated. The tables are also restricted. Although the format and index data are used by many routines, only SEARCH is permitted to obtain it. SEARCH then relays the data to the using routine. In a similar manner, the device-handling routines have been collected in INPUT and DISPLAY to simplify the message analysis and file-handling subsystems. Both units provide adapters to accept unique device formats, but (as shown for INPUT in Fig. 1.10) all activity common to input or output is handled by a single program. A common set of editing functions, such as "blank deletion," "$ insertion," "decimal point alignment," or, more elaborately, "spelling correction," serves all input devices; QUERY does the same for output displays. The INPUT and DISPLAY units are treated as tightly bound units so that the conversion routines within them need not contribute to subsystem complexity. Unfortunately, the multiple device types complicate the actual I/O programs.

To examine the effect of the design decision, the weights for Fig. 1.8 and Fig 1.9 are compared in Table 1.5. These weights are obtained by drawing the free-body diagrams of the elements and calculating the input and output interface weights (Fig. 1.11) for each element. All explicit information available in the specification is used. Thus in element 7 of the logical subsystem, ADD A FIELD, the aggregate output data interface weight is 5, representing 1 for the special interface between ADD A FIELD and SEARCH for updating the audit trail, plus 4 for sorting out all possible uses of the FORMAT output by the four successor processing programs. If you did not know UPDATE was directed only to SEARCH, you would have to assume both UPDATE and FORMAT could serve five sinks, yielding a

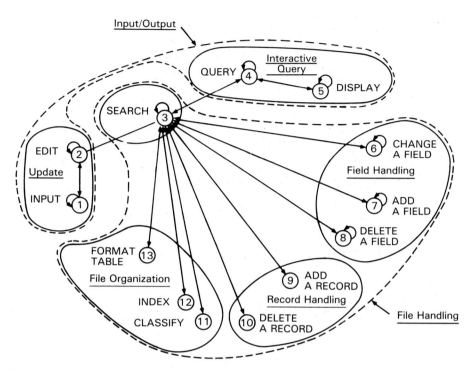

Fig. 1.9 Information retrieval—Structured subsystem.

TABLE 1.4.   INFORMATION RETRIEVAL—STRUCTURED SUBSYSTEM

Module	1	2	3	4	5	6	7	8	9	10	11	12	13	Sum
1	1	1												2
2	1	1	1											3
3			1	1		1	1	1	1	1	1	1	1	10
4			1	1	1									3
5				1	1									2
6			1			1								2
7			1				1							2
8			1					1						2
9			1											1
10			1											1
11			1											1
12			1											1
13			1											1
Sum	2	2	11	3	2	2	2	2	1	1	1	1	1	31

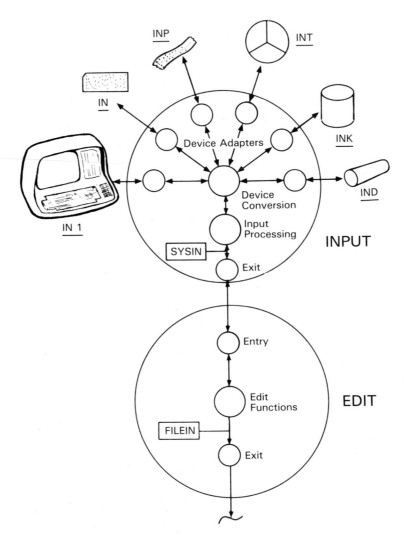

Fig. 1.10 Information retrieval—Common interface.

weight of 6.67. As the results show, the structured design simplifies most of the elements and reduces the total degree of difficulty by 20 percent. Since SEARCH originally handled all the data items when it responded to queries, it need not grow significantly in order to serve as a focus. Performance may suffer because there is so much switching back and forth to SEARCH; however, it is better to start with a clean design and later tune it for performance than to concentrate on performance and end up with an unmanageable design.

Henry and Kafura [20] discuss a complexity measure based on the number of control flows and data structure references of an element:

$$\text{complexity} = \text{length (fan-in} \times \text{fan-out)}^2.$$

Length is an optional factor representing element size. Fan-in is the sum of input controls and data structures referenced by the element. Fan-out is the sum of the output controls and data structures updated by the element.

TABLE 1.5.   COMPARISON — LOGICAL SUBSYSTEM VS. STRUCTURED SUBSYSTEM

Element	Weight	
	Logical subsystem	Structured subsystem
1 INPUT	17.42	17.38
2 EDIT	12.00	10.00
3 SEARCH	20.40	25.80
4 QUERY	12.17	12.17
5 DISPLAY	15.33	15.33
6 CHANGE A FIELD	10.26	7.50
7 ADD A FIELD	14.46	7.83
8 DELETE A FIELD	12.60	7.17
9 ADD A RECORD	12.00	8.00
10 DELETE A RECORD	10.83	7.33
11 CLASSIFY	7.00	7.00
12 INDEX	14.33	6.33
13 FORMAT TABLE	14.50	6.50
Sum of Element Weights	173.30	138.34

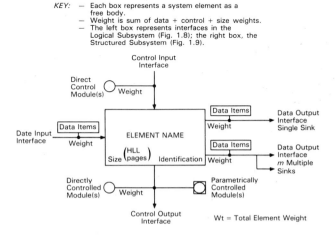

Fig. 1.11 Information retrieval — Element weights.

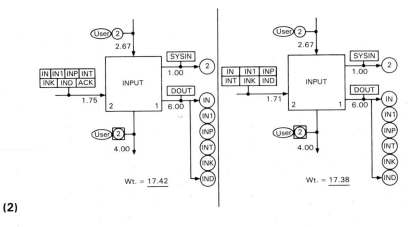

(2)

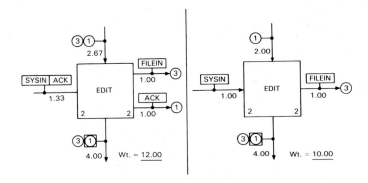

(3)

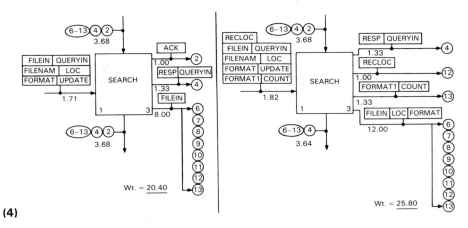

(4)

Fig. 1.11 Continued.

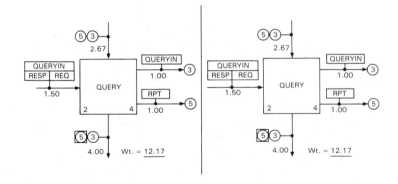

(5)

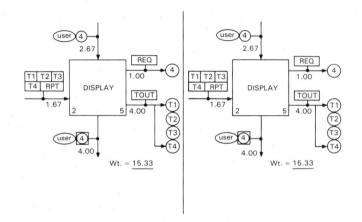

(6)

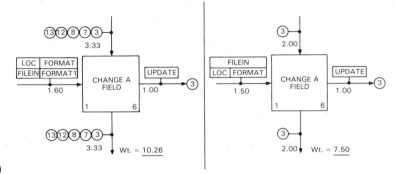

(7)

Fig. 1.11 Continued.

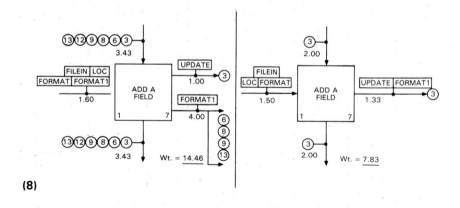

(8)

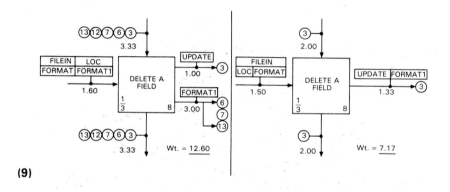

(9)

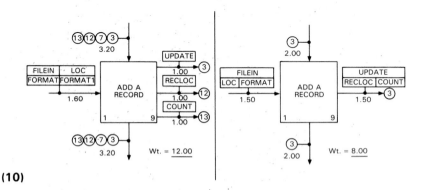

(10)

Fig. 1.11 Continued.

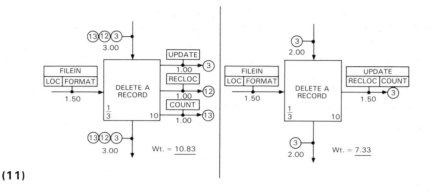

(11)

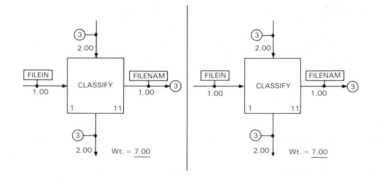

(12)

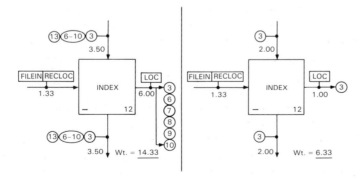

(13)

Fig. 1.11 Continued.

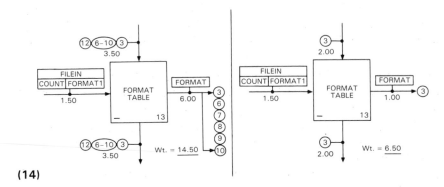

(14)

Fig. 1.11 Continued.

Roughly speaking, length is the same as size in Fig. 1.11; fan-in is the number of sources of control and data (generally shown as circles in Fig. 1.11); fan-out is the number of sinks. For example, element 7, ADD A FIELD, would measure:

complexity of logical system $= 1 (7 \times 11)^2 = 5929$
complexity of structured system $= 1 (2 \times 2)^2 = 16$

In Fig. 1.11, elements 12 and 13 have zero length, which causes a problem when length is a multiplicative factor. If length is ignored, the complexity of element 7 is unchanged, but the complexity of elements 12 and 13 becomes a dominant aspect of the logical system. The wide range of results obtained from this measure makes it difficult to tell the significance of a given element's weight. Nevertheless, the authors predict that, in a system, the elements with high complexity values will contain more errors than average as evidenced by a higher number of changes and modifications. They tested this hypothesis on the UNIX operating system and validated their measure when the UNIX modules with the most changes scored highest in complexity. The best correlation was obtained from the metric $(\text{fan-in} \times \text{fan-out})^2$. When applied to Fig. 1.11, this metric shows the structured system to be 40 percent better than the logical system.

The same system design can be represented by a tree structure as in Fig. 1.12. This diagram shows how elements are grouped into packages. It has the same form as an organization chart and can be useful in deciding which organizational group will be assigned responsibility for each package. Note that the system described by the tree is not the same as the system in Fig. 1.9. The tree only allows for minimal coupling, so it does not show the interactions between such elements as 9 and 12. Instead, it introduces dummy elements A through I which act as collecting nodes for lower level

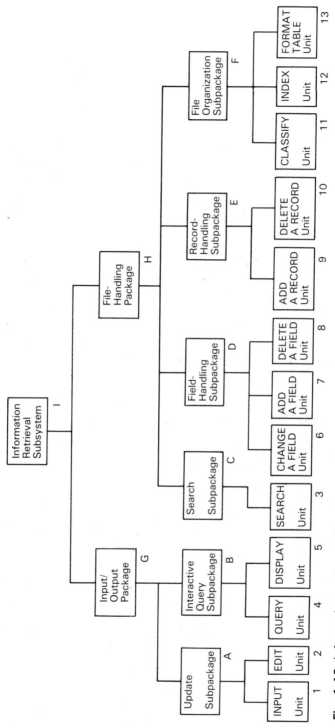

Fig. 1.12 Information retrieval—Tree diagram of structured subsystem.

49

elements. If A through I are designed as real modules through which data and control must pass, the tree diagram will be a complete and accurate description of the system. If A through I are not real modules, the tree diagram is not complete and must be supplemented by the basic system diagram; otherwise, developers will lose track of key interactions.

The coupling in the structured system can be seen in Fig. 1.13, which shows the data and control flow among subsystems. The internal structure of each of the subsystems is hidden. At least in an ideal implementation of the structure shown in the figure there would be no coupling that is not in the picture (i.e., SEARCH has only one direct control interface out to FIELD HANDLING, subsequent routing is handled in some way by a supervisor within FIELD HANDLING). The Henry and Kafura metric fails to give satisfactory results for this level of packaging. It exaggerates the I/O complexity because it treats control and data interfaces as equally complex. McCabe [21] would measure the complexity of this structure by a simple formula:

$$V = e - n + 2$$

where complexity, V, is the number of linearly independent circuits in the connected graph which has e edges, counting parallel lines connecting two vertices as one edge, and n vertices.[10] (Given a structured flow chart, V is the number of predicate nodes plus 1.) McCabe's experience is that V should be 10 or less to keep complexity under control. In Fig. 1.13, $V = 5 - 6 + 2 = 1$ which fits the guideline. Compare this to Fig. 1.7 where $V = 80$, and Fig. 1.8 where $V = 29$, and Fig. 1.9 where $V = 9$. McCabe's measure shows the structuring steps are progressively improving the system based on a guideline for maximum acceptable coupling. Since several different structures can have the same value of V, weights can be used to find the preferred alternative.

The different subsystems carry comparable weights, which is desirable.[11] Each subsystem represents roughly the same degree of difficulty (except for I/O device code) and could be implemented by groups of similar skill and productivity. The greater complexity of SEARCH is highlighted, pointing out where special skills and management attention are required. In this example, the calculation of complexity weights provided a test of the ef-

---

10. The formula is actually $V(G) = e - n + 2p$ where G is a connected graph containing p connected components or subgraphs. p is taken as 1 in the text.

11. Here the free bodies to which weights are assigned are a level higher than those tabulated in Table 1.5. The weight of a higher-level module is not the sum of the weights of its lower-level components (compare FIELD HANDLING, WT = 9.16, to CHANGE A FIELD + ADD A FIELD + DELETE A FIELD, WT = 22.50). It is independently calculated and should only be compared to other modules at the same level.

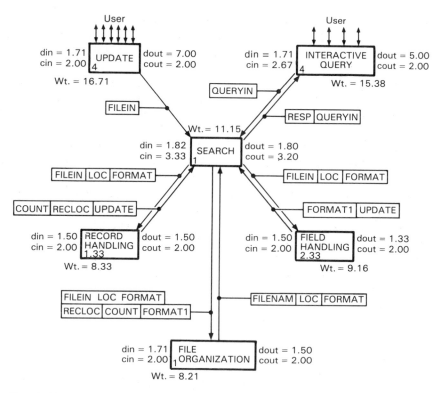

Fig. 1.13 Information retrieval—Package coupling.

fectiveness of design decisions. Good decisions reduce complexity, but design is still an art. Complexity measures and design methodologies help you tell when you are moving in the right direction, but they do not tell you what decisions to make.

1.4   SYSTEM INTEGRITY

A useful concept presented in Part 1 is that a program system exists only in its documentation. A system has *integrity* when it is complete and its completeness is clearly exposed in the system documentation. A delivered system has integrity when it does everything the documentation says it does *and* when everything it does can be understood by referring to the documentation. A system has integrity when it fulfills the expectations of a knowledgeable user. "Integrity" is different from "utility." There is no guarantee that a system that has integrity will do a useful job. Utility depends on whether the system requirements were chosen well, with respect to the environment at the time of delivery. On the other hand, a system with a high degree of utility must also have integrity. Otherwise, the user will have no confidence in the system and will question the results, reducing their value to the organization. "Integrity," as just defined, is also different from "trustworthiness" in the sense of file security or privacy. Yet, here too, if the system requirements properly define the level of security desired, then the delivered system must have integrity to insure that the built-in protective devices function properly at all times.

System designers are the only ones who deal with the system as a unit prior to final integration tests. They design for integrity by keeping the system objectives within their conceptual ability and by meticulously examining all possible system interactions. Not all designers can do this. Many competent programmers lack the self-knowledge or the patience with detail that is required. Those that are competent to design systems are very careful to study the scope of their assignment to be sure they either can handle it as one system or partition it into several smaller systems. They also recognize that system requirements change with time. They phase system implementation so that each deliverable subsystem preserves system integrity while poorly defined or changing requirements are postponed to a later phase.

Designers who bite off more than they can chew will fail to define some of the system interactions. They define only what they can see in the limited time they are able to spend on design, but, lacking the conceptual ability to see the whole picture, they omit key relationships. Later, these omissions are discovered by the implementers in the form of unexplained or illogical behavior of system elements during integration tests. Notice that this is the earliest that missing interactions can be detected. Up to this point, the separate program units will be self-consistent. Only when two or more units are tested together are interface problems uncovered.

1.4.1 Module Size

Ferdinand [22] suggests a guideline for modularizing a system so as to reduce the expected number of errors. He shows analytically that a system of N elements will have a minimum expected number of errors when it contains modules whose average size is the cube root of $2N$, thus,[12] when

N is 13, the optimum module size is 3 elements;

N is 100, the optimum module size is 6 elements;

N is 62,500, the optimum module size is 50 elements.

---

12. Ferdinand relates the expected number of errors to a graph $m = kn^u v^n$ where n is the number of nodes and m is the total number of nodes/interrelationships/dependencies/etc.; k is a constant; u and v are parameters describing the system structure. Typically $u = 2$, $v = 1$. This can be interpreted as a maximal graph as defined earlier. When more than one edge in each direction is allowed, $v > 1$. Graicunas' organizational relationships are of this type (see Part 1). Ferdinand's formula fits the $u = 2$, $v = 1$ case only; it is, however, consistent with practical experience.

Compare these numbers to the guidelines mentioned earlier:

- In the information system example, $N = 13$ and the packages (Fig. 1.9) had no more than three program units each.

- In the references to organizations in Part 1, a manager of one hundred people was advised to organize first-level department with a span of control no more than six.

- Structured programmers working in large projects are advised to limit a block of programming to one page—about fifty lines.

Thus, the guideline offered by Ferdinand tends to confirm conventional wisdom.

Since individuals differ in innate and acquired ability to handle a particular job, different people should be given different modules, none larger than $(2N)^{1/3}$, to fit their ability. In addition, when N is very large the cube root of $2N$ exceeds the limits placed on the size of modules by prudent managers. A manager of 1000 people should not accept first-level departments averaging 13 people. Neither will the manager of a 1,000,000 statement program system consider an average program unit size of 125 acceptable when a page limit of 50 has been adopted as a management standard. In both cases, the module complexity is too much to handle reliably. These situations are resolved by top-down hierarchical design, using the Ferdinand guideline as a limit of module size at each level of the hierarchy. In this way, manageability is designed into the system by minimizing the error propensity of the design.

1.4.2 Dynamics of Module Complexity

Schwartz [23] points out that the difficulty of completing a module correctly is an exponential function of the *local context complexity* of the module. The local context complexity is more or less the same as the total free-body complexity discussed in section 1.2.4. Schwartz's point is that, if module A has a total weight twice that of module B, then A will be, say, four times as hard to build—not twice as hard; more than twice as hard. He goes on to point out that there are two facets of local context complexity that change dynamically as development proceeds. The *external irresolution* complexity that represents the still-to-be-resolved design details when work starts will be eliminated as work progresses. Offsetting this, however, is the increase in complexity due to changes in specifications for the module and its neighbors. Schwartz calls this the *accumulated external complexity*. In order to prevent total complexity growing unmanageable he suggests:

- Early definition of module interfaces with particular care to freeze the "external environment" of the most complex modules
- Implementation of the most complex modules first.

These rules are compatible with top-down implementation. They lead to small modules of limited complexity and they resolve interface issues early to forestall the accumulation of complexity as the programs grow.

1.5   WORKLOAD AND COMPLEXITY

Several assumptions simplify the analysis of system workload by making it possible to relate workload to the number of program units in the deliverable end product. These assumptions are:

- The system is conceivable and can be built.
- The system design has strong binding and weak coupling.
- Each program unit in the design can be built by an individual, i.e., its total complexity is within the programmer's grasp.
- Each group of programmers can be managed by their first-level manager; i.e., the total complexity of the group activity is within the manager's conceptual ability.

The first assumption is more a matter of belief and self-confidence than anything else. It is often not evident at the start of a project that the system cannot be built [24]. Indications of a problem will surface during system design when it turns out that a portion of the system cannot be defined because the designers cannot understand it or because an invention is required to solve the problem. If either condition occurs, work should stop while the original system requirements are reexamined and simplified. Alternatively, work can continue toward a conceivable end product that will not meet the requirements but that may be a suitable substitute.

The second and third assumptions can be controlled by choosing a design approach that tests coupling and measures complexity down to the level of each program unit. Individual variation among programmers will lead to some cases in which a program unit is too complex. This will force some redesign and increase the workload; however, in large projects the exposure can usually be anticipated by applying a safety factor to the estimate.

The sum total of all the program units within one manager's span of control will often be excessive. But, just as a programmer concentrates on only one program unit at a time, a manager controls only those units that are active at one time. Elements that have not yet started and elements that have been finished do not require much manager attention. The manager has to plan ahead and be prepared to reactivate units when a change occurs in the design, but most of the manager's attention can go to the *effective interactions*—those that are associated with the active units. *In general, if, at all times, the number of effective interactions at each level of the system is within the span of control of the manager at that level, the system is manageable.*

1.5.1   Workload

Given these assumptions, program system workload is a function of n, the number of program units, and i, the number of interactions in the design. Workload is expressed in programmer-months or some similar labor units. To convert n and i to labor, a productivity factor must be introduced. Typically, productivity factors have wide ranges, reflecting the high degree of variability among individual programmers. For instance, a widely used commercial information systems guideline is that a typical program unit takes one programmer four to eight weeks, a productivity of one or one-half unit per programmer month. Any particular project can be estimated more accurately by using accumulated local experience. Whatever value is selected for productivity, p, the work required to write the program is n/p with an allowance for variability. System integration, test, and documentation are not accounted for; neither are the administrative support nor the management hierarchy. Since all these activities are related to i rather than n, it can be seen that the estimates for large systems would be too low by a wide margin. A complete estimate should have the form:

$$E = (n/p) + f(i)$$

where $f(i)$, expressed in labor units, represents the workload of management and support. Unfortunately, there is no reliable data to show what $f(i)$ is. Very few published project histories exist; the available sources are of questionable statistical value because the data categories are not well defined. They lack the detail to show what types of activity went into the total effort or how many effective interactions there were at each stage of the project. The best one can say after examining the records is that: "On project X, K labor units were spent over T months to deliver a system of n instructions." If $\bar{y}$ is the average number of people on the project, then:

$$K = \bar{y}T \text{ people-months.}$$

Total workload, K, is usually available from cost accounting records covering system development. (K as used here excludes project definition and continuing maintenance.) Job duration, T, is either recorded or is easily recalled by people associated with the project. Sometimes T is unknown and the only staffing level the records refer to is the peak population, y'. (Average population is often not available because, as an after-the-fact number, no one took the trouble to record it. People tend to remember how "big" their job was and often make a point of it in project records.) In general:

$$y' = \frac{3}{2}\bar{y}$$

and

$$K = \frac{2}{3}y'T.$$

Large jobs involve more than one department in an organization; therefore, even though K or T may be known, no one recalls y' or $\bar{y}$. In this situation, it is likely that at least one person had cognizance of all the programming design and implementation and can recall the peak number of *programming professionals* y'_{prog}. The relationship between y'_{prog} and y' is a function of project size and complexity. One model of this relationship is based on analysis of a number of IBM projects (over one hundred). It reflects the cost of supporting multiple releases of a program system and it includes a factor related to project organization as a surrogate for project size.

$$y' = (\frac{3c + L - 1}{2})y'_{prog}$$

similarly,

$$\bar{y} = (c + \frac{L - 1}{3})y'_{prog}.$$

Parameter c represents the effort required to generalize the product:

$c = 1$ for special-purpose end products for single customers.

$c = 2$ for general-purpose end products for a market containing many customers.

Parameter L is the actual number of levels of management in the project organization. (L approximates $[\log y']$; that is, the next integer larger than the logarithm to the base 10 of the project peak population.) Interactions within the organization contribute to complexity; L represents the effect.

The purpose of these guidelines is to provide a very rough method of estimating project requirements when only limited planning data on schedules or resources are available. In Table 1.6, the characteristics of four projects are shown.[13] The table shows how the population is divided between programming, management, and other support. Even though complexity grows as the square of the number elements in a system, the workload necessary to manage complexity in a well-designed system does not increase as the square. Equating programmers to elements it is clear from Table 1.6 that Project C does not have 625 times the workload of Project A, even though C has 25 times as many programmers. The effect of complexity does increase workload, but, in a well-designed system, each participant has a

---

13. The three smaller projects are typical of projects observed over a period from 1965 to 1973 in the IBM Federal Systems Division. During this period, improved programming techniques were experimentally introduced. Each of these jobs was performed for a single user. The largest project is patterned after IBM's OS/360 development in which the requirements of a very broad set of users were met by making the design as general purpose as possible. The workload shown covers the period of program design, implementation, and test of the complete system. Maintenance and upgrade are not included.

TABLE 1.6.   WORKLOAD PATTERNS

	Project A	Project B	Project C	Project D
Peak Population	6	36	250	1350
Programmers	4	18	100	300
Managers	1	6	50	150
Support	1	12	100	900
Average Population	4	24	167	900
Duration (months)	12	18	36	36
Workload (people-months)	48	432	6000	32,400
Levels of Management (L)	1	2	3	4
Generality (c)	1	1	1	2
Peak/Average	1.5	1.5	1.5	1.5
Peak/Peak Programmers	1.5	2.0	2.5	4.5
$\dfrac{\text{Workload (py)}}{\text{Programmers}_{peak}}$	1.0	2.0	5.0	9.0

manageable assignment so that local context complexity need not be a factor in total system workload. Only if an element gets out of control will its complexity affect the rest of the system. The effect of complexity, then, is measured in orders of magnitude and is quantified via exponential functions; i.e., logarithms.

The last row of the table shows the ratio of workload stated in people-years, $K/12$, to the peak programming staff. This ratio is handy in evaluating an estimate that says, "I need so many programmers to develop so much code." The ratio quickly explodes the programming number to a project number. Considering the size of the ratio for large jobs, such a rule-of-thumb is almost essential.

The guidelines fit the table which, itself, is only broadly representative of programming systems experience. More detailed models of project life cycles are given in Chapter 3.

1.5.2   Changes in Workload

Referring back to the assumptions behind workload estimating, it is important to recognize that an estimate depends on the quality of system design. The program units must be the right size for the programmers and the managers must be given manageable assignments. They can do everything within their span of control and conceptual ability. Anything outside their range cannot be done no matter how much effort they expend. As a consequence, a poor design (or an unexpectedly low skill level) can cause an estimate to blow up. The effects can be surprising. Take the case where one manager is unable to control an assigned subsystem.

n = elements in system

s = elements in manager's subsystem

p = programmer productivity

a = workload expansion factor

Estimated labor units = $a(n/p)$

When the subsystem of s elements is recognized as a problem, it will either have to be reassigned in the belief that a new manager can do the job or redesigned to create two subsystems. Together, the two new subsystems may have s elements. More likely, m coordinating elements will have to be added, so now the total system has $n + m$ elements. Each of the m additional elements adds potential interactions at the lowest level of design. Since the development is partly complete, it is much more difficult tracing and/or blocking potential interactions at this stage than it was during initial design. In fact, m' elements may eventually have to be added to fix up the consequences of the first redesign decision. (Such recursive system growth will be ignored here. The related problem in programming system estimating and maintenance is discussed in later chapters.)

The status of the workload when s fails and r other elements remain to be done looks like this:

1. Work completed $a[(n - r)/p]$
2. Work wasted $a(s/p)$
3. New work required $a[(s + m)/p]$
4. Work remaining $a[(r + s + m)/p]$
5. Revised estimate of total workload (1) + (4)
   $E' = a'[(n + s + m)/p], a' \geq a$

The work done on the original s elements was, in effect, wasted. The total workload has increased by an amount equal to the number of elements in the revised design. In addition, the relative amount of management and support may increase depending on how the project organizes to handle the problem.

The cost of the wasted effort plus the cost of the replacement effort is referred to as *scrap and rework* in some cost accounting circles. A safety factor should include the amount by which a cost estimate is increased to allow for scrap and rework. The amount is determined from past experience and is usually given as a percent.

Brooks's warning against throwing in more "warm bodies" to solve a system problem [2] agrees with item 5 above. When a system becomes unmanageable, adding a lot of people merely makes the situation worse. They increase the workload still more when tasks are created to keep them busy. They also force a' to increase as extra management and support is added to keep things straight. A much better approach to the problem is to slow down the activity and simplify the problem so it can be solved with the same or fewer people. In other words, some slack should exist in the original project schedule to provide time for scrap and rework and, of course, to cover the variability in the original estimate. These points are discussed further in Chapter 3.

1.6 SUMMARY

A system is a structured assembly of heterogeneous elements that interact cooperatively to satisfy a set of functional and performance objectives. The elements can be individually simple, but when they are assembled, the aggregate is complex. Interrelationships are established among the elements which must be controlled for the system to be manageable. By imposing structure on the elements and by minimizing the coupling between elements, a system architect can reduce complexity and improve the system. A well-structured system is easier to understand, to build and operate, to modify, and to expand. Many structures are possible; therefore, it is useful to have some guidelines for comparing alternatives to find the design that is least difficult to implement. One set of guidelines has been presented which uses data coupling, control coupling, and program unit size to establish weights that can be summed to measure the relative complexity of a design. Additional guidelines relate complexity to workload. In the process, it becomes clear that complexity is a natural constraint on the size of a project. Some projects are just too complex to succeed.

The interesting thing about complexity is that, regardless of the nature of a system, its manageability is governed by the same constraints. In particular, Miller's "magical number seven" [25] keeps reappearing as an upper bound on the number of independent subordinates controlled by a single supervisor. The most effective social groups, be they software projects, school systems, business organizations, governments, or sporting clubs, are the ones with clearly identified leaders of various ranks supervising small groups of subordinates. As a result, some of the most innovative concepts for supporting large organizations, such as matrix organizations, are primarily management systems that preserve the effectiveness of small groups within increasingly complex large groups.

The naturalness of hierarchical organization can be traced back to the way primitive tribes arranged their affairs. In Europe, for instance, around the third or fourth century A.D., the basic unit of a barbarian tribe was the family. Several families would establish a cluster of houses for protection. This village with its neighbors formed a political unit called a "hundred." Hundreds were grouped into counties which, taken together, covered the territory of the tribe headed by a prince or king. Not only the size of the social units but their geographic distribution was structured. Christaller's Central-Place Theory [26] showed that tribes set up towns so as to equalize the distribution of people, goods, and resources. As a result, the towns tended to be equidistant. Recent archeological digs confirm Christaller's data. For example, Marcus [27] found a rigidly hierarchical lattice of sites in Yucatan, Guatemala, and Honduras. The ancient towns were arranged around four primary centers. Each primary served five to eight secondary centers, each of which, in turn, had a like number of tertiary villages.

Here, in the seventh to tenth centuries, a prototype social structure had evolved naturally into a hierarchical organization. Without the benefit of management science, the Mayans found an effective structure that had a limited span of control at each level. Is it coincidence that the span of control was the same as that now recommended for programming departments? Is it coincidence that the tribal complexes consisted of roughly equal elements? Or is the central-place theory one more example of the natural bounds on complexity in well-structured systems?

EXERCISES AND DISCUSSION QUESTIONS

1. Classify each of the following as a system or a nonsystem. Explain why you classify each item as you do.
   a. automobile
   b. fuel pump
   c. wheel
   d. book
   e. shelf of books in a library
   f. public library
   g. football game
   h. suit of clothes
   i. electoral campaign
   j. tool kit
   k. COBOL/FORTRAN/ALGOL/PL/I
   l. an ADD instruction.

2. The human body is a complex system.
   a. Name three subsystems of the human body. Why is it useful in biology and medicine to isolate such subsystems?
   b. Considering the hardware (physiology) and the software (mental processes), is the human body a conceivable or an inconceivable system, in your opinion?

3. A data-processing application requires a sort step. You are asked to select any one of three packaged sort programs. Which will be the least complex? Given the application flow:

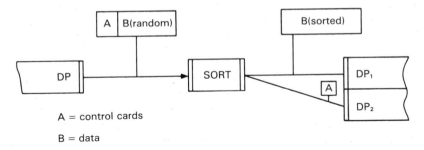

A = control cards

B = data

A = control cards
B = data
The control cards, identified by an A in position 1, are to be separated from the data, sorted in ascending sequence using a two-character transaction code in columns 13–14 as the key, and stored on tape or disk for program DP_2. The data is to be sorted in ascending sequence on a sixteen-character key consisting of record positions 1–10 and 21–26. Position 1 may contain any character other than A. The data is to be stored on tape or disk for program DP_1, which will start execution as soon as SORT is complete.

Assume A records are fixed length 60 characters and B records are fixed length 256 characters. The file is normally contained on one reel of tape, but occasionally runs to two reels. Assume you have all the physical resources required.

The available sort packages do the following:

a. SORTSEQUENCE takes an input stream of any length and sorts it into a single sequence. Records in the input stream must be fixed length; the length must be given in a header record. Record lengths up to 20,000 characters are allowed. All records will be sorted on a single key (given in the header record) which may consist of up to 100 characters from up to five fields anywhere in the data record. Multiple tape files are accepted as input when the MTF bit is a "1" in the header and a trailer record indicates the end of file.

b. SORTFILE takes an input stream not exceeding one physical tape or disk and sorts the input data into one or more sequences. Each record must contain a transaction code in position 1 and a length code in position 2–4. Alternatively, the length of record for a transaction code can be given in a header identified by zero in position 1. Maximum record length is 1000 characters. The header is required to specify key location, sort sequences, and error controls. In the absence of a header for any transaction code, records will be sorted in ascending sequence on positions 3–15. Duplicates will be retained. Sorted records will be stored on a physical device of the same type as the input device. An index to the file locations will be placed at the origin of the output device.

c. SORTGENERATE   takes an input stream of any length and composition and sorts it to meet specified conditions. Control cards are required which specify input characteristics, sort controls, and output characteristics. Part of the control cards will be analyzed in pass 1—GENERATE—to produce an optimal sort program to be executed in subsequent passes. The user must supply input transaction codes, record keys, record lengths (variable length records are allowed), number of records per transaction code, number and names of physical devices used for input and output, resources available for intermediate merge passes, sequences desired per transaction code, error conditions for duplicates, missing keys, prohibited keys, and length violations. Parameters in the control cards designating key location are passed directly to the pass 2 sort program.

4. Table-driven control is intended to increase system integrity by preventing one module from modifying another. The table places control information in a common data area. How can you ensure that the table is not accidentally or intentionally changed to contain incorrect data?

5. You discover a program module 2000 lines of code in length. It has an easily corrected bug. What are the pros and cons of breaking the module into smaller modules (of 30 to 50 lines each) as you fix the bug?

6. The weight of the information retrieval subsystem designs given in the text was calculated from module layouts which show exactly where each data item went. Alternatively, the data outputs can be lumped as though all data items go to all sinks. The resulting values are given below:

Module	Logical subsystem Explicit value	Lumped value	Structured subsystem Explicit value	Lumped value
1	17.42	19.75	17.38	19.71
2	12.00	12.67	10.00	10.00
3	20.40	26.07	25.80	26.34
4	12.17	12.84	12.17	12.84
5	15.33	17.00	15.33	17.00
6	10.26	10.26	7.50	7.50
7	14.46	16.13	7.83	7.83
8	12.60	13.93	7.17	7.17
9	12.00	13.50	8.00	8.00
10	10.83	12.33	7.33	7.33
11	7.00	7.00	7.00	7.00
12	14.33	14.33	6.33	6.33
13	14.50	14.50	6.50	6.50
Total	173.30	190.31	138.34	143.55

a. What are the benefits, if any, of using the explicit approach instead of the lumped approach?

b. Module 3, SEARCH, actually lumps FILEIN LOC FORMAT on the data output interface to modules 6 through 13 when modules 11–13 have no use for LOC or FORMAT. What are the pros and cons of the design as shown?

REFERENCES

1. Aron, J. D. "Apollo Programming Support." *Software Engineering Techniques.* Edited by J. N. Buxton and B. Randell. Brussels, Belgium: NATO Science Committee, April 1970.

2. Brooks, F. P., Jr. *The Mythical Man-Month.* Reading, Mass.: Addison-Wesley, 1975.

3. Lorin, H., and Deitel, H. M. *Operating Systems.* Reading, Mass.: Addison-Wesley, 1981. Also, Auslander, M. A.; Larkin, D. C.; and Scherr, A. L. "The Evolution of the MVS Operating System." *IBM Journal of Research and Development* 25, no. 5 (September 1981).

4. Preparata, F. P., and Yeh, R. T. *Introduction to Discrete Structures.* Reading, Mass.: Addison-Wesley, 1973.

5. Sackman, H. *Computers, System Science, and Evolving Society.* New York: John Wiley and Sons, 1967.

6. Beer, S. *Platform for Change.* New York: John Wiley & Sons, 1975.

7. Burchard, H. "A-Warning Proves a Blunder." *The Washington Post,* February 21, 1971.

8. Flagle, C. D.; Huggins, W. H.; and Roy, R. H. *Operations Research and Systems Engineering.* Baltimore: The Johns Hopkins Press, 1960.

9. Molnar, J. P. "The Telephone Plant of the 1970s." *Bell Laboratories Record* 49, no. 1 (January 1971).

10. Reed, R. "Oh, What a Lovely Murder: A Chat with Cinema's Mr. Macabre." *The Washington Post,* June 11, 1972.

11. Alexander, M. J. *Information Systems Analysis.* Chicago: Science Research Associates, 1974.

12. Thierauf, R. J. *Systems Analysis and Design of Real-Time Management Information Systems.* Englewood Cliffs, N.J.: Prentice-Hall, 1975.

13. Jones, J. C. *Design Methods.* London: John Wiley & Sons, 1970.

14. Myers, G. J. *Reliable Software Through Composite Design.* New York: Petrocelli/Charter, 1975; and Myers, G. J. "Characteristics of Composite Design." *DATAMATION* 19, no. 9 (September 1973).

15. McCririck, I. B., and Goldstein, Robert C. "What Do Data Administrators Really Do?" *DATAMATION* 26, no. 8 (August 1980).

16. Aron, J. D. "Fitting MIS into the Organization," in *MIS: Information Systems for the Manager.* Washington, D.C.: The Institute of Management Science, Washington, D.C., Chapter, 1970; and Aron, J. D. "Information Systems in Perspective." *Computing Surveys* 1, no. 4 (December 1969).

17. Date, C. J. *An Introduction to Database Systems.* Reading, Mass.: Addison-Wesley, 1981.

18. Busacker, R. G., and Saaty, T. L. *Finite Graphs and Networks—An Introduction With Applications.* New York: McGraw-Hill, 1965.

19. Elson, M. *Data Structures.* Chicago: Science Research Associates, 1975.

20. Henry, S., and Kafura, D. "Software Structure Metrics Based on Information Flow." *IEEE Transactions on Software Engineering* SE-7, no. 5 (September 1981).

21. McCabe, T. J. "A Complexity Measure." *IEEE Transactions on Software Engineering* SE-2, no. 4 (December 1976). See also, Berliner, E. "An Information Theory Based Complexity Measure." AFIPS Conference *Proceedings 1980 NCC.* Arlington, Va.: AFIPS Press, 1980.

22. Ferdinand, A. E. "A Theory of System Complexity." Joint National Meeting ORSA, TIMS, AITE, November 8–10, 1972, Atlantic City, New Jersey; Ferdinand, A. E. "Quality in Programming." IBM Systems Development Division Technical Report 21.485, Kingston, New York, IBM Corporation, June 1972.

23. Schwartz, J. T. "On Programming. An Interim Report on the SETL Project, Installment: Generalities." Courant Institute of Mathematical Sciences. New York: New York University, February 1973. Also, "Principles of Specification Language Design with Some Observations Concerning the Utility of Specification Languages." *Algorithm Specification.* Edited by R. Rustin. Englewood Cliffs, N.J.: Prentice-Hall, 1972.

24. Grosch, H. R. J. "Why MAC, MIS and ABM Won't Fly (Or, SAGE Advice to the Ambitious)." *DATAMATION* 17, no. 21 (November 1, 1971). Also, Broad, William J. "Computers and the Military Don't Mix." *Science* 207 (March 14, 1980).

25. Miller, G. A. "The Magical Number Seven, Plus or Minus Two: Some Limits on Our Capacity for Processing Information." *The Psychological Review* 63, no. 2 (March 1956). This article also appears in *The Psychology of Communication.* Baltimore: Penguin Books, 1969.

26. Berry, B. J. L., and Harris, C. D. "Walter Christaller: An Appreciation." *Geographical Review* 60, no. 1 (January 1970).

27. Marcus, J. "Territorial Organization of the Lowland Classic Maya." *Science* 180, no. 4089 (June 1, 1973).

2
Total System
Behavior

There are many ways of looking at a system. Goethe said, "The conclusions of men are very different according to the mode in which they approach a science or branch of knowledge; from which side, through which door they enter."[1] Each point of view is like a new dimension and, in fact, every system is multidimensional. Managers look at a system differently from designers whose viewpoint is different from that of evaluators, and so on. At any given time, each individual concentrates mainly on one facet of the system to understand it in depth. The limited conceptual abilities of human beings force them to focus their attention in this manner. Nevertheless, by consciously introducing structure into the system, they can control a complex project. The structured point of view permits them to look at a limited amount of data and draw conclusions about broad aspects of the project [1].

Two generally useful structures are the hierarchy and the time sequence. *Hierarchical structure* breaks the system into smaller subsystems. It displays *interactions* clearly at every level of the system and has several advantages for analysts:

- Each level of the hierarchy can be dealt with as an entity without the need for details about lower levels.

- The rules for structure interactions that apply at one level apply to all levels so that uniform analysis and design techniques can be used.

---

1. J. W. V. Goethe, *Theory of Colors* (Cambridge, Mass.: MIT Press, 1970).

- Any element at one level of the system can be extracted and treated as a free body as long as its interface characteristics are not changed. In other words, changes within an element need not affect anything outside the element. This permits team members to proceed in parallel. (A strict hierarchy in which program nodes call only lower nodes has this property. General hierarchies exist which permit calls upward and sideways in which case there may be external effects of internal changes.)
- The hierarchy implies a chain of command which is useful in making design and organizational decisions.
- The hierarchical structure is easy to document since element relationships can be completely described level by level.

Time-sequence structures display *activities* effectively. By relating the elements of a system to a time scale, schedules and estimates can be prepared. Analysts can then see:

- Who is assigned to each task
- Which activities can be done in parallel and which must run in sequence
- The critical path in the schedule
- What has been done and what remains to be done
- Which tasks are currently active.

Together, hierarchies and time-sequence structures can be used to record system data in such a way that, no matter what point of view is being taken to produce the data, the record accurately portrays the real system.

The point of view taken thus far in this book is that a program system is a hierarchy of interacting *programs*. This is an important technical point of view, but it ignores many facets of the development process. The most obvious omission is people. Programs can only be built if there is an organization in place to build them. The role of people in the development process is by no means limited to programming. All sorts of other interactions among people inside and outside the project must be considered. Personal style in management, design, or implementation—even in interpersonal relations—must be harnessed to advance the project. External pressures and internal conflicts of interest must be prevented from distorting the project. Different motivators must be provided as the program system develops because each stage of the process calls for a different emphasis on what people are doing. Choices must be made as to the timing of personnel changeovers so that the best management is in charge of the best mix of people at each stage of the developing system.

Not everyone would emphasize hierarchical structures so much. Typically, people emphasize the one or two areas of activity that are most important to each individual personally. In this chapter, several such points of view will be covered, including the system development considerations related to: (1) people, (2) hardware and software, and (3) tools and techniques. Later chapters will offer guidelines for dealing with each of these aspects of a system as part of a cohesive development life cycle.

2.1 PEOPLE

An observer looking at a program system through special glasses that filter out everything but the people developing the system will see:

- Analysts—gathering data on system requirements, preparing requirements documents, determining potential solutions to system requirements, and making trade-off analyses to select the best approach

- Programmers—planning and designing programs, writing programs for the deliverable system, writing programs to assist other programmers, writing programs to test the end items, writing programs to assist the project control office, maintaining existing programs or improving the computer facility program system, preparing software models and evaluation tools to predict system performance, teaching, etc.

- Clerks—preparing correspondence, typing and distributing system documentation, keypunching computer inputs, filing, and carrying jobs to and from the computer

- Managers—supervising development groups, support groups, and control groups, negotiating scopes of work, establishing commitments, and implementing policy

- Other development project personnel—computer operators, marketing representatives, standards and procedures monitors, technical writers, layout and graphics specialists, human factors engineers and test subjects for on-line applications, experts in math, physics, economics, or other appropriate subjects

Separate from this group, but of no less importance, are the prospective users of the system. Individual users may not get personally involved in development activities; their requirements will be presented by intermediaries. The quality of user participation in program system definition and development will vary greatly according to how well the intermediary understands, supports, and represents the user.

Surrounding the development group are additional support activities: financial planners and accountants, long-range business planners, administrative and technical staff people, personnel staffs, facilities management and maintenance people, and many others. All of them will be maintaining a constant dialogue with the development team, often providing a check-and-balance on project decisions. Budget variances will be questioned by

Finance who will ask the responsible manager for a plan to compensate for
the variance. When a manager plans to promote a programmer, without a
change in work scope, someone from Personnel may intervene to find out
why, all of a sudden, the job has been reclassified. Or perhaps a manager
who plans to install an additional program checkout computer will clear the
order through Finance and Procurement only to find that Facilities will not
or cannot provide space for it. Each of these situations can be resolved
through negotiation, but only at the expense of additional effort on the part
of each individual. As emphasized earlier, the communications between the
development groups and the peripheral groups represent bona fide system
interactions.

Some of the people relationships are external to the project; they represent various demands, pressures, or suggestions passed to the project
through the manager or through direct contacts between project members
and outsiders. Internal relationships are the ones put in place by the project
manager plus those that existed previously or arise spontaneously.

2.1.1   Lines of Authority

Consider a large project to develop a real-time multiprocessor system program for air traffic control in the United States. The customer is the federal
government. The project is the responsibility of a prime contractor who has
subcontracted various parts of the programming to the companies who
manufacture the special radars and displays attached to the multiprocessor.
There are several development groups, each with its own support organization. The prime contractor supplies additional administrative people to coordinate the subcontractors and to provide a single project interface with
the customer. The formal line of authority flows from the prime to the subs.
This fairly clean interface is complicated by a number of *"invisible"* rela-
tionships that exist in the overall environment. Each affects the decisions of
the program system manager:

■ Political relationships   As a national program, air traffic control requires not only the support of Congress but also that of the state and local
officials whose jurisdictions cover major air terminals. Political support is
based on initial forecasts of system delivery dates. Key supporters advertise
the forecasts as firm commitments in order to convince their constituents to
support the program. Unfortunately, if any slippage occurs the officials are
embarrassed and may bring pressure to meet the original date at the expense
of performance. They may even withdraw their support and, with it, the
funds to complete the project. A second exposure affects long projects that
span an election year. If the incumbents lose their seats to an opposing
party, there is the risk that the new officials will restructure the system to be

able to claim it as their own conception. They could also kill the project because they consider it unjustified or simply because they must fulfill a campaign pledge to economize.[2]

■ Organizational relationships   Within the customer's organization are groups with special interests in engineering, research, operations, or finance. Each group is concerned with the effectiveness of air traffic control as measured by their standards. One of the groups is the official interface with the prime contractor, but all of the others usually have enough access to the development team to make their views known. The result is that conflicting demands are made on the developers. It may be that the operations people want an input based on an existing radar, whereas the engineers want to design a new radar and the researchers want to be able to experiment with a variety of sensing systems. Ordinarily, normal procedures for deciding which path to follow will lead to a single customer position. It is also possible, however, for a power struggle to develop within the customer's organization that prevents the decision process from working. This invariably delays the development project.

■ Labor relations   The air traffic control system is operated by professional controllers who have contributed substantially to the technical statement of requirements for the system. The controllers have nontechnical interests as well. Their concerns with job security, job complexity, and employee responsibility relate to the impact of an automated system on them as individuals. They express their concerns through a labor organization, which has no official status in the development project but that has a definite influence on project decisions.

■ User relationship   Users of an air traffic control system include pilots and passengers. Their main concern is flight safety without regard to cost—or so it would appear. More accurately, the users want to improve safety and, at the same time, increase air traffic, but they do not want to increase the cost of flying. Thus a system design in which system programs have been improved at the expense of a special hardware device in every plane represents a trade-off that might be unacceptable to small plane pilots. They have an association to voice their protest. Likewise, a design that limits traffic would draw criticism from the airlines and the public. They, too, have effective representation.

These relationships influence the requirements, constraints, and policies established by the customer and passed on to the project manager. They are invisible because the project manager is unaware of the true source of the

---

2. Many government projects are designed to complete a major operational milestone prior to an election. The practice ensures that the expenditures will have a pay-off.

customer's orders. In a few cases, a policy will make no sense. It will appear entirely arbitrary and unjustified. Sometimes, the problem is due to the customer's not thinking through the issue. Joint discussions with the project manager could lead to a better definition, but there are times when attempts to understand the policy will be unsuccessful and a project manager who pushes too hard will be turned off. In these situations, the project manager should realize that the customer has issued an edict in order to satisfy irresistible demands from external sources. Unless the edict is intolerable, the manager should fit it into the system.

How can an invisible relationship be so powerful? Figure 2.1 suggests an answer.[3] The individual system programmer gets direction from above and, in addition, communicates with a limited number of support groups. At a higher level of the system, the project manager nominally takes direction only from the customer's representative; however, for practical purposes, all of the many direct interest groups associated with the project and a still larger number of indirect groups affect the manager.

Management *direction and authority* potentially constitute the power to make and enforce decisions regarding the duties of subordinates. Management direction and authority should flow down the chain of command in the form of *orders*. *Information* should flow down, up, and sideways. Occasionally the two concepts become confused when a routine information exchange is interpreted as an order. This can happen accidentally, as when a casual comment by a high-level manager is taken as an order by a junior department member. All remarks of high-level managers carry the stamp of authority simply because junior people may not feel free to question or discuss them. Experienced managers should avoid accidents of this type by clearly identifying orders and by always using the chain of command for propagating orders. They should also watch their words in mixed meetings of various department levels. Intentional confusion of authority also occurs. Since *communication* is indispensable at all levels of a system, there are always avenues of access between different interest groups and individual development team members. For instance, sometimes a user will tell a programmer what is needed, fully intending the programmer to inter-

---

3. Baram [2] writing in 1973 about the relationship between technology and society reflects the current view that indirect interest groups will gradually achieve a direct control of technological decisions through legal and governmental processes. In other words, the "public" will have a direct, formal role in assessing technology that impacts the quality of life. His model of the process is quite similar to Fig. 2.1. The influence of ecological groups in the United States in the 1970s fit Baram's model, although economic concerns weakened the influence in the early 1980s. A more sustained example of public influence occurs in those countries where labor organizations are mandatory and there are procedures for labor to participate in management decision making.

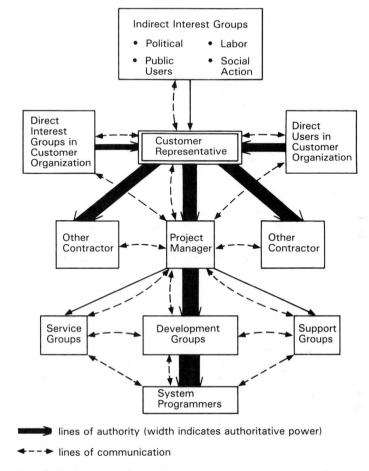

Fig. 2.1 System of people.

pret the information as an order. Of course, the user has no direct authority over the programmer; he or she is simply trying to bypass the normal chain of command. In the process, the user may generate both technical and budget problems. The appropriate protection against this behavior is: (1) a strong chain of command, (2) a reporting system to show exactly what is going on, (3) a clear set of procedures governing who is authorized to do what, and (4) an enforcement plan to make the procedures work. Inexperienced programmers or those who normally work alone may see such procedures as unwelcome constraints. Experienced team programmers see them as an aid to meeting their objectives.

Project managers, themselves, may get confused about their authority. They realize the need for timely, controlled communication of technical and administrative data, and they know there is a selling job to be done as well.

- The sponsors must be continually motivated to support the project. Managers motivate them by presenting achievement reports and requesting concurrence with future plans.

- Users have to be prepared for the introduction of the system. Managers see this is done through teaching, distributing reports, meeting with user groups, advertising, and other forms of communication.

Being the focal point of these communication processes, some managers fall into the trap of thinking that they are actually running the show. The fact of the matter is that they have no authority at all over the direct and indirect interest groups. At best, they can win the interest groups over to their way of thinking by good communication.

When a good relationship exists, decisions are the result of mutual agreement. Then the distinction between lines of authority and communication lines becomes unimportant. When a project manager has not established rapport with his counterparts, conflict can be generated. The symptoms of a poor relationship are pretty easy to identify. One symptom is common: Given a specific requirement by the customer, the project manager decides to provide something different. Usually, the project manager knows how to improve on the specification; nevertheless, this is a mistake on the part of the project manager. Instead of ignoring the authority of the customer, proper behavior would be to explain to the customer why the original specification is deficient and why the proposed solution is preferable. Then, after the customer has evaluated the alternatives and decided which way to go, the project manager should abide by the decision.

Another symptom of a poor relationship is a decision by the project manager to satisfy the requirement of some interest group without coordinating with the customer's representative. The decision may be technically acceptable, but, in making the decision, the project manager risks upsetting the balance among the interest groups. The customer has gone to a lot of trouble to satisfy the conflicting interests of all parties by giving concessions in some areas in order to protect plans in other areas. Wherever possible, the customer made these tradeoffs without getting the project manager involved in the politics. It is very important that no additional concessions be made without a thorough analysis of their impact; therefore, the customer does not want to be bypassed by the project manager.

2.1.2   User/Buyer Relationships

A special type of external relationship similar to the customer/interest group relationship can exist in the customer's organization. This is the case where the customer is represented by two people: the *user* and the *buyer*.

Both are in direct contact with the project personnel, but only the buyer has authority over the project manager. The distinction occurs in many organizations:

- In government contracting, the procurement procedures are so detailed that only specialists can implement them properly; therefore, procurement offices are established to negotiate and administer contracts with vendors. This leads to efficient contract administration, but it forces the ultimate user of the product to work through the procurement officer to have his or her requirements reflected in the contract.

- In business data processing, the user is often a functional department manager such as the Personnel Manager. To make sure the user defines jobs that meet the local standards for establishing data bases and scheduling production computer runs, a control group is often established to "buy" the appropriate package from a systems or applications programming group on behalf of the user.

- Where several user departments are jointly sponsoring a new data-processing system, a "steering committee" may be set up to represent the users. The committee will usually have one part-time member from each interested department. Because of its makeup, a steering committee tends to limit its role to review and decision making. It seldom provides technical leadership.

- In computer companies, software systems may be included in the sales catalog. Here, the user is the unknown customer who will eventually buy the computer. Again, an intermediary is established; in this case, a product planning or product marketing group that negotiates with the development organization for the best customer-oriented software.

Each of these situations creates a problem for the project manager. As shown in Fig. 2.2, the user/buyer distinction tends to create two bosses.

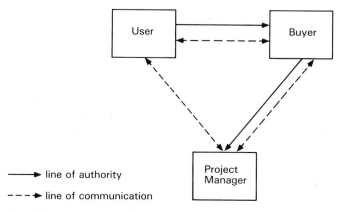

Fig. 2.2   System participants.

Only the buyer is authorized to direct the project manager and to control funds, but the user is the sponsor of the project and the only person who can tell if the product is any good. That makes it important for the project manager to respect the user's wishes.

In the preceding examples of "users," it is obvious that the user is often diffuse. One or more departments want to obtain a new data-processing system for any number of *end users*—the department members or department clients who will ultimately use the system. The "user" is many voices trying to speak as one (or remaining silent). The buyer, on the other hand, is quite often one person. The project manager may find it easier to respond to the buyer because the buyer's objectives are more easily obtained and clearer than the "user's."

If communications were perfect and motives were never influenced by job objectives, the user/buyer relationship would be transparent; i.e., the project manager would think he or she was talking only to the user. That is not the way things work, however. The user's requirements are vaguely stated and subject to change. When the buyer freezes the requirements into a contractual document, the words do not—and cannot—represent perfectly what the user wants. Furthermore, the user is interested in function, performance, and quality, regardless of cost. The natural tendency of the user is to find ways to improve the system as it grows. When this happens, project costs increase and the contract period lengthens. The buyer, on the other hand, is motivated to administer the contract as written, controlling cost and schedule above everything else. A natural tendency is to delete function in order to achieve or improve on cost objectives.

Obviously, the buyer can be too conservative and reject changes that are critical to the success of the system. Similarly, the user can be reckless and make requests that explode the cost and complexity of the system. Together they form a check and balance on the content of the contract; yet their interaction frequently squeezes the project manager to agree to something without knowing whether it has been fully agreed to by both. Each will try to make the project manager an ally in the negotiation with the other, and whichever one loses an argument may blame the project manager for the outcome. There are two ways the project manager can provide self-protection: (1) establish strong change control procedures to prevent one party from modifying the job without the knowledge of all parties, and (2) participate in disputes only to the extent of making a fair presentation of the facts on both sides of the issue. This helps avoid accusations of bias or favoritism. Taken together, these two points show that the project manager is playing by the rules to do the best job for all concerned.

When an impasse is reached, as happens only too often, the project manager in a contract environment has a clear obligation to take direction from the official contract administrator. Even though the user's arguments are compelling and, perhaps, consistent with the project manager's own ideas, the buyer has the last word according to the contract.

In the absence of a contract, it is not so obvious how to resolve an impasse. Take the complex situation that can occur in a computer company where the programming project manager works for an engineering laboratory manager. System program requirements reach the project manager from several sources. Some come from in-house users who do the company's own data processing; some come from large customers who take the initiative to make their needs known. The bulk of the requirements, however, come from the product planning arm of the company. The planners have surveyed the market and boiled down the inputs to a priority list that they believe will lead to the largest sales volume. What does the project manager do when the priority list includes items that engineers think are impractical and omits items the engineers think are essential? It is probably unwise to accept the engineers' position just to please the boss. If the market data is correct, such a decision may lead to poor sales. Neither the engineers nor the planners have the clear-cut authority to make the decision. Therefore, a control procedure is required that *escalates* the decision to a higher level—to a manager with authority over both departments (Fig. 2.3) or to a steering committee. This may appear to inflate the problem out of proportion, but it is necessary. Otherwise, a decision will be made at the lower level on the basis of local interests and the outcome may be wrong for the company.

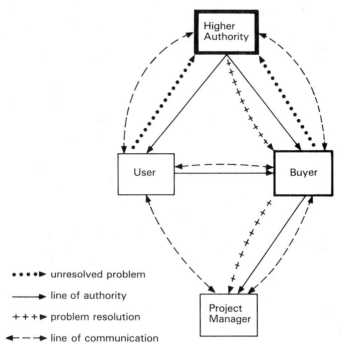

• • • • ► unresolved problem

——————► line of authority

+ + + ► problem resolution

◄ — — ► line of communication

Fig. 2.3 Problem resolution.

2.1.3   Internal Relationships

Within a project, numerous relationships affect the decisions of the project managers. The relationships, which constantly change in character and impact as the job progresses, sometimes support management and sometimes constrain it. In Chapter 5, the relations between managers are discussed, both with respect to managers in the same group and managers in separate groups. Line and staff relationships are also covered in Chapter 5 in conjunction with the overall dynamics of organization behavior. Problems that arise when one group hands responsibility to another on the completion of a phase of the project are discussed in later chapters. The appearance of handover problems in so many places emphasizes the dynamic nature of project management, as well as the importance of a clean, recognizable transfer of responsibility. Manager-employee relations show up in several chapters, particularly Chapter 5.

2.1.3.1   Goals and measurement

Relatively few factors govern the relations among the people within the organization. Chief among these is the nature of the goals and measurements applied to each person. While it is standard management practice to motivate everyone to put out a maximum effort ''for the good of the project'' or ''for the good of the company'' or ''for the national interest,'' these goals are too remote from everyday affairs to overcome individual self-interest. As Herzberg [3] points out, people are complex; they respond simultaneously to many motivations. At any given instant they will act in accord with the net positive or negative motivation provided by the situation and the environment. Furthermore, most people place a higher weight on advancing their personal interests than on supporting someone else's goals. Translated into organizational terms, this means that: ''I will help you when it's good for me and I will oppose you when your actions are bad for me.'' Within a direct chain of command, this motivation can be turned into a strong desire to do the job one is assigned because the manager who assigned the job also controls the employee's salary and advancement. It is perfectly clear to the employee that an outstanding response to the manager's request is worthwhile.

No such ''carrot and stick'' motivator exists between independent groups (unless they report to the same manager). Thus a computer center manager does not provide support to a development manager because the development manager controls the computer manager's career. The support is provided because it is the computer manager's job to support all development projects. The computer manager's goal, as stated here, conflicts with the development manager's goal. The computer manager is measured on the ability to provide support equitably to all requestors. The development manager is measured on how well the development project is run. Both define all their actions in terms of the goals they are measured on. Thus, "excellent turnaround for development programmers" may mean "users should receive their results in twenty-four hours" to the computer manager and "one hour" to the development manager. Similar conflicts arise in any interaction between a project team (devoted to one task) and a functional organization (supporting many projects). The conflicts are resolved or, at least, controlled by higher authority placing priorities on the various projects. This changes the function manager's goal; measurement is no longer based on equitable support to all users, but is now based on providing a graded level of support in which the highest priority user gets preference. At the same time, it tells all other development managers why they are unable to get immediate response from the computer center. *Priority setting* makes it possible for groups whose goals conflict to work together effectively.

It is often desirable to change conflicting goals to compatible goals. This is done by explaining to everyone involved that "for the duration of this project I am going to measure your performance in terms of your support to the project." The employees really have to believe the manager means it. Once they accept this redirection, they tend to respond well because they know their rewards depend on it. While this sounds like Pavlovian stimulus-response behavior modification repugnant to the individual, in practice it is ordinary people management. It works because people in teams develop converging interests as they build experience. Note that this technique does not require any reorganization. People in any group can be motivated to support another group by setting their goals to make self-interest merge with project objectives. Of course, this method can complicate a manager's job when half the department is working toward one goal and the rest toward another.

Each individual has both stated and tacit goals that motivate his or her actions. Each group also has goals—almost always stated rather than tacit—to which its actions are directed. The general objectives of the group are handed down in the form of mission statements and job assignments from higher management, usually after discussion with group members. The more detailed, specific objectives are usually developed within the group and represent how the group wants to carry out its assigned responsibilities.

2.1.3.2 Negotiation with peers

Considering that sooner or later every project manager will need help from a group whose goals are incompatible, there must still be a way to operate. The project manager lacks the authority to direct the other group to respond. An appeal to higher management will not work since the higher manager established and obviously supports the goals of the two groups that are in conflict. That leaves cooperation often achieved through *negotiation.* The thought that there has to be a give-and-take among peers within an organization is surprising to some people, especially new second-level managers (see Chapter 5), yet it takes only one conflict to impress a manager with the need for negotiation.

"I want Jack to give me three of his best people for six months but he won't do it. He claims they are needed to meet the schedule he has accepted for his own job. Yet both Jack and I recognize the importance of the overall project our jobs are supporting. Maybe we can work toward a mutual agreement where he'll let me have one of his people full-time and the others part-time if I promise to help him by modifying one of my tasks slightly so it will do part of his job as well." There are several points of interest hidden in this scenario:

- Negotiation requires mutual agreement among peers (or individuals temporarily acting as peers such as a manager and an employee working out the employee's objectives for the next year).

- The result of negotiation is usually a plan that is less than optimal in the eyes of all negotiators, even though all agree it is the best plan for the organization as a whole.

- The negotiation is usually related to resources, budgets, or schedules and tends to correct an imbalance caused by poor planning somewhere along the line (not necessarily by the negotiators—the problem may have been imposed on them).

- All parties to a negotiation must be prepared to give up something in order to gain something.

Further, it should be noted that the conflicts leading to negotiation are the natural consequence of system complexity. There is no implication that one party is trying to take advantage of another. There is no reason to suspect that dishonest plans or actions led to the imbalance addressed by the negotiators.[4] A complex system by its very nature leads to oversights, omissions, and incorrect assumptions during planning. Understanding this, negotiators can establish a cooperative atmosphere in which everybody is trying to arrive at the best solution for the system within the constraints placed on individual components.

2.1.3.3 Interface Agreements

In a smoothly running project, every system task is identified and assigned to someone. It takes a lot of planning, direction, and negotiation to reach this point. Even then, changes to the system requirements or specifications

---

4. In this book, management methods are presented for coping with complexity under normal conditions. Dishonesty, concealment, and personal antagonism are personnel problems addressed and eliminated by management methods such as those in Levinson [4]. They are not further addressed here.

will force new assignments to be made on a continuing basis. It is not enough, however, to assign a task to someone without explaining how the task is related to other elements of the system. There are many dependencies within the system affecting schedules and technical decisions. If B's task needs the results of A's task before B can proceed, there is not only a system dependency but also a personal relationship—the success of B depends on the performance of A. If the day arrives when B is to start and A is not finished, B is going to jump all over A. Furthermore, if A is able to say "Don't blame me. I never promised you anything on this date," a serious project management problem can develop. Individuals will lose confidence in the support they can expect from their associates. Conscientious individuals will start to provide their own support, duplicating what someone else is assigned to do and raising project cost. Less concerned individuals will develop a "who cares?" philosophy, waiting until their support arrives and ruining both the project schedule and the budget.

The solution to this potential problem is to define tasks as assignments to individuals and to document each task assignment in such a way that: (1) the assignee must *commit* to a specific result on a specific date, (2) the assignee knows who needs the result and when, and (3) the people who need the result know when it is committed for delivery.

These interface agreements prevent A from saying, "Don't blame me." Failure to deliver on time is a black mark against the delinquent. On the other hand, there is no point in using the interface agreements to point the finger at poor performers. The proper function of the agreement is to fix the commitments between people so they can monitor progress and adjust to problems before it is too late.[5] Thus, B can go to A and say, "You've committed to deliver a product to me in three weeks. Are you going to make it? Will it do everything described in the interface agreement? Do you expect any problems which are going to affect my plans?" Depending on the answers, B can cooperate with A and, perhaps, others to come up with a new plan that will preserve the total system schedule.

2.1.4 Focus of Management Attention

As soon as a project manager gets all the people interactions under control it will be time to adjust to the changing conditions of a dynamic system. Each decision of each person in the system is situation dependent. Consciously or unconsciously, each decision-maker asks:

- What are my goals at the moment?
- What action will do the most for me right now?
- What additional actions will position me most favorably tomorrow?

---

5. The important concept of commitment is addressed further in Chapter 4.

At the start of a project, when only the manager and a few designers are involved, the answers to these questions run along these lines:

- Goals   Plan and design a system that can successfully be built to the user's requirement.

- Action now   Structure the design so all the system interactions are clearly identified. This permits assigning the units to the development team with confidence that they can be assembled into the final product later.

- Future   Prepare a test plan and carefully document all system units and interfaces so the project can be controlled.

These points stress the importance of getting the system interactions right. The concept of "span of attention" says that a manager's attention must be focused on a limited number of things at one time. Putting two and two together, most managers during the design phase concentrate primarily on the interactions among units. Since interactions among units imply interactions among designers, the management of system structure consists of reviews and discussions in which the team as a group searches for omissions, errors, and opportunities for improvement in the system design.

As the design phase nears completion, individual units are assigned to individual implementers, and gradually the character of the project changes. From a small team activity, the project rapidly grows into a large set of individual activities. At this stage a manager's goal is to lead the developers to build the system units correctly and economically. The focus of management attention is now placed on manager-employee relations aimed at setting objectives, guiding and motivating individuals, arranging for support services, reviewing progress, etc. In addition, this is the time to inspect program units to see that they have the accuracy and quality required. In contrast to the design phase, managers concentrate on system units during implementation, not on system interactions. Their attention is directed to component details, not to system structure. They are concerned with people, not architecture.

At the end of the implementation phase, management reverts to its original focus on interactions. Here, as package integration and tests begin, the assumption is that all the units submitted for integration have been completely debugged. The only remaining errors are expected to occur between units because of problems in the definition or interpretation of interaction specifications. Finally, as summarized in Fig. 2.4, the product is released and subsequent maintenance and upgrade requires equal attention to structure and detail.

Two generalizations are worth stating regarding the changing focus of management attention:

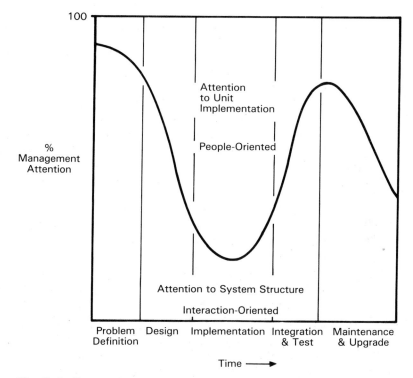

Fig. 2.4 Focus of management attention.

- Managers must be able to shift their focus as the project moves forward. If they cannot do it, they will not succeed. If it is known that a good design manager cannot also lead an implementation team, a suitable replacement should be brought in at the end of the design phase.

- Negotiations among managers should take into account the current phase each one is concerned with. By knowing where a manager's attention is focused, you can better understand his or her goals and motivations.

2.2 HARDWARE AND SOFTWARE

Project managers want to think of their project springing full-blown out of nothing without any constraints. The fact of the matter is that the constraints are numerous and varied. Some of them are discussed in section 2.1, but many project managers do not worry about people relationships; they are confident that their natural charm and unparalleled technical depth will cause each conflict or negotiation to come out the way they want it to.

In this section, a set of constraints is introduced that is not so easily dismissed. The constraints consist of hardware, in development, installed, or on order; and software, inherited from previous systems, specified by the user, or available from a library.

There is a strong resistance to modifying commercial hardware. This attitude is probably based on the practice in the data-processing industry of building general purpose computers to be used without modification. The hardware is offered as a package with a set of systems programs that can be adapted to a specific application. This practice is good for the majority of users. It creates a sharp line of demarcation between the vendor and the user. It assigns system responsibility to the vendor and application responsibility solely to the user. The traditional practice is changing as more and more users tackle complex systems and data-processing vendors supply a catalog of hardware and software components that can be mixed, matched, and modified to meet the specific needs of a single customer. It may then be necessary to allow modifications to the "hard" elements of the system. (Advances in microcode and microprocessors, covered later, facilitate modifications.) Until that time comes, the inviolate rigidity of hardware will force the program subsystem to absorb all the impact of device incompatibility, timing requirements, functional capability enhancements, and other application-dependent requirements. Program system design should take into account the difficulty and cost of modifying existing hardware and system programs. As a general rule, applications programmers should avoid changing anything below the system program user interface. Systems programmers in an information system department can make local modifications to vendor software, but should avoid changing hardware since they may interfere with system performance, maintenance, and vendor engineering upgrades. Systems programmers in a vendor organization work much closer to raw hardware and can influence its design. Their problem is that new hardware is often unavailable when they want it.

Modifiability of hardware versus software is illustrated in Fig. 2.5. The thickness of the walls around the various subsystems indicates their relative *impermeability to change*. The public utility transmission subsystem is unlikely to change regardless of what happens in the rest of the system. The centralized host computer is less likely to be modified than its software which, in turn, is less likely to be modified than the application programs that use it. Several types of input/output devices are shown, ranging from *hardwired devices* to completely programmable devices. Examples of the former are on-line disk or tape units.

Devices of this type have fixed characteristics that are controlled by host software and personalized by host applications. Hence, if you want to modify their behavior you do it by revising a program. *Intelligent I/O* has some built-in control and personality, noted in the figure as firmware, as

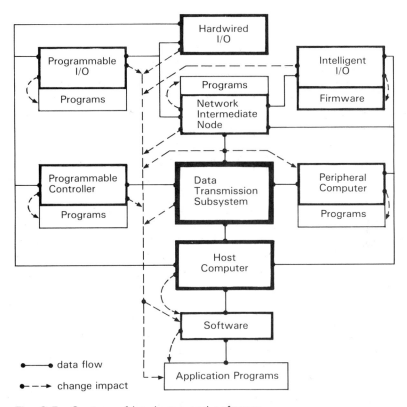

Fig. 2.5 System of hardware and software.

proposed by Opler [5]. The vendor can change the device by changing the firmware. Users, in general, can only modify the behavior of the device by changing host applications. In either case, the change is made by revising a program rather than physically altering the hardware. The third type of I/O is designed with a programming language and a means of loading and storing programs so that the user can program it directly. In this respect, a *programmable I/O* device is a small computer. Other similar units in Fig. 2.5 are the programmable controller, the network intermediate node, and the peripheral computer. Each of these can be attached to I/O or other computers by direct connection or via a data transmission link. In some cases, the unit may have multiple connections to peers, although many computers lack the parts or the software controls to support more than one connection.

A *programmable controller* is a computer with some firmware provided to drive various I/O devices. It also provides limited facilities for user application programs, usually written in a macrolanguage and assembled on a supporting host computer. Once set up with its application programs, the controller acts as a special-purpose device and is infrequently reprogrammed. Controllers are specified when system control is centralized but system components are geographically distributed. A *network intermediate node* is a computer, with or without full user programming support or firmware, distinguished by its primary use as the buffering and switching node in a data transmission subsystem. In some networks, the network intermediate node is directly attached to a host computer and is considered to be part of the host data-processing subsystem. As with a programmable controller, the node is generally initialized and left alone.

A *peripheral computer* is a computer with self-sufficient programming and operating facilities. It could be a host computer but often, as shown in Fig. 2.5, is a junior member of a hierarchy of computers. For example, a mini-computer controlling a process might be scheduled and provided with data by a higher-level maxi which, in turn, is managed by a large data processor. The latter is the host; the others are peripheral computers hierarchically subordinate to the host. At times, a peripheral computer will be used as a programmable controller or network intermediate node simply because it is the most economical unit available. More generally, the peripheral computer is selected because it can be programmed conveniently by the user. It is well suited to functions that are likely to require minor changes. It is the preferred unit in a system with decentralized control where each processor is independent but all the processors cooperate in a system network. When any one of these compute units is subordinate to another, changes in its behavior affect both its attached devices and the unit it is attached to. A subordinate unit is typically so limited in its capacity and flexibility that changes in its behavior require external support. Most often, the external support must come from the host software and application programs.

The ability to change a system component varies over the life of the component [6]. When a piece of hardware is being designed, there is a reasonable opportunity to change the design to accommodate different or additional features. Once the hardware has been released to the manufacturing department, changes become too costly and too disruptive of the manufacturing process to be considered. Absolutely essential changes are postponed until the hardware is built. They are then added as modifications to the existing box. In this form, the changes are always slightly awkward since they are not totally integrated with the basic design. The effect of jury-rigging the modification is generally seen in the form of performance degradation and increased maintenance cost. When the hardware box contains firmware, it is somewhat easier to make a modification; easier in the sense of requiring less mechanical effort or parts replacement. The firmware can usually be replaced by reloading a special storage unit. Extensive changes to firmware are hazardous, though. Since the microcoded programs are effectively an extension to the hardware, they must not contain any errors. Yet, as everyone knows, exhaustive testing of large programs is prohibitively expensive. Firmware can only practicably be changed by the original vendor who has the full test bucket used for the base product. Thus, once the hardware and firmware exist, changes to them for the benefit of a single project are avoided.

As an existing product ages, two factors further militate against changes. One is that the user generally lacks the intimate knowledge of the unit to write reasonable and reliable change requirements. The other is that so many people have become used to the unit behaving as it does that a change can interfere with their efficiency. Because of the first factor, changes to the data transmission subsystem, particularly a public telephone subsystem, are almost never advisable unless they are transparent to the rest of the system. In the case of terminals used by clerical personnel trained to enter data in a particular format, the second factor applies. Here, a change that reduces the amount of input may be feasible, but the cost of retraining the operators plus the cost of errors due to a change in format may offset the expected savings.

In summary, the hardest subsystems to change are the hardware and the procedures. The longer they have been in use, the more difficult it is to justify changing them. Therefore, if modifications to a system's function or performance are required, it is appropriate to try to make the changes by modifying only the software; in fact, changes should be limited to the application program system if possible.

"Software" turns out to be a more apt name than was originally intended. Early users of the term were trying to distinguish programs from products that could be touched and handled. The latter were already called "hardware," so "software" was the obvious antonym. In the context of a total system, software also happens to be the most malleable, most easily penetrated component of the system. The name fits perfectly.

2.2.1 Major Constraints Impacting Software

Whether a system is new or is simply an upgrading of an existing capability, several constraints are imposed by the hardware and software.

Schedule constraints

In at least half the data-processing systems development projects involving large teams, new hardware is developed as well as new software. Vendors who make hardware are in this category as are government agencies that specify unique hardware for military needs, telecommunications, and traffic control. Many business firms are also included as they build special purpose process control systems, reservation systems, and banking systems. Although it would be logical to design a hardware/software system *in toto* from the top down, the state-of-the-art does not allow it. The usual methods of system development start out as top-down efforts, but, as soon as the hardware has been specified, all attention turns to detailed hardware design. Software development is placed in suspense until the hardware is finalized, then software can proceed, using simulated hardware up to a point. Sooner or later, the software must be checked out on real hardware. Therefore, the delivery date for tested software is always later than the ready date for hardware. By-products of this state of affairs include two additional constraints:

- Last-minute changes are applied to the software since it is the only subsystem still under development.

- Test time is often truncated for the software in order to meet delivery commitments.

Both of these by-products increase the probability that the software will contain errors. These problems affect a vendor creating a new product line. They also affect a user who, for instance, is adding on-line terminals to an installed system. In both cases, a hardware commitment must be made before a detailed software subsystem can be completed. (A partial solution to the problem involves using higher-level languages to develop the software. This allows some software work to proceed in parallel with hardware planning. Of course, the value of this approach is reduced if no compiler is planned for the target machine or if the applications are highly machine-dependent.)

Budget constraints   Programming takes the brunt of budget constraints as a consequence of schedule constraints. By the time programming is well under way, the budget is substantially used up. Managers exert strong pressures at this time to avoid overruns. All the pressure is applied to programming implementation and test because that is where the current expenses are incurred. Yet, the programmers are also being forced to absorb all the changes due to problems in other subsystems; therefore, the programmers are least able to predict the cost of their subsystem and most likely to exceed their original cost estimates. Clearly, strong budget controls based on realistic estimates (and charge back procedures to bill the requester for changes) should be applied throughout a project to avoid making the programmers look like villains when, actually, they are victims.

Modularity constraints   A common constraint affecting program design is one resulting from inadequate or unbalanced hardware capabilities. For instance, a particular program function, such as a polling routine, may naturally take 1000 bytes of storage for itself plus 100 bytes for each device it polls. It would need 11,000 bytes to hold input strings for 100 terminals. If the box on which this program runs provides only 5000 bytes for polling, some of the terminal input space must be placed in bulk storage. In addition, the polling program may grow to 2000 bytes after the roll-in/roll-out capability is added. In this example, the mismatch between the predetermined size of a hardware component and the nominal size of a program results in extra programming cost and undoubtedly worse performance.

Recoverability constraints Any system that passes data from one subsystem to another must maintain some sort of audit trail in case a subsystem fails. The audit trail can consist of very simple procedures, such as keeping redundant copies of data or building in error control and acknowledgment routines. The idea is to: (1) know that a process has been completed correctly, and (2) be able to reconstruct a process that fails. The constraints in this area show up when a design for recoverability overloads one or more system components. Either the system capacity must be increased or recoverability compromised.

Compatibility constraints *Compatibility* is often essential to orderly growth. Compatibility is a very strong constraint. Thus two disk drives are not compatible if the user must reformat data files to change disks. Two processors are not compatible if timing differences on one cause errors in programs that run correctly on the other. Two programs are not compatible if their outputs can differ for given inputs. The mechanism for achieving compatibility is not important. It can be done by substituting proportionately faster circuits (or program routines), by emulating, by adding adapters, or any other method that is invisible to the user. The key point is that the user must see exactly the same results regardless of which system is running the job.

In practice, large high-speed computers tend to have more storage and I/O devices than do small slow-speed computers. That, in itself, presents no problem as long as the large system contains a subset identical to the small system. Then a program written for the small system will run on the large system and, at worst, some of the large system capacity will be wasted.

The situation begins to get sticky when systems programmers extend the operating system to accommodate the additional devices that can be attached to the large computer. The operating system they install on the large machine is different from that on the small machine due to new interactions. Perfect compatibility requires that there be no effect on user programs due to these interactions, but perfection is seldom achieved.

Rather than risk the loss of an investment in existing programs, users may avoid problems by restricting the flexibility of the systems programmers. Many users refuse to install a new version of an operating system unless it is completely compatible with their current version. In doing this, they sacrifice some growth capability, but they protect their bread-and-butter operations.

Eventually, growth pressures and changing conditions in the environment justify the design of a replacement system. At this time, compatibility becomes just one factor in the overall cost tradeoff. Nevertheless, it is a big factor when media conversion, reprogramming, and retraining are taken into account. That is why standards for character codes and programming languages are attractive; they minimize the cost of conversion. That is also why, even in major new systems, the procedures followed by the people in the system are disturbed as little as possible.

2.2.2   Example: Constraints in a Banking System

A trend toward on-line banking systems in the 1970s [7] shows how various constraints finally focus all change activity on the system software.

Banks process customer deposits and withdrawals. They make loans, handle checks and other transfers of funds for their depositors, manage investment portfolios, and carry on other financial activities. The pressure for on-line banking comes from the part of the business conducted between individual customers and branch office tellers. By giving the tellers immediate access to the master depositor accounts, the bank can give better service to the customer. The customer spends less time waiting in line and can get all kinds of information about an account in a few minutes. The bank benefits by reducing the cost per transaction since one teller can serve more customers with the on-line system. On-line banking received its impetus from banks in Europe, Japan, and Canada where a single national bank may have thousands of tellers. The benefits of going on-line were substantial for them. U.S. banks have relatively fewer branches due to legal restrictions, so they waited several years for the cost of such systems to come down.

All the banks had manual systems of some sort before going on-line. Typically, each teller would have an accounting machine to record transactions and update both a file card and the customer's pass book. All the transactions would be sent to a central location at the end of the day. There they would be posted to the master files in a batch.

Insofar as possible, the on-line system manager was constrained to order one standard type of teller terminal and use an existing central processing system for the master files. Because the number of terminals needed by any one of the large banks represented a huge sale for many companies making accounting machines or other keyboard devices, it was not difficult for the banks to solicit competitive bids for terminals. The result of the competition was often an award to a terminal vendor different from the central computer vendor. The large number of terminals also justified programmable controllers to handle clusters of terminals in a branch bank, perhaps doing a small amount of editing or calculation on transactions before shipping them to the host via telephone lines. Intermediate network nodes, acting as concentrators or multiplexers, as well as buffers and switches, would be used to organize data streams into efficient formats for transmission or computing. All of these items were as likely to come from terminal or communications companies as from computer companies. Other hardware, such as hardwired readers for magnetically-encoded or optically-encoded checks, intelligent inquiry consoles for loan officers and investment managers, or bulk storage devices for the bank's master account, could also come from diverse sources.

All the hardware procurement decisions would have been made and the devices ordered before the programmers were on board. When they started their design, they would try to use existing programs—unsuccessfully. The number of terminals might exceed table and buffer capacity, there would be no routine for communicating with the multiplexer, there would be no provision for automatically writing duplicate files, and recovery procedures would not be secure enough for the bank's purposes. So the programmers would design solutions to these problems. Next, they would calculate the time to process an on-line teller transaction. When they would count the number of disk accesses they would find, they could not handle the peak load.[6] That required a new priority dispatching procedure in the operating system. Then they would discover that the teller terminal must be disabled by the operating system long enough for the transaction to be processed and an acknowledgment returned to the teller. That interfered with the continuity of the teller's dialogue with the customer, so tellers had to be taught a new procedure. Most of these requirements could have been eliminated by adding features to the hardware, but that was not done. The sequence of decisions in a data-processing system freezes the hardware and the basic system procedures early. Corrective changes must be made through the software. The result would be a specially tailored application system unique to the bank.

2.2.3 Interface Modules

Programming may be required to compensate for incompatibilities in the hardware. Although much of the hardware used in data processing can be connected by standard plugs and sockets, the standard interface does not ensure that the devices are compatible. For instance, a string of bits issued by a processor to an output device may be interpreted one way by one type of device and differently by other devices. Both a printer and a graphic display may interpret the first sixteen bits in a string as a command; however,

---

6. The same overhead incurred once for a batch of items is incurred once for each on-line transaction. It is not unusual to find on-line transactions taking ten times as long to process as the equivalent item in a sorted batch.

the printer may read the bits as a command to "skip two lines" and the display may read them as an "erase screen" command. At a higher level, the message format displayed to a teller may not be the format transmitted by the terminal (Fig. 2.6). Programmers working with transformed data of this type must be careful to modify the transformation routine whenever they have cause to modify either the display or transmission data formats.

In a user/server relation (as shown in Fig. 1.4), the transformation is done in the adapter that is an integral part of the user code. In a peer relation or when many users access a standard server, it is convenient to build a bridge that does the transformation in an independent *interface module*. As shown in Fig. 2.7a, an interface module, either hardware or software (or

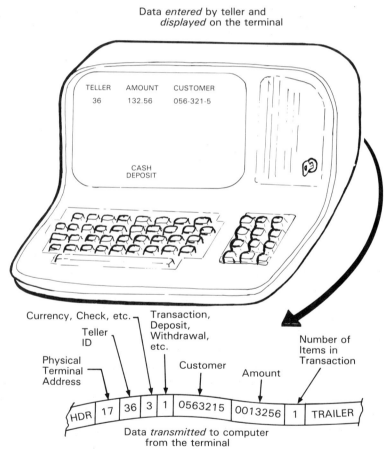

Fig. 2.6   Data transformations.

even a manual procedure), can be placed between any two modules, A and B. The function of the interface module, $_AX_B$, converts signals from A into the form required by B. The signals can represent either data or control information. Most such modules are designed and built to convert in only one direction; two-way conversion is handled by packaging two one-way converters together. Simple interface modules that only convert characters from one form to another (e.g., telegraphic Baudot code to computer EBCDIC or ASCII code) and match timing signals are often referred to as "stunt boxes" when in hardware or "conversion routines" when in software. Other interface modules such as the one that transforms the message formats shown in Fig. 2.6 are described by their function, i.e., "Teller Terminal Display to Transmission Format Converter."

A particular advantage of an interface module is that it isolates modules on one side of the interface from changes in modules on the other side. Thus if a bank decides to postpone its final choice of a teller terminal while it experiments with half a dozen candidates, an interface module can shield the teller data-processing routines from the terminal device routines. This

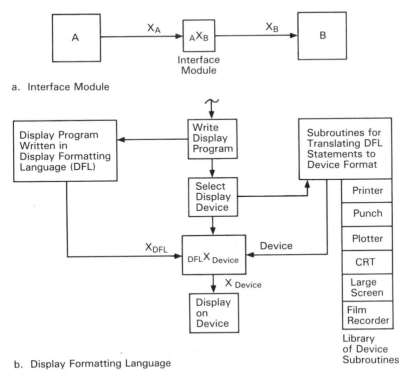

a. Interface Module

b. Display Formatting Language

Fig. 2.7 Interface modules.

technique, illustrated in Fig. 2.7b, was used in the Display Formatting Language (DFL) [8] on Project Apollo. Programmers and Apollo mission controllers who had to develop graphic displays were given DFL for that purpose. The language provided display-oriented macros that were easy to learn and use. A repertoire of subroutines was written to convert the DFL statements into commands to operate various installed and proposed display devices. Each subroutine provided one function of the type:

$$\text{DFL}X_{\text{Device}}$$

The subroutines formed a library. By slipping the right control card in with a run, a programmer could call on whichever one of the subroutines was most appropriate at the time. The user would designate the primary display unit and one or more alternates. If the primary display were intended for a large screen to be delivered six months in the future, the programmer could still see what the display images would look like by designating an available printer as the alternate. The technique of using an interface module separates the programming activity from the installation planning activity. It permits programmers to progress without depending on the delivery of specific hardware devices. When the hardware finally is delivered and checked out, installation of the programs debugged using DFL proceeds rapidly. Similar techniques are used in computer networks to do protocol conversion permitting devices of different types to communicate over a common link.

2.3   TOOLS AND TECHNIQUES

DFL increased the productivity of programmers by generalizing the output interface of the Apollo system. Programmers found DFL useful enough to want it in their bag of tools, available in a standard form in the computer facility. A support group was assigned to maintain DFL and show programmers how to use it. Money was included in the project budget to allow system-wide use of the DFL tool. It was a tool that interacted with the programs being developed, with the schedule of the project, with the computer use plan, with the training plan, etc. DFL illustrates that a tool used in a system is part of the system and must be considered as a contributor to system complexity as well as to system productivity.

A tool is designed to be used for a specific purpose and it must be handled according to instructions. Improperly used it can cause more damage than it is worth. Carpenters learn this early when they are taught how to use a tool, such as an adze for squaring off logs. The adze is built something like an axe with a horizontal cutting edge. The carpenter straddles the log and wields the adze in an arc, following through between the legs. Properly used, the adze rapidly produces a neat plane surface on a large log or plank.

Improperly used, the adze is dangerous. A misstroke can cut too deep and spoil the surface beyond recovery. More important, a loose grip, a glancing blow, or bad aim can turn the cutting edge into the carpenter's leg with bloody consequences. The carpenter has to be convinced that the benefit of using an adze exceeds the cost of buying and caring for one and, in addition, exceeds the cost of a mistake. Not surprisingly, the adze is found in relatively few carpentry kits.

Tools used in programming projects are similar to tools in a carpenter's kit. Each has an initial procurement cost, each has a continuing maintenance and update cost, and each requires proper training before use. The project must be adjusted somewhat to fit the tool. And, in spite of the precautions taken by the toolmaker and the user to avoid misuse, the tool can cause irreparable damage. A tradeoff analysis comparing the costs and potential risks to the potential benefits is a prerequisite to a commitment to a specific tool.

There are three dominant reasons why managers authorize the use of tools:

- Increase productivity.
- Improve quality.
- Improve resource and schedule control.

Really, all three are only different aspects of a single reason for justifying the expense of a tool; namely, that the value exceeds the cost.

Tools generate value by increasing the useful output obtained from a given unit of work. For a program system costing $60,000,000 containing one million lines of code, the cost of production would be $60,000 per thousand lines of code, or $60,000/KLOC.[7] Programmer productivity for this project may be 2500 instructions per programmer-year or 0.4 programmer years/KLOC. (At $60,000/person-year, 1000 person-years expended, 400 programmer-years, 600 support-and manager-years, as per Project C in Table 1.6.) A similar project using a tool that improves the productivity of programming and testing 25 percent should spend proportionately less. Allocating the 25-percent saving to programming and the test portion of support (200 tester-years) and leaving everything else the same, the project would use 850 person-years, costing only $51,000,000 plus the cost of the

---

7. The scale factor KLOC has been recommended for measuring many aspects of program development because it is based on a measurable characteristic of actual programs [9]. Although "lines of code" is defined in various ways (to include or exclude comments, to include or exclude instructions resulting from macro expansion, etc.), the number of source lines in a specific program can be determined simply by counting. The cost elements of the project that produced that program can be stated as $/KLOC, person-months/KLOC, defects/KLOC, etc., facilitating comparisons across products.

aid. In most organizations, an aid costing less than $9,000,000 would be attractive if it could ensure the indicated personnel savings.

An improvement of 25 percent in programming and testing is a very large improvement. Most aids do not promise that much; in fact, most aids do not *promise* any improvement. The value of an aid is almost always based on consensus opinion rather than on quantitative factors. Each aid is promoted by its originator on the basis of common sense and demonstration. Thus a technique such as structured programming is presented as "a logical way to write programs." A program is presented in two versions, one structured, the other not. If it is not obvious to the observer that the structured version is better, the demonstrator will ask a few questions about the program's function. The observer will find it easier to answer the questions by reading the structured version. In time, the observer will become convinced that structured programming has merit, arriving at this conclusion at about the same time as the bulk of his or her colleagues. Most techniques gain acceptance in a similar way. Initially, someone originates the technique to solve a practical problem. It works; so the originator or an associate uses it, becomes devoted to it, and proceeds to promote it outside one's immediate area. For a while, there is little response other than admiration for a resourceful problem solver. Gradually, a few more people independently pick up the technique until a ground swell of enthusiasm sweeps the technique into wide use. At this time, each new user adopts the technique because "everyone is using it; it must be good." And so it is. The technique would have been abandoned early if it were inadequate. Interestingly, it is usually after the widespread acceptance of the technique that people start to measure its effectiveness. The data obtained can be used to suggest areas for improvement but are too late to affect management decisions regarding the technique's value.

Various tools for software development are discussed or referenced in this book. In dealing with tools that help an individual working alone [10], the pros and cons of each tool are reasonably self-evident. The tools used by people on medium and large projects (including many already discussed) interact in more complex ways and may be harder to evaluate. For instance, an on-line programming system that allows a programmer to type in a source program, edit it interactively, and compile and run it without leaving the office may cut many days off the schedule for producing the unit of programming. Yet, with one hundred programmers on a single project, it may not be economically feasible to give everyone a terminal. This may cause queues to build up at each terminal and may force some people to leave the office to find an available terminal. This takes away much of the convenience and immediacy of on-line operation. A project that depends on interactive methods with no backup technique may be out of business when the support computers are not available.

Another factor affecting the large groups may be the inability of one computer to handle the whole workload. As will be seen later, the integration of a large program system using classical methods chews up many hours of computer time. The interactive terminal user generates the heavy integration and test workload by submitting completed program units for integration. The user then must compete with the integration workload in order to get time for editing and debugging interactively the program unit currently being worked on. When the workload fills the computer, the terminal response time gets worse and worse until it is no longer efficient. When the workload overflows the computer, a new problem develops—there is no longer a convenient way to refer to all parts of the system. A new communication and control procedure is needed to bridge the gap from one computer to the other. This is a quite difficult and expensive step; yet, without it, the basic interactive terminal loses some of its capability.

On large projects, the set of tools that was appropriate for small jobs must be augmented by additional tools designed just for large projects [11]. Most such tools emphasize standard ways of doing things and standard ways of describing things so everyone on the project can understand what is going on and so deviations from the plan are easy to spot in areas of: (1) analysis and design, (2) development and test, and (3) status control.

2.3.1 Analysis and Design

The steps in a project (Table 2.1) proceed from a general problem statement to a more specific requirements document showing exactly *what* the system must do. The analysts who develop the detailed requirements select what they believe is the minimum set of necessary, feasible items. System architects respond to the requirements by specifying what will be built—often a subset of the requirements statement—and how it will look to the user. The purpose of this step is to specify the external interfaces of the system and to allocate system functions to either side of the interfaces. From this point, the internal design of *how* the new system will be built can proceed step-by-

TABLE 2.1. PROGRAM PROJECT STEPS

Problem Statement
Objectives
Requirements
Architecture
High-Level Design
Detailed Design, Code, Debug
Integration, Test, Release
Operation, Maintenance, Upgrade
Termination

step. When the design is detailed enough to identify program units, the units are assigned to individuals who build them and submit the results for integration, test, and release to operations, followed, in most cases, by a period of maintenance and improvement. The large number of people involved in these activities makes it very difficult to have direct communication between all of the implementers and the key analysts and designers. The analysts/designers, knowing that they are writing specifications for people they may never meet, need a way of writing requirements/specifications that is unambiguous and easy to understand. The method should be particularly good for describing interfaces. It should be easy to maintain and modify and should be in a form that supports simulation. The components of such a tool are an analysis/design language, an automated specification program, a simulation capacity, and a methodology for ensuring complete, consistent results. Everyone must learn the language (which may be a programming language or simply a uniform way of writing specs). The other components are used mainly by the analysts/designers. The automated spec is a means of monitoring programs written by the implementers to see that they use the names and linkages called for by the spec. The output of this program can go back to the implementers to help them see where they went wrong. The simulator exercises a model of the system to check that, if all the specs are followed, the system will work. Simulation results are the designers' proof to the implementers that the spec is valid and should be obeyed. Now, even though no single designer or implementer understands the whole system, there is a single baseline spec that everyone can refer to in order to resolve questions.

2.3.1.1 Analysis and design languages

Languages for system analysis must work in the managerial as well as the technical areas of system development. They must cope with poorly defined user requests, unsolved technical problems, and arbitrary resource constraints. The indefinite nature of these aspects of analysis tends to result in more text segments—explanations of assumptions or justification of decisions—than are found in finished programs. Still, to improve clarity, traceability, and testability, and to maintain positive control of the contents of the requirements at all times, systems analysis languages have been developed. One example, based on the *Problem Statement Language/Problem Statement Analyzer (PSL/PSA)* originated by the University of Michigan *ISDOS* project [12, 13], is contained in *REVS* [14]. REVS is a *r*equirements *e*ngineering and *v*alidation *s*ystem developed by TRW for use in large real-time systems. The language component of REVS is *RSL*. RSL deals with system entities, messages, activities, and paths (R-nets) from an input interface to an output interface. (See Section 4.1.3.4 for an example.) The R-nets are constructed according to a small number of rules for where to start and how to proceed. The result is a requirements statement document that can be analyzed for completeness by the REVS support facilities. The specific TRW system has added capability for building models and executing simulations from the requirements and evaluating the feasibility of meeting the system performance requirements. All of this is embedded in a REVS library facility, which has a flexible inquiry capability permitting managers to investigate project status from a variety of viewpoints. It is significant that REVS includes "engineering" in its title. Experience with the hardware portions of large systems led engineers to adopt formal procedures for defining the project. REVS carries engineering discipline over to software activities. It is both a documentation language and a decision support tool.

A second analysis approach is *SADT,* the *structured analysis and design* technique of SofTech, Inc. Devised by Ross [15], SADT offers a graphic language, as it were, to show the functions to be performed by a system. As a graphic language, SADT is primarily a manual system although it carries enough descriptive data to justify on-line database support. Great emphasis is placed on the identification scheme used to label activity or data boxes and the arrows that connect the boxes, showing inputs, outputs, controls, and proposed mechanisms for implementation. As a result, SADT permits multiple hierarchical views of the system to be correlated with one another. Each viewpoint supports one important aspect of requirements analysis. It is often easier to develop the requirements in one class if the requirements of another class are separated out. Thus software requirements to satisfy all members of a user's group may provide one viewpoint and a huge list of functions to be performed. Different requirements as presented by a developer reflect concern for compatibility, economy, useability, and other factors that make up a smaller list of functions. SADT permits both analyses to proceed and then provides the means for bringing them together in order to decide on the list of functions to be adopted, which may be a compromise between the two viewpoints. The reference system that supports multiple views also provides the data needed to check the requirements document for completeness and consistency. SADT differs from REVS in that the analysis and design stages of a project are both supported by SADT. In fact, SADT methodology encourages iteration between requirements analysis and design at appropriate points. One such point is when analysis stops at an obstacle that could be removed by a design decision. For example, detailed requirements for the content and visual quality of a display may depend on knowing what physical device is to be provided by the implementer.

Generally, all analysis and design techniques including SADT postpone such decisions as long as possible. SADT, however, is very flexible in this respect, whereas some design techniques assume that analysis is complete before design starts. In the latter group are the design methodologies strongly influenced by the structure of commercial information systems departments where analysis is often done by one part of the organization—design by another. The analyst skills stress subject area experience (financial, personnel) and design skills stress data-processing experience. The departmental split permits economic justification for new work to be done by the analysts to avoid make-work tasks originating in the programming department. Within the programming department there is a need for tools, which raise the performance of all the staff up to an acceptable average. For this reason, design approaches such as Jackson's [16], Langefors' [17], and Warnier's [18] give rules for converting from the design language to actual programs.

Languages exclusively for program design have not achieved wide acceptance. Unlike procedural languages such as PL/I or COBOL, design languages do not have an agreed-upon core vocabulary. As a result, there is no one design language that everyone recognizes as the best. APL has been advanced by its advocates as the best available design language, yet APL is used more to evaluate designs and to create models for analysis than it is to document designs. The power of set operations available in APL is the basis of *SETL,* advanced by Schwartz [19] as a program development language. Less comprehensive proposals such as the *Module Interconnection Language (MIL)* suggested by DeRemer and Kron [20] tackle less of the development process, concentrating in this case on formalizing interface designs. It may be that no standard design language will ever exist because it is not needed. The evidence for this comes from the increase in informal program design languages that mix natural language (e.g., English) descriptions with statements in a high-order structured programming language (HOL) such as PL/I, ALGOL, structured COBOL, or structured FORTRAN. The informal approach builds on the work of Dijkstra [21, 22], Wirth [23], Mills [24], and others whose emphasis on top-down development makes good use of mixed format. The most successful informal languages or *pseudo-codes* establish a small number of key words/commands which are, in effect, the names of the basic control structures of structured programming [25]. Design is more concerned with the flow of control and data among program units than with the internal behavior of the units; therefore, it is natural and effective to use a design language that highlights control structures. Flow can be verified by deleting the natural language and compiling the remaining statements. It is a straightforward step to proceed from the pseudo-code design to a formally coded program.

2.3.1.2 Automated Specification

An automated specification is a specification written in a formal language and stored on-line. An automated specification tool is a program that can scan and manipulate the spec. The tool can also scan programs written in a formal language, preferably the same language used for the spec. The purpose of the tool is to compare a completed program unit to the spec and determine that, for each control statement, identifier, or variable in the spec, there is a corresponding, correctly named entry in the program. The tool will flag program references that have no counterpart in the spec. Deviations such as this are brought to the attention of both the programmer and the designer (or design control group) to ensure that the deviation is explained or corrected [26].

The choice of an informal design language makes it more difficult to build an automated specification tool. In order to verify that a program agrees with the spec, the tool must be able to recognize corresponding names, dimensions, displacements, and the like. Informal design languages do not have built-in enforcement procedures to require all programmers to use the same conventions. Obviously, rigorous rules take away much of the informality. Sooner or later, however, all references to the same object in a system must be reduced to a common base, usually in the specification for a program unit. Thus an automated specification tool would apply primarily to the lowest level of design definition. The designer can use any technique for draft specifications. The final specification must be free of natural language and contain only legitimate statements in a programming language. To make the spec self-documenting, appropriate comment statements should be included. The resulting spec is compilable because it uses HOL statements exclusively. At this stage, all system references must agree with the standard references in the glossary of system names and synonyms. As a design, however, the spec lacks the detail necessary to make the program units function.

As more is learned about proving the correctness of programs, it is likely that both designs and coded program units will be checked for correctness. To do this, assertions regarding the intended behavior of a program must be included in the spec. A *proof mechanism* built into the automated spec tool would test the assertion by carrying out the logical steps described by the spec or the completed program. The results would be particularly useful in large programs with many internal branch points. It is easy for the designer to get confused in such circumstances. Unfortunately, the state-of-the-art of correctness proofs does not span large enough program systems to solve the designer's problem [27]. Future promise of proof tools nevertheless justifies the adoption today of the discipline of making appropriate assertions as an aid to program verification. Once made, the assertions will be a useful aid to inspectors who examine the design and code at appropriate points in the project. The assertions will clarify the programmer's intent better, perhaps, than the program text.

2.3.1.3 HIPO

A simple procedure for preparing design specs so they are readable, well-organized, systematic, and useful to programmers is *HIPO* [28]. HIPO is a documentation technique for displaying *H*ierarchy, *I*nput, *P*rocessing, and *O*utput. It parallels top-down design by proceeding from overview to detail (Fig. 2.8). Two types of charts are used. One is a tree structure representing the program system structure (Fig. 2.9a). It is the index to the process dia-

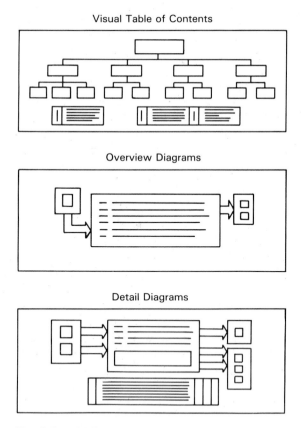

Fig. 2.8   HIPO top-down structure. From "Management Overview," reference [50], reprinted by permission of IBM Corp.

grams (Fig. 2.9b) which show inputs, process, and outputs and below, if necessary, additional information (such as assertions, management guidance as to schedules, resources, etc., or technical guidance such as standards or macros to be used). The detail diagrams can be filled in with English or pseudo-code or POL statements. The purpose of HIPO is to provide a graphic view of a complex system without getting lost in the detail. HIPO does not give guidance in how to design; it simply documents the design. In this respect, HIPO is less sophisticated than the design techniques already mentioned. It is also simpler and cheaper. Being easy to use in any hierarchical environment, HIPO can help overcome the communication problems that often hurt projects.

HIPO is quite similar to an approach taken by the System Development Corporation when they prepared a planning guide for the use of the U.S. Naval Command Systems Support Activity [29]. Prepared in 1965, the

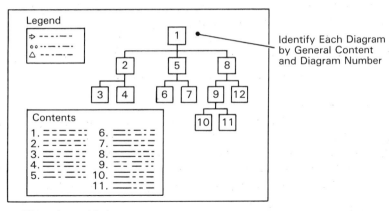

a. Hierarchy and Index

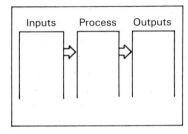

b. Detail Diagram

Fig. 2.9 HIPO charts. From "Management Overview," reference [50], reprinted by permission of IBM Corp.

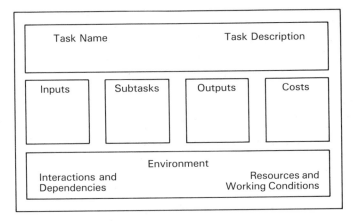

Fig. 2.10   SDC task breakdown diagram.

guide gave Navy project leaders instructions for managing a complete programming life cycle. In most respects, it is valid today. It is mentioned here
because the main technique for showing the steps in the life cycle is remark-
ably like HIPO. The life cycle is treated as a sequence so no tree-structure
diagrams appear; however, each detail diagram looks like a HIPO chart
with the addition of cost and environment data (Fig. 2.10). It is clear that
the HIPO technique is useful and flexible and, indeed, meets a need for
more systematic design documentation [30].

2.3.1.4 Modeling and simulation

A design language and some means of design verification give a degree of
control over the functions of the system being built. These tools do not deal
with system performance. Modeling and simulation are required to predict
performance. *Modeling* consists of building a description of the system design in which all the key parameters are present. The model is intended to
act as the real system would. In some cases, the model is a set of equations
that can be solved exactly by mathematical methods. More often, the model
is nondeterministic. Its behavior must be determined by exercising it. *Simulation* consists of feeding realistic inputs to a model and observing the
model's behavior. Most useful models represent hardware/software systems in the sense that they include information about hardware function,
speed, and capacity, plus information about software function, path
lengths, and control disciplines. Simulation runs can then show what happens when a given distribution of input transactions is processed by the software on the hardware. Depending on the detail of the model and the capability of the simulator, the results of simulation may be anything from a

simple output distribution to a history of all delays, resource assignments, instructions executed, or other internal data. Since the simulator can be a program itself, it can be designed to run on an available computer while simulating a nonexistent planned hardware/software system.

Analytical models represent the design in equations. Simulation models represent the discrete steps executed in a procedure; although, for computing efficiency, all the steps in a fixed path will be aggregated into a single step in the model. An analytical queuing model of a network intermediate node, for example, uses a continuous equation based on average message arrival times and average message service times to predict node performance. Internal node features, such as a priority queue which processes all waiting messages with priority 1 before handling any messages of priority 2, are ignored or, at best, approximated by skewing the statistical distribution of service times. A simulation model of the same box would take a message stream (which can range from a statistical distribution to an actual stream produced by a network simulator or an operator) and trace it through the explicit sequence of buffer stages, priority interrupts, services routines, etc., in the node. Thus a complex interaction between, say, modem delays and message lengths would be apparent in the discrete event model where it would be smoothed over in the queuing model. The degree of precision in a discrete event model is up to the developer. An actual operational system is a discrete event model with 100 percent fidelity. The amount of detail is governed by the objectives of the simulation, the quality of the available data, and the budget.

In general, analytical models are used to obtain rough, "ballpark" estimates and simulation models are used for fine tuning. Ballpark estimates are of greatest value early in a project when few implementation details are settled. As each design problem surfaces, alternative solutions will be proposed and a decision will have to be made to select a course of action. At this point, an analytical model is useful to answer the question, "How will the system behave, given proposal X, assuming reasonable values for all other relevant system features?" By changing the model to represent each proposal in turn, the relative effect of each can be determined. The margin of error is high, but the information obtained will still help guide the designer to better solutions.

An accepted design must be controlled to tighter tolerances. Here is where the discrete event model comes in. It is constructed exactly like the system design. For each element in the design there is a corresponding element in the model, and for each control sequence in the design there is a corresponding control sequence in the model. In fact, if the design is written in pseudo-language or POL, it is already the skeleton of the model. To complete the model, all you do is enter performance factors for each element or control sequence. Early in the design stage, it is necessary to guess at the performance factors. Educated guesses as to the path length, real memory size, and virtual working set size of each section of the program are best made by using similar existing programs for reference. As the project advances, the early estimates can be improved by the programmers and, eventually, exact measurements can be made of completed program units. The model gets better as it matures. During early design, results from simulation runs provide only ballpark figures, perhaps 50 to 100 percent from the true values.[8] By the time the system is ready for delivery, simulation can predict consistently within 5 to 10 percent of actual performance. In complex systems, simulation results may sometimes surprise the designers because they exhibit behavior due to subtle system interactions the designers never thought about. Guest, Lai, and Loyear, in their report on the extensive simulation of the intelligent controller subsystem in a banking system [31], show that such surprises are usually helpful.

The main drawback of modeling and simulation is high cost. Even when the original design serves as the model, there is a large cost associated with obtaining performance factors, updating the model, and running some number of simulations. There are only a few people doing system design so that the added cost of modeling during the design stage appears to be doubling project cost. In fact, like most of the best tools, simulation requires an early expenditure to avoid a much larger expenditure later. Thus, $20,000 to $50,000 worth of systems modeling that selects a successful design alternative may avoid $1,000,000 worth of rework on a system that fails to pass its acceptance test. On a large system such as the Apollo programming effort, some 2 to 4 percent of project cost went into modeling and simulation of the program system. The percentage appears to be very affordable; in fact, Apollo had over 20 professionals working on a continuous basis. However 2 to 4 percent of a small project may mean one part-time analyst—not enough to do a comprehensive job. The critical mass of a group capable of modeling a complex system and preparing simulation runs for multiple studies is three to six people. Such a group can support projects of at least a couple of hundred people. Systems modeling groups are infrequently found in smaller organizations. They are found, however, in large organizations in which there are few if any large projects. In these cases, the systems modeling group looks for the common thread linking the projects and tries to build models that can be used over and over again with minor changes to fit each project.

One such situation, in a large computer manufacturing firm, led to the development of three basic models by three analysis groups in different lo-

---

8. The accuracy of simulators early in the design stage is not actually known because there is never a fully executable version of the system represented at that time in the model.

cations. In principle, the models could be linked together; in practice, two of the three were developed in the same language and could be linked to each other but not to the third. Each model was intended to serve a different purpose. Together, the three could cover most of the system analysis needs of the projects being served.

One model, call it OS-SS, was a detailed discrete event model of the main operating system used in company projects. The second, DES, was a discrete event model of each of several programmable controllers and displays with detailed treatment of message handling in the company's standard network architecture. The third, SELL, was a gross discrete event model of network flow dealing with system engineering aspects of links and loads. All three models could: (1) simulate a complex data-processing network, (2) use a simple input description language to speed up problem setup for a simulation run, and (3) be supported by simulators that kept a wide variety of measurements for later analysis.

With SELL, an expert systems team could quickly compare a current system to a proposed system. Using the input preparation aid, the project team would describe their current system (in terms of hardware configuration, system software, and application mix—the last summarized in terms of user program path lengths and database accesses). A simulation run would then show how the current system should perform (batch throughout, end user response). The project team could check the results against their own current system measurements. Then the proposed system was described and a second simulation run to produce performance data for it. After comparing the two runs, the project team could modify their proposed system changing only the relevant parts of the simulation input. Several proposals could be examined in a couple of days. (As "SELL" implies, the simulator was also used by the manufacturer to sell computers. The use of SELL permitted the customer to understand current and planned systems in detail. The tool provided a convincing comparison using the customer's own data.)

OS-SS and DES were used by designers concerned with building on an existing system base. OS-SS focused on host computers. It covered every significant OS function in detail. Only after many simulation runs demonstrated that a detailed portion of the model was stable enough to be replaced by a shorthand representation was the model simplified. As a result, any change to OS potentially forced OS-SS to change. The advantage of this level of detail lay in being able to determine quite accurately what changes in performance would be caused by a change in OS. In addition, the model helped identify the source of some performance problems. In an OS development shop, OS-SS could help designers minimize execution path length and delays due to contention as the OS evolved. In an OS user shop, OS-SS could eke out additional work on a nearly saturated processor. OS-SS did not ignore the system outside the host. It simply treated everything outside as a delay function; i.e., when the host sent a message to a network node, the simulator would send the message, wait a certain length of time determined by the delay function, then create a response to the message at the host input interface.

DES was very much like OS-SS, but it focused on everything but the host. Actually, DES was intended to be a library of modules, one for every controller, I/O device, and processor in a network. With any one module, you could solve design problems as with OS-SS. With all the modules, you could run a detailed version of SELL.

The ultimate goal of a systems analysis group is to be able to pick a modeling and simulation approach in which the cost and effort of problem solving is appropriate for the value of the problem to be solved. The gross level of SELL is appropriate for general system flow questions, "How many IMS transactions can my system process per hour with my present batch load, 100 terminals, 10 controllers, and 90 percent of the IMS responses in less than 5 seconds?" The gross level of SELL with certain points of interest represented by the detail level of OS-SS or DES, plugged into SELL can deal with, "If batch and interactive messages share the same links, what sort of congestion can I expect in the network and is there some way I can reprogram the network intermediate nodes to reduce the congestion?" The detail level of OS-SS and DES would answer, "Would my jobs run faster if I let each one do its own database management instead of using a database management system?" "How much memory should my controller have if it will typically handle four user programs of type X?" "How much space can my controller operating system use if I must leave space for four user programs of type X?"

2.3.1.5 Benchmarks, prototypes, phased implementation

Managers who are frightened by high initial costs sometimes try to get performance data by other means. Some of them try to predict the performance of a proposed system by using a benchmark [32]. A benchmark is a hardware selection aid. It is not a recommended design tool; neither is it cheap. A *benchmark* consists of a defined set of jobs with input and database given and output either known or easily checked. A *benchmark test* is a timing run in which the standard job stream is executed against the clock. Obviously, to be valid the test must execute actual programs, but since there are no programs available during the design stage, a benchmark at this point must be built of programs from some earlier system. The only condition under which the benchmark will predict the performance of the new system is that the new system will be identical to the old one. Yet, if you know that to be the case, you do not have to run the benchmark at all.

Benchmarks are poor design tools because they are poor representations of the system to be built. When used as aids to computer selection, this major disadvantage gets cancelled out. When several bidders are given the same problem, they all start from scratch. The best benchmark result, while a poor indicator of ultimate system performance, may be an acceptable indicator of the best proposal. In this case, the benchmark is not expected to be a precise model of the new system. As long as it is in the same class, it can be used to distinguish among bidders. It is thereby possible for government agencies and computer companies to build a library of standard benchmarks to be used for comparing one generation of computers to a predecessor or to compare one line of equipment to a competitive line [33].

A *prototype* is a small version of the planned system [34]. It may be an inexpensive subset of the planned system which merely omits functions. In this form, it can be profitably used to check a particular design decision at the module level. It can also be used to improve early requirements definition. The prototype may also be completely different from the planned system. Such a prototype—a "quick and dirty" version—is discarded after it is studied. In this form, it is worth little. People who build "quick and dirty" prototypes believe they can study the prototype and learn something about the ultimate system. The economics of prototypes, however, result in small, limited packages that are not at all representative of the desired end product. The key to their problem is that they intend to throw away the prototype; therefore, they cannot afford to invest much in it.

A primary reason benchmarks and prototypes fail as design and development tools is that extrapolation in the software business is very unreliable. When you use program A as a reference to predict something about program B, you must rely on A and B being largely alike. No one wants to spend a lot of money to get a B that is just like the A he or she already has. B must have added value due to more functions or better cost/performance. Usually, B is either larger than A or different from A. Fig. 2.11 illustrates that, while you could predict B from A if they were alike, you cannot predict B from A when they differ, and you cannot predict B accurately when it is larger than A. The last case is the most common and the most likely to cause expensive errors. The picture shows B twice as large as A, but, following the *square law* of complex systems [10], B is four times as complicated as A. In a sense, when you use A as a reference, you are ignoring 75 percent of the problem. Most estimators would predict B to take twice the resources of A. A safer estimate would be four to one. Even then, the estimate is based on the often invalid assumption that the large unknown part of B is qualitatively like A. This picture applies whether you are predicting performance, estimating workload, or setting schedules. Overreliance on an existing reference system will lead to large understatements of results.

As a design and development tool in database and communications-based system, modeling and simulation are substantially more useful than any level of benchmarking or prototyping as long as the model is faithful to the design and is kept current. This is feasible when the model is the byprod-

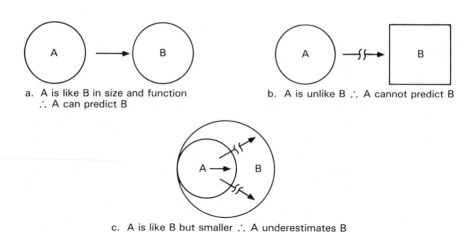

a. A is like B in size and function
   ∴ A can predict B

b. A is unlike B ∴ A cannot predict B

c. A is like B but smaller ∴ A underestimates B

Fig. 2.11   Predictability using a reference system.

uct of design. The model can be kept current as a byproduct of design control. In these circumstances, one use of the model on a sizeable job (say, twenty runs to evaluate alternate design proposals) can be expected to take ten to fifteen analyst-weeks and thirty to sixty hours of CPU use (not counting connect time when interactive terminals are used during simulation).

The weaknesses of throwaway prototypes are avoided in a related development method called *phased implementation*. Phased implementation also starts by building a small version of the planned system, but this version has two important characteristics: (1) it is delivered to the user as an operational package, and (2) it is built within an architecture that will permit major modifications and additions.

The purpose of the phased approach is to get something in the customer's hands in order to study the true operational requirements; then, using the first package as the base, build a second package more responsive to the customer's needs. Little effort is wasted. The inevitable changes requested by the customer are handled at phase changeovers. In the process, the customer gets an interim capability of recognizable value.

2.3.2 Development and Test

Two major types of development and test tools are important: tools that increase individual productivity and quality, and tools that increase project productivity and quality. When the two types of tools are coordinated, the total value of the resulting development support system is enhanced.

Many people have contributed to the state-of-the-art in programming technology. Acceptance of a comprehensive set of consistent techniques followed practical demonstrations such as those reported by Harlan Mills and Terry Baker of the IBM Federal Systems Division. [35]. Sources include a variety of books [10, 22–24, 36–48] and other materials [49–57],[9] discussing improved programming technologies (IPT) at a basic level. In 1978, IPT included a variety of techniques mostly related to the unit design, coding, and debugging phases of programming but already reaching out in both directions to include analysis and design techniques and test techniques. The term, IPT, is a catchall covering the currently recognized techniques for improving some phase of the program development process. On the IPT list in 1978, were:

- Structured programming
- Code reading
- Top-down development and step-wise refinement
- Structured design
- Pseudo-code program design language
- HIPO
- Chief programmer teams
- Development support libraries
- Structured walkthroughs
- Inspections

Each year, some of these items such as structured programming become so common in daily use that they are no longer considered "improved" technologies. Others are dropped for lack of effectiveness. New items will constantly be identified, proven by experiment, and added to the IPT list to maintain the stream of progress.

When these tools are all used on a project, the net result is expected to be an improvement in both the individual and the project aspects of productivity and quality. The reason is that the methods tend to build in quality from the beginning, eliminating the need for much of the costly scrap and rework that characterizes the tail end of many projects. Such results are "expected" but, unfortunately, not proven. It is improbable that a sound, repeatable experiment will ever be conducted to test the hypothesis that IPT is better than old methods.[10] Nevertheless, experienced managers are adopting IPT widely because, at a minimum, they find it decreases their risks. Without going into much detail, it is possible to see why.

---

9. The references contain a sample of IBM items readily available to this author. There are, of course, other sources for vendor manuals and reports.

10. A controlled experiment would require at least two independent developments of the same large-scale system. Such an experiment is uneconomic. Furthermore, the normal variance in programmer skill can cause major productivity/quality differences regardless of tools used by two independent groups. If one group does the job twice, the experiment also fails because the knowledge gained on the first version will dominate the factors contributing to productivity/quality in the second version.

2.3.2.1 Structured programming (SP) vs. unstructured programming

Structured programming applies a few simple rules of good programming that result in an easy-to-read code. The programs are designed to have one entry and one exit. They are written in execution sequence and, when properly indented on the page, the programs can be read like a book. There are no illogical branches to arbitrary points elsewhere in the program. Insofar as possible, the program is modularized in a hierarchy to permit each module to be written on one sheet of paper. Lower-level modules are written on separate sheets and referenced by name in the parent.

Managers are not comfortable managing products they cannot understand. They can understand structured code. They know that most discussion about programs takes place at the level of functions which are often recognizable as substructures of a good program. Therefore, SP makes it easier for: (1) a manager to talk to a programmer, (2) a writer to document the program, (3) a diagnostician to trace an error and apply a modification, and (4) a programmer to write the program correctly in the first place.

2.3.2.2 Code reading vs. no code reading

It is well known that the originators of a document are poor proofreaders of the result. For one thing, enough of the material is retained in the writers' memory that that they see what they expect to see rather than what is written. (Thus the redundant "that" in the previous sentence is easily overlooked in proofing.) Retention is even more pronounced when copying data, particularly numbers. A keypuncher is so likely to make the same error on the second reading of a source document that it is normal to use a second person to verify the cards produced by the first. The same is true in publishing where an editor proofs the galleys prepared by a typist.

Proofreading by the buddy-system was also common in the early days of computing when programmers wanted help or wanted to show off good code. The practice ebbed as programming workload grew. Programmers no longer felt they could afford the time to help others. Code reading came back into style when it was pointed out that the practice (1) catches more errors than many other methods, and (2) leads to better structure and more understandable programs.

The value of independent verification has been extended to the analysis and design activity in SADT. An integral part of Ross's method is the thorough review of each graphic document leading to an exchange of corrections, modifications, and suggestions between the reader and the author.

2.3.2.3 Top-down vs. bottom-up

Top-down design successively refines the solution to a problem resulting in a tree structure of well-designed modules. Top-down implementation consists of verifying the design as it is constructed. In the early stages, the design consists mainly of some data structures, some processing functions identified by name but with no supporting code, and a hopefully well thought out block diagram relating the data and the functions. "Executing" the design at this level shows whether the relationships in the block diagram are valid. Omissions can be found and incomplete or illogical paths can be identified. Top-down implementation requires that this level of design be in a programming language. Stubs are placed in the design to represent missing detail. (A stub is like the sign at a bridge under repair: "Arkham Bridge Out! Take Detour." It tells you where you are and where to go next. Executing a path in a partially completed design which should, say, invoke subprogram ARKHAM—not yet written—causes the stub to return a message showing that the proper path was followed, the bridge to ARKHAM was reached, but ARKHAM was not executed. Then the stub will provide an exit which either simulates the expected ARKHAM exit or returns to the invoking program or terminates the execution.) As lower levels of the design are coded, top-down implementation tests the correctness of processing modules as well as checking the system flow. In theory, when all program units are coded, the entire system will run correctly with no further system integration or testing.

In practice, it is often hard to find the "top" [10]; e.g., the one and only root of the tree from which all branches grow. As a result, there is no guarantee that a project can proceed top-down. If it can, the result will be savings certainly of money, possibly of time. In addition, the product will probably have fewer defects than a traditional bottom-up implementation. The bottom-up approach defers execution until design is complete and program units have been coded. Then, with the help of throwaway drivers, the units are debugged, integrated, and tested. Structural flaws can remain hidden all the way through the project only to show up during tests as serious defects with no simple cure. Bottom-up methods use a lot of scaffolding to help support their bricks. The scaffolding is then thrown away and sometimes the building collapses too. Top-down methods build a sound skeleton strong enough to support bricks and the designers know it ahead of time. Furthermore, by verifying the design as it is developed, top-down implementers avoid the excessively high costs of changing a finished project.

2.3.2.4 Structured design vs. unstructured design

Structured design refers to the conscious control of binding and coupling. Independent modules are truly independent and dependent modules have explicit interfaces and parameters. As a result, programmers can work on individual modules without fear of modifying other people's work.

Structured design also relies on explicit development of models of system data and system functions. Completeness can be checked by mapping the data models onto the function models. Maintenance is also improved by virtue of the clean interfaces that facilitate diagnosis and tend to pinpoint the source of a problem.

2.3.2.5 Program-design language vs. free-form design

One project that got into trouble was audited by a team of experts to see what was required to complete the job. There were some fifteen people in four groups working on what they said was a structured top-down design. The auditors found each group using a different technique for design—flowcharts, PL/I, prose, and assembly-language. No one knew what the others were doing, nor could the auditors figure out the design status. Here was a clear case where the lack of a uniform design language resulted in a project failure. The audit team recommendation was adopted; the project was taken away from the fifteen people and reconstructed by another group at another location. The procedural discipline of a program design language avoids such trouble.

2.3.2.6 HIPO vs. flowchart

The combination of functional data with procedural and managerial data gives everyone on a project a better view of what to do, when to do it, who is affected, and where each activity fits into the overall project. Simple flowcharts describe program structure but not project structure. Simple activity charts show project structure but not program structure. HIPO or its equivalents show both.

2.3.2.7 Chief programmer teams vs. other organizations

Chief Programmer Team operations allocate tasks on the basis of skills and focus attention, via the chief programmer, on top-down implementation. It is easier to use IPT in a team organization. Communiction is simpler, takes less time, and is more effective in a team. The team is a hierarchy headed by the chief programmer but, because it is small, personal relations can be excellent. Small teams can also operate effectively without a chief programmer because communications lines are short. Nevertheless, there is a lack of focus on the hierarchical nature of the program system, making it somewhat more difficult to manage a top-down implementation. Large groups tend to lose the focus altogether and act as collections of peers with individual goals instead of a team with a single goal.

2.3.2.8 Development support libraries vs. private code

When work in process is collected in an on-line library rather than kept in the programmer's desk, several benefits appear. The official record of the system is accessible to all programmers and managers. Less time is spent handling card decks and tapes. Code reading is supported by current output listings. Interactive code, debug, and test aids can be installed. Skilled librarians can enter, maintain, and retrieve library records, as well as run tests as requested and distribute the output. Ultimately, delivery of the program package can be made automatically from the library.

2.3.2.9 Structured walkthroughs vs. checkpoints

A checkpoint is a date in a project schedule when an activity is to be completed and management intends to check that it is done. To avoid the problems caused when an activity is complete but wrong, the structured walkthrough converts the checkpoint into a careful examination of the completeness, accuracy, and general quality of the work product. The reviewers are often part of the development team. In the review of a program unit, the programmer who did the work under review walks through the program step-by-step, explaining how the program works and how the test plan will verify the program functions. A sample input is traced through the program. The reviewers then critique the work and recommend what, if anything, the programmer should correct, change, or restudy. Different aspects of a project draw attention at different stages of development, as shown in Table 2.2. The whole process is quite informal. It relies on peer pressure from the reviewers on the developer to produce a high-quality product.

2.3.2.10 Inspections vs. structured walkthroughs

The success of a structured walkthrough depends on the personal relations within a project. Some walkthroughs are more successful than others. With respect to program unit evaluation, the more formal, more costly technique of inspection overcomes the variability of walkthroughs [46]. Inspections

TABLE 2.2. STRUCTURED WALKTHROUGHS AT PROJECT CHECKPOINTS

	Project checkpoints		Items to be reviewed via a structured walkthrough
Major project checkpoints	End of system planning		Project plans System definition Task identification
	Major technical review		Functional specifications Work assignments Schedules
	Multiple minor checkpoints	Detailed design	Internal specifications HIPO package
		Coding	Uncompiled source listings
		Documentation	User guides Programmer maintenance manuals • Internal specifications • HIPO package
	End of development		Deliverable product • Code • Documentation

From "Code Reading, Structured Walkthroughs, and Inspections," reference [50], reprinted by permission of IBM Corp.

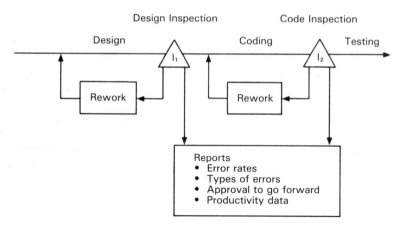

Fig. 2.12 Inspections. From "Code Reading, Structured Walk-throughs, and Inspections," reference [50], reprinted by permission of IBM Corp.

use a review team chaired by a moderator who organizes the review and re-ports the results. The team members are the designer, implementer, and tester of the program being inspected, plus other technical experts or affected parties as necessary. Usually, four people are plenty. When an activity satisfies the project exit criteria for design completion or code comple-tion, the moderator conducts an inspection (Fig. 2.12). The inspection pro-cedure follows a set pattern in which the design (at inspection I_1) or the code (at inspection I_2) is read and analyzed for logic and accuracy. Errors are identified (using a checklist to help). Based on the error rate, the moderator can either authorize the activity to proceed or send it back for rework. In-spections are an explicit management tool. They capture quality data for management analysis and they result in management decisions affecting project schedules. Whereas walkthroughs were said to occur at checkpoints, inspections occur at milestones. The distinction between a checkpoint and a milestone is that the former verifies that an event occurred, and the latter verifies the occurrence *and* requires a management decision to proceed or modify the project plan.

2.3.2.11 Support tools

Much of the basic library of a program development organization provides support to the programmers. Compilers and assemblers support the deci-sion to use a higher-level language. Trace programs, measurement aids, and utilities support program analysis, manipulation, and storage. Over and above these common tools are program systems designed solely to make programming easier and more reliable. The general characteristics of these support systems are:

- Interactive facilities that help the programmer compose a program and coach him or her in local procedures and use of the tool
- Displays supplementing keyboard terminals to provide quiet access to a limited segment of a program or document, plus the ability to access a hard copy of the full listing when needed
- Central files of project control information, data set definitions, where-used tables, etc.; an appropriate database management system (DBMS) to build, access, and change the files; and a data dictionary program to describe the contents of the files
- Library services for storing programs, isolating work in process from released programs, and retrieving programs or program segments for authorized users
- Text preparation services for editing programs and preparing system documentation
- Test execution facilities based on a simple command system for selecting test cases and programs from the library and running a sequence of tests
- Facilities for simulation and performance measurement
- Facilities for generating test cases
- Facilities to collect system measurements and user statistics for management reports.

Attempts to organize all these functions in a single system lead to extremely large support facilities which become development problems themselves. Therefore it has been recognized that the best support system is a collection of individual tools that have been designed to work together within a common architecture. It should be possible to link the tools together automatically to produce a useful sequence of operations such as program entry, compile, test case generation, link edit, load and execute, file program and tests for future use, and prepare and release results.

By planning the approach around separate tools, the full capability of a support system can be obtained by a development shop that cannot afford to build its own. Pomeroy [58] listed some of the tools that were commercially available in 1972. Since then, the list has expanded to include various on-line systems, display processors, structured programming aids, syntax checkers, database managers, text processors, test generators, command systems, and reporting aids [59]. The major drawback is that these tools are seldom designed to a consistent architecture even within a single vendor's catalog. On the other hand, it is not hard to modify the output of one to satisfy the input requirements of another.

An organization with many programmers simultaneously coding, debugging, testing, and shipping programs will have one or more computers dedicated to the support system. Most organizations will have to use their operational computer. In either case, the preferred way to protect one activity from another when they share a single CPU is to use a virtual machine operating system. Such a system creates an artificial machine environment for each user. As a result, the operational version of an installation OS can be isolated from the version used by developers. This is particularly helpful when the OS itself is being modified.

A great deal of the benefit from a support system comes from its library capabilities. It is the repository of all the project data. All project personnel can be given access to project data to learn it, to use it, to work on it, or to analyze it for design or management reasons. Nothing gets lost in a programmer's desk. "Private" code becomes "public" code. All the communications links needed to move the project forward can be provided through the support system. These capabilities appear in various degrees in the large CLEAR/CASTER system used in IBM program development [60], ISDOS under development at the University of Michigan [61], and in the Bell Laboratories Programmer's Workbench [62].

2.3.3   Applicability of Technical Tools

Development and test tools, particularly structured programming, are better established than analysis/design tools. The reasons for this are based on the characteristics of the program development life cycle discussed in the next chapter. Briefly, the most obvious place to look for the source of program errors or cost overruns is to the individual programmers. When this was done in the late 1960s it became immediately apparent that the large number of people who entered the field since 1960 were not doing basically "good" programming. In the 1950s, programmers carried a task from start to finish by themselves. They did structured programming and stepwise refinement without thinking about it. It was a natural way to work. The relatively simple jobs at that time did not have obscure or convoluted structures. In the 1960s, individual jobs were fewer (except for the special case of personal computing) and team jobs failed to give individuals a context in which to develop "good" habits. Techniques such as structured programming were rediscovered by theoreticians who, fortunately, explained their ideas in a teachable format. Then, when the team programmers learned how to distinguish "good" programs from "bad" ones, the largest part of the quality and cost problems was solved—or so it seemed. In fact, the progress made with improved programming techniques served to highlight the fact that good programmers cannot compensate for poor designs. This discovery led to the development of improved design methodologies that could interface with and take advantage of improved programming techniques.

Still there were serious problems, now due to the frequent changes and mis-understandings arising from poor requirements statements. So in the 1970s, work on requirements analysis techniques accelerated. (See Chapter 4.)

2.3.3.1 Scope of selected tools

Tools developed for specific purposes tend to be efficient only within the limits of their design even though they may be used elsewhere. By analogy, FORTRAN fits well in mathematical problems but is clumsy as a commer-cial data-processing language. REVS, which was built to help requirements writers, is not promoted as a design tool. SADT is offered to cover both analysis and design but does not claim to be a programming tool at the im-plementation level. HIPO exhibits a different type of specialization. It ad-dresses only documentation and does not have the functional sophistication of the design approaches. HIPO, however, requires practically no invest-ment by the user. Self-teaching is quite feasible. It does not do much but what it does is important, of wide use, and economical. So far, simplicity and economy coupled with formal rules and standard procedures charac-terize IPT tools. Other analysis/design/development/test tools tend to be more sophisticated. They give the user freedom of action to express his or her own style in the "art" of analysis and design. The price of such flexibil-ity is that they cost more to acquire and use, and generally require a training course to be used properly.

None of these tools is necessarily important to a programmer working totally alone, particularly when the programmer is the only person that will ever use the program. The tools pay off best in team projects, either me-dium-sized projects where analysis and high-level design may be merged, or large-sized projects where more specialization of skills is found. A method such as REVS is probably of greatest interest in large projects where re-quirements analysis is a special skill separate from design. SADT would be more suitable in medium-sized projects, as would Jackson or Warnier ap-proaches. Further, the stress on good documentation and control tech-niques lets all the tools contribute to better maintenance and other follow-up activities.

2.3.3.2 Benefits of IPT

Efforts to put a price tag on the benefits of IPT have been largely unsuccess-ful because of the lack of controlled experiments. It is equally risky to draw conclusions from isolated examples where productivity and/or quality im-proved simultaneously with the introduction of IPT. Analysis of such cases often shows other factors also contributed to the improvement; principally, the increase in the average level of experience of the staff over the period of the sample. For instance, a trend observed in United States data for the period 1974–1976 will reflect the fact that there was little hiring or employee turnover among programmers for those years. The same people were being observed for three years. Even though there is no proof that experience improves productivity and quality, it is highly probable that if an improvement is observed it is as much due to experience as anything else. The most believable data would have to come from very large programming organizations (over 300 programmers) that have many jobs in process and have converted some, but not all, to IPT. In this case, the numbers would be large enough to allow averaging over aggregates of individuals and jobs. The mix of characteristics of all the IPT jobs can be assumed to be the same as the mix for all the non-IPT jobs. Now, if a trend is observed in production rates, error rates, or resource utilization rates, it could be attributed to IPT.

There is no such clear-cut experimental analysis to this author's knowledge. Very good analyses, however, are attributable to Fagan [51] and Jones [9]. Both had access to extensive production and maintenance records on numerous program systems; however, the data that had been collected was not complete nor was it consistently defined. Therefore, many of the analytical results represent the investigator's insight and consensus opinions. Fagan observed the programming locations of IBM in Kingston and Poughkeepsie, New York; Jones observed a smaller group at IBM San Jose but augmented his data from other sources. Fagan predicted that structured programs undergoing design and code inspections will have substantially fewer errors per KLOC than structured programs without formal inspections. His measurements show that inspections I_1 (design) and I_2 (code) are the key to the saving. They catch errors early and avoid error propagation. Both inspections occur before any significant machine time is used; that is, before program unit debugging starts. Fagan also finds a 20-percent saving in the coding portion of development. Jones, working from a different database and a planning model, compared IPT projects with other methods: an "old style" in which program unit debugging was the earliest quality control, an "OS/360 style" in which design verification was also done, a "structured style" combining design verification with top-down design and structured programming, and a "modern style" where inspections supplement the structured style. Jones also found about 40 percent reduction in errors/KLOC when comparing OS/360 style to modern style. Savings in post-release service are projected by Jones ranging from 40 to 95 percent of the four-year cost of fixing errors in program products with many users. Considering that in four years, service of OS/360 style programs uses one-third as many programmer-years and one-and-a-third as many computer hours as the total initial development of the type of products Jones is concerned with, IPT savings represent big money.

The effects of four different quality control approaches are shown in Table 2.3. Using Jones's old style as a base, the errors found in a project are

TABLE 2.3.   QUALITY CONTROL—PERCENT OF ERRORS
FOUND BY FOUR QUALITY CONTROL APPROACHES

Quality control approach \\ Project stage	Design	Code	Debug	Test	Post-release	System errors
		(% errors found in each stage)				(relative to old style)
Old Style debug, test	0	0	15	60	25	100
OS/360 Style design review debug, test	20	0	15	50	15	98
Structured Style IPT with walkthroughs	25	20	15	35	5	58
Modern Style IPT with inspections	45	25	7	20	3	55

allocated to the development cycle stages: design, code, debug, test, and post-release. Thus, in old style no errors are found by explicit quality controls until the debugging stage. There, 15 percent of the errors are found; 60 percent are found in system integration and test; and 25 percent of the errors remain for users to find. By contrast, most of the erors are found in the unit design and code stages when the modern style is followed. The table entries for old style and OS/360 style are interpreted from Jones's data. The structured style is an average of data from several sources where IPT was used but inspections were not used because the project team preferred structured walkthroughs or even less rigorous reviews. Modern style is an average of Jones, Fagan, and other sources which reflects a range of optimism allocating from 25 to 55 percent of the errors found to the design stage.

An important feature of the various techniques is the cascade effect of early error detection [63]. An error eliminated during program unit design tends to forestall additional errors later. As a result, the total number of errors encountered in a modern style project is less than in an old style project. As IPT adds more techniques, especially those related to package design, the cascade increases. Some experts in large system design predict that IPT eventually will be ten times better than old style. Here, a more modest improvement of 45 percent is projected based on what has been achieved to date.

It is possible to see the dramatic value of IPT by using the cost of fixing an error detected in a given stage (Table 2.4) to estimate the relative costs of each quality control approach. Remember that the cost of an error is proportional not only to the difficulty of finding a solution (fix) but also to the

TABLE 2.4. QUALITY
RELATIVE COST OF FIXING
AN ERROR

Stage	Relative cost
Design	0.3
Code	0.5
Debug	2.5
Test	21.0
Post-Release	36.0

number of people whose progress is stalled while waiting for the fix. During design there are only a few people involved and they know their product intimately. During test there are many people involved who, at best, know only a small part of the product. After release, the errors are reported by users who submit incorrect and duplicate reports to maintenance teams who may be quite unfamiliar with the nuances of the product design. These factors account for the huge increase in cost per fix at later stages. If you were to translate the relative factors to dollars, you would immediately see the benefit of cleaning up errors early. Using the values in Tables 2.3 and 2.4, Table 2.5 presents the relative cost per stage and the total cost per project of quality control. The multiplication of *project errors* times *percent per stage* times *cost per stage to repair* is carried out to decimal values to be consistent with Tables 2.3 and 2.4. The totals are rounded off since the original data, while taken from actual environments, is not precise. Still, there is a 7:1 improvement in quality projected over the period 1960–1976. If the trend is consistently maintained, the vendor's costs will continue to go down but the main beneficiary will be the user who will have fewer problems. For every twenty-five errors that reached the customer under the old style, only two to four should reach the customer today, and still fewer in the future. This speaks well for the quality control aspect of program development, but it does not address other issues of productivity and cost.

Using the same data as Fagan and Jones, Horne in early 1976 set out to show the effectiveness of IPT in terms that nonprogramming managers would understand. This objective would require statistically valid results large enough to be convincing. This objective was not achieved for a variety of reasons, the most important of which was that the source data had not been obtained for the purpose of this study. Most of the data was used by local managers to track departmental performance. Horne needed to draw general parameters out of data that was collected for local, specialized purposes. She had collected a considerable amount of data on IBM system control programs (e.g., MVS, VS1) and application programs (e.g., IMS, health industry packages, government and commercial contract programs).

TABLE 2.5. RELATIVE COST OF FIXING ALL ERRORS

Project stage / Quality control approach	Design	Code	Debug	Test	Post-release	Total project
		(cost relative to old style)				(rounded value)
Old Style	0	0	37.5	1260.0	900.0	2200
OS/360 Style	5.88	0	36.75	1029.0	529.2	1600
Structured Style	4.35	5.8	21.75	426.3	104.4	560
Modern Style	7.425	6.875	9.625	231.0	59.4	315

Cost entries are product of errors per stage times cost from Tables 2.3 and 2.4.

In this list were very large complex programs, widely distributed programs, small simple programs, and one-user programs. The data included varying degrees of detail on program size, size of changes to existing programs, IPT used, programmer-months, estimated difficulty, productivity, errors found before and after release, and other items; however, the data was unreliable. Measurements were not consistent and were not well defined. For example, one program appeared in four reports, each of which gave different size, productivity, cost, and error rates per KLOC. "Productivity" was sometimes limited to KLOC/programmer-month and in other cases covered KLOC/project personnel-months, but it was hard to tell which was which. The IPT usage reports were often subjective. You could not tell if a project reporting IPT usage understood the techniques claimed. For instance, inspections are different from walkthroughs but few people were aware of the difference. The applications people did not report cost or post-release errors. Reports for new programs were intermixed with reports for new releases of old programs. In fact, in the total KLOC in the programs surveyed there were far more KLOC of old code than there were new or changed KLOC. To complicate matters, the individuals who collected the data were no longer around so it was difficult to clarify issues of definition and scope.

Nevertheless, in the analysis by Horne and this author it was possible to sustain the belief that IPT improves the program development process based on the following indications (as opposed to proofs):

1. For projects of comparable difficulty, IPT increased productivity.

2. Managers were willing to commit to higher productivity on new projects, increasing the KLOC/programmer-month used in their estimating tables.

3. Managers were willing to commit to fewer errors/KLOC in post-release code because they had confidence in their quality control techniques.

4. Managers were convinced that IPT helped them and they were voluntarily adopting the techniques.

On the negative side, the indications were:

1. It is so far not possible to separate the benefits of one technique from another.

2. Unusually high productivity (found in a few 1–5 programmer projects) is due more to outstanding programmers than to IPT.

3. Determining the effect of IPT (or any other process modification) on quality probably requires about two years of post-release error data. However, when trends have been established for several programs, it should be possible to model the results to predict quality in other programs given only pre-release error data.

4. For every set of data supporting IPT, there is a counterexample.

5. The range of results with IPT overlaps the range without. Since the data is statistically weak, no conclusion can be drawn about the average results due to IPT.

6. If IPT data solidifies so improvement in the averages can be seen, the effect on process measurements may remain invisible because the savings can be masked by other factors.
   a. The cost of system support, integration, and release may dwarf the cost of new code, so IPT benefits appear negligible.
   b. The savings due to IPT may be immediately reinvested in additional program functions; i.e., total outlay is not reduced.
   c. The reduction in errors/KLOC may be accompanied by an increase in KLOC so the user sees no change in practice.
   d. The savings in programmer-hours may simply reduce programmer overtime without changing salary costs or programmer population.

An interesting sidelight of the Horne study was due to an attempt to fit curves to the data. The purpose was to be able to predict costs and error rates by class of program, difficulty, and workload. The form of the curves that best fit the data was parabolic;

$$y = k\,(A)\,(\Delta A) + a$$

where y is the number of errors in the delivered package, and A is the size of the package in KLOC (or modules) which in the study ranged from about 30 KLOC to 200 KLOC. The packages were mostly part of one system of some 2000 KLOC but, unfortunately, the data available did not cover all parts of the system. ΔA is the number of new or changed KLOC (or modules); ΔA

equals A for a new program; it may even exceed A when an existing program is drastically modified and extended. k is a factor (errors/$KLOC^2$) related to programmer productivity, and a is a constant (errors) related to design quality and process management. The equation reflects the discussion of Chapter 1 by implying that errors are caused by complexity, A^2, and the workload due to handling a portion of the package, $\Delta A/A$. Their product is $(A)(\Delta A)$.

The values available for y, A, and ΔA were for such a limited set of packages that values of k and a derived from curve fitting would be of no general use. Nevertheless, the curve fitting exercise provided some useful insights into error sources. The packages used in the analysis were done in different places by different types of programmers. When it was noticed that k and a calculated for all packages as a group led to very large deviations between model results and actual reported data, particularly for large packages, the input was regrouped by developer. The result of this step was to produce distinctly different values of k and a by program type (operating system management, database management, communications management) and by location. In the parabolic equation, the variable portion, $k(A)(\Delta A)$, of the error model can be interpreted as the number of errors delivered in a program system due to programmer activity. The constant portion, a, which should be zero, is the number of delivered errors due to the development process. The surprise was that in this model when $k = 0$ (i.e., each programmer did a perfect job of program unit coding and debugging), a was nonzero. The process itself was introducing a certain number of defects, on the order of 20–140, for the user to find.

If the analysis is correct, these system errors must be due to: (1) inadequate design, (2) errors put in after unit debugging, and (3) the nature of test and release activities [64]. IPT is expected to improve design and minimize the test and release activities. Support tools that hold the system online can reduce handling errors after unit debugging; therefore, the new technology may get a down to zero where it belongs.

A different approach to evaluating IPT was taken by Hunter and Reed [65] who subjectively rated the use of IPT on a large project at Barclays Bank Ltd., in the United Kingdom. They found significant but unquantified gains in product quality, enhanced personnel skills and motivation, and about 25 percent better productivity than on other jobs with which they were familiar. The techniques used wholly or in part were:

- Structured design
- Pseudo-code program design language
- Structured programming
- Top-down implementation and testing
- Development support library

- Librarians
- Walkthroughs
- Team operations

The project received advice and assistance from the group who wrote the IPT manuals [50]. As a result, the joint Barclay-IBM team was able to get off to a fast start. At the end of the project, a set of questions was prepared to show where IPT made a difference. The strong positive bias of the answers showed that IPT had been a success in this particular project. A summary of the questions covering manageability, productivity, maintainability, and reliability shows how the qualitative assessment turned out (Table 2.6).

TABLE 2.6.   SUBJECTIVE EVALUATION OF IPT

Manageability	Yes	Yes due to IPT	No	No effect
• Are major schedules being met more often?	(√)	( )	( )	( )
• Are budgets being met more often?	(√)	( )	( )	( )
• Are milestones and checkpoints easier to set up and to enforce?	(√)	(√)	( )	( )
• Are intermediate project milestones and checkpoints being met more often?	(√)	(√)	( )	( )
• Do project managers get better status reports to track progress?	(√)	(√)	( )	( )
• Is the developing system more visible, centralized, and open to inspection?	(√)	(√)	( )	( )
• Is the user more involved with the system development effort?	(√)	(√)	( )	( )
• Can changes be made to the developing system more easily?	(√)	(√)	( )	( )
• Can part of the system be exercised and shown to the user before the end of the project?	(√)	(√)	( )	( )
• Are project managers more confident about their ability to manage and is their job satisfaction higher?	(√)	(√)	( )	( )
• Are analysts and programmers more satisfied with their jobs?	(√)	( )	( )	( )
• Can people be phased into projects more easily?	( )	( )	( )	(√)
• Are clerical tasks easier to delegate?	(√)	(√)	( )	( )
• Is the user more satisfied?	(√)	(√)	( )	( )
• Is the chief executive more satisfied?	(√)	(√)	( )	( )
• Is the DP manager more satisfied?	(√)	(√)	( )	( )

From I. C. Hunter and J. N. Reed, "An IPT Project—Results, Conclusions, and Recommendations," reference [65], reprinted by permission of IBM Corp.

TABLE 2.6. continued

Productivity	Yes	Yes due to IPT	No	No effect
• Is there less confusion between users and DP?	( )	( )	( )	(√)
• Is the identification of responsibilities more sharply defined?	( )	( )	( )	(√)
• Can analysts and programmers find what they need to know more easily?	(√)	(√)	( )	( )
• Can programmers schedule their time more effectively?	(√)	(√)	( )	( )
• Does the system need fewer drivers than similar systems produced in the past?	(√)	(√)	( )	( )
• Is there less throw-away code?	(√)	(√)	( )	( )
• Is the amount of machine test time less?	(√)	(√)	( )	( )
• Can machine time now be scheduled and used more effectively?	(√)	(√)	( )	( )
• Is machine turnaround time less of a productivity bottleneck?	(√)	(√)	( )	( )
• Can test data and test cases be generated more systematically?	( )	( )	( )	(√)
• Does it seem that DP is producing more output for a unit of time?	(√)	( )	( )	( )
• Does it seem that DP is producing more output for a unit of cost?	(√)	( )	( )	( )

Maintainability & Reliability	Yes	Yes due to IPT	No	No effect
• Does the developing system seem to have fewer errors?	(√)	(√)	( )	( )
• Does it take less time and effort to fix the errors that do occur?	(√)	(√)	( )	( )
• Is it taking less machine time to find and fix errors?	(√)	(√)	( )	( )
• Are the errors that occur less catastrophic than in the past?	( )	( )	(√)	( )
• Is integration test less traumatic than in the past?	(√)	(√)	( )	( )
• Once into operation, does the system have fewer errors?	(√)	(√)	( )	( )
• Does it take less time to make a maintenance change?	(√)	(√)	( )	( )
• Is the documentation more meaningful on this system?	(√)	(√)	( )	( )
• Is the documentation easier to update?	(√)	(√)	( )	( )
• Do programmers show less reluctance to maintain someone else's code?	(√)	(√)	( )	( )
• Is there less of a stigma surrounding maintenance?	( )	( )	( )	(√)
• Are fewer programmers required to maintain this system than similar systems?	(√)	(√)	( )	( )

The conclusions of this study parallel those given earlier:

- IPT provides a framework for project development that is better than the traditional approach and should become the standard [66].
- The techniques are not a "miracle formula" for a successful project. Without a sensible schedule, strong technical leadership, and competent design and programming, a project can fail with or without IPT.
- Ideally, projects should introduce most of the techniques together, starting as early in development as possible. The techniques fit naturally together and in some cases depend for their success on being used in conjunction with others.
- A subset of the techniques can easily be used as a starting point. It should consist of structured programming (including pseudo-code), use of a development support library approach, and walkthroughs.
- Standards in many cases need to be altered to accommodate development along IPT lines.
- The overhead cost of learning the techniques is almost certainly recovered inside one year.
- IPT is not a rigid or inflexible set of rules; rather, it is a group of related concepts and techniques. It is natural and inevitable for different projects to use and interpret IPT somewhat differently.

Taking advantage of the plusses of IPT, it is likely that modern style program development will lead to quality and productivity improvements. IPT—taken as the list of design and programming techniques in section 2.3.2—should generate about 40 percent improvement of the old style of 1970 [65]; that is, 40 percent fewer errors found during development and more than a 40-percent reduction in errors in code released to users (because of the cumulative effect of early discovery). Project resource requirements per KLOC should also go down. The range of 1–4 KLOC/programmer-month (before adjusting for system support, system test, release, and maintenance) is achievable.[11] This outlook is within the range of the technology forecast for 1985 made by the Air Force Systems Command in its 1972 study "Information Processing/Data Automation Implications of Air Force Command and Control Requirements in the 1980s (CCIP–85)" reported by Boehm and Kosy [67]. However, Boehm [68] notes that such productivity had not been achieved as of 1981. The industry average productivity in KLOC per person-month continues to improve 3 to 4 percent a year, but this improvement may be entirely due to achievements of the industry leaders.

---

11. The increase is attributed to IPT but includes programming languages, design aids, and reuse of common functions (macros/library programs).

2.3.4 Status Control

There is a certain excitement in applying the best technology to develop the best possible product. It is easy to get caught up in the excitement and spend so much time polishing and tuning the product that you miss the delivery date. Every project operates under constraints involving time and money. They cannot be ignored. Yet in a complete system, it is just as hard to know where you stand with respect to the constraints as it is to know whether the components have been properly designed. Status control tools help show where you stand.

The basis of most status control tools is simple accounting. Status control is concerned with costs of labor, materials, facilities, and with inventories of people, programs, hardware. Above all, it is concerned with the variance between the planned expenditures and inventories and the actual status of the project costs and inventories at all stages of the project. Variances are signals to the project manager that action is required.

The main difference between status control in program projects and the usual financial accounting controls is that the programs that make up the deliverable product are often hard to describe in quantitative terms. This characteristic became evident in the early 1960s when a reasonable number of large software systems were underway. Managers at that time found no one in their project could tell them how much of the system was complete or when it would be finished. The "95 percent complete" problem arose: Routine reports would show the project to be 95 percent complete after, say, twelve months work, but the system would not be ready for delivery for another twelve months. The reporting system was only showing how much of the budget had been spent in the first twelve months; namely, 95 percent of it. There was no correlation between the rate of expenditure and the technical accomplishment. Project overruns were common at this time but the status control system, based solely on cost data, was unable to predict the overrun. It did not even alert management to the exposure.

To correct the weakness of cost reporting, two things have to be done. First, a means of reporting technical progress has to be developed. Second, a means of relating cost data to technical progress has to be found. The solution to the first problem is to abandon the practice of reporting "percent completion" and base all reports on the 100-percent completion of readily identifiable small tasks. Definitive events are substituted for judgments. The solution to the second problem is to key all cost reports to the same small tasks used for technical reporting. This procedure gives a useful picture of progress in a large project because the sum of the task reports is a valid estimate of the percent of completion of the project as a whole. In other words, when a project consisting of one hundred tasks reports that fifty tasks representing 60 percent of the projected workload have been finished, there is reason to assume that the project is about 60 percent complete. Of course, the actual status of the overall project depends on whether the fifty tasks were finished on time and within budget. If, on the average, they met their planned targets, then it is possible to assume that the remaining tasks will also be on target unless some problems have been identified by the task managers. In this way, task completion reports and variance reports show how well the project is progressing along its plan and provide a basis for forecasting the future course of the project. The technique is not perfect. None is. The deficiency of this approach is that it only points out potential overruns or slippage due to technical problems. It does not provide any estimate of the cost or time involved in fixing a problem should one arise. Furthermore, it is difficult to define tasks clearly in the areas of planning, design, and general support. Suggestions on minimizing the number of undefined activities are given in section 2.3.4.2.

2.3.4.1 Configuration accounting

The procedure that makes status control possible can be called the *configuration accounting* element of *configuration management*. The "configuration" being managed is the entire system project. It includes the inputs, the deliverables, the people developing the deliverables, the support structure, and anything else that tangibly interacts with the project. Configuration accounting keeps track of the status of every system element, showing

- Who is responsible for the element
- Who depends on the completion of the element
- What the current status of the element is
- What the history of the element has been
- How much resource has been budgeted for the element
- When the element is due to be finished
- What the element's official nomenclature (part number) is

In order to work effectively, the configuration accounting system must be built on some obvious prerequisites:

- A system development plan must exist that identifies the accountable tasks and shows who is responsible for each task.
- Responsible individuals must commit to accept their responsibility.
- Changes to the plan must be controlled.
- The sum of the task budgets must be less than or equal to the system budget.

- The critical path, taking into account all schedule constraints, must be shorter than or equal to the project schedule.

- The accountable tasks must be identifiable and their completion must be measurable.

- Each accountable task must be small compared to the size of the overall system.

As noted, each of these items is obvious but each has been overlooked or violated in more than one major project. The list can be a useful reminder during project planning.

2.3.4.2 Task identification

The program unit is a suitable task for medium and large systems. The program unit is the work of an individual; therefore, it is possible to develop unambiguous reports about the task by speaking to one person. It is not necessary to interpret the possibly different inputs of several people. Program units tend to be in the range of 400–1000 lines of code. Medium to large systems tend to exceed 50KLOC, so there are over 50–125 program units in a system—a large enough number to permit averaging techniques to operate. The design, coding, and debugging of a program unit take four to eight weeks in general. This is a short time span compared to the twelve to twenty-four months duration of the typical project. Furthermore, there is a definite end to the program unit development. The unit programmer must release the unit to someone else when debugging is completed. At this point, other programmers and test teams are free to use the "complete" unit in their activities. By instituting a simple but formal reporting procedure, the completion event can be recorded. In a project with computerized library support, the completion of each program unit/task can be recorded automatically as the program unit leaves the programmer's private workspace and enters the system library. The activities in program unit development—unit design, coding, and debugging/unit test—also make feasible tasks when formal inspections are used to denote completion of each activity.

The characteristics that make the program unit suitable for identification as a task are not found in many other aspects of system activity. The program unit permits effective reporting throughout the portion of the development cycle that deals with unit programming and much of the subsequent package testing period when units are combined and exercised. Some other reporting basis is required for the less well-defined design and support activities. Depending on the nature of the activity, various pseudo-tasks can be established:

- Design activity, which is done by small groups and produces a document as its output, can be set up as one task for each planned document. Thus there could be a "system design" task or a "package *n* design" task. Such tasks are bigger than program units in terms of resources used and time allotted; nevertheless, they have clear start and stop criteria that permit them to be elements of a task reporting system.

- Design support activity such as modeling and simulation can be tracked by setting up each independent activity as a task. This method applies to simulation runs, test runs, tradeoff studies, document preparation, etc. It helps to subdivide these activities where feasible into one-person tasks, but it is not essential. On the other hand, it is essential to identify the output of the activity, usually a report or document, in order to pinpoint the completion date.

- General support activities, particularly those provided by a large support group such as a computer center, are impractical to track as tasks. Quite often, the individuals providing a particular type of support change from day to day so that reporting by task involves complicated time recording. Although such time recording may be required for accounting purposes, it is generally too cumbersome for tracking technical status. It is preferable to key the support activity to some more easily identifiable task and report it as a burden on the basic task. In this way, clerical support can be reported as, say, 10 percent of project cost allocated to each task in proportion to the number of project personnel working on the task. Computer operations personnel can be reported as X percent of the cost of one unit of computer time to be billed to computer users in proportion to the number of units of computer service actually used. Documentation can be reported as X hours (of editing, typing, layout, etc.) per KLOC. This technique can also be applied to other overhead functions: management, planning, facilities maintenance, document reproduction, etc.

In each case, an effort should be made to determine whether the activity, in the project at hand, can be readily measured as a task. If it can, make it a task. If it cannot, treat it as burden on other tasks.[12]

Guidelines such as these produce reports consisting of task names, start and stop dates planned, start and stop dates achieved, cost of the direct ef-

---

12. Jones [9] is strongly opposed to the use of ratios and apportionments for planning estimates. He is right in showing that ratios such as "Design = 30 percent of Schedule" are too general and may not fit two successive projects. He is also right in saying that, if you plan forty pages of documentation, you should cost out the work to produce the forty pages rather than allocate 5 percent of project cost to documentation. Nevertheless, if you have no prior experience data to guide your estimates, ratio methods are acceptable while you build a database for future projects.

fort (that is, of the resources applied by the person or group assigned the task), cost of the indirect effort (the burden added to the direct effort for services from other groups), and comments regarding the impact of any variance between the plan and actual achievement.

2.3.4.3 Coordinated reports

Given the need for task reporting, it is appropriate to select report formats that clearly and accurately display all the data needed by managers. Several different formats are generally required: one to highlight schedule, one for cost; one for dependencies, one for workload, one for workload assignments, and others focusing on system views important to management. The various reports should be designed so that they are consistent; consequently, coordination is required to ensure that standard nomenclature, numbering techniques, report closing dates, and conversion routines are used.

To illustrate, the information retrieval subsystem shown as a hierarchy in Fig. 1.12 is repeated with new labels in Fig. 2.13. The hierarchical labeling scheme shows that information retrieval is the first subsystem in some larger system. The subsystem has been initially designed to have two packages, six subpackages, and thirteen units. Each unit is small enough for one programmer to handle as shown in the rough estimate of workload in Table 2.7. Again, the example is grossly oversimplified. So, even though it may strike you that one programmer can do this subsystem in six months, accept the estimates for their illustrative value. You will notice immediately that one more level has been added to the subsystem hierarchy. As a result of a package design review, it was decided that each input adapter should be treated as a separate system element. The modularity of the system is improved by this decision and should make it easier to change one input device or terminal without touching the others. The time projected for each program unit ranges from two to eight weeks. The short tasks are obviously considered easy. The File Organization subpackage, though, is considered hard. It has relatively little code, but each of its units presents a design problem. The CLASSIFY unit requires analysis of various word-processing algorithms, entailing some library research, generation of some sample data streams, and some experimentation. The INDEX and FORMAT TABLE units involve a great deal of coordination with other units and constant verification of formats and definitions. SEARCH is also a coordinating unit and, regardless of how long it takes to code, SEARCH will probably be the last unit to be finished. Up until the end, changes in other units will potentially modify SEARCH so the SEARCH programmer must be available to review the changes and react as necessary.

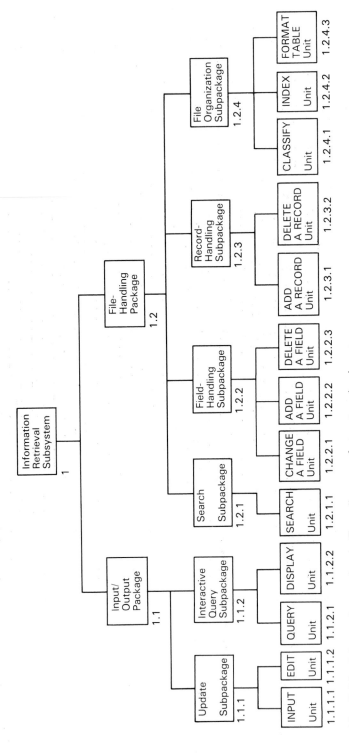

Fig. 2.13 Information retrieval—Tree diagram of structured subsystem.

TABLE 2.7.
INFORMATION RETRIEVAL—
ROUGH ESTIMATE OF PROGRAMMER WORKLOAD

Hierarchical identifier	System element/ Program unit	Lines of code		Weight	Weeks
		Source	Object		
1	Information Retrieval Subsystem				
1.1	Input/Output Pkg.				
1.1.1	Update Subpkg.			(17)	
1.1.1.1	INPUT Unit	120	210	17	6
1.1.1.1.1	IN		65		2
.2	IN1		65		2
.3	INP		65		2
.4	INT		65		2
.5	INK		65		2
.6	IND		65		2
.2	EDIT Unit	120	600	10	8
1.1.2	Interactive Query Subpkg.			(15)	
.1	QUERY Unit	120	600	12	8
.2	DISPLAY Unit	120	200	15	6
.1	T1		100		3
.2	T2		100		3
.3	T3		100		3
.4	T4		100		3
1.2	File-Handling Pkg.				
1.2.1	Search Subpkg.			(11)	
.1	SEARCH Unit	70	350	26	8
1.2.2	Field-Handling Subpkg.			(9)	
.1	CHANGE A FIELD Unit	50	250	7½	4
.2	ADD A FIELD Unit	50	250	8	4
.3	DELETE A FIELD Unit	20	80	7	2
1.2.3	Record-Handling Subpkg.			(8)	
.1	ADD A RECORD Unit	50	250	8	4
.2	DELETE A RECORD Unit	20	80	7	2
1.2.4	File Organization Subpkg.			(8)	
.1	CLASSIFY Unit	60	300	7	8
.2	INDEX Unit	—	20	6	6
.3	FORMAT TABLE Unit	—	20	6½	6
Total Workload		800	4000		96

2.3.4.4 Activity network chart

The data in Table 2.7 give the range of time required to develop the information retrieval program units; namely, eight to ninety-six weeks. One person presumably would take ninety-six weeks to code and debug the units, not counting any time used for integration and test. A team of twelve might do the code and debug work in eight weeks. Or would it? Possibly not. There are dependencies among the units that imply some sequencing of work. The constraints due to sequential relationships may extend the project beyond the eight weeks estimated for the longest task. It is necessary to lay out an implementation plan showing the dependencies, including communications and coordination requirements, to determine how long the critical path actually is and what steps might be taken to improve it. The critical path is seldom obvious. Even small projects have enough interactions to obscure some of the dependencies. The recommended method for finding the dependencies is to draw an *activity network chart.* In such a chart, *activities* are represented by arrows that start and end at *events,* represented by circles. The starting event of an activity represents the completion of all activities that are prerequisites to the activity. The ending event of an activity represents 100 percent completion of the activity. When the activity arrows are labeled with estimates of the time they are expected to take, it becomes clear that the earliest completion time for the project is determined by the longest essential path from start to finish. This is the *critical path.* All other paths contain slack; that is, their activities can take a little longer than estimated without affecting the project completion date. It is often possible to use that slack to redirect resources to the critical path and shorten it.

The calculations for schedule and cost optimization of an activity network can become difficult; however, tools are available, including PERT/TIME and PERT/COST, for doing the arithmetic and drawing the graphs [69, 70]. In spite of on-line support tools, these analytic methods are not used much in programming projects for a number of reasons, the most important of which is that the cost of maintaining the project activity network is large compared to the value of the calculated results. Other contributing factors are the relative inflexibility of resources that makes reallocation awkward (how can a programmer change tasks for two to three days and be useful?) and the complications introduced by the iterative nature of programming (PERT assumes loop-free networks). A good design also contributes by reducing the sequential dependence among events. Hence, interest in maintaining an activity network wanes after its initial use. Nevertheless, the first use is significant. The activity network chart is the only report format that explicitly shows the sequential relationships among activities. Without this information, the development plan can be way off the mark.

A partial activity network based on Fig. 2.13 is shown in Fig. 2.14. One of the advantages of drawing such a chart is that it forces you to think through many details that are otherwise overlooked.[13] The new activities in Fig. 2.14 are the results of this need to explain the activities step by step. For example, a decision has been made that certain data items must be defined before the SEARCH unit can be designed. Some additional data items must be defined before the rest of the File-Handling Package can be designed. These definition activities take time, estimated at one-half week each, and must be shown in the network chart. A whole new package has also been added—the System Tests package. It reflects the need to develop and check out test cases before testing of the deliverable packages can start. A rough estimate is that the System Tests package will take 8 weeks, 3.8 for design, 0.2 for inspection, and 4.0 for coding and debugging.[14] Next, each package consisting of several units must be tested as an integral package. This time must be estimated as must the time to integrate and test File Handling with I/O. The workload is now larger than the range suggested by Table 2.7, but the elapsed time may not be large because the network shows that many activities can proceed in parallel. There are only a few points at which the parallel activities have to be synchronized. Event 17 shows that all the deliverables should be designed and inspected to provide the basis for evaluating the design of the system tests. Events 13 and 15 show that the design and inspection of the master input and display units must be completed before work starts on the subordinate I/O adapters. And, of course, the tests at 38, 39, and 40 require the availability of all the components to be tested.

---

13. A specialist in the author's organization was once assigned to introduce PERT into a number of projects in response to government requirements. His efforts were uniformly unsuccessful until he adopted the following approach:
1. Using his authority as a technical staff manager, he asked a project manager to explain the major aspects of the project.
2. That night he developed an activity network chart in as much detail as he could legitimately generate.
3. The next day, he went back to the PM saying, "You know my expertise is in management techniques not in your project. As an aid to understanding what you told me I put it in a form I am used to. I wonder if you would look at the chart and tell me if I got it right?"
4. The PM agreed to help and, in going over the activity network chart, he said, "Yes, that's exactly right"; "By George, you even have some things in here I hadn't mentioned"; "Say, this activity here governs the schedule for my most important deliverable. I didn't realize that"; and finally, "Do you mind if I keep this chart, I think it will be useful. When did you say you were running a PERT course?"

14. In Fig. 2.14, an estimate for each activity is given in (weeks) below the activity line. The estimate for each subpackage, above the activities, is the sum of design (D), inspect (I), code and debug (C). Time to define or test (T) is additional. The events are numbered arbitrarily here. They should be numbered to agree with hierarchical identifiers in practice.

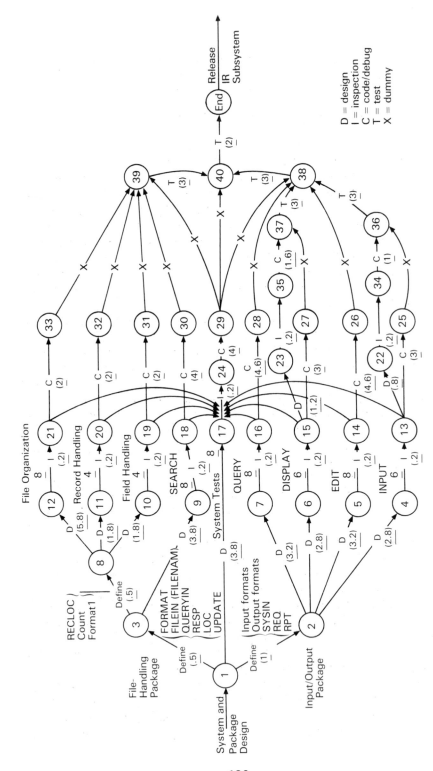

Fig. 2.14 Information retrieval—Partial activity network.

The critical path in this activity network is found by tracing all the paths from event 1 to event 40. The longest path is the critical path shown in Fig. 2.15. It requires 16.2 weeks. The network chart is so dense and cluttered that it would be hard to trace the paths directly. Instead, the data contained in the chart is tabulated for easier analysis. For this small chart, Table 2.8 lays out all paths formed starting at event 1. The table shows the time required to reach each event node (row entry) from each possible predecessor event (column entry). Thus, row 10 shows there is one path to event 10; it arrives via one intermediate node, event 8, and takes an estimated 2.8 weeks. Event 17 can be reached via nine paths, ranging from 3 to 7 weeks in estimated path length. Event 24 follows event 17 and has a path length of 7.2 weeks found by taking the longest path to event 17 and adding the activity duration of the System Tests inspection. It does not take much searching to discover that the design activity of the File Organization package is a bottleneck. It controls the critical path. If you could justify removing the dependency between events 17 and 21, you could save 2.5 weeks. Or could you? To find out, return to Table 2.8 and cross out the entry in row 17, column 21. This makes the path through SEARCH the longest route to event 17, giving event 17 a new path length of 4.5 weeks. Tracing the rest of the route via event 17 shows the expected reduction of 2.5 weeks:

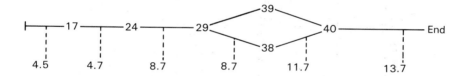

This is no longer the critical path, however. Since events 38 and 39 can now be reached in 8.7 weeks instead of 11.2 weeks, the critical path has switched to the I/O Package. Its path takes 10 weeks to reach event 38. With the subsequent tests, it requires a critical path of 15 weeks to reach the end event:

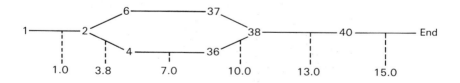

As shown here, the critical path is generally not obvious from visual scanning of a network; neither is the effect of a design change on the critical path readily apparent. A methodical analysis supported by a computer program is recommended for dealing with activity network charts.

TABLE 2.8. CRITICAL PATH IDENTIFICATION

Successor Events	Predecessor Events																			
	1	2	3	4	5	6	7	8	9	10	11	12	13	14	15	16	17	18	19	20
1																				
2																				
3	.5																			
4		3.8																		
5		4.2																		
6		3.8																		
7		4.2																		
8			1																	
9			4.3																	
10								2.8												
11								2.8												
12								6.8												
13				4																
14					4.4															
15						4														
16							4.4													
17	3.8												4	4.4	4	4.4		4.5	3	3
18									4.5											
19										3										
20											3									
21												7								
22													4.8							
23															5.2					
24																	7.2			
25													7							
26														9						
27																7				
28																	9			
29																				
30																		8.5		
31																			5	
32																				5
33																				
34																				
35																				
36																				
37																				
38																				
39																				
40																				
41																				

Table entries represent estimate in weeks to reach any node (successor event) via a path through the predecessor event.

21	22	23	24	25	26	27	28	29	30	31	32	33	34	35	36	37	38	39	40
7																			
			11.2																
9																			
	5																		
		5.4																	
			7										6						
				7										7					
					9		9	11.2							10	10			
								11.2	8.5	5	5	9							
								11.2									14.2	14.2	
																			16.2

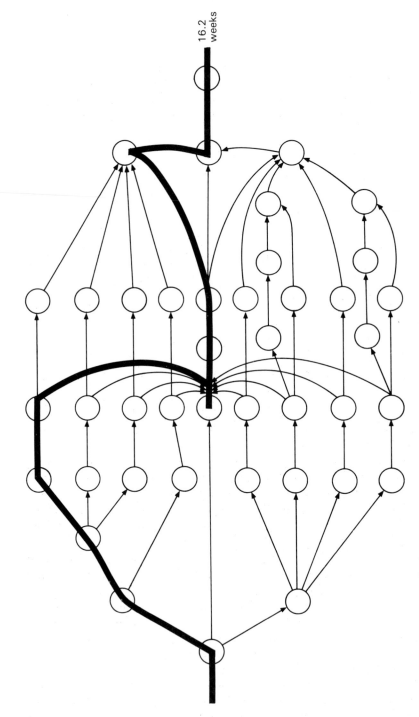

16.2 weeks

Fig. 2.15 Information retrieval—Partial activity network critical path.

The activity network has exposed some hidden relationships in the project plan and it has provided a basis for assigning parallel tasks. The schedule determined by analyzing the network is a very rough estimate of the time required for the project. In the specific case of the example, the schedule of 16.2 weeks is probably an underestimate.

Two factors have been ignored so far. First, no resources have been considered. The example assumes that all the people needed to do the activities are available at the right time. With this assumption, it would require twenty-two programmers during the fifth week to do the job. (Remember, each of the subpackages contains several program units. In the fifth week, there are twenty-two units active: Input plus its six adapters, Edit, Display plus four adapters, Query, System Tests, Search, all the File-Handling and Record-Handling units (5), and the Classify unit.) Yet the project hardly calls for such a large group. Twenty-two people would generate a great deal of idle time—over 60 percent of the time they are assigned to the project would be wasted if all twenty-two were there 16.2 weeks. Obviously, a resource plan is required in which a tradeoff is made between the number of people and the schedule.

Second, the charts show no dates. Therefore, schedule conflicts are not apparent. Suppose the project inspections were to be led by a trained inspector from another department. Each inspection takes a whole day according to the chart. At least the inspection leader must be present all day. Thus there will be some obvious conflicts. For example, three field-handling and two record-handling units will be ready for inspection on the same day, but they cannot be inspected on the same day. Five different days are needed. If they are consecutive, the inspections will end 3.8 weeks after the project start date; that is, events 19 and 20 now have a path length of 3.8 instead of 3.0 weeks. As soon as these events occur, the inspector can go to work on Input and Display that are ready. Of course, if the inspector has commitments to support other projects, further schedule delays must be planned.

A related problem is the schedule delay caused by iteration. When a unit fails an inspection or a test, it is necessary to backtrack and redo some or all of the earlier steps. Since the frequency and amount of rework is unknown, no estimates are given. As noted before, automated PERT analyses do not handle looping of this sort. Consequently, it is necessary to make an educated guess, based on past experience, of the amount of schedule delay due to iteration. This is usually handled as a contingency factor expressed as a percentage of the overall schedule.

2.3.4.5 Work breakdown chart and schedule bar chart

To overcome the fact that an activity network based solely on functional relationships is not a good resource management tool, two other charts are used: a *work breakdown chart* to show who will do each task and a *bar chart* to show when the events will occur. Figure 2.16 shows the format of these convenient charts. Coordinating the activity network chart with these two additional charts leads to a manageable performance plan. The work breakdown corresponding to the functional breakdown of Fig. 2.13 allocates each program unit to some organizational entity. In line with the rule "maximize binding, minimize coupling," all the related programs are given to one person or one team, when possible. Often the workload for a cohesive package is too much for one team to handle. In this case, the package is broken up and distributed to several groups and some allowance is made in the plan for the extra cost of this decision due to the increase in project communications.

As a practical matter, all three charts have to be developed at the same time. An initial activity net will show the functional dependencies dictated by the nature of the job. Work assignments will add resource dependencies which modify the activity net. The bar chart schedule will show further dependencies caused by resource conflicts. After an initial pass at the plan, the coordinated development of all three charts takes into account job content, resource availability, task assignments, and schedules. When contingency factors are added, costs can be estimated, then various plan alternatives can be investigated to improve the schedule or the cost.

For example, the information retrieval task has been assigned to Lucy Lee, an experienced programmer currently managing eight other programmers and a secretary. She has been asked to plan the job with her present department. A quick review of the situation shows her personnel situation:

Lucy Lee	manager/experienced programmer
Marge Constant	secretary/librarian
Jim Stone	database programmer
Dave Johnson	database programmer
Jean Fabre	database programmer—promoted out now
Elaine Brown	experienced programmer
Paul Worth	experienced
Georgianne Green	experienced
Mel Minkus	experienced—transferring out now
Harv Cox	database programmer transferring in twelve weeks
June Smith	trainee—available in four weeks
Tom Simmons	trainee—available in four weeks

Because of transfers and promotions that have already been committed, Lee has only two experienced database programmers and three programmers

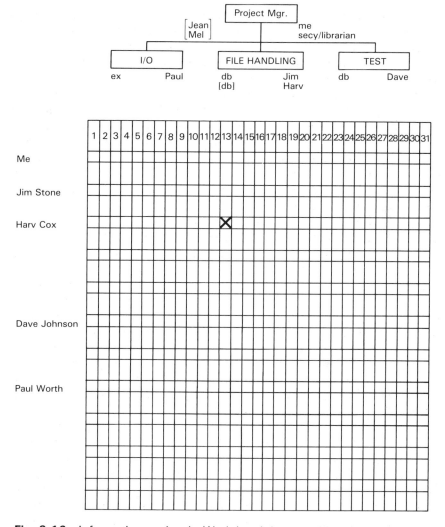

Fig. 2.16 Information retrieval—Work breakdown and bar chart schedule —Basic layout.

with other application experience available permanently. Cox is a database man but he is only available for twelve more weeks. Two experienced programmers are leaving now to be replaced by trainees who graduate from programmer's school in four weeks. Lee has identified three major areas in the project: I/O, File Handling, and Test. She wants to put an experienced person in charge of each area. Since the database issues will arise in File

Handling and Test, she mentally assigns Stone to the former and Johnson to the latter. Worth is the most experienced of the other programmers. He gets to lead the I/O team. These three, with Lee, will do the top-level design, including system input definitions and refine the plan. There are three experienced programmers left, plus two trainees. I/O consists of four major paths which could run in parallel; File Handling has four paths also. They cannot all run simultaneously. Lee can immediately see that the 16.2 weeks proposed for unlimited resources will stretch to some longer schedule.

The workload estimate (Table 2.7) shows that I/O involves 52 weeks of program unit effort; File Handling takes only 44. The Test activities were not estimated. Using her experience, Lee judges that the complexity of the system test cases is roughly equal to the data interface complexity of the deliverable units. The amount of test case code to be written will be about equal to the amount of deliverable code. Judging that the data complexity is about half the system complexity, she guesses that the test effort will take about 48 weeks—half the system effort. The total effort is now looking more like 18 to 19 weeks with no allowance for schedule problems. Lee provides for some slippage and sketches out a worksheet for seeing who can do what (Fig. 2.16). As she fills in the worksheet, she tries to match her people with the work. Cox goes into the File-Handling team because of his database experience, but he is given things he can finish within twelve weeks; preferably, tasks that are not central to system behavior. For the key tasks such as the SEARCH unit, Lee assigns an experienced programmer who will be available throughout the project (and after release, if possible) to handle questions that arise when using the system. For the time being, Lee plans to be the inspector herself. She has done it before and believes it gives her better management control.

Step by step, Lee sketches in specific tasks for each person. The activity net shows task dependencies. The personnel plan shows at least some of the resource dependencies. (Vacations, for example, are not shown.) The workload estimates influence the number of people per task. All the units in Table 2.7 were one-programmer tasks. Systems Tests, however, are undefined. It is estimated that they consist of some number of small activities that can be done in eight weeks, consuming forty-eight programmer-weeks; i.e., six programmers would be required to actually finish in eight weeks. With these points in mind, Lee reserves week 1 for design and definition by herself and the three team leaders (Fig. 2.17). She then assumes that Stone will tackle the SEARCH unit and be generally responsible for system control functions. (Note that Stone spends a whole week with the team leaders even though SEARCH could have started halfway through the definition activity.) Cox can start on Field Handling or Record Handling—no, he may not finish Field Handling in time and Record Handling does not use his database background very well. He is a good candidate to do the intellectually difficult CLASSIFY unit. It is reasonably independent of other units.

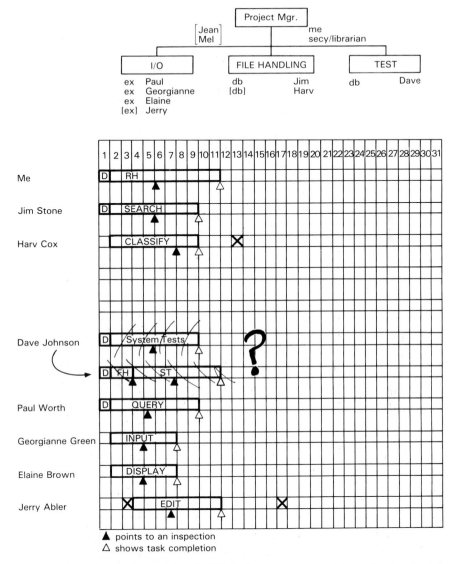

Fig. 2.17 Information retrieval—Work breakdown and bar chart schedule —First attempt.

In addition, it is on the critical path. Cox may be able to accelerate the schedule compared to someone without his knowledge. In Lee's opinion, QUERY is the toughest single I/O unit. Worth can do that. INPUT and DISPLAY are top-down implementations with a lot of activity in each sub-subpackage. They should start right away. Green and Brown are assigned to

Worth's team to get this going. EDIT is still unassigned. If Worth does it, it will be week 13 before the System Tests inspection can occur. That's bad. Somehow, Lee has to assign someone to EDIT. The trainees are not going to be ready to undertake such a responsibility—they should be reserved for the adapters and test cases where they can be well supervised by an experienced programmer. Lee cannot do it herself and also be available for all the inspections, not to mention running the department. She presents this situation to her manager with a plea for more help. He understands the problem and makes the arrangements for Jerry Abler to be borrowed from another department. Abler will be available to Lee's project during weeks 3 through 16. He is given the EDIT unit. Lee assumes he will be effective in week 4 even though he arrives ready to go in week 3. There are still two activities unassigned. Lee decides to do Record Handling herself. To allow for her other duties, she assumes she will take 2 1/2 times as long as had been originally estimated. What should she do with Field Handling? Johnson could do part of it. He doesn't have to start the Systems Tests design much more than four weeks before the inspection. The earliest inspection date so far looks like week 8. Johnson cannot finish much in four weeks, though. That is a problem.

This impasse leads Lee to abandon her first attempt and take another approach. Leaving the overall structure of the system as it is, she decides to concentrate on design until all units are designed and successfully inspected. With a thorough design, well documented, anyone could implement a program unit. The approach is consistent with top-down implementation. Although Lee's department has never done a job this way, her manager's two other departments have tried the approach and it worked.

The top-down plan (Fig. 2.18) leaves SEARCH with Stone but requires him to design the FORMAT TABLE unit before coding SEARCH. Cox is still assigned to CLASSIFY. Green joins Stone's team to design the three Field-Handling units and then code them. When this team finishes its File-Handling units, the programmers start coding test cases previously designed by Johnson.

On the I/O side, Worth designs the QUERY/DISPLAY units and Brown designs the EDIT/INPUT units. The coding of these units and the subsidiary adapters is spread out among the four team members with one piece left over—a display adapter. It is assigned to the trainee, Smith, who will be on Johnson's team. When Abler arrives, he is given design responsibility for Record Handling and he is asked to supervise the trainee, Simmons, who will code the two Record-Handling units. Johnson is the System Tests designer; he has until week 10 to finish the design. INDEX is still unassigned. Lee decides that it is a good task for a trainee, so she asks Johnson to delay the test case designs in order to design INDEX and then supervise Smith who will code it. As she makes these assignments, Lee juggles the in-

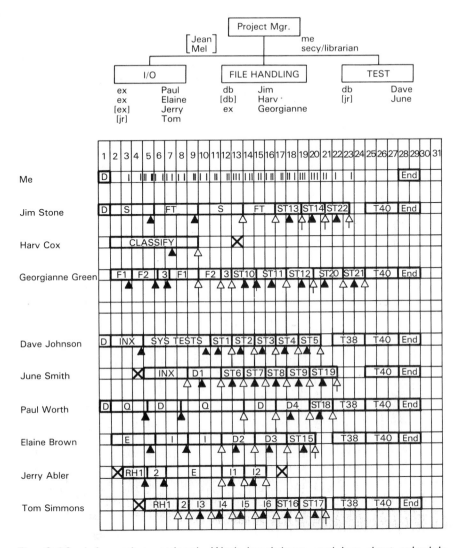

Fig. 2.18 Information retrieval—Work breakdown and bar chart schedule —Second attempt.

spection dates so they do not conflict and she schedules her own time to fit the inspections.

The result of the second attempt at a plan looks good to Lee. She finds that she can schedule all design inspections, including CLASSIFY, prior to the System Tests inspection, as required by the activity network event 17.

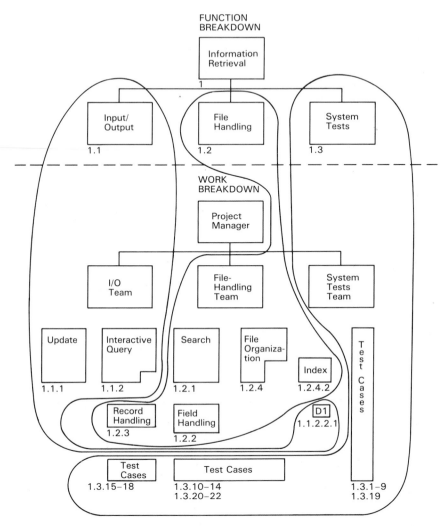

Fig. 2.19   Information retrieval—Function vs. workload breakdown.

Unfortunately, the assignments are not all within the appropriate teams (Fig. 2.19). Stone will have to rely on Johnson's support for INDEX and on Worth's supervision of Record Handling. Worth finds a portion of his responsibility assigned to Johnson's trainee. Johnson has test cases spread all over the map.

Lee, herself, is very busy with inspections. She chose to be the inspector before she realized that there were 46 separate units called for. Not only is her time eaten up, but some of the inspections have to be delayed until she is available. Fortunately, she did not volunteer to program anything herself in this plan. In several places, she allowed more time for a task than had been estimated in the activity chart. The trainees were given a little extra time to do their first job and Johnson was given all the slack available to do the System Tests. In fact, having estimated that twenty-two test cases would be required (averaging two weeks each to design, inspect, code, and debug), Lee thinks Johnson will need all the time he can get for design. The resulting schedule makes good use of everyone's time. There is little remaining slack or idle time, yet the completion date is not nearly as good as Lee had expected. The end date is now twenty-nine weeks after the start, not counting the time that has been spent planning and not counting potential computer time delays. That is half a year. If vacations, holidays, sickness, and other nonproductive hours are added at a typical ratio of 44:52, the project will probably span thirty-four weeks. What started as a seemingly simple programming task has grown quite large. The plan is not inefficient. It is the natural outcome of a project approach which involves:

- Dependencies among tasks
- Resource constraints and mixed skills
- Resource conflicts
- Interface communications among coupled activities
- Management and supervision of team members

If one person could have done the entire job, a great deal of the project effort devoted to communications and coordination could be dropped. The moment the decision was made that a team approach was necessary, project-oriented costs were inevitable. In this example, the costs are largely hidden because the working programmers carry the extra load themselves. In large projects, management, clerical and administrative support, project control, system test, and computer operations are often split out. The special groups established to do this work are called *indirect* because they do not generate the basic deliverables. The ratio of indirect people to direct people ranges from 1:3 for a small project (less than a dozen people total) to as much as 10:1 for a very large multiuser operating system project (hundreds of people). Lee's project has the equivalent of four to five people doing indirect work all or part of the time, slightly more than one third of her eleven people.

2.3.4.6 Development plan

Lee now has the basic data for managing her project. The planning charts can now be combined into a control document called the *Development Plan*. This document will be updated weekly and will serve as the communications medium for Lee's group and as the reporting mechanism (in abbreviated form) for her manager. The Development Plan shows what must be done and what has been accomplished as of each update. The hierarchic identification scheme organizes the report by function and permits quick references between related activities. A combination of presentation formats is used:

1. Lists: to give a compact, organized set of formatted data; e.g., list of deliverables, list of program units, list of tests

2. Activity networks in graphic or list format: to show interfaces and dependencies

3. Bar charts: to show status versus time[15]
   a. arranged by task to show start date, end date, current status, schedule changes
   b. arranged by individuals to show assignments, schedule of performance, planned absences, current status, schedule changes, total people required each week
   c. arranged by support resource (computer, typing pool) to show requirements, commitments, current status, schedule changes due to unfulfilled requirements, total resource of each type required per week
   d. arranged by critical event (inspection, test, decision milestone) to show whether events occur as planned

4. Arrays: to show relationships such as which test cases must be run with each program unit

5. Budget variance reports: to show how well the expense plan is being followed.

6. Narrative: to cover requirements, changes, problems, reports.

These charts, and others as necessary, should exhaustively list the items to be managed. Information about a program unit, therefore, should include name, ID, description, responsible programmer, estimated core requirement, source instructions, running time, schedule for development and test, predecessor and successor programs, parent and child programs, etc. With all these data in one place, well-indexed and easily segmented, weekly project meetings can be held which review the status of the plan and quickly pinpoint issues to be resolved by the responsible individuals.

---

15. The various uses of bar charts follow the ideas of Henry Gantt [71].

2.4   SUMMARY

Every system contains diverse components. Some components are easier to modify than others; therefore, system design is constrained from the outset to use certain components as is and modify the remainder to tailor the system to the user's requirements. Software typically bears the brunt of modification. Consequently, software tends to be the subsystem that is finished last. Software determines the critical path in the system development schedule (i.e., the time to build the system if everything goes well) for two reasons:

- Software development cannot start until the hardware specifications are firm, frozen, and, if possible, demonstratable. Software being developed to support new hardware products can be severely impacted. It is not unusual for specially designed hardware to deviate in some way from the pre-production specifications. Programmers want to program the delivered version not the planned version. In some cases, the programmers cannot proceed beyond high-level design until the first unit of special hardware is available.

- Software development cannot end until the system has been integrated and tested. Given that the software is the subsystem that will be changed to correct problems, it is clear that any problems found during system integration and test result in new and additional tasks for the programmers.

In an effort to reduce total schedule duration, tasks are done in parallel; however, inter-task dependencies interfere with parallel implementation activities. Obviously, if task B depends too heavily on task A, B must be delayed until A is either finished or completely defined. Opportunities for parallel implementation are increased by uncoupling the system components. The prerequisite for uncoupling is a firm system architecture defining interfaces and protocols for communicating across interfaces. Techniques that facilitate parallel implementation are the use of higher-level languages (to reduce dependence on hardware characteristics), interface modules (to insulate a module from changes in its peers), and simulation (to represent interactions by models in advance of getting the real things).

Problems that arise during system integration and test can be very difficult and time consuming. Such problems expose omissions and deviations from the original system design. Clearly, when the problem is a deviation in hardware that must be corrected by changing the software, it will be a new task for the programmers, unanticipated in the original software design. Although software schedules normally include a contingency factor, particularly difficult problems may require an effort considerably in excess of the amount provided in the estimate for programming. An overrun will occur and, in most cases, the programming team will be blamed for the project being late and costing too much. There does not appear to be any practical way to shift the blame, say, to the hardware developer whose deviation from specs caused the problem. Managers, unless enlightened by previous projects, associate the overrun with the group that finishes last. Programmers as a group have a bad name in some organizations simply because the organization has inadequate system management resulting in overruns at the end of the project. Programmers may not be blameless regarding system problems, but they certainly deserve some credit for ultimately bringing the system to an operational level. For their own protection, software managers should educate the system managers to recognize the real source of problems early in the life cycle so they can be attended to during system and subsystem design.

Software managers also protect themselves by selecting a suitable kit of development support and status control tools. The right tools increase productivity and improve project control. Every tool has a cost but, surprisingly, some of the most effective tools are also the easiest to acquire, learn, and use.

Figure 2.20 shows some well-known development tools and techniques in a chart which, in the author's opinion, represents value versus cost. The greatest relative value comes from tools and techniques (such as structured programming in a high-order language [72]) which are reasonable to expect every programmer to learn. Other tools (such as interactive programming using on-line time-sharing support or a comprehensive virtual machine development system) have high value, but they cost more to use. In line with earlier observations, inspections are rated as more valuable than walkthroughs albeit at extra expense. Top-down implementation is rated high value at moderate cost with the proviso that the technique may not apply to all projects. HIPO is rated higher than a program design language, although many people would disagree. The reasoning here is that HIPO is a superior documentation aid when compared to other such aids whereas no one program design language has emerged as clearly superior. For similar reasons, no single analysis and design tool is plotted. The roughly oval area indicates that, the value of such tools depends on how well they fit a particular project. Until this class of tools has been used enough to generate a consensus opinion about the value and cost of each particular tool, it would be premature to be specific. The banana shape assigned to modeling and simulation has a different purpose. In general, the value of such techniques is proportional to the effort applied; therefore, assuming consistent quality of implementation, the more you spend, the more you get in return. That guideline does not apply to the expensive class of benchmarks and throwaway prototypes since they are poor representations of the system under de-

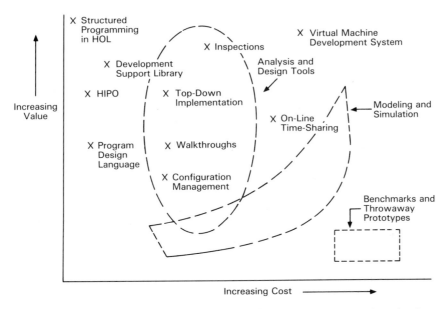

Fig. 2.20   Relative value of development support tools (subjective view).

velopment.[16] A complete development support system dedicated to a single project has a large fixed cost. For this reason, such systems are found only in projects large enough to spread the fixed costs over a number of programmers. Thus each tool or technique will be of great value to some projects and little value to others.

There is a trend to define simpler tools that can be used without relying on large computers or large tool-building staffs. Kernighan and Plauger [73] have shown what can be achieved by defining commonly used program functions, rather small and simple to start with, and combining the basic functions in the form of macros or routines into larger and more powerful tools. Their approach would apply to any organization where there was enough commonality of program function to justify on-line support. For economy, such an approach relies on a small computer or on a time-shared region of a large computer. When the programmers are writing programs for a different machine, there must be an easy way to move the results from the development support system to the user environment. Hence, one attri-

---

16. Throwaway prototypes, used only for study and predictions, should not be confused with the first phase of a phased implementation. In the latter case, the first phase is not thrown away; it serves as the base for subsequent phases. Phased implementation has high value, but it is omitted from the chart since it is more a management technique than a development support tool.

bute of a good tool is that it be flexible enough to be easily transportable from one environment to another.

Status control tools should have the same general attributes as development support tools. A flexible status control tool is one that permits a data set to be displayed in a variety of formats. For example, a computerized development plan could consist of a project database stored under the control of a database management system (DBMS). Different data mappings could be used to extract selected items to be formatted for the project manager's bar chart or fewer items to go into the highlights report for higher management or all the detail for a single program unit presented in the format requested by the unit's programmer.

In addition to being flexible, good tools have the following attributes:

- Simple: well-defined functions that are easy to understand and use
- Well-documented: readily available, readable manuals
- Teachable: supporting training materials (classroom course outlines self-teaching materials, reference manuals, built-in user assistance)
- Appropriate: language and terminology suitable for user; i.e., business-oriented users need tools based on business terms not on scientific notation
- Procedural: standard step-by-step procedures that guide the user and minimize mistakes
- Inexpensive: economical with respect to direct cost, on-going usage cost and resource consumption, cost of backup capability, cost of delay due to tool lead time.

In Chapter 1 the argument that complexity is a function of size was illustrated using only the elements of a program system. In this chapter, the lesson has been that in a total system, a program system can be no more than a subsystem. Other subsystems, including both deliverable items (such as hardware and vendor software) and nondeliverables (such as tools and the people involved with the project), conspire to increase the complexity of the system development project. The burden is on the project managers to find a way to control the project so as to complete it successfully in spite of all the complexity. They do this by:

- Identifying all the elements in the system
- Structuring the elements
- Eliminating unnecessary elements
- Establishing a baseline system specification and a plan of action
- Establishing a change control procedure

- Focusing attention on only those elements that are currently active
- Shifting attention as the project progresses
- Measuring progress versus the plan
- Modifying the plan to fit the situation

Of course, this is only a partial list of a manager's duties. It highlights those things that are most clearly affected by the interactions within the system. Of additional interest is the attitude management should adopt when making decisions. Basically, managers should be bold in design but conservative in implementation. Their goal should be to maximize chances for success and minimize risk of failure. They should use methods that are known to work. They should reuse good programs. They should protect product quality by adopting proven standards as well as by extensive testing. At all times they should know what will happen next. No surprises. With that level of control, they can cope with the problem of complexity.

EXERCISES AND DISCUSSION QUESTIONS

1. Discuss the changing balance of power in the following situations:
   a. Executive/Legislative/Judiciary checks and balances in the Watergate affair. The role of the public.
   b. Consumer/Supplier/Government relationships in the oil and natural gas areas due to
      1) escalation of oil prices by the Organization of Petroleum Exporting Countries
      2) an unusually long cold spell which can exhaust gas supplies
      3) environmental impact studies which prevent accelerated development of alternative energy sources.
      How do these global events affect day-to-day management decisions?

2. You are contractually responsible for delivering a program system to the user of a new type of computer. You have written the program in a higher-level language as directed and tested it on your in-house computer. You have been unable to test it on the user's machine because the compiler is not available. The compiler was committed for delivery last month by another contractor. It now looks like it will be six months late. Your contract runs out in three months. What should you do?

3. Your installed system includes remote controllers and display terminals. The controllers have programmable read-only stores which can store small programs and execute them faster than if they were in regular memory. You have been asked to design and implement a new display format for the terminals. It requires conversational prompting of the user and involves the use of predetermined keywords and pointers to fill out the format. Under what conditions would you put this program in the host, the controller application program area, or the controller read-only store?

4. Improved Programming Technologies (IPT) are discussed in the text as they apply to new program developments. How applicable do you think the following techniques are to the modification of existing programs that did not use the techniques originally?

    a. structured programming
    b. code reading
    c. top-down development
    d. structured design
    e. pseudo-code
    f. HIPO
    g. team operations
    h. development support library
    i. inspections

5. You are in the ninth month of a twelve-month project. A total of 80 percent of the deliverable modules have been written and 10 percent have been tested. Are you on target? Ahead? Behind? Do you have a problem?

6. Project status reports are prepared Friday morning for collection by 4 P.M. Consolidated reports are run over the weekend and available at 1 P.M. Monday for the weekly staff meeting. Due to absences and late reports, some 20 percent of the data are missing from the weekly summary. Should the management team:

    a. postpone the staff meeting until all the data are in?
    b. postpone discussion of the areas affected by the missing data?
    c. use last week's data for the affected areas?
    d. extrapolate this week's data for the affected areas based on the trend to date?
    e. rely on verbal input from the managers of the affected areas?
    f. take some other course of action?

7. Lucy Lee planned her information retrieval project as a top-down implementation.

    a. In her plan, she spends the first week reviewing the initial design and defining data. Subsequently, she inspects each detailed unit design (I_1). She did not allow for code inspection (I_2) prior to debugging. Assuming each deliverable unit and each test case has a code inspection, redo the schedule.

    b. Draw the activity network chart corresponding to the plan in Fig. 2.21 to show resource dependencies as well as task dependencies.

    c. Lee's manager tells her that his two other departments required six weeks training before doing a top-down implementation. Without such training, he doubts that Lee's group can do an adequate job of documentation and hand-off among team members. He asks her to estimate the delivery schedule according to her original approach, where the same person designs and codes each unit whenever possible. Draw up a plan with this constraint.

    d. Lee's manager supports her top-down approach and tells her that his experience shows that design is often done faster when related activities are done by the same person. Lee agrees and cuts 40 percent off the design time for Query/Display, Edit/Input, the Field-Handling units, and Format Table. She leaves all others alone. Draw up a revised plan reflecting this change.

REFERENCES

1. Gorn, S. "When The Chips are Down." Also, Schwartz, J. T. "What Constitutes Progress in Programming?" In ACM Forum: The State of Computer Methodology. *CACM* 18, no. 11 (November 1975).

2. Baram, M. S. "Technology Assessment and Social Control." *Science* 180 (May 4, 1973).

3. Herzberg, F. *Work and The Nature of Man.* Cleveland, Ohio: World Publishing, 1966.

4. Levinson, H. *The Exceptional Executive: A Psychological Conception.* Cambridge, Mass.: Harvard University Press, 1968. Also, Newman, W. H. *Administrative Action: The Techniques of Organization and Management,* 2nd ed. Englewood Cliffs, N.J.: Prentice Hall, 1963.

5. Opler, A. "Fourth Generation Software." *DATAMATION* 13, no. 1 (January 1967). Also Chroust, G., and Mühlbacher, J. R. *Firmware, Microprogramming, and Restructurable Hardware.* Amsterdam: North-Holland Publishing, 1980.

6. Aron, J. D. "Commercial Data Processing Machines in Government Applications." *AFIPS Conference Proceedings* 40, Spring Joint Computer Conference, 1972. Montvale, N.J.: AFIPS Press, 1972.

7. Banham, J. A., and McClelland, P. "Design Features of a Real Time Check Clearing System." *IBM Systems Journal* 11, no. 4 (1972). Also, *DATAMATION* 22, no. 7 (1976) Special Feature on Electronic Banking; and *Computer Decisions* 8, no. 3 (1976) Features on Electronic Funds Transfer (EFT).

8. Weiler, P. W.; Kopp, R. S.; and Dorman, R. G. "A Real-Time Operating System for Manned Spaceflight." *IEEE Transactions on Computers* C-19, no. 5 (May 1970).

9. Jones, T. C. "Measuring Programming Quality and Productivity." *IBM Systems Journal* 17, no. 1 (1978).

10. Aron, J. D. *The Program Development Process Part I—The Individual Programmer.* Reading, Mass.: Addison-Wesley, 1974.

11. Boehm, B. W. "Software Engineering." *IEEE Transactions on Computers* C-25, no. 12 (December 1976).

12. Teichroew, D., and Hershey, E. A. III. "PSL/PSA: A Computer-aided Technique for Structured Documentation and Analysis of Information Processing Systems." *IEEE Transactions on Software Engineering* SE-3, no. 1 (January 1977).

13. Winters, E. W. "An Analysis of the Capabilities of Problem Statement Language: A Language for System Requirements and Specification". *Proceedings: COMPSAC 79.* Long Beach, Calif.: IEEE Computer Society, 1979.

14. Bell, T. E.; Bixler, D. C.; and Dyer, M. E. "An Extendable Approach to Computer-Aided Software Requirements Engineering." Also, Alford, M. "A Requirements Engineering Methodology for Real-Time Processing Requirements." Also, Davis, C. G., and Vick, C. R. "The Software Development System." *IEEE Transactions on Software Engineering* SE-3, no. 1 (January 1977).

15. Ross, D. T., and Schoman, K. "Structured Analysis for Requirements Definition." Second International Conference on Software Engineering, October 1976. *IEEE Transactions on Software Engineering* SE-3, no. 1 (January 1977). Also Ross, D. T., and Brackett, J. W. "An Approach to Structured Analysis." *Computer Decisions* 8, no. 9 (1976).

16. Jackson, M. A. *Principles of Program Design.* New York: Academic Press, 1975.

17. Langefors, B. *Theoretical Analysis of Information Systems.* Philadelphia: Auerbach, 1973. Also, Langefors, B., and Sundgren, B. *Information Systems Architecture.* New York: Petrocelli/Charter, 1975.

18. Warnier, J. D. *Logical Construction of Programs.* Leiden, Netherlands: H. F. Stenfurt Kroese, B. V., 1974, and New York: Van Nostrand-Reinhold, 1976. Also, Warnier, J. D. *Logical Construction of Systems.* New York: Van Nostrand-Reinhold, 1981.

19. Schwartz, J. T. "Principles of Specification Language Design with Some Observations Concerning the Utility of Specification Languages" in *Algorithm Specification.* Edited by R. Rustin. Englewood Cliffs, N.J.: Prentice-Hall, 1972.

20. DeRemer, F., and Kron, H. H. "Programming-in-the-Large Versus Programming-in-the-Small." *IEEE Transactions on Software Engineering* SE-2, no. 2 (June 1976).

21. Dijkstra, E. W. "Notes on Structured Programming." The Report 70-WSK-03. Eindhoven, Netherlands: Technical Hochschule, April 1970.

22. Dahl, O.-J.; Dijkstra, E. W.; and Hoare, C. A. R. *Structured Programming.* New York: Academic Press, 1972.

23. Wirth, N. *Systematic Programming: An Introduction.* Englewood Cliffs, N.J.: Prentice-Hall, 1973.

24. Linger, R. C.; Mills, H. D.; and Witt, B. I. *Structured Programming: Theory and Practice.* Reading, Mass.: Addison-Wesley, 1979.

25. Van Leer, P. "Top-Down Development Using a Program Design Language." *IBM Systems Journal* 15, no. 2 (1976).

26. Hamilton, M., and Zeldin, S. "Higher Order Software—A Methodology for Defining Software." *IEEE Transactions on Software Engineering* SE-2, no. 1, (March 1976).

27. King, J. C. "Program Correctness: On Inductive Assertion Methods." *IEEE Transactions on Software Engineering* SE-6, no. 5 (September 1980).

28. "HIPO—A Design and Documentation Technique." Installation Management Series, Form GC20–1851. White Plains, N.Y.: IBM Corp., 1974. Also Katzan, H. *Systems Design and Documentation: An Introduction to the HIPO Method.* New York: Van Nostrand-Reinhold, 1976.

29. Barr, L.; LaBolle, V.; and Willmorth, N. E. *Planning Guide for Computer Program Development.* Report No. TM–2314, Santa Monica, Calif: System Development Corp., 1965.

30. Jones, M. N. "HIPO for Developing Specifications." *DATAMATION* 22, no. 3 (1976). Also, Stay, J. F. "HIPO and Integrated Program Design." *IBM Systems Journal* 15, no. 2 (1976).

31. Guest, J.; Lai, S.; and Loyear, R. L. "Simulation Technique of a Distributed Intelligence System." 1975 Summer Computer Simulation Conference. LaJolla, Calif.: Simulation Councils, Inc., 1975.

32. Benwell, N., ed. *Benchmarking-Computer Evaluation and Measurement.* Washington, D.C.: Hemisphere Publishing, 1975. Distributed by John Wiley & Sons, New York.

33. Lucas, H. C., Jr. "Synthetic Program Specifications for Performance Evaluation." *Proceedings of the ACM Annual Conference,* 1972. New York: Association for Computing Machinery, 1972.

34. Wilkes, M. V. "Software Engineering and Structured Programming." *IEEE Transactions on Software Engineering* SE-2 (November, December 1976).

35. Mills, H. D. "Software Development." *IEEE Transactions on Software Engineering* SE-2, no. 4 (December 1976). Also, Mills, H. D. "Top-down Programming in Large Systems" in *Debugging Techniques in Large Systems,* edited by R. Rustin, Englewood Cliffs, N.J.: Prentice-Hall, 1971. Also, Mills, H. D. "Chief Programmer Team: Principles and Procedures." Report FSC 71–5108. Gaithersburg, Md.: IBM Federal Systems Division, 1971. Also, Mills, H. D. "Mathematical Foundations for Structured Programming." Report FSC 72–6012. Gaithersburg, Md.: IBM Federal Systems Division, 1972. Also, Mills, H. D. "How to Write Correct Programs and Know It." Report FSC 73–5008, Gaithersburg, Md.: IBM Federal Systems Division, 1973. Also, Mills H. D. "On the Development of Large, Reliable Programs." *Proceedings of the IEEE Symposium on Computer Reliability.* New York: IEEE, 1973. Also, Mills, H. D., and Baker, F. T. "Chief Programmer Teams." *DATAMATION* 19, no. 12 (1973). Also, Baker, F. T. "Chief Programmer Team Management of Production." *IBM Systems Journal* 11, no. 1 (1972). Also, Baker, F. T. "System Quality Through Structured Programming-Programming." *AFIPS Conference Proceedings* 41, Fall Joint Computer Conference 1972. Montvale, N.J.: AFIPS Press, 1972. Also, Baker, F. T. "Structured Programming in a Production Environment." *IEEE Transactions on Software Engineering* SE-1, no. 2 (June 1975).

36. Brooks, F. P., Jr. *The Mythical Man-Month.* Reading, Mass.: Addison-Wesley, 1975.

37. Reynolds, J. C. *The Craft of Programming.* Englewood Cliffs, N.J.: Prentice-Hall, 1981.

38. Conway, R., and Gries, D. *An Introduction to Programming*. Cambridge, Mass.: Winthrop, 1973.

39. Dijkstra, E. W. *A Discipline of Programming*. Englewood Cliffs, N.J.: Prentice-Hall, 1976.

40. Kernighan, B. W., and Plauger, P. J. *The Elements of Programming Style*. New York: McGraw-Hill, 1974.

41. McCracken, D. D. *A Simplified Guide to Structured COBOL Programming*. New York: John Wiley & Sons, 1976.

42. McGowan, C. L., and Kelly, J. R. *Top-Down Structured Programming Techniques*. New York: Petrocelli/Charter, 1975.

43. Myers, G. J. *Reliable Software Through Composite Design*. New York: Petrocelli/Charter, 1975.

44. Weinberg, G. M. *The Psychology of Computer Programming*. New York: Van Nostrand-Reinhold, 1971.

45. Yourdon, E., and Constantine, L. L. *Structured Design*. Englewood Cliffs, N.J.: Prentice-Hall, 1979.

46. DeMarco, T. *Structured Analysis and System Specification*. New York: Yourdon, 1978.

47. Special Issue: Programming. Articles by Brown, P. J.; Yohe, J. M.; Wirth, N.; Knuth, D. E.; Kernighan, B. W.; and P. J. Plauger, edited by P. J. Denning. *ACM Computing Surveys* 6, no. 4 (1974).

48. *Symposium on Structured Programming COBOL—Future and Present*. New York: Association for Computing Machinery, 1975.

49. "An Introduction to Structured Programming in COBOL," GC20-1776. "An Introduction to Structured Programming in PL/I," GC20-1777. "HIPO—A Design and Documentation Technique," GC20-1851. "OS Development Support Libraries," GC20-1663. "Improved Programming Technologies—An Overview," GC20-185. IBM Installation Management Series. White Plains, N.Y.

50. "Management Overview," GE19-5086. Also, Partch, H. B. "The Programming Dilemma: Maintenance vs. Development," GE19-5085. Also, "Code Reading, Structured Walk-Throughs, and Inspections," GE19-5200. IBM World Trade Corporation. Improved Programming Technologies Series. Copenhagen, Denmark.

51. Fagan, M. E. "Design and Code Inspection to Reduce Errors in Program Development." *IBM Systems Journal* 15, no. 3 (1976).

52. Greaves, T. J. "Learning to Use Structured Programming or, How to Think in a Structured Manner," TR54.043. IBM Corp., White Plains, N.Y., 1974.

53. Opdyke, H. G. "An Approach to Team Programming," TR00.2613. IBM Corp., White Plains, N.Y., 1975.

54. Stevens, W. P.; Myers, G. J.; and Constantine, L. L. "Structured Design." *IBM Systems Journal* 13, no. 2 (1974).

55. Thomas, D. J. "A Definition of Top-Down Programming System Development," TR00.2562. IBM Corp., White Plains, N.Y., 1974.

56. Waldstein, N. S. "The Walk-Thru, A Method of Specification, Design and Code Review," TR00.2536. IBM Corp., White Plains, N.Y., 1974.

57. Waldstein, N. S., and Alulis. R. J. "The Library Controller," TR00.2633. IBM Corp., White Plains, N.Y., 1975.

58. Pomeroy, J. W. "A Guide to Programming Tools and Techniques." *IBM Systems Journal* 11, no. 3 (1972).

59. *Software Directory. Vol. 1—Data Processing Management. Vol. 2—Business Applications.* Carmel, Ind.: International Computer Programs, Inc. Published in January and July.

60. Brown, H. M. "Support Software for Large Systems," in *Software Engineering: Concepts and Techniques.* Edited by J. N. Buxton, P. Naur, and B. Randell. New York: Petrocelli/Charter, 1976.

61. Teichroew, D. "Information Processing Systems Analysis and Design." Progress Report C00-25-44-1. Michigan University, Ann Arbor, Michigan, January 1–September 30, 1975.

62. Thomas, R., and Yates, J. *A User Guide to the UNIX System.* New York: McGraw-Hill, 1982. Also, Dolotta, T. A., and Mashey, J. R. "An Introduction to the Programmer's Workbench" and companion papers. *Proceedings of the 2nd International Conference on Software Engineering.* Long Beach, Calif.: IEEE Computer Society, 1976.

63. Lattanzi, L. D. "An Analysis of the Performance of a Software Development Methodology." *Proceedings: COMPSAC 79.* Long Beach, Calif.: IEEE Computer Society, 1979.

64. Myers, G. J. *Software Reliability: Principles and Practices.* New York: John Wiley & Sons, 1976.

65. Hunter, I. C., and Reed, J. N. "An IPT Project—Results, Conclusions, and Recommendations." Report SETR-77-008. IBM United Kingdom, Ltd, 1976.

66. Hsia, P., and Petry, F. E. "A Framework for Discipline in Programming". *IEEE Transactions on Software Engineering* SE-6, no. 2 (March 1980).

67. Boehm, B. W. "Software and Its Impact: A Quantitative Assessment". *DATAMATION* 19, no. 5 (1973). Also, Kosy, D. W. "Air Force Command and Control Information Processing in the 1980s: Trends in Software Technology." Report R-1012-PR. Santa Monica, Calif.: Rand Corp., June 1974.

68. Boehm, B. W. *Software Engineering Economics* Englewood Cliffs, N.J.: Prentice-Hall, 1981.

69. Moder, J. J., and Phillips, C. R. *Project Management with CPM and Pert.* New York: Van Nostrand-Reinhold, 1970. Also, Whitehouse, G. E. *Systems Analysis and Design Using Network Techniques.* Englewood Cliffs, N.J.: Prentice-Hall, 1973.

70. Ackoff, R. L., and Sasieni, N. W. *Fundamentals of Operations Research.* New York: John Wiley & Sons, 1968.

71. Clark, W. *The Gantt Chart.* London: Sir Isaac Pitman and Sons, 1938.

72. Shaw, M.; Almes, G. T.; Newcomer, J. M.; Reid, B. K.; and Wulf, W. A. "A Comparison of Programming Languages for Software Engineering." *Software-Practice and Experience* 11, no. 1 (January 1981). Also, Metzger, J. R., and Barnes, B. H. *Decision Table Languages and Systems.* New York: Academic Press, 1977.

73. Kernighan, B. W., and Plauger, P. J. *Software Tools.* Reading, Mass.: Addison-Wesley, 1976.

3
The System Development Life Cycle

The life cycle of a complete program system follows the same steps as a program unit, but the issues that are important at each decision point in the cycle are often different. For this reason, the life cycle of a programming system will be covered in some detail in this and subsequent chapters. Specifically, the following sequential stages in the cycle are covered:

Concept Formulation: Output—System Objectives

Project Definition: Output—Design Requirements Baseline

Project Implementation: Output—Deliverable End Product

- Design: Output—System and Package Design Specifications
- Development: Output—Debugged Program Units
- Test: Output—Deliverable End Product

Operation, Maintenance, and Upgrade: Output—Operational System

Termination: Output—Project Archives

3.1 THE LIFE CYCLE

The *life cycle* consists of the steps a project follows from its original conception to its termination. Although every project has a life cycle, few managers bother to formalize the process. Exceptions are found in large companies, whose procedures are for internal use only, and in government, where the procedures are published and used as a means of managing subcontractor performance [1].

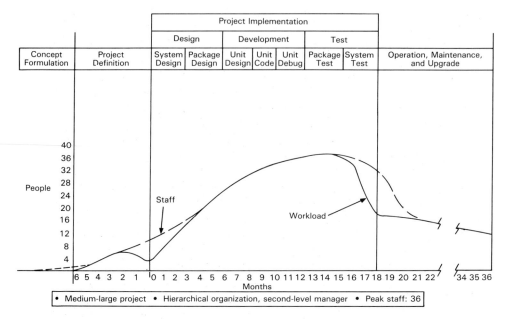

		Project Implementation							
		Design		Development			Test		
Concept Formulation	Project Definition	System Design	Package Design	Unit Design	Unit Code	Unit Debug	Package Test	System Test	Operation, Maintenance, and Upgrade

- Medium-large project • Hierarchical organization, second-level manager • Peak staff: 36

Fig. 3.1   Program system development life cycle.

A picture of the life cycle is often useful as an aid to planning and estimating. Figure 3.1 is characteristic of moderately large programming projects that use a normal pyramid organization and bottom-up system integration and test; it shows how resources build and fall over the life of the job. The solid line represents the people required by the workload, and the dashed line represents the probable number of people assigned to the project as a result of recruiting schedules. With such a chart, given the scheduled delivery date and the peak personnel required, the project manager can budget weekly resource requirements, set up a recruiting plan, determine when to schedule reviews, and make various other routine decisions related to resources and time.[1] Since the chart shows all the people assigned to the job, the picture can be subdivided to show the portion of the people actually programming—programmers, analysts, etc.—as opposed to those providing support (Fig. 3.2). Note that in this chart only the upper portion repre-

---

1. The life cycle chart has a different shape for different organizational and support setups. The case shown is representative of the most common approach to program system development since about 1963. Newer methods, such as top-down implementation, tend to flatten out the peak of the chart. (See section 3.2.1.) The relationship between project size and project schedule also affects the shape of the curve, as shown in section 3.2.2. The area under the curve is the total project resource requirement.

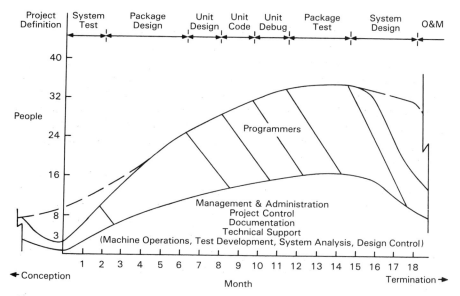

Fig. 3.2   Programmers vs. support.

sents sequential steps in the life cycle. The lower portion covers a variety of overhead support activities that span several stages in the dynamic process. Furthermore, as the slanting boundaries indicate, even the dynamic process does not consist of clearly distinct steps. Each stage overlaps its neighbors to some extent. In practical terms, when there are many people on the project some finish their assignments sooner than others. Some program units will be completely debugged before others are coded. As a result, some programmers will be available to form the nucleus of a test team while the rest of the programmers are still coding and debugging.

    Only one phase of a project is shown in the life cycle charts. Good design frequently dictates *phased implementation* [2,3]. This requires some overlap of life cycles, as in Fig. 3.3. Clearly, the total labor force peaks at a higher level than the Phase I labor force. On the other hand, judicious selection of functions assigned to each phase, accompanied by careful planning, can level off the peak labor force requirement. Starting about the time Phase I is in test, Phase II can begin. Hopefully, the Phase II buildup can be staffed with people coming off Phase I, although it requires skillful management to make sure the people available for Phase II have design talents. The factors affecting the division of a requirement into phases are discussed in general in later chapters but, since the factors are very dependent on the specifics of a particular system, no detailed recommendations regarding phasing are made.

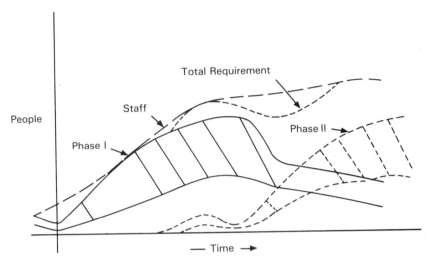

Fig. 3.3 Phased implementation.

In a large organization with several multiphase projects underway, the phenomenon of specialization is readily apparent. In contrast to very small jobs where one person does everything, large teams tend to distinguish among job types and individual responsibilities. Specialization initially addresses issues of professional expertise. As specialists are trained, they gradually reinforce their skills by clustering in centers of competence. It then becomes apparent that the dynamics of project staging and phasing concentrate on certain skills at certain times so that specialists can be shifted from one project to another. When the schedules permit, time-sharing the specialists is more attractive than assigning them to jobs outside their specialty. Finally, managers notice that specialization can be used to create a check and balance system that leads to better products. This is accomplished by assigning responsibilities in such a way that the results of one specialty area are evaluated by members of another area.

The effect of these management attitudes on program development shows up in the job categories that are found in many organizations. On the left side of Fig. 3.4 is a typical job structure for the professionals in a medium-sized team showing which project stages they are responsible for. The user is responsible for originating the problem and setting the objectives for what is wanted. The project team includes all the other skills. Systems analysts and designers determine what will be delivered and specify how it will be built. In this group, an individual may be an analyst or a designer or may do both tasks as required. Individual programmers build the end product. Test specialists test it. (This group is sometimes merged

Project Stages

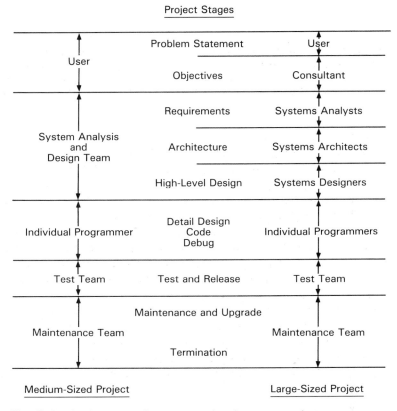

Fig. 3.4   Assignments in program development projects.

with the programmers, but when it is separate it is an excellent quality control check on the other groups.) Then a maintenance team takes care of the end product.

Larger teams recognize more specialties, as shown on the right of Fig. 3.4. Here, the user is still expected to originate the problem, but he or she may not be able to state the objectives without the help of a consultant. The objectives go to a system analysis team—no designers—where a requirements statement is developed. The highest level of design is performed by architects who are specialists in system structure more than algorithms and processes. Their work is turned over to system designers who carry the specifications to lower levels but do not write programs. As before, individual programmers, testers, and maintainers carry the job to completion. The changing specialties reemphasize the dynamic nature of the life cycle and the need for the management team to adapt its behavior to the current situation at all times.

The purpose of the system development life cycle chart is to keep the entire project in front of the eyes of management. Under normal conditions, each person focuses on the current task with only a little time devoted to preparing for the next task. This near-term concentration may be efficient for the moment, but it can lead to major problems later. The chart is a reminder that the project has many aspects beyond those of immediate concern. It helps a person with tunnel vision move off to the side far enough to see that the tunnel pierces a mountain. An individual programmer may get by perfectly well by simply going through the tunnel producing one isolated program unit. The project manager, on the other hand, has to be aware of the mountain to know its character and dimensions.

There is an old story that illustrates the value of getting the big picture: A building contractor decided to interview some of his construction workers one day to bolster employee relations. He went over to a group of three bricklayers and talked to each one separately. He asked them what they were doing and how they liked the job. The first man commented that he was laying 133 bricks that day and he liked the work fine as long as the foreman didn't bug him about lying in the shade when his quota was laid. The contractor figured this fellow to be a slacker who tried to get by with the absolute minimum effort. But his brickwork was good and there was no cause to criticize the man. The second bricklayer explained that he was building a loadbearing exterior wall with matching ornamental face bricks. He liked the job fine because he could see the results of his work when he was done. This response impressed the contractor. The man showed an interest in his work. He appreciated quality and structural integrity and he knew the purpose of his task. The contractor made a note to keep an eye on this fellow because he was a good prospect for the next promotion opportunity. The third bricklayer was asked the same questions. He answered that he was helping to build a great cathedral that would last a thousand years and be the new focal point of community activity. He was proud to have a responsible role in constructing an edifice devoted to the public good. The contractor fired him. Not only were his courses of brick uneven and spattered with mortar, but he was supposed to be building a garage.

The contractor had the big picture; the employees did not. The best of them showed a conscientious and reliable approach to his piece of the job. The minimum performer contributed not because he tried very hard but because the system development process had been set up to succeed as long as he did not do substandard work. The process was not flexible enough to absorb the impact of the third man. His misdirected energy was impacting the development plan and interfering with the work of the rest of the team.

The contractor's counterpart in program system development is the project manager or, more broadly, the management team. Managers must have the big picture in order to lay out a system development life cycle that will produce the desired product, even when individual workers have limited knowledge of the whole system.

Corresponding to the life cycle is a management procedure. For each stage in the life cycle the management procedure calls for certain inputs, activities, and outputs. Reviews and decisions are scheduled events within the procedure. Thorough documentation makes the management procedure work. (One version of a documentation approach is presented in this chapter. It provides for the data and milestones appropriate to most projects. Managers of small- and medium-sized projects will be able to omit some portions of the documentation.) The value to the project manager is [4] that the procedures provide:

- Aid in controlling commitments in the area of design, performance, schedule, size, effectiveness, and cost
- A basis for making decisions
- An historical reference

By following the procedure, the manager is constrained to make commitments only after determining what is to be done (requirement) and how it is to be accomplished (specification/plan). The manager is forced to monitor project status and decide, at key milestones, whether to continue as planned, alter the plan, or scrap the project. The orderly structure of the procedure provides a permanent record of the project that can be analyzed after the project has been completed. Although the hindsight gained by this historical analysis does not guarantee that future projects will be flawless, it does point out trouble spots and suggest how to avoid them.

3.1.1 Concept Formulation

The original idea that sets the project development activity in motion is usually conceived by one or more people who are trying to solve a rather broad problem. They have identified a specific operational requirement that cannot be satisfied by any means currently available; neither can they make the requirement go away. They therefore consciously attempt to formulate a solution. The solution may be obvious; particularly, if several other organizations have faced the same situation, solved it, and made their experience available. Sometimes the solution is not obvious, but an easy nontechnical approach can be based on sound management experience. For example, a programmer training problem may be alleviated by standardizing on one higher-level language in place of three or four languages currently in use. Concept formulation in this case will normally be done by the key managers with minimal technical assistance. In fact, the decision may be made in a single sitting.

The case where the solution is unobvious and outside the experience of the organization requires a more extensive concept formulation effort. Technical studies must be made, often with the assistance of outside consultants, to determine how to solve the problem. The results of such studies will demonstrate whether a concept exists[2] that appears to be economically feasible and that would satisfy the requirement. More precisely, the study will formulate an itemized description of the system requirement and show that all of the items on the list could be built and presumably could be integrated.

At this stage, the requirements to be met by the total system will have been pinned down and could be documented. The details of the subsystems and lower-level packages remain undefined. At best, some guesswork and some experience will have been combined to show that it is feasible to satisfy the system requirement. The statement of the system requirement, called the "system objectives" document, is a statement of direction, setting out *what is wanted:* what the program system should accomplish. *System objectives* state the objectives of the system in terms of technical, operational, and mission-oriented requirements of the system as a whole. The document is not very detailed; it emphasizes the significance of the requirements to the organization or the business.

In the previous chapter, an on-line banking system was introduced to show how various constraints affect system software. The same example illustrates several aspects of the concept formulation stage of system development. Remember that the problem is to improve customer service. The solution is to build an on-line system for banking activities that are currently done manually or by batch data processing. The major questions to be answered are:

- How long should a teller transaction take in order to improve customer service?
- Can an on-line system process transactions fast enough to satisfy the service criterion?

It is not hard to see how to answer these questions. Start by observing the current system. Measure the time taken by various teller activities, and survey customer satisfaction. You can anticipate a correlation between customer waiting time and customer satisfaction. By classifying customer responses you may find that during a busy hour:

---

2. The study may also show that no concept exists for solving the problem within the constraints imposed by the situation. It is possible that a concept exists and has been implemented elsewhere by unknown methods; yet the development team is unable to invent their own solution concept. These cases generally call for a new start: restating the requirement or seeking additional advice and assistance.

95 percent of all customers were in the bank (in a queue or being served) less than five minutes.

50 percent of all customers were in the bank (in a queue or being served) less than two minutes.

10 percent of all customers were in the bank (in a queue or being served) less than one minute.

95 percent of all customers required less than five minutes of teller service.

50 percent of all customers required less than one minute of teller service.

10 percent of all customers required less than thirty seconds of teller service.

80 percent of all customers were dissatisfied with the speed of service.

15 percent of all customers were indifferent.

5 percent of all customers were satisfied.

Analysis of such data might suggest that the satisfied customers came from the class of customers whose time in the bank was small (e.g., they did not have to wait for a teller to become available) and whose service time approximated their time in the bank (e.g., they did not waste time). It seems that a system that could handle one customer per teller every thirty seconds for most types of transactions would be a great improvement. The assumption can be tested by running a couple of experiments in which special manual support is provided to a branch to speed up teller processing and again surveying customer attitudes. Simultaneously, estimates based on existing programs can be made of the computer time required for various transactions. The processing time must be substantially less than thirty seconds for the system to work. A real test of feasibility requires analysis of a queuing model to determine that all tellers, while processing a variety of transactions during peak periods, can maintain an average service rate of thirty seconds per customer.

Notice that the answers obtained by these means merely show that on-line banking is feasible. No in-depth design has been done so that there is considerable risk that the actual system will be inadequate. Nevertheless, the system objectives document permits further work to proceed. The nature of the objectives in this case are:

- To increase productivity in terms of business volume per employee
- To increase customer satisfaction in terms of total time per transaction
- To obtain a service advantage over competitors

The type of criterion accompanying these objectives would be, for example, "for 95 percent of the transaction types A through F, total processing time must not exceed thirty seconds."

During concept formulation, an effort is made to forecast the cost of the system being described. However gross the cost estimate is at this early stage, it should be compared to the supposed value of the system to see if the project is worthwhile. This exercise requires considerable judgment. The cost figures are always optimistic at this point simply because no one can foresee the complexity that may be introduced as the details of the design are developed; neither can anyone guess how many changes will occur during the life of the project to affect its cost. Generous allowance should be made for complexity, change activity, and other factors (such as the inflation rates of the economy) when estimating the system cost. Value is even harder to quantify. Usually the system is intended to reduce cost or increase productivity (output or business volume per unit of cost). If the system achieves this objective, the user may increase profit as a result. Nevertheless, the value of the program system is measured by the change in some hard-to-measure, hard-to-predict activity. Adding to the difficulty of quantifying value is the likelihood that emotions have influenced the system requirement. When a chief executive says, "I am convinced that we can double our volume if the computer can handle orders in one second instead of ten seconds," a certain intangible value is placed on making the system meet a one-second response time objective. It is unfortunate that several years later when the same executive criticizes the amount spent on the order-processing system there is no way to prove that the amount was justified in relation to the executive's goals. Allowing for these special situations, the concept formulation stage of a project should produce a properly qualified quantitative cost justification for the system.

Concept formulation supports a decision to proceed or not to proceed to a formal project. The output of the concept formulation stage is a pair of documents typically containing very general data which will be refined in later stages of the product:

System objectives
- preliminary objectives for the program subsystem
- initial project justification

Project definition plan
- firm plan for Project Definition Stage
  people
  tasks
  budget
- tentative plan for project life cycle through all stages

These documents are reviewed by all the responsible parties, including the support groups, the financial department, the managers of activities that can be impacted by the planned system, as well as the managers who placed the requirement. The review should produce a third document—the review report—which contains the management decision and, if necessary, a list of changes required to the objectives and plan.

Management approval at this point represents conditional approval of the development project. Final approval is inappropriate since there has been no real work done to design the system and estimate its cost.

The stages of the life cycle can be characterized, á la HIPO, by their inputs, outputs, and processing activities. Concept formulation is treated this way in Fig. 3.6, following an index to the life cycle stages in Fig. 3.5.

3.1.2 Project Definition

The next stage in the project is to analyze the system objectives in order to define the requirements in detail and prepare some preliminary design specifications (Fig. 3.7). This work is sufficiently time consuming on a large project to warrant assigning it to a team brought together for the purpose. The team could be the cadre for later development activity if final approval is given. When the team comes from within the organization, it is assigned the responsibility for project definition without any intervening delay; however, for program systems of any size, the number of people required may not be available in-house. Certainly the rapid buildup implied in the

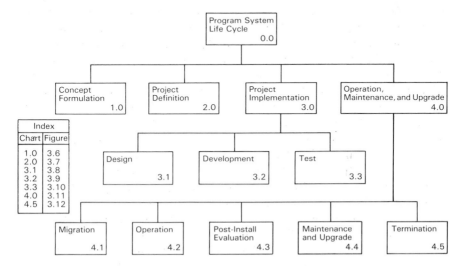

Fig. 3.5 Program system life cycle stages.

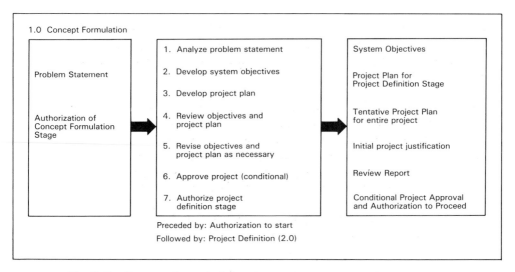

1.0 Concept Formulation

Problem Statement	1. Analyze problem statement	System Objectives
	2. Develop system objectives	Project Plan for Project Definition Stage
	3. Develop project plan	
Authorization of Concept Formulation Stage	4. Review objectives and project plan	Tentative Project Plan for entire project
	5. Revise objectives and project plan as necessary	Initial project justification
	6. Approve project (conditional)	Review Report
	7. Authorize project definition stage	Conditional Project Approval and Authorization to Proceed

Preceded by: Authorization to start
Followed by: Project Definition (2.0)

Fig. 3.6 Concept formulation stage.

life cycle curve of Fig. 3.1 may not be possible without using an outside pool of talent, such as found in a software house or a service bureau.

If the development responsibility is to be contracted outside the organization, it is normal to issue a *request for proposals (RFP)* to obtain the best offer from among several qualified competitive vendors. The RFP process, assuming adequate time for study, proposal preparation, proposal evaluation, vendor selection, and contract negotiation can take three to twelve months. Some large companies use the RFP internally so one division of the company can obtain a development estimate when another division is the developer. A few companies use noncompetitive RFPs or RFQs (request for quotation) to establish a price from the single vendor they normally work with. Most companies and government agencies use the RFP to obtain multiple competitive bids. The lowest, technically responsive bid wins the job; more precisely, the winner is the bidder with the best score on a rating scale that considers multiple factors including responsiveness, cost, technology, and past performance.[3]

---

3. For very large systems, some organizations, notably the U.S. government, select two or three bidders to do parallel project definitions. The competition during this stage is expected to increase the quality of the project definition and reduce the risks associated with implementation. The method is expensive but, where properly used, it is only a fraction of the total system cost. As insurance for the success of the total system, it is a good investment.

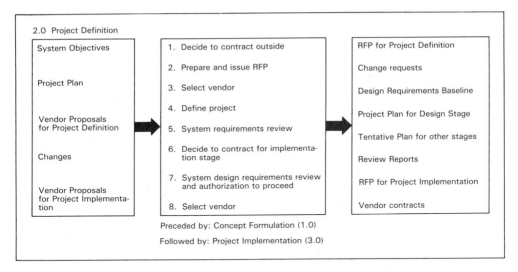

Fig. 3.7 Project definition stage.

The information contained in the RFP includes all the relevant data used to generate the system objectives, the objectives document itself, and descriptions of the procedures vendors must follow in responding and in performing. The response to the RFP contains the vendor's firm proposal for performing the project definition and a plan for doing the subsequent development. (This is the first revision of the project plan produced in the concept formulation stage.) The firm proposal can serve as the basis for negotiating a contract covering project definition. The plan for later development can be used to gauge the ultimate cost and feasibility of the project. At this point, if the independent judgment of the vendors shows the project will be much more expensive than predicted by the concept formulation effort, the decision to proceed should be reconsidered. This is particularly true when the vendors are more experienced in the area than you are. (Wide variance among vendors is a warning that your RFP is incomplete or ambiguous.) After responses to an RFP are reviewed and the winning bidder selected, the total system as described in the system objectives document is subjected to a top-down analysis to eliminate frills ("nice-to-have" requirements) and add essentials that were overlooked during concept formulation. The goal of the analysis is to produce a far more detailed *design requirements baseline*. This is a statement of *what is to be provided*, as opposed to what was wanted. The design requirements baseline goes into the detailed function and performance requirements of the subsystems and smaller packages. That is, it describes how each of these components must look to the user and to each other. it does not say how they must be built, although the builders quite often accept the structure of the baseline functions as the architecture of the product. The baseline should be sufficiently detailed to convey the needs to be met, but the requirements should be written to allow the developer maximum technical freedom. The contents of the baseline document are organized the same way as the subsequent design specification document described in section 3.1.3, but they necessarily contain less detail and do not include certain sections.

In the banking example, concept formulation addressed general questions regarding customer service and technical feasibility. Project definition would go into secondary questions such as:

- Should a customer get the same fast service at all branch offices, or can a distinction be made between transactions at the customer's local branch and transactions elsewhere?

- Should an on-line system provide the file integrity and data privacy the bank has in its batch system?

- Does the operation of on-line terminals by branch personnel require any procedural or organization changes in the bank?

- Assuming service is so good that we acquire new customers, can the on-line system keep up with the growth of our business?

The questions probe topics such as centralization vs. decentralization, fiduciary responsibility, and growth potential. The answers may all be favorable from a technical standpoint; they may or may not be acceptable to management.

Inevitably, the design requirements for a complex system will contain hidden flaws that interfere with the implementation of the system. Such flaws are not always serious. The design requirements baseline is a document that will be studied, interpreted, modified, and negotiated by people. If they do their job properly, they will find the flaws and fix them. In the process the baseline will be updated until it is the best statement of requirements for the system against which the end product is to be checked for compliance and suitablility.

Two things that happened in the banking environment illustrate the limitations of initial studies. In one case, the program path lengths used to estimate processing time were all based on simple batch programs without shared files. The new system used a database management system and a single-integrated database. In the new system, more instructions were executed by the database manager than by the old application programs. When the new system ran, the queue buildup started much sooner than expected and the service objectives were not met. In the second case, service was improved by a factor of 4 for the average customer; however, customer satisfaction got worse. The problem was psychological rather than technical, and it escaped detection during concept formulation and project definition because of the nature of the experiments. A customer under the old system would come into the bank, get in a queue for a teller, wait a bit until reaching the teller, then give the teller a transaction to process. The teller would check the papers, leave the window, go to a tub file to collect the customer's records (or phone another office for them), return to the window to make some entries, stamp some papers, and issue a receipt or an updated account book. At least thirty seconds, or, more often, several minutes, would be required by the teller. During the initial studies, the teller was augmented by a processing team that simulated an on-line computer. The significant characteristic that the old system and the experiments shared was that all the processing activity was visible to the customer. Seeing how busy the teller was, the customer did not feel that his or her time was being wasted. Later, when the new system reduced the time in the bank to thirty seconds, the customer would come into the bank, be directed to a teller, find no queue, hand in a transaction, and watch the teller key the data into an on-line terminal. Then there would be a ten- to twenty-second wait. With nothing else to do, the teller might ask about the weather or try to be pleasant in some other way. Finally, the completed transaction would be returned by the terminal and the customer could leave. When surveyed, however, the customer had two complaints: First, his or her time had been wasted by the teller who was passing the time of day instead of working; second, he or she had been unnecessarily restricted by the queue supervisor (a sign saying "Wait Here" which permitted the customer to get the first free teller). In the customer's opinion, service had not improved.

These examples do not imply that concept formulation and project definition were inadequate in the banking environment. Rather, they show that no amount of study will answer all questions. New information will turn up at all stages of development that will affect system behavior. The early stages need only support the decision to proceed to design; the life cycle provides flexibility in later stages to absorb changes.

In parallel with the development of the design requirements baseline by the systems analysts, the project definition team should prepare a detailed plan for the design stage, covering cost estimates, schedules, resources, milestone decisions, documentation and test development, reviews, and, where applicable, market forecasts. Each of these points is laid out in detail so managers can control performance during the design stage.

In addition, tentative plans are made for subsequent stages to describe the project life cycle in the light of the new information provided by the project definition.

Midway in the project definition stage it is appropriate to review progress and see that the work is going in the right direction. In Fig. 3.7 this event is called the *system requirements review*. At the end of project definition a more thorough review of the *system design requirements baseline* verifies that the work is complete and responsive to the systems objectives. The plan for design and implementation is also reviewed and, if it is acceptable both technically and economically, approval to proceed is given. This approval is final but revocable; i.e., it is a decision to start developing the system subject to cancellation if technical or financial problems crop up. Completion of project definition then represents:

- Acceptance of the design requirements baseline
- Approval of the plan for the design stage
- Conditional approval for the whole project
- Authorization to start the design stage

These decisions have been reached by an orderly process of analysis which converted the very general system requirement into a vehicle for design and a baseline against which to evaluate results. The procedure gives management the means to [5]:

- Identify system requirements in a systematic manner on a total system basis, including hardware, software, procedures, data, facilities, and personnel.
- Develop design requirements consistent with schedule, performance, and cost constraints.
- Integrate considerations of reliability, maintainability, produce-ability, procure-ability, safety, and human factors.
- Establish a baseline requirement that will be the forcing function on design.
- Establish the information needed to tie together plans for system test and installation.
- Provide a single source of documentation for evaluating the system design to ensure that the total system objectives are met.

Authorization to proceed from project definition to design changes the character of the project in many organizations. Prior to this point, the project has been run on a task force basis without any firm commitment to carry the project to completion. Once implementation has been authorized, it is necessary to put together a formal organization with a budget and authority to recruit, place requirements on support groups, lay out schedules, negotiate changes to the baseline, etc. Again, it is useful to request proposals to determine how close the implementer (from within the firm or from a contracting organization) can come to the plan laid out by the project definition team. Separate RFPs are often issued for each subsystem while responsibility for total system integration is either retained by the user or assigned to a contractor specializing in systems integration and management. Thus a large data-processing system may be built by the combined talents of a computer company, a peripheral device manufacturer, a communications utility, a software vendor, and a management consultant all coordinated by a project office set up in the user's information systems department. There are advantages to having one group do the whole job; namely, better communications and more time spent productively, and a better focus on the problem with less energy devoted to management of conflicting interests. However, large projects can exceed the capability of any one group. Considering the potential cost advantages of competitive bidding, many experienced systems managers assemble subsystem implementers from various sources based on cost and quality considerations.

When the RFP route is followed, it is not uncommon that the proposal responses supply some good ideas for improving the design requirements. Therefore, even before project implementation begins there can be changes to the baseline. From here on out, the scope of work consists of the

Baseline + Changes.

The original baseline should be preserved and all the changes should be explicitly documented. This makes it easy to back off to an earlier set of requirements if some changes turn sour. The explicit records also make it possible to keep track of budget exposures and, in a contract environment, provide a basis for negotiating the cost and fee of the vendor. In addition to the changes that modify the current baseline, there will be some changes that are deferred to a later release of the product. The deferred changes are usually product enhancements whose added value will make the later release more attractive to users.

3.1.3   Project Implementation

Once the team is formed, implementation starts in earnest. *Implementation,* in the context of program system development, means building the program system. (Each field of activity uses words to fit parochial interests. "Implementation" to an Information Systems Manager means installing a new operational system. To a staff manager, "implementation" means activating a new policy or procedure. In this book, "implementation" means design, development, and testing of program systems.) Looking at the program subsystem, the first step is the design of the programs. This is a high-level structural design done by a small team. It goes over the same ground as the previous stage, but now the purpose is to determine *how* to supply the requirements. System Objectives said *what* was wanted. Design Requirements said *what must be provided* to satisfy the objectives. Sometimes more is provided than is needed to satisfy the user. This approach may be the best cost tradeoff (as when general purpose packages are used instead of writing new code). Sometimes less is provided than is wanted because, on inspection, the objectives cannot be met within the applied constraints.

3.1.3.1 Design

The small team that designs any level of a system should not exceed five people. If one person could do the whole design, so much the better; the result would be simple, self-consistent, and probably efficient. Where a design team is needed, it must be kept small so that the people can function as a unit. The upper limit of five people is arbitrary but practical. No matter how large the project, a group of this size can structure the top few levels. Then each of the lower-level packages can be assigned to a second-level design group if necessary. Thus one design team can generate work for several other teams, leading to the rapid buildup in resources shown (in the life cycle chart) as package design starts.

The activity of the designers leads to a *design specification*. A program system design specification contains structural information showing system data structures and control interfaces, package functions, and performance requirements. This part of the spec is the system architecture. The remainder of the spec covers system test plans, and system design standards and conventions. It also lays out a plan for package design. Package designers produce specifications that contain similar information regarding the structure of lower-level units (Fig. 3.8). At the bottom of the hierarchy of structured design is a set of documents describing what each program unit must do. These documents are the instructions to individual programmers who will develop the program units.

To control the design process, formal reviews are scheduled. A *preliminary design review (PDR)* is held to evaluate the completeness, quality, feasibility, cost, and suitability of the system design specification. Then each package design specification is given a *critical design review* (*CDR*). The PDR not only examines the design specification, it also compares the specification to the design requirements baseline. The two must agree, meaning that differences should be corrected by adopting changes to either the spec or the baseline. Since the user understands the baseline, the PDR gives the user his or her best, and possibly last, chance to effectively influence the implementation process. (Later reviews may be too detailed for the user to deal with at a managerial level.) If the PDR raises unanswerable questions about feasibility or cost, a decision can be made to redo the system design, restate the objectives, or abandon the project. Going from system to pack-

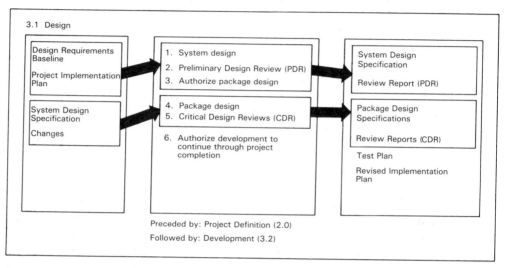

Fig. 3.8 Project implementation stage—Design.

age design entails a bigger expense so the project should not proceed until the PDR gives a green light. Similarly, the CDRs occur at the boundary between design and development, where cost again leaps up. The main new information available in a CDR is a reliable estimate of development cost. If the project cost estimate exceeds the project budget, the decision to proceed must be reevaluated. After CDR, reviews and inspections concentrate on program unit progress and quality. During the period of programming and early testing, no new management data will be generated that will show unequivocally that the project is on safe ground. The CDR decision, therefore, is essentially an irrevocable commitment.

Unfortunately, CDR is not one point in time as is PDR [6]. Each package design is completed on its own schedule and reviewed right away. That means that quite a few packages will have passed into the development stage before the last CDR is finished; therefore, the project manager should keep a running tally on project cost. One useful tally compares the original cost estimate (at PDR) to three forecasts:

- Low forecast—Assume original cost estimate can be improved as much as the maximum improvement seen so far in any CDR.

- Average forecast—Assume original cost estimate will vary as much as the average of all packages that have passed CDR.

- High forecast—Assume original cost estimate will be exceeded as much as the worst package seen so far in any CDR.

Many project managers know from experience that cost estimates tend to grow; they just do not know how much. These managers will ignore the low forecast, plan to the average, and treat the high forecast as an upper bound that might be reached if costs are not carefully watched.

From the previous remarks, it becomes apparent that more is going on during the design stage than design. It is during this period that all the plans are prepared for the remainder of the project. Hence, a management and administrative cadre must exist in addition to the design team. This group recruits the people for later stages, converts the design specifications into resources and schedules, organizes reviews, meetings, negotiations, etc., and generates the project control procedures. Insofar as possible, the people responsible for management and administration are distinct from the designers; otherwise, the designers would be unable to concentrate on the technical issues.

3.1.3.2 Development

When individual units of programming are specified, they are handed off to individual programmers. The move from design to development changes the focus of manager attention. Attention shifts away from architecture and planning toward production and control (Fig. 3.9). Not only are the deliverable units of code under way, but test cases and support programs are also being built during the development phase. Most of the people doing this work are newcomers to the project, as are the additional administrative and operations support people. Control of the many and varied activities calls for standards and procedures that protect the structure of the system. As long as the individuals observe the rules such as "Use PL/1," "Observe Naming Conventions published in the Data Dictionary Standard," "Obtain manager's approval before releasing your program unit to the master public library," they are free to be as creative as they can be in the design and implementation of the units they are responsible for. Any ideas they have that affect other units, however, must be examined by a control group to see that they are improvements, not potential problems.

In the system design stage, when everyone works in one small team, control is self-imposed. In the package design stage the nucleus of system designers is still close at hand so that changes are easily recognized. These benefits of teamwork are lost when a large number of unit programmers get to work. They did not participate in the design so all they know about the system is contained in the specifications they have been given plus whatever overview was presented in their indoctrination course. It is simply not possible for them to be aware of the impact of their individual decisions on the rest of the system. Consequently, control can no longer be self-imposed by the development team. Instead, a control group must be established with

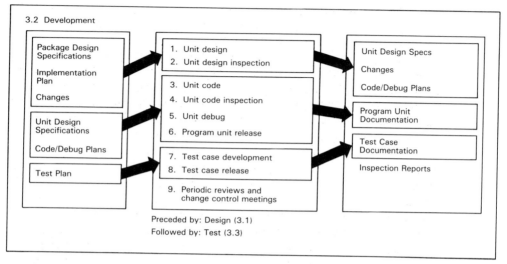

Fig. 3.9   Project implementation stage—Development.

responsibility for continually checking the work in progress against the design specification and the design requirements baseline.

In a similar manner, other activities lead to the formation of specialty groups. Whereas the design teams could write their own documentation (except perhaps for help in editing and style), the development teams cannot. Unit programmers can only describe what they know; namely, the unit they are working on. A collection of such unit writeups is not a coherent description of the system. It takes someone else to integrate the pieces into a useful whole that will mean something to the ultimate user. Other activities calling for such a system overview include system performance analysis, modeling and simulation, project control of schedules and resources, design control, and, of course, management. Not all specialty groups exist for this reason, though. The computer facility is set up for efficiency. The test teams are separate from the programmers to preserve their independent judgment. Support tool developers remain separate because the subsystems they are working on are independent of the main project design specification. Regardless of the reason for their existence, these groups require supervision. Those that do not have unit tasks but provide a service require a different kind of supervision from the developers. Consequently, management during the development stage consists of administering a large number of diverse activities, all of which are interrelated and all of which are constrained by a common schedule and budget.

It is during the development stage that *contention* first becomes a management concern. Before this time, the few conflicts that might arise over computer time or typing support can be worked out within the design team. The organization and size of the development stage preclude simple solutions. For one thing, control of the support facilities has moved out of the programming group into the specialty groups. This requires negotiation between two managers whenever an individual is dissatisfied with support services. A second type of problem arises from the fact that all the activities are related. Frequently, one program unit cannot be started until another unit assigned to someone else is completed. Delays can also be caused by change proposals that take a week or two to evaluate. Imaginative managers try to plan work and education so as to fill most of the dead waiting periods, but they cannot fill them all. Boredom and inactivity create personnel problems. Individuals begin to blame each other for delays. Actually, the managers are to blame if anyone is. They set up the project. The delays are primarily due to the level of resources they provided and to the way they assigned units of work. It is their responsibility to manage the people problems that arise from that plan [7].

Unit programming within the development stage follows the guidelines for unit design, coding, and debugging. Each task is a program unit built by one person. The more units there are, the better the support tools the project can afford. That means that large projects will tend to automate more of the editing, debugging, and library functions. They will also rely on more automated control techniques.

Given a good project plan and a good set of design specifications, managers can concentrate on monitoring quality and timely completion of events during the development portion of project implementation. The plan should clearly show all significant events: when they should occur, what they consist of, who is responsible, who depends on completion of the event, and what the budget targets are. Since all of the activities covered by the plan may vary from their targets, frequent reviews are needed to avoid accumulating small variances into a major problem. *Weekly coordination reviews* are appropriate to bring the small variances to light and to recommend changes to the plan to adjust the important variances. These meetings usually deal with checkpoints and milestones. Each manager reports on any departures he or she has noted or expects to occur. The other managers, particularly those affected by the problem, evaluate the impact so the management team can decide whether corrective action is needed. A good log of the meeting provides continuity from week to week and keeps decisions from getting "lost." Action recommendations are formalized in *Change Requests,* which go before a Configuration Control Board for detailed technical and management assessment before they are adopted. Supplementing these meetings are the technical reviews and inspections of the growing body of code. Code inspections mostly affect the unit or package of code under analysis; however, they may also uncover interface problems or problems due to late deliveries by others resulting in Change Requests.

Recurring activities are not easily handled in a HIPO-style diagram; neither do they fit well into activity networks or even lists of calendar events because they are not dependent on predecessor events. Weekly meetings go into the implementation plan as a standard management practice. The management team must support the practice in order for the technique to be effective. When they do participate regularly, they help to avoid the surprises so commonly catastrophic in projects that lack good internal communications.

3.1.3.3 Test

By following the guidelines for unit programming, an individual programmer is justified in assuming that the successful completion of debugging is the end of the task. When the unit is part of a system, that assumption is often not valid. Perfect units do not necessarily work when they are integrated with other units. The usual reasons for trouble are:

■ *Poorly designed unit requirements*—the fault of the package designer (or the lowest-level designer above the unit programmer) due to inexperience or lack of information about the system as a whole. Example: In a distributed banking system, a unit is defined that posts transactions against a database for local customers. However, the design that calls for this process to be done in a small remote controller does not specify program size constraints so the unit programmer assumes the entire working memory of the controller is available. In fact, the controller is meant to be multiprogrammed and the program unit will not fit the space available.

■ *Poorly defined interactions with other units*—the fault of some designer in the hierarchy, usually at a fairly high level of the hierarchy. The error represents lack of thoroughness on the part of the designer. Since every interaction involves two elements, there is a check and balance available when the two elements belong to different designers. Even then, there may be subtle interactions the designers overlook. Example: A large bank has remote controllers spread over a wide geographic area, connected by telephone lines. The system design (using a standard line control called SDLC) permits up to eight messages to be sent from any source to any one destination before an acknowledgment must be received. In other words, the ninth message will be queued until one or more acknowledgment message returns from the destination showing that the first eight arrived all right. If no acknowledgment is received within two seconds, the original messages will be retransmitted on the assumption that the first try failed. This method assumes a leased line network dedicated to the bank, but the communication subsystem, for economy, was changed to a vendor's shared networking utility which queues messages at intermediate nodes when traffic is heavy. As a result, the two-second deadline in the banking system could often be missed even though the original messages arrive at the destination. The acknowledgments would simply be late getting back. Unfortunately, the source would still create duplicates after two seconds, causing confusion at the destination and incidentally adding to the traffic overload.

■ *Poorly understood requirements or interactions*—the fault of the requirement setter or designer who is unable to write a clear and unambiguous design document. Personal communication between designer and implementer can sometimes correct the problem. Example: To adjust service to meet changes in workload, a designer calls for a program that periodically rearranges a priority table. The spec says that the highest priority must go to transaction types which in the last hour "have exceeded ten per minute average and requested data base access (DBMS) or had to be routed to a different computer." This can mean: (1) (greater than 10/min AND DBMS) OR (routed elsewhere), (2) (greater than 10/min) AND (DBMS OR routed elsewhere). Using Boolean connectives, it is easy enough to establish a convention for picking either (1) or (2).[4] Written out in words, the meaning is ambiguous yet easy to clarify by contacting the designer.

■ *Incomplete system and package design*—fault of the system and package designers. Incomplete design is the combination of avoidable omissions due to careless work and unavoidable omissions due to lack of information or inability to predict system behavior. Avoidable omissions are addressed by management leadership and structured design methods that facilitate verification of completeness. Unavoidable omissions are corrected when they are found by Change Requests and redesign. Example: An avoidable omission in some banking designs is the failure to add up the total storage requirement for programs coresident in the remote controllers to see if they fit. Errors in hardware orders (and cost estimates) result. An unavoidable omission in the same environment is the failure to accurately predict the extent of the rise in customer transactions due to the improvement in customer service. This omission will only be detected after the system is in use. System overloads will occur that eventually require a bigger central processor.

■ *Overdesign*—fault of the designers at all levels who do not pay attention to details of related modules. Overdesign results in unnecessary code and, usually, performance penalties. Example: In a period following a few serious user problems due to errors in data processing, a company had a major campaign to improve system integrity. Most designers and programmers interpreted this as a requirement for data checking. They responded by putting data verification routines at the input interface of every program unit. As a result, it was possible to have a sequence occur: Read Employee

---

4. Most programming languages would select (1) as the correct meaning.

Record, Execute Employee Verification Program, Execute Employee Time Card Calculation (but first recheck to see if employee name is valid), Execute Employee Deductions (but first recheck to see if employee name is valid), etc. Such sequences, occurring in systems programs as well as applications, can only be entered under controlled circumstances (i.e., the employee name *is* valid). Once in the sequence, further verification of the control parameter merely adds to the execution path length.

■ *Poorly designed tests*—the fault of the test designer. Tests may indicate problems that are not really present. The tests in such a case are testing against an incorrect set of criteria. Tests may also fail to find problems that are present, again because of poor test design. Example: To determine whether a banking system could provide ten-second responses to 95 percent of the transactions under peak load of ten transactions per second, a test is set up using a driver. The driver is a small computer programmed to simulate the network of terminals. The maximum capacity of the driver is seven transactions per second. Running at this rate, system performance is measured and the results adjusted linearly to represent a load of ten transactions per second. In fact, the main processor begins to saturate at eight transactions and is unable to handle the peak load. This test is poorly designed because it fails to stress the system.

If the system structure was perfect, most of these troubles could not arise. Then a perfect unit would always integrate successfully on the first attempt. Top-down implementation strives to reach this state of control by essentially doing integration and test as the project proceeds. By contrast, bottom-up implementation collects a group of units into a package or subpackage before running tests. Later, groups of packages are integrated until the whole system can be tested as an entity. At each step along the way problems are detected that cause the status of the project to fall back, or regress, to some earlier tested level. The problems must be fixed. If they are within a unit, the unit programmer makes the fix; however, interaction problems require design changes plus unit repairs and even new unit development. This takes a lot of people: the test team, the unit programmers, the designers, and all the support people. Even when some people do double duty (e.g., a unit programmer doubles as a test team member), the number of people needed during the test stage hits a peak. Translated to money, a bottom-up implementation costs more than an equivalent top-down implementation.[5]

---

5. Top-down implementation is used effectively on small- and medium-sized jobs where the entire job is comprehensible to the designers and managers. Large and very large jobs lack this property and proceed from the bottom up, although the lowest-level components may themselves be sizeable packages built top down. The discussion of team capabilities in Chapter 5 probes why this is true.

The purpose of the test stage is to verify that the packages and then the total system meet the current design requirements baseline (Fig. 3.10). Testers should not have to do any debugging. Managers are charged with seeing that program units are completely debugged according to an agreed-upon plan worked out by each unit programmer. The test team should be able to assume that any problem detected during package integration or test is a fault in the specifications, not just sloppy programming. Diagnosis and correction of faults is more effective in such an environment.

The mechanics of testing are not very different from debugging except that large systems require more planning, more people, and more difficult detective work. Testing does differ from debugging in one important respect. Testing determines only whether the system, as built, satisfies its requirements. It is not concerned with how cleverly the design specification has been handled unless the method of implementation is relevant to meeting a requirement. A tight response time requirement may lead the test team to study the design spec to see where the delays are. Even in a case such as this, it should be enough for the test team to explain carefully what aspect of the test failed. The design and development team can figure out why. At the level of a program unit, the distinction between a requirement and a specification is not so clean. Consequently, most debugging runs evaluate the quality of the implementation at the same time they check the program against the requirements. By separating the concepts of debugging and testing, it is possible to lay out a test plan that can be staffed by nonprogrammers or, at least, by people unfamiliar with the internal details of the programs being tested. [8].

Integration of program units into packages and packages into a system is primarily a scheduling and library management problem. The integration team works with both implementers and testers to determine when each unit is due for completion and to fit the units into a schedule for integration and regression testing. The *integration* step collects related modules and produces working packages. In some cases, this entails adding simulated modules or drivers to the available deliverable units. The integrated package can accept inputs, execute its limited functions, and produce outputs. The test plan, of course, must anticipate what capabilities will be available at various dates so the tests scheduled at that time are appropriate. Then large quantities of machine time must be committed to support the numerous integration and test runs.

Testing is both progressive and regressive. It is progressive in the sense that each set of tests is designed to verify more and more of the system. It is regressive because each test can disclose flaws in parts of the system that had passed earlier tests. *Regression testing* consists of falling back to the earlier test level and retesting affected modules after fixes have been applied.

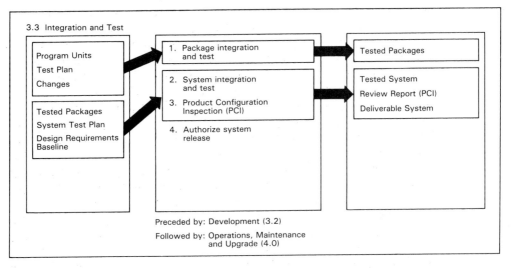

Fig. 3.10   Project implementation stage—Integration and test.

Table 3.1 shows how a single program unit, C1.1.1, may be affected during the integration and test stage. The unit is part of subpackage C1 in package C in system S. The system will use an operating system VS release 3 which does not become available for testing until late in the system development plan. VS release 2.6 must be used for earlier tests. The first set of integrated tests is made on a base containing packages A (input), B (data structure) C1, C2, and D1 (temporary output). The tests disclose an error in the data format C1.1.1 uses to pass data to C1.2.1. A fix is applied to C1.1.1 and the new version is released for integration. Nothing else has changed in test 2 (except for other fixes in the base elements) and the test succeeds. Next, a new base is integrated containing components of packages E and G. Test 3 shows a problem between E1.3.4 and C1.1.1. Before C1.1.1 is fixed, a new base is integrated and test 4 is run. Of course, the known problem reoccurs. (The situation would be more complicated if the known problem did not occur in test 4.) Test 5 introduces the third version of C1.1.1 and runs all right. When VS3 arrives, a new base is integrated containing all of E and G and part of F. VS3 now causes problems in C1.1.1 (and many other units) because it is not completely compatible with VS2.6. These problems are cleaned up in the fourth version of C1.1.1 and no further problems are traced back to that unit.

Tests 2, 5, and 7 are reruns of a given base to check the effectiveness of corrections made to program units. In practice, the cost of full-scale tests is so high that tests, 2, 5, and 7 would not be run. That means that simple program unit fixes will be mixed with new, untested units in each new test. Such

TABLE 3.1.   REGRESSION TESTS

| Test no. | Integration base | | | Program unit C1.1.1 version | Source of errors in C1.1.1 |
	Level	Contents	OS		
1	1	A,B,C1,C2,D1	2.6	1	C1.2.1
2	1	A,B,C1,C2,D1	2.6	2	None
3	2	A,B,C1,C2,D1 E1,G1,G2	2.6	2	E1.3.4 interface
4	3	A,B,C,D,E,G1,G2,G3	2.6	2	E1.3.4 interface
5	3	A,B,C,D,E,G1,G2,G3	2.6	3	None
6	4	A,B,C,D,E,F1,G	3	3	VS3
7	4	A,B,C,D,E,F1,G	3	4	None
8	5	S_1	3	4	None

a violation of the concept of controlled testing is common; it complicates the detective work by which errors are found.

Because regression testing very often uncovers errors in previously tested packages, it is not sufficient for a package to pass one set of tests. It must pass all tests in which it is involved in any way. Therefore, the earliest formal test that can be conducted on the finished programs is the *system test*. The system test starts when all packages can be integrated and run together. It is permissible to test packages in a simulated environment, but it is more effective to test the system in a real environment. By setting this rule, it is possible to observe the effects of operator behavior, real time constraints, machine availability, and other environmental factors. The formal test conducted at this time is a *product configuration inspection* (PCI). It is a comprehensive review of the system in operation, the system documentation, and the deliverable program package. Attention is paid to how well the design requirements have been met; that is, the test verifies that everything called for is present (an accounting of the configuration) and that it can be used (a human factors test of quality). Useability implies not only that the program can be initiated and run by following the instructions, but also that the user can install this program and make it work in the environments for which it was designed. A high level of detachment is required to judge the useability of a system. For this reason, the system test should be conducted by people who have not been involved in the development. They can be the people who have been writing test cases in parallel with the program development. Where the organization can afford it, they should come from a completely independent system assurance group.

At the completion of system test, a *deliverable system package* is ready for release to the user. The decision to release concludes the implementation stage of the life cycle.

3.1.4 Operation, Maintenance, and Upgrade

Delivery of a program package is the point at which the implementation team turns responsibility over to the user. The cleanest example of this occurs when a software vendor's contract ends after a successful PCI.[6] An equivalent situation occurs when a computer vendor places a program system in a library. Unknown users will order copies of the package. The users are on their own with regard to installing the system. Of course, a complete program package will be self-explanatory. It will contain instructions for generating the appropriate system for a subset of the modules in the package. There will be user manuals, education materials, and examples of how the system works. What will not be in the package is the know-how that is in the developers' heads. Sometimes a user can buy this know-how in the form of consultations or classroom instruction; other users will have to acquire the know-how by experience.

For simplicity, a look at the post-release activities of an organization that develops a system for its own use will show what goes on, in general, during operations, maintenance, and upgrade. Figure 3.11 breaks these activities into five categories of migration, operation, post-installation evaluation, maintenance and upgrade, and termination. (The fact that each activity can be shown in more detail by a lower-level chart or hierarchy of charts is shown by the labels in parentheses.)

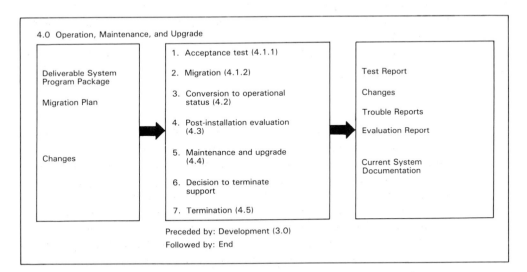

Fig. 3.11 Operations, maintenance, and upgrade.

---

6. It is common practice to terminate software development contracts after PCI. It would make more sense to extend them to cover conversion, installation, and user education.

The first activity is acceptance. The mere fact that the system meets its own requirements according to the PCI is no assurance that the user will find it acceptable. The incumbent manager in the user shop may not have been a party to the requirement-setting procedure. Sometimes circumstances change unexpectedly so requirements agreed upon only a few weeks ago are no longer valid. Some managers naturally doubt that the tests run by an independent team are relevant to their department's needs. For reasons such as these, plus the more practical reason that the system must be useable in the user's unique environment, an acceptance test is scheduled. Whereas the PCI can be conducted in the developer's facility, acceptance tests should be run in the user's facility with the normal facility staff. A formal acceptance document is generated (particularly when contracts are involved) to acknowledge the transfer of responsibility from the developer to the user when the acceptance test succeeds.

In parallel with acceptance testing, training and conversion can start, following the plans for these activities that should have been developed as part of the overall system plan. The procedures for conversion include those described in [9]; however, just as a *system acceptance test* is more formal than a program unit *suitability test, system conversion* is more extensive than *unit conversion*. In fact, the term *system migration* has come into use to describe the process. In the process of designing a complex system and building it over many months, certain assumptions are made regarding the hardware and software the system will require. Before the system is accepted, the user probably has no need for some of the items. For instance, a batch facility needs no interactive terminals before it has an interactive programming system to control the terminals. Furthermore, the larger and more complex the new system is, the more significant the new requirements are likely to be. Any attempt to make all the changes at once is too risky. Experienced installation managers will lay out a plan that introduces one new feature at a time until the system "migrates" from its present configuration to the desired one. The first step may be to install the operating system required by the system under development. Next, the special access methods for new storage devices or terminals can be added to the operating system (even though the devices are not attached). New usage accounting routines can be prepared. Schedules can be changed to reflect the priorities planned for the new system. All the associated procedures can be written and staffed through the approval cycle. The new hardware can be checked out a piece at a time. Then normal conversion procedures can be followed, with parallel runs providing system integrity until cutover to the new system is authorized.

In [9], only one program unit was considered so the complexity of conversion, while not negligible, could be planned to take only three or four parallel runs spread over several accounting periods to see the effects of different input streams. Migration to a complex system takes longer. Depending on system size, complexity, and novelty, the migration period can span several months of continuous parallel operation before cutover. In some cases, migration takes one to two years of step-by-step conversion before the full capability of the new system is realized. This was the case with large banks in Europe, Canada, and Japan which had to install thousands of terminals in hundreds of branches without interfering with customer service. Only when the new system is a separate and distinct facility (e.g., when no conversion is required) can migration be avoided. The original system plan must forecast the migration cost in order for the user to budget for this period. Such costs include space for temporary hardware, more frequent system generation runs with accompanying user problems leading to job reruns, potentially higher job costs due to increased system overhead before all system functions are installed, etc. This is the price paid for nondisruptive growth to a new capability. Assuming that the new capability is cost-justified, taking all expenses into account, the price is worth paying. Otherwise, a hasty conversion may result in system failures that balloon system costs beyond control.

After conversion and after the system has settled down to the point that all its important features are in routine use, a post-installation evaluation review should be held. The purpose of the evaluation is to determine if the system is satisfactory. Of equal importance, the lessons learned in developing the system can be recorded for future use. The results of the evaluation are a key input to, and often the trigger for, the next phase of development of the system.

Once installed, the new system does not just sit there. It requires constant attention, called *maintenance and upgrade* activity. The two terms are conjoined since the dividing line between fixing errors and adding new features is never clear. In theory, the delivered system does everything it is required to do. The system test demonstrated this. Therefore, any problem must represent a new requirement, yet if the system gives the wrong results, it must contain an error. Rather than argue over the precise meaning of an error versus a new system feature, it is easier to erase the distinction between maintenance and upgrade activities.[7] Maintenance and upgrade is usually assigned to a group of people as a level of effort. They do as much as they can—never all that is desired—to make the system effective. They handle requests according to urgency without segregating them by type. When a "trouble report" is received it is assigned to someone in the group who will eliminate the "trouble." The remedy may be an error correction, or a new feature, or simply some instruction to the user regarding how to avoid the

---

7. Data on the exact nature of each change made to a released system are useful to management. In particular, they want to know which changes are essential, which enhance performance, and which provide new function. The data help them control the level of effort for maintenance and upgrade and also give some feeling for the quality of the earlier system design and development effort.

problem. Likewise, a Change Request submitted by a user who thinks a new feature is needed may be handled in various ways by the maintenance and upgrade group according to whether the feature exists already or can justifiably be added.

As implied here, many problems are not problems at all. They are merely misinterpretations or uneducated conclusions on the part of the user. Yet the concept of change says that, as time passes, the environment and the requirements of the user will both change. As a result, many bona fide requests for help arise, saying, "The system as it works today does not do what I want done. Let's change the system rather than tie my hands due to its inadequacies." The cost of satisfying such requests is seldom quantified. Two generalizations that have been useful over the years are:

- *For systems programs,* vendors of general-purpose program systems plan a maintenance and upgrade level of effort at about one-third the peak level during development; that is, a project of 150 people may require 50 people for maintenance and upgrade. (This guideline does not cover the addition of major new functions such as would require phased implementation.) The pure maintenance portion is shrinking due to improved programming techniques so the total maintenance and upgrade workload is trending downwards.

- *For applications programs,* commercial information systems departments devote about one-half to two-thirds of their staff to maintenance and upgrade activities [2, 10]; that is, two-thirds of the staff is working on the library of existing programs and only one-third is developing new programs. The actual ratio of new development to maintenance and upgrade depends on the average useful life of the programs in the library. Useful life, in turn, depends on the nature of the business the library serves.

The commercial environment must respond to rapid changes caused by business conditions or regulatory requirements. This tends to account for the higher rate of activity compared to a vendor who is only obligated to correct errors but can control the number of new features allowed. (In practice, vendors find it is good business to offer more functions and better performance in multiple releases; therefore, the number of people assigned to a major system may remain at peak levels for a number of years.)

As a final observation, programs offered without maintenance and upgrade have a short life [11].

Maintenance and upgrade activities have most of the characteristics of development. Each proposed change must be reviewed and evaluated before it is authorized. Additions to the system must be fully debugged before they are integrated; then they must be fully tested in regression fashion before being released. This process has one additional facet during maintenance and upgrade. Since the system is operational and there is, presumably, scant free machine time, great care must be exercised in switching from the running version to the upgraded version. The availability of a tested feature is not a sufficient excuse for installing the feature. Each new release requires all the steps of conversion, including suitability tests, announcement, training, procedure update, etc. Conversion is not difficult for most of the upgrades but it does cost time and money; therefore, a schedule of upgrades should be prepared that clusters tested changes to minimize the actual number of releases during the year. The final decision to make a system upgrade should reflect the current priorities in the organization, as well as the problems that might result from a faulty conversion. One or more post-installation evaluations can lay the groundwork for judging the value of upgrading a given system when the exposure to all other installed systems is considered.

3.1.5 Termination

Sooner or later, a project should end. In theory, every project *must* end; in practice, some projects drag on in the maintenance and upgrade stage forever. That is, someone is always assigned to handle trouble reports and change requests. It is wiser to plan on terminating support for a given system at a specific point in time. Use of the program package need not end at the same time. The function performed by many programs, particularly those in public libraries, remains useful long after support has been withdrawn. By that time, however, the program has stabilized to the point that no additional support is needed, even by the most inexperienced users. By documenting this state, the support team can turn to their next assignment (Fig. 3.12).

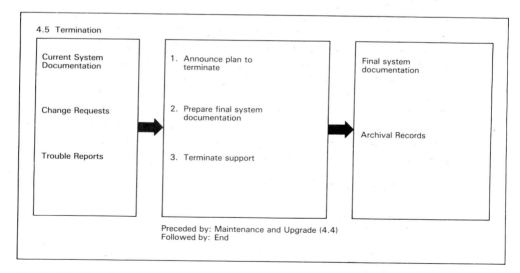

Fig. 3.12 Termination.

Termination of a project should be scheduled to coincide with an event such as:

- Installation of a replacement system
- Installation of incompatible hardware
- Discontinuance of operational use of the system

When the frequency of changes falls below some predetermined level, the cost per change rises rapidly because the programmers doing maintenance lose their intimate knowledge of the system. At this point, termination is also justified.

Quite commonly, projects are terminated when the resources supporting them are needed elsewhere. This is the wrong way to pick a termination date because it ignores the user's requirements. Along these lines, a general-purpose program installed in many places can not be terminated on the day that its successor is released. The coincident schedule only works for a one-user case. When there are many users it is necessary to support the original system for six to twelve months after the successor is released so all users can migrate to the successor. In summary, the system development cycle should be terminated when the system is no longer needed or when it is so stable that additional modifications are not justified.

3.2   CHARACTERISTICS OF THE LIFE CYCLE

The curve of Fig. 3.1 shows the buildup of people over time for a moderately large project. The assumptions behind this curve are:

- The organization is a pyramid hierarchy with two levels of management.
- Peak staff is thirty-six people during the test stage.
- A single deliverable program package is to be released.
- Implementation is scheduled to take eighteen months following a six-month project definition.
- People are available as needed and can be reassigned at will.
- The implementation schedule is allocated

  10 percent to System Design
  25 percent to Package Design
  10 percent to Unit Design
  10 percent to Unit Code
  10 percent to Unit Debug
  17 1/2 percent to Package Test
  17 1/2 percent to System Test
- Maintenance will be provided for eighteen months.

There are a lot of variables in this list of assumptions: schedule, recruiting flexibility, organization, etc. What is shown, then, is a typical, manageable plan for a thirty-six-person project spread over eighteen months. A change in any of the assumptions will change both the shape and the area (= cost) of the curve. In the absence of any better plan, managers can use the typical curve as a guideline and then work out the detailed variations as the project is defined. The guideline is also useful to the pricing and budget departments since it helps them lay out the requirement for funds early. In fact, many multiproject organizations prepare standard planning aids, based on curves such as Fig. 3.1, showing the resources by month as a percent of the peak [12]. Then they can budget any single-release job in the same class by multiplying the peak staff count on the planned job by the monthly ratios. (In the next section, some planning data of this type is given to illustrate the point. Note, however, that the data are idealized representations of the author's experience. They should not be used without careful correlation with your experience.)

3.2.1 Staff Buildup

The rate at which people join the project is based on two factors: (1) the work to be done, and (2) the ability to absorb more people. The concept of span of control suggests that the size of a group working together on one task should be less than seven people. Concept formulation, project definition, system design, and the design of each package are covered by this guideline. Unit design, coding, and debugging are, by definition, tasks for individual programmers and take four to six weeks per unit. Support personnel, particularly those in centralized service department, are usually figured as a ratio of the line development people or, where possible, in terms of support hours per KLOC.

Concept formulation requires typically seven or less people. No people are assigned to concept formulation in those cases where the project is a logical follow-on to an existing activity. The decisions in this case are made by the existing managers as a normal part of their job. The upper limit of seven members reflects the fact that, even for very large systems, the system concept should be within the grasp of one person. Put more than seven people together and it becomes almost impossible for them to arrive at a single concept they all understand. An optimum concept formulation team for a large project has three to five people. The stage will last up to a year or two, during which only a short time is needed to frame the concept. The rest of the time is taken up with defining a mission, surveying organization attitudes, considering whether a system is needed, and lining up management support. Even when temporary consultants are used, concept formulation can be inexpensive. Excluding massive weapons systems so big as to require legislative approval, it is reasonable to formulate a system concept in six to eight people-months spread over various periods of time [13].

The number of people required during project definition depends on the circumstances. Project definition is more costly than concept formulation. The analysis, the tradeoff studies, the documentation, and the planning all take a substantial amount of detailed, specialized work. Model construction calls for some experts who know the application subject area very well, and others who know math, others who are good at using a computer language for modeling. Occasionally, one individual is available with all these skills. More often, a team of specialists must be formed for the intensive effort of producing a baseline and a plan. The nuclear team is again small, three to five people, but it may have the support of many more people to do specific tasks. A large system definition can span many months. Typically, three to twelve months are required, not counting the time reserved for proposal review and contract selection or for the system design requirements review. If these periods are included, project definition can span six to twenty-four months for the typical large information system (25 percent less if no RFP were issued).

Staff peaks about two-thirds of the way through the project definition stage. The number of people at the peak depends on the complexity of the job.[8] The peak staff during project definition is about one-sixth the peak staff expected during development, if this is primarily a programming job. These numbers are not valid for every project; they are merely illustrative of the way in which the project is staffed. It builds up rapidly to bring together a team of specialists, primarily analysts. After completing its primary outputs—the baseline and the plan—the staff can shrink. The specialists can return to their home departments. Only the management and key technical people are needed to form a nucleus around which the design team will form. (In some cases, where it is easier to absorb the cost of standby personnel than to obtain new people, the full peak staff is retained. Since not all are needed for the start of the next stage, they can devote their time to training and setting up a suitable set of development controls.)

Entering the implementation stage, there need be only a few people on board. A rapid buildup starts immediately, meaning that someone must be concerned with recruiting, training, and making task assignments while the key designers structure the system. To do this, some administrative support must be provided from the very beginning of the project. The rate of build-

---

8. For example, a twelve-month definition stage may start with a small team that identifies a sequence of analyses and models it wants. Perhaps some survey data must be acquired. The small team generates work for, say, four other teams and requires perhaps one person in support of each four professionals. It may average four people the first three months (proposal evaluation), sixteen people the next nine months, hitting a peak of twenty-five in the ninth month and tapering off to seven in the twelfth month. This type of project definition supports a large project for which some 150 people will be needed at the peak of the implementation stage.

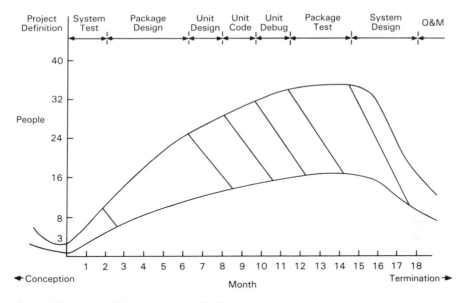

Fig. 3.13   Second-level project—Buildup.

up shown in Fig. 3.13 (the implementation portion of Fig. 3.1) assumes that people are readily available; i.e., no carry over from project definition is shown. This assumption is only valid in large programming organizations where the total number of programmers far exceeds the number needed by any single project (or where a contractor has been hired to supply the people). Otherwise, the rate of buildup is limited to what is achievable. Clearly, the staffing plan should be approved before the implementation stage begins. In fact, if the staff buildup cannot be assured, the capability of the organization to handle the project is questionable.

For the particular case of Fig. 3.13, the month by month staffing is given in Table 3.2. It is typical of jobs run by a second-level manager. That is, if the job is suitable for a second-level organization, the life cycle shown is typical. Roughly half the people provide support to the other half. During system design there is an average of seven people: four designers and three management and support people (Fig. 3.14a). The project total is shown at the left of the second-level manager's box. At the right of each box is the number of people assigned to that group. The four designers specify three packages, one per first-level department. A fourth first-level department is set up to provide support including project control and test development (Fig. 3.14b). The first-level managers are counted as line developers; all higher-level managers and their staff are included with support totals. Since the organization continues to grow as it progresses, there will be people on

TABLE 3.2.   STAFFING A SECOND-LEVEL PROJECT

Event	Staff	% schedule	Month	Staff	Recruiting activity
Start system design	3	0	0	3	+3
			1	7	+4
			2	11	+4
Start package design	10	10	3	15	+4
			4	19	+4
			5	22	+3
			6	25	+3
Start unit design	25	35	7	28	+3
			8	30	+2
Start unit code	30	45	9	31	+1
			10	32	+1
Start unit debug	32	55	11	34	+2
			12	35	+1
Start package test	36	65	13	36	+1
			14	36	—
			15	36	—
Start system test	36	82.5	16	34	−2
			17	26	−8
			18	18	−8
Release system	18	100	36	12	−6
Terminate project	12	200			

board in each stage who are in training for their assignment in the next stage. Thus starting in the package design stage additional programmers will join the project in a nonproductive role. To prevent these individuals from distracting the designers, some managers create one additional first-level department, which is the staging point for new arrivals. Here, indoctrination and training plus various support activities occupy the recruits. When program units have been specified, these people implement them, calling on the support of project resources and central services as well (Fig. 3.14c). Still more people will be needed to test the system raising the peak staff to thirty-six during testing. In the example, some fifteen unit programmers devote 5.4 months to implementation. This suggests that the package designers exploded the three packages into various lower levels until they had specified eighty-one units (at one programmer-month per unit).

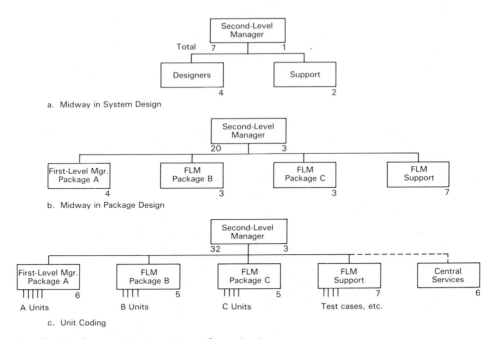

Fig. 3.14 Second-level project—Organization.

The shape of the life cycle curve for the typical second-level project fits the workload and requires a moderate but consistent recruiting effort. The largest monthly shifts in population occur at the end of system test. New assignments must be available for the people coming off the job since they must leave to avoid a budget overrun. In many organizations, rapid changes in permanent staff headcount create management problems that are harder to handle than financing the cost of a less drastic approach. Software vendors will try to schedule several projects so they overlap in such a way as to allow people to move from one to another with only minor fluctuations in total headcount. Users with small staffs and only one major project lack the opportunity in balance staff this way. They often turn to software contractors who will provide the staff on a temporary basis and, in addition, offer to manage the job.

Small projects run by a first-level manager have a different shape, as in Fig. 3.15, a six-person implementation over a twelve-month period. In many cases this curve would be flat, reflecting the fact that a first-level team is often assigned as a team. When this happens, there will be extra people at each end of the cycle. In a small group this presents no serious problem. It is certainly preferable to breaking up an existing team.

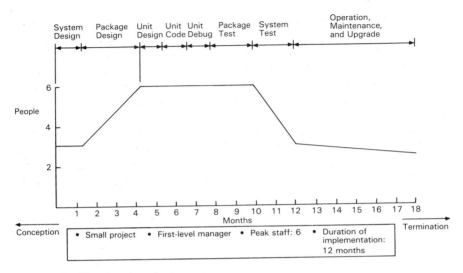

Fig. 3.15 First-level project.

Large projects sweep to a peak much faster than smaller jobs. System design starts with a few people as before, but many more packages are defined. Each package spawns relatively more units than would be the case in a smaller project, so relatively more people are needed in a large job than at the comparable point in a smaller one. A three-year project with a peak staff of 250 people is sketched in Fig. 3.16 with its monthly staff level given in Table 3.3. A larger portion of the schedule has been allowed for test in this example. As a result, there are almost four months for system design, nine months for package design, and only eight months for writing the programs. This leaves eight months each for package test and system test, acknowledging the greater complexity of a system of this size. Another feature of the example is that the recruiting load is immense at first and keeps up the pace for many months. For a project this large, thirty to forty people would have been involved in project definition. Of these, some five designers and ten support people are carried over to the development stage.[9] A fast buildup is needed to obtain the package designers (and lots of project planning and control people). Once they are assigned, there is a slight slowdown until the designers have produced enough unit specifications to justify completing the complement of unit programmers. Thus the project grows 67 percent in the first two weeks and only 30 percent in the fourth two weeks.

---

9. All 40 project definition people can be carried over in a training status at an additional cost of 50 people-months. This is a small factor in the 5790 people-month project.

TABLE 3.3.   STAFFING A HIGHER-LEVEL PROJECT

Event	Staff	% schedule	Month	Staff	Recruiting activity
Start system design	15	0	0	15	+ 15
			2	25	+ 10
			4	35	+ 10
Start package design	32	10	6	50	+ 15
			8	65	+ 15
			10	85	+ 20
			12	110	+ 25
Start unit design	120	35	14	145	+ 35
Start unit code	174	42.5	16	190	+ 45
			18	220	+ 30
Start unit debug	220	50	20	235	+ 15
Start package test	240	57.5	22	250	+ 15
			24	250	—
			26	250	—
			28	250	—
Start system test	250	80	30	250	—
			32	235	− 15
			34	180	− 55
			36	125	− 55
Release system	125	100	48	100	− 25
			60	75	− 25
			72	50	− 25
Terminate project	50	200			

Between the fourteenth and sixteenth weeks another 30 percent addition brings forty-five people to the project. The rate of growth here is moderate, but adding forty-five people to any project is a major effort. In this particular aspect of project management, the need for a strong and experienced support organization is obvious.

One more life cycle chart is interesting. In Fig. 3.17 and Table 3.4 the moderately large project of Fig. 3.1 is replanned using top-down implementation which, by spreading integration and test throughout the project, allows fewer people to do the same scope of work. It avoids the accumulation of complexity that is typical of bottom-up implementations. Problems are resolved when they occur; therefore, separate integration and test teams are

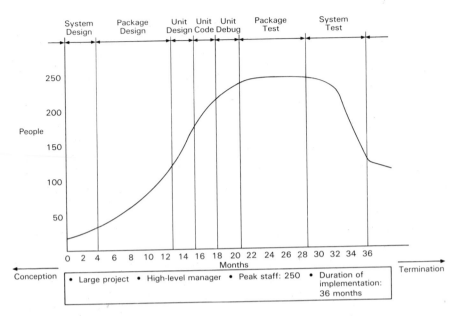

Fig. 3.16   Higher-level project.

not needed. Test cases are inherent in the design so another support activity shrinks. Even documentation is simplified because it can easily be done in parallel with programming instead of being pasted together from unit descriptions during the test stage. In the table, recruiting is spread more or less evenly. It can be argued that recruiting can be postponed to the sixth or eighth month while reducing the administrative workload on the cadre. While this is theoretically true, practical experience dictates that it is better to gradually add people as they become available than to try to schedule a mass movement. This practice does, however, dilute the cadre's attention to design and implementation. The total implementation workload in Table 3.2 is 467.5 people-months[10] for a peak staff of 36 in month 13. The equivalent cost of Table 3.4 is 266 people-months with a peak staff of 19 in month 12. The saving for the example is over 40 percent of the traditional method.

---

10. This is the sum of the average headcount each month ignoring changes within a month. (In month one the average is $(3 + 7)/2 = 5$ people months.) Implementation starts and ends with zero headcount; month zero has 1.5 people-months. Month 18 has 9 people-months for implementation and an additional 9 people-months for post-release support. The curve is based on a limited number of small to medium projects which claimed to be and appeared to be run top-down.

TABLE 3.4. STAFFING A TOP-DOWN IMPLEMENTATION

Event	Staff	% schedule	Month	Staff	Recruiting activity
Start system design	3	0	0	3	+3
			1	6	+3
			2	8	+2
			3	10	+2
			4	11	+1
			5	13	+2
			6	14	+1
			7	16	+2
			8	17	+1
			9	17	—
			10	18	+1
			11	18	—
			12	19	+1
			13	19	—
			14	19	—
			15	19	—
			16	18	−1
			17	18	—
			18	9	−9
Release system	18	100	36	6	−3
Terminate system		200			

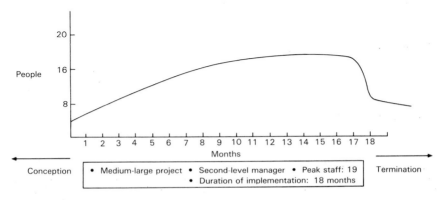

Fig. 3.17 Second-level project—Top-down implementation.

No comparable figures are offered for small or very large jobs. The unity of a small team often permits it to capitalize on efficient methods without fanfare. The likelihood that an experienced small team is already doing top-down implementation is too high to expect significant savings if they are told to do it. Furthermore, reducing the size of a functioning first-level team may reduce its capability to produce. If top-down methods can increase the productivity of such a team, it is better management practice to increase the work scope of the team. At the other extreme, there is inadequate evidence that very large jobs are amenable to top-down implementation. Since no one ever does the same job twice to produce comparative data, it would be overly speculative to quote a potential savings due to top-down implementation.[11] Undoubtedly, the potential is there, but it is probably hidden at the package design level. It can only be quantified when the project is so organized as to isolate each package as an independent subsystem with its own life cycle.

3.2.2   Schedule Flexibility

The examples, showing a small project taking twelve months, a moderately large one taking eighteen months, and a large one taking thirty-six months, have been offered without explanation. There is no explanation, really. The schedules were selected because they seemed reasonable. Why is that? Each manager has an intuitive idea of how long it takes to do certain things as well as how many things can be handled at once. Applying these unstated ideas, the manager arrives at a smoothed-out life cycle that fits neatly into the planning structure surrounding the project. For example, the author asked between 500 and 1000 IBM programming managers attending project management courses, "How long was the schedule for the last project you were on?" The answers tended to follow the pattern of Fig. 3.18. The most noticeable feature of this chart is that most projects are scheduled in semi-annual units. Managers tend to round off their plans to fit accounting periods. It is quite unusual for a proposal to offer a thirteen-month schedule; yet, twelve-month schedules are very common. In phased implementations, 6- and 12-month phases are routine. Similarly, long jobs do not start out with twenty-five-month schedules. They are scheduled to take twenty-four months or, if there are many exposures, thirty months.

---

11. An attempt to run an orbit determination project with two independent teams—one of about twenty people using old methods, and the second with two to four people experimenting with new methods—failed as a comparison test. The customer was not a full party to the experiment so he dealt only with the low-risk, contract-bound, old-style group. As changes arose, the old-style group modified their work plan and gradually diverged from the new-style team.

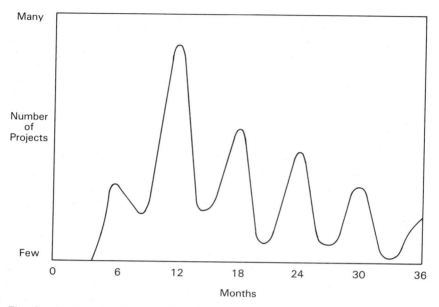

Fig. 3.18 Length of planned projects.

The U.S. government, which is a major buyer of large program systems, and many large corporations plan all their budgets on a twelve-month fiscal year. They then permit major budget adjustments at mid-year and minor changes quarterly. The accounting system that goes with fiscal year planning makes it easier to control major projects on an annual basis than on any other time span. For instance, all the planning forms and reports are set up for annualized entries. As a result, it is a convenience of some significance for a project manager to fit the project schedule into the fiscal pattern. As the project moves ahead, realistic changes to the schedule are made which are free to depart from the pattern. The net of this is that most managers have learned to select the optimum period of performance for a project from a limited set of desirable schedules.

3.2.2.1 Feasible schedules

The compromise between administrative objectives and technical project requirements is effective because, as Pietrasanta shows, there is a range of possible schedules for any job [14]. Within a narrow portion of the range, as indicated in Fig. 3.19, there are several minimum cost choices for project length. Beyond that range, there are many options that cost somewhat more because they introduce inefficiencies. Normally, a manager forms an initial idea of what the project schedule should be by laying out an activity plan.

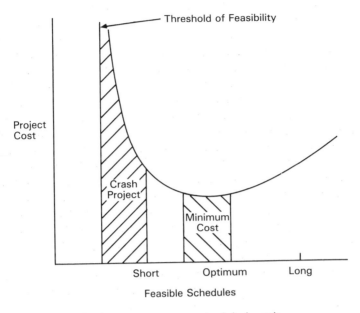

Fig. 3.19   Project cost versus schedule length.

This establishes a feasible schedule. The manager then adjusts it to fit a convenient accounting period. If, in doing this, the schedule is overextended there is a strong likelihood that there will be less work to do than there are people to do it in some part of the schedule. Thus the incremental cost of a longer than optimum schedule is due to underutilization of resources. The evidence of this is the gradual loss of focus and enthusiasm that accompanies boredom. Programmers can be found reading the newspaper. Tasks that can be done in ten days are delivered after fifteen days. Approval cycles stretch out until the change review procedure begins to look like a bureaucracy instead of an action organization. In extreme cases of stretched schedules, the development team members lose sight of the purpose of the job and start making dumb mistakes, doing things out of context with the system objectives.

Shorter than optimum schedules pay a much higher cost penalty due to an increase in unproductive energy. Since it takes more people to do the same amount of work on a short schedule, there is more friction and disorganization than there would be on the optimum schedule. Work is required to overcome the natural disorder among so many people. This amount of work is unproductive because it only organizes the group to do the job; it does not produce any system components.[12] The amount of efficiency lost

---

12. Note the analogy to *entropy* in thermodynamics.

due to tightening the schedule is unknown for programming projects because of the lack of large-scale controlled experiments in the field. It cannot be ignored, however. Suppose, for instance, that the loss of efficiency were related to the complexity of management which, in turn, is related to the number of people on the job. If the work required to deliver the system is the product of the average population times project duration, $k = \bar{y}T$, the optimum schedule will minimize the work:

$$k_0 = \bar{y}_0 T_0 = \min k.$$

Therefore, a shorter schedule, $T_i < T_0$, results in $k_i > k_0$; $\bar{y}_i > \bar{y}_0$. The work required is k_0; namely, the minimum effort to do the job. The work expended is k_i. The difference is due to the lower efficiency of the short schedule. This can be expressed as:

$$k_0 = k_i\left(1 - \frac{\text{unproductive effort}}{\text{applied effort}}\right).$$

The optimum workload is the project manager's best plan. The efficiency factor is a function of complexity which is based on the assumptions:

- Applied effort is proportional to the complexity of a system with $\bar{y}_i$ elements.
- Unproductive effort is proportional to the ratio of the complexity of k_i to k_0; that is, all the extra complexity leads to unproductive effort.
- The proportionality is exponential in that each additional person added to the project compounds the problem.

An expression can be constructed having these characteristics:

$$k_0 = k_i\left(1 - \frac{\ell n\left(\frac{\bar{y}_i^2}{\bar{y}_0^2}\right)}{\ell n\, \bar{y}_i^2}\right) \quad ;$$

$$\bar{y}_0 T_0 = \bar{y}_i T_i\left(\frac{\ell n\, \bar{y}_0}{\ell n\, \bar{y}_i}\right) \quad ;$$

$$\frac{\bar{y}_0}{\ell n\, \bar{y}_0} \times \frac{T_0}{T_i} = \frac{\bar{y}_i}{\ell n\, \bar{y}_i} \quad ;$$

from which the average headcount and total workload of the shorter than optimum schedule can be calculated.

Table 3.2 gave the life cycle for an eighteen-month optimum schedule which produced a 467.5 people-month system. Using the logic of the preceding equations, what would the same job cost on a twelve-month schedule?

$$\bar{y}_0 = \frac{467.5}{18} = 26 \qquad T_0 = 18 \qquad T_i = 12$$

$$\frac{\bar{y}_0}{\ell n \, \bar{y}_0} \times \frac{T_0}{T_i} = 11.97 = \frac{\bar{y}_i}{\ell n \, \bar{y}_i}$$

$\bar{y}_i = 46$ people approximately.

In this case, 77 percent more people are required and, even though the job is six months shorter, the work done amounts to 552 people-months, almost 20 percent more than the optimum. An attempt to drive the job down to six months total would require an average of 113 people. At this point, it is probably unrealistic to agree to staff and manage the original task.

Similar results are obtained when the thirty-six-month plan of Table 3.3 is shortened, although the percent impact on this large project is less dramatic. The impact on the top-down implementation of Table 3.4 and the small job of Fig. 3.15 is worse than on the eighteen-month medium-scale project. In these two projects, however, the guidelines may not even apply. The top-down implementation grew to nineteen people in the optimum plan. Although the rule-of-thumb that peak population is 1.5 times the average does not apply to top-down jobs due to the leveling off of work assignments, the ratio is still greater than one. As a result, the job in Table 3.4 when squeezed to twelve months requires an average of twenty-eight and a peak of thirty to forty people. No one is sure that a clean top-down approach can be managed on that scale. When the FLM job is squeezed one-third to nine months, it ceases to be an FLM job. The average population grows to nine with a peak of fourteen. An additional layer of management is needed and the overall impact of the accelerated schedule is much worse than that predicted by the guidelines.

3.2.2.2 Crash projects and infeasible schedules

Very short schedules may still be feasible but are probably uneconomical. Pietrasanta calls these "crash projects." In line with the concept of complexity, Brooks explains that crash projects are dominated by communications; i.e., interactions [15]. This makes crash projects virtually unmanageable unless they are perfectly planned and executed. Unfortunately, most crash projects are really infeasible projects run by an unqualified manager. What leads to these situations is the overwhelming desire on the part of the user (or a vendor trying to please or impress a user) to have a system delivered on a certain date. The normal project definition procedure under the direction of a competent manager reports back that the schedule cannot be met. At this stage, instead of reanalyzing the requirements, the user asserts some authority and says, "It *can* be done—but not by you!" Then the organization is searched for some other candidate, usually a strong daring, leader-type, who is willing to stand up and say, "I can do it!" Of course, the new volunteer cannot do it. In fact, people who enjoy challenges like this usually have left a trail of failed projects behind them. The more wily among them have transferred out of each failure before the finger of guilt was pointed at them. Even if they are marked individuals, however, all they need do is volunteer at the right time to get another crack at a crash project.

The subsequent history of the project follows the sad pattern shown in Fig. 3.20. Here, an optimum project plan (light dashed line) representing the schedule which minimizes project cost (solid line) is rejected. The desired schedule is much shorter but may still be feasible at higher cost. Unfortunately, the manager who knows the most about the job is not the manager in charge of the new plan. What *may* be feasible in theory may be *infeasible* in practice for the new manager operating under intense pressure.

It is clear that a crash plan (heavy dashed line) must be devised. The new manager knows that a lot of people will be needed. Assuming they can be found, they are brought on board (A). There has been no time to design any tasks for them, so most of them are just drawing pay while awaiting instructions. Meanwhile, the design stage gets under way. It is a confused operation because it is overstaffed. The confusion leads to bad design decisions reflected in awkward designs with more modules and interactions than are really needed. Given a normal concern for system integrity, there will be enough review activity to catch the most blatant design errors. However, by the time these are fixed, half the schedule will be eaten up (B). In addition, an estimate of what it will take to implement the design will show that it is impossible to finish on time.

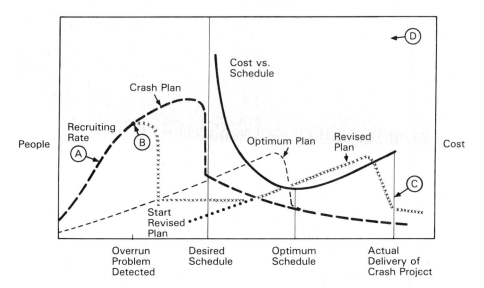

Fig. 3.20 Crash project.

Significantly, on an infeasible project the evidence of late delivery is detected at point B. It was known before the project started, but no one wanted to believe the original estimate. Now they have to believe it and try to make up for lost time. Unfortunately, little can be salvaged from the work done up to B. A new project plan is required (x's). If the system requirements are unchanged, the new plan will probably look like the original optimum plan. It will be penalized by virtue of the existing staff. It does not make sense to reassign everyone, so instead of a clean start (dots), a nucleus of people is retained while the project is redone. When the new plan is approved, the delivery date will be C and the cost will escalate to D.

In other words, do not plan jobs on a crash schedule.

3.2.2.3 Adjusting to schedule constraints

The example just given illustrates bad judgment. There are cases where a very short schedule is mandatory but manageable. In general, these cases occur in deadline situations where the delivery date is fixed by some external force. In commercial systems, new laws are periodically published calling for compliance on a certain date. In the United States, such laws constantly affect payroll and labor accounting systems. The best example of deadline scheduling in the scientific/engineering field has been in the spaceflight area. Here, the relative position of the launch site (i.e., the Earth) and the target (i.e., the Moon, the Sun, a planet) is critical to the success of the mission. Certain shots can only be made once or twice a year when the conditions are just right to open a narrow "window" to the target. The shot must go at that moment or be delayed a year.

So far, time has been traded for people (and cost). Even though the tradeoff has not been completely efficient, it has been possible to adjust to various schedules by changing the manning level. If the delivery date is fixed and the manning level for that schedule is unmanageable, the project will fail. Something else must give. The only variable left is function.[13] If you think of the system development life cycle as a spring, you can shorten the schedule by anchoring the left end and pushing on the right end. Where you do this, the middle pops up; i.e., the shorter schedule takes more people. If you do not want more people, you must push down on the spring at the same time you push from the right. What comes squooshing out the sides is the workload represented by the area under the spring. Headcount and schedule determine the achievable workload; therefore, headcount can be reduced to a manageable level by reducing the workload. This can be done

---

13. Quality can be sacrificed; however, it is not smart to do so. Neither can the saving gained by such a tradeoff be quantified; therefore, it is not treated as an option here.

by negotiation with the user as long as it is possible to prioritize the project requirements. Then the lowest priority functions are eliminated until a satisfactory project plan can be drawn [16].

3.2.2.4 A life cycle model

The life cycle observed in program development projects is not unique to software. Similar curves are well known in hardware projects. Norden [17] showed that labor force buildup and phase down in large hardware development projects follows a model derived from reliability theory. In hardware projects the overall plan is the sum of overlapping subcycles for planning, designing, building and testing a prototype, engineering release to manufacturing, some redesign, product support, and value engineering. Each of these subcycles starts small as the work to be done is organized and people build the understanding of the problems to be solved. The staff grows as the backlog of work builds. At the same time, people learn how to handle the work better and their rate of problem solving improves. Soon the backlog starts to shrink and the staff, working at high efficiency, also shrinks. Each of the subcycles in Norden's Life-Cycle Model is described by the equation:

$$y' = 2\,k\,a\,t\,e^{-a\,t^2}$$

where

y' = people-months per month or approximately the number of people on board at time t. (In the following discussion y' will only be used for the population onboard in the month, t_{peak}.)

k = total people-months in the subcycle.

$a = \dfrac{1}{2t_{peak}^2}$ = parameter indicating the "crashiness" of the project plan.

t = months from start of subcycle.

t_{peak} = month in which population peaks.

This is a differential equation. When integrated, it gives the cumulative people-months used through month t. This is the

Applied Effort $(t) = k\,(1 - e^{-at^2})$.

In the early stages of a subcycle it is possible to forecast peak population, total workload, expenditure rate by month, and possible slippage. History data establish the relations between the successive subcycles in the typical hardware project. Thus data from the planning subcycle can lead to forecasts of total project behavior.

The life cycles generated by the model look very much like Fig. 3.1. In fact, in 1959 Pietrasanta and Schreiber found the model applied rather well to program development projects. The single-purpose character of program development makes all activity from beginning to end a homogeneous problem-solving effort, according to Norden. The resulting life cycle corresponds to a single cycle of the model. This is fortuitous for established data on definition, design, development, test, maintenance, and upgrade are not available. No clear line is drawn between design and development; consequently, data on subcycles would be of questionable value in any case.

The fact that software life cycles look like Norden's curves does not mean that software projects have the same characteristics as hardware. The hardware environment is more mature. It is more mechanized due to the constraints of standard tools and manufacturing facilities. A hardware prototype is a stepping stone to the manufactured product. The corresponding software entity is the one and only manufactured product. As a result, one would expect to see differences between hardware and software due to different staffing rates and different processes. Table 3.5 compares the four projects from Tables 3.2, 3.3, 3.4 and Fig. 3.15 to highlight the points in which the Life Cycle Model (LCM) confirms the empirical model. The peak HC and peak month were taken from the tables; they reflect management and recruiting constraints observed in practice. The short schedules discussed in section 3.2.2.1 are included with estimated peak month data. Total workload, k, for the entire project was computed; i.e.,

Case 1: $y' = 36$ $t_{peak} = 13$

Total Workload, $k = y'/(2\,a\,t\,e^{-a\,t^2}) = 771.6$ people-months to termination.

Applied Effort through month 18 = 771.6 $(1 - e^{-at^2}) = 475.7$ people-months to release in month 18.

The results are driven by the choice of peak month data. Nevertheless, the agreement between the two sets of data is very good at several points. The estimate of total project workload is essentially the same for two traditional style projects; however, the model tends to overestimate the workload to release. To see why, compare the monthly staff levels of the Second-Level Traditional cases in Table 3.6. Here, the pragmatics of the empirical model are apparent; a sharp drop off when the product is released, a gradual reduction in maintenance and upgrade resources, and an arbitrary cutoff date selected by management. By contrast, the Life Cycle Model is an analytic curve with a well-formed peak and a smooth decline to a long tail. LCM projects a longer schedule and permits fractional headcounts (indicated by dashes in the table where LCM figures are rounded to the nearest integer). In addition, LCM does not indicate when release [R] occurs; the

TABLE 3.5. LIFE CYCLE MODEL APPLIED TO PROGRAM PROJECTS

| Program project type | Months to | | Project peak | | Workload to | | | |
| | Release | Termination | Month | HC | Release | | Termination | |
					EMP	LCM	EMP	LCM
Second-Level Traditional	18	36	13	36	467.5	476	737.5	772
	12	24	8	69	552	615	900	910
Third-Level Traditional	36	72	22	250	5790	6691	8940	9068
	24	48	16	398	6360	7090	10340	10499
Second-Level Top Down	18	36	12	19	266	254	401	376
First Level	12	24	4	6	62	39	92	40

HC = headcount
EMP = empirical model
LCM = Life cycle model in which
  y' = HC on board in peak month = $2\, kate^{-at^2}$
  y = workload in people-months through time $t = k\,(1 - e^{-at^2})$

curve assumes that there is only one activity in the cycle and it ends at the end point [T]. For this reason, some people have treated the peak month, *, as the month of release. When this is done, the estimate of the workload to release is:

$$\text{Applied Effort} = y' = k(1 - e^{-a\,t'^2}) = k\,(1 - e^{-1/2}).$$

The result understates the development workload. (In the cases shown, the peak occurs about two-thirds of the way to release. The workload through the peak is only about 58 percent of the workload to release; it is not a useful measure.)

If you have done enough project planning to have determined the peak month and peak staff level, you can probably draw the life cycle curve. Its area will be close to k, which you can calculate from the peak data. That is the workload to termination. Workload to release is 60 to 70 percent of k for medium- to large-sized jobs. The remaining effort applied to post-release activities should be planned according to local guidelines in preference to the LCM headcounts.

The influence of the "crashiness" parameter is seen in the short schedule. The LCM produces an asymmetrical curve with a front-end load; i.e., there is relatively more work in the early months. Shortening the schedule increases the front-end load, eventually exceeding the limits of a feasible staffing plan. As a result, the LCM tends to overestimate workload to release. The deviation from normal staffing practice increases as schedule

TABLE 3.6.   STAFFING PLAN—EMPIRICAL VS. LIFE CYCLE MODEL

Second-level program project (traditional)

MONTH	Optimum schedule (18 mo.)				Short schedule (12 mo.)			
	EMP HC	LCM HC	EMP Effort	LCM Effort	EMP HC	LCM HC	EMP Effort	LCM Effort
0	3	0			3	0		
1	7	5	5	2	10	14	6.5	7
2	11	9	14	9	20	28	21.5	28
3	15	13	27	20	30	40	46.5	62
4	19	17	44	36	40	50	81.5	107
5	22	21	64.5	55	50	59	126.5	161
6	25	24	88	78	62	65	182.5	223
7	28	27	114.5	104	67	68	247	289
8	30	30	143.5	133	69*	69*	315	358
9	31	32	174	164	69	68	384	426
10	32	34	205.5	198	66	65	451.5	493
11	34	35	238.5	232	50	61	509.5	556
12	35	36	273	268	35 (R)	56	552 (R)	615
13	36*	36*	308.5	304	34	49	586.5	668
14	36	36	344.5	340	33	43	620	714
15	36	35	380.5	375	32	37	652.5	754
16	34	34	415.5	410	31	31	684	788
17	26	33	445.5	443	30	25	714.5	816
18	18 (R)	31	467.5 (R)	476	29	20	744	838
19	18	30	485.5	506	28	16	772.5	856
20	17	28	503	535	27	13	800	870
21	17	26	520	562	26	10	826.5	882
22	17	24	537	587	25	7	852	890

216

896 900 904 906 908 909 910 . . . 910

876.5
900

T

5 4 3 2 1 1 1 | | | | | | | | | | | | | | | | | | . . . |

24
23

T

610 631 650 667 682 696 708 718 727 734 741 746 751 755 758 760 762 763 764 765 766 767 768 . . . 772

553.5 569.5 585.5 601 616 631 645.5 659.5 673.5 687 700 713 725.5 737.5

T

22 20 18 16 14 13 11 10 8 7 6 5 4 4 3 2 2 1 1 1 1 1 1 . . . |

16 16 16 15 15 15 14 14 14 13 13 13 12 12

T

23 24 25 26 27 28 29 30 31 32 33 34 35 36 37 38 39 40 41 42 43 44 45 . . . 8

pressures and the stress on management increase. In Table 3.6, the optimum schedule to release is roughly the same for both the empirical and the LCM approaches. After release, LCM is misleading because it ignores the fast drop off of staff headcount. In the short schedule, the prerelease staff levels are much higher than appropriate in the LCM. The estimates provided by the LCM will aggravate the problems in crash projects due to excess people. Given free access to qualified people, it is probably feasible to do a project in two-thirds to one-half the optimum schedule ($a = 2$ to 4 times optimum a). Shorter schedules invite failure. Unfortunately, it is rarely possible to apply this guideline since few projects have a well-defined optimum nor are qualified people readily available. The rule is best used as a reasonableness test of the project manager's schedules and budgets. Returning to the shape of the LCM curve, the examples show that in the range of feasible schedules the LCM deviates only about 10 percent from the empirical curve. That is close enough for guidelines such as these. Incidentally, the LCM staffing rate for the "optimum" schedule is so close to the empirical plan that it increases your confidence in the optimality of the eighteen-month schedule.

Top-down implementation is an even more homogeneous activity than traditional bottom-up development. Nevertheless, k in the top-down example understates the empirical figure for total project workload. Workload to release does compare well with the empirical data. The reason for this is that the tail of the empirical plan is a guess and is apparently inflated. It is based on the usual rule that HC at release is one-half peak and HC at termination is one-third peak. Since top-down methods are less error-prone, the maintenance and upgrade effort should be no worse than in traditional projects. The LCM in this case suggests that it is the empirical model that is wrong; the top-down approach is even better than expected.

The last example is the first level manager's project. The LCM does not work in this situation. The unique characteristic of the FLM project was that it represented the work of a FLM group. The size of the group determined the number of people-years expended. Excess resources were applied simply because the people were available and it was deemed better to keep the group intact than to splinter it. LCM says, "Theoretically, you could have done the job with less than half the effort." The FLM would agree, in principle. In practice, though, the first-level manager paid a premium to buy teamwork, control, and confidence in meeting his or her commitments.

The LCM is an attractive planning aid for large organizations. It permits staff evaluations of many projects using a few simple data items. The U.S. Army Computer Systems Command has made such use of it where Putnam [17] has extended Norden's work. The LCM is a special case of the family of probability density functions known as Weibull distributions. The functions, common in reliability theory, have time series counterparts called

Rayleigh functions found in financial and personnel planning. Putnam's Rayleigh functions

$$y' = 2\,k\,a\,t\,e^{-a\,t^2}$$

are exactly like Norden's LCM. In the process, Putnam points out some interesting characteristics of the variables.

$$k = \text{total workload}$$
$$t' = \text{peak month}$$

$$\frac{1}{2t'^2} = a = \text{``crashiness''}$$

as before. In addition,

$$t_d = \text{time to release};$$

$$\frac{k}{t_d^2} = \text{``difficulty''};$$

i.e., the larger this parameter (or ak) is, the greater the difficulty of the project; and

$$\frac{k}{t_d^3} = \text{``capability''};$$

the value of this parameter is related to the capability of the development team to succeed in this class of projects. The Computer Systems Command (CSC) history of some fifty systems of various sizes and types provided some interesting information about these parameters. First, as is obvious, both difficulty and capability are affected more drastically by a schedule reduction than by a headcount change. (Putnam makes no interpretations about schedule extensions. He does note that, for practical purposes, large systems are planned to take at least two years to termination and not more than five years. New versions are built to extend system life.) Second, "difficulty" is inversely related to productivity. This result is also obvious but is seldom tested. Putnam plotted

$$\left(\frac{k}{t_d^2} \right)$$

for completed projects versus delivered statements per people-year and found an excellent fit. From this plot, estimating factors can be obtained for predicting the resources required for future CSC projects. Third, somewhat surprisingly, "capability" is a classification constant. That is, for all CSC projects, when k and t are expressed in people-years and years respectively:

$$\frac{k}{t_d^3} = \text{either 8, 15, or 27.}$$

The constant 8 correlated with hard, complex projects starting from scratch. The value 15 occurred with new stand-alone, noncomplex, systems. Easy projects built on an existing base were in the third capability class. Although 8, 15, and 27 are local results for CSC, they are structurally similar to such standard estimating rules such as "delivered statements per programmer per month will be

$$\left. \begin{array}{l} 125 \\ 250 \\ 500 \end{array} \right\} \text{ when the task is } \left\{ \begin{array}{l} \text{hard, complex} \\ \text{medium, less complex} \\ \text{easy, not complex} \end{array} \right\} \text{."}$$

The ratio 1:2:4 among classes is almost 8:15:27. The CSC constants do not fit the examples of Table 3.5; that may simply indicate that the CSC experience does not consist of such cases. Actually, CSC projects tend to be second-level jobs much longer than eighteen months. Nevertheless, the "capability" parameter shows that classification is possible and that the number of job and team classifications in any one environment is small. Furthermore, team capability improves in quantum jumps; i.e., a team that has established credentials in class 27 is not expected to do well on a hard project but, eventually, should move up to tackle class 15 jobs. At the same time, the team should perform better on class 27 jobs. As an example, a software house has successfully done a number of easy jobs. A typical assignment might have been one involving 700 people-years spread over three years, capability 27. As they gained experience and built an internal team knowledgeable in the type of work offered them, and as they built the right set of support tools and techniques, they found their productivity drastically improved. The first evidence was a significant underrun on a routine project. Soon they will adjust their estimating parameters and start bidding to do the same class of jobs in the same time with only 400 people-years.

The usual warning must be stated here: Quantitative guidelines based on concepts and random samples are subject to large errors; use them with caution. In this chapter, the discussion of life cycle models has significantly omitted any discussion of the type of program system being built. Clearly, the development process depends in some way on the nature of the job being done [18]. The models, therefore, can only be approximate. Nevertheless, analysis of the behavior of life cycles provides considerable insight into how to plan and manage team projects.

3.2.3 Life Cycle Handovers

A simplified picture of the changing conditions in the system development life cycle is shown in Fig. 3.21. The chart has been highlighted to emphasize certain handover events that affect everyone on the project and contribute to changing the focus of management attention.

When the design requirements baseline is completed during the project definition stage, a series of events takes place. The project definition team is

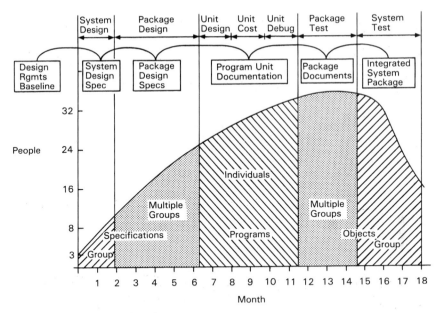

Fig. 3.21   Life cycle handovers.

dissolved with only a few, if any, of the technical members of the team available for system design. Further, there is a delay while the baseline is studied by upper management, prior to their approving the design stage. Add to this the time required to solicit proposals and select a development organization (when the contract route is followed). By the time system design starts, no one on the project has a fresh, personal knowledge of the design requirements. The ability to proceed is wholly dependent on the quality of the information in the design requirements baseline document. The handover of this document from the project definition stage to the system design stage is a critical link in the life cycle. Subsequent document handovers are equally important. The concept that documents are the only embodiment of a programming system, discussed in [9], applies to these life cycle handovers. Looking at the rate of staff buildup in the life cycle, it is obvious that each month new people arrive. They learn what is going on by talking to the old-timers and by studying the project documents. The old-timers are flexible and can provide useful insights. The documents, though, are always available; therefore, they are the primary means of passing information to the newcomers.[14]

---

14. While "documentation" normally refers to hard-copy printed material, it may also include on-line computer databases structured to support inquiry and on-line training.

Handovers occurring at the transitions between life cycle stages do not only disseminate the work of a small group to the members of a larger group. They also trigger changes in the mode of operation of the project. For instance, the handover of the system design specification to the package designers signals a shift from a one-group, tightly knit, idea-generating activity to a multigroup, more loosely organized activity. Both stages share a common interest in that they are concerned with top-down design resulting in a specification. Only the system designers, however, have first-hand knowledge of the full system requirements. The package designers have first-hand knowledge of one package and second-hand knowledge of the overall system. As a result, many questions arise during package design that can only be answered by cross-communication among the package design groups. This suggests that tools and techniques used during the design stages should support both group teamwork and inter-group communication. On small projects, a good set of project documents plus effective working relations among the team members is sufficient. Large projects require early formalization of on-line documentation, interface management, and change control procedures.

At the next stage, specifications are distributed to individual programmers who are going to work by themselves. Each unit is supposed to be insulated from its neighbors so that extensive intra-group communication is less important than it was during design. The unit designer is the unit implementer; hence, no handovers are needed until the unit is finished. Because of the partitioned nature of the project at this stage, it is feasible to introduce tools that increase the productivity of individuals. The most notable tool in this category is interactive time-sharing [9].

As the units enter test there is another handover. This time the recipients are not only unfamiliar with the units in detail, but some of them are not even familiar with programming. They are test personnel who treat the programs as *objects* to be combined in various ways and run with previously prepared test cases. The kind of tools they need are automated libraries with good storage and retrieval facilities, remote job entry support for good test turnaround, and various project controls over integration sequences and test schedules. The same tools carry over into the system test stage when the main change is that user personnel may join the test team.

In a sense, the character of the life cycle is a closed loop. It starts with a single, small-group activity and ends with a single, larger-group activity. In between, the work grows to a group of groups, then to many individual tasks, reconsolidating to a group of groups. The closed pattern is not uniform, however. At the start, the activities are *descriptive,* specifying things about programs. In the middle, the activities are *constructive,* building the programs themselves. At the end, the activities are *evaluative,* testing the programs as parts of a system.

3.2.4 Life Cycle Dynamics

The environment surrounding a program system constantly changes. User requirements change as it becomes clear that the program system permits the user to operate differently and more effectively. New requirements arise when the user has installed the basic system and finds time to analyze new computer applications. Sometimes the user's business changes during the life of the program system. Such was the case with the trend to on-line banking. All the existing centralized software either had to be modified to handle terminals or it had to be replaced. A business decision must be made in such cases to determine if it will pay to change the program to reflect the change in the environment.

In general there are four major reasons for modifying a program:

1. To correct an error
2. To improve an existing capability
3. To add a new capability
4. To improve performance

The majority of known errors will be approved for fixing. Occasionally, errors will be ignored on the basis that they will rarely occur.

When user feedback shows that an existing capability is no longer useful, it is normal for the developer to modify the program design to adapt to the new environment. Rarely will users be told to "take it or leave it." Therefore, program improvements are common.

New capabilities will also be authorized when they are projected to increase the value of a program (in terms of revenue, extended life, competitive appeal, or customer satisfaction).

Performance improvements are governed by technical considerations and environment. It usually gets harder to improve performance as a program ages. As a consequence, performance improvements are more common in the early releases of a program system. Later, their cost appears disproportionate to the promised gain. A larger computer starts to look like a better approach.

Historically, program developers have been more willing to make changes than to stabilize their product. Under the circumstances, systems grow bigger and more complex, calling for more and more effort to avoid errors.

Multiphase projects bring growth under control by limiting the amount of effort involved in any particular release. One way of doing this is to define Version 1/Release 1 as a base containing all technically essential capabilities plus the minimum set of capabilities needed to sell the product. The base, Version 1, is periodically enhanced with maintenance releases. Ostensibly, a maintenance release merely fixes errors. In practice, most releases also modify capabilities. Ideally, the addition of new capabilities is scheduled for Version 2. Version 2 would contain all the improvements to Version 1 plus the new functions and, possibly, major revisions to some of the basic modules. Version 1/Release 1 would be like a new automobile. Version 1/Release 2 would correspond to the same car after it had received the manufacturer's ninety-day warranty service. Version 1/Release 3 might correspond to the same car after a recall to replace a weak steering column cotter pin, which the owner scheduled to coincide with an 18,000-mile checkup. Version 2 would be the next year's model: same chassis, same engine, new transmission, new upholstery, plus some things that were not available before—electronic ignition, built-in diagnostic computer, and safety air bags. Both Version 1 and Version 2 are the same type of car, say a Chevrolet Citation. There is so much fixed investment tied up in plant, tools, spare parts, etc., that the manufacturer is reluctant to scrap the Citation X-body model and build a new offering from scratch. Similarly, a major operating system such as OS/MVS is likely to be improved rather than scrapped and replaced. Sooner or later, though, system maintenance will become a problem. The system will either become technologically obsolete or uneconomically complex, necessitating replacement.

Replacement in the past tended to coincide with the installation of a new computer. Each generation of computers introduced new performance advantages that could only be realized with new programs. More recently, compatible families and high-level languages have made computer replacement less of a factor in deciding when to replace a program. Now it is appropriate to compare the life cycle cost of extending an existing system to the cost of creating a new system.

Little data exist to help a manager make the decision. Ongoing costs of the existing system can be projected, but costs of the replacement are hard to agree on. Furthermore, no good forecasting and marketing techniques are known that will demonstrate the value of the new system versus the old one.

Most methods are indirect and favor extending the existing system. For example, a replacement payroll was estimated to cost eight people-years or (at the time) $240,000. The only tangible savings were a fifteen-minute per week reduction in run time, elimination of about eight hours per week of system analyst "handholding" necessary to get the existing system to run correctly, and about half-time for one maintenance programmer. At prevailing rates, the savings were only $28,800. Since the payroll worked despite its poor quality, there was clearly no economic advantage to writing a new system. In this case, though, the payroll *had* to be replaced because company pay practices and government tax rules changed so much the program became obsolete. Replacement economics are even worse for companies that supply software at no charge to support revenue-producing hardware. Any value, say in terms of hardware sales due to software capabilities, is intangible because there is no way to prove that the hardware sales would have been lower without this specific software package. At least there is no way to prove it to the salespeople and the hardware engineers who are contending for budget dollars to improve their own area of the business. Only where the programs are sold as products on their own merits is the tangible value (i.e., income) hopefully going to exceed the cost of development plus maintenance. More and more vendor software is being unbundled to take advantage of objective cost data. But most program managers are unable to base replacement decisions solely on tangible values; they must rely instead on intangibles such as cost and quality trends or customer satisfaction.

Steps in the direction of providing more solid bases for management decisions have been taken by Lehman, Belady, and their colleagues [19]. Their programming research is concerned with the evolutionary pattern of program systems. By taking a system view, they have generated some useful insights into program system life cycles and, quite possibly, have laid the groundwork for analysis of system dynamics in broader areas than programming. They started their work with a detailed analysis of the maintenance releases of IBM's OS/360 (twenty releases over a ten-year period). This study supported some hypotheses that were confirmed by analysis of several other projects. OS/360 was very large and could be a pathological case. The other projects, however, were smaller. Several companies were involved so the results are not simply a reflection of IBM's project management procedures. Different computers and different languages were also involved. Nevertheless, the results of the studies showed that all of the systems had similar characteristics in the maintenance and upgrade stage of their life. In particular,

- All systems grew in size throughout their life.
- The rate of growth slowed as the system evolved.
- The rate of maintenance work on the system was relatively stable.
- Intervals between successive releases lengthened.

These conclusions fit the expected characteristics of a system as discussed in Chapter 1. Version 1/Release 1 has a certain inherent complexity and usually contains some residual errors. Release 2 is an attempt to reduce the number of errors. In addition, Release 2 may modify an existing capability. Both activities can generate new errors, and uncorrected errors from Release 1 will remain. If you concentrate only on system errors (i.e., errors that affect more than one system element), you expect to find many fixes taking the form of new modules that act as adapters or bridges between affected components. That is one possible reason for system growth. The addition of new modules to handle new function is another obvious reason. But every new module increases system complexity; therefore, successive re-

leases become more difficult. Each release takes longer to accomplish because, even though the time to make one change may be constant, the interactive effect causes more modules to be handled in each successive release.
The consistency of life cycle behavior is not easy to observe since any one
stage of the cycle may appear to deviate from the predicted pattern and
overlap between stages obscures the long-term trends. After a series of releases, however, it is possible to detect the trends.

The measure of complexity, C_R, used by Lehman and Belady for the
post-release stage is given as the number of modules handled to generate a
new release divided by the total number of modules in the system. (They
chose "module" rather than "statement" or "instruction" because modules in OS/360 were well-defined entities, easily tracked through the development process. There were enough modules to permit statistical analysis of
a reasonable size population.) C_R is an abstract of the complexity measures
of Chapter 1. A single change will affect one or more modules as can be
determined from a connection matrix. C_R simply counts the number of
modules affected by the specific changes made for one release. The rate at
which C_R grew in OS/360 as indicated in Fig. 3.22, which shows the value of

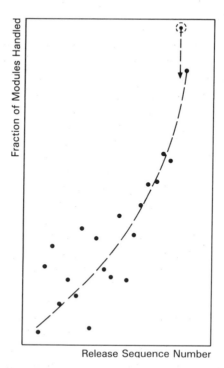

Fig. 3.22   Complexity growth (OS/360).
L. A. Belady and M. M. Lehman, "A Model of Large Program Development,"
IBM Systems Journal 15, no. 3 (1976).

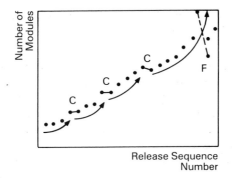

Fig. 3.23 System consolidation (C) and fission (F).
L. A. Belady and M. M. Lehman, "A Model of Large Program Development,"
IBM Systems Journal 15, no. 3 (1976).

C_R just prior to each release. While the curve is smooth, the values are quite scattered. This local variation is related to two characteristics of the process that serve to stress the invariance of the basic conclusions made by the research team.

1. An effort to conserve effort and minimize complexity by restricting growth in the nth release will simply cause the $n + $ 1st release to exceed the average.

2. It is necessary to stop for a breather periodically. After several stages of growth, a consolidation step (C), consisting of various local structure improvements, is required (Fig. 3.23). At some point, indicated by the arrow in Fig. 3.22, following Release 20, fission (F) occurs creating a completely new version; i.e., the system is so complex, it must be restructured or somehow simplified if it is to remain viable.

To summarize their findings, Belady and Lehman postulate three laws of Program Evolution Dynamics:

I   *Law of Continuing Change:* A system that is used undergoes continuing change until it is judged more cost effective to freeze and recreate it.

II   *Law of Increasing Entropy:* The entropy of a system (its unstructuredness) increases with time unless specific work is executed to maintain or reduce it.

III *Law of Statistically Smooth Growth:* Growth trend measures of global system attributes may appear to be stochastic locally in time and space, but statistically, they are cyclically self-regulating, with well-defined long-range trends.

For OS/360, the data support the laws. The number of modules handled per release kept growing (Fig. 3.24a) representing continual product change. The number of different modules handled was approaching 100 percent

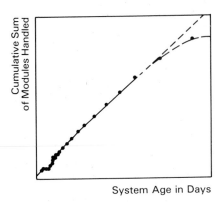

a. Modules Handled Per Release (OS/360)

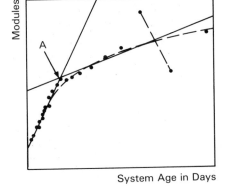

b. System Growth: Modules in System by Release (OS/360)

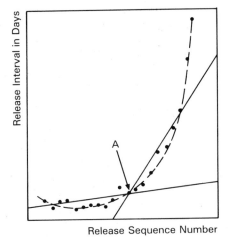

c. Interval between Releases (OS/360)

Fig. 3.24 Program evolution dynamics.
L. A. Belady and M. M. Lehman, "A Model of Large Program Development,"
IBM Systems Journal 15, no. 3 (1976).

when fission occurred. Obviously, if you have to handle every module in the
system to produce a new release, you should consider replacing the system.
Not shown in the chart is the number of times a given module was handled.
Due to interactions, a module can be affected by changes to other modules
and, consequently, be handled several times per release. Some feel for the
effectiveness of the system structure can be obtained by examining the distribution of module handlings. The more compact the set of modules affected by a change, the more likely the system is well designed. For example,
in the information retrieval example of Chapter 1, two system designs were

presented. The logical subsystem of Fig. 1.8 had eight modules communicating with Module 13—the Format Table. One of the eight was the Format Table itself. In the structured subsystem of Fig. 1.9, only SEARCH communicates with FORMAT TABLE. If a change in the procedure for accessing FORMAT and COUNT data becomes necessary, each of the using modules will be affected. In addition, each affected module can reflect the change back to the source and to any of its neighbors according to the design decisions made in implementing the change. Table 3.7 enumerates one possible cascade of changes for each of the information retrieval designs.

TABLE 3.7. EFFECT OF STRUCTURE ON MODULE HANDLING (cascade effect of changing FORMAT TABLE module in Information Retrieval System)

Module	Initial change	First level	Second level	Third level	Module handlings	
			Interactive effects			
1						
2						
3		13			1	
4						
5						
6		13			1	
7		13			1	
8		13			1	
9		13			1	
10		13			1	
11						
12		13	7,8,9,10		5 }	2/3 of total handlings
13	x	13	7,8,9,10	12	7 }	
					18	

a. Logical Subsystem

Module	Initial change	First level	Second level	Third level	Module handlings	
1						
2						
3		13			1	
4						
5						
6						
7						
8						
9						
10						
11						
12						
13	x		3		2 }	2/3 of total handlings
					3	

b. Structured Subsystem

The locality of change is much better, of course, in the structured design. There, the module handlings were concentrated on 15 percent of the modules in the system. In the logical system, the modules handlings were distributed across 60 percent of the modules in the system—a gross measure to be sure, but one worth watching as a gauge of the increasing entropy in a long-lived system. It can help trigger the decision to replace a system with a re-structured version.

Lehman and Parr [19] suggest tracking an arbitrary ratio based on the observation that in many systems the majority of the activity affects a minority of the system. Following this observation, the data to track is the ratio formed by dividing the number of modules involved in 2/3 of the module handling by the number of modules in the system. To do this, arrange the system modules in order of handling frequency. (Table 3.7 is in this order with high frequency at the bottom.) Starting with the highest frequency, count the modules representing 2/3 of the module handlings. (In Table 3.7a, two modules represent twelve out of eighteen module handlings; in 3.7b, one module is handled twice in a total of three handlings.) Divide the count by the total number of modules. (In Table 3.7a, 2/13; in 3.7b, 1/13.) If the result is more than 1/3, begin to worry. If it is considerably more than 1/3, do something to improve the system structure. (Neither Table 3.7a nor 3.7b is a problem at present.)

Other factors to watch are the rate at which the system grows and new features are released. In Fig. 3.24b and c, the complexity of OS/360 is reflected in the slowing rate of adding new modules and the increased time required to ready a new release. At point A, around Releases 12–13, an inflection in these curves occurred. That was the signal that management attention to system dynamics was important. Beyond that point, system maintenance cost due to complexity grows too fast. It interferes with the release of system improvements. More and more of the project budget goes to the structure-related activities of documentation, administration, communication, and learning, and less money is available for the progressive work of error correction and system enhancement. Neglect of the structure-related activities merely creates a backlog of problems that increase the future cost of keeping the system alive.[15]

The systems view behind the study of program dynamics searches for invariant characteristics of *system* behavior independent of system type.

---

15. A potential effect of neglecting such things as documentation and communication is that the point is reached where no one on the project is certain any more about what the system does or how it is used. Consequently, the individual can no longer be sure that a compatible replacement can be built. This complicates the re-placement decision by limiting the choices to: (1) preserving the current system regardless of cost, or (2) designing an incompatible replacement with obvious marketing risks.

Thus, Belady and Lehman intend to extend their methods beyond programming to other systems including social and economic systems. Reverse flow also exists. In spite of obvious differences between the engineering and production activities of hardware and software, there is a continuing influence on software procedures from hardware sources. The influence is often due to the fact that software organizations are surrounded by or subordinate to managers with extensive hardware experience. The value of procedural discipline on the hardware side is reason enough for those managers to try to apply it to the software. Engineering management techniques are not directly transferable to software, but the life cycles have analogous stages and the signals available from data on system dynamics have similar uses. It took about two years to modify military and space agency procedures to accommodate programming in the 1965–1966 time period. It took the large hardware/software vendors about the same length of time to set up similar procedures. IBM, for instance, developed a comprehensive phase process that covered software over several years in the late 1960s.[16] If you were to compare the resulting life cycle to the engineering life cycle found in a standard text such as Chestnut [20], the similarities would be obvious. The same thing would happen if you looked up the types of life cycles followed by commercial systems analysts [8, 13, 21]. Their methods are essentially unchanged from pre-computing days. Where engineering, applications analysis, and programming differ from one another, specific management and technical tools are called for. It appears, however, that in those gross areas of similarity a single theory of system dynamics may apply to all.

3.3 SUMMARY

Initially in this chapter, the life cycle was introduced as a useful tool for visualizing a dynamic process. It lays out the steps in a project so as to emphasize the sequence of activities, but it also shows resource requirements at each step and allows the resources to be subdivided into skill categories. Used in conjunction with other tools, the life cycle helps with project planning and estimating. In a given organization where numerous projects are started each year, standard templates can be drawn representing the shape of the life cycle, under local conditions, for each class of project. Then, as a first approximation, a new job can be quickly sized and a tentative schedule

---

16. In the mid 1970s, IBM changed its packaging and release procedures to permit major components to be independently released. This change from a single, integrated system release philosophy resulted in new procedure guides being developed in 1975–1976. The original phase process was new and it took time to figure out what would work. The revised process was much easier to postulate, but it took time to get the necessary agreements and migration plans in place before it could become effective.

can be selected by referring to the template for the class of projects it belongs to. The shape of the life cycle indicates when people will be required by a project and when they will be free for reassignment. The shape and dimensions can be converted into approximate project costs as well.

At the end of the chapter, it began to appear that the life cycle is more than a useful graphic tool. It is a representation of a portion of a possible theory of system dynamics for software. Observers who, over the years, watched how programs were developed—mostly in large projects in large organizations—saw the same things over and over again. They saw that projects proceed from concept to objectives to justified requirements, then to design specifications, program development, integration, and test. The delivered end product would go into operation and immediately generate maintenance and upgrade requirements. As the change requests came in, a new release of the product would be built. Periodically, the product would be restructured in a new version, which was the deliverable end product of a second project. Thus the life history of a major software product was a sequence of overlapping project life cycles. Over the long term, the program system continually grew, becoming less well structured as it grew, and requiring a constant amount of attention to system changes and system structure.

The rate at which a delivered end product grows and deteriorates depends on its original quality. Quality is built in to each program unit by individual programmers using good programming and design techniques. Quality is built in to the system by the project team using good communication techniques. In the life cycle, communication is achieved by handing specific documents over from stage to stage. A management system explains the stages of the life cycle and provides the formats to be used by the team for their documentation. The larger the project, the more detailed are the documentation requirements. There is a great likelihood that someone working on a small piece of a large program system will be unable to get help from any source other than the documentation. The documents may give a narrow view of the system, primarily because the writer and the reader concentrate on their narrow area of responsibility. System quality requires a broad view as well to ensure that interrelationships are defined and properly implemented. Frequent reviews are held to get the broad view and the cross-communication that are necessary to a healthy project.

EXERCISE AND DISCUSSION QUESTIONS

1. Compare the skills recruited each month in the project of Table 3.2 with those in the top-down implementation of Table 3.4.

2. As a rule-of-thumb, 2/3 of every mature applications programming group is committed to maintaining and upgrading existing programs. Is this reasonable? (Assume that the number of new applications requested annually is constant and that application life averages three years.)

3. For the projects of Tables 3.2 and 3.3 calculate the total workload, average headcount, and peak headcount for delivery schedules 2/3, 1/3, 1/6 of the optimum schedule given in the tables. Which of these shorter schedules is feasible in your opinion. Why?

4. List the essential documents in a team programming project. Which of these should be in the hands of the individuals who are writing program units?

5. Show why the Norden Life Cycle Model, $y = k(1 - e^{-at^2})$, predicts that workload through the peak month is only 58 percent of the workload through release for program projects.

6. Calculate the capability parameter

$$\frac{k}{t_d^3}$$

for the project schedules in Exercise 3. The U. S. Army Computer Systems Command found the parameter takes on the values 8, 15, or 27 in their environment. Larger values represented easier jobs and/or more capable development teams. Reversing the logic, you could assume that a large value is an indication of how easy a job must be in order to be successfully carried out with a given project plan. Considering the Army experience, do the values of the capability parameter in Exercise 3 change your opinion regarding the feasibility of the short schedules?

7. How would you use an interactive display terminal during:
    a. Design stage?
    b. Development stage?
    c. Test stage?

8. What is the most influential factor governing the resource buildup in a project?
    a. System dynamics
    b. Life cycle model
    c. Project requirements
    d. Resource availability

REFERENCES

1. *Configuration Management Practices for Systems, Equipment, Munitions, and Computer Programs.* Military Standard MIL–STD–483 (USAF). GPO 1971 –433–698/9514. Washington, D.C.: U.S. Government Printing Office, December 1970. Also, Bersoff, E. H.; Henderson, V. D.; and Siegel, S. G. *Software Configuration Management: An Investment in Product Integrity.* Englewood Cliffs, N.J.: Prentice-Hall, 1980. Also Chase, W. P. *Management of System Engineering.* New York: John Wiley & Sons, 1974. Also Metzger, P. W. *Managing a Programming Project.* Englewood Cliffs, N.J.: Prentice-Hall, 1981. Also Horowitz, E., ed. *Practical Strategies for Developing Large Software Systems.* Reading, Mass.: Addison-Wesley, 1976.

2. Mills, H. D. "Software Development." *IEEE Transactions on Software Engineering* SE–2, no. 4 (December 1976).

3. Turn, R.; Davis, M. R.; and Reinstedt, R. N. "A Management Approach to the Development of Computer-based Systems." Proceedings 2nd International Conference on Software Engineering. New York: IEEE, Inc., 1976.

4. Bevier, R. B. "System Program Development." Presentation to GUIDE XXVIII meeting held June 1969. IBM Technical Report TR00.1817. Poughkeepsie, N.Y.: IBM Corp., December 1968.

5. *System Engineering Management*. Military Standard MIL–STD–499 (USAF). GPO 1971–433–698/9374. Washington, D.C.: U.S. Government Printing Office, July 1969.

6. Piligian, M. S., and Pokorney, J. L. "Air Force Concepts for the Technical Control and Design Verification of Computer Programs." AFIPS Conference Proceedings, vol. 30, 1967 SJCC. Washington, D.C.: Thompson Book Co., 1967.

7. Hicks, H. G. *The Management of Organizations: A Systems and Human Resources Approach*. New York: McGraw-Hill, 1972.

8. Shaw, J. C., and Atkins, W. *Managing Computer System Projects*. New York: McGraw-Hill, 1970.

9. Aron, J. D. *The Program Development Process Part I—The Individual Programmer*. Reading, Mass.: Addison-Wesley, 1974.

10. Runyan, L. "Applications Development: Software Still a Sore Spot." *DATAMATION* 27, no. 3 (March 1981).

11. Robinson, H. W. "Unbundling and the Independent Service Companies." *DATAMATION* 16, no. 3 (March 1970).

12. Kornreich, D. W. "Utilization of 'Normalized' Data for Defense Contracts." *IRE Transactions on Engineering Management* EM–9, no. 1 (March 1962).

13. Hice, G. F.; Turner, W. S., III; and Cashwell, L. F. *System Development Methodology*. 2nd ed. Amsterdam: North-Holland Publishing Co., 1974. New York: Elsevier North-Holland, 1978.

14. Pietrasanta, A. M. "Resource Analysis of Computer Program System Development," in *On the Management of Computer Programming*. Edited by G. F. Weinwurm. Princeton, N.J.: Auerbach Publishers, 1970.

15. Brooks, F. P., Jr. "Why is the Software Late." *Data Management* 9, no. 8 (August 1971).

16. Aron, J. D. "Estimating Resources for Large Programming Systems," in *Software Engineering Concepts and Techniques*. Edited by J. N. Buxton, P. Naur, and B. Randell. New York: Petrocelli/Charter, 1976.

17. Norden, P. V. "Project Life Cycle Modelling: Background and Application of the Life Cycle Curves." *Software Phenomenology*. Working Papers of the Software Life Cycle Management Workshop, Fort Belvoir, Va.: HQ US Army Computer Systems Command, 1977. Also, Putnam, L. H. "A General Empirical Solution to the Macro Software Sizing and Estimation Problem." *IEEE Transactions on Software Engineering* SE–4, no. 4 (July 1978).

18. Parr, F. N. "An Alternative to the Rayleigh Curve Model for Software Development Effort." *IEEE Transactions on Software Engineering* SE–6, no. 3 (May 1980).

19. Belady, L. A., and Lehman, M. M. "A Model of Large Program Development" *IBM Systems Journal* 15, no. 3 (1976). Also, Lehman, M. M., and Parr, F. N. "Program Evolution and its Impact on Software Engineering." *Proceedings 2nd International Conference on Software Engineering.* New York: IEEE, Inc., 1976.

20. Chestnut, H. *Systems Engineering Methods.* New York: John Wiley & Sons, 1967.

21. Rubin, M. L. *Introduction to the System Life Cycle.* Handbook of Data Processing Management, Vol. 1. Princeton, N.J.: Brandon/Systems Press, 1970.

4
Project
Definition

System development proceeds in a stepwise fashion from the original formulation of a system concept. Breaking the underlying concept into successively more explicit requirements is called *system analysis*. Data are collected and analyzed, the major components of the system are identified, and
the system structure is defined. This process examines all aspects of the system; e.g., personal and political interactions as well as hardware and software [1]. The output of the analysis is a system objectives document in the
concept formulation stage and a systems design requirements baseline document in the project definition stage. These documents will inevitably talk
about *objects* such as computers, terminals, and operating systems, and
processes such as addressing and editing, rather than *intangibles* such as
useability. Nevertheless, a complete analysis will have considered the intangibles and the documentation will explain their effects on the decisions
leading to the baseline.

4.1 SYSTEM ANALYSIS

The fundamental method of system analysis is to apply common sense to a
complete statement of a problem. Large systems tend to frustrate analysts
who take this approach because it is so hard to obtain a complete statement
of the problem or even the objectives of the problem solution. In those cases
where time and money are available to get the information, the analysts
may find that they cannot individually comprehend all they have acquired;
neither can they act as a team with but one mind capable of taking a com-
mon-sense approach. As a substitute, each analyst must focus on a subset of
the problem—usually with suboptimal results—and make mutual tradeoffs
with the results of the rest of the team.

The inability of one person to do the whole job undoubtedly leads to the numerous changes that occur throughout a large system's life cycle. New information keeps appearing and old decisions are seen in a new light, justifying changes to the design requirements baseline. Although the system proceeds generally in a top-down manner, the changes constantly interrupt progress and introduce bottom-up activities with associated feedback and cycling at higher levels. Meanwhile, managers try to keep the whole staff busy. For this purpose, a best guess is made as to which system elements are least likely to be affected by the change. These elements are continued without interruption. At some later time, if it turns out that these elements have been affected by the change, an effort will often be made to use the completed elements anyway, patching them up as necessary. The undesirable effect this approach has on program quality and maintenance cost is well known, but its importance is not well understood; managers continue to try to protect their schedules by taking risks regarding where changes will impact work in progress.

4.1.1   Setting Requirements

It is always useful to distinguish between analysis and design. Analysis sets requirements by defining *what* should be done. Design provides solutions by defining *how* the requirements will be met. Keeping the two activities separate leads to a requirements document that can be used to verify that the deliverable end product is acceptable. Separation is always useful but not always essential [2].

In the special case of, say, an engineer who uses a terminal to produce an on-line program to solve a problem, the engineer does not have to write down a requirements statement. One-person jobs, particularly very short jobs, can get by on the problem-solver's memory, his or her ability to grasp all the requirements, and the use of common sense. Larger jobs, though, need documented requirements as the basis for communication and negotiation among the multiple participants in the project. Generally speaking, then, the system analysis activity produces a document. The contents of the document are *requirements statements* and *rationales.* The requirements statements are of the form: "The system must handle 200 transactions per hour (as defined in Section C) with an average response time of two seconds; 95 percent of the transactions must be completed in less than 3.5 seconds," or, "Daily customer account balances shall be computed for each transaction in sequence with appropriate overdraft penalties being assessed whenever the current balance falls below the account minimum balance." The rationales explain why the less obvious requirements are there; e.g., "analysis of revenue indicates that income from overdrafts will be 0.3 percent higher if overdrafts are processed as they occur instead of being assessed on the daily closing balance." Such an explanation gives the designer flexibility. It tells what an overdraft is and how it is recognized, yet it allows the designer to decide whether to calculate a penalty when an overdraft is recognized or to flag the event and defer the calculation to a more convenient point. The requirements document should not tie the designers' hands. It should leave as many implementation decisions to designers as possible. (In later stages of the project, the rationales are invaluable in giving new team members an understanding of the system.)

Looking back at the performance requirements that referenced a definition "in Section C," it may occur to you that the examples seem to get very long and involved. You may feel like the English farmer who was struggling with paperwork from the Common Market. He wondered why it took only 56 words for the Lord's Prayer and 300 for the American Declaration of Independence but it took 26,911 words to explain the Common Market export rules for duck eggs.[1] This is the difference between broad statements of principle and detailed explanations of implementable and enforceable requirements. There is no way short of exhaustive documentation to make a complex requirement or specification unambiguously clear to the imperfect souls who have to understand it.

Because this is the case, analysts must test each requirement by asking themselves:

- What does this requirement statement mean?
- What else could it mean?
- What should it say to mean what is intended and no more or less?

They should ask their colleagues to interpret the statements, too. As a general rule, if someone misinterprets what you write, you should rewrite it. It is your error, not the reader's. This rule may not apply to poets or novelists, but it certainly applies to analysts and designers whose sole purpose is to pass clear and definite data on to other people via the written word.

A second set of questions guides the stepwise refinements of the analysis. These questions serve to separate the requirements into five categories:

- Essential requirements—The problem cannot be solved if these requirements are not satisfied.
- Justified requirements—Nonessential requirements that have a cost, performance, safety, useability, or reliability justification.
- Desirable requirements—Nonessential requirements without an explicit justification.
- Undesirable requirements—Nonessential requirements which, if satisfied, would interfere with solving the problem.
- Nonrequirements—Irrelevant requests.

---

1. Peterborough, "London Day by Day," *The Daily Telegraph,* December 17, 1976.

Each analyst's answers to such questions should always be checked by colleagues; otherwise, an essential requirement may be deleted because it is not essential to the piece of the system a given analyst is studying.

Some examples of these points can be seen by sketching the process of system analysis in a particular case. Consider the problem of "computer networking." It involves a software vendor's decision to offer products that support networks of computers. The problem arises because data processing has grown to the point where many users have computers at multiple locations. Furthermore, they have integrated key databases at selected locations. They see a clear need to tie all their locations together with communications links so as to give all locations access to all data. As a byproduct, they expect to be able to balance workloads by shipping jobs from one location to another. When many such users ask their computer supplier to provide computer networking, the problem starts to take shape.[2]

The objective for computer networking as it was simply stated in the mid-1970s was to "permit any data processing end user to talk to any other." This is, of course, a very conceptual objective. More specific information is needed to know what is actually required.

4.1.2   Defining the Problem—Task Force Approach

The software supplier given the conceptual requirement for computer networking will follow an orderly sequence of events in order to make a business decision: Should the company satisfy the requirement? A similar but less complicated sequence of events will support decision making in other organizations. The difference in the two cases is that the supplier must balance the needs of many diverse users, whereas other organizations can usually limit the number of requirements sources.

---

2. The networking example is based on a real situation. It is substantially abridged since the actual case ran to many volumes of requirements, specifications, and deliverable items. In the abridged version, you may note inconsistencies or errors. They are not put in on purpose but they do represent a basic problem related to program systems. If the case study is big enough to be a useful illustration, it is too big for one person to handle alone—including this author. What may seem perfectly logical at one point may contradict something elsewhere, just as the results of two analysts may conflict. Two analysts observing good review discipline will recognize and reduce their conflict. An author representing both analysts will often fail to recognize the conflict and it will end up in the example. A similar problem occurs in the classroom where a group of students emulates a much larger programming team. Many problems will be overlooked with the potential effect of convincing the students that large projects are not as hard as professional programmers say they are.

This particular example deals with vendor activities. It is directly applicable to programming professionals employed by or consulting with computer manufacturer's and software vendors. Most of the key points apply as well to Information System department activities, which represent the largest pool of programming professionals.

Initially, an alert company will observe a developing trend before it matures into a requirement. Routine tracking of the state-of-the-art in research and development revealed interest in networking several years before it became an area of interest to commercial data-processing customers. Major experiments centered on university activities (including the nationwide US ARPANET [3]) were well publicized and generally successful. Seeing this, the data-processing supplier tries to develop a thorough understanding of the meaning of the trend. Various methods are used to do this preliminary work.

1. Independent consultants are hired to survey the state-of-the-art and prepare a forecast of technical and marketing trends.
2. In-house projects are initiated to:
   - study and report on the technology vs. company capability
   - survey the market opportunities in the company's business area
   - assess the potential opportunity for the company to enter a new business area.
3. Surveys are made (by the company salespeople or an outside consultant) of the company's customers regarding their need for the new technology and when they might acquire it.
4. Product development plans are evaluated to see how the company might fit the new technology into its strategic plan.

As these activities proceed, top management interest grows until it demands a business decision. Now the emphasis will be on speed to arrive at a company position before someone else preempts the market opportunities. To get the best advice in the shortest time, the top managers may set up a *task force*. This is a special group led by a senior manager, usually selected from the department responsible for products related to the new technology. The task force members represent all the departments involved either with the new technology or with business practices. Thus there will be scientists and engineers, product planners, specialists in applications and user requirements, sales forecasters, lawyers, financial specialists, and others. By concentrating these diverse skills on a single question, top management can get a well-balanced recommendation quickly.

Several guidelines are applicable to task forces to ensure their effectiveness:

- Task forces advise; they do not manage. The diversity that strengthens the quality of task force recommendations prevents a task force from leading the implementation of the recommendations.
- The scope and duration of a task force should be strictly limited. A task force interferes with the normal conduct of business. It can be tolerated only while it is focused on a single issue with a near-term deadline. Further, its effectiveness as a focusing mechanism will be diluted if it looks at more than one issue.

- Within the authorized scope of investigation, a task force should be given extraordinary power to obtain data and access to key people. The risk of incorrect results justifies giving the task force all the information it needs, even though such information may be withheld from the individual members in their own departments. (Members may have to sign confidentiality agreements to prevent leaks from reaching the home departments.)

- The task force should be as small as possible. Too many cooks spoil the broth. Instead of taking someone from every involved department, take members from key groups but make sure they obtain inputs from the remaining groups. (Every organization has key people who know what's going on and keep in touch with each other. Allen and Cohen [4] call them "technical gatekeepers." They make good task force members.)

- Assign a task force manager; provide clerical and administrative support.

- Pick a leader as task force manager—someone who can merge the members' diverse interests and make progress toward a goal.

- Relieve the members of all other duties for the duration of the task force. (This is not done very often and may not be necessary; however, the task force results will be more thorough, better justified, and available sooner if the members do not have to divide their efforts.)

- At the completion of its work, the task force should formally report to the manager who convened it (and others as directed) and then disband.

Following these guidelines, the data-processing supplier can convene a task force to: "Recommend whether our company should provide computer networking products or services and, if yes, recommend what we should provide." In this question, the product area is limited to computer networking.[3] The task force is not asked to recommend an alternate product plan if computer networking is a poor idea. The area of networking, however, is left open. Recommendations are permitted regarding new data-processing products, including computer programs, communications products, design and installation services for network owners, construction and operation of a networking service as a company subsidiary, or similar offerings. The question asks for a plan of action to support a positive recommendation, but here, too, is a constraint. The requested plan is to relate to the recommended products or services only, not to peripheral issues; in particu-

---

3. "Networking" is used for multicomputer connections to distinguish them from a "network" consisting of a single host and its tree of subordinate units.

lar, the company's management structure. The task force may find that a new communication processor is required that combines the features of products presently built by two independent divisions of the company. This belongs in the recommendation. The task force may believe that the only way to proceed to get the new box is to merge both groups into one division. This organizational recommendation does not belong in the report. The company executives did not ask for advice on this point. In general, purely managerial questions related to policy, organization, personnel appointments, and other judgmental topics are not good subjects for task force action. Task forces are valuable in areas where an extensive amount of technical, operational, or business data is involved. Key managers cannot acquire the data personally so they use a team to give them a well-digested summary. Judgmental decisions do not require such detail and can be dealt with directly by the responsible managers.

Five steps characterize the task force activity:

1. Plan the task force schedule and outline the final report format.
2. Collect relevant data.
3. Analyze the data and agree on recommendations.
4. Develop an action plan to support the recommendations (assuming action has been recommended).
5. Prepare and present the task force report.

The time required for each step depends on the subject and the location of the activity. As a general rule, what takes one week to accomplish in one location takes two to three weeks to accomplish if trips to one or more other locations are required within the home country (two weeks within most European countries, three weeks in United States). It will take four to six weeks if transoceanic travel is required. If international airmail is used instead, it will still take four to six weeks to send inquiries, clarify questions, and get the response. Allowing for such variables, steps 1 and 2 should be allotted about 40 percent of the schedule. Steps 3 and 4 will overlap and interact. They get about 40 percent or a little more. Step 5 gets the rest of the time; however, report writing can start in step 1. By outlining the format of the final report at the start, bounds are set on the task force output. The team can fill in the report as it goes, leaving the conclusions and recommendations to the end of steps 3 and 4 and leaving the executive summary and presentation charts until step 5. The final report might have the outline given in Table 4.1. It should be terse and graphic because many key managers will only scan it; yet they must understand the conclusions and recommendations. Presentations of the report will probably be allocated three hours at middle-management levels, and one hour or less at top management levels; thus there must be versions of the report that make all the key

TABLE 4.1. SAMPLE TASK FORCE REPORT FORMAT

Section	Contents
1	EXECUTIVE SUMMARY
1.1	Introduction
1.1.1	Objectives
1.1.2	Approach
1.1.3	Overview of Subject Area
1.2	Conclusions
1.3	Recommendations
1.4	Action Plan
2	CAPABILITIES AND NEEDS
2.1	General Observations
2.2	Capability Assessment
2.2.1	Technical Capabilities
2.2.2	Marketing Capabilities
2.2.3	Resource Availability
2.3	Needs
3	MARKET EVALUATION
3.1	Market Structure
3.2	Growth Trends
3.3	Competitive Outlook
3.4	Sales Estimate
3.4.1	Current Plan
3.4.2	Increment Due to New Offerings
4	COST ANALYSIS
4.1	Cost of Proposed Plan A
4.2	Cost of Proposed Plan B
...	
4.n	Cost of Proposed Plan N
5	CONCLUSIONS AND RECOMMENDATIONS
5.1	Conclusions
5.1.1	Capability for New Offerings
5.1.2	Value of New Offerings to Market as a Whole
5.1.3	Alternative Proposals for New Offerings
5.1.4	Value of Alternatives to Company
5.2	Recommendations
5.2.1	General
5.2.2	Specific
5.2.3	Priorities
6	ACTION PLAN
6.1	Tasks
6.1.1	Assumptions
6.1.2	Objectives
6.1.3	Criteria for Assignment of Tasks
6.2	Schedules
6.3	Resources
APPENDICES	
A	TASK FORCE MEMBERS
B	SOURCES OF DATA
C	BACKUP MATERIAL
C.1	Explanatory Information
C.2	Detailed Action Plan Task Descriptions

points via charts that can be grasped in those time periods. In each case, as detail is eliminated from the presentation, the key points must be carefully retained.

The outline given assumes that the task force is looking at the computer networking situation for which sales and cost data are important. In other situations, these sections are omitted and a more general value analysis is inserted. For instance, a task force was asked to recommend which algorithm should be used for path prediction of an early moon mission. At that time there were several candidate algorithms and no experience with actual moon flights. A small team of experts was assembled to select the "best candidate." The value analysis appropriate in this case was to estimate the accuracy of each algorithm with respect to computation time and computer storage requirements. No direct conversion to dollars was made, but the ranking that resulted was based on the relative importance of the time and storage factors. Another type of value analysis involves displaceable costs. In the case of selecting a high-level programming language, the most valuable language may be the one that minimizes programmer hours for a typical set of jobs displacing the need for additional programmers.

The report format is part of the task force plan; the task force will:

- Make a recommendation supported by an action plan
- Present the results in an appropriate form to various levels of management
- Consider the capability of the organization to meet the identified needs
- Assess the value of meeting the needs
- Estimate the cost of meeting the needs
- Consider alternate plans for meeting all or part of the needs
- Give a plan for implementing the recommended alternative

The first stage of work is to review what is known about the problem. Usually the task force members have to supplement their own knowledge and experience by talking to other people. Interviews are scheduled with each of the key people who can contribute, including managers whose functions would be impacted by the task force recommendations even if they know nothing about the subject. They are included to get their opinion on the effects of the impact and also to get them to start thinking about how they would react if the task force report is adopted. Additional data are available from existing files and on-line databases. Certainly, customer and sales data should be available; however, the task force may want to look at the data in a new way. This would require programming and clerical support over and above that needed for task force administration.

For efficiency, the task force members disperse so each one collects data from a different organizational segment or subject area. Weekly meetings or even daily meetings are needed to coordinate this activity; otherwise, the members will start to duplicate each other's work. They may also get into too much detail and fail to move on to the next important topic. The coordination meetings help to keep everyone current and avoid such problems. Each meeting can also be a replanning meeting to decide whether the data collection stage is complete. By comparing notes, the members can agree on whether the added value of further interviews justifies the effort. At the end of the activity, there should be a record of all the data sources:

- Task force members
- People interviewed
- Reports obtained
- Literature references

The raw data in the form of longhand notes does not become part of the report, but it should go into the archives.

To do the networking concept formulation, a task force of sixteen people plus support was required. The group took eight weeks to complete its report. During this period one team member acted as a coordinator of schedules and information exchange. The project required extensive travel to understand the worldwide capabilities and needs of a large company. This task force consumed some twenty-five people-months. At least as much effort was provided by interviewees, forecasters, product specialists, and others who supported the team. The report recommended product development and led to a six-month project definition activity carried out by existing development and marketing departments. The scale of this case is large, but the procedures apply elsewhere. If you shrink the task force down to one person you have the typical commercial system analyst. Medium-sized projects are distinguished only by the amount of effort and the time required, not by a different set of system analysis procedures. For example, a medium-sized aerospace company took less than three people-months spread over two months to formulate a concept justifying the merger of their payroll and personnel data processing into a single employee-number database system. Key concerns were feasibility, savings potential, and unique features of the company's major locations. The task force members were the company Information Systems manager (chairman) plus a key person from each location Information Systems group. Following a ''go'' recommendation, the location members of the task force became the project definition leaders at their location.

4.1.3 Organizing the Data

The statement that computer networking will ''permit any data processing end user to talk to any other'' is too general to be instructive. The picture of networking (Fig. 4.1) generated by such a requirement statement is without form or content. More detail is needed. As data are gathered, it will be ob-

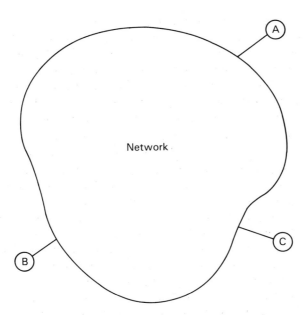

"Allow any end user, A, B, or C, to talk to any other."

Fig. 4.1   Networking — Gross problem statement.

vious that each potential user has a specific set of needs for his or her environment. For example, a manufacturer may have multiple locations that are relatively autonomous, yet they operate on a common product database. It appears feasible to unify the independent locations to save communications cost and share data or applications. However, a closer look shows that each location has built up a unique configuration over a period of years so that today there is little system commonality (Fig. 4.2).

This company's networking requirements include the ability to incorporate the diverse hardware and software already in place. In addition, migratability must be assured without affecting the autonomy of each location. A company that had a history of more centralized data-processing planning might not have these concerns. Consequently, the requirements that are collected have varying degrees of importance to the potential customers. The relative importance must be estimated for each requirement as it is determined.

The sum total of user inputs plus the inputs from technical experts leads to a better set of computer networking objectives (Table 4.2). The new list is still very general and is probably too rich to do all at once. The data must be organized better to show what the underlying structure of the requirements is. Organization is also required simply to handle the data in large systems.

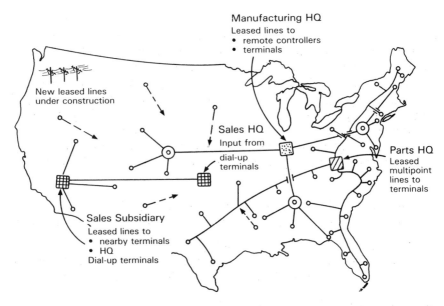

Manufacturing HQ
Leased lines to
 • remote controllers
 • terminals

New leased lines
under construction

Sales HQ
Input from

dial-up
terminals

Parts HQ
Leased
multipoint
lines to
terminals

Sales Subsidiary
Leased lines to
 • nearby terminals
 • HQ
Dial-up terminals

Fig. 4.2   Networking—Typical in-place networks.

4.1.3.1 Structure

To organize the data structurally, it helps to divide the objectives into classes. For the list of Table 4.2, five classes can be selected:

1. Configuration—to include objectives related to component compatibility and diversity, migration, and reconfiguration.
2. Control—location of control points, scope of control, types of control function, optimization.
3. Usage—applications, user interfaces, useability, accounting.
4. Performance—reliability, speed, predictability.
5. Availability—modularity, continuous operation, backup.

The choice of the categories should be based on the state-of-the-art. In other words, pick the areas that have been identified by others as critical to design and planning. In the absence of such guidance, you will have to define the categories based on your analysis of the critical areas. Both approaches were applicable to the networking case. University networks had already highlighted configuration, control, and performance as important factors [5,6,7]. On the other hand, the university environment represents a subset of the usage modes and availability requirements that a computer company is interested in. So two more classifications emerge. Yet, when the

TABLE 4.2.   NETWORKING OBJECTIVES

Objectives

1. Permit any end user to connect to and communicate with any other end user. For example, any terminal must be able to connect to any host computer. The objective is to allow physical and logical resources to be shared.

2. Provide clean interfaces between end users and transmission facilities. Failure of any element should not cause failure in other elements.

3. Move information consisting of data messages or data segments and control messages from source to destination accurately, completely (without loss or duplication), and in the sequence of transmission.

4. Support all of the following modes of dp use:
   a. Transaction processing (by host subsystems such as a database manager)
   b. Remote job entry to batch processing from workstations or peer computers
   c. Message switching via intermediate nodes
   d. Interactive computing
   e. Interactive preparation of programs for dispatch to batch
   f. Distributed processing (program-to-program communication, either vertically in a hierarchy or horizontally among peers)

5. Support hardware and software of all major vendors. A single computer must be allowed to use multiple access methods.

6. Permit backup resources to be substituted for failed resources without disturbing other resources. Also permit resources to be added or removed from the network without affecting network operation.

7. Provide means for authorizing users to access various resources; however, do not make authorization mandatory.

8. Provide means for data security (such as encryption).

9. Operate without a dedicated network manager; i.e., distribute control.

10. Provide means for usage, performance, and accounting data collection by end user and by resource.

11. Provide for predictable transmission delays between source and destination.

12. Minimize migration time and effort for network owner and for users.

objectives are allocated to classes, as in Table 4.3, there is still too much overlap. The same objective appears in several classes. Further structural breakdown is needed. To discriminate between configuration and control, a set of definitions would be useful to explain what types of configurations are intended and what is meant by "control." The task force defined five types of networking to highlight various options:

Type 0—no networking: single host tree structure

Type 1—shared transmission facility: two or more single host trees sharing communications via a multiplexing arrangement

Type 2—multiple tree peer coupling: two or more trees with host-to-host connections

Type 3—multiple tree direct routing: two or more trees with host-to-host and terminal-to-any-host connections

Type 4—mesh network: any user to any user connections

Types 0 through 3 assume that control resides in the user's computers or in a separate network manager's computer. Furthermore, each host owns some set of controllers and terminals that can only communicate with other devices via their host or with their host's permission. Control is strongly hierarchical. Type 4 does not require any particular host/terminal assignments; however, it implies that control is somehow hidden inside the transmission network. In practice, this might mean that each of the end users is owned by a network node which is a computer dedicated to data transmission and control. Data flow in this case is from node to node and amounts to Type 2 networking. The characteristics of the five networking types are shown in Fig. 4.3 where dashed lines represent control message flow (requests for connection and authorizations to connect) and heavy solid lines represent data message flow. Thus, in Types 0, 1, and 2 two classes of end users are distinguished, the hosts (rectangles) and the terminals (circles); terminals talk only to their designated hosts. In Type 2, hosts can talk to each other on a peer basis. Then, in Type 3, while retaining the two classes of end users, the networking design permits terminals to send messages to any destination after requesting their host to set up and authorize the direct path.

TABLE 4.3.   NETWORKING—CLASSIFIED OBJECTIVES

	Objectives	Configuration	Control	Usage	Performance	Availability
1	Connect-ability	x	x		x	x
2	Interface	x	x	x		x
3	Message flow		x	x	x	
4	Modes of use		x	x	x	
5	Diversity	x	x		x	
6	Backup	x	x			x
7	Authorization		x			
8	Security		x	x	x	
9	Distributed control		x			x
10	Statistics		x	x	x	
11	Predictability				x	
12	Migratability	x				

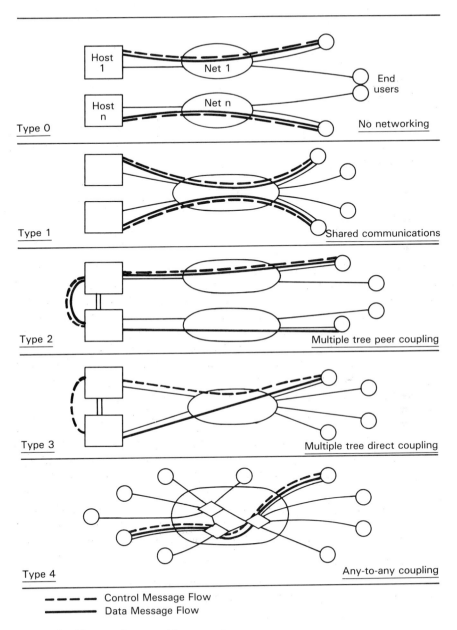

Fig. 4.3   Types of networking.

The authorization is the result of host-to-host peer communication which arranges for the destination end user to accept the connection. In Type 4, the end user classes can be ignored since the network nodes (diamonds) can set up the connections.

In defining the types of networking, the analysts looked ahead to postulate how a networking system might be designed. Purists would argue that analysts should avoid such behavior. For most analysts, however, it is appropriate, if not necessary, to use all available sources of information. When confronted with a problem statement, the analyst must break it down based on facts and experience. In new areas, there are few facts and no directly applicable experience. It becomes natural, therefore, to clarify the problem statement by trying to guess how to solve the problem. You can see this process operate when you solve a brain teaser problem such as: Find the numbers corresponding to the letters in:

$$
\begin{array}{r}
Q\;U\;I\;L\;T \\
+\;\;G\;I\;V\;E\;S \\
\hline
S\;T\;A\;T\;U\;S
\end{array}
$$

First, you guess; then you use brute force, trying all combinations. This gets tedious, so you start to search for algorithms such as "if T + S = S, then T = 0" or "if Q + G = ST, then S = 1." Eventually, you get:

$$
\begin{array}{r}
23570 \\
+\;85461 \\
\hline
109031.
\end{array}
$$

Systems analysis benefits from a similar process. When a set of requirements is vague or confusing, it helps to slip out of the analyst's role into the designer's role to ask, "What would the requirement mean if I had a solution that worked in such-and-such a way?" "If the first S in STATUS must mean 1, then mustn't a requirement of the problem be that either Q or G is at least 5 to produce a carry?" "If I were to build a Type 2 network would it permit any end user to communicate with any other?" There is no reason to discourage such flipping back and forth between analysis and design when the purpose is to refine the analysis. There is, however, a need to prevent the analyst's hasty and incomplete design speculations from becoming design decisions that interfere with the thorough design of the next stage of the project.

Following this line of attack, it appears that the requirement for any end user to communicate with any other can be met with networking Types 2, 3, and 4, given enough physical interconnections. However, Types 2 and 3 emphasize host control while Type 4 emphasizes network control. This exposes the need for a requirement statement dealing with the ownership characteristics of the information system to be served by the network. If the main purpose of the net is to share resources owned by the data-processing departments of a single firm, host control will be preferable. It leaves all data-processing decisions in the hands of dp personnel and protects the applications from idiosyncracies of the network. A different conclusion would be reached by a communications supplier whose purpose is to serve many unrelated users. As a "networking utility," this supplier would prefer to set up a standard interface that anyone can adapt to by small modifications to their software. Host control tends to increase the cost of attaching diverse devices to the network; all devices have to be architecturally compatible. Network control tends to increase the cost of application programming. New error routines are needed to compensate for the fact that devices formerly owned by the application are now owned by the network. The two approaches represent different philosophies of networking. The analysis must state which one applies.

Suppose host control is preferred because the market survey shows an abundance of prospective sales to multiple location corporations versus only a few to networking utilities. Should Type 2 or Type 3 be requested? This depends on the performance requirements. Another look at Table 4.2 shows that there is no performance requirement explicitly stated. Performance is simply implied by other requirements such as the need for interactive modes of use. A reasonable interpretation of the implied requirements is that performance should be at least as good with networking as it is without networking. This can be stated:

> "Performance requirement 1: For each mode of use, the average message transit time between a host and a terminal must be constant regardless of network configuration."

> "Performance requirement 2: The average number of instructions executed per data message must not be increased (in any host) due to networking."

Type 2 networks pass all messages through the hosts (at least two and maybe more, depending on the available paths) between the source and the destination. Clearly, Type 2 networking increases message delays and uses up host capacity. Even if the delays can be offset by using faster communication lines, the loss of capacity would be a problem. Type 3 networking avoids the problem. The analyst need not select Type 3 in the requirement; a designer will naturally pick a Type 3 solution to meet the stringent conditions. If the designer cannot find a solution at all, the requirement will have to be modified and a change to the baseline will have to be requested.

4.1.3.2 Content

Wordiness is apparent in the performance requirement. The general point of the requirement is that the user does not want to pay for networking in terms of lost throughput. Throughput depends on many factors: some, such as multiprogramming, have no bearing on networking. A subset of relevant factors has to be selected, in this case message transit time and instruction executions, which can be related to networking performance. But having gone that far, it becomes evident that still more words are needed to explain what is meant by "message," "transit time," "average transit time," "instructions per data message," and so on. The requirements will grow as they become more specific. Simultaneously, the description of each requirement will grow to contain the type of information needed to verify the system design at a later date. As an example, an expansion of the first performance requirement might look like this:

> "Performance requirement 1: For each mode of use, the average message transit time between a host and a terminal must be constant regardless of network configuration.

> Priority: 2

> Discussion: In a tree network, message transit time is measured from the time output execution starts at the source until the message is time-stamped at the destination. Errors and retransmissions do not affect transit time. Average message transit time is the time for a repeatable string of messages of equal length to be transmitted to one terminal type over one line type averaged over the number of messages sent. The string of messages should be randomly addressed to the full set of terminals of the selected type that can be attached to the source host. When the source host and its terminals are attached to a larger network, the same message string may follow new routes over network-provided links with potential delays at network nodes. Assuming that link speed compensates for route delays, the requirement says that the average message transit time for the repeatable message string will be the same (or better) in the networking configuration as it is in the tree configuration. This should be true regardless of the number of other users of the network or the number of nodes in the network.

> Justification: The additional cost of networking (due to network hardware and overhead expense) is primarily amortized against new applications requiring access to remote resources and by line sharing among existing and new applications. Line sharing among existing applications may become uneconomic, however, if networking reduces message throughput or user response. Therefore, line sharing must assume constant behavior for existing applications."

This brief statement of a requirement contains a discussion of what is wanted and a guide to the importance of the requirement. Hints for setting up tests to see whether the requirement has been met are indirectly included in the discussion. Importance is shown in two ways: priority with respect to other requirements and value to the user. No effort is made to show how the requirement would be changed if the present version is unachievable. Such alternatives require too much anticipation of design. Rather than prejudge alternatives, it is preferable to keep the design within reasonable bounds by management techniques such as design reviews. Cost and schedule estimates presented by the designers will show whether a requirement is achievable in practice. Pending such feedback, the analysts should rely on their normal professional judgment to determine if a requirement is reasonable.

The ultimate content of an individual requirement concerns function or performance or some other attribute that is observable in the delivered product. To identify the attributes, several types of structuring representing several points of view are used.

- The state-of-the-art in technology and competitive marketing compared to customer long-range plans leads to the original concept formulation.

- Analysis of in-house capabilities vs. what would be needed to respond to the concept narrows down the scope of the problem to a subset appropriate to the firm.

- Market or user evaluation further narrows the scope by showing where to put emphasis in order to maximize revenue or benefits to the firm.

- Cost analysis is used to select out the portion of the applicable market or user set to maximize return on investment.

- Classification of the major features of a system solution helps analysts look thoroughly at all topics.

- A definitional structure helps clarify the features of interest.

- Classification of the functional and performance requirements keeps related items together and supports complete and consistent analysis.

Within these structures, a detailed list of requirements, such as Table 4.4, can be constructed that expands into a file of requirements statements, each containing: (1) what is wanted; (2) a priority rank; (3) a discussion of what is wanted, where necessary; and (4) a justification.

4.1.3.3 Formalism

Requirements statements that contain the right information could theoretically be written in longhand on any piece of paper. In practice, more discipline is required. As a minimum, the format should be standard within a

TABLE 4.4. NETWORKING—CLASSIFICATION OF REQUIREMENTS LIST

Requirement	Priority	Configuration	Control	Usage	Performance	Availability	Other
1. Connectability							
a. Support diverse communications links	1						
1) Dial/leased point-point/leased multidrop	1	x					
2) All speeds	1				x		
3) Terrestrial/satellite	1				x		
4) Half and full duplex	1				x		
5) Voice network/data network	1	x					
b) Provide addresses and paths for	1						
1) Application—application same host	1						x
2) Application—application different hosts	1	x					
3) Application—terminal	1	x					
4) Terminal—terminal	2	x					
c. Support redundant and multiple connections	2						
1) Multiple trunk lines between two points	2				x		
2) Multiple hosts/terminals per communications processor	2					x	
d. Provide both operator and program-controlled reconfiguration	1		x				
2. Interface							
a. Separate network from end user	1					x	
1) Front-end communication processor	1						x
2) Application program interface	1			x			
b. Support device independence with standard interface	1						
1) "Virtual" terminal	1	x					
2) Self-identifying terminal	1		x				
c. User specified data link control	2	x					

TABLE 4.4.   CONTINUED

Requirement	Priority	Configuration	Control	Usage	Performance	Availability	Other
d. Interconnection of independent networks, common addressing	3	x					
e. Substitution of independent network function for equivalent layers of user network	3	x					
f. Support multiple independent enterprises on same network	2			x			
g. ASCII code option	1			x			
3. Message Flow							
a. Variable length messages	1			x			
b. Sequential delivery of message segments	1		x				
c. Multiple user priorities	1				x		
1) Control and statistics at highest priority	1		x				
2) Priority within user	1				x		
3) Priority between users	2				x		
d. Data transmission integrity	1						
1) Acknowledge correct receipt	1		x				
2) No duplicates	1		x				
3) No lost messages	2		x				
e. Store and forward service	1						
1) Hold messages for future delivery	1			x			
2) Broadcast to multiple addresses	3			x			
3) Deliver to alternate addressee	2			x			
4) Queue until destination free	1			x			
4. Modes of Use							
a. Session connection via log on	1						
1) User logs on interactively	1			x			
2) System establishes session automatically	1			x			
b. Transaction routing by user-supplied header	1			x			

TABLE 4.4. CONTINUED

Requirement	Priority	Configuration	Control	Usage	Performance	Availability	Other
c. Application types coexisting	1			X			
1) Interactive computing	1			X			
2) Interactive inquiry	1			X			
3) Remote job entry	1			X			
4) Message switching	2			X			
5) Batch processing	1			X			
6) Bulk data transmission/data set transfer	2			X			
7) Image processing	3			X			
8) Load leveling among hosts	2			X			
d. Queue management	1		X				
e. User exits	1				X		
5. Diversity							
a. Hardware of all vendors	1	X					
b. Software of all vendors	2	X					
c. Multiple access methods in one host	1		X				
d. Mixed communications modes	2	X					
e. Mixed modes of use	1				X		
6. Backup							
a. Alternate path routing	1						
1) To bypass link failures	1					X	
2) To avoid delays	2				X		
b. 24-hour operation	1					X	
c. Fast recovery	1					X	
1) Automatic switchover to spare unit	1					X	
2) Reload and recover 90% of failures in 5 minutes	1					X	
d. Isolate problems	1					X	
1) Route around failed units	1		X				
2) Mean time to system failure—ten years	2					X	
e. Alternate network control points	1					X	
f. Restart to point of failure	2						X
g. Notify users of failures, lost messages, recovery options	2		X				

TABLE 4.4.   CONTINUED

Requirement	Priority	Configuration	Control	Usage	Performance	Availability	Other
h. Nondisruptive recovery	1					x	
1) No interruption to service during recovery	1					x	
2) No interruption to service due to addition or deletion of network resources	1					x	
7. Authorization							
a. Maintain index of authorized connections	2		x				
1) Index under control of network operator	1		x				
2) Aliases permitted	2		x				
b. Verify authorization before connecting	1		x				
c. Notify user of need for authorization	2		x				
8. Security							
a. Provide code conversion service	2						
1) Encryption (follow Federal Standard FIPS Pub. 46)*	3			x			
2) Data compression/compaction	2				x		
b. Protect data and applications against unauthorized access (misdelivery, snooping)	1			x			
c. Protect access keys	1		x				
d. Disconnect users who attempt to violate rules	2		x				
e. Record attempts to violate security	2		x				
9. Distributed Control							
a. Provide for multiple control points	1		x				

*Data Encryption Standard, FIPS Publ. 46. U.S. Department of Commerce, National Bureau of Standards. Springfield, Va.: National Technical Information Service, U.S. Department of Commerce, 1977.

TABLE 4.4. CONTINUED

Requirement	Priority	Configuration	Control	Usage	Performance	Availability	Other
1) Permit one system control point/operator	1		x				
2) Permit multiple peer control points	1		x				
3) Permit subsystem hierarchies to act as single host trees	2		x				
4) Permit alternate control point to take over function of failed control point	1					x	
b. Permit network operator or operators to	1						
1) Control system or subsystem resources	1		x				
2) Initialize resources and shut down resources	1		x				
3) Obtain status information	1		x				
4) Set and modify priorities/authorizations	1		x				
5) Initiate diagnostic routines	1					x	
6) Reconfigure system or subsystem	1		x				
7) Act as a user	1		x				
c. Single set of network commands	1		x				
10. Statistics							
a. Collect status information on resource utilization	1						
1) Accounting and billing data	1			x			
2) Performance data	1				x		
b. Dynamically tune network	2				x		
c. Record statistics by time, resource, user	1			x			
1) Report to central point to consolidate	1			x			
2) Display on request	1			x			

TABLE 4.4.   CONTINUED

Requirement	Priority	Configuration	Control	Usage	Performance	Availability	Other
d. Provide user exits for specific data collection	1		x				
e. Monitor line quality	2				x		
11. Predictability							
a. Provide means for user to see how long on average an activity will take	2				x		
b. Maintain constant average message transit time	1				x		
c. Minimize user path length due to networking	1				x		
1) Instructions per data message same as in tree	1				x		
2) Instructions for control and log-on not greater than 110% of path length in tree	1				x		
3) Host path length to be independent of message routing	1				x		
d. Maintain constant average system behavior (delay, response time) over an 8-hour shift	1				x		
e. Provide display of current queue lengths	2				x		
f. Provide design aids/tools	1				x		
12. Migratability							
a. Support old and new versions of modified resources	1	x					
b. Provide test mode to permit duplicate subsystems to co-exist (one operational, one test)	2	x					
c. Permit installation of new resource without change in any other resource	1						x
d. Provide installation and test aids	1	x					

project. Readers will find it easier to use the requirements documents if they know where to look for the requirement itself versus the priority or the justification. Test personnel, for example, are interested in the precise wording of what is wanted. Their tests will be written to verify that the requirement as stated is satisfied in the final product. Rationales are of little interest to testers except when they supply hints as to what to look for in tests of human factors requirements. Designers need all the data in the requirements document, but their focus of interest varies. At first they want to know why a requirement is listed; at another time they will want to know how important a requirement is. Standard document formats let them focus quickly on the data they need.

A second formality consisting of standard identification rules keeps the work of several analysts under control and provides an audit trail for the life of the project. Naming and numbering conventions are adopted, which give each requirement a unique name and identification number. Usually, it is appropriate to structure the numbering rules to expose the hierarchical structure of the requirements themselves. Thus the requirement to permit networking end users to be connected via diverse communications links might be identified as:

R1a   Support Diverse Communications Links.

The requirement to support all speeds could be:

R1a2   All Speeds.

And the requirement to support 9600 baud links could be:

R1a2.4 9600 Baud.

The scheme where "R" represents "requirement" and the following sequence identifies a particular entry in the requirements list is only one way to keep track of separate entries, yet it illustrates some of the attributes of a good identification scheme:

- Permanence—The identification numbers can be assigned early in the project and remain valid throughout the project. The category symbol R represents a requirement, S could represent a specification, T a test. The item R1a2.4 can lead to a design specification S1a2.4 for 9600 baud links. The presence of 9600 baud support can be tested by test specification T1a2.4.

- Auditability—Correlation of requirements, specifications, tests, and deliverable end products checks the completeness of the end product.

- Extendability—The use of separators (such as a decimal point or a change from numeric to alphabetic) permits new entries and more detail to be added.

- Hierarchy—The identifier can be interpreted to represent the hierarchical structure of the subject matter.

- Printability—All the symbols used can be found on standard office machines.

The scheme also illustrates some attributes of less general value:

- Sequence—Numbers or letters can be interpreted as sequences at a given level. R1a2 can be interpreted as following R1a1 and preceding R1a3 (in time or in importance). Using identification numbers to represent sequence in project documentation carries a risk. Sequences of implementation and sequences of end product execution change as the project matures. Identification numbers should not change. If they do, auditability may be lost and all the accounting-like controls built around the ID numbers suffer.

- Diversity—One identification number can contain more than one type of information. In addition to being a unique pointer to an element of documentation or code, the ID number can show priority, who is responsible for the element, whether synonyms or substitutes exist, etc. Manual systems should avoid diversity in numbering schemes because it leads to very large ID numbers and manual errors. (Even in the example, R1a2.4 is clumsy in a manual system.) Automated systems can cope with diversity better and may be able to search or arrange data more effectively when complex IDs are provided.

- Recognition—Mnemonic symbols can be used instead of coded numbers and letters to make the ID number a brief descriptor; i.e., R.COMM.DIV instead of R1a. Mnemonics get long and complicated, however, and are not always as obvious as their originator thinks.

The same identification scheme should be used throughout the life cycle of the project. Uniformity simplifies record keeping and avoids confusion. Uniformity also facilitates automation in projects large enough to justify computerized control systems.

4.1.3.4 Methodology—REVS

Automation leads to additional formalities: a language for writing requirements, conventions for graphic display of requirements and their relationships, standardized reports, and conventions for consistency and logic checks of requirement lists. The Software Requirements Engineering Methodology (SREM) developed for the U.S. Ballistic Missile Defense Advanced Technology Center [8, 9, 10, 11] describes a full-scale automated system. SREM emphasizes techniques that are easy to use and that enhance the creativity of the analyst (or requirements engineer in the terminology of the report). Included in the system are numerous tools. Among them are:

1. Procedures for requirements decomposition
2. Procedures for managing the requirements process
3. A requirements statement language, RSL
4. A requirements engineering and validation system (REVS) containing:
    - A translator of RSL
    - A central relational database manager, ASSM
    - A set of tools for processing data in the ASSM consisting of such things as:
        a. interactive graphics capable of displaying and editing line drawings of flow diagrams
        b. automated simulators capable of tracing flow or checking algorithms
        c. structure checkers
        d. data usage checkers
        e. file search and report generators

The language is extendable. The tool kit permits the user to add special tools. As a result, SREM makes it possible to do much of the requirements job on line. In particular, SREM supports management of the detailed levels of system analysis after the data-processing requirements are agreed to and when it is necessary to get down to specific cases regarding what is wanted. At this point in a project many people are working and the need for control is great. This is when it is possible for several analysts to use the same term for different purposes; for example:

> "R4c2.3 Sequential Inquiry. The receipt of an *input message* from an inquiry station will suppress further input from that end user until a response has been sent to and acknowledged by the end user."

> "R4c3.1 Segmented Input. An *input message* from a remote job entry station consists of one or more message segments bounded by distinctive header and trailer symbols."

> "R4c7.4 Screen Input. An *input message* from an interactive graphic station consists of a fixed number of bits (determined by device type) transmitted as k segments where k is the message length divided by the smallest node buffer size permitted by the networking configuration."

The first analyst is thinking of short, one-segment inquiries that always generate an answer. This individual wants to make sure the answer is received before the user can ask another question. The second analyst is concerned with large jobs that have to be segmented to pass through the network. Clearly, the RJE function cannot afford to suppress all but the first segment in a transmission, yet a design that satisfied R4c2.3 might do just that. Similarly, a design that satisfied R4c7.4 might ignore all but the first k segments of a long transmission. Or a design based on R4c3.1 may cause the input process to look for headers and trailers that are not present in inquiry or screen input. *Input message* does not have one common meaning in the three examples; however, the analysts are unaware of the conflict. In a system such as REVS, conflicts can be found by compiling a dictionary of terms. For example, the database can be sorted on names, and each occurrence of a name can be checked to see what it means in context; multiple meanings can be eliminated by finding new unique names. The resulting dictionary can be used to verify that all new requirements attach the proper meaning to their terms.[4]

With the data under control it is safe to refer to data elements by name, knowing that the name's meaning can be obtained on request from the dictionary. In RSL a new element can be defined and added to the dictionary like this:

```
DEFINE ELEMENT_TYPE: INPUT_INTERFACE (*A port that
    accepts data*).
```

The element "INPUT_INTERFACE" is treated like a noun in English. It is user-defined. RSL also has some standard element types: DATA, ALPHA (for functional processing steps), and R_NET (for processing flow specifications). RSL considers "elements" to be language primitives. There are four primitives: "elements" and "relationships" that act like verbs, "attributes" that act like adjectives to describe the elements, and "structures" that are like flow charts. With these primitives and user-defined extensions, RSL can express requirements statements completely and unambiguously as, for example, in Fig. 4.4. Here, ORIGINATING_REQUIREMENT, DATA, FILE, MESSAGE, ENTITY_CLASS, ALPHA refer to named elements such as ADDRESS, ALT_ADDRESS, LOGICAL_UNIT. The names are unique references. Even after the requirements grow and are reshuffled to keep all MESSAGES in one place and ALPHAS in another, it is possible to scan on the key ADDRESS to see where it is used. The attributes DESCRIPTION and ENTERED BY offer the freedom of natural language to supplement the formal entries. Relationships between data elements and files or associations of data elements that make up an entity such as LOGI-

---

4. Text-processing programs exist to do this type of data organization. They are used quite widely to provide data management and control of the operating programs in a data-processing installation. Here, terms used in financial and administrative applications have very specific meanings that are valid for many years. As new applications are developed it is necessary to verify that data references are properly defined; otherwise, misleading reports can be generated and, worse, a portion of a database may be wiped out by incorrect update procedures.

```
ORIGINATING_REQUIREMENT: R3e3.
    DESCRIPTION:         "DEFINES DELIVERY TO ALTERNATE ADDRESS."
    TRACES TO:           ALPHA ALTERNATE_DESTINATION.
                         MESSAGE ALTERNATE_DELIVERY.
                         MESSAGE TROUBLE_REPORT_TYPE_ALT.
    ENTERED BY:          "N. BROWN, JUL 76."

MESSAGE: ALTERNATE_DELIVERY.
    PASSED_THROUGH: SESSION_PRIMARY.
    MADE_BY:             DATA SESSION_ID, DATA SEQ_NO, DATA ADDRESS,
                         DATA ALT_ADDRESS, DATA REASON_CODE,
                         DATA TIME_STAMP.
    TRACED_FROM:         R3e3.

MESSAGE: TROUBLE_REPORT_TYPE_ALT.
    DESCRIPTION:         "EXPLAINS REASON FOR REROUTING."
    PASSED_THROUGH: SYSTEMS_SERVICES_CONTROL_POINT.
    MADE_BY:             DATA ADDRESS, DATA ALT_ADDRESS,
                         DATA REASON_CODE, DATA TIME_STAMP.
    TRACED_FROM:         R3e3.

DATA: STATION_CONTROL_BLOCK.
    INCLUDES:            NAME, ADDRESS, CLASS, FEATURES.

FILE: ADDRESS.
    CONTAINS:            DATA NAME, DATA SYNONYM, DATA ADDRESS,
                         DATA ALT_ADDRESS, DATA BROADCAST_ADDRESS.

ENTITY_CLASS: LOGICAL_UNIT.
    ASSOCIATES:          DATA STATION_CONTROL_BLOCK, DATA END_USER,
                         DATA AUTHORIZATION, FILE ADDRESS.

ALPHA: ALTERNATE_DESTINATION.
    INPUTS:              ADDRESS, UNABLE_TO_TRANSMIT, RETRY_EXHAUSTED.
    OUTPUTS:             ALT_ADDRESS, NO_ALT.
    DESCRIPTION:         "FINDS NEXT AUTHORIZED ALTERNATE ADDRESS, IF ANY,
                         TO PERMIT TRANSMISSION TO PROCEED."
    ENTERED BY:          "T. PIERCE, JAN 77."
```

Fig. 4.4 Formal requirements language.

CAL_UNIT are visible as are the paths from original requirements to detailed entries. When the flow chart structure (the R_NET in RSL) is added to show the flow from input to output via the ALPHAs, the requirement is complete. This method of documentation has the advantage of combining a degree of formal rigor with sufficient discursiveness to meet the needs of almost any requirement. It has the disadvantage of being somewhat unnatural to write and potentially cryptic for anyone but a well-trained analyst to read.

4.1.3.5 Methodology—SADT

Different people have different styles leading some to prefer free text, others to prefer formal text, and a large number to prefer pictures and diagrams. Graphic methods can be used in combination with text methods to produce well-balanced documentation or, with proper training, graphic methods without text will suffice. In the latter case, the analysts and designers who use the method must be skilled at functional decomposition so that they can express their ideas within the bounds of the symbol and page sizes available. The skill is similar to that of a structured programmer who is asked to limit all programs to one page. After a little practice it becomes easy and the resulting programs are well-structured and of high quality.

The SADT method [12] referenced in Chapter 2 uses diagrams as its basic documentation device. Primitives such as those used in RSL appear in SADT as boxes, arrows, positions, and structures. Perhaps structure receives more emphasis in SADT than in REVS since every diagram tends to show the immediate neighbors of an entity. For example, the single element, ALPHA:ALTERNATE_DESTINATION, of Fig. 4.4 would probably never appear in isolation in an SADT diagram. Instead, the box representing that process would be shown as part of a sequence of processes, such as in Fig. 4.5. In this activity diagram each symbol has the meaning shown in Fig. 4.6a. A collection of such activity boxes in a structured analysis represents one view of the system from the standpoint of what it does. Data boxes, such as in Fig. 4.6b, can be structured to describe the system from the point of view of what data are processed. The two views taken together give a means of checking accuracy and completeness. Properly done, there will be an arrow in the activity model for each box in the data model and vice versa. In addition, all elements except the initial and terminal elements will be connected to a labeled entity. Management accounting data can be constructed from the labeled structure.

The format of the boxes is intentionally rigid. Each side of the box represents an interface: input (I), control (C), output (O), or mechanism (M). The ICOM formalism helps identify elements; for instance the output "No alternate" in Fig. 4.5 is element 3O2. It is the second output of Box 3. The convention "left to right, top to bottom" is used to number boxes on a page and arrows on an interface. Obviously, the labels can be omitted from the diagram without losing the ability to identify elements, but the more important reason for the ICOM formalism is to force the analyst into thinking through the real purpose of a requirement. What inputs are involved? Of these, which inputs control or trigger the activity? What outputs are desired? Are there any implementation constraints? SADT does not require an answer (thus some interfaces may have no arrows); however, SADT leads the analyst through a four-item checklist for each box that is constructed.

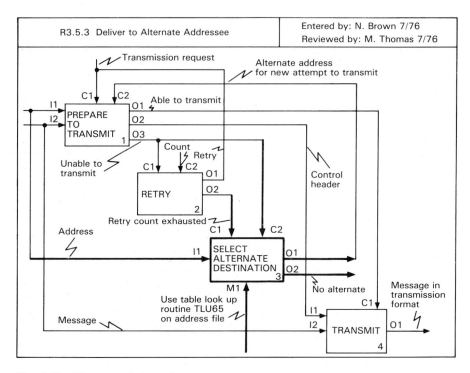

Fig. 4.5   Diagram of a requirement.

In Fig. 4.4, the process ALPHA:ALTERNATE_DESTINATION followed some data and message definitions, but the reason why the surrounding materials is relevant is not self-evident. In Fig. 4.5, the equivalent activity, SELECT ALTERNATE DESTINATION, highlighted in heavy lines makes somewhat more sense. Nevertheless, the simple diagram of Fig. 4.5 is pretty cluttered, illustrating some of the limitations of graphic methods. This particular diagram has been drawn to point up both good and bad features of graphics. On the good side, the activity of interest is shown in context. If you were to isolate just the box and its attached arrows on a separate sheet, you would not know where anything comes from or goes to. Of course, the next step in functional decomposition of the requirement will be to expand Box 3 on a separate sheet into the three or four subactivities that comprise it. The loss of continuity between pages will still be a problem. It already is with respect to arrows 1I1, 1I2, 1C1, 2C2, 3O2, and 4O1. Each of these connects to something off the sheet.[5] You

_____

5. Arrow 3M1 is also unconnected. Representing guidance to the designer, this mechanism is not necessarily tied to any higher-level diagram.

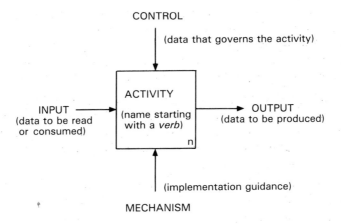

a. Activity Box

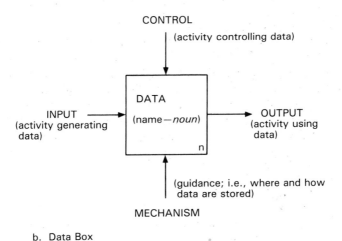

b. Data Box

Fig. 4.6   Building blocks in SADT.

must realize that Fig. 4.5 is diagram R3.5.3, the expansion of a box in a higher-level diagram R3.5 where, for example, 1O3 is a request to transmit data which had been held for future delivery. Thus R3.5.1O3 becomes R.3.5.3.1C1.

The graphic diagram helps clarify data usage. The fact that ADDRESS is associated with MESSAGE, but not part of it, is shown by the arrows 1I1 and 1I2. The fact that it is specifically ADDRESS that is provided to Box 3 is also clear. Likewise, even if the header portion of the transmitted message had not been renamed "CONTROL HEADER," 1O2/4I1, it would be recognized as a new header different from ADDRESS. In fact, if 1O2 had been called "ADDRESS," the reviewer would have been prompted to ask the analyst why two apparently different items have the same name. Distinctions between data and controls show the analyst's intent. 1C1 is a TRANSMISSION REQUEST that is a trigger initiating the sequence of activities in R3.5.3. The second control, 1C2, is ALTERNATE ADDRESS supplied by Box 3. Since the primary ADDRESS, 1I1, was not a control, why is ALTERNATE ADDRESS treated this way? From the diagram it is not clear. All you can tell is that analyst Brown looked at ALTERNATE ADDRESS as a control over the behavior of Box 1, and reviewer Thomas agreed with that view. You would have to look deeper into the expansion of PREPARE TO TRANSMIT for an answer. Here you would probably find that, when an alternate destination is selected, the analyst expects Box R3.5.3.1 to produce supervisory control message explaining the extraordinary decision to reroute. Two such messages were mentioned in Fig. 4.4. Arbitrary decisions of this type generally require narrative explanation; graphics cannot convey the reasons behind their structure very well.

Graphics suffer from other artistic weaknesses. Miller's "magical number seven" dictates that no more than seven or so independent entities be presented in one display [13]. Ross, in explaining SADT, limits diagrams to six boxes. It can be argued that the information content of Fig. 4.5 is more or less than the limit. Certainly, you cannot grasp the full meaning of the diagram in one look. Some study is required. Even observing a left-to-right, top-to-bottom rule for cascading the boxes down the page, there appears to be a lot of backtracking and crossing of paths. What would happen if there were six boxes with more than three arrows on each interface? Clutter and crowding would become real obstacles. As it is, the labels on each arrow have been placed badly. A label should be a clue for the eye, leading the eye to pertinent information. In this way, labels 1O1 and 1O3 are well placed to show the outputs of Box 1 but 1O2 is too far away. Unfortunately, a well-placed output label can be poorly placed with respect to the related input. 1O3 is also 3C2; the reader concentrating on Box 3 has to do a lot of scanning to learn what initiates the action of Box 3. Optimum placement of all the information in a complex graphic is next to impossible; therefore, the information transfer capability of complex system diagrams is limited. A picture is still worth a thousand words in the right circumstances. The trouble with Fig. 4.5 is that words are not conveyed well by a picture. Only the flows and element relationships are easily grasped from the diagram.

This leads to one more difficulty with graphic methods that affect projects which intend to automate the requirements and specification document files. Diagrams such as Fig. 4.5 require two types of data that are usually stored separately, making retrieval slow and awkward. The two types of data are, first, the information contained in the diagram, and, second, information about the drawing itself. Box 3 might be represented in the first database as:

```
ACTIVITY BOX 3  SELECT ALTERNATE DESTINATION
INPUTS          1  ADDRESS
CONTROLS        1  RETRY COUNT EXHAUSTED
                2  UNABLE TO TRANSMIT
OUTPUTS         1  ALTERNATE ADDRESS FOR NEW ATTEMPT TO
                   TRANSMIT
                2  NO ALTERNATE
MECHANISM       1  USE TABLE LOOK UP ROUTINE TLU65 ON
                   ADDRESS FILE
DESCRIPTION        FINDS NEXT AUTHORIZED ALTERNATE
                   ADDRESS, IF ANY, TO PERMIT TRANSMIS-
                   SION TO PROCEED
ENTERED BY         T. PIERCE, JAN 77
```

This format is quite similar to the RSL equivalent of Fig. 4.4. In the REVS system, the RSL text would be accompanied by a structure diagram, but the diagram would label only the boxes (ALPHAs) and the key decision paths. SADT displays all of its data on the diagram so it is representative of the class of graphics which would involve much more information in its structure file; for instance:

```
ELEMENT BOX3, X62Y23, SIZE B, LABEL 3, I1, C2,02,M1.
ELEMENT ARROW 3I1, BRANCH 1I1, SOURCE X, LABEL 3I1,
        POINTER 2, SIZE C, PROX 1,3
ELEMENT ARROW 3M1, SOURCE X, LABEL 3M1, POINTER 2,
        SIZE C, PROX 3, ABOVE 4I2.
```

While these examples are not taken from an actual system, they show some of the graphic problems. The Box 3 entry gives X and Y coordinates for placing the box. Obviously, someone has sketched the diagram by hand to decide what X and Y are. The other entries let the graphic support programs decide where to put symbols. They give guidance such as "place the label of arrow 3I1 (which, by the way, is a branch of 1I1 which starts off the page) equidistant from Boxes 1 and 3. You will find the label in the descriptive database under Box 3. Add a pointer of Type 2. Use type size C for the label." Arrow 3M1 is specified as being close to Box 3 (the proximity specification, PROX 3) and above Arrow 4I2. Any position selected by the program that satisfies these conditions is acceptable. If you think about it, though, even these loose specifications must be based on an initial sketch unless, perhaps, the analyst is building the diagram interactively at a display console.

4.1.3.6 Methodology—summary

REVS was introduced in Chapter 2 as a variant of PSL/PSA. The University of Michigan research in PSL/PSA has shown that over thirty different system requirements analysis aids can be expressed in PSL/PSA. Even the graphic systems such as SADT can be represented in PSL/PSA. The central attribute of PSL/PSA that makes this possible is its database management capability. PSL/PSA is based on a relational DBMS. PSL is a language of entities, relations, classes, and structures. PSA is a tool kit for processing a relational database. All generalized DBMSs have three important properties:

1. The functions of database management are independent of the meaning of the data in the database; i.e., the "entities" can be requirements or specifications or test cases, etc.; it makes no difference to the database manager.

2. Data are stored and processed in a form dictated by the DBMS, but it can be accepted or delivered in other forms as required by the user; i.e., a DBMS can have text or graphic or coded input and output, conversion from one form to another occurs at the I/O interface.

3. The functions of database management are independent of the specific hardware/software implementation; i.e., a request for a report showing all named elements used by a process should produce the same result regardless of where and in what order the data are stored and regardless of what data-processing system the DBMS is running on.

These properties make it feasible for PSL/PSA to be used in all stages of the project life cycle by allowing the database to evolve as specifications, code, tests, etc., are added. The analysis tools would also evolve since project personnel need different kinds of support at different stages. Early on, structural information is most useful. Later, completeness checks and simulations are important. Then quantitative data about path lengths and execution times is requested. A single DBMS can support all such needs, although no single system has been developed that does it all. Rather, the DBMS approach has been applied separately to requirements analysis (REVS, SADT) and to development (CLEAR/CASTER). In the one case, the tools for analysis stress documentation and logical control of requirements; in the other, they stress documentation and inventory control of deliverable programs. Current approaches also emphasize user convenience and local needs. Some users want graphic I/O. Others want text I/O with automated support of performance simulation. As a result, no one approach is widely accepted. PSL/PSA could be the basis for one approach tailored as necessary for local needs, but other experimenters can show that PSL/QBE is equally valid. In this case, the analysis of the database would be done with a Query-By-Example (QBE) package. One could draw the conclusion that, as a minimum, a project support tool kit should consist of:

1. A generalized DBMS
2. A problem statement language selected for ease of use and adaptability to project working methods
3. A project management discipline which produces consistent use of the tools

In the requirements analysis stage, such a tool kit would provide:

1. Standardized format
2. Standardized naming and numbering conventions
3. Maintenance of project files, automated where possible:
    - Requirements index
    - Data definitions
    - Requirements statements
    - Structure diagrams
      a. logical structure
      b. information flow
    - Management information
      a. "where used" file
      b. configuration accounting
      c. "who is responsible" file
4. Formal language (supplemented by narrative)
    - Requirements statement language
    - Diagrammatic method
5. Tools
    - Accounting
    - Simulation
    - Editing and display formatting
    - Test data generation
    - Structure and usage checking
    - Information retrieval and reporting

To be really useful, the tool kit should be:

1. Easy to learn
2. Easy to use
3. Inexpensive to acquire or build basic capabilities
4. Incrementally extendable (when cost justified)
5. Applicable to all stages of project life cycle
6. Suitable for automation

4.1.4   Analyzing the Data

Common to each of the examples in the previous section is a very low level of detail. Much analysis must have taken place before a requirement for alternate delivery due to transmission blockage could be written. In practice, formal procedures have their greatest value at the detailed level while ordinary narrative is acceptable in the early stages of generalized activity. Therefore, typical examples of formalized requirements will deal with details. The details in turn are the end product of the analysis process obtained by decomposition of the original problem statement. Two very strong biases exist among analysts that tend to separate all analysis and design techniques into two classes: (1) Process-oriented, and (2) Data-oriented. There is great overlap between the two—it is perhaps correct to say that the classes are points of view rather fundamentally different methodologies.

In the history of computing, *process-oriented analysis* developed first as scientists and engineers began to attack previously unattainable problems with the new, expensive computers. These problems had no established databases. Often, they led to extensive computation on a very few inputs to produce a few output numbers. A good example of this was weather prognostication circa 1960. About 1300 input values fed a set of equations which exercised the largest computer available for an hour and a half to produce enough output values to draw one weather chart. Naturally enough, the meteorologists concerned with this problem focused their attention on the equations: "What must be done to be able to draw a weather chart?" Answers to a *"What must be done?"* question are activities and processes. Except for the initial input, the data handled by the system are defined to meet the needs of the processes. The descendants of the early process-oriented analysts are found today in all the areas where new, untried problems are being solved. Included in this set of problems are many large, interesting projects related to space flight, networking, military operations, and computer operating systems.

Data-oriented analysis grew out of the manual and punched-card accounting procedures of ordinary business operations. It flowered when computerized database management systems made integrated files practical. For a data-oriented analyst, the purpose of a data-processing system is to build on existing files to make appropriate data available when needed. File integrity is very important. Manipulation of very large files that cannot be easily reformatted dictates that system procedures be designed to fit the data, not the other way around. Thus it is natural for the data-oriented analyst to ask, *"What data must be handled?"* The answer will define data structures. Then, given the data structures, it will be possible to define the functions that transform the data from one state to another. As indicated by its origins, data-oriented analysis is the dominant approach in business data processing, finance, logistics, and information retrieval.

There is usually a strong correspondence between the key parameters used to manage a business and the major data items used in data processing. For this reason, the common "business factors" are often the nucleus of a *data dictionary*, which grows to include all data items relevant to the business. Each item is defined as to meaning, usage, format, source, when generated, when destroyed, etc. All synonyms for a given piece of data are cross-referenced. Programs are available that automate the data dictionary. Analysts can then refer to existing definitions, avoid creating conflicting or misleading dictionary entries, and take advantage of the similarity between managers' terms and computer database field names.

The attitude of the data-oriented analyst is clearly visible in the guidelines adopted in dp applications departments [14, 15, 16]. Collins [17], for example, separates system analysis into an investigation stage and an analysis stage. This is a useful insight because it reminds the analyst that it is often unwise to simply describe a current process and redo it on a new machine. By calling for an analysis of the results of the investigation, Collins lays the basis for improvements over the existing applications. His two stages lead to project flows of the following type:

1. Systems Investigation
   - Develop and agree on project objectives
   - Investigate existing functions and department responsibilities
   - Investigate and define existing information systems
2. Systems Analysis
   - Analyze business into major systems
   - Define control variables
   - Analyze existing information systems by comparing to conceptual model of management control
   - Rank strengths and weaknesses of existing systems
3. Systems Design
4. Program Implementation
5. Operation, Maintenance, and Upgrade

The key word here is *existing*. The procedure is based on a conceptual environment in which all new developments are incremental changes to existing systems. The concept is consistent with compatible growth, feasible objectives, and economy. Even when no existing systems appear to be in place, the procedure leads the analyst to look for them and may prevent awkward oversights, as, for example, assuming that a terrestrial communications system uses only telephone wires when, in fact, the telephone company has an automatic switchover to satellite link to back up land line outages. Most of the time, the procedure is used in dp applications where there really are major existing systems that dominate all new planning.

Missing from the preceding project flow is a key step in system definition; namely, the synthesis of the new system. Collins includes this step in "System Design." The goal of separating requirements setting from specification writing calls for a discrete system synthesis step leading up to the release of a requirements statement. Later, designers will synthesize additional system views to respond to the requirement. As usual, the purpose of synthesis during the analysis stage is to determine *what* the new system must do. The purpose of synthesis during the design stage is to show *how* the proposed system elements satisfy the requirements. Project flow can now be revised to:

1. Systems Investigation
   - Develop and agree on project objectives
   - Investigate existing functions and department responsibilities
   - Investigate and define existing information systems
2. Systems Analysis
   - Analyze business into major systems
   - Define control variables
   - Analyze existing information systems by comparing to conceptual model of management control
   - Rank strengths and weaknesses of existing systems
3. Systems Synthesis
   - Define new functions necessary to meet project objectives
   - Define requirements for new system or systems to meet project objectives
4. System Design, etc. . . .

During the investigation, emphasis is on documentation techniques for gathering data, organizing data, and supporting the preparation of a description of the existing information systems. Information systems departments tend to formalize their own version of standard documentation aids. The system study recurs often enough in a large organization to justify actually printing a stock of planning sheets. Various types of forms exist, each reflecting the personal taste or experience of the originator. The successful documentation procedures share a common approach to what data are needed. The Study Organization Plan published in 1961 by IBM[6] identified the following inputs as necessary to understand the existing system:

- Resource usage—Describes the organizational framework and costs of the activities covered by the system study (Fig. 4.7).

---

6. The Study Organization Plan consisted of one IBM Form C20-8075 and several related reports. All are out of print. Glans et al. [14] cover the basic SOP methods in expanded form.

Fig. 4.7 Resource usage sheet.
Study Organization Plan IBM Form C20-8075, 1961.

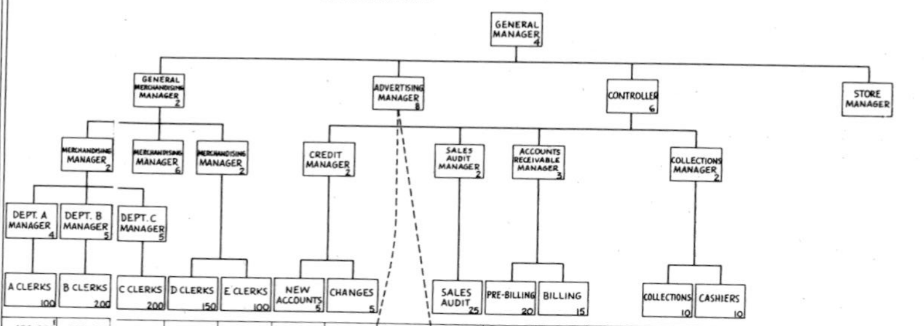

RESOURCE USAGE SHEET

Study ___ASSOCIATED RETAILERS, INC.___
Analyst ___L.H. BAKER, JR.___
Date ___29 FEB 61___

NOTES:

3. THESE FIGURES SHOW ONLY A FEW OF THE ORGANIZATIONAL COMPONENTS. THE TOTALS WOULD BE LARGER IF ALL COMPONENTS WERE INCLUDED.

4. THE VALUES FOR THIS ACTIVITY WOULD BE ENTERED IN THE SAME MANNER AS THOSE FOR CHARGE ACCOUNTS—EXCEPT THAT NOT ALL OF THE SAME ORGANIZATIONAL COMPONENTS WOULD PARTICIPATE.

NOTES

1. THE PERSONNEL COST FOR THE SALES CLERKS IS THE AVERAGE NUMBER OF CLERKS X $4500

2. NEW HIRES ARE SENT TO TRAINING CLASSES. THIS COST IS THE AMORTIZED COST PER ATTENDEE.

- Activities—Each activity in the system is described in terms of operational flow, input/output characteristics, file usage, frequency, applicable deadlines, and elapsed time for present operations, particularly manual operations (Fig. 4.8).

- Operations—Lists inputs and outputs, processing steps and the events which trigger them, and frequency of each operation (manual or automated) in each information system application. The resources applied to each operation are also included (Fig. 4.9).

- Messages—The details about message content, layout, distribution, media, frequency, where used, etc., are given and a sample copy is attached.

- Files—Gives the details of file content, media, index structure and location, sequence, labels, volumes, record format, where used, etc.

The analysis step evaluates the input data to complete the understanding of the existing system and to place the new objectives in perspective. The synthesis step recombines the system elements produced by analysis into a set of requirements for the new system to satisfy the new objectives. Ample weight is given to the stability of the portions of the existing system that need not change. In fact, the new system may be burdened by constraints imposed by the existing system such as file organizations or operator responsibilities. The new system, therefore, is more likely to be an evolutionary upgrade of the existing data-processing system than to be a completely new replacement.

A bias toward either process or data orientation can influence the ability of project members to understand a given methodology. It is not surprising to find each methodology aimed at a single type of user to minimize the difficulty of teaching or using the method. REVS and SADT lean in the direction of process-oriented analysts. The Jackson and Warnier design techniques mentioned in Chapter 2 are data-oriented. As design techniques, they do not claim to be analysis tools; however, they assume that an analysis has been done that describes a set of databases and a set of requirements for information to be obtained from the databases. As in almost all aspects of system development, the best analysts will use all appropriate techniques. They will take a data-oriented approach to view requirements from one angle and a process-oriented approach to get a different view. SADT explicitly encourages such behavior. All the other methods permit it.

4.1.4.1 A process-oriented example

Networking has already been named as a large, interesting project suitable for process-oriented analysis. Networking does not rely on the existence of any databases, although it may define requirements for new databases. It is

Fig. 4.8 Activity sheet.
Study Organization Plan IBM Form C20-8075, 1961.

FUNCTION: POSTING A/R
FREQUENCY: DAILY
INPUTS: 2000
CONDITIONS

DAY	AVG.	AVG.	PEAK	PEAK	AVG.	AVG.	PEAK	PEAK
WEEK	AVG.	AVG.	AVG.	AVG.	PEAK	PEAK	PEAK	PEAK
CYCLE BEING BILLED?	NO	YES	NO	YES	NO	YES	NO	YES
KEYS 1-3	1D	1D	1D	1D	1D	1D	1D	1D
3-6	1/2D	1/4D	1D	1/2D	1D	3/4D	2D	1 1/2D
7-12	1 1/2D	1 1/4D	2D	1 1/2D				
13-18								
19-24			REMAINDER FILLED IN THE SAME WAY					
25-26								

FUNCTION: BILLING
FREQUENCY: 20 DAYS PER MONTH
OUTPUTS: 3000
CONDITIONS

DAY	AVG.	PEAK	AVG.	PEAK
WEEK	AVG.	AVG.	PEAK	PEAK
KEYS 26-27	1D	1 1/2D	2D	2D
27-28	1D	2D	2D	3D
28-32	1D	1D	1 1/2D	2D
TOTAL 26-32	3D	4 1/2D	5 1/2D	7D
26-13 (AVERAGE PAYMENT RECEIVED)	18D	19 1/2D	22 1/2D	25D
SEE NOTE			1060	1060

INPUTS

KEY	NAME	SOURCE	AVG. DAY AVG. WK.	PEAK DAY AVG. WK.	AVG. DAY PEAK WK.	PEAK DAY PEAK WK.	SEE NOTE
2000	CHARGE SALE	CUSTOMER	15K/D	30K/D	45K/D	60K/D	1030
		FREQUENCY	143D/YR	143D/YR	13D/YR	13D/YR	1040
2010	RETURNS	CUSTOMER					
		FREQUENCY					
2020	PAYMENTS				REMAINDER FILLED IN THE SAME WAY		
		FREQUENCY					
2030	FILE CHANGES						
		FREQUENCY					

OUTPUTS

KEY	NAME	DESTINATION	AVG. DAY AVG. WK.	PEAK DAY AVG. WK.	AVG. DAY PEAK WK.	PEAK DAY PEAK WK.	SEE NOTE
3000	BILLS	CUSTOMER	15K/MC	30K/MC	20K/MC	35K/MC	
		FREQUENCY	165D/YR	55D/YR	15D/YR	5D/YR	1050

FILE USAGE

KEY	FILE NAME USG. NAME	NO. OF MESSAGES AVG.	NO. OF MESSAGES PEAK	ACCESS RANDOM OR CYCLE	ACCESS TIME		SEE NOTE
4000	CUSTOMER	500K	550K	RANDOM	≤ 1MIN.		
4010	CUSTOMER	500K	550K	CYCLE	1D		
4020	1 CYCLE CUSTOMER	25K	40K	CYCLE	1 CYCLE PER DAY 20 CYCLES PER MO.		

FLOW DIAGRAM

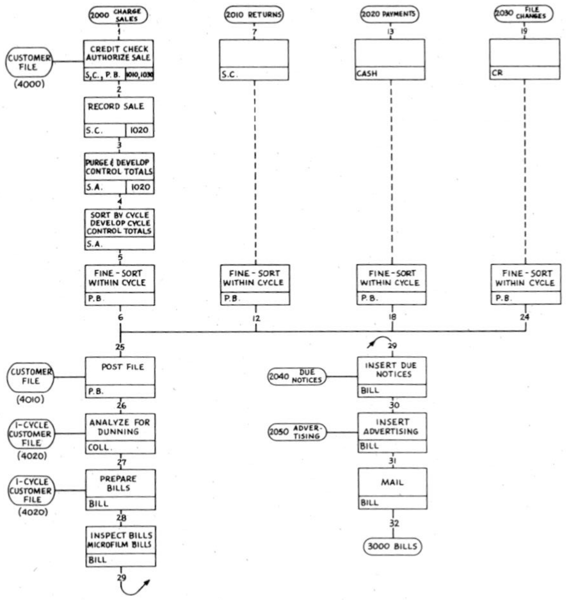

NOTES

1010 - UNIT AUTHORIZER IS SUPERVISOR OR CREDIT MANAGER IF NECESSARY, DEPENDING ON AMOUNT OF SALE.

1020 - UNDER PRESENT SYSTEM, MEDIA FROM A REGISTER INCLUDES CASH SALES, CHARGES, COD, LAYAWAYS, VOIDS, ETC. ALL MEDIA FROM REGISTER ARE BALANCED TO THE REGISTER TOTAL; TOTALS ARE DEVELOPED FOR MERCHANDISE AND NON-MERCHANDISE CLASSES, AND MEDIA SEPARATED BY TYPE. CAUTION SHOULD BE USED IN ANY ATTEMPT TO SEPARATE THESE OPERATIONS FROM THE TOTAL JOB.

1030 - AT PRESENT, ONLY 60% OF CHARGE SALE TRANSACTIONS ARE AUTHORIZED WITHOUT APPROVAL OF UNIT AUTHORIZER.

MO 8 - 4608

NOTES

1040 - THERE ARE 302 WORKING DAYS PER YEAR IN THIS OPERATION.

1050 - THERE ARE 240 WORKING DAYS PER YEAR IN THIS OPERATION.

1060 - DELAY IN BILLING DURING THE CHRISTMAS PEAK RAISES ACCTS. RECEIVABLE INVESTMENT BY $500,000.

NOTES

LEGEND BOX

ORGANIZATIONAL COMPONENTS

S.C. - SALES CLERKS
S.A. - SALES AUDIT
P.B. - PRE-BILLING
COLL. - COLLECTIONS
BILL. - BILLING
CASH. - CASHIER
CR. - CREDIT OFFICE

KEY NUMBERS

1 - 999 Between Operations
1000 - 1999 Notes
2000 - 2999 Inputs
3000 - 3999 Outputs
4000 - 4999 File Usage

ACTIVITY SHEET

Analyst: LH BAKER, JR.
Date: 29 FEB 61
Study: ATLANTIC DISTRIBUTORS, INC.
Activity Name: CHARGE ACCOUNTS

Fig. 4.9   Operation sheet.
Study Organization Plan IBM Form C20-8075, 1961.

IBM   Operation Sheet

OPERATION	ID NO.	TRIGGERS, INPUTS AND OUTPUTS — NAME AND QUALIFICATIONS	RECEIVED FROM OR SENT TO	VOLUME AVG	PER	ELAPSED TIME	ID NO.	PROCESSES — DESCRIPTION AND QUALIFICATIONS	FREQ	RESOURCES ID NO.	TYPE	UNIT TIME AVG	TOTAL TIME AVG	PER
014 011 BILLING (KEY NOS. 27-28)	T1	RECEIPT OF IQ I1					P1	COUNT TRANSACTION SLIPS	1/I1	X1	CLERKS (5)	20 MIN OP		
	I1	CUSTOMER RECORD	COLLECTIONS	20K	D	0	P2	COMPARE COUNT TO NUMBER OF TRANS- ACTIONS ON CUSTOMER RECORD	1/I1	X2	XEROX COPIER (2)		13H	D
	I2	TRANSACTION SLIP		60K	D	0								
	R1	CUSTOMER RECORD	ANALYSIS SECTION OF BILLING	20K	D	7 MIN	P3	RETURN CUSTOMER RECORD AND TRANS- ACTION SLIPS TO COLLECTIONS	1/I50I1					
	R2	BILL		60K	D	7 MIN		DEPT. FOR ERROR TRACING AND						
	R3	TRANSACTION SLIP		60K	D	7 MIN		CORRECTION.						
	R4	ERROR SHEET	COLLECTIONS SUPVR	5	D	8H	P4	ENTER ACCOUNT NUMBER AND NATURE OF ERROR ON ERROR SHEET.	1/I50I1					
							P5	XEROX BILL FROM CUSTOMER RECORD	1/I1					
							P6	ATTACH TRANSACTION SLIPS TO BILL	1/I1					
							P7	ENTER INITIALS ON CUSTOMER RECORD	1/I1					
							P8	SEND CUSTOMER RECORD, BILL, AND TRANSACTIONS SLIPS TO ANALYSIS SECTION	1/IOI1					
							P9	SEND ERROR SHEET TO ANALYSIS SUPVR.	1/D					
014 021 BILLING (KEY NOS. 28-29)	T1	RECEIPT OF IOI1					P1	INSPECT BILLS FOR LEGIBILITY AND ATTACHED TRANSACTION SLIPS	1/I1	X1	CLERKS (2)	2 MIN OP		
	I1	CUSTOMER RECORD	FILE SECTION OF BILLING	20K	D	0	P2	RETURN CUSTOMER RECORD, BILL, AND TRANSACTION SLIPS TO FILE SECTION.	1/700I1	X2	MICROFILM CAMERA		4H	D
	I2	BILL		20K	D	0								
	I3	TRANSACTION SLIP		60K	D	0	P3	ENTER FILE CLERK INITIALS AND NATURE	1/700I1					
	R1	CUSTOMER RECORD	COLLECTIONS	NOTE 1		1H		OF ERROR ON ERROR SHEET.						
	R2	BILL	MAILING SECTION OF BILLING			5 MIN	P4	MICROFILM BILL	1/I1					
	R3	TRANSACTION SLIP				5 MIN	P5	SEND BILL AND TRANSACTION SLIPS TO MAILING SECTION.	1/IOI1					
	R4	ERROR SHEET	FILE SECTION SUPVR	2	D	8H	P6	SEND CUSTOMER RECORD TO COLLECTIONS.	1/250I1					
							P7	SEND ERROR SHEET TO FILE SECTION SUPVR	1/D					

① VOLUME HAS CYCLIC FLUCTUATION:

FREQ	165D/YR	55D/YR	150D/YR	5D/YR
VOLUME	15K/D	30K/D	20K/D	35K/D

BILLING DEPT. — SCHULTZ   ASSOCIATED RETAILERS INC.   CHARGE ACCOUNTS

29 FEB 61   LH BAKER JR.   PAGE 6

very important, however, to decide what the capabilities of a networking product line should be. Such decisions were required to produce Table 4.4.

A sample objective from Table 4.2 can illustrate the process: "Support hardware and software of all major vendors." The broad objective should be satisfied to the extent that the support cost is justified by expected revenue. This objective will lead to requirements for compatibility with some products, interfaces with others, and no special effort for the rest of the multitude of computer hardware and software on the market. The question is how to select the products that fall into each of the three classes. The answer requires some data about major vendors and their products, about how the products are used, about the distribution of products by type of customer, and about the existing interconnectability of the products. Assumptions will have to be made about future changes in the market. The cost of providing compatibility or interfaces will have to be estimated. Then decisions must be made regarding the desirability of providing support for all, less than all, or none of the other vendors' products.

Following Quade's advice [1], the analysts faced with answering the question raised by the objective of broad-based product support will concentrate first on formulating the problem clearly. They will develop their understanding of the problem in its system context. In this case, the system context is a proposed but undefined networking environment. Therefore, the aspects of the problem to focus on are those related to interconnected data-processing facilities. To size each market category, various alternative hypotheses are set forth and evaluated:

■ Hypothesis 1—*All data-processing machines have equal reason to be connected to all others; therefore, any investment in compatibility should be proportional to the number of machines in existence or projected for the future.* This hypothesis leads to a ranking of industry data obtained by market research. Using some basis for relating cost to return, the ranked list can be cut into, say, three parts. The highest part of the list justifies investing in full compatibility because there are enough machines of each type to expand the networking vendor's market if the machines can talk to his or her competitor's machines. The next lower group is numerous enough to justify providing a simple way for competitors to attach to the networking vendors facilities. The lowest group is considered economically unimportant.

■ Hypothesis 2—*The networking vendor, N, can maximize sales by providing unique facilities to connect N machines but not competitive machines.* If this hypothesis is valid, no market research is required. The ranking need only be done for *N*'s own products to determine which *N* machines should be allowed to interconnect.

■ Hypothesis 3—*Only some portion of existing data-processing machines have a need to be interconnected. These machines exist exclusively in com-*

panies that have two or more physical computing sites separated by more than a mile. This hypothesis is a narrower version of Hypothesis 1. It excludes multiple computers locally interconnected by cables and it excludes connections among companies each of which has only one computer site. Market research at a much more detailed level is required to handle this case.

- Hypothesis 4—Hypothesis 1, 2, and 3 assume that "networking" provides intelligent information transfer between end users; i.e., a connection between a program and a remote terminal conveys all the control information needed to activate and manage the program and the terminal as well as the data to be processed or displayed. An alternative approach based on the telephone business would be *to transmit only data, leaving all dp controls to the user.* Such an approach requires a standard interface for the user to access the network. The primary cost consideration is whether the user must bear all the expense of adapting to the interface (limiting sales because some users will not go to that much trouble for such a low level of service) or whether N should invest in adaptation facilities. N's investments again could be evaluated from a market study as in Hypothesis 1.

Of these four alternatives, the first meets the objective best, but it is very broad; the second is totally unresponsive to the objective, but may be a good business choice; the third is partly responsive and seems to be realistic; the fourth is totally responsive, but not exactly in N's line of business. The analysts favor Hypothesis 3, but keep all options open as they study the available market data. They set out to find out how many customers fit the description of a multicomputer, multisite company. The number of customers today must be projected somehow to predict how many there might be during the life of the networking product line. This forecasting exercise is best handled by a model. Quade reminds the analyst to emphasize the question, not the model. The model should be an aid to the thought process, not a substitute for it. Too much attention to model detail will often suboptimize components of the problem while distorting the overall system.

The type of model applicable to sizing the networking market opportunity is quite simple—as are most initial analytical models. It merely extrapolates the present market situation, according to assumed growth rates. From published data or from a private survey, the present market is characterized by a matrix such as Table 4.5. It shows how many companies fit various categories of size, connectivity, and dispersion. The matrix is based on the analysts' explicit assumptions that:

- Networking is primarily of interest to companies with multiple sites and many terminals.

TABLE 4.5. NETWORKING—MARKET SURVEY SUMMARY

Current year	One location		Two locations		More than two locations	
	Number of companies	Number of computers	Number of companies	Number of computers	Number of companies	Number of computers
Two or more large computers plus large net A	none	none	500	5,000	1,000	15,000
Two or more large computers plus small net B	500	3,000	2,000	10,000	3,000	30,000
Intermediate computers plus large net C	500	600	1,000	3,000	2,000	10,000
Intermediate computers plus small net D	5,000	6,000	2,000	6,000	2,000	10,000
Small computers plus net or any computers without net E	10,000	12,000	4,000	10,000	1,000	5,000

- A company with only two sites may be able to use a simpler networking architecture (Type 2) than a company with three or more sites (e.g., no addressing, no alternate routing, simple error recovery).

- The type of application that justifies remote access from all parts of a company is most often found on a large computer.

- A company with a large present investment in dp is more likely to pay for networking than other firms (e.g., with a relatively small increase in total expense, networking permits resource sharing that can avoid a large increase in expenses).

The actual data obtained is more finely segregated than shown. "Large," "intermediate," and "small" have to be clearly defined. Software must be identified. The data should be broken down by vendor or at least into "N" data and "other" data. N's data is probably more accurate than the data obtained for other vendors; it can help set the bounds on market projections. But data on other vendor's products are needed to assess the value of supporting non-N systems. The quality of the data available is usually low, ranging from field reports to pure guesses. As with many decisions in the software business, the quality of data supports only simple analyses rather than elaborate statistical computation.

More assumptions are required about the matrix so the analysts can project from the base data.

- Some companies will grow up a row each year.

- Some companies will move one column to the right each year.

- The number of computers per company will grow over the years.

- The number of companies in the matrix will grow over the years.

The growth rates in these assumptions are found by selectively interviewing customers, by referring to industry forecasts, and by examining historic growth. Once a growth rate (or range) has been agreed on, it is a straightforward arithmetic job to calculate the corresponding matrices for the next five to ten years.[7] The numbers in the matrix rows A–D represent the gross potential for networking. The analysts must next decide: (1) what the likelihood is that the potential customers will actually buy something from some vendor, and (2) how many of those will buy from N. The gross potential is reduced to: (1) the market opportunity which is further reduced to (2) a sales estimate. The sales estimate will determine how much investment is

---

7. Projections from data of this type magnify the inherent survey errors. The projections are good enough for planning operations over the next two years. They are useful for strategizing and requirements setting over five to ten years, but they have very low credence beyond five years in the dynamic data-processing industry.

warranted in networking. Suppose the projection shows, for the year 19XX, that 10,000 companies (40 percent of row A, 25 percent of B, 10 percent of C, 5 percent of D) are networking prospects, but 1,000 of them have only one location and 3,000 have only two locations in 19XX. Can one set of networking requirements satisfy all the prospects? Will a telephone company solve the networking problem for one location companies that want to share lines or data with other companies? If we assume that it is cheaper to connect two computers than it is to connect more than two, should we define Type 2 requirements for the 3,000 companies? Is it possible that among the 6,000 companies with more than two computers there are some who would actually interconnect pairs of related computers rather than interconnect everything they own? If so, is the Type 2 solution the one N should offer? If the N product, Ⓝ, supports interconnection of all types of computers, will N benefit enough to recover expenses or, will the benefits go to other companies? What happens to the sales estimate for Ⓝ when all major vendors offer networking solutions and the best prospects have some computers from each vendor installed?

As questions arise, analysts provide answers based on available data and good judgement. In the process, competitive strategies and tactics are evaluated. All alternatives are given a fair analysis. Wherever possible, uncertainties are made explicit, such as the uncertainty about how many of the computers in a multicomputer company really need to be interconnected and what the resulting networks will look like. This may call for an investment in market research or joint application studies. Suboptimization should be avoided and detail postponed. For example, N may have an excellent communications access method, ⓃAM. It may be logical to plan networking around ⓃAM. But it is better to keep the analysis open to other possibilities. A more general requirements statement will result, giving the designers more freedom of action. Their solution may still be based on ⓃAM, but it will probably be flexible enough to coexist with other access methods and to accept ⓃAM's replacement at some future date.

The types of conclusions reached by the networking analysts are given in R5-Diversity in the requirements list of Table 4.4. The market analysis showed a high degree of vendor diversity among the top prospects for networking. Networking implies that for each end user who wants to communicate there must be another end user to talk to. The analysts realized that if both end users had to have N's hardware there might not be enough customers. Therefore, they set requirement R5a—Support Hardware of All Vendors—at the highest priority. As the project proceeds and support costs are better known, R5a will have to be reexamined to limit development expense. R5b shows a lower priority for the support of the software of all vendors. The designers will interpret that as meaning that they should establish stable program interfaces and protocols to permit anyone to use N's networking support but ⓃN will not provide the attachment software itself. R5c says two things. More than one access method must be supported for networking and at least two access methods must be simultaneously operable in one host (without interfering with each other). The designers will assume this requirement refers only to N's access methods, namely ⓃNAM and its two or three most popular predecessors. R5d, like R5a, says networking should coexist with the communications links the customer already has (and implies that it should permit other types of connection such as satellite links). R5e says that the networking design must support the modes of use (given in R4) in the same network and in a single host. Some of the conclusions of the analysts working on R5 show up elsewhere. R2d recognizes the probable existence of X and Y networking solutions and suggests (priority 3) that N's solution include gateways to allow communication with X and Y networks. R2f gives priority 2 to the interconnection of multiple enterprises (companies) on a single network. This decision offers something to the one-site prospects who want to share communications resources, even though it may have been a response to requests from very large companies interviewed in a market survey. R4c8 also supports the lower end of the market spectrum by allowing independent users to negotiate capacity-sharing agreements implemented via networking.

4.1.4.2 A data-oriented example

Assume a bank wants to set requirements for a distributed demand deposit system. At present, the bank has a single computer center with three large computers linked to each other and to a large disk storage bank. Transactions consisting of deposits, withdrawals, inquiries, and credit checks originate at terminals connected to one of the hosts. That host edits the transactions, processes inquiries, and checks credit. It routes deposits and withdrawals to the second host. The third host does unrelated work but is on standby to replace either of the first two machines. Batch input to the customer files involves loan processing, check reconciliation, automatic deductions to pay customer bills, and interest calculations. The same file is used for bank studies related to customer income brackets, economic behavior, and demography. Growth in customer activity at the bank is projected at 5 percent a year over a five-year period. This will overload the processors in two years. Thus the bank ran a study to lay out a plan of action to prevent customer service problems. The study recommended offloading the host processors by installing controllers in branch banks to handle all the terminals and process deposits and withdrawals. The primary objective of this approach was to maintain good customer response times.

The system analysts who are assigned to this project start with a major database in place. Database processing is done using a standard vendor-supplied database management subsystem that runs on all three hosts. The data dictionary associated with the DBMS describes all the data items used for database processing. The database is obviously too large to fit in a controller so, at most, a small piece can be distributed. Furthermore, the database serves many centralized applications that need not be changed as a result of redesigning the demand deposit system. Finally, the central database has an elaborate set of security and protection procedures that allow for recovery of the bank's business after a catastrophe; the procedures cannot be compromised. Under such conditions, the analysts are naturally going to think in terms of minimizing the impact on the main database caused by the distributed system design. Their first set of assumptions will be that the main database is fixed but that additions to its format and size are permitted and that subsets may be copied to a remote controller. However, the meaning of terms in the data dictionary cannot be changed without the concurrence of all users. Their second set of assumptions will be that the functions of a demand deposit system are fixed and completely defined by the present banking system; however, the implementation of the processes may be changed. Their third set of assumptions is that the integrity of the banking functions is critically important, that the operators in the system are hired for clerical/teller skills not for dp skills, and that system integrity must be largely provided by the dp system itself. In each analyst's mind is a general picture of the demand deposit activity. It consists of a customer giving a transaction to a teller who submits it to the demand deposit program where changes are made to the database (sometimes) and a set of reports is generated from the database. Among the reports is a receipt or a transaction acknowledgment for the customer to carry away.

The distributed system requirements will depend on the volume of transactions of each possible type per teller per branch per peak hour of the day projected for future years. This information is generated like the market data in the networking example. The requirements also depend on which database operations can be performed in the branch. From the set that *can* be offloaded, an analyst can select the functions that *should* be offloaded to improve customer service. Note that the analyst makes a choice based on the objectives of the project. The choice may be influenced by knowledge of computer execution times but the analyst tries to avoid making design decisions. Therefore, the requirements may call for something to be placed in a controller that leads to inefficiency in system performance. If so, the designers who receive the requirements statement will point out the problem and request a change.

One approach to selecting the functions to be offloaded is to trace what must happen to each transaction as it passes through the system. Starting with the highest volume transaction, a deposit, the flow may consist of:

1. The customer fills out a deposit slip with name, account number, items to be deposited, and total value.

2. The teller checks items against the total and, if correct, accepts the deposit by giving the customer a receipt.
   a. Where necessary, the teller will look up the customer's account number.
   b. When the total is wrong, the teller will ask the customer to agree with the correct total.
3. The customer account balance is increased by the total cash deposited.
   a. Each deposit item is listed as a separate record in the customer's current activity file.
   b. Each check deposited is marked "no funds"; the amount of the check is *not* added to the account balance.
   c. Each item is time-stamped for audit purposes and for interest calculations.
4. Checks deposited are batched for transmission to a clearing bank to obtain funds represented by the checks; when a check clears, the "no funds" marker is erased and the customer balance is adjusted.
5. The bank branch account balance is increased.
6. The bank balance is increased.
7. At the end of the month, a customer statement is produced showing each item in sequence by date.

Looking at the flow, an analyst can see that by separating own-branch customers from foreign-branch customers, it becomes feasible to maintain information about own-branch customers locally. Customers from foreign-branches will still require help from the central site (or, via networking, from the customer's own-branch). An adding machine capability can do total checking in Step 2. A customer name/account file can do Step 2a. A customer master file can do Steps 2, 3, and 5. Since the bank collects all checks physically at the center for clearing, it may be better to do Step 4 at the host. The host must do Step 6. Step 7 can be done either at the host or the branch. The maximum offloading would place the customer master file for a whole month in the controller. Only at the end of the month would the whole file be used (except to answer inquiries). On other days, deposits can be handled given only the previous day's balance. In any case, the full master file will be retained in the central database for security, protection, and other purposes. The picture developing in the analyst's mind shows a central database containing all customer information as of midnight each day. Before dawn, each branch controller receives a copy of the master file for its customers. The information sent to the branch includes customer name, account number, account balance, value of checks not yet credited to balance, list of such checks giving amount and bank codes, account restrictions such as maximum loans permitted, and a list of adjustments so far this month such as penalties for overdrawal, interest accrued, or bills paid. The branch will always maintain its customer name/account list permitting a completeness check of the daily file. During the day, all deposits will be accepted and recorded in the branch controller. At closing time, the new customer file, including the day's transaction details, is shipped to the central master file, and a copy is set aside in the branch for recovery purposes. At the end of the month, the host computer sends all statement records to the controller which works after hours to print the statements.

The types of requirements generated by this thought process are statements about:

- Controller storage capacity
- Time available to load storage
- Number of transactions of each type per hour
- Response time allowed for each transaction type
- Data recovery requirements
- Communications among branches and between a branch and the host
- Input formats dictated by customer and teller ease of use considerations
- System capability when host fails or when branch controller fails

The requirements state what the demand deposit system design must do to improve customer service. The framework of the analysis was based on data structures: record formats, transactions, and operations on key information fields.

4.1.5 Establishing Requirements

A common characteristic of systems analysis is that it produces imperfect requirements. Errors are made in large systems because conflicts are not apparent to the different analysts who prepare the requirements statements. Omissions are due to the fact that the analysts have an incomplete set of data to work with. Other problems are due to imperfect analysts—those who do not understand the situation and those who understand it but warp it to fit their own value judgments. Within the list of Table 4.4 are some examples of what can go wrong.

- Requirement 1a3) may conflict with 11b. If the standard of performance is based on telephone lines using terrestrial links, a network based on satellite links may appear slower due to the fixed transit time up to and down from the satellite.

■ Requirement 1b1) is obviously not a networking requirement since it only applies to one host. The item actually anticipates a design decision that, in order to satisfy 1b2), every application must be addressable as an end user. The user may get 1b1) free as a byproduct of the networking design, yet, by making it a requirement, the analyst may force the designer to place some network routing functions in the host that good judgement would put in a front-end processor. In other words, the non-networking requirement can lead to an uneconomic networking implementation.

■ Requirement 2a1) also dictates design. A front-end processor may be an excellent way to handle network control and flow, but that is for the designer to determine. The developer may want a front-end processor in the product line for business reasons; the network designer may want such a box, too. In either case, a separate analysis and justification process is probably warranted before investing in such a potentially expensive box.[8]

■ There are so many priority 1 items that the priority scheme offers little flexibility. The priority 3 items are either future needs (like 4c7)), technically infeasible (like 2e), or just nice to have (like 2d). Many will probably be dropped. Priority 2 items should at least influence the system architecture and may be implemented, sometimes at the expense of more difficult priority 1 items. Certain priority 3 items should also be covered in the architecture. This applies to items like 8a1), which would be priority 1 if presently untested customer or government attitudes toward security become mandated requirements. Since it is an integral part of system architecture it must be considered now if ever.

■ Requirement 3c3) asks for priority between users. Priority is easy to handle when all priorities are authorized by one controller. Who is the controller who will assign priorities to separate users in a multi-enterprise networking utility (2f)? The designers will have to have more input on what is meant by 3c3).

■ Requirements 1b4) and 4c7) are examples of simply stated requirements that imply the existence of hardware that can do what is requested. Development of such hardware is probably outside the scope of the networking project. The detailed requirements statement will have to name the specific devices that are intended:

    1. Which terminals are intelligent enough to store the addresses of other end users?

---

8. Sequential decisions in large organizations contribute to the long lead time for systems implementation. In the example, a networking solution that requires a front-end processor may face a delay in the design stage while the processor is justified, authorized, and designed. Later, there may be delays in testing due to unavailability of the finished processor. The degree of economic and technical risk a company is willing to take determines whether the sequential activities will be overlapped.

2. Which devices handle photographic half-tone images? How fast are they?

8a1), on the other hand, is specific because a reference to a standard is provided to show what type of device is meant.

■ The modes of use in 4c can interfere with system performance, depending on the mix of message traffic competing for network resources. As design proceeds it will be necessary to give the network manager the ability to tune system flow to fit the mix according to local installation rules. This will expose an omission in 3c regarding the need for priorities among modes of use to supplement user priority.

■ Diversity, class 5, is redundant with classes 1, 2, 4, and 12. If the analysts do not see that the class 5 requirements can be better handled within the detailed statements of other classes, there may be a lack of understanding among the analysts.

■ Items 7c and 8 may conflict. Some security approaches refuse to tell a user why a connection failed. Snoopers are known to have used such feedback to break the security algorithm.

■ Class 10 requirements may so load the system as to interfere with performance.

■ Requirement 12c deals with situations such as upgrading a database manager, call it DBMS1, to a new version NAM. If DBMS1 is installed on four hosts that talk to each other, it is required that NAM be installable on one host and talk to DBMS1 on the other three. The conversion to NAM would proceed one machine at a time. The networking design should not prevent this. Yet, there is nothing the network designer can do to guarantee that the DB developer will give NAM the ability to talk to DBMS1.

None of these examples will necessarily be evident to the analysts at first. For that reason, the requirements document produced by the analysts is only a baseline—the *Design Requirements Baseline*. Change control procedures permit flaws to be corrected, omissions to be analyzed, misunderstandings to be clarified, and the results of tradeoff decisions to be formalized. Approved change requests become part of the requirements document that retains its value throughout the project as a guide to design and as the authoritative basis for system and acceptance tests. By allowing for future changes, it becomes feasible to give the analysts free rein to include all the requirements they believe to be justified in the initial requirements statement. Establishing requirements, then, becomes a process of defining what it takes to meet an objective, evaluating alternative approaches, discarding unnecessary items, giving preference to items with a favorable economic justification, and compiling the results in the Design Requirements Baseline.

The emphasis in Table 4.4 is on requirements set by the developer of a general purpose program for multiple users. In the completed design requirements baseline there will be requirements for:

- Function
- Performance
- Operational characteristics
- Conversion and migration
- Education and training
- Installation
- Documentation

The developer concentrates on the requirements necessary to make the product succeed. This leads to requirements for ease of migration from the existing systems of likely users. Other migration paths may be given low priority. Educational materials and course outlines, as well as documentation for user personnel, are spelled out in the requirements to the extent necessary. The final package should be the minimum package that meets the project objectives, sells the package to the user, and provides the user with the means to make the package work effectively.

A single-user program system has a similar list of requirements applicable to the user's environment. For instance, a bank planning to distribute data-processing functions to its branches will distinguish between central site functions and branch functions in its requirements statements. Branch functions might be further broken down to distinguish between large, intermediate, and small branches and between branches close to the central site versus those at a distance affecting communications media. Where a general-purpose product vendor will establish communication network interfaces, the individual user must establish both the interfaces and the network configuration in order to estimate system cost. The requirements for database structure and for user input/output formats must all be specific to the bank. Performance requirements obviously must be stated in terms that fit the branch banking operation. Operational requirements must consider bank employee skill levels, operating schedules, and vital records. These requirements will influence the design of the system regarding:

- User-machine interaction
- Availability/reliability
- Backup/recovery

The bank's conversion and education requirements should be tailored to the bank's method of operating and should be laid out to fit a schedule that is consistent with the bank's concept of system stability. The same level of detail with regard to the bank's people, its hardware and software, its buildings, its budget, and its operating deadlines will be reflected in the installation and documentation requirements.

Fortunate users will find that their very specific requirements are a perfect subset of some vendor offering. They can use the commercial product and save development expense and time, but they still have to manage the steps necessary to introduce, install, and cut over to the new product. Most users will have some essential requirements that no commercial offering can handle; i.e., the most applicable commercial product will require tailoring to fit local needs. These users must first make a tradeoff decision whether to acquire and build on a commercial offering or to do the whole system from scratch. The economic benefits of using a fully supported commercial system may lead to some compromises in the user's requirements. Whichever way the tradeoff decision falls, the user has a program development project to manage.

4.2 TRADEOFF STUDIES

The networking analysts would have liked to specify separate requirements for a Type 2 networking product line and a Type 3 networking product line. The total cost of two endeavors was so much higher than N had in mind that the analysts settled for a single requirement that could be met with a Type 3 solution. They made a tradeoff decision. Knowing they could not have both Type 2 and Type 3, they chose Type 3 because it was a better response to the objectives of networking.

Many decisions involve the choice of one solution from a set of feasible solutions when multiple solutions are not simultaneously achievable. When the feasible solutions are otherwise equal, the best one is the least expensive one. In the more common case when the feasible solutions offer different functions, performance, or quality, a *tradeoff decision* selects the best choice as the solution that offers the best compromise between system capabilities and resource availability. The choice of only one solution sacrifices the features offered by other solutions. You choose A at the expense of B. The tradeoff involves the merits of A compared to the merits of B. The decision must take into account the features of each component, its cost, and its effect on the system in the absence of the other component. It does not make sense to tradeoff a system function against its prerequisite function; one is useless without the other. Small dependencies between functions can be eliminated, however, by making the remaining component self-sufficient at extra cost. Every tradeoff decision, then, involves pluses and minuses for each feasible solution.

The basis for a tradeoff decision is the objective to be met. In a classical example of elementary linear programming, nuts of various types are to be mixed to maximize the seller's profit. Profit is the seller's objective. Given the cost of each type of nut, the profit on plain peanuts, cashews, hazels, as well as various mixed nut packages, and the amount of each type of nut available, a linear program calculates an optimum solution. Requirements tradeoffs are not so neat. All the inputs are either subjective judgments or approximations generated by modeling and simulation. The objective is also vague—"maximize customer satisfaction." Nevertheless, the normal way to make tradeoffs in the software process is to assign numbers to all key factors and calculate a quantitative figure or merit for each of the alternatives.

For the networking example, the objective that "any end user can talk to any other" translates for tradeoff studies to "create a business opportunity that will maximize revenue and profit for N by permitting any end user to talk to any other." The analysis produced sales estimates by product for various types of customers. The sales estimates can be converted to revenue by estimating the price of each product. Relative profit can be found by subtracting an estimate of project cost from revenue. Table 4.6 shows the possible lifetime revenues for each potential solution and for the unachievable situation where both solutions are offered.

Given the cost of $60 million for Type 2, $200 million for Type 3, and $240 million for both, the best business choice is clearly the Type 3 networking solution. In fact, it is preferable to doing both solutions even if resources were available. Of course, in this illustration the numbers are chosen to make the answer obvious. In practical situations, the choice is not as easy. In particular, if the two alternatives differ by only 10 to 20 percent, you cannot choose between them. When that happens, additional evaluation criteria must be found. Uncertainty may still remain, in which case it is advisable to start designing for both alternatives. As more system information is developed, one approach will become clearly more desirable than the other or it will become evident that either one will do. The final decision should be made before leaving the system design stage to avoid unnecessary expense. There are many examples of large risky hardware projects—mostly aerospace and weapons systems—where competitive alternatives have been carried in parallel through prototype development. This is uncommon in software projects because the cost of a prototype is large compared to the cost of the final product. Occasionally, two similar software projects run in parallel, but this is usually due to actual competition; that is, two independent project managers work on similar programs hoping that theirs will "win" acceptance. If the two competing managers had a common superior, it is unlikely that both projects would proceed beyond the system design stage.

TABLE 4.6.   NETWORKING REVENUE—PRODUCT LIFETIME

revenue in millions

Type	One location	Two locations	More than two locations
A	—	80	80
B	—	149	110
C	—	19	19
D	—	5	2

a. Type 2 Networking   Total   464

	One location	Two locations	More than two locations
A	—	432	896
B	—	660	1200
C	—	104	224
D	—	20	22

b. Type 3 Networking   Total   3558

	One location	Two locations	More than two locations
A	—	307	981
B	—	389	1226
C	—	65	235
D	—	13	22

c. Type 2 and Type 3 Networking   Total   3238

Assumptions used to construct this table:

- Average product life: 80 months
- 3,000 companies out of 10,000 prospects would buy a Type 3 (N) solution.
  1,000 would buy a Type 2 solution.
  3,500 would buy one solution if both were available.

Type 2	"2-location" customers	"More than 2" customers	Revenue per month per system
A (very large)	125	125	$8,000
B (large)	310	230	6,000
C (medium)	60	60	4,000
D (small)	60	30	1,000

- Type 3

A	270	560	$20,000
B	550	1000	15,000
C	130	280	10,000
D	100	110	2,500

- Both

	Type 2/3	Type 2/3	Type 2/3
A	230/100	70/585	$8,000/20,000
B	560/100	230/930	6,000/15,000
C	115/ 35	60/270	4,000/10,000
D	95/ 25	35/ 95	1,000/2,500

The data are imaginary, but the relations between entries are representative of real forecasting situations.

4.2.1 System Tradeoffs

The decision to build a Type 3 networking system for economic reasons is a system tradeoff affecting all subsequent activity. Hardware and software tradeoffs are subsystem decisions. Since subsystem decisions satisfy local objectives they may conflict with the objectives of other subsystems and the overall system. Ideally, system tradeoff decisions should precede subsystem decisions. In practice, tradeoffs are made in waves. Major system tradeoffs affecting policies and long-term commitments are made first. Then subsystem tradeoffs proceed in a top-down manner. Each decision can create a conflict with prior decisions. The conflicts flow back up the hierarchy to be resolved by a revised decision at some higher level. The change then flows down and the process continues until a mutually compatible set of decisions has been made.

Within the very broad guidelines of the system objectives, system tradeoffs are made to optimize the contribution each subsystem makes to the total system. The governing factors tend to be budget, schedule, constraints due to existing system components, compatibility, and the environment the completed system will operate in.

Recall that the development life cycle is drawn as a convex curve. Think of it as a pile of sand. If you try to shorten the delivery schedule by pushing from the right, the pile gets higher. You have traded time for cost. And, as shown in Chapter 3, if you squeeze too much, the pile gets so high it becomes unstable. A reverse tradeoff corresponds to shoveling sand off the top and throwing it out to the right; resources are thus traded for a longer schedule. A tradeoff between advanced techniques and skill mix is possible where resource cost is cut by substituting a small number of technology specialists for a larger number of generalists or by using a tool that increases productivity. This approach might be likened to consolidating the sandpile by pouring water on it and tamping it down. The fourth type of tradeoff consists of removing some of the sand and trucking it away altogether; i.e., doing less work. This amounts to cutting out some of the job requirements. It reduces resource requirements and preserves the schedule. Other tradeoffs substitute existing commercial packages for new developments or substitute money for in-house resources by hiring subcontractors.

The subsystems of concern in a system tradeoff are big. Elimination of a whole subsystem may be unnecessary. A little trimming here or there may suffice. Two approaches to trimming constitute partial tradeoff decisions.

- The *implicit approach* spreads the impact of the fund shortage to all subsystems. Given costs totaling $10M and a budget of $8M, upper management can arbitrarily allocate 80 percent of the requested funds to each subsystem manager with instructions to do the job with that much money. This approach forces every subsystem manager to cut back somewhere. Sometimes, economies are found that permit all requirements to be satisfied. At other times, one or more of the subsystems may be starved for funds leading to potential system failure or cost overruns or loss of the subsystem. The trouble with this approach is that the tradeoff decisions are made at a low level and may be invisible to upper management until a crisis occurs. The decisions of upper management are then dictated by the circumstances and are usually costly for the system. It should also be clear that the arbitrary squeeze has the worst impact on the best performers. That is, all the managers who submitted inflated budgets can absorb the 20 percent cut simply by tightening up their plan. The efficient managers who had no fat in their budgets may be unable to do their assigned work with less money.

■ The *explicit approach* reduces cost by deleting requirements or substituting cheaper solutions at the subsystem level. Given the same 10:8 cost problem, each subsystem manager is asked to propose changes that will reduce his or her subsystem cost by 20 percent or more (usually more, say, 30 percent). The proposals are then evaluated and a set selected that generates the needed 20 percent savings. The advantage of this approach is that the system definition is clear throughout. There are no surprises due to hidden decisions made as the project proceeds. There are added advantages in the type of tradeoff encouraged by this approach. Subsystem managers tend to delete items that could be added to a later release; they then protect the system by designing an interface for the future addition. They also tend to substitute less costly implementations, particularly when the value of the alternatives is fuzzy. As an example, in networking an original plan to analyze network traffic in order to balance traffic flows and prevent messages from getting trapped in loops may be scrapped in favor of a plan that ignores flow control. The second plan may be much cheaper and, although it will not perform as well as the first, it may be perfectly acceptable in lightly loaded networks. Some customers may never have a flow control problem. Those that do may be able to solve it by increasing the network hardware capacity. In the future, flow control may become a general problem. At that time the more sophisticated implementation could be released, using funds generated by the base networking system.

The possibility of substituting extra network capacity for software flow control illustrates a hardware/software tradeoff. This very common type of tradeoff moves function out of one subsystem into another. In the exchange, an objective is realized. For example, a computer manufacturer may find it easier to recover the cost of a function by incorporating it in hardware. On the other hand, the manufacturer may decide to strip out as much as possible from the hardware to lower the entry price for customers with simple needs. All the sophisticated functions can then be packaged into software modules and only the people who use a function would pay for it.

Sometimes a novel feature is put into the hardware subsystem to improve the protection of the owner's proprietary rights. At other times, a function is frozen in hardware to improve reliability. Functions that are likely to be modified end up in software. Functions that are hard to define often end up as manual procedures in the human operator subsystem.

4.2.2 Hardware Tradeoffs

The type of hardware tradeoff most familiar to experienced programmers is the "space/time" tradeoff. The requirement for the tradeoff arose because of the relatively high cost of hardware in early dp systems. To limit hardware expense, programmers were asked to squeeze their programs into the minimum core storage space. The consequence of this approach was that the program execution time would increase (due to multiple pass programs on machines with no auxiliary storage or due to access time when auxiliary storage was available). The tradeoff decision was made to select the right balance between storage hardware and program design to meet the user's response time requirements. As hardware technology improved, hardware costs came down and the space/time tradeoff had diminishing importance. Old habits live on, however. Project managers took it for granted that they should economize on storage. The effect of this approach was to drive up the cost of many large program systems. As Boehm [18] reported in 1973, the effort to find techniques for fitting a large program into a saturated machine can multiply total system cost by as much as eight times.

Conditions became favorable in the early 1970s to support a change in attitudes. Hardware prices, which had been improving every year, began to reach low enough levels that hardware no longer dominated system decisions. At the same time, virtual operating systems and virtual storage had the effect of giving the programmers as much "capacity" as they wanted. As a result, many people stopped worrying about the space/time tradeoff. That was a mistake. Although the cost factors had changed for the better, new, troublesome performance factors arose. The dimensions of the program space available to each programmer were almost unlimited, but the performance of the program depended on the size of real memory relative to the total size of the working set of all active programs. Compounding this problem was the discovery that interactive on-line systems generated far more computer work than had been expected. The most direct solution to the problem was to get more hardware. Space was now less expensive so the space/time tradeoff for a virtual system would initially favor more memory. This decision reduced paging and reduced the number of operating system instructions executed. If response time was still not good enough, a faster compatible processor would be installed. But in the complex environment of a virtual system with multiprogrammed interactive subsystems, a faster processor was not always the answer—response time could be limited by disk channels or communications line speed. Simple answers to space/time questions were no longer sufficient. Multiple tradeoffs between subsystems were necessary to remove a bottleneck which, when removed, would create a bottleneck somewhere else, etc. Tradeoffs of this complexity can only be made intelligently during or after system design.

One hardware tradeoff that should always be deferred as long as possible is computer selection. It is preferable to have a firm system design in hand when ordering hardware; otherwise, the actual design may be unwisely constrained by the hardware [19]. Obviously, it is not always possible to defer computer selection. When a new program system is to be added to existing hardware, compliance with the constraints must be a requirement. Also, when a major long lead-time activity is planned—such as the development of a new product line by a manufacturer—the architecture of the planned hardware must be treated as given. A third case occurs when a system is planned for a well-defined application area—say, citizen protection where small computers in police cars will give better emergency response capability—and a huge quantity discount is available if a five-year supply of machines is ordered now. At these times, the hardware decisions are based on subjective judgments regarding compatibility, MIPS, storage capacities, channels, devices, existing software support, maintenance support, vendor history, etc.

When two or more off-the-shelf computers could fit the job objectives, a tradeoff among these subjective characteristics must be made. Various methods are available to make such a tradeoff.

For example, consider the following operational requirement: "Develop a commercially viable family of computers for the sensor-based market that can be produced within three years. Appropriate software support is to be provided." Typical figures of merit for the proposed system might cover:

- Performance—The capacity of the system for handling the required inputs and producing the required outputs at the appropriate rate.
- Deliverability—The ability to produce, test, and deliver the whole system on schedule.
- Implementation risk—The ability to build all the components to perform as required.
- Growth potential—The ability to handle an increase in workload or a reduction in system response time.
- Development cost—The estimated cost to build and install the system, including contingencies for changes and technical risks.

- Customer support—The effort required to train the customer to use and maintain the system properly.
- Maintenance cost—The cost of keeping the system operable in the light of system reliability and repair/replace policy.

Other aspects of the system can also be selected for analysis. In general, it is sufficient to select the important aspects—those that carry weight in a management decision regarding the system worth.

In this example, there are probably industry source materials that give quantitative data on sensor characteristics (signal levels, data rates, coding schemes) and response time requirements. A formula might be selected to express, say, the performance of the system in terms of computer speed (*PI*), I/O bit rate, and the number of separate sensors that can be serviced by one computer. *PI* is modeled as

$$PI = \log\left(\frac{a \cdot b \cdot c \cdot d}{h}\right)$$

where

a = maximum internal storage in words
b = word size in bytes
c = number of bytes addressed in an ADD instruction
d = number of instructions in the machine repertoire
h = fastest time to fetch and completely execute one ADD instruction.

Using this formula for all hardware alternatives produces a relative performance measure based on easily determined data. The index is a reasonable measure of "compute" performance when there is no significant file handling.[9] Parameters a, b, c describe the depth and breadth of the machine with respect to the precision of data, the size of problems, and the length of instruction sequences. Parameter h describes built-in performance features such as instruction overlap. Parameter d represents the ability of a programmer to find an optimum instruction sequence for a given problem; i.e., the more instructions there are the more opportunities exist for optimization. The model is used for both binary and decimal machines:

---

9. This formula is an example only. It is based on a more elaborate formula used successfully by the author to compare processors of all manufacturers from 1955 to 1971. The purpose of this unpublished work was to explain "price/performance" as a measure of user trends; i.e., why did users buy machines with similar ADD times but widely different prices? (See Exercise 6 at the end of this chapter.) A different formula based on main memory size, direct access storage capacity, and date of system introduction is discussed by Cale et al. [20]. Date of introduction is a surrogate for the state-of-the-art and, hence, for the improvement in architecture and component speeds that are represented by explicit factors in *PI*.

	a	*b*	*c*	*d*	*h*	*PI*
Binary parallel machine A	131	4	4	90	2	4.97
Decimal serial machine B	65	1	,4	140	20	3.26
Binary parallel machine C	262	8	8	90	2	5.88
Decimal serial machine D	524	1	4	140	4	4.86

Taking the logarithm reduces *PI* to a convenient range. In interpreting *PI*, a difference of 1.0 between two machines means that one is ten times more "powerful" for straight computing than the other. Thus machine B is well behind the others as can be expected because of its slow add time and small memory. Looking at machine D, though, it appears that a decimal serial machine can be competitive with machine A if the price is right. Machine C shows the wide range of performance that can be achieved by varying storage capacity and word size. Of course the sensor-based application may not be able to use words longer than four bytes since its data precision is limited. Thus the interpretation of the formula must take into account all known characteristics of the problem. Having normalized the *PI* calculation, the model builder can add in the effects of I/O rates and sensor capacity to come up with the composite model:

Figure of merit $= e \cdot k \cdot PI$

where

e = I/O bit rate
k = number of sensors that can be attached.

Similar models could be devised for maintenance cost (based on statistical failure rates, repair times, repair costs), development cost (based on component counts, instruction counts, average unit cost of each component type, etc.), and other key aspects of the system.

Now the models are exercised to produce cost, time, and performance envelopes characterizing each alternative over a range of conditions. A tradeoff analysis is performed on the results to select the one alternative that best satisfies the effectiveness measures. If no single alternative is best, an arbitrary selection can be made. Or, where the budget will permit, two or three candidates can be carried forward through additional analysis until one emerges the winner. The key to the tradeoff process is establishing a measure of effectiveness that is highest for the system that fulfills the most important objectives of the system. Thus, if Table 4.7 lists the values and the figures of merit associated with the sensor-based system (after dropping machine B), it is clear that alternative C is a better choice for this requirement than A or D. Referring back to the discussion of change, however, there is no guarantee that the values set during project definition will not change in the judgment of executive management before the system is complete. Once an approach has been selected, it is relatively difficult to modify

TABLE 4.7. SELECTION BY WEIGHTED FIGURE OF MERIT

Aspect	Value	Approach A Raw merit	Approach A Weighted	Approach C Raw merit	Approach C Weighted	Approach D Raw merit	Approach D Weighted
Performance	25	1.0	25	3.0	75	3.0	75
Deliverability	20	2.0	40	1.0	20	1.0	20
*Implementation Risk	5	10.0	50	5.0	25	7.0	35
Growth Potential	15	1.0	15	2.0	30	1.0	15
*Development Cost	10	5.0	50	4.0	40	3.0	30
Customer Support	18	1.0	18	3.0	54	2.0	36
*Cost of Maintenance	7	1.0	7	4.0	28	6.0	42
Totals	100	18.0	205	22.0	272	23.0	253

*Merit is inverse of cost or risk.

it later to fit a different set of values. While it can be modified to do a different job, the odds are that it will appear to do it more expensively than necessary if it is measured against any set of values other than the one it was selected to meet. The effect of changing values is easily seen using the same figures of merit in Table 4.7. Suppose the most important aspect of the sensor-based system is not to provide outstanding performance for all applications but to get a working system on the market as soon as possible. This objective might lead to a new set of values:

Performance	10	} Trade performance for early delivery.
Deliverability	35	
Risk	13	} Trade some of the installation support
Growth	15	that ensures full use of all system func-
Development Cost	10	} tions for high confidence that the job
Customer Support	10	can be done as planned.
Maintenance Cost	7	

The weighted totals for the three approaches are:

A = 292   C = 258   D = 263

and approach A now looks best.

A study by a joint Army/Navy committee [21] looked at nine different machines to select a candidate for a common architecture for military use. Key criteria were the need for efficient real-time interrupt handling, virtual memory, program protection, floating point arithmetic, and several other architectural features. Six of the machines lacked some of these features and were eliminated in Step 1 of a four-step selection procedure:

Step 1   Test against absolute criteria—pass or fail

Step 2   Measure performance and capability against standard benchmarks—rank by results

Step 3   Evaluate support against a standard and estimate cost of bringing up to standard—rank by cost

Step 4   Calculate system life cycle cost based on previous results—rank by quantitative score

Very simple benchmarks were used consisting of twelve small, kernel programs that were written and run under controlled conditions. The process was not trivial since great care was required to get comparable results by expressing the various factors in common units; a simulator was actually used to obtain the benchmark statistics. The results permitted rankings to be made of storage requirements, memory activity, and processor activity in each machine averaged over a number of sample test cases. At the end of Step 2, the three candidate machines each had a single figure of merit. Step 3 then determined whether each candidate had the basic support (twenty-eight tools including compilers, debugging aids, database manager, etc.) required for military use. If any support item was missing, an estimate was made of the cost of obtaining it. The total cost of support became a second figure of merit for each candidate. The ranks in Step 3 were different from those in Step 2. Step 4 considered what a typical military project would cost using each candidate. The final ranking was able to point to the architecture of one of the candidates as the best because it had the highest quantitative score overall. (Unfortunately, all three finalists were within 15 percent of the mean score. This fact plus the judgments used in selecting the factors opened the study to criticism and provoked a few letters to the editor of *DATAMATION* after the report was published [22]. Furthermore, some people thought the tests had selected a standard military *computer* when, in fact, the tests merely recommended a standard *architecture*.) Under the conditions of uncertainty faced by the committee, their methodology was appropriate. Their objective was to identify an architecture for common use. That they did. In the process, they eliminated some candidates for cause and used a weighting system to compare the others. They used the available data in a reasonable manner and actually went much farther than most project managers would to arrive at a rational conclusion.[10]

---

10. Subsequently, the U.S. Department of Defense adopted a set of standard computer architectures for various operational requirements [23]:
- MIL-STD-1750 (1979)—Air Force avionics applications and other 16-bit requirements.
- MIL-STD-1862 (1980)—Army military computer family and Air Force 32-bit requirements.
- AN/UYK-43 (1980)—Navy large 32-bit shipboard computers (successor to AN/UYK-7 (1970)).
- AN/UYK-44 (1980)—Navy shipboard 16-bit minicomputer (successor to AN/UYK-20 (1973)).
- AN/UYS-1 (1981)—Navy advanced signal processor.

The average computer user has only a general idea of the workload characteristics of his or her environment. In this case, a full-scale benchmark may be necessary for computer selection. It would consist of a representative sample of actual current workload to be run either on the actual candidate machines or on valid models of the machines. The result of the benchmark is a performance figure relevant to the sample run. By relating the performance to the price of the configuration used, a so-called "price/performance" number can be assigned to each type of hardware evaluated. The price/performance so obtained applies only to the benchmark. Since the implementation of the benchmark on various machines may have been more or less efficient, the price/performance rating includes a variable factor due to the effectiveness of the benchmark team (either as expert programmers or as expert salespeople). Furthermore, the results can be extrapolated only to similar future workloads. These limitations suggest that benchmarks are not worth a great deal of money. A thorough evaluation of system features by a good analyst, accompanied by a few measurement runs to verify assumptions may be more useful and less costly than a full-scale benchmark.

The types of hardware data that are most likely to affect system performance are:

- Arithmetic speed—Stated in terms of add time or, preferably, average execution time for an instruction mix (raw speed)

- Storage size—Number of digits or bytes of real memory available (affects paging and references to external storage)

- Arithmetic word size—Number of digits or bytes in the operand of an arithmetic instruction (affects number of instructions to be executed)

- Instruction repertoire—Number of valid instructions available (also affects number of instructions required for a computation)

- Bandwidth—Number of bits per microsecond the computer can handle, usually measured by the product of the fastest storage (or cache) cycle and the width in bits of the main data transfer bus (sets limit on total activity; i.e., a 10 megabit I/O channel will overload a 6 megabit bandwidth CPU, so will ten 1 megabit I/O channels running simultaneously)

- Disk transfer rate—Number of bits per microsecond available from fastest disk device (affects average delay due to disk references)

- Channels—Number of simultaneously operative channels (affects maximum rate of external reference)

- Auxiliary storage capacity per disk—Number of bits in the largest disk (affects search time and ability to handle any size program or data set)

- Interrupt mechanism—Existence of interrupt mechanism and time required to service preemptive interrupt (affects multiprogram performance)
- Lock mechanism—Existence of lock mechanisms and time required to service resource locks (affects multiprocessor performance)
- Device addresses—Number of devices than can be attached to computer (affects network configuration)
- Modem and line—Maximum speed supported and data link control standard (affects network response time)
- Device storage capacity—Buffer size and memory size (affects functions that can be offloaded from host and determines time required to service device)
- Device intelligence—Programmability or built-in program function (affects offloading).

Many other factors are relevant. Hardware support for paging, microcoded routines for array processing, look ahead features for staging memory transfers, or prepositioning access arms are all important, albeit less easy to quantify for comparison purposes. Important in another sense are hardware maintenance features and vendor maintenance history, availability of backup features such as switches and battery-powered memory dumps, compatibility with an existing machine, deliverability, etc.

A review of each of these factors with respect to the objectives of a project will support the selection of the hardware mix that best satisfies the important system requirements, usually at the expense of less critical items. Still, the project manager will have little idea how the hardware will actually perform because the selection technique has so far omitted software considerations. Most machines are completely redefined by their software; therefore, it is essential to decide what software environment is required.

4.2.3 Software Tradeoffs

Because software masks hardware function, it is possible to select hardware that is inherently right for a job only to find that it is unsatisfactory in operation. Most often, the trouble is the consequence of poor judgment in the tradeoff between general purpose and special purpose software. General purpose software is built to satisfy the largest set of user requirements and may sacrifice performance. Special purpose software aims at a narrow user set and may sacrifice growth capability and other factors. The economics of maintaining complex special purpose software tend to be unfavorable because of the narrow user base. Because of this, project managers prefer general purpose solutions. It should be taken for granted that programming will be done in a standard, vendor-supported high-level language, that a vendor's operating system will be used, and that commercially available database managers and utilities will be obtained. An obvious exception occurs when the purpose of the project is to create software for a new machine and no suitable program exists. Even in this case, high-level language and commercial software can be used to support development of the specialized products.

4.2.3.1 Language

The selection of source language is discussed in [24]. There, a number of criteria identified by Sammet [25] are given with the intent that each be weighted. The weighted average is a figure of merit for the language. Five types of criteria are given: technical factors, human factors, efficiency, compatibility, and cost. An individual will score the criteria of each type according to personal preference. A project manager will score them differently. The criteria that tend to dominate language selection for team projects are those that improve quality and reduce cost. Pass/fail criteria include the requirement for structured programming syntactic elements, interactive capability, history of support, and expectation of future support. Beyond these tests, the major factors to be evaluated are related to how many of the project team know the language, how easy it is to learn and use, and how good its compilers are with respect to debugging and transportability across machine types. These points do not emphasize efficiency; an implicit tradeoff is made that gives a low weight to code optimization. For the majority of application programs, this tradeoff is acceptable because most compilers produce good code to start with and because the application code often represents less than half the problem execution time anyway—the rest being used by the operating system. On the other hand, for many real time projects and for many operating system developments, compiler output is not efficient enough to meet performance requirements. In such projects, explicit tradeoff decisions must be made such as:

- Use assembly language instead of high-level language at the expense of coding productivity and potential loss of quality and structured programming benefits.
- Use a high-level language for initial code development, then hand-tune object code at the expense of productivity, quality, and documentation accuracy.
- Develop an optimizing compiler specifically for the project at the expense of increased cost and potential schedule delay.
- Relax performance requirements (from, say, 95 percent of all responses within two seconds to 90 percent) at the expense of decreased user satisfaction.

Whichever basis for tradeoff applies to the project, the decision will impact the organization for several years.

4.2.3.2 Operating system

Operating systems are evaluated in terms of the services they offer, their scheduling mechanisms, their path lengths, and their storage requirements. Whether selecting an OS as the basis for an application system or setting requirements for the construction of a new OS, the same types of tradeoffs apply. The important criteria vary from one OS to another according to its objectives. For example:

■ Microprocessors may be used primarily for single, special functions programmed by the user. In this case, the OS may be a very basic control program that permits hardware initialization, program loading, device control, signal generation, and limited diagnosis.

■ Small processors used for small business data processing or machine tool control may include the basics plus some simple I/O routines, an assembler or compiler for a high-level language subset, a simple scheduler, an interrupt handler, some standard application programs, and a package of utilities. The user is expected to do little or no programming in the small business application where canned programs are available. The user is expected to do a great deal of programming at the assembly language level in the machine tool application. Numerous "hooks" are provided for the latter situation so the user can modify the OS.

■ Large, general purpose processors supporting many applications and many users require operating systems that minimize user concern with the computer. The OS with general purpose, interactive tools can be both an executive program and a development support system. Many services are included in a large OS. Multiple versions of each service are also provided such as compilers for many languages, disk access methods for various storage structures, communications access methods with and without queuing, etc. Comprehensive support for multiprogramming batch and interactive users is provided. With so many features, an OS is exposed to undesirable component interactions. So even more functions are added to allocate resources efficiently and to protect users from each other or from system errors.

■ Large, special purpose systems such as airline reservations systems place a higher value on response time than on development support. Airline project managers want as many services as they can get, but they do not want them badly enough to affect transaction volume or response.

If the same list of objectives were presented to managers of development for four different computer environments:

■ The microprocessor manager would delete all requirements that were not essential to making the micro run.

■ The small processor manager would delete as many redundant requirements as possible (i.e., one compiler instead of four) and as many nonessentials as the user representatives will agree to. At the same time, the manager will ensure that interfaces are provided to permit the user to add anything he or she wants. To help the small business user, the developer may provide an ease-of-use interface with self-teaching, conversational features.

■ The large, general-purpose processor manager will attempt to provide all requirements, eliminating only those that fall below the budget cutoff line and those that conflict with a more important item. However, only high-level user interfaces may be offered so as to prevent users from tinkering with the OS itself.

■ The large, special-purpose system manager will assume that a general-purpose processor is available (perhaps on a backup machine) and will eliminate every requirement that does not support the special purpose mission; however, the individual will develop an interface to facilitate communication between the special OS and its general-purpose neighbor.

The main difficulties in OS planning are due to the complexity of the product. It is not always possible to know whether or not two requirements conflict. Models built by the system designers will eventually detect conflicts. This leads to a greater need for iterative analysis and design in the OS area than in simpler projects.

Two characteristic tradeoffs in programming systems occur repeatedly in general-purpose OS planning. One deals with system growth capability and the other with execution time. System growth capability implies that a design permit growth and, moreover, anticipate growth by incorporating architectural features of the ultimate system in the base. Execution time implies that the user be given the opportunity to get at raw machine speed when appropriate. Some examples will show the possible situations that arise;

■ A requirement of networking is that the addition of new nodes be permitted at any time. To do this, the original system must have a standard network architecture that permits expansion of address tables, dynamic modification of network configuration, and connection of future new products. This will result in extra code to produce standard headers in conflict with a requirement for minimizing path length and storage.

■ A requirement for future multiprocessing may have the current effect of reducing MIPS because extra overhead is incurred by checking to see if there is multiprocessor resource contention, even when there is only one processor.

■ A requirement for device-independent code may increase the I/O path lengths to translate from symbolic device names to actual device IDs, even when the user knows the device ID.

■ A requirement for queued access to communications may duplicate the queuing in a user's program.

The nature of the tradeoffs arising from these situations is to decide whether it is more important to provide one solution for all users or to provide many user options. A single solution is sometimes cheaper, but it will be unsatisfactory to some subset of users. Often the dissatisfied users are experienced and sophisticated. The installations are finely tuned and their requirements relatively precise. They are also equipped to modify the general-purpose program to their own needs. They can bypass or eliminate unused code and put in their own high-speed routines or add their own special functions. Having done this, though, they create an added maintenance burden for themselves and the developer.

A design that contains many selectable options permits the user to generate a system to meet his or her needs. The cost of the multiple options, when designed in at the start, can often be competitive with one, more difficult general-purpose solution. A second approach requires a hierarchical design that permits the user to work at any level of the hierarchy. This approach, which is consistent with the design concepts of many OS builders, would, for instance, have READ/WRITE routines to move bytes to and from an I/O device. At a higher level, a SEND/RECEIVE routine would set up whole records with appropriate headers before issuing the READ/WRITE command. SEND/RECEIVE could in turn be part of a GET/PUT which handles record sequencing and queuing. Then, instead of telling the user that GET/PUT commands must be issued, it is possible to tell him or her how (and when) to use the lower-level commands as well. The extra flexibility provided by these methods increases the number of system elements to be managed. When the user takes advantage of the flexibility, there will be additional management problems in education, maintenance, and field support. Such problems can be reduced by restricting access to low-level interfaces to "authorized" users.

4.2.3.3 Quality characteristics

Boehm et al., reporting on studies performed at TRW [26], define a number of factors that affect *software quality*. Quality, in its broadest sense, includes everything that contributes to successful use of a software system. There are relationships among quality characteristics. The relationships form a tree (Fig. 4.10), showing which characteristics are prerequisites of others. The most fundamental characteristics are the ones that are easiest to quantify and measure; therefore, they can be stated as unambiguous requirements. There is a definite cost benefit in having testable quality requirements; namely, quality control eliminates errors early in the project when the cost of fixing errors is low.

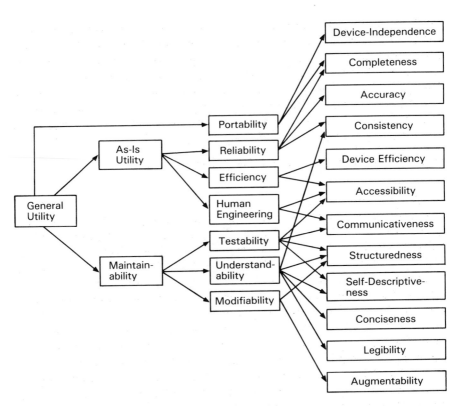

Fig. 4.10   Software quality characteristics tree.
B. W. Boehm et al., *Characteristics of Software Quality* (Amsterdam and New York: North-Holland, 1978).

The quality characteristics defined by Boehm et al. are:

- *Accessibility:*   Accessible code facilitates selective use of its parts. (Examples: variable dimensioned arrays or symbolic names for constants.)

- *Accuracy:*   Accurate outputs are sufficiently precise to satisfy their intended use.

- *Augmentability:*   Code is augmentable to the extent that it can easily accommodate expansion in component computational functions or data storage requirements.

- *Communicativeness:*   Communicative code facilitates the specification of inputs and provides outputs whose form and content are easy to assimilate and are useful.

■   *Completeness:*   Code is complete when all its parts are present and each part is fully developed. This implies that external references are available and required functions are coded and present as designed, etc. Completeness implies self-containability and robustness.

■   *Conciseness:*   Concise code contains no excessive information. This implies that programs are not excessively fragmented into modules, overlays, functions, and subroutines nor that the same sequence of code is repeated in numerous places, rather than defining a subroutine or macro; etc.

■   *Consistency:*   Internal consistency implies uniform notation, terminology, and symbology within the code; external consistency means that the content is traceable to the requirements.

■   *Device-Independence:*   Device-independent code can be executed on computer hardware units other than its current one; i.e., any tape or disk that is available can be used to store a file.

■   *Efficiency:*   Efficient code fulfills its purpose without waste of resources. This implies that choices of source code constructions are made in order to produce the minimum number of words of object code; or that where alternate algorithms are available, those taking the least time are chosen; or that information-packing density in core is high. *Device-efficiency* means that each device or physical resource is used as intended; i.e., its advantageous features are optimized consistent with its role in the system.

■   *Human Engineering:*   Code is human-engineered to the extent that it fulfills its purpose without wasting the users' time and energy, or degrading their morale, or misleading them.

■   *Legibility:*   The function of legible code is easily discerned by reading the code. (Example: complex expressions have mnemonic variable names and parentheses even if unnecessary.)

■   *Maintainability:*   Maintainable code facilitates updating to satisfy new requirements or to correct deficiencies. This implies that comments are used to locate subroutine calls and entry points, visual search for locations of branching statements and their targets is facilitated by special formats, or the program is designed to fit into available resources with plenty of margins to avoid major redesign, etc.

■   *Modifiability:*   Code is modifiable to the extent that it facilitates the incorporation of changes, once the nature of the desired change has been determined. Note the higher level of abstractness of this characteristic as compared with augmentability.

- *Portability:* Portable code can be operated easily and well on computer configurations other than its current one. This implies that special language features, not easily available at other facilities, are not used; or that standard library functions and subroutines are selected for universal applicability, etc. Portability applies to computers of different types; i.e., a portable program can be moved from a Burroughs machine to a comparably sized Univac machine.

- *Reliability:* Reliable code can be expected to perform its intended functions satisfactorily. This implies that the program will compile, load, and execute, and that the program will continue to operate correctly, except for a tolerably small number of instances, while in operational use.

- *Self-Descriptiveness:* Code is self-descriptive to the extent that it contains enough information for a reader to determine or verify its objectives, assumptions, constraints, inputs, outputs, components, and revision status.

- *Structuredness:* Structured code has a definite pattern of organization. This implies that evolution of the program design has proceeded in an orderly and systematic manner and that standard control structures have been followed in coding the program, etc.

- *Testability:* Testable code facilitates the establishment of verification criteria and supports evaluation of its performance. This implies that requirements are matched to specific modules or diagnostic capabilities are provided, etc.

- *Understandability:* Understandable code is clear to the inspector. This implies that variable names or symbols are used consistently, modules of code are self-descriptive, and the control structure is simple or in accordance with a prescribed standard, etc.

- *Useability (As-Is-Utility)* Code is usable to the extent that it is reliable, efficient, and properly human-engineered. This implies that the function performed by the program is useful elsewhere, is robust against human errors (e.g., accepts either integer or real representations for type real variables), or does not require excessive core memory, etc.

The structural relationships found among these characteristics are described by the authors:

> . . . if a program is Maintainable it must necessarily be Understandable and Testable; e.g., a high degree of Maintainability implies a high degree of Understandability and Testability.

We also began to find that there was another level of more primitive concepts below the level of Understandability and Testability. For example, if a program is Understandable, it is also necessarily Structured, Consistent, and Concise (three of the original characteristics) and additionally Legible and Self-Descriptive (two additional characteristics not implied by the three above). We were thus generating some additional characteristics and finding that the entire set of characteristics could be represented in a tree structure, in which each of the more primitive characteristics was a necessary condition for some of the more general characteristics.

The Software Quality Characteristics Tree . . . reflects the actual uses to which evaluation of software quality would be put. In general, when one is acquiring a software package, one is mainly concerned with three questions:

- How well (easily, reliably, efficiently) can I use it as is?

- How easy is it to maintain (understand, modify, and retest)?

- Can I still use it if I change my environment?

Thus, As-is Utility, Maintainability, and Portability are necessary (but not sufficient) conditions for General Utility. As-is Utility requires a program to be Reliable and adequately Efficient and Human-Engineered, but does not require the user to test the program, understand its internal workings, modify it, or try to use it elsewhere. Maintainability requires that the user be able to understand, modify, and test the program, and is aided by good Human-engineering, but does not depend on the program's current Reliability, Efficiency, or Portability (except to the extent the user's computer system is undergoing evolution).

The lower level structure of the characteristics tree provides a set of primitive characteristics which are also strongly differentiated with respect to each other, and which combine into sets of necessary conditions for the intermediate-level characteristics. For example:

- A program which does not initialize its own storage is not Portable even though it may be completely Device-Independent.

- A program using formats such as 12A6 is not Device-Independent, and is therefore not Portable, even though it may be Complete.

- A program which is Device-Independent and Complete but is not Accurate, Consistent, Device-Efficient, Accessible, Communicative, Self-Descriptive, Structured, Concise, Legible, and Augmentable still satisfies the definition for Portability.

The primitives have little overlap, but they may still conflict. Thus a Complete program may be Reliable and Portable, but the fact that it is self-contained and may incorporate all its own function support may interfere with Maintainability and Efficiency. Particularly when the program is an element of a system, it may execute code that duplicates system routines. When a system characteristic is changed, maintenance fixes may be required in both the system routine and the self-contained program. A decision is required to establish the relative importance of each quality characteristic leading up to a tradeoff between conflicting properties. In an example of how to rank quality characteristics, the authors used the objective of reducing project cost by catching errors early. Using a database for error types associated with a previous study [18], the team determined how effective each quality characteristic would be in advancing the point of detection of various types of errors. Altogether there were 224 types of errors. The frequency of each type of error would affect the total expected savings due to improved detection but, ignoring that point, the more error types a quality characteristic corrected, the more important it would be. Table 4.8 shows the ranking of the nine characteristics that improved error detection. The first value shown is the number of error types corrected by a given quality. The second value is a normalized number representing how much earlier in the life cycle an error type would be detected if the given quality had been present. Not surprisingly, the results show that primitives related to Reliability and Testability have the most effect on the objective of the example.

TABLE 4.8.   ERROR CORRECTION EFFECTIVENESS OF QUALITY CHARACTERISTICS

Primitive quality characteristic	Number of error types corrected	Relative life cycle value
Completeness	37	62
Consistency	34	89
Communicativeness	17	35
Structuredness	2	2
Self-Descriptiveness	1	4
Conciseness	1	4
Accuracy	1	2
Accessibility	1	2

B. W. Boehm et al., *Characteristics of Software Quality* (Amsterdam and New York: North-Holland, 1978).

To carry out this study, the primitive characteristics were described in terms of "metrics." These took the form of statements or questions regarding some observable feature of a program that would show whether the program exhibited the specified characteristic. An example for Self-Descriptiveness is shown in Table 4.9. The advantages of the metric approach are that the qualities are well defined and nonoverlapping, and that the metrics form useful checklists for reviewers, analysts, and designers.

TABLE 4.9. PARTIAL CHECKLIST OF METRICS FOR THE QUALITY CHARACTERISTIC: SELF-DESCRIPTIVENESS

Self-Descriptiveness	

Definition: A software product possesses self-descriptiveness to the extent that it contains enough information for a reader to determine or verify its objectives, assumptions, constraints, inputs, outputs, components, and revision status.

Checklist: a. Does each program module contain a header block of commentary that describes: (1) program name, (2) effective date, (3) accuracy requirement, (4) purpose, (5) limitations and restrictions, (6) modification history, (7) inputs and outputs, (8) method, (9) assumptions, (10) error recovery procedures for all foreseeable error exits that exist?

   b. Are decision points and subsequent branching alternatives adequately described?

   c. Are the functions of the modules as well as inputs/outputs adequately defined to allow module testing?

   d. Are comments provided to support selection of specific input values to permit performance of specialized program testing?

   e. Is information provided to support assessment of the impact of a change in other portions of the program?

   f. Is information provided to support identification of program code which must be modified to effect a required change?

   g. Where there is module dependence, is it clearly specified by commentary, program documentation, or inherent program structure?

   h. Are variable names descriptive of the physical or functional property represented?

   i. Do uniquely recognizable functions contain adequate descriptive information (e.g., comments) so that the purpose of each is clear?

   j. Are adequate descriptions provided to allow correlation of variable names with the physical property or entity which they represent?

B. W. Boehm et al., *Characteristics of Software Quality* (Amsterdam and New York: North-Holland, 1978).

4.2.4 Capability Tradeoffs

When it is necessary to eliminate or modify job requirements in order to live with a firm budget and schedule, several new considerations are useful. The requirements statement at this stage contains only essential and justified requirements. Yet something must go. Again, a ranking scheme will arrange the list of requirements in order of importance. Since each requirement has a positive value in terms of importance to the success of the system and return of cost, some additional basis is needed to discriminate among the capabilities requested. The new factors to consider are:

■ The feasibility of producing the capability (including an assessment of the ability of your team to do the job)

■ The degree to which the capability—if built as planned—will satisfy the user

■ The effectiveness of the capability in the environment provided by the rest of the system

To illustrate how some of these factors appear in practice, consider the networking requirement 11b. It says that the system must maintain a constant average message transit time. A specific user requirement included within this general statement is that "the system must support all attached printers at their maximum rated speed." In other words, a 1000 lpm printer should run at 1000 lpm regardless of where it is located in the network. You can imagine ways of doing this by using very fast communications links, or by batching messages in blocks, or by dedicating a path to a device. But these approaches are either not wise or not within the power of the networking developer to enforce. In point of fact, there is no good way to guarantee that the rate at which messages are delivered to a printer will always match the printer's speed. Network configuration and traffic conditions will ultimately determine printer speed. The requirement can be marked "not feasible" and converted to a guideline to remind designers not to create obstacles to printer performance. A similar requirement for a database and data communication (DB/DC) system might call for average response to a trivial message of X seconds. Since average response depends on the way the DB/DC program shares resources with other multiprogrammed applications, it may vary widely. Here, rather than expend a great deal of effort to find a DB/DC "fast path" at the expense of maintainability and security, it may be adequate to convert the requirement to a conditional specification that promises the desired average response only when the DB/DC program is running at the highest available priority on the machine.

User satisfaction is highly subjective. The factor is most often relevant in leading-edge applications where a computer method is to replace a well-established manual method. One case involved the use of a sophisticated computer output plotter for making maps. The plotter had superior precision and line quality so that the maps it drew looked as though they had been drawn by a cartographer—with a few exceptions. The plotter was capable of drawing straight lines between two points and printing a variety of letters and symbols. The straight lines could be made short enough to approximate most curves. However, when it came to lettering, problems arose. A good map has names positioned next to the feature named. When two names fall in the same area, they are either displaced or interleaved to make both legible. Thus, "ST. LOUIS" would be horizontally sited next to the city symbol; "MISSISSIPPI RIVER" would wind its way along the river symbol; "MISSOURI" and "ILLINOIS" would be widely spaced across the state areas; and none of these characters would interfere with each other. A human cartographer has no great trouble doing this because everything completed is always visible. The computer found it virtually impossible. It was not able to align the river and state names suitably in a sequence that would always permit the remaining symbols to be plotted. The maps drawn by the computer were definitely inferior visually and could not compete with good cartographers. On the other hand, by relaxing the requirements for visual aesthetics, the mapping application found a home in applications where fast updates were valuable, as in aeronautical charting and city planning.

A similar application had less ultimate success. For a number of years, a great deal of outstanding scientific attention was paid to mechanical translation. The thought of being able to automate the translation of all the technical literature into all the major languages had great appeal. Demonstrations of the capability to translate had been getting consistently better when, in 1966, a committee of the U.S. National Academy of Sciences assessed the situation. This group, chaired by J. R. Pierce, found that machine translation was not as good as human translation and found no indication that it would ever be as good. Machine output always required post-editing and, in some cases, was misleading in its choice of word meanings. While supporting scientific research in linguistics, text handling, and automatic translation, the committee said: "The motive for doing so cannot sensibly be any foreseeable improvement in practical translation. Perhaps our attitude might be different if there were some pressing need for machine translation, but we find none" [27]. That conclusion was backed up by the interesting information that human translators were not only better, but they were cheaper than the mechanized process of manual data entry, computer processing, and manual editing. Furthermore, there were about 500 interpreters looking for work. Following this study, the requirements for machine translation slowly died because the product was not the best solution to the user need.

The DB/DC example shows that a system with a high-priority real-time application sharing the same machine with a lower-priority DB/DC program may impair the effectiveness of the DB/DC response time. Another type of internal conflict due to a program acting as though it owns the system resources also occurred in a DB/DC program. Here, the DB/DC requirement for fast response led to a program module that maintained an optimally arranged I/O queue. The queue was on disk arranged in the predicted order of events and the disk access arms were repositioned after an access to reduce the time required for the next access. Unfortunately, the DB/DC program shared the disk with other programs. When they made a disk reference, they invalidated all the optimization work done by the I/O module. Thus an intended performance improvement became, in practice, a performance degradation. Even less foresight was used in a sewage plant control application. In this case, sensor devices were placed at key points in a sewage disposal plant. The sensors were connected to a process control computer that monitored plant efficiency and controlled sprays, gates, chemical releases, etc. The cost of this system was to be offset by reducing the plant staff. The only staff members affected were the monitors, one per shift, who checked gauges and adjusted controls every hour or so. The planners failed to notice that their sensors replaced only about two-thirds of the gauges in the plant. The other third still had to be monitored and it would still take one monitor per shift to do it. The process control computer represented a net additional cost to do only part of the job.

These examples all raise the question, "If we provide the function, will our solution be the best solution for the user?" When the answer is no, an otherwise justified function becomes a candidate for elimination or redefinition.

Timing enters into one more class of tradeoff decisions. When a developer plans a product to be offered for a price, he or she expects to establish a cash flow that pays for the original development and finances both maintenance and follow-on developments. Often, the follow-on project is an enhancement of the first offering. Now the question is what functions to put in the separate versions of this product line. The first offering has to be rich enough in function to draw customers. If competition exists, the first version will probably have to at least match the competitive functions. Say it costs $100,000 to produce and support the first version. There are 1000 customers who are expected to buy it for $150 apiece generating $150,000 spread over some period of time. Inflation, the cost of borrowed money, profit for the stockholders, and variations from the forecast of sales may leave $25,000 to invest in version 2. Ideally, you would like each successive product to generate more revenue per dollar spent so the business can grow. Most software products do not work that way, however. The base product will contain all the functions some customers will ever need. Additional functions are mainly of interest to a sophisticated subset of users. Hence, version 2 is unlikely to increase the customer set to 2000. It is more likely to increase the customer set to 1100 of whom only 400 of the original forecast upgrade to version 2 while 100 new customers buy the product because of the new function offered. To recover the $25,000 from these 500 customers will require a price of $50. A growth plan may make $100 a more reasonable price. In either case, this figure is an increment over the $150 for version 1.

Obviously, version 2 must have some dramatic new capability to convince someone for whom version 1 is currently acceptable to pay a 30- to 70-percent price increase. Having thus set the stage for a very tough business environment, what options are available to the project manager? He or she can put all the planned functions in version 1, price it to maximize gross profit, and use the income to build a completely different product with a large forecast. Every product would have only one version with periodic maintenance releases. This approach fails to build repeat business. It is also vulnerable to competition. The manager can put only essential functions in version 1 and schedule major performance, capability, and ease-of-use items for later versions. The weakness here is that the first version may not attract enough customers to produce the cash flow needed to build version 2. Either approach is risky. The second offers more opportunity for reacting to changes in market requirements and for taking advantage of improvements in technology. The tradeoff decisions are very difficult because there is so little data to work with. For each function, a decision must be made to put it in version 1 or hold it back. Furthermore, every deferred function must contribute a quantifiable benefit to the user. It is necessary to explain the incremental cost of version 2 in terms of the hard savings in some aspect of user operations. Thus a database compression function that "saves 30 percent of storage space and reduces average access time by 15 percent" can be evaluated by a version 1 user. A new version that improves the quality of code in the system cannot be evaluated. If anything, that type of change will look like a way to get the user to pay the vendor to reduce the vendor's maintenance cost.

4.2.5   Tools and Techniques Tradeoffs

One tradeoff decision related to tools and techniques is illustrated in Fig. 2.20. This chart compares the cost and value of selected items. The tradeoff implied by the chart is between value received and expense incurred. When selecting the tools and techniques to use on a project, budget will be a constraint. The project budget is limited by the resources available and the expected project benefits. Tentatively, an arbitrary portion of the total project budget is earmarked for aids and tools. It is often about 10 percent of the programmer budget and rarely as much as the total of programmer salaries.

In any particular organization, the tentative allocation for aids and tools tends to be based on local history.

Since aids and tools displace the need for additional programmers, it would be preferable to plan programmer requirements and aids/tools requirements jointly. The budget for aids/tools would then be the amount needed to minimize overall expense and/or project time. Such planning is not normally done at the start of a project since firm commitments to an aids/tools approach require more study than is available before initial budget commitments are authorized. Therefore, the starting budget for aids/tools is arbitrary.

After eliminating the approaches you cannot afford, it is appropriate to look at one or more items to adopt as project standards. The cost-related condition for adoption is simple: The total actual outlay for tools and techniques must be less than or equal to the amount budgeted for this type of support. The evaluation of this condition is not so simple. The value of each item includes such intangibles as improved quality, readability, and predictability. Value also includes more tangible advantages such as time saved or reduced maintenance cost. To the extent that a cash value can be placed on the tangible advantages, it is reasonable to ask whether the amount budgeted for tools should not be augmented by some portion of the saving.

In numerical terms, suppose the project budget allocates $25,000 for purchases, training, and operation of aids. You have looked at Tool Set A which consists of languages and documentation aids and at Tool Set B which includes A plus an on-line library and test support system. You estimate the cost of A as $1,000/month over the life of the project. B would cost $3,000/month. The plan spans eighteen months. However, you strongly believe that, using B, you can finish in fifteen months. In either case, you expect to have ten people on the job in the last stages of work (at $3,000/programmer-month).

Tool set	Cost/mo.	Cost/project	Savings	Net cost
A	1,000	18,000	—	18,000
B	3,000	45,000	90,000	(45,000)

Given these assumptions, the potential saving due to early completion more than pays for the more costly set of tools. Even if you only achieve one month improvement in the schedule, Tool Set B (at a net cost of $15,000) looks more attractive than A.[11] But before you decide, examine the cash

---

11. Any decision based on estimates or projections is subject to error. As indicated here, a *sensitivity analysis* is called for. Ask "How much would the answer change if each of the assumptions is wrong by X percent and Y units?" The consequences of being wrong should be known before the decision is frozen.

flow. At present, only $25,000 is earmarked to pay for tools. At $3,000/month, you will use up the budget in less than nine months, well before the project is finished. Clearly, to select Tool Set B you must convince your manager and your controller to change the budget to $45,000. You must replan the job and *commit* to the early date and the projected savings.

A second tradeoff regarding tools and techniques involves value versus time. A new and unfamiliar method takes time to learn and additional time to become proficient. Since improper use of a tool or technique reduces its value to zero, short cuts in the learning process are not recommended. Selection of a method implies that you have plenty of time allocated in the schedule for learning.

Third, a tool or technique must be compatible with your environment. Compatibility is easiest to achieve on brand new systems. Existing systems, with their existing code and databases, their existing machine configurations and operating procedures, and their ingrained programming techniques, are hostile to some types of changes. As an example, it is hard to enforce a structured programming standard on a task that consists of maintaining existing unstructured code. It is also difficult to introduce on-line development support when the only available hardware is fully utilized for daily operational processing. When you attempt to slip a new method into a hostile environment you have to make compromises that tend to reduce the value of the new method. Therefore, you should limit new tools and techniques to those that are suitable for the environment. If necessary, defer new methods until you start a brand new project.

Two specific situations to look for when evaluating environmental conditions are *cohabitability* and *portability*. The first term means that all the tools used on a project must be able to "live together." The second term means that the tools applicable to one project should also be useful on the next project. An example of tools that cohabit might include a system with a PL/I subset for design run interactively under a virtual system that has the ability to talk to both the development support library and the installation's batch facility. The programmers in this situation would work with PL/I plus a command language and would think they were dealing with a single, integrated support system. A similar support system using APL for a design language but not supporting shared files lacks cohabitability. Programmers using the facility would have to re-create their programs in the language used for library and batch operations and may have to go to extra trouble to restructure source code and data each time a file moves from the working library to the batch test stream. The last step becomes a portability issue when the support system used on machine X for one project must run on a different machine Y for a second project.

4.3   WRITING A PROPOSAL

System analysis results in a set of requirements that is intended to satisfy the users' objectives. Some things that were originally requested have been deleted for economic, technical, or other reasons. Normally, the users do not participate directly in the analysis. They wait for the results. If they like the results, they will let the project proceed; otherwise, the users will ask for changes or perhaps even kill the project. To avoid the latter alternative, the system requirements baseline is presented for review as a *proposal*.[12] The implications of the term "proposal" are: (1) that the requirements are offered for approval and are therefore subject to modification, and (2) that the requirements document is supported by a selling effort. The proposal sells itself when it contains enough information on benefits, costs, and tradeoffs to convince the user that the system will be a good investment.

It is appropriate to prepare a proposal even in the informal, noncompetitive environment of an in-house project. The proposal reinforces the user/server relationship by documenting the plans of the project team (server) in terms the user can understand and evaluate. The proposal can also strengthen the rapport between the user and the project team. A good proposal says, "Here is what I am going to do to satisfy your needs." Without salesmanship, a requirements list merely says, "Here is what I am going to build—take it or leave it."

The value of the selling effort increases as the degree of competition increases. The easiest situation occurs when the job is pre-sold. This is most common in a data-processing department charged with doing all the program development for its company. In other situations good proposals are relatively more important.

■ Unsolicited in-house proposal—In the uncommon case where a data-processing department has run out of work, a proposal is written to recommend to management the best job for the department to undertake. The proposal must show that the money spent on data-processing will be more productive than if it is spent elsewhere.

■ Competitive in-house proposal—Some organizations control cost by creating competition between internal groups or between an internal group and outside vendors. The internal group most closely associated with the problem area has an advantage over the competitors and should win the job. Nevertheless, their proposal must show that they will do a better job in order for them to win the assignment. "Better" in this case usually means "less expensive."

---

12. Much of the material in this section comes from the *Proposal Manager's Handbook,* an internal document of the IBM Federal Systems Division prepared initially in 1970.

■ Unsolicited proposal to another organization—A software house in business to develop programs for others specializes in areas that stress its capabilities. Through market studies and calls on prospects, likely customers are identified. Unsolicited proposals for specific deliverables in the area of specialization are sent to these prospects. Preparing an unsolicited proposal is easier than preparing one that the customer requests. You are working in a field in which you have some expertise and are preparing the proposal according to your own schedule. There is time to ensure that it is complete in every way. As the originator, you are already sold on the validity and worth of the program and your motive is to convince the customer to finance the program as a worthwhile solution to his or her problem. You work very closely with the customer in order to build interest, but you protect your competitive position by getting the customer to agree to respect your proprietary rights in the proposal.

The evaluator of your unsolicited proposal is in a more difficult position. That individual must evaluate the feasibility and worth of an idea about which he or she may be poorly informed or is only casually interested in. The evaluator may have given very little thought or consideration to the idea. To evaluate your proposal fairly, he or she may have to look at the problem and subject matter from an entirely new viewpoint. With luck, the prospect will buy sole source; i.e., from the proposer. More likely, if the prospect is a large company with software purchasing experience, other vendors will be invited to submit competing proposals. The original proposer maintains a competitive advantage by virtue of being closer to the customer and to the problem. In the time allotted for the submission of competitive proposals, the originator can improve the existing position while all others have to generate their offer from scratch.

■ Solicited proposals—Solicited proposals are written in response to a statement of a technical problem or task in which the customer feels that a vendor may have both an interest and a capability. Unlike unsolicited proposals, the proposal originates not with the proposal manager or team, but with the person or agency to whom the proposal is directed. The customer is already convinced that the work should be done (this may have resulted from your, or a competitor's, pre-proposal activity, or from some pressing operational requirement).

Solicited proposals also differ from unsolicited proposals in funding. The writer of an unsolicited proposal knows how much he or she wants for doing the work, whereas the writer of a solicited proposal knows only that the customer has a sum of money available to perform the work—how much is the question. For solicited proposals, you must determine how much the work is worth.

Perhaps the greatest difficulty in writing a solicited proposal is the time limitation. Invariably, the imposed deadline allows much less preparation time than you desire and certainly less time than that allowed to prepare an unsolicited proposal.

The format of a solicited proposal is often rigidly prescribed by the customer in a request for proposal (RFP). The purpose of uniformity is to make it easier to compare the competitive submissions. Since formalism tends to be restrictive, it is always a challenge to sell the unique advantages of your solution in the proposal document. Consequently, winning proposals are the culmination of a well-planned marketing effort.

Marketing is the eyes and ears of any business organization. Regardless of where the marketing responsibility lies, one of its key objectives is to determine where and when new business opportunities will appear. If marketing efforts are effective, it will be possible to know ahead of time when requests for assistance will occur and thus allow sufficient time for planning and other pre-proposal activities.

The objective of pre-proposal activities is twofold: first to obtain as much information as possible on what will be requested, what the funding limitations are, how to respond, and what the chances for a win will be; second, to provide as much information to the customer as possible on the benefits of doing business with your organization. The only opportunity to accomplish these objectives, on a direct basis, is before an RFP is generated. Most marketing people will tell you that if you have done no pre-proposal work or if the issuance of an RFP comes as a surprise to you, then you are by definition ill-prepared to bid on the job and the chances of winning are poor.

Your chances of winning will be high if the RFP reflects your thinking on the problem. A "white paper" can be the link in a sales campaign that presents your thoughts in a convincing manner. Submit the white paper well before the proposal is due so your customer is familiar with your approach and, hopefully, sold on it before seeing your bid. Such a paper is developed purely as a technical paper and does not offer any financial or resource information. It must demonstrate your understanding of the problem, the proposed concept to be followed in solving the problem, the method by which the approach will be carried out, and the benefits that this approach will provide for the customer. A good rule to follow in developing such a paper is to think of it as a "technical proposal" to be included in a formal proposal submission. Although the purpose of such a paper is to create customer interest, it is important to realize at the same time that the customer will expect you to be able to develop the capabilities you are proposing. Therefore, it is necessary to keep the suggested approach reasonable and not to go overboard with elaborate recommendations that may not be feasible.

4.3.1 Proposing Only What Is Required

The objective of the proposal is to win the job by demonstrating a thorough understanding of the problem and convincing the prospective customer of your capability for solving it efficiently and effectively. This simple and obvious objective is often misunderstood by vendors. Some believe it means "Win" period. They are likely to overstate benefits and understate costs. If they win, the result may be a severe overrun and a highly dissatisfied customer. Fortunately, their proposals will appear unsound compared to realistic bids. Other vendors will be excessively cautious and lose to a low bidder. A third type of loser is a "know-it-all." Based on one's experience, capability, product line, and intuition, the know-it-all proposes what the customer "needs" rather than what the customer wants. The expression, "You're trying to sell me a Cadillac when I want a Ford" is a reminder that most know-it-alls offer too much function at too high a price. Others offer a new high-risk technology when the customer has asked for a proven off-the-shelf package.

It is always possible prior to the release of an RFP to show poorly informed customers why they need more than they think they do. This is one of the reasons to put recommendations into an early "white paper." Once the RFP is issued, the bidder's only concern should be how to respond most effectively. He or she must read the RFP carefully. No matter how much previous contact has occurred with the customer, the bidder cannot presume to know what the RFP says until it has been read. The user and the buyer are often different people with some conflicts of interest. The RFP is released by the buyer; therefore, it reflects the buyer's interests as well as (or in place of) the user's. Competitors will probably bid the minimum system that is responsive. A higher bid, made in an effort to improve the system's capability, will probably lose the business. The best way for you to serve the customer is to win the business with an explicitly responsive proposal that sells a solution. It offers the best price. In addition, it presents recommendations for improving the system, which become the subject for future negotiation. This approach makes the bid competitive. The customer can see from this proposal the advantages of modifying plans. He or she will not be surprised later on if the changes become necessary. The buyer's can see that the bidder is not making a low bid with the intent of escalating the cost once the job has been awarded.

Should you bid at all? This depends on your need for the job and numerous other considerations:

- Does the customer have funding and is he or she ready to buy?
- What is the total sales potential and what is it going to cost to win? What is the follow-on potential?

- What are the benefits (other than sales and revenue) with respect to reputation, maintaining or improving technological capability, and competitive position for other/future programs?

- Is it consistent with your business strategy?

- Who are the key personnel (or agencies) and what is your working relationship with them? What is their attitude toward you and your reputation with them?

- Who is your competition? What related contracts are they involved in that gives them an advantage?

- How do you compare with the competition? What are your strengths and weaknesses?

- What are the legal and contractual problems? What type of contract is required?

- Can you be responsive to the requirements? What tradeoffs or alternatives are possible?

- What are the deliverable items, schedules, milestones, and acceptance criteria?

- What are the risks; i.e., system guarantee, delivery schedule, performance specifications, and availability of qualified personnel and resources?

- Will you require subcontract support (make or buy)? Will you require a team-mate? What facilities are required?

- What is the win strategy? Is a qualified proposal manager/team available?

- Is there enough time to write a good proposal?

Assumptions are made on each of these points and a scorecard is constructed to evaluate both the probability of winning and the business risk of performing should you win. Given many proposal opportunities, you rank them as in any tradeoff to arrive at a decision to "Bid" or "No Bid" each one. (See section 4.4.2.)

4.3.2   Proposal Activities

The decision to bid sets into motion a procedure involving all the key areas of the business. A large proposal illustrates this best since a dedicated proposal team can be justified. Small proposals are similar, but the proposal manager draws on the support of various groups as needed; only he or she is assigned full time to the proposal. Assume you are the manager of a proposal in response to a U.S. military RFP. You are responsible for all of the activities in Fig. 4.11. You are not responsible for the actual bid decision.

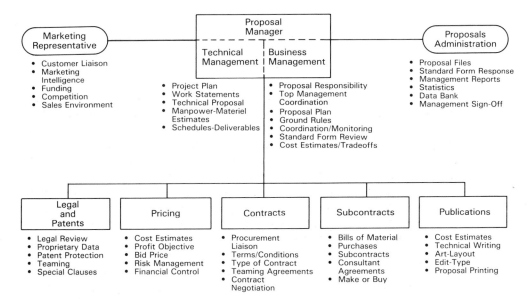

Fig. 4.11 Proposal activities.

Your team consists of yourself and two full-time people. You have access to company lawyers and contract, pricing, and purchasing specialists. An editor has been assigned in the technical publications department to help you get your proposal set up and printed in a hurry. Time will be a critical commodity because only thirty days have been allowed by the customer for RFP responses.

Your first task as proposal manager is to confirm that you have the complete RFP. It may consist of several volumes. You should then thoroughly read the entire RFP and use the support (e.g., Marketing, Contracts, Legal) available to ensure that you understand all aspects. Key items are:

■ Due date—This is the key date upon which you base your schedule. Bids received after the *exact* time specified are not accepted.

■ Agency—Although the location to which the proposal is to be delivered is identified in the RFP, you must obtain additional information about the agency involved. Has it awarded contracts to you in the past? Are you currently under contract to this agency? What type of awards does it normally make? What other RFPs have you received from it?

■ Special conditions—What are the conditions under which the work will be performed? For example, does the customer indicate or imply that the contractor needs to perform near the customer's location? Will equipment be provided or does the contractor furnish it? Is the delivery schedule tight and will you be dependent upon fast delivery by subcontractors? Does the customer require patent and data rights clauses in the contract that may be objectionable if you bid proprietary technology? Much of this type of information may not be included in the customer's statement of work but may be included somewhere in the total RFP.

Often, the customer will schedule a bidders' conference to bring together all of those bidding to ensure that they have a proper understanding of the requirements. You and your technical and marketing representatives should attend. At the conference, you and your competitors can ask questions of individuals directly concerned with preparation of the RFP. These same people will probably evaluate your proposal and award the contract.

Questions may be asked about gray areas in the technical statement of work, required formats, pricing data, and the exceptions or deviations to the contractual terms and conditions. In addition, competitive intelligence data can be gathered that may affect the total marketing approach to the program. Information on strengths and weaknesses can be obtained from paying close attention to the questions asked by the competition; teams can be identified and technical approaches to be used by the competition can sometimes be predicted.

Without waiting for the bidders' conference, you should lay out your plan for producing the proposal. To save time, you should assemble all the players, including the representatives of the functional organizations that will support you. At the meeting, you explain how and what you are bidding, what support will be required in the proposal effort, and what the proposal schedule is. During the meeting, all representatives will be expected to commit their departments to both the requirements and the schedule. This discussion will lead to action:

- Resolve schedule conflicts and get commitments.
- Identify the constraints involved and assign responsible individuals to obtain the necessary commitments and approvals.
- Develop a schedule for key milestones with the help of a proposal specialist (Fig. 4.12).
  a. Due date for submitting proposal
  b. Start date and time for normal, safe, assured delivery; also consider how to handle the worst possible case and still ensure delivery
  c. Start date for documentation coordination and review
  d. Date for input to the technical publications groups
  e. Date for cost estimates to Pricing
  f. Freeze date on all changes to the plan and/or configuration
  g. Date for statements of work to Purchasing for vendors/subcontractors
  h. Date for management review of technical/management proposal
  i. Date for consolidation of all written inputs to the proposal

Fig. 4.12   Proposal flow.

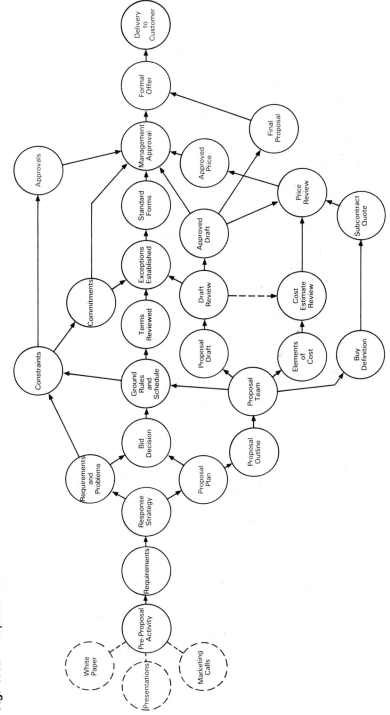

Review and discuss the entire detailed proposal outline with your team. Redefine and reinterpret intent if necessary. Fill in missing areas, if any. Require that your team members tell you immediately when and if they deviate from the outline and also what assumptions they are making. Evaluate assumptions in light of conflict with the RFP, proposal plan, and company restraints.

Organize the proposal team with lead people responsible for various areas of the work. Proposal development cycles are too short to allow the luxury of a gradual buildup. The entire team must be on board very early and functioning as an integrated unit. Give clear work assignments to every individual on the team. Be ready to change the work assignments as other things (e.g., technical approach) change. Assign responsibility by subject matter. This makes an individual responsible for all references to a given subject wherever they may appear in the proposal. The objective is consistency. Plan to have key people you expect to use on the project itself involved in the proposal effort. If the use of a Chief Programmer (CP) Team is anticipated, the CP should be part of the proposal team. The ability to accomplish these objectives is one of the key benefits derived from proper pre-proposal activities.

All these points can be summarized by a single word: *plan.* A proposal effort should be planned, just as a project should be planned. In fact, the very tight time restrictions during the proposal phase make planning all the more imperative.

Win or lose, you and your company must know why. If the proposal loses, ask the customer for a debriefing. This meeting should provide specific information on price, technical approach, performance, labor force, reliability, economy of operation, and delivery schedule. In discussing these specific items, try to discern what the winner did with respect to engineering contribution to the problem, alternative approaches, reliability, etc. This information should be studied carefully since you will probably compete against the same companies again. If the proposal wins, find out what your advantages were. Let your associates know about them; they might be able to adopt them for another win.

4.3.3 Proposal Content

The proposal must clearly and concisely define your understanding of the RFP requirements. Some members of the customer's evaluation team may not have participated with you during your pre-proposal activities; in fact, some of the evaluation team members may have participated with a competitor on a similar effort. It is therefore, essential that your description of the RFP requirements be complete, even though you may feel that you and the customer have a common understanding.

4.3.3.1 Selling the benefits

Every proposal is assumed to provide an acceptable product or technology. To give the proposal sales impact, stress the features the customer wants, e.g., reliability, simplicity, state-of-the-art, unique concept, low production costs, and so on. Your efforts in gathering information from pre-proposal contacts or from careful review of the RFP should result in a list of key features to be stressed in the proposal. Merely stating in your proposal that you will provide these key features is not enough. Your whole proposal, from beginning to end, must reflect your intention to provide these features and show that they are uppermost in your mind. If, for example, low cost is significant, show how each stage of your planned development cycle will address cost reduction. Discuss the various approaches you have considered and rejected in the proposal. Show the tradeoffs that have been made and present convincing arguments that yours is the best approach.

The emphasis in these examples is on the merit of your approach. Program development proposals deal with high-risk, expensive projects. The customer must have confidence in the developer. You build confidence through personal contact in the pre-proposal effort and through the presentation of facts and accomplishments in the proposal. A soft-sell builds the lasting relationship you want. Hard-sell techniques, such as might apply to program product advertisements or catalog blurbs, are often a negative influence in development proposals. Following this line of reasoning, you make your best sales points in the technical sections of your proposal. The most important points in the customer's evaluation procedure are: (1) your qualifications, and (2) your technical approach. In the evaluation of U.S. military contracts (hardware as well as software), the customer looks for the following indicators:

- Qualifications
    1. Specific experience of the key people who will work on the project; related projects completed by your organization.

    2. Technical organization
        a. Proposal structure—showing how you think and communicate and showing your depth of understanding of the problem area.
        b. Project structure—indicating whether you know how to organize to get results and whether you view the key aspects of the problem the way the customer does.
        c. Company organization—showing whether there is sufficient breadth and depth in the company to back you up if the project encounters difficulties.

    3. Special equipment and facilities. The fact that you own or have access to special facilities relevant to the job implies a commitment on your part to the subject area.

4. Analytical capacity. Special people, like special facilities, show you know what it takes to produce results in the subject area.

5. Level of effort/support. Your estimate of what resources are needed to do the job compared to the customer's estimate is a clue to your understanding of the job. You do not have to agree with the customer's estimate as long as you give good reasons for your estimate. When subcontractors are supporting you, the customer will also check to see if you have proposed a management system to control the overall effort.

6. Track record and current strength. Past performance and current financial soundness show that you can undertake the job and complete it. Some small software houses cannot handle the added burden of a large, new project.

■   Technical approach

1. Understanding the problem.   Many good approaches are presented for the wrong problem. The first prerequisite in preparing a responsive approach is understanding the problem. Some RFPs state the problem poorly. Often it is wise to have several people read and submit separate summaries of the RFP to the proposal manager to ensure that the real problem has been recognized.

2. Soundness of approach.   The manner in which a problem is approached usually determines how successfully it is solved. A proposal should substantiate the technical soundness of its approach thoroughly enough to demonstrate feasibility and probability of successful results.

3. Compliance requirements.   Often, small details or nontechnical requirements (e.g., reporting schedules, technical and cost proposal format, and submission schedules) are easily overlooked. A proposal will be penalized for their omission. They are necessary and cannot be randomly omitted.

4. Special technical factors.   Consideration is given to simplicity of design, ease of maintenance, unique ideas, configuration, reliability, and related items applicable to the particular program. Unique ideas are desired. By including a discussion of relevant ideas, you can accomplish several objectives.

   a. The effort you put into the analysis shows your interest in the subject.

   b. By comparing technical ideas, discarding some and ranking the others, you can lay the groundwork for a follow-on contract to develop the most promising ideas.

   c. By showing the benefits of the idea you propose to implement, you sell your approach.

TABLE 4.10.   FACTORS CONTRIBUTING TO PROPOSAL WINS AND LOSSES

Reason	Type of items procured		
	Major systems	Studies	Components
Only responsive bidder	5	7	6
Best technical proposal	43	47	19
Best management capability	21	14	18
Related experience	9	16	8
Best quality assurance	4	0	10
Most responsive to schedule	7	4	18
Most reasonable price	11	12	21

a. Factors Contributing to Acceptance, Percent

Reason	Type of items procured		
	Major systems	Studies	Components
Nonresponsive to RFP	15	21	3
Not technically acceptable	55	41	35
Weak management and organization	3	14	22
Lack of related experience	0	5	0
Quality assurance disqualification	10	0	11
Unacceptable schedule	9	0	16
Unreasonable price	8	19	13

b. Factors Contributing to Rejection, Percent

The relative importance of some of these factors in a study of some 300 military systems of all types ranging from $25,000 to multimillion-dollar jobs is shown in Table 4.10.

4.3.3.2 Completeness

The RFP may specify the format of your proposal. Some elaborate RFPs spell out what every table or chart should look like and even how many pages are permitted in each section of the response. Lacking such guidance, you should design your proposal to be as complete and clear as possible. Completeness involves responding to each and every point in the RFP *plus* organizing the proposal to fit the audience. The latter point results in a proposal that has at least three parts:

1. An *Executive Summary* contains a concise statement of what you are offering, how you are going to manage the project, what key assumptions affect the validity of your offer, and why you should win the job. The actual business offer is usually made in a cover letter signed by the bidder's authorized executive.

2. A *Technical Proposal* expands on the executive summary to show your statement of the system requirements, your technical approach, your description of what the resulting system will consist of, and your project plan. The project plan is your *statement of work* (SOW) which breaks your work into tasks and gives milestones. It also explains the deliverables and sets the criteria for testing the acceptability of the deliverables. The SOW includes your statement of the customer's responsibilities, too. In most programming projects, the performance of the developer is dependent on parallel tasks being performed by the user.

3. A *Management Proposal* covers the "qualifications" data listed previously. In addition, pricing details, proposed progress reporting procedures, and contract terms and conditions can go in this section.

Other sections covering definitions of terms, "white papers" or other preliminary documents, proposed alternatives, etc., can be added as appendixes. By breaking the proposal package up this way, you can style each section differently. Give the executive an overview, emphasizing results and benefits in nontechnical terms. Give the operational managers an in-depth technical document. Give the buyer's evaluation team the information they need to assess your competence and reliability.

Complete responsiveness requires that you answer every request in the RFP. Negative answers are appropriate; omissions are not. For instance, if you have proposed a disk database system with no tape drives, do not ignore the RFP question, "What tape specifications apply?" Answer either "No tapes are required" or give the specifications of the tape for the type of processor you will use. The people who receive the proposals may get only a subsection to evaluate. Therefore, the supplies specialist who is checking on the inventory management implications of the proposal may not know about your disk-only design.

Most RFPs require that you describe the problem areas involved in developing particular items and proposed solutions. Any component of your product that has not been successfully demonstrated by previous tests and that has to be substantiated by testing or other means during the program is "something to be worked out," and the customer must be told how you intend to do it. In demonstrating capabilities related to problem solving, two types of problems should be discussed: (1) actual problems to be faced and worked out because of new concepts, or (2) advanced technology and potential problems that could exist had they not been solved in previous problems.

One of the most important aspects of the program plan is the description of the number and types of tests to be performed. Convince the customer that the tests to be performed are adequate to do the job and are not more than necessary. When the number and types of tests are defined in the RFP, it is advisable for you to analyze these requirements to determine if you believe they will meet program objectives. If you agree, say so; otherwise, suggest a different number of tests.

A weakness of many proposals is the presentation of time schedules and milestones. It may be difficult for the customer to determine that the proposed time schedule is sound and realistic from a brief listing of events. Discuss in your proposal the schedules and milestones based on experience to show that they are arranged logically and can be met during contract performance. When the time schedule has been established by the customer, it is equally important that you verify in your best judgment that it is realistic. If it is not, you should clearly state the reasons why the schedule cannot be met and propose alternative approaches whereby the customer's objectives can be met within a reasonable time frame. Generally, the customer is aware of the degree of risk involved and, if you do not mention it, your understanding of the situation may be questioned.

4.3.3.3 Clarity

Clarity is also important. The proposal should be precise and unambiguous so that the buyer understands your offer exactly as you mean it. Clarity is, of course, a matter of judgment. You, as the proposal manager, must make that judgment as the proposal develops.

Read each page for meaning, intent, and compliance with the proposal plan and outline. Be concise. Be consistent in the use of terminology and acronyms. Check for vague and ambiguous terms. Use mandatory statements when they are required: in English *shall* is binding, *should* expresses a declaration of purpose, and *will* expresses futures. Your proposal is a legal document which *will* be incorporated into the contract and, *shall* be used to resolve disputes, if any arise. Sometimes certain seemingly innocent absolute words and phrases have lasting customer and legal implications in terms of making commitments. When responding to an RFP, use, "We believe our response satisfies your mandatory requirements" rather than, "We meet your mandatory requirements." It not only sounds better but creates a certain aura of assurance through modest understatement. Specifically avoid, or at least be very careful, using terms such as *insure, always, never, any, guarantee, warranty, all, every, will,* and *we* (when it means you together with the customer). They can be troublesome as they leave the extent of your obligation open to the customer's interpretation.

Consider *all:* "The system will detect all errors in the input and notify the operator with recommended action" versus "The system signals the operator and recommends action when it detects an input error." Coding to find every conceivable error is difficult, if not impossible. The word *determine* illustrates something else. Even though you might have good customer rapport and control, it is necessary to be sensitive to the customer's prerogatives. You *document, record, study, analyze, compile, identify, gather, summarize,* and *report* requirements, but you do not *determine* them. You *recommend, suggest,* and *submit* systems to meet requirements and let the customer *determine* the one he or she needs. You can, however, determine how to build the system the customer selects to meet the stated requirements. You are the expert in developing systems that meet certain objectives and adhere to certain constraints.

In the role as systems assurance manager for program development projects performed by the commercial contracting services department of IBM, T. A. Humphrey reviewed many proposals. Invariably, he had to recommend wording changes. His objective was to assure that his organization could do the proposed work within the terms and conditions offered. The changes he recommended tended to improve the *precision* of the commitment statements and *place limits* on the amount of work involved. As an example, he reviewed the following description of a requirements definition task:

> Requirements definition is the first technical activity. The purpose of this activity is to determine what kind of system support the user departments desire. This activity consists of the following detail steps.
>
> ■ Define the objectives of the functional units that are planned to be supported by the system under design.
>
> ■ Identify each functional subunit and establish an interview guide for that unit.
>
> ■ Conduct an in-depth interview of the functional subunit. Establish information received and information delivered. Determine the processing steps performed on the input to produce the required output and determine the stored information requirements.
>
> ■ Assess the information received in the interview above. Determine why functions are performed as they are. The "why" can usually be divided into two classes:
>
> 1. Business environment and resulting policy decisions. The project team will offer consulting guidance, where appropriate, in these areas.
> 2. Constraints of existing tools. The project team will make recommendations for more effective tools.

- Review the above assessment with the resultant recommendations with appropriate functional personnel. *Iterate until agreement is reached.*

- Identify and *define all problem areas and requirements.*

- Classify the above problem areas and requirements by various *parameters such as* functional organization, common data usage, timeliness and response requirements, etc. This classification step is a necessary prelude to full understanding and the subsequent support definition.

- Organize the assembled data into a logical whole with all integral parts defined and related.

Looking at the italicized phrases, he noted that: (1) the iteration could be an endless cycle, (2) the proposal offered to define the undefinable—"'all' problem areas and requirements,' and (3) the classification by parameters was open-ended because only examples were given. These problems could be corrected by: (1) setting a fixed number of review meetings followed by an escalation to higher user management for a decision, (2) defining only "problem areas identified during the system analysis," and (3) classifying "by the parameters Functional Organization, Common Data Usage, Timeliness, Response Requirement, and such other parameters identified as significant during the system analysis." These changes close the open ends or permit the bidder rather than the user to decide when the task is finished. Incidentally, Humphrey also pointed out that, from a selling standpoint, this example is weak. It does not even mention the user or the application. It could apply to anyone. Thus it fails to show the bidder's special interest in the customer's problem.

The value of precise wording can be seen in another of Humphrey's examples from an actual proposal to design and install a time-sharing system. The original wording aggregates details and specifics and, while not inaccurate, the generalized statements fail to tell the customer what he or she is buying. Compare the original version to the new version after system assurance review:

ORIGINAL VERSION

Prepare a profile of each prospective terminal user group and their projected activities defining their functional and performance requirements for time-sharing. Among those to be considered are: current time-sharing users in L-Properties and L-Corporation, the system control terminal operator, and program development personnel.

NEW VERSION

Interview each prospective terminal user group and collect the following information:

    For current time-sharing users:

    a. Number of programs to be converted

    b. Sizes of largest programs—No. lines of code

    c. Language(s) used

    d. Data File Requirements

        – Record sizes

        – File sizes

    e. Frequency and duration of time-sharing usage

    f. Relative frequency of usage of catalogued programs vs. one-time jobs—for FORTRAN only

  For Programmers:

    a. Number of programs to be catalogued

    b. Average size of programs—No. of lines

    c. Language(s) used

    d. Anticipated frequency and durations of system use

    e. Size of largest program to be invoked—probably a compiler

    f. Number of programmers to be served

  The users to be interviewed are:

    a. Financial Planning—L-Corporation

    b. Economic and Financial Planning—L-Properties

    c. L-Services Systems Development.

By listing specific things to be done, this proposal not only limits the bidder's obligations but also gives a much clearer view of what a user "profile" is for each of the two major classes of users. The New Version reflects the experience of a bidder who knows time-sharing systems.

4.3.4 Management Approval

A good proposal satisfies the customer and leads to a profitable venture for the bidder. A good test for a proposal is to be able to certify that, "This proposal is accurate, complete, correct, and free from exaggeration or omission that would make the proposal misleading." Under the time pressure of most proposals, however, the draft is not always as good as it should be. As protection against offering an unprofitable or infeasible statement of work (SOW), the bidder establishes a formal procedure to ensure that the draft is carefully reviewed and approved before the proposal leaves the shop. Call it a "DCA" procedure to emphasize that it is concerned with *d*ocument *c*oordination and *a*pproval.

The DCA is usually a serial process involving review and approval by the proposal manager, technical management, marketing, contracts, counsel, controller and general manager—in that order. On occasion, to expedite the process, nontechnical and technical signoffs are obtained in parallel. In a crisis, the DCA process involves a sign-off meeting. There are generally only two circumstances under which a sign-off meeting is held: (1) insufficient time for a serial or parallel sign off, and (2) proposal complexity requires everyone to be present to handle questions. (The same DCA process can apply to all business commitments, contracts, purchases, and proposals. Time is less of a constraint in such cases; therefore, the only excuse for a sign-off meeting for a contract or a purchase is that it is convenient to bring the key people together regularly to deal with such matters.) Review and approval can be expedited by letting management and staff know what is being done by providing an abstract of the RFP and draft copies of the proposal for review. The staff can begin to resolve problems early to allow sufficient time for changes before the DCA. The DCA is a poor time to begin solving problems. Decisions made in this environment may not always be compatible with good business judgment.

Management concern during the final approval of the proposal is directed toward the following questions:

- Is the statement of work specific?

- Is a schedule included; does it identify the duration of discrete efforts and include milestones and delivery dates?

- Are support items clearly identified as to what is required, when it must be available, who provides it, and what the result is if it is not provided as required?

- Do we give a precise description of deliverable items?

- Do the acceptance criteria indicate what constitutes completion of the effort, terminating our obligations under the contract?

Lacking time to read a large proposal in detail, the executive managers will concentrate on the transmittal letter that constitutes the formal offer to provide services and/or equipment under terms mutually agreeable to the customer and the bidder. This letter can only be signed by an authorized official of the bidding company. Once signed, it binds the company to honor the offer if the customer accepts it.

The letter should summarize the bidder's offer and should provide the customer with all the basic information needed for quick reference. If everything but the letter were thrown away, the customer should still be able to determine what would be done, the cost and terms of the contract, and whom to call for more information. The following can be used as a guide for letter content:

1. Identification of the service or product
2. The bidder's unique qualifications for being selected
3. Type of contract upon which the offer is based
4. Period of performance
5. Financial information
6. When the offer expires
7. Whom to contact for contractual/technical information
8. Concluding statement
9. Reference to separate proposal notes

As proposal manager you should satisfy yourself that the proposal meets the objectives of the plan you established at the beginning of the proposal effort. At this point, you can stand up in front of your general manager to sell what you believe is a winning proposal. You will have the support of the staff to show that you are making an acceptable business offer that meets the legal, contractual, and financial requirements of your organization. It is now up to the general manager to decide whether to submit the proposal and make the commitment it implies.

4.4   COMMITMENT AND RISK

Each individual in an organization has a designated job with defined functions and all the responsibility and authority that goes with that job. The proposal manager's job is to produce a proposal. The general manager's job is to assess business opportunities and risks and commit company resources to the best opportunities. In her paper, "The Meaning of Responsibility in Business Management" [28], Follett presents the idea of function, responsibility, and authority being the three inseparables of business organization. She then points out that within an effective organization ultimate responsibility is cumulative and shared. "An executive decision is a moment in a process." In other words, the basis of every decision consists of the accumulated work of various line and staff groups. The executive decision is the contribution of the individual whose function it is to approve or disapprove the proposed course of action.

The general manager signs the proposal (or contract or purchase order) because he or she is authorized to commit the company. The proposal manager does not have that authority. The proposal manager can organize and manage the proposal effort, and can decide whether the resulting document is ready to go to top management for sign off.

The general manager knows the overall resource plan. He or she can: (1) determine how many proposals are outstanding, (2) compare the opportunity and risk of the new proposal against all other opportunities, (3) assess the company's ability to absorb the risk, and (4) juggle projects to avoid or compensate for risk. Therefore, the general manager is the best person to assess the commitment offered in the proposal from a business viewpoint. The general manager who is consistently right will be a success in a healthy company; otherwise, he or she might ruin the company and fall with it.

The proposal manager stands or falls on the quality of the proposal. In business terms, his or her success depends on winning the job.

4.4.1   What Is a Commitment?

In the described cycle, a proposal manager *proposes* to commit the organization's resources, reputation, and future health. The general manager *makes the commitment.* The project manager *accepts* and *implements* the commitment. The managers of support functions likewise accept and implement the subcommitments for their area. The meaning of the *commitment* is that the committed party will do everything that is explicitly stated in the proposal (or, in practice, in the contract resulting from and incorporating the proposal). In addition, the commited party will do what is implied in the proposal/contract as interpreted according to the rules of good business practice in the country. That is all—but that is enough.

The explicit activities cover all deliverables and include the criteria for determining when the committed party has discharged the responsibility. In a good proposal these points are quite clear. That is why the use of a formal proposal is recommended even for in-house projects. The proposal establishes the basis for a clean relationship between the user and the server, uncluttered by misunderstandings. Nevertheless, some organizations have difficulty understanding what their commitments entail. This is particularly true in service groups who normally work on a *best-efforts* basis. That is, they do what they can within the limits of time and resource. They intend to deliver a completed product at the end of the allotted time but, if they fail to finish, they do not feel obligated to do anything about it. Such is the case when a sales organization *volunteers* to help develop a customer's program but has to stop work to tend to a critical sales situation elsewhere. When such a group accepts a *firm commitment* to produce and deliver something by a certain date, they often fail to put the proper management controls in place to ensure that the commitment will be met. They continue to operate on a best-efforts basis. In a contract environment, they can be held liable for damages if they miss the committed date. Best-efforts are not good enough unless the contract explicitly states that the work product will be a best-effort.

Some commitments are particularly difficult to manage. For this reason, proposals and contracts should avoid them. The "key personnel" clause is an example. Most customers will try to get a vendor to specify by name the key people who will work on a job. If they succeed in getting the names in the contract, obviously those specific individuals must work on the job and, by implication, are unavailable for other assignments. Naturally, they are the vendor's best people, known to the customer by reputation or previous contact. Few vendors can accept the loss of flexibility caused by locking the best people into one project. Neither will they want to block career opportunities for these people by tying them to a long-term assignment. Thus the key personnel clause is to be avoided.

Another trouble spot occurs in the description of acceptance tests. If no criteria are given, good business practice would imply that the customer should decide if the product is acceptable. Rather than treat such an important point in a vague manner, some explicit criteria should be proposed. Then the question will be whether to test with a mutually acceptable test data script or with live customer data. Live data are highly unpredictable and may lead to unsatisfactory and expensive tests; therefore, the vendor should plan to commit only to scripted test data.

A third sensitive area deals with customer participation. Every good proposal spells out what the customer must do in order for the proposal to be valid; however, the level of detail is not always adequate. For example, a common RFP requirement is that the vendor submit all specifications to the customer for review before the vendor starts work on the specified items. The proposal response offers to submit the specs for review but usually fails to say how long the customer can take to complete the review. Consider a vendor commitment to do a job in twelve months during which the customer must conduct four reviews of unknown duration. The vendor expects each review to take a week; in fact, each takes two months and the vendor defaults on his or her commitment. To correct this, vendors try to word their commitments to provide some protection: "Specs will be submitted for review: one week is allowed for review, delays beyond one week will extend the contract completion date day for day" or "If a review is not completed in one week, vendor will start work, customer agrees to accept all costs for such effort even if the task is subsequently disapproved."

Another aspect of customer participation is the degree of support he or she provides. Most vendors who work on a contract basis like a clean separation between the user and the server, between the customer and themselves. Their preferred interface is the requirements baseline document and their preferred method of management is via change proposals, reviews, and approvals, all properly documented. This type of management system avoids the confusion caused by "private treaties" between individuals in the two organizations. It helps control projects where the user must perform some part of the work. Documented assignments, specs, and delivery dates permit careful tracking of every task and tend to encourage the user to meet the obligations. Nevertheless, the user is not as tightly bound as the vendor unless the contract makes vendor performance contingent on user performance. The more normal relationship is a best-effort for the user and a firm commitment for the contractor.

Attitude is important when accepting a commitment. On a best-efforts job the appropriate attitude is, "I think the objective is achievable and I am going to do my best to accomplish it." On a job with firm deliverables and dates, the attitude must be, "I have studied this job carefully and have defined the commitment in such a way that I know I can do the job; therefore, I shall accomplish it."

4.4.2   Assessing Risk

In making a commitment, it always help to have thought through the consequences of failure. In every undertaking there are risks and uncertainties; therefore, in every decision the questions are, "How big is the potential payoff compared to the risk?" and "Can we accept the consequences of failure?" A conservative executive is inclined to limit commitments to situations where the project payoff is assured to the extent that some minimum benefit is expected even if all the possible exposures occur. A more aggressive executive will be willing to take a loss occasionally to achieve higher potential benefits. In this case, the cost of the project exposures must not exceed the benefits achieved on other projects; i.e., the total benefit achieved over all projects must exceed some minimum objective. A speculator may go still further and make a commitment that carries exposures that can bankrupt the firm. Each executive is operating rationally within the guidelines for his or her particular environment.

Using "risk" in its broadest sense, risk assessment evaluates exposures. Management action can then deal with the exposures. Risks should be stated in terms of money, where possible, so executives can rapidly interpret them. This is true of technical risks as well as business risks. For each type of exposure, an assessment of risk should be made and an action plan should be put in place to control the exposure; e.g.,

- Technical Risks
    1. Environment: Is it familiar?
       Action: Allow time for training and familiarization
    2. Function: Is it feasible? Can you do it? Does it require any special equipment that you lack?
       Action: Quality control
    3. Performance: Can you predict performance? Will it be adequate?
       Action: Continuous prediction/measurement using models and simulated environmental tests

4. Availability: Can you predict availability? Will it be adequate?
   Action: Recovery procedures
5. Testing: Is input data pre-tested? Do you conduct tests or does user do it?
   Action: Detailed test plan early in life cycle

- Business Risks
  1. Schedule: Is it feasible? Are there buffers for contingency? Is there a penalty for late delivery?
     Action: Lay out optimum plan and request additional resources and time for deviations
  2. Customer participation: Do you depend on customer output? Can customer do his or her part of the job?
     Action: Clear-cut job definition and interfaces, plan for monitoring progress
  3. Delivery: What constitutes acceptance? Are the deliverables defined?
     Action: Precise statement-of-work
  4. Terms and conditions: Type of contract? User reviews or special clearances? Work at your location or user's?
     Action: Adjust SOW and schedule to fit conditions

Software contractors involved in many jobs develop internal checklists that simplify the process of risk assessment. In the checklist, each risk factor that has proven to be significant in the past is broken into typical categories such as:

1. Contract Type (check one)
   a. Fixed price   ( )
   b. Cost Plus Incentive Fee (CPIF)   ( )
   c. Cost Plus Fixed Fee (CPFF)   ( )
   d. Time and Materials   ( )
2. Data to Be Used in Acceptance Test (check all applicable)
   a. Input data will be pre-tested   ( )
   b. Input data will be untested   ( )
   c. Input source will be automatic   ( )
   d. Input source will be manual—contractor personnel ( )
   e. Input source will be manual—customer personnel   ( )
   f. Input rate will be script controlled   ( )
   g. Input rate will be source controlled/random   ( )

The elements of such a checklist depend very much on the company's experience; therefore, no list can be offered here as a standard. The usual method of weighting the entries and calculating a figure of merit is used to evaluate the checklist output.

Pressure of time and the desire to simplify decisions cause managers to boil down the results of risk assessment to single figures of merit. They want to know what are the chances a proposal will win. Will the commitments be fulfilled? What is the impact of missing the targets? One organization deals with these questions by automating the risk assessment questionnaire. Each element is assigned a weight based on its significance in the past. Based on the answers to the questionnaire, an estimate of "actual risk" is then extracted from a table, as is an estimate of the "importance" of the element. The product of element weight times actual risk times importance gives a number representing the exposure due to that element. For example, the element Customer Personnel carrying a *weight* of 9 (on a scale of 10) is associated with questions such as:

Customer Personnel   (check all applicable)
None required	( )
Less than 15% of project total(X)	
15% to 30%	( )
Greater than 30%	( )
Separate task	( )
Skilled	(X)

The computer program refers to an *actual risk* table containing the values:

0	Skilled, separate task
1.0	(Not skilled, separate task) or (Skilled, not separate task)
1.5	Not skilled, not separate task

The *importance* table has four values:

0	No customer personnel
0.5	Less than 15% of project total
1.0	15% to 30%
1.5	Greater than 30%

The element exposure as checked is $9 \times 1.0 \times 0.5 = 4.5$.

Given adequate experience data, a single risk value can be produced by adding up the element exposures as in Table 4.11. In the contract environment, "No Bid" situations arise. The tables have been constructed to contain values greater than 1.0 as No Bid flags. When such a value is read, management knows that, historically, this factor led to failure. In this example, the element System Performance is a potential "show-stopper." Before making a commitment, top management will want to see a plan for reducing the risk in this area to a manageable level. The action plan can consist of assigning special skills, requesting more time, changing the performance objectives, etc.; actions that tend to raise cost or reduce responsiveness.

TABLE 4.11.   A RISK EVALUATION

EVALUATION: proposal to be prime contractor for requirements definition, system design, program development, and system integration. Area is new to project team. Schedule is tight. Customer and subcontractors: 30 percent of total. Hardware and support software are new releases.

	Weight	Actual risk	Importance	Score
Vendor team	8	.75	1	6.0
Customer personnel	9	1	1	9.0
Customer approvals	2	.25	1	0.5
Project requirements	6	.75	1	4.5
Design specifications	4	.90	1	3.6
Test facilities	4	.50	.75	1.5
Hardware (vendor)	4	.50	.50	1.0
Software (vendor)	6	.50	.50	1.5
Hardware (other)	6	0	0	0.0
Software (other)	10	0	0	0.0
Installation premises	2	1	1	2.0
System integration	6	1	1	6.0
System performance	8	1.5	1	*12.0
System acceptance	6	1	1	6.0
System availability	5	.20	.30	0.3
Work premises	4	0	1	0.0
Project management	10	.50	1	5.0
Risk Score				58.9

*Potential show-stopper

The organization using this technique has selected the table entries so that the result, the Risk Score, can be used directly as a price uplift factor. If the price of a particular job would normally be $100 and the risk score is zero, $100 can be bid with confidence. If the risk score is 10, $110 would be bid. On the average, the job would be profitable at that level. A risk score of 58.9 would result in a bid price of $158.90. Again, that price should be a financially safe offer, yet it may be much too high to win the business. Consequently, the company will normally look for business with lower risk scores. Note that in each case a bid of $100 is possible. If all of the exposures are avoided, the job will succeed. Risk uplift simply recognizes that tougher commitments increase risk and that high risk jobs command a higher target profit. In-house jobs, lacking the profit objective, must compensate for risk either by relaxing job constraints or by completely redefining the job. Some risk is desirable because it challenges the development team to become more proficient. Excessive risk is an invitation to failure.

4.4.3   Limiting Liability

The buyer in a contract environment recognizes that there is a possibility that the winning bidder will fail to do the job. Only rarely does the buyer want to pay the cost of a failed project. Sometimes it is unavoidable, as is the case in high-technology areas where the project is essentially experimental. (It is obviously unavoidable with respect to in-house projects.) In general, though, the buyer will insist on some form of risk sharing whereby the contractor will not be paid (or will pay a penalty) for nonperformance. The contractor, most naturally, will try to limit the liability. The first and most effective means of limiting liability is the contract. With very precise statements of the extent of guarantees and warranties on the work done, the contract can be the best protection. When liability cannot be eliminated, the contractor seeks the minimum exposure by trying to restrict the penalties to actual hardship endured by the customer.

If the job can be completed but not on time, the customer loses some benefits expected from the system. Benefits are hard to calculate precisely. In particular, it is hard to claim that a program system projected to have a net value of $250,000 per year will be worth $1,000 a day starting the day it is accepted. For this reason, penalties for late delivery tend to have nominal values such as $100 a day for every day of slippage. An exception to this guideline occurs when the customer has migrated to a new configuration and has restructured internal responsibilities by the date called out in the contract. Here, the cost of new unutilized hardware, software, and personnel can be calculated. The contractor may be required to reimburse the customer for these costs each day they are present but not utilized.

When the project is delivered but fails, the customer has to consider whether to let the contractor fix it or whether to start over again. In the first case, the buyer will want to withhold payment or may want to force the contractor to pay the cost of redoing the job even if another contractor is given the assignment. Contracts exist with such clauses.

The greatest exposure arises from *contingent liabilities* whereby the customer suffers a loss through the use of the contractor's product. As an example, a demand deposit system is built for a bank. Once installed and running, teller response time improves as expected; however, at noon every day, lunch hour crowds overstress the system. Not only are depositors annoyed by the slow service but some deposits get lost, creating inaccurate balances. The bank feels the contractor is to blame and sues for the estimated cost to the bank of real or anticipated business losses.

Program development is, and probably will remain, a complex undertaking. The interaction between the user and the system changes as experience with the system functions is acquired. For this reason, it is rare that the initial description of the system is valid throughout the life cycle. The concept of *Baseline + Changes* is a means of coping with the fluidity of the real-life situation. A good contract permits changes and anticipates the cost of changes. A good contract also limits liability to the explicit commitments covered by the current version of the contract document. Unforeseen contingencies should be excluded by appropriate wording. Foreseeable contingencies are negotiable; however, a project manager should avoid them because the cost associated with contingent liabilities can be open-ended. A more appropriate offer would be to fix problems caused by defects in the product. In the bank, if deposits are lost because of incorrect checking routines in the program, the contractor could provide correct routines. If the deposits were lost because tellers made out deposit receipts with the intent of entering the data after the crowd dispersed, but then misplaced the inputs, the contractor is not at fault. The contract can be negotiated so the contractor pays costs in the first situation but not the second. Such a contract, where the contractor must "make good" on commitments, bears a high premium. Normally, the scope of work would have to score very low on the actual risk scale to qualify for consideration of such an agreement.

Far more common are liability clauses restricted to specific observable results such as delivery date, and average number of test transactions correctly processed per minute. Careful explanation of each commitment and its associated acceptance criteria is needed in the body of the contract. Every change must be incorporated promptly in the document as well, thereby limiting liability effectively. The contract document establishes the best working relationship between the customer (user and buyer) and the developer.

In-house projects do not involve contracts nor do they involve the legal or financial aspects of liability. Nevertheless, they have all the other characteristics of commitment and risk. Here, too, an effective relationship between the user and the developer must be based on mutual understanding of what is to be built and what the exposures to success are. A "document of understanding" similar to a contract is recommended for in-house projects. It can be the basis for more successful projects.

4.5   SUMMARY

As pointed out earlier, a contract formalizes many of the activities in a software project. It certainly clarifies the relationships between the developer, the user, and the buyer. For these reasons, the contract environment has been used here as the basis for discussing the concept formulation and project definition stages of a project. Even in the absence of a contract, as in a typical internal project, the formalities and guidelines covered in this chapter are useful.

The need for program development originates with the formulation of a concept and the preparation of system objectives. If the estimated value of the conceptual system is attractive compared to the estimated cost, project definition can be started. During project definition the objectives are reduced to requirements. The system analysts who do this separate essentials from nonessentials and provide a detailed, justified list of requirements for the designers. The Design Requirements Baseline (incorporating authorized changes) is the basis for soliciting proposals, negotiating contracts, and testing the end product for completeness and contract compliance.

The procedures for system analysis are the same whether one person does the work or a whole team is involved. There are two main approaches to analysis: process-oriented and data-oriented approaches. The first approach is more effective in real-time systems where there is no significant existing database and where the system can be described as in terms of a transaction flowing through a sequence of processes. The process requirements are defined first by the analysts, who then establish database requirements to fit the processes. A data-oriented approach builds on existing databases—which may or may not be automated in the existing system—and then sets requirements for processes to fit the databases. Both approaches can be used in the same system where appropriate. Either approach implies some consideration of the ultimate system design by the analysts. As a rule, it is a good idea to test and improve requirements by mentally picturing how the requirements will be met. On the other hand, it is definitely a bad idea to write the requirements in such a way that they prevent the system designers from finding the best possible ways to build the system.

System analysis usually starts with the advice. "Don't worry about cost. Just come up with the best set of requirements to meet our objectives." This guidance encourages brainstorming, novel and original thinking, breadth of investigation, and long-range planning. However, when the analysts reach the point of justifying the requirements list, they find out that there is indeed a limit on allowable cost. The budget for the project is roughly fixed, either by limits on available resources in the company or by the estimated value of the end product. Furthermore, the budget is usually much less than the total cost of all the justifiable requirements. At this point, tradeoffs must be made. The quality of cost and value estimates is statistically poor early in the life cycle, so tradeoff techniques tend to be simple weighted ranking methods. Each feature of the system is assigned a number representing its relative value. When the features are arranged in numerical sequence, items at the bottom of the list can be given up in order to preserve those at the top of the list.

In the contract environment, the contractor submits a proposal, usually in competition with other bidders, explaining how he or she would respond to the design requirements baseline. The proposal is a bridge between the project definition and project implementation stages of the life cycle. It serves to show whether the proposer understands the requirements, whether there is a reasonable plan for meeting the requirements, and whether personal experience qualifies him or her for the job. In a competitive situation, the best bidder can be selected. In-house jobs may allow no such choice but the proposal can still serve its purpose. If the internal development manager prepares a proposal/plan showing a lack of understanding of the job, it is possible to go through another iteration of problem definition, or consider an outside contractor. (To avoid conflicts of interest in an information systems department where analysts and developers all report to the same manager, proposal evaluation can be done by a steering committee. This is particularly valuable on large jobs where an interdepartmental task force was convened to formulate the system concept. Task force members or their managers can form a steering committee that monitors the system throughout the life cycle. The steering committee recommends actions to be taken by general management. Thus the committee effectively evaluates the proposals.)

A proposal is an offer to do a job. Aside from its legal implications, a proposal is a statement of what the proposer is ready to commit to do. A well-written proposal is responsive to the requirements, clear and precise, realistically priced. It provides advice for the user regarding changes or improvements to the baseline. It itemizes user/buyer responsibilities demanded by the proposer. It takes into account the risks associated with the commitment the proposer is offering to make. When accepted by the user/buyer, a well-written proposal can be a sound basis for preparing a revised design requirements baseline and negotiating a firm agreement to proceed with project implementation.

EXERCISES AND DISCUSSION QUESTIONS

1. In recruiting analysts for a large project, what professional attributes should you look for in the candidates?

2. What sources of information within a bank must be analyzed to generate the requirement that "daily customer account balances shall be computed for each transaction in sequence with appropriate overdraft penalties being assessed whenever the current balance falls below the account minimum balance"?

3. Can a justified requirement be an undesirable requirement? Why?

4. A university has 300 rooms of various size in 28 buildings on a 3,000-acre site. There are 200 classrooms (30 seminar rooms, 10 to 15 people; 50 classrooms, 25 students; 100 classrooms, 40 students; 20 classrooms, 80 students); 30 laboratories (5 physics, 5 electronics, 7 chemistry, 4 biology, 4 mechanics, 5 multipurpose); 30 terminal rooms (25 have 6 terminals, 5 have 20 terminals each); 35 study and student recreation halls; and 5 auditoriums (3 at 200 seats, 1 at 300 seats, 1 at 2,000 seats). There are 7,000 students expected next year. Approximately 1,250 courses are to be offered for a total of 550 classroom and 200 lab hours per week. You are to chair a task force to define a resource allocation system to assign classroom and lab space.

   a. Who should be on the task force?

   b. Who should be interviewed?

   c. Name two published sources on classroom scheduling.

   d. Write a representative set of system objectives.

   e. Write a representative requirement statement for scheduling terminals. Assume 40 percent of the students use terminals regularly; i.e., 2 to 3 hours a week.

   f. Outline the task force report.

5. Critique the following networking requirements:

   a. "It should be possible for multiple customers to share a common network to reduce communication costs. This capability will require special considerations in:

      1) Extending security/privacy (by node, by application).

      2) Accounting (detailed network usage by users, by time of day).

      3) Network management (central control of some network functions, multiple control points for others).

      4) Common job control definition, etc.

     Priority: 2

     Discussion: These same functions are required for the divisions within a multi-division company but the concept is clearer if multiple customers are considered.

     Justification: It is likely to be cheaper for small companies with a few very widely spaced locations to buy service from a networking utility than to build an in-house network."

   b. "The network user should perceive a logical address independent of the physical address being used by the network.

     Priority: 1

     Discussion: Users should not have to know anything about network structure in order to send messages.

     Justification: Maintenance of directories of physical addresses imposes cost and delay on all users which will cause some of them to reject the service."

   c. "It is desirable to block small messages together in one transmission segment. Several techniques are possible including:

      1) Hold transmission until an entire block is filled.

      2) Hold transmission for a maximum time interval (send a segment every n seconds).

     If blocking is done on the sending end, then deblocking is done on the receiving end.

Priority: 2

Discussion: It is acknowledged that while block/deblock increases transmission efficiency, it does have an effect on response time. Therefore, it should be provided as a user option.

Justification: Improved line utilization.''

   d. ''Compaction and compression should be provided as user options.

Priority: 2

Discussion: Both are used to eliminate any character or number which occurs more than x (three) consecutive times and are used to increase transmission efficiency. It could represent significant savings provided the time to compress and expand at the other end were not too great.

Justification: Clearly, compression/compaction are required for bulk data and image transmission.''

   e. ''The network should have the responsibility for restarting to the point of failure for any hardware, software, or line interface problem. If the user chooses, no messages will be lost. The user may define messages (e.g., some interactive transactions) which for performance reasons are not backed up 100 percent.

   In addition to no messages being lost, no duplicates should be created. Requirements for no lost messages or duplicates may be impossible to achieve. It may be acceptable to provide tools that would aid in the determination and correction of lost/duplicate message traffic.

   1) A forced IPL should be avoided if possible. This slows down the restart and destroys other data.

   2) It may be possible to handle some aspects of the restart in an application.

   3) Checkpoint/Restart of the host access method is a prerequisite.

Priority: 1

Justification: Though restart may not be unique to networking, networking may complicate the restart over simple tree network restart.''

   f. ''The network will have to be constructed gradually. It is visualized that the first CPU to use the network would have its terminals connected to a remote node or possibly two and that these terminals function effectively before moving forward. Nodes would continue to be added one at a time as would other CPU's. Each node will have to be tested to assure that the links operate satisfactorily and that routing tables and recovery routines are operational.

   By the very nature of a data network, it would have to function with multiple operating systems and access methods in addition to program products. Implementing a network should not require changes to any existing application programs.

   For large organizations, a test network would have to be established to permit modification of programming systems in the node and complete testing prior to introduction into the operational network. Diagnostic routines for the customer and field engineering should be thorough and easily usable.

The network should be independent of releases of programming systems in the CPU as well as in the nodes. That is, applications and operating systems in the CPU should be changeable without impacting the network. Also, different release levels of the program driving the nodes should co-exist within the network to permit a gradual conversion to a newer release.''

6. In a rational marketplace, consumer decisions are based on value. When consumers replaced second-generation computers with third-generation systems they must have perceived greater value in the new machines; i.e., price/performance had improved. It can be assumed that microprocessors have less capability than miniprocessors, which have less capability than large general-purpose processors—even if machines in each category have the same add time. Thus performance is not easily quantifiable. To assist in computer selection, an analyst constructs an algorithm that reflects marketplace behavior and ranks machines in price/performance order. The analyst hypothesizes that the following formula is a fair measure of hardware price/performance in general situations:

$$P/P = [\frac{a \cdot b \cdot c \cdot d \cdot e \cdot \log (f \cdot g)}{h \cdot i}]$$

where

a = internal storage capacity, maximum, in bytes
b = memory word size, in bytes (1 in a byte-oriented machine)
c = number of bytes in ADD operand (arithmetic word size)
d = number of instructions in repertoire
e = maximum number of bytes per second transferred from auxiliary storage (all channels operating) not to exceed computer bandwidth
f = maximum disk unit capacity in bytes
g = number of channels
h = average instruction time (default value = average add time)
i = price of typical configuration

The factors were chosen because they are published by vendors and periodically collected in references such as *Computer Review.**

a. Test this hypothesis against half a dozen machines including a micro, a mini, and a large machine.
   1) For machines of the same vendor, does the formula confirm the spectrum of price/performance of a compatible line?
   2) For machines of various vendors, does the formula confirm your opinion of relative price/performance ranks?
b. What is the consequence of ignoring software?
c. What type of decision, if any, does the formula support?

Computer Review and *Minicomputer Review* published three times a year by *GML* Corporation, Lexington, Mass.

7. Analysis of an installed system shows that, at present volumes, response time is adequate but that projected volumes will overload the system. Two solutions have been proposed to handle the volume increase without affecting response time. Solution A proposes to expand the existing processor to a multiprocessor at a cost of $1,000,000 (covering planning, installation, and use for three years). Solution B proposes to revise the system programs to reduce their average path length by 40 percent. The cost of B is estimated to be $800,000 (covering the development life cycle including three years of maintenance).

  a. which solution is more attractive: the hardware solution, A, or the software solution, B? Why?
  b. Your organization has been through many similar situations. Past experience shows that hardware costs differ by 0 to + 19 percent from the estimate, primarily due to unanticipated software changes caused by new hardware. Programming costs differ by − 10 percent to + 50 percent from the estimate, primarily due to specification changes during development. With this information, would you pick A or B? Why?

8. Compare proposal Executive Summary A to Executive B. B is better. Why? How would you improve B?

EXECUTIVE SUMMARY A

The ABLE Corporation proposes to provide Bee Manufacturing with those services necessary to design the required system support for the material control, purchasing, and sales analysis areas. Information for this proposal was gathered over several meetings with members of the staff at Bee Manufacturing.

Support for the material control area will encompass the timely flow of transactions to update a material database. Reporting from this database will then be on an inquiry, exception, or cyclical basis. For those items that are forecastable, tools will be provided for forecasting and order point/order quantity control. A majority of parts are not forecastable, but are dependent on usage in a higher level. For these parts the project team will develop a requirements planning subsystem. A purchasing system will be developed, along with a sales analysis system that will provide the necessary support for forecasting.

ABLE's proposed approach to the system design offers significant benefits to Bee Manufacturing;

  a. The application of a dedicated contractual group to the development of the intended system provides assurance of continuity of purpose, minimal distraction, and an earlier implementation.
  b. Bee Manufacturing will be relieved of the necessity to add permanent employees for the peak labor force and special skills requirements of a manufacturing based system.
  c. The ABLE Project Manager will develop detailed work plans, review progress, take corrective action where necessary, and provide Bee Manufacturing with status reports.

This particular proposal relates to the detailed analysis of functional requirements and the design of a Material Control System. This effort can be defined as Phase 0 of the development cycle. The prime objective of Phase 0 is to provide those specifications that will lead to orderly and effective accomplishment of design and implementation. There are three major tasks in Phase 0; a brief description of those tasks follows.

Task 1—Project initiation and planning
The major objectives of this task are to establish the procedures for communications through the project administrator, identify the personnel who will serve as information sources, orient the ABLE project team to Bee Manufacturing's present material control system, and allow a review of the status of existing operations, procedures, and organization.

Task 2—Requirements Definition
The major objective of this task is to establish, in user terms, the functions to be supported by the system. To accomplish this, the existing material control system will be analyzed in detail. This detailed information plus new system requirements will serve as the basis for the System Requirements Report.

Task 3—General system definition
The major objective of this task is to prepare a System Concept Report for review and concurrence by Bee Manufacturing. This report will define the general system organization, functional flow, and database structures. A description of the major functional systems and their interrelationships will be included. The PROCON Program Products will be evaluated at this point. These program products contain varying amounts of material control philosophy. The project team will match the philosophy base of the packages with the material control philosophy of Bee Manufacturing. The project team will then evaluate such factors as package fits, package flexibility, implementation time requirements, and economics. Based on this analysis, ABLE will recommend optimal and balanced implementation to meet the specific requirements of Bee Manufacturing.

EXECUTIVE SUMMARY B

Bee Manufacturing has discussed with ABLE their management need and operational need for improving efficiency and responsiveness in material control, purchasing, and sales analysis. ABLE has formed a general understanding of your objectives through three meetings in September with Messrs. Dubya, Echs, Wye, and Zee.

ABLE proposes to initiate work toward your desired improvements by performing a requirements analysis in the stated areas and to then recommend which of those requirements could be enhanced by automation. We will conclude this contractual effort, which we call Phase 0, with a general concept design for a Material Control System including purchasing and sales analysis.

We currently believe that consolidating your material control, purchasing and sales analysis data into a single information bank is important groundwork for improving efficiency. We have observed that your present system retains essentially the same kind of data in several places. In addition to causing redundant effort, this practice risks making decisions on out-of-date or incompatible information. Automating this consolidated database should improve the timeliness by which new information can be assimilated and processed, and should, therefore, increase the likelihood of making decisions on the latest and most compatible information. Available forecasting and economic order quantity techniques can be considered for the automated database system. We believe steps can also be taken to include some forecasting capability for components whose requirements are governed by forecasts of larger items.

ABLE believes that by selecting our proposed approach you will acquire an increased system development capability without a permanent increase in your development staff, and will be relieved of many of the managerial details of project development.

There are three steps in our approach to recommending a concept design.

Task 1—Project initiation and planning

This task sets up working relationships with your project administrator, identifies your personnel who will serve as information sources, and orients the ABLE team to the existing operations, procedures and organization of your present material control system.

Task 2—Requirements definition

This task establishes, in Bee Manufacturing terminology, the functions in your current system. Your existing material control system will be combined with your new system requirements and presented for your review in the System Requirements Report.

Task 3—General system definition

This task considers the total requirements of your material control system and recommends those that appear suitable and cost effective for automation. These recommendations are formulated into a general design and documented in a System Concept Report for your review and concurrence. This report defines the general system organization, major processing components, general flow of data and data storage components.

ABLE's PROCON Program Products will be evaluated by matching their capabilities to the material control needs of Bee Manufacturing. Based on suitability, flexibility, and implementation time, ABLE will recommend what, if any, role PROCON can play in a balanced implementation meeting the specific requirements of Bee Manufacturing.

9. The original project description and statement of work for the proposed installation of a time-sharing system based on TSO are shown below followed by new versions resulting from a system assurance review. Separating the two proposals are a series of discussion questions regarding the changes made to the original version.

ORIGINAL PROPOSAL
Section 1
Project Description

1.1 INTRODUCTION

Successful installation of the Time-Sharing Option of Operating System/370 (TSO) and its associated Program Products can be a complicated, time-consuming procedure. In view of the urgency expressed by LANCO Services personnel concerning the installation of TSO, it is important that this work be performed by people who are familiar with TSO and experienced in its installation. ABLE is well qualified to perform this service for LANCO.

1.2 PROJECT OBJECTIVES

The fundamental goal of this project is to install and deliver to LANCO Services an effective time-sharing system utilizing TSO and several Program Products. This installation is planned to occur within a time frame necessary to support the pressing needs of LANCO time-sharing users. This system will be designed to service both professional programming personnel as a program development aid and the problem solvers at LANCO Properties and LANCO Corporate Headquarters currently employing outside time-sharing services.

1.3 TASK OBJECTIVES

Task 1—Requirements Definition
The objective of this task is to determine and document the functional and performance requirements of each group of users of the time-sharing capability to be provided by LANCO Services. The current activities of these users will be studied as well as the characteristics of the Miami Datacenter OS/370 environment. These requirements will be documented in the Installation Plan described in Task 2.

Task 2—System Definition
The primary objective of this task is to define the implementation of TSO and associated Program Products which satisfies the requirements defined during Task 1. This will be expressed in terms of the features of TSO to be provided and an Installation Plan for installing and demonstrating TSO and the associated Program Products. This Plan will be submitted to LANCO Services for their review.

Task 3—TSO Installation
The purpose of this task is execution of the Installation Plan developed during Task 2. TSO and the associated Program Products will be installed and tested to verify their proper operation. Terminal users and operators will be trained. On the basis of the functional demonstration specified in the Installation Plan, the time-sharing system will be turned over to LANCO Services for productive use.

Task 4—System Measurement and Tuning
The objective of this task is to assist LANCO Services Technical Support personnel in applying system measurement techniques to the functional time-sharing system delivered at the end of Task 3 and to assist in making adjustments where necessary to improve system performance.

Section 2
STATEMENT OF WORK

2.1 INTRODUCTION

This section describes the tasks ABLE will perform in the installation of TSO, the project's deliverable items, a planned project schedule, and the responsibilities of LANCO Services in support of this project. Certain assumptions upon which we have based both the scope of this project and our estimates are also included.

2.2 TASK DESCRIPTIONS

Subject to the provisions of the Agreement for ABLE Contract Services, ABLE will perform the following tasks:

Task 1—Requirements Definition
Prepare a profile of each prospective TSO terminal user group and their projected activities defining their functional and performance requirements for time-sharing. Among those to be considered are: current time-sharing users in LANCO Properties and LANCO Corporation, the system control terminal operator, and program development personnel.
Analyze current data-processing operations to determine present system loading. This information will later be combined with the projected TSO loading to provide a basis for system generation planning.

Task 2—System Definition
Define features of TSO and supporting Program Products that satisfy the above requirements and recommend to LANCO Services which licenses for Program Products to procure in conjunction with TSO.
Define educational requirements for terminal users and system operators and develop appropriate training materials.
Define system control procedures such as accounting and recommend what course LANCO Services should pursue in implementing these functions.
Develop conversion plans for each prospective terminal user to ease the transition from that user's current mode of operation to TSO.
Prepare an OS/370 system generation specification to satisfy the current data-processing environment with the addition of TSO as determined in Task 1. The extent to which the performance requirements will be satisfied will, of course, be dependent upon the actual system loads encountered and the hardware resources available.
Prepare a detailed Installation Plan describing the requirements identified in Task 1, the system definition derived in Task 2, and a detailed work plan for

Task 3. The Plan will describe the criteria for demonstrating the completeness of the installation. This Plan will be submitted to LANCO for its review and approval.

Task 3–TSO Installation

Generate OS/370 and TSO and test for proper function. The Program Products procured by LANCO Services will be included in the system library and verified.

Conduct a terminal users class for both programmers and problem solvers. The subjects to be covered will be TSO concepts, the TSO command language, and LANCO installation procedures.

Train system operators in TSO initialization, operational monitoring, termination, and recovery procedures. They will also be instructed in the application of LANCO installation procedures.

Demonstrate the tested functional TSO system in accordance with the agreed upon criteria in the Installation Plan. The system will be turned over to LANCO Services Operations and Technical Support personnel for productive use.

Task 4—System Measurement and Tuning

For a period of thirty days and for a maximum of five person-days, following the delivery of the system to LANCO Services, ABLE will periodically measure TSO performance and make adjustments to improve it. These adjustments will, of course, be constrained by the functional requirements of the system and the availability of required hardware resources.

2.3   PROJECT DELIVERABLES

Subject to the provisions of Paragraph X of the Agreement, the following items are planned for delivery to LANCO Services Project Administrator:

1. *TSO Installation Plan:* This document will contain the following sections:
   a. Profile of each user of time-sharing services as defined in Task 1 of the Statement of Work.
   b. Description of the current OS/370 installation at LANCO Services and a definition of system loading.
   c. List and description of features of TSO and supporting Program Products to be installed at LANCO Services.
   d. Plan for time-sharing education for users and support personnel at LANCO, including a general description of each required course.
   e. Procedures for converting each current time-sharing user to TSO. These procedures will be a list of the steps each user should take to convert his or her data and operation.
   f. A detailed task list and schedule for generation and testing of TSO and the supporting Program Products.
   g. A list of the functions to be demonstrated to LANCO as evidence of completion of the installation. Each function will be described in terms of the operation that will be performed and the expected results.

2. A tested, functioning time-sharing system built around the Time Sharing Option (TSO) of OS/370.
3. Training materials for terminal users and system operators as prepared and used in the training courses in Task 3.

2.4   RESPONSIBILITITES OF LANCO SERVICES

ABLE's performance of the Statement of Work is contingent upon LANCO Services assuming the following responsibilities:

1. LANCO is to designate a Project Administrator to serve as the coordinator between ABLE and LANCO Services. He or she will be responsible for providing the ABLE project team with required information, for making decisions relative to the technical performance required, and for granting or obtaining approval of items submitted for concurrence.
2. LANCO is to provide ABLE personnel access to all documents, data, personnel, and facilities necessary to complete the tasks described in 2.2.
3. LANCO is to provide ABLE with whatever computer time is required.
4. LANCO is to procure licenses in order to use the Program Products necessary to satisfy the requirements of the system.
5. LANCO is to convert the listing programs and data as required to operate under TSO.
6. LANCO is to define and implement security measures to protect programs and/or data from access by unauthorized persons.
7. LANCO is to provide user training required beyond that discussed under 2.2 above.
8. LANCO is to provide any secretarial, clerical, keypunch, or reproducing services that may be required. In addition, LANCO will provide work facilities for the ABLE team consistent with those provided its own personnel performing similar work.
9. LANCO is to define, procure, and install any communications facilities required to implement TSO.

2.5   PROJECT ASSUMPTIONS

The scope of the effort ABLE is proposing herein and the cost of that effort have been predicated on certain assumptions, as follows:

1. That OS/370, TSO, and associated Program Products will be used without modification.
2. That no original programming effort will be required of ABLE personnel assigned to this project.

2.6   PROJECT SCHEDULE

Figure 2.6-1 is the schedule for ABLE's performance of the tasks described in Section 2.2 above (omitted).

Read the revised version of the proposal, given below; then, referring to the original proposal, answer the following questions:

a. Does paragraph 1.1 address LANCO and LANCO's problems?

b. What is an *effective* time-sharing system (1.2)?

c. When will the proposed time-sharing system be operational?

d. In paragraph 1.2 does the phrase "designed to service" mean there is some doubt that the system "will service" LANCO's needs?

e. What is the scope of the document referred to in Task 1?

f. Does Task 2 "define requirements" or "define an installation plan"?

g. Is it important to specify what LANCO uses the time-sharing system for after they accept it?

h. What does "functional" mean in Task 4?

i. In Task 2 of the SOW, should ABLE develop conversion plans for "each prospective terminal user"?

j. In Task 3, what will ABLE do if LANCO does not agree that all the recommended Program Products are necessary? Does paragraph 2.4.4 answer this question?

k. Is it meaningful to measure and tune TSO rather than the overall LANCO system of TSO plus batch plus other interactive programs, if any? (Task 4)?

l. How will ABLE and LANCO resolve any disagreement regarding the acceptability of the test and demonstration plan (paragraphs 2.2 Task 3, 2.3. f and g, 2.4.1)?

In the following revised version, a number of phrases have been italicized. These are candidates for further improvement. What changes do you suggest?

REVISED VERSION
Section 1
PROJECT DESCRIPTION

1.1   INTRODUCTION

LANCO Services personnel recently expressed to ABLE their urgent need to install the time-sharing option of Operating System/370 and its associated Program Products. Since installing TSO can be a complicated and time-consuming procedure, it is important that the work be performed by personnel familiar with TSO and its installation. ABLE has such personnel and is proposing to accomplish this installation for LANCO.

1.2   PROJECT OBJECTIVES

Mr. Blanque of LANCO Services has stated the urgent need for TSO. To meet this need ABLE will install a time-sharing system utilizing TSO and other appropriate Program Products on an expedited installation plan (estimated as 90 days from start of contract performance). This system will be a program development aid for your professional programming staff and an in-house problem-solving facility for your employees currently using outside time-sharing services. We will survey user needs before generating the TSO system. Following installation we will review the first 30 days of use to retune TSO performance balanced against existing operations.

Since your TSO performance characteristics will depend on many factors whose average effect may not be readily apparent in the first 30 days, you should plan to continue this performance tuning for 6 to 12 months.

1.3   TASK OBJECTIVES

Task 1—Requirements definition
This task analyzes and documents the functional and performance requirements of your present and potential time-sharing users. The current activities of these users and the characteristics of the Miami Datacenter OS/370 environment will be studied. These activities and characteristics will be documented as requirements and constraints in the Installation Plan described in Task 2.

Task 2—System definition
This task defines the implementation of TSO and associated Program Products consistent with the requirements recorded during Task 1. This definition will list the features of TSO to be provided and *contain the Installation Plan* for installing and demonstrating the TSO system. *This plan will be submitted to LANCO for review.*

Task 3—TSO installation
This task executes the Installation Plan. The TSO system will be installed and tested to verify proper operation. Terminal users and operators will be trained. The functional demonstration will be conducted as specified in the Installation Plan. After demonstrating the functions and criteria given in the plan, the time-sharing system will be turned over to LANCO.

Task 4—System measurement and tuning
This task assists LANCO Technical Support personnel in applying system measurement techniques to the time-sharing system and in making adjustments to improve system performance.

Section 2
STATEMENT OF WORK

2.1   INTRODUCTION

This section describes the tasks ABLE will perform in the installation of TSO, the project's deliverable items, an estimated project schedule, and the responsibilities of LANCO Service in support of this project. Certain assumptions upon which ABLE has based both the scope of this project and its estimates are also included.

2.2   TASK DESCRIPTIONS

Subject to the *provisions of the Agreement for ABLE Contract Services,* ABLE will perform the following tasks:

2.2.1 Task 1—Requirements definition

2.2.1.1   Interview each prospective TSO terminal user group and collect the following information:

- For Current Time-Sharing Users:
  1) Number of programs to be converted
  2) Sizes of largest program (# lines of code)
  3) Language(s) used
  4) Data file requirements
     a) record sizes
     b) file sizes
  5) Frequency and duration of time-sharing usage
  6) Relative frequency of usage of catalogued programs vs. one-time jobs (for FORTRAN only)

- For Programmers
  1) Number of programs to be catalogued
  2) Average size of programs (# lines)
  3) Language(s) used
  4) Anticipated frequency and duration of system use
  5) Size of largest program(s) to be invoked (probably a compiler)
  6) Number of programmers to be served

The users to be interviewed are:
  1) Financial Planning—LANCO Corporation
  2) Economic and Financial Planning—LANCO Properties
  3) LANCO Services Systems Development

2.2.1.2   Collect the following information about current data-processing operations at the Miami Datacenter.
  1) List of OS routines which are transient and resident
  2) List of DASD device and channel utilization as determined from SMF
  3) Core map of current system (including problem regions)
  4) Estimated current CPU utilization as determined from SMF

2.2.1.3   Establish communication between ABLE and LANCO to *review the requirements definition, select the requirements applicable to Task 2, and determine change control procedures.*

2.2.2 Task 2—System definition
2.2.2.1   Based on the requirements defined by LANCO in Task 1, summarized in matrix form, define the features of TSO and supporting Program Products *that satisfy* these requirements. Recommend to LANCO Services which licenses for Program Products to procure in conjunction with TSO. The Program Products to be considered are:

> ANS COBOL Compiler and Library
> TSO COBOL Prompter
> Code and Go FORTRAN IV Compiler
> FORTRAN IV G1 Compiler
> TSO FORTRAN Prompter
> Structured Programming Facility
> BASIC-VS
> TSO Assembler Prompter

TSO Data Utilities
COBOL Interactive Debug
STAT/BASIC
MATH/BASIC

2.2.2.2   Prepare class outline for terminal users and system operators classes and develop *appropriate* training materials.

2.2.2.3   Prepare OS/370 system generation parameters to satisfy the current data-processing environment with the addition of TSO as determined in Task 1.

2.2.2.4   Prepare specifications for testing and demonstrating the time-sharing system. These specifications will define that data representing problems or source programs which will be entered through the time-sharing system as a functional demonstration of each product. The test will create its own data where necessary. *The standard test procedure will be to enter data through one or more time-sharing Program Products and execute the resulting program.*

2.2.2.5   Prepare an Installation Plan describing the requirements identified in Task 1, the system definition derived in Task 2, and a detailed work plan for Task 3. *The Plan will describe the criteria for demonstrating the completeness of the installation. This plan will be submitted to LANCO for its review.*

2.2.3 *Task 3—TSO installation*

2.2.3.1   Generate OS/370 and TSO and test according to the test plan defined under Task 2.2.2.4. The Program Products procured by LANCO Services will be included in the system library.

2.2.3.2   *Conduct a terminal users class* for both programmers and problem solvers. The subjects to be covered will be TSO concepts, the TSO command language, and LANCO installation procedures. *This will be a half-day class.*

2.2.3.3   *Train system operators* in TSO initialization, operational monitoring, termination, and recovery procedures. They will also be instructed in the application of LANCO installation control policies and procedures. *This will be a half day classroom training and twenty hours of on the job training.*

2.2.3.4   Demonstrate the time-sharing system made up of TSO and those Program Products selected in Task 2 in accordance with the criteria in the Installation Plan. Upon completion of the demonstration, the system will be turned over to LANCO Services Operations and Technical Support personnel for productive use.

2.2.4 *Task 4—System measurement and tuning*

For a period of thirty days and for a maximum of five person-days, following the delivery of the system to LANCO Services, ABLE will provide interpretation of SMF output to determine:

1) Excessive device contention
2) Excessive calls for transient routines and insufficient use of resident routines
3) Time-sharing region core utilization
4) "Think time" (time between terminal ready and enter key depressed) distribution.

Where these areas are different than those predicted in Task 2.2.1.2, ABLE will also provide within the limits of the hours available:

1) Re-allocation of time-sharing data sets by device and channel
2) Adjustment of transient vs resident routines
3) Time-sharing region size adjustment
4) Adjustment of number of time-sharing regions

2.3   PROJECT DELIVERABLES

Subject to the provisions of the Agreement, the following items are planned for delivery to the LANCO Services Project Administrator:

2.3.1   TSO Installation Plan—this document will contain the following sections:

2.3.1.1   *Profile of each user* of time-sharing services as defined in Task 1 of Statement of Work. This will be a matrix of the information as determined in Task 1.

2.3.1.2   Description of the current OS/370 installation as per items collected in Task 2.2.1.2.

2.3.1.3   List and description of features of TSO and supporting Program Products to be installed at LANCO Services.

2.3.1.4   Class outlines for users and support personnel at LANCO.

2.3.1.5   A schedule for generation and testing of TSO and the supporting Program Products.

2.3.1.6   A list of the functions to be demonstrated to LANCO as evidence of completion of the installation. *Each function will be described in terms of the operation that will be performed and the expected results.*

2.3.2   *The demonstrated time-sharing system.*

2.3.3   *Training materials*—for terminal users and system operators as prepared and used in the training courses in Task 3.

2.4   RESPONSIBILITIES OF LANCO SERVICES

ABLE's performance of the Statement of Work is contingent upon LANCO Services assuming the following responsibilities:

2.4.1   LANCO is to designate a Project Administrator to serve as the coordinator between ABLE and LANCO Services. He or she will be responsible for providing the ABLE project team with required information, for making decisions relative to the technical performance required, and for granting or obtaining approval of items submitted to LANCO for concurrence.

2.4.2   LANCO is to provide ABLE access to all *documents, data, personnel, and facilities necessary* to complete the tasks described in 2.2 above.

2.4.3   LANCO is to provide at no cost to ABLE *whatever computer time is required* during prime shift at the LANCO Miami Datacenter. Specific estimates for hands-on and on-line time will be included in the Installation Plan described under Task 2.

2.4.4   LANCO is to procure licenses in order to use the Program Products necessary to satisfy the requirements of the system.

2.4.5   *LANCO is to convert existing programs and data as required to operate under TSO.*

2.4.6   *LANCO is to define and implement backup, accounting, and security measures as required.*

2.4.7   LANCO is to provide user training required beyond that discussed under 2.2.3 above.

2.4.8   *LANCO is to provide any secretarial, clerical, keypunch, or reproducing services that may be required.* In addition, LANCO will provide work facilities for the ABLE team consistent with those provided its own personnel performing similar work.

2.4.9   LANCO is to define, procure, and install *any communications facilities required* to implement TSO:

2.5   PROJECT ASSUMPTIONS

The scope of the effort ABLE is proposing herein and the cost of that effort have been predicated on certain assumptions, as follows:

2.5.1   That OS/370, TSO, and associated Program Products will be used without modification.

2.5.2   That no original programming effort will be required of ABLE personnel assigned to this project.

2.5.3   LANCO review and approval will take no longer than five working days for requirements selection in Task 1 and for the Installation Plan in Task 2. Delays will be reflected in the completion date day-for-day; moreover, delays in approval will reduce the duration of Task 4 one day for each day of delay beyond fifteen working days. The validity of system tuning will be correspondingly affected.

2.6   PROJECT SCHEDULE

Figure 2.6.1 is an estimated schedule for ABLE's performance of the tasks described in Section 2.2 (omitted).

REFERENCES

1. Quade, E. E. *Analysis for Public Decisions.* New York: American Elsevier Publishing Co., 1975.

2. Bell, T. E., and Thayer, T. A. "Software Requirements: Are They Really a Problem?" *Proceedings 2nd International Conference on Software Engineering.* New York: IEEE, Inc. 1976.

3. Abramson, N., and Kuo, F. F. *Computer-Communication Networks.* Englewood Cliffs, N.J.: Prentice-Hall, 1973.

4. Allen, T. J., and Cohen, S. I. "Information Flow in Research and Development Laboratories." *Administrative Science Quarterly* 14, no. 1 (March 1969).

5. Sanders, R. W. "A Possible Structure for Designing Computer Communication Networks and the Near-Term Possibilities." *Second USA-Japan Computer Conference, 1975.* Montvale, N.J.: AFIPS, Inc., 1975.

6. Criteria for the Performance Evaluation of Data Communications Services for Computer Networks. *NBS Technical Note 882.* U.S. Department of Commerce, National Bureau of Standards. Washington, D.C.: U.S. Government Printing Office, 1975.

7. Blanc, R. P., and Cotton, I. W. *Computer Networking.* New York: IEEE Press, 1976.

8. Davis, C. G., and Vick, C. R. "The Software Development System." *IEEE Transactions on Software Engineering* SE-3, no. 1 (January, 1977).

9. Alford, M. "A Requirements Engineering Methodology for Real-Time Processing Requirements." *IEEE Transactions on Software Engineering* SE-3, no. 1 (January, 1977).

10. Bell, T. E.; Bixler, D. C.; and Dyer, M. E. "An Extendable Approach to Computer-Aided Software Requirements Engineering." *IEEE Transactions on Software Engineering* SE-3, no. 1 (January, 1977).

11. Dreyfus, J. M., and Karacsony, P. J. "The Preliminary Design as a Key to Successful Software Development." *Proceedings 2nd International Conference on Software Engineering.* New York: IEEE, Inc., 1976.

12. Ross, D. T. "Structure Analysis (SA): A Language for Communicating Ideas." *IEEE Transactions on Software Engineering* SE-3, no. 1 (January 1977). Also, Ross, D. T., and Schoman, K. E. "Structured Analysis for Requirements Definition." *IEEE Transactions on Software Engineering* SE-3, no. 1 (January 1977).

13. Miller, G. A. "The Magical Number Seven, Plus or Minus Two: Some Limits on Our Capacity for Processing Information." *The Psychological Review* 63, no. 2 (March 1956).

14. Glans, T. B.; Grad, B.; Holstein, D.; Meyers, W. E.; and Schmidt, R. N. *Management Systems.* New York: Holt, Rinehart and Winston, 1968.

15. Hartman, W.; Matthes, H.; and Proeme, A. *Management Information Systems Handbook.* Apeldoorn, The Netherlands: N.V. Philips-Electrologica, 1968.

16. Langefors, B. *Theoretical Analysis of Information Systems.* Philadelphia: Auerbach, 1973.

17. Collins, J. H. "The Application of the Systems Approach to the Design of Computer Based Data Processing Systems." *Journal of Systems Engineering* 4, no. 2 (January 1976).

18. Boehm, B. W. "Software and Its Impact: A Quantitative Assessment." *DATAMATION* 19, no. 5 (1973).

19. Aron, J. D. "Commercial Data Processing Machines in Government Applications." *AFIPS Conference Proceedings* 40, Spring Joint Computer Conference, 1972. Montvale, N.J.: AFIPS Press, 1972.

20. Fedorowicz, J. "Comments on Price/Performance Patterns of U.S. Computer Systems." *Communications of the ACM* 24, no. 9 (September 1981). Also, Cale, E. G.; Gremillion L. L.; and McKenney, J. L. "Price/Performance Patterns of U.S. Computer Systems." *Communications of the ACM* 22, no. 4 (April 1979).

21. Burr, W. E., and Smith, W. R. "Comparing Architectures." *DATAMATION* 23, no. 2 (February 1977).

22. Bartik, J. J. "Let Me Interrupt" and Parlette, R. R. W. "Criteria Clarified." Letters, *DATAMATION* 23, no. 5 (May 1977). Also, Entner, R. S. " 'Architecture' Answers" and McElbone, D. H. " . . . and More." Letters, *DATAMATION* 23, no. 6 (June 1977).

23. IBM Federal Systems Division. *Technical Directions* 7, no. 2 (Summer 1981).

24. Aron, J. D. *The Program Development Process: Part I—The Individual Programmer.* Reading, Mass.: Addison-Wesley, 1974.

25. Sammet, J. E. "Problems in, and a Pragmatic Approach to, Programming Language Measurement." *AFIPS Conference Proceedings* 39, Fall Joint Computer Conference. Montvale, N.J.: AFIPS Press, 1971.

26. Boehm, B. W.; Brown, J. R.; Kaspar, H.; Lipow, M.; MacLeod, G. J.; and Merritt, M. Y. *Characteristics of Software Quality.* Also, Thayer, T. A.; Lipow, M.; and Nelson, E. C. *Software Reliability: A Study of Large Project Reality.* Both published by Amsterdam, The Netherlands and New York: North-Holland Publishing Co., 1978.

27. Automatic Language Processing Advisory Committee. "Language and Machines: Computers in Translation and Linguistics." Publication 1416. Washington, D.C.: National Academy of Sciences, 1966.

28. Metcalf, H. C., and Urwick, L. *Dynamic Administration.* The Collected Papers of Mary Parker Follett. New York: Harper & Row, 1940.

5
Project Management and Organization

The problems of managing programming teams surfaced as soon as projects grew to require teams. As early as 1963, leaders in the field recognized that programming was advancing rapidly in terms of technology but was stagnant in terms of management practices. That year, some twenty managers met near Washington, D.C., to discuss the issues. The largest current systems, both government and commercial, were represented. The proceedings [1], which summarized the three-day symposium, cover two major topics: Management Planning and Control, and the Production Process. What is notable, however, is that under both topics the bulk of the discussion centered around how to manage. Then, as now, success in a large program development project was more dependent on management than on technology.

Management was difficult for three reasons. First, the earliest applications of computers were completed by individuals so no one developed any experience in managing others. Second, the personal and unstructured character of programming technology did not appear to fit the textbook management processes. Third, programmers were in great demand and many took advantage of this fact to indulge their individualism and resist management direction. The first problem was overcome by time. The second problem is in the process of being overcome by the development of more structured programming methods. The third problem essentially solved itself when demand slackened and the maturing programmers made a career commitment to their work and came to appreciate the benefits of teamwork. Still, program project management is difficult. It lies near one extreme of a spectrum of management environments. Program project management is largely concerned with the intellectual product of a group of people—not so much as the management of research but far more so than

369

the management of hardware development or manufacturing. In the latter cases, many tools exist to produce the desired results. Some activities are almost mechanistic. Planning and controlling such projects is significantly helped by the ability to measure and predict progress. Software development has not advanced that far and, if you look at software as more abstract than hardware, it may never reach the same degree of formalism. Software management can be expected to continue to be more concerned with people than with tools. Tools and procedures exist, as shown in earlier chapters, but they focus on assisting in the production of intellectual output. Except for the computer systems needed to develop, test, and execute code, most software tools and procedures involve documents rather than machines—plans, reports, program listings, standards, and the like. Such aids are aimed at communication among team members. The goal is to make the combined output of many people as coherent and effective as if it were the work of one person.

Most authors writing about management define *management* to fit the purpose of their text. A 1954 definition by the U.S. Air Force said "management is defined as a process of organizing and employing resources to accomplish predetermined objectives. A manager is a person who makes things happen, through the efforts of other people" [2]. Andrews [3] later defined management as "leadership in the informed, planned, purposeful conduct of complex activity." *Leadership* brings more life to the *process*. Dale [4] emphasized the *people* aspect by quoting Dean J. L. Hayes of Duquesne University. Hayes told a seminar audience in 1960 that, although new managers often hear "management is getting things done *through other people*," experienced managers hear the same words as "management is *getting things done* through other people." The first interpretation implies authoritarianism; the second interpretation implies a team led by a decision-making manager cooperating to reach a goal.

Dale, himself, follows the accepted practice of describing management in terms of the functions of a manager.[1] His seven functions, broadly defined, are:

- *Planning* Deciding what to do, setting objectives, selecting the means for meeting the objectives, subdividing the activities to fit the capabilities of the people

- *Organizing* Deciding what positions must be filled and what the duties and responsibilities of each position are, specifying clear lines of communication and reporting relationships

---

1. Dale's seven functions of management are a modification of Gulick's list [5], which is known by the mnemonic, POSDCORB, for *p*lanning, *o*rganizing, *s*taffing, *d*irecting, *c*oordinating, *r*eporting, and *b*udgeting. Dale treats budgeting within planning, coordination within organizing, and reporting within "control." The last is one of three new terms Dale has used.

- *Staffing* Selecting the right person for each job, providing for successors, training
- *Directing* Providing day-by-day direction and leadership for subordinates, telling them what to do and helping them do it, motivating
- *Controlling* Measuring progress and evaluating how well jobs have been done, seeing that the operating results conform to plan
- *Innovating* Finding and applying new ideas to improve operations and create opportunities
- *Representing* Representing the organization in dealings with other groups

These points include the key topics of management as developed over the years by Fayol, Taylor, Follett, Urwick, and many others [6]. *Control* is separated from *planning* as advocated by Taylor, yet the functions can be performed by the same person, as pointed out by Drucker [7, 8]. Control also implies measurement-by-objectives [8] and the use of quantitative techniques to support measurement and evaluation, and to build a base for decision-making [9]. *Staffing* recognizes the responsibility of management to perpetuate itself in order to ensure continuity in achieving the objectives. The functions of *direction, organization,* and *staffing* show the influence of Follett [10] and the human relations movement [11, 12] which relies on informed cooperation rather than "power." *Innovating* leads managers to use methods that encourage creativity. *Representing* the projects reminds managers that projects exist in a dynamic environment requiring each project team to communicate with many others.

The functions apply to management at all levels:

- Executive level or top management   Responsible for final business decisions, policy, long-range plan
- Higher-level or middle management   Responsible for administering the business, short- to medium-term outlook (Some authors use the term *administration* as a synonym for management when talking about this group).
- First-level management   Responsible for managing the people who actually carry out the operations of the business, short-term outlook

The relative emphasis placed on various management functions at each level depends to a large degree on the portion of time the manager devotes to direct supervision of subordinates. Direction consumes the most time at the first level, as indicated by Fig. 5.1. The guideline for span of control limits the number of people a manager supervises to less than seven. The chart shows that, in fact, the number should decrease at higher levels. The rule is often violated at the executive level. The people reporting to an executive are expected to be self-directed, leaving the executive free to plan

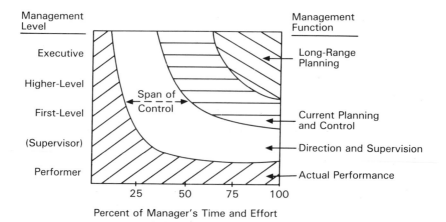

Fig. 5.1   Distribution of effort.
W. H. Newman, *Administrative Action: The Techniques and Organization of Management* (Englewood Cliffs, N.J.: Prentice-Hall, 1963). Reprinted by permission of Prentice-Hall, Inc., Englewood Cliffs, N.J.

and control [13]. In many industries, notably in manufacturing, the role of a supervisor or foreman has been created to improve the direction of large numbers of workers. Very little planning is expected of the supervisor who is usually carrying out the orders of a first-level manager. There is no good analogy for this job in programming. So-called "project leaders" or "team leaders" in programming are actually first-level managers. They have simply not yet been given the permanent job title of "manager."

Note the tradeoffs implied by the chart. A first-level manager with too many programmers will not be able to do much technical planning and control because he or she will be spending so much time directing the others. Likewise, if it is necessary for a higher-level manager to spend a substantial amount of time performing, say on a task force or calling on customers, his or her span of control should be reduced. The proper balance among management functions depends on the situation. An improper balance will lead to low quality results in the neglected areas.

5.1 PROJECT MANAGEMENT

The team brought together to carry out a project is a microcosm of its parent organization. Depending on the project size, one or more levels of management are organized in a hierarchy. It is through the organizational hierarchy that requirements are converted into action plans. The nature of the decisions at each point of the hierarchy depend on the level and role of the decision-making manager. Thus a first-level manager (FLM) at the base of the organizational pyramid is involved in different issues from those facing a higher-level manager (HLM).

The first-level manager manages the people who do the work. To accomplish this job, the FLM must be technically competent to show the workers what to do and to evaluate their output. In other words, a programming FLM must be a competent programmer. Since most FLMs are promoted from the ranks, it should be easy to meet the technical requirements of the job. It might be harder to find candidates who can carry out the other functions of a manager. Management experience is not acquired by nonmanagers.

This last point has been a source of considerable difficulty in the programming business. The extremely fast increase in demand for programmers that occurred in the 1960s set a pattern that persisted in the 1970s. In 1966, the pattern consisted of hiring college graduates (none of whom had any specific computer training since such courses were rarely offered at the time), teaching them a programming language, and immediately assigning them to write programs. As time passed, some of the employees found programming boring. They left the business or sought assignments in marketing or administration—areas where their natural curiosity about people and their interest in variety and fast-paced activity could be served. The remaining programmers, as a group, tended to be less gregarious, more interested in solving problems through to conclusion, and quite happy with the details of coding and debugging. Although it was not noticed much at the time, the people who left programming possessed more of the attributes associated with managers than the ones who stayed. The ones who stayed spent about five years programming before they became candidates for management positions. Then, when the time came, two types of employees were selected for promotion: the best performers who were little interested in managing and the few remaining "management types." The latter group lacked the self-confidence to get out of programming and into another line of work, yet, in the absence of better candidates, they were picked to be FLMs. Overall, the quality of management at the first level was weak during the mid-1960s. The good programmers in management preferred to do the critical programming themselves rather than delegate. (They were not acting as Chief Programmers, merely as individuals.) They were particularly weak in carrying out their staffing responsibilities. The consequence of this behavior was a poorly trained cadre of programmers entering the 1970s. A second consequence of this approach to promotion was that the best programmers tended to be diverted from technical activity. By 1970, it was common for ten- to fifteen-year veterans currently occupying management or administrative positions to bemoan the lack of progress since "their day." Few of them realized that this lack of progress was mainly due to their own redirection into management and the effect of their lackluster management performance on the young people that followed them.

The response to the problems was to develop training programs to teach existing managers how to do their job. As a first step this dammed the flood of new problems. Next, consideration was given to the kinds of project control mechanisms that could be adopted to cushion the effect of a manager's inexperience. To reduce the losses of potential manager candidates in the first few years of employment, more attention was given to making the programmer's job interesting and to provide opportunities for initiative and responsibility by nonmanagers. The latter involved not only giving each programmer more freedom of action but in setting up temporary project leaders for small teams. Finally, after the management crisis was addressed, some attention was paid to the technical side of the business. Methods were studied for capitalizing on the strengths of a very strong programmer without burdening that individual with management activities. (The Chief Programmer concept is such a method.) An increasing interest in making software development look more like hardware development with its standards, practices, and underlying scientific disciplines was another outcome of the technical concern. (Introduction of IPT and configuration management techniques resulted, for example.)

The historical trends were noted by W. A. Weimer, among others. He was managing an important IBM programming center where he had the opportunity to validate trends through interviews and employee meetings. In the course of his studies he collected data from both managers and programmers. A clear conclusion of the study was that some people thought of themselves as professional programmers; others considered themselves managers. There was considerable evidence to show that if either individual were forced to develop the aptitudes, attitudes, and interests of the other, performance would drop. Accepting that as the case, top management should see the need for a dual ladder of promotion, separating the opportunities of the technical professional from the managers. One would not have to become a manager to advance. On the other hand, no arbitrary obstacles would be placed to prevent someone from changing ladders. This approach allows people to capitalize on their strengths. There is a danger that junior employees will be stereotyped as "technical types" or "manager types" and that assignments based on the stereotyped image will fail to develop valuable skills. Most organizations use appraisal and counseling techniques to avoid such waste. Appraisal and counseling create a good understanding of an individual's capability and aspirations. With understanding, a manager can avoid such mistakes as turning a strong technical professional into a weak manager.

What are the clues that distinguish between people most likely to fit one ladder or the other? Weimer listed some of the attributes observable in the first few years of a programmer's nonmanagerial employment. His list, given in Table 5.1, is not exhaustive. Characteristics such as productivity, self-sufficiency, and general attitude are also important. Nevertheless, the list is a very good representation of the attitudes of experienced managers. Since it is these managers who make promotions, the bias generated by their attitudes and reflected in their behavior is relevant. In other words, an employee with the characteristics of a professional manager is much more likely to be promoted to a management position than an employee whose characteristics fit the professional programmer list.

5.1.1   First-Level Technical Manager (FLM)

Using the attributes of Table 5.1 to select new FLMs, the next step is to teach the recruits how to manage. That entails two types of courses: administrative and technical. It has always been common practice for new managers to go to classes to learn the personnel, financial, and administrative policies and procedures of their organization. These classes mix programming managers with engineers, sales managers, administrators, etc.; they are not designed to teach aspects of technical management. Programming managers also attended technical courses but these dealt mainly with techniques for writing programs. Starting in the 1960s, a series of programming project management courses added specific training in the duties of a FLM as a manager in a programming environment. The course outlines concentrated on system theory, development life cycles, technical planning, and resource management.

In one such course, the instructor made it a practice to ask the students (all managers with varying amounts of experience) what they thought the duties of a first-level manager were. Class consensus was normally obtained on the major management functions of planning, organizing, staffing, directing, controlling, innovating, and representing. They had already learned these in the manager's administrative course. On other items there was no consensus, most probably because each student's answers were based on personal experience and the spectrum of prior experience was wide. However, among the items suggested were management methods that have since become accepted as improved techniques.

- Planning
    1. Review technical alternatives to determine a course of action based upon technical implications and business objectives.
    2. Develop and recommend long- and short-range objectives, policies, and plans designed to produce the best results attainable from the group within the assigned area. (FLMs include long-range objectives in their charter even though they do not give them much attention.)
    3. Select project standards and tools including language, on-line support, documentation format, and analysis aids (consistent with overall project if the assigned area is a subset.)

TABLE 5.1.   ATTRIBUTES: PROGRAMMER VS. MANAGER

Professional programmer	Professional manager
1. *Communication* Good writer; insists on accurate, thorough documentation of detail; may dislike public speaking assignments	Good verbal communicator; sometimes tends to be less than thorough in documentation of detail
2. *Attention to detail* Likes to become immersed in detail-type assignments; likes the idea of becoming a specialist in a given subject	Usually dislikes detail; sees himself or herself as a generalist and therefore searches for a variety of assignments
3. *Attitude toward the organization* Dislikes structured environment; has difficulty keeping communication channels open with all his or her staff counterparts	Builds contacts in various organizations naturally; seems to always know whom to call to get an answer to a question
4. *Technical aptitude* Strong aptitude for and interest in technology; good analytical capability in technical matters	May or may not be strong technically; makes a real effort to understand rather than analyze; knows how to use technical advice from experts
5. *Aptitude for administrative and planning work* Capable of doing thorough and accurate administrative work but does not enjoy it	Strong aptitude for this kind of work; quite interested in it
6. *Interest in people* Usually more interested in concepts; tends to be impatient with people less capable than himself or herself; seeks out peers who can contribute to his or her knowledge	Quite interested in people and their development and training; looks for the best in people, even those not outstanding technically; shows interest in family affairs and outside interests of his or her people
7. *Judgment* Good technical and analytical judgment	Good judgment on matters of planning and strategy
8. *Self-motivation* Good in programming assignments; needs guidance and prodding in planning and staff interface assignments	Good in planning and staff interface assignments; needs guidance and prodding in assignments demanding precise technical detail

TABLE 5.1.   CONTINUED

Professional programmer	Professional manager
9. *Risk-taking*	
Takes few if any chances; usually will use the trial and error approach only when he or she is sure of his or her ability to correct problems that arise; tends to be a perfectionist	Will take the chance of being wrong; is happy if he or she is right at least half the time; sometimes impatient with the perfectionists in the group; may be more interested in games such as poker as opposed to bridge or chess
10. *Desire to make a contribution to his or her profession*	
Discipline-oriented; wants to document new findings and new techniques; is frustrated when time does not permit his or her contributing to the programming profession	Goals-oriented; prefers to document new ways to approach problems; often will write critiques of the education program or organizational structure for in-house improvements

4. Determine resource requirements and develop plans, schedules, and cost data for the assigned project. Submit realistic budgets, as required, reflecting anticipated income and/or expenditures. (While few managers denied their responsibility for developing a resource plan, many believed that budgets are actually created in the financial department and imposed on project managers. This belief is compounded in the software business by a tendency for projects to fit schedule and budget constraints. The managers confused the delivery deadline and the dollar limits with their own plan for achieving these objectives.)

5. Estimate workload to be assigned to each programmer. (Inexperienced managers agreed with this statement without qualification. Experienced managers restated it to read "Obtain estimates of workload from each programmer for the tasks assigned, balance the load on each programmer, rework these estimates into a departmental estimate, and report the departmental estimate to higher management." This is a technique of participative management. Experienced managers know that an employee is the best judge of his or her own work. These managers do not tell a programmer how long a job will take; they ask. If the estimate is unacceptable, some management action is required. The end result is a set of assignments that the employee accepts as a commitment.)

6. Schedule machine requirements for program debugging. (This duty was considered menial by some and significant by others. The latter group included more experienced managers who knew that it was essential to have machines available at the right times. Sometimes it takes considerable planning and negotiation to achieve this and it warrants the manager's attention.)

- Organizing
  1. Determine what jobs must be filled.
  2. Assign responsibility clearly so that subordinates know what they are expected to do, the extent of their authority, and the standards by which they will be judged; provide adequate guidance, counsel, and supervision, but give them sufficient authority to carry out their assignments and make decisions.
  3. Coordinate the activities of individuals on the team.
  4. Establish project leaders where appropriate to lead small teams on specific tasks.
  5. Develop organizational support for small teams and chief programmer teams as necessary. (These last two points were obviously supported by managers who had prior success with teams. They were ignored or considered drawbacks to FLM authority by others.)

- Staffing
  1. Staff the organization with capable people, train subordinates in the competent performance of their duties, periodically appraise their performance, and develop suitable replacements, including a successor. (Many managers felt they lacked the authority to staff their organization. They believed their HLM was going to give them only those people who could be spared elsewhere. This undoubtedly happens to managers who fail to aggressively seek out the right people for the job at hand. In general, though, the first-level managers are considered the only individuals qualified to set requirements for their staff, to recruit, and to evaluate their people.)
  2. Encourage and praise initiative, imagination, and resourcefulness; develop employees by advice and example in the exercise of judgment.
  3. Delegate wherever possible; teach prospective new managers and technical leaders how to manage and how to lead.

- Directing
  1. Assign tasks, obtain assignee's commitment, and provide technical direction. Unsnarl day-to-day operating problems without playing nursemaid; let subordinates solve as many of their own problems as possible.

2. Act as a trouble shooter to resolve critical problems. Step in and program when necessary. (On the basis that if all else fails the manager must personally lead the group to the objective, everyone agreed to this duty. There was no consensus, however, on how to determine that the time for such drastic action has come.)

3. Participate as well as direct. (The right level of participation maintains the FLM's technical competence and self-confidence as a programmer. Having been recently promoted from the ranks, most FLMs wanted to stay technically active so they readily agreed to this point. However, there were holdouts who reached their management position without ever having been programmers. Assuming that they must be qualified to hold their position and fearing embarrassment if they tried to catch up with their subordinates, these managers did not accept this as an appropriate duty.)

4. Set up mechanisms to foster good project communication, conduct regular group meetings, enforce change control procedures, and demand up-to-date documentation.

5. Insulate the group from unnecessary intrusions and excessive non-productive activities.

6. Insist on adherence to the current baseline design while encouraging constructive design change.

7. Supervise task interfaces. (The general consensus was that managers should control interfaces since no single programmer is in a good position to keep track of all the programmers' activities. The dissent on this point came from managers who intended to select one person as a technical assistant to supervise interfaces. In most organizations, however, FLMs are not authorized to have technical assistants.)

8. Understand and comply with established policies, procedures, and instructions and ensure that subordinates do likewise; and recommend changes when it appears that existing policy is no longer appropriate. (There were widely mixed reactions to two aspects of this item. Most managers were reluctant to follow standards set by anyone but themselves, their immediate superiors, or their customers. They were generally unable to justify their reluctance except by the unsupported claim that their project was unique. Second, a number of managers, particularly those in very large corporations or in civil service, were hesitant to agree that a first-level manager could *or should* try to effect changes in obsolete or onerous policies.)

9. Make provisions for the monitoring of test results; assuring adherence to the test plan while allowing for unique situations that don't fit the plan.

10. Schedule so as to minimize overtime and so as to leave time for employee self-development. (Aside from the need for vacations and sickness absences, many managers advised leaving up to 20 percent of available time for employees to read, attend meetings, write papers, etc. Almost an equal number of managers disagreed. The latter group felt that self-development should be done on the employees' own time. Furthermore, they frequently expressed the opinion that some level of overtime should always be planned to make certain that everyone is putting out his or her best effort.)

11. Institute adequate safety measures in the work area through elimination of potential hazards and safety education of subordinates in work practices and use of equipment.

12. Motivate employees through prompt and fair salary reviews, appraisal and counseling, definition of worthwhile tasks, participation in project decisions, and friendly and fair supervision. ("Manager types" emphasized these points, reflecting their orientation toward people. "Technical types" frequently felt that the opportunity to do an interesting job was sufficient motivation. They seemed not to recognize that what interested them might not interest the team members.)

- Controlling
  1. Determine status by discussion with team members.
  2. Ensure that the assigned project meets objectives and is completed according to schedule within assigned costs.
  3. Review the quality of the program by reviewing designs and by reading all or part of the code generated by the team. (Various levels of thoroughness were proposed. Good programmers who had become managers believed that code scanning was essential to quality control and employee growth. Chief Programmers read code as a requirement of their structured programming approach. Others sampled code at random and sat in on code inspections. The poor programmers and nonprogrammers did not read their employee's code and did not believe their time should be spent in that way.)
  4. Alert management as early as possible to problems that could materially affect objectives, schedules, and costs. (The emphasis here was on striking a balance between problems the team could solve and those requiring HLM attention. At the same time, experienced managers pointed out the importance of clear status reports that paint an accurate picture.)
  5. Control cost, performance, function content, quality, schedule, and standards. (All agreed on the basics of control. Disagreements related to the degree of formal control employed. Some managers believed in "back-of-an-envelope" methods supported by experi-

ence, intuition, and fast reaction. Others insisted on regular reports and analyses leading to trends, forecasts, and advanced planning. Either approach apparently works for a good manager; however, a weak manager needs rigorous aids.)

6. Ensure documentation of project activity including deliverables and appropriate reports.

- Innovating

1. Detect the need for and propose modifications in plans and operating methods that will result in improvements within the department.

2. Keep informed on developments affecting the assigned area and, to the extent possible, utilize these to the benefit of the project; and allow time for seminars, classes, conferences, reading technical papers, etc.

3. Solicit, reward, and use (appropriate) creative ideas, while at the same time knowing when to stop "improving" and start delivering.

- Representing

1. "Sell" HLM on the advisability of proposed actions.

2. Know what support is available from other departments and obtain it when required.

3. Negotiate with other programming personnel at the same level to assure integration of assigned project with the larger mission.

4. Cooperate actively with associates, both line and staff, to further the attainment of project objectives.

5. Ensure adequate and controlled communication with counterparts in the customer's organization.

6. Arrange for technical reports and papers that explain the lessons learned from the project activity. Exchange technical information with customers and professional groups. (All managers agreed on the importance of proper program and system documentation. They also agreed on the need for good communication with the customer. But when "communication" was extended to include professional society participation and development of technical reports for publication in a professional journal, most managers were unwilling to agree that they should lead their people in this area. This is probably due to an overemphasis on getting a job done and a lack of concern about the technology employed in the process.)

7. Do "completed staff work"; i.e., when reporting to higher-level management, always analyze available alternatives and propose a course of action stated in a form that will be clear to the HLM. (Everyone agreed on the importance of this vertical communication process but few knew what it entailed.)

Significantly, most FLMs singled out *communicating* as a key function of management. Although communication and communication skills are prerequisites of the seven basic functions, it is not unreasonable to add communicating as an eighth function. The FLM's task in this area is to let the team know where they stand—as individuals, as members of the team, as participants in the project, and as a subset of a system environment.

The list of FLM duties is supplemented by all of the administrative chores assigned to every manager in an organization. A first-level manager is a very busy person; yet, in spite of the scope of duties facing a new manager, very few first-level managers fail. Their success seems to be based on the fact that the problems they face are small, concrete, and local. Therefore, as long as they act to resolve a problem their chances are very high of finding a suitable solution before the problem gets out of hand. In addition, they get a lot of help from their HLM.

5.1.2   Higher-Level Technical Manager (HLM)

The distinction between a first-level manager and all higher-level managers is that the first-level manager supervises technical professionals and the higher-level manager mainly supervises managers. The subject matter at the first-level is programming technology. Higher up the subject is management. A consequence of this difference is seen in Fig. 5.2 to be a shift in the amount of direct attention paid to subordinates (vertical arrows) versus the amount devoted to peers (horizontal arrows) in the system hierarchy. The width of the arrows represents the amount of time and effort associated with each interface. Fig. 5.2 is another way of looking at the distribution of effort in Fig. 5.1. At the lowest levels, the assigned task is coherent and, often, self-contained as far as the assignee is concerned. Higher up the ladder, system complexity leads to more and more external activities.

The relationships at higher-levels involve significantly more negotiation. In order to control system interactions and simultaneously shield the lower-level managers from the need to resolve problems due to interactions, the HLM negotiates a mutually acceptable position with his or her counterparts. This takes more and more effort as one proceeds up the organizational pyramid because the concepts at high levels are poorly defined and hard to understand. In addition, the managers at high levels are strong enough to protect their area of responsibility from the impact of arbitrary directives. Each problem arising at these levels must be thoroughly evaluated in the light of its relation to all parts of the project. Then, by mutual agreement, one or more of the subsystem managers will accept the responsibility for a change in his or her area that will contribute to the solution to the problem. There develops a strong feeling of teamwork in this process, and each manager recognizes that he or she can be effective only by cooper-

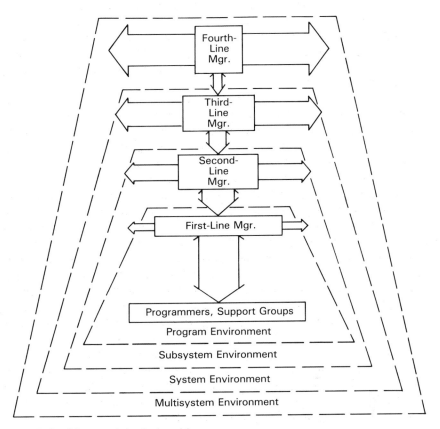

Fig. 5.2 Managerial relationships.

ating with other managers. The first time a newly-promoted second-level manager realizes that some of the near-dictatorial power he or she had as a first-level manager has been lost, it is quite a shock. Soon the individual realizes that the complexity of large systems is so great that no other method of operations could hope to achieve adequate control.

The duties of a higher-level manager are less precise and longer-range than those of a first-level manager. As a result of working with managers rather than with technologists, the duties emphasize plans, controls, and communications rather than programming. There are often nonmanagers (besides a secretary or clerk) reporting to a HLM; these people are generally senior technical people who require little direct supervision. In some departments, an HLM may also be the FLM for some task-oriented professionals. They will tend to distract the HLM from the primary duties of higher-level management. These duties include:

- Plan, organize, staff, direct, and control tasks within the area of responsibility; innovate; represent the organization.
- Be particularly sensitive to interfaces between subordinates, with parallel departments, and with the customer.
- Manage against plan using predominantly nontechnical summary data (such as status of events and accomplishments).
- Use intuitive ability to probe sources of information to evaluate where the project stands.
- Supervise the manner in which the lower-level managers administer their departments, help them grow as managers; replace them, if necessary.
- Plan for contingencies.
    1. Allow slack time in the resource plan so there is a reserve capability to handle problems and emergencies.
    2. Constantly ask "What if . . . ?" questions to develop alternate plans to meet contingency requirements.
    3. Build a technically competent organization that can perform in a changing environment.
- Teach subordinates to report in meaningful terms; make meaningful summary reports to HLM.

Given the lengthy list of FLM duties, most higher-level managers would say, "Well, I do all those things, too." The difference in the two lists is that experienced managers take such things as "delegate" as too obvious to require repeating. In addition, they recognize that they should not personally do such things as "review code." By contrast, they need to be reminded of the importance of managing interfaces and of preparing backup plans.

One new duty has been included in the list that marks the distinction between management levels. After the suggestion that the HLM learn how to measure status from nontechnical reports comes the recommendation that the HLM use judgment to evaluate the data. Although judgment cannot be taught, a manager who has it can put it to good use. The HLM gradually forgets the specifics of programming due to lack of practice and because there is no time to really absorb the changes in the technology. This makes the individual less effective as a judge of details within his or her area. The HLM must rely on subordinates to control the details. Then he or she must concentrate on evaluating the first-level managers. For a thoughtful, competent manager this is easier to accomplish than one might expect. It turns out that the organizational structure that isolates the HLM from the actual implementation effort positions him or her to evaluate the implementation. However, the HLM has access to information, strategies, executive thinking, etc., to which the FLM is not privy. In typical "can't see the forest for the trees" fashion, an FLM is often unable to spot the broad consequences of the team's work. The HLM can pick up these consequences more easily. The trick is to establish good enough communications between the two managers so that information about the "forest" is actually discussed. This can be done by directing the discussion to the *purpose* rather than the *mechanics* of each of the FLM's activities. It can also be done by drawing analogies between the current activities and past activities that the HLM was directly involved in. By drawing on experience, the HLM can often recognize courses of action that turned out badly in the past and, therefore, might be ill-advised in the present situation. A third method of establishing communication is to challenge the FLM's approach. The purpose of the challenge is to force the subordinate manager to justify the course of action and, in so doing, clarify it for the HLM. (In each case, the HLM must show that his or her main objective is to help the FLM do a good job. Improperly handled, the attempt to establish communications may give the subordinate the feeling that the HLM lacks confidence in him or her.) The consequence of effective HLM support is that a well-prepared FLM will make a presentation to the HLM, knowing full well that the HLM is less familiar with the situation than the FLM. The HLM will draw the key issues out of the presentation, integrate them mentally with additional facts about the project, about past history, and about the state-of-the-art, and reach conclusions that make sense. The FLM will leave the meeting impressed with the HLM's mental ability to understand the details and wondering "Why didn't I think of that?" with respect to the HLM's recommendations.

The HLM does not, in fact, understand the details; he or she understands the *context*. A given context calls up stored models of related situations that have been acquired over the years, often unconsciously [14]. These models lead the HLM to focus on certain bits of data that experience have shown to be important. As a result, the HLM deals with a smaller quantity of data than the FLM. He or she analyzes the key data with respect to a broader set of situational models than the less-experienced FLM knows about. The HLM's conclusions, therefore, can be completely outside the range of conclusions the FLM would reach. The conclusions will not necessarily be right, but they will be relevant. Through this type of exchange, the FLM begins to acquire the breadth of knowledge that he or she will use as an HLM. Unfortunately, the process is not one that can be taught in a classroom. Most HLMs cannot explain how they arrived at a given conclusion. The ability is acquired through experience and exposure to more experienced people. Two guidelines may help accelerate the process:

1. Make a *conscious effort to remember* the facts that apply to each situation.

2. Take time to *review past experience* periodically to determine what facts appear to have influenced the outcome of a situation.

5.1.3   Functional Manager

The generalization that HLMs lose touch with technology details does not entirely apply to functional managers who head groups of specialists. Functional managers are found both in line and staff positions [15]. In the line, they manage such activities as the system analysis department, the publications shop, computer operations, and accounting. On high-level staffs, they have authority over specialized activities performed by people distributed among the line organizations. Real estate decisions, advertising, accounting practices, and employee appraisal rating procedures are typical of the activities a corporation may assign to a staff manager specializing in the topic. In the programming environment, decisions regarding tools and techniques, hardware/software purchases, and standards are sometimes set up under staff functional managers. The staff functional manager does not manage the employees in the groups under his or her "dotted-line" authority.

One common characteristic of functional management is that the function is a service to some other group. In the case of a staff, the function may also coordinate the activities of other groups. A primary duty of a functional manager is to develop standards of service that convince the other groups that the function is worthwhile. The standards should be based on:

- Technical competence
- Technical leadership
- Standards of performance (such as turnaround time and cost-effectiveness)
- Consistency of functional guidance
- Fair service for all requests (within a priority system)

5.1.4   Communication Responsibilities

Communication is the essential glue that holds a project together. At the same time, it is a source of complexity and contradiction that can tear a project apart. Communications processes must be properly managed to prevent disruptive effects.

5.1.4.1 Unity of command

An organization hierarchy structured in the form of a pyramid or tree has one chief. The structure provides unity of command; in fact, each person in the organization has one and only one boss. Strict observance of the chain of command minimizes confusion. On the other hand, the length of the chain of command can delay decisions.

The chain of command can complicate coordination among groups at the same level who do not report to the same manager. Fayol, who included unity of command among his principles of organization, proposed the use of bridges or gangplanks to permit information to flow horizontally within the levels of a tree [16]. He still retained the idea of one boss. An employee could talk to and work with anyone, but could take direction only from his or her manager. The difficulty with this approach is that it permits *treaties*—informal agreements between individuals—to affect an employee's workscope and commitments without the manager's knowledge. To guard against undesirable treaties, the concept of unity of command can be strengthened by teaching all employees that:

- They should take *direction* only from their manager.
- They may *contact* anyone in the organization when necessary to do their job as long as:
    1. They keep their manager informed.
    2. They refer all requests for action to their manager for decision.
    3. They refer all potential or actual disagreements to their manager for resolution.
    4. They refer all recommendations for deviation from their plan or from existing standards or policies to their manager for action.
    5. They use common sense and good judgment to ensure that the contacts are useful in furthering their assigned job.

These guidelines should not be treated as restrictions. They are aids to communication that tend to strengthen the team and avoid the possibly undesirable effects of uncoordinated individual actions.

5.1.4.2 Departures from unity of command

Employees have a natural respect for the authority of their manager based partly on the desire for reward, partly on fear of punishment, partly on the desire to accomplish the task, partly on the desire to be a good team player, and hopefully on the manager's leadership. Whatever the reason, this built-in responsiveness simplifies a manager's job. A side effect of employee willingness to take direction leads to a common violation of the normal chain-of-command. It occurs when a higher-level manager happens to drop a suggestion to a programmer in the course of a friendly discussion. This happens a great deal in organizations where the managers are strong technically and, as one expression has it, have "carried their hobbies along" with them. They are so interested in using (or showing off) their experience that it is perfectly natural for them to turn a casual conversation into a discussion of a specific programming task. When the conversation is with a programmer, though, anything the HLM suggests could be interpreted as a direct order by the programmer. The problem is compounded because it does not occur to the HLM that some friendly hints could possibly be treated as anything more than shop-talk. As a result, the fact that the programmer is implementing the suggestion never gets recorded and remains outside the scope of the project control procedures.

Functional management violates the unity of command principle. An employee receiving functional direction from a staff manager also has a line manager. The line manager is usually responsible for evaluating the employee's performance and initiating salary increases and promotion. Self-interest forces the employee to exert some effort to please the line manager. At the same time, the employee has to follow the direction of the functional manager. There is no way to eliminate this division of loyalty as long as the employee has two bosses. To minimize the undesirable effects, it is possible to:

- Restrict the role of the functional manager.
    1. Make all communications from the functional manager go through the line manager.
    2. Limit the functional manager to setting objectives and prescribing requirements; let the line manager be responsible for implementation.
    3. Limit the scope of functional manager authority to tasks that represent only a portion of an employee's job.
- Have the functional manager and line manager cooperate in measuring and appraising employee performance.
- Spell out clearly the subject areas in which the functional manager is the ultimate authority versus those where the line manager has the last word.

A clever employee will still play the two bosses off against each other. Managers must cooperate to avoid such manipulation; they must also cooperate to avoid every small disagreement being escalated to their mutual superior somewhere high in the chain-of-command. Through cooperation they can attempt to make the functional arrangement behave almost like a unified command where each employee takes direction from only one person.

5.1.4.3 Participative management

By referring to *subordinate* and *superior,* it is possible to convey the idea of a hierarchy in which some people have authority to direct others. There is no implication in the use of these terms that a ''superior'' is better than a ''subordinate''; neither is there an implication that there is any constraint on personal friendships and personal contacts in the team. The whole idea is to bring out the importance of the chain of command as a tool for controlling a complex system. Similarly, the terms *direct* and *control* imply that managers have the responsibility for getting things done—that large projects are not the result of committee action, they are the result of the coordinated activity of individuals, each assigned tasks by the management team. This concept that is so clear throughout industry and government and, particularly, the military has not been clear to all programmers.[2] One explanation of this paradox is that many programmers entered the field directly from college where, if they had any organizational experience at all, they have been exposed to a research organization. It is not unusual for a "manager" in a research lab to be junior to the scientists reporting to him or her [17]. This is an extreme example of the dual-career ladder. It works in research because scientists gain seniority from their scientific accomplishments which are, for the most part, self-initiated. In addition, there are rarely any rigid time schedules associated with the work. The FLM in a research lab, therefore, may not always direct the work in the same sense as a development manager. Instead, the manager administers the department and encourages decisions by consensus. The FLM is concerned with meeting the needs of the scientists and guiding them into directions set by the Chief Scientist, but he or she need not directly supervise their activities. At the same time, there is no complex system activity in the lab to demand stronger chains of command. Each task is supervised by a technical expert. Systems are synthesized by interconnecting separate tasks (bottom-up design) and removing discrepancies during system test. Several research-based organizations, such as Bell Laboratories, MITRE Corporation, RAND, Illinois Institute of Technology, etc., have been associated with major data-processing applications. Their employees occasionally express surprise at the concept of true line authority for a manager. When they recognize that the development process is, indeed, different from independent research, they begin to understand the value of focusing both responsibility and control on the managers. (They may, however, insist that their managers be the most technically distinguished project members.)

The emphasis on manager authority can be carried too far. No manager is always right. An authoritarian forcing subordinates to do as they were told fails to take advantage of the tremendous help available through teamwork. Good managers are also good leaders. They encourage teamwork and esprit de corps. They listen to their people and encourage them to speak out. When they are going to make a decision they first consult with the team to gather all the information they may influence the situation. Then they make the decision and issue the necessary instructions. If their

2. The concept is rejected in some countries where management by committee or consensus is encouraged as a policy.

subordinates do not agree with the instructions, the managers listen to the complaints and either change their position based on the new inputs or stick by their original decisions. People who work for these managers participate in the decision-making process and seldom feel as though they are being "ordered around." The manager is a true focal point.

5.1.4.4 Information flow

Information consisting of orders and other data flows through the organization. Orders follow a path defined by the control structure of the organization. The control structure is a graph, usually a tree rooted in the executive suite. Other data can follow any path from one individual to another. Normally, such other data flow only between people who have occasion to communicate because of mutual interests or physical proximity. Quite often, management must stimulate communication between people who are working on related activities but who do not bother to talk to each other.

At one time, isolation seemed reasonable. In tracing the trends in organization theory, Scott [11] notes that traditionalists supported a clean tree-structured chain of command that minimizes the need for cross talk. Moreover, they believed that employees were only motivated by self-interest, i.e., if you paid well, you could expect your employees to do what you told them to do. Information flow in this environment consisted of orders flowing down and status reports flowing up. No effort went into explaining why the orders were issued nor how each task related to the bigger picture of a system. This technique had succeeded over the years. The characteristics of this approach are a strong discipline and a system of rewards and punishments. Around the turn of the century, Taylor's school of "scientific management" concentrated on defining the best ways of implementing these characteristics. Effort went into "standardizing" employee behavior to achieve a technically effective operation. The work environment also drew a lot of attention. The management process, however, remained impersonal. Based on later studies, including the famous Hawthorne investigations initiated by Mayo's group at Harvard, a new school of thought arose. It was concerned with human relations. The Hawthorne investigations were conducted by the Western Electric Company at its Hawthorne plant in Chicago [18]. They were motivated by the observations made in a normal scientific management study of the work environment in this telephone equipment manufacturing plant of 30,000 employees. In the study, a control group continued to work under normal conditions while the environment for the test group was altered. The observations showed that improved lighting was followed by higher output for the test group. However, the output of the control group also rose. Furthermore, after a later test in which lighting was decreased, productivity went up in both groups. Some factor other than physical comfort was affecting employee efficiency.

The company decided to find out what the unknown factor was. Their action was to sponsor a massive series of investigations lasting from 1927 to 1932 and beyond. The primary finding was that employee emotions, attitudes, and social groupings dominated their behavior. Apparently the lighting tests were influenced because the employees were part of a "select" test or control group. In the later, lengthy Relay Assembly and Bank Wiring investigations sustained improvements following each environment change were not achieved. But positive effects were traced to employees' role as test subjects—they liked the responsibility, they enjoyed the team aspects, they appreciated the interest supervisors showed in each person as an individual, and, in spite of close supervision, observation, and measurement, they felt "freer" in the test room than on the general shop floor. Among the recommendations to management was the advice to improve communication among managers and workers so as to capitalize on the teamwork potential in the group. Hence, information flow expanded to cover more information about the project, its purpose, the interrelationships among the team members and other groups, the work plans, the work methods, etc. Information flow was more extensive, more participative, and more personal. The Hawthorne studies, among other things, confirmed Follett's point [10] that leaders are influenced by their group, or, as Seckler-Hudson [19] put it, "The leader both leads and follows." Participative management helps the employees enjoy their work, yet it takes nothing away from the authority of the leader.

Manley and Dunne [20] noted that an alert project manager can tell when things are not going well if he or she pays attention to what is being said within the project. Eight warning flags project danger ahead. They all take the form of "if only . . ." statements.

1. "If only they would get off my back."

2. "If only they would give me some muscle."

3. "If only they would talk to one another."

4. "If only there were more hours in a day."

5. "If only they would ease up on specs."

6. "If only they would make a decision."

7. "If only my team had let me know of the problem."

8. "If only they would sit on this information until we can work it out."

"They" means "my HLM" in most instances. Warning number 3 refers to the group of HLMs at the next higher level above the speaker. Warning number 8 refers at times to a subordinate who is in the position to "blow the whistle" on the speaker's failures. More often, warning number 8 refers to the speaker's HLM who is about to take a corrective action.

5.1.4.5 Organization control

The project manager is controlled by the direct chain-of-command plus all the direct and indirect interest groups associated with the activity. The *management system* is the collection of directives, procedures, and assignments that explains how an organization operates. The system contains job descriptions, responsibilities and authority associated with each job, interface definitions, and procedures for passing information and control across interfaces. Powers reserved by each level of management are specified when the mission and scope of lower levels of management are written. Consequently, the management system tells each manager what he or she can and cannot do. To further clarify the instructions, each job is explained in context with the overall organization and the measurements that will be applied to the manager's performance. The types of verbs used to describe position responsibilities include:

- *Do*—carry to completion
- *Set*—set objectives for others
- *Approve*—authorize plans of others

Interlocking relationships require:

- *Concur*—agree with plans of others or force escalation
- *Review*—review plans of others and suggest improvements

Each of these verbs, with the exception of *review,* denotes a positive action. As a result, approval and concurrence procedures can slow down the decision process. For example, in a large programming organization the management system may require all third-level management appointments to be approved by two levels of management (fourth and fifth levels) with the concurrence of the VP, Programming. The manager who wants to make this appointment must justify it to his or her boss and to the VP, then wait for them to act. Approval may be given on the spot, but the VP may delay concurring until after a business trip. The appointment should be held in suspense until the VP either concurs or does not. A good management system, however, provides instructions on delegating authority and on time limits for approve/concur actions so unreasonable delays can be avoided. The management system can be summarized in a chart showing all the activities of the organization and, for each activity, which manager has responsibility for *do, set, approve, concur,* and *review* action.

5.2 PROJECT ORGANIZATION

Implicit in references to "chain-of-command" and "hierarchy" is the concept of a standard pyramid organization. In this concept, there is one top-level manager to whom everyone reports through the management structure. Some resources may not report directly to the project manager. For very large projects, the direct resource control available to the project manager may be small indeed. This was anticipated in Fig. 5.2, which showed substantial management attention to coordination with other groups. The requirement for horizontal communication between groups is a function of project size and complexity. Horizontal communication weakens vertical communication. The power and authority a manager has to control his or her area of responsibility is diluted when project complexity forces negotiation of each decision with other groups. Knowing this, it is possible to lay down a few simple guidelines for organizing a project.

1. Try to organize the entire project as a tree structure.
2. Failing this, establish small groups dedicated to the project, even though they may report to unrelated organizations. Give each group well-defined responsibilities, measurements, and interfaces.
3. If it is not possible for all the subgroups to be dedicated to the project, establish user-server relationships. With project groups as users and external groups as servers, define the interfaces and responsibilities of each. Document the agreed-upon commitments and manage the commitments in lieu of managing the external resources.
4. At all stages avoid confusion by providing job descriptions for each manager and each subgroup.

Guidelines such as these permit flexibility in building an organization, but they ensure that the dilutive effect of complexity is balanced by the strengthening effect of project controls.

5.2.1 Types of Organization

The guidelines try to keep the project structure simple. The first guideline produces a tree-structured hierarchy known as a *project-oriented organization*. It places all the project resources under the line control of the project manager. Needless to say, this structure is preferred by project managers. In its simplest form, it consists of several identical development groups plus a staff. The development groups are also project-oriented organizations with unique deliverables and all the resources to do the job. The technical and administrative staffs support the project manager; together they constitute a project office. Three variants of this simple structure are a typical FLM department (Fig. 5.3a) where the manager has development professionals and no staff (or only clerical support); a basic applications development shop (Fig. 5.3b) where various large and small applications are assigned to development groups but no applications are split among groups; and a system development shop (Fig. 5.3c) consisting of a team of teams each working on a component of the same system. A fourth variant is very common (Fig. 5.4); it consists of different kinds of departments only some of which

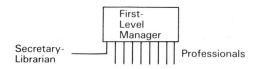

a. FLM Department

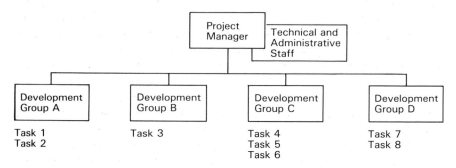

b. Applications Development

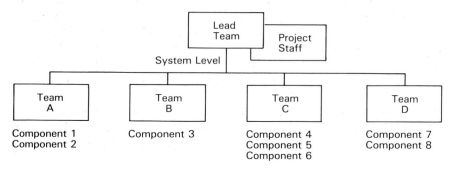

c. System Development

Fig. 5.3 Project organization.

are project-oriented, yet all the resources belong to the project manager. The inner structure of this mixed organization has two departments organized around special skills; namely, computer operations and system test/evaluation. Overall, the mixed structure has the same advantages as other project-oriented organizations. These advantages include clean lines of authority and clear interfaces. Since all resources are available within the organization, the project manager has maximum flexibility to address problems as they arise. Subordinate managers have well-defined responsibilities and can focus all their attention on their specific part of the project. The

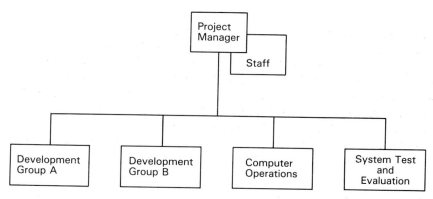

Fig. 5.4   Mixed organization.

customer also has only one interface—the project manager—to deal with. Because the entire team is working toward one and the same end, the project manager finds that all the textbook methods for building loyalty and esprit de corps work well.

If the project-oriented organization has such merit, why consider any other? Because the project-oriented organization has a few drawbacks. One is cost. In order to have the resources available when they are needed, the project manager has to pay to keep the resources around when they are not needed. Another drawback is quality. Individuals in a large project-oriented organization may be more distinguished by their ability to contribute to the team than by their ability to write good programs.

Functional organization is used to overcome the drawbacks by creating critical masses of people with related skills. Robb [in 19] contrasts project and functional approaches to subdividing a large group into smaller, more manageable units. The project approach leads to small units whose general characteristics are similar to the whole. The functional approach leads to dissimilar small units, each of which concentrates on one function. As an example, Robb describes emergency support organized to feed a community following a disaster. In a project approach, the top emergency relief officer assigns a unit leader to each household to obtain, deliver, prepare, and serve food and clean up after meals in the assigned house. All the houses in a block are grouped under a second-level block leader and higher groupings are organized until the whole community is taken care of. In a functional approach, the top relief officer would set up a provisioning corps to obtain and deliver food, a kitchen corps to prepare meals, and an operations group to run one or more mess halls. All the people in the community would be brought to the mess halls for meals.

The functional groups can reduce cost by serving multiple projects. They improve quality by gathering the experts in a topic together in one department where they complement each other and build the technical capability of the group. Functional departments are not project-oriented. Serving all users, they tend to give lower priority to each user than the user wants. Nevertheless, a functional approach is recommended for certain aspects of program development such as computer operations and publications.

The functional organization has several attributes:

- Special skills are required to do the assigned work.
- The skills are discipline-oriented and more or less application-independent.
- The employees can back each other up but are not readily interchangeable with other departments.
- The functional group requires at least a minimum number of people (critical mass) to be effective.
- The average level of performance in the group is higher than that achieved by nonspecialists.
- The employees maintain proficiency in the latest aspects of their specialty.
- There is more than one potential user of the functional group.

With these attributes, a small functional group can serve a large number of projects, delivering high quality at low cost.

An example of the value of special skills involved a complex data classification algorithm in an information storage and retrieval system. The design had occupied two analysts for three months. At a quarterly review of their job they explained that their solution was too slow to be useful. A senior mathematician at the meeting reframed the problem as a matrix computation and showed in a few hours how to solve the problem in a very satisfactory manner. Obviously, if he had been asked to help at an earlier date there would have been significant savings. In this case, nonspecialists used up six people-months. (If they had understood the subject better, they would have recognized that they were stuck and they could have, at least, alerted their manager. As it was, they thought they were solving their problem.) If a specialist had been available and this were the only problem to be solved, the individual would be idle for at least six months out of the year, and more probably, for all but one day. On the other hand, if one problem arose from each of fifty projects, the person might be occupied most of the year. Therefore, the specialist is more valuable when he or she is in a functional organization that supports all project managers. In practice, this individual's manager will try to limit tasks to 60–80 percent of available time in order to leave plenty of time for the specialist to enhance his or her knowledge of the discipline.

The net benefit of using the functional department in appropriate situations is substantial. This conclusion is clear when the critical mass involves a facility such as a computer or a printing press. The project manager who needs a whole computer will seldom agree to let the programmers use it at will; instead, the computer will be set up in a special department to schedule efficient use of the hardware. The project manager who needs less computer time will usually turn to a central facility belonging to a service group. Buying time from them is cheaper than paying for a whole machine that exceeds the department's needs. The same applies to publishing project documentation. It is very difficult for a single project to generate the volume to compete with a centralized service facility. Coupling with this the fact that few project managers understand the intricacies of publishing and printing, it is unusual to see this function in a project organization. The result, as shown in Fig. 5.5a, is that projects tend to modify their structure to include some functional elements and to procure some services from functional organizations outside the project. The personnel department is included in the list of functional service groups to highlight the fact that the pure project organization probably never occurs. Even under the tightest project structure some things such as personnel, finance, and public relations may be separated into functional departments.

Project-oriented and functional organizations are quite different in their methods of operation. They are sufficiently different that conflicts arise. The project-oriented manager mobilizes resources to achieve his or her primary objective—completion of the project. The functional manager's objective is to provide the best service to all projects at minimum cost. Nothing can prevent peak loads from occurring, however. The functional manager learns the hard way that he or she can never satisfy all the customers and, in general, not even one of them can be satisfied for very long. However, by combining advanced planning, contingency planning, and open-minded negotiation, every job can be done satisfactorily at a net saving. The delays due to sharing functional resources are easier to manage than the problems resulting from letting less proficient project personnel handle the task.

In Fig. 5.5a, the Project Manager has direct control over Computer Operations, and is in a position to establish and enforce the user-server agreements between the development groups and the computer group. Something more along the lines of a contract is needed to obtain enforceable commitments from the technical publications and systems analysis departments.

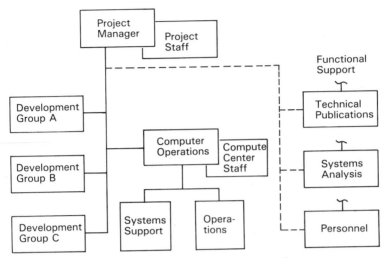

a. Mixed Project-Oriented Organization with Functional Support

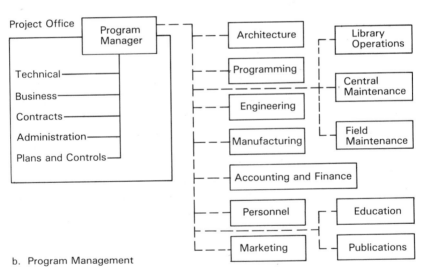

b. Program Management

Fig. 5.5 Functional organization.

The extreme case of functional organization can be called *program management*. As shown in Fig. 5.5b, the project/program manager in this case owns none of the project resources, except for the project office. The manager procures everything from other departments, using the project office to plan, monitor, coordinate, and control. This matrix structure grew up around hardware procurements where existing plants and assembly facilities were used. There was no reason to duplicate the facilities; furthermore, it was impractical to build a project team more skilled in operating those facilities than the existing management and work force. Only a small management and control group was sufficient to coordinate the output of a number of functional groups. Interestingly enough, many of the functional groups, such as the plant manufacturing electronic power supplies, would create internal project-oriented groups, say for the "XYZ Co. low voltage, ruggedized unit."

In very large organizations, the matrix structure has the advantage of tightening control without much additional cost. Two effects that contribute to improved control are: (1) decoupling of function, and (2) contention. Evans [21] assumes that the separation of line and staff is clean with only minor redundancies. True separation, while difficult, can be achieved through careful organization design supported by a management system that explicitly assigns authority and responsibilities to each department. The result is a modular structure exactly like a program system design: tightly-bound, loosely coupled units. An organization of people differs from a program structure in one respect. People often want to expand their role beyond the confines of a specified job. A programmer may want to add capabilities to his or her package. A test manager may want to build fixes to errors found in test before returning units to the developers. A team chief may want a computer dedicated to the team. Within the fixed resources available to the organization, growth plans such as these can lead to conflict. Conflict is resolved by a contention process that pits the multiple hierarchies against each other until an acceptable tradeoff position is reached.

Matrix structures can be efficiently controlled by their built-in check-and-balance systems [22]. They are particularly important in very large organizations (nations, multinational companies, major corporations). The only drawback is that they are difficult to implement. Managers have to be trained to operate effectively in a matrix environment.

A special case of the functional organization is the *mission-oriented organization*. A typical functional organization is a center of excellence to which project managers voluntarily turn for expert assistance. The people are carefully selected for their skill in a discipline, which is usually application-independent. In the case of a mission-oriented organization the people are not necessarily specialists but the organization is directed to specialize in a single subject area such as Sorting or Compiler Engineering. Within a company, the group with the Sort mission writes all Sort programs required by all the projects in the company. To justify having a mission-oriented Sort group there would have to be a continuous, heavy load of sorting work. A project manager, in this situation, may be ordered to use the mission group. The purpose of the mission assignment is the same as any functional organization: to provide the best service at minimum cost. This is achieved by building an experienced team and keeping it together for many years. The need to preempt work arises because: (1) the tasks are interesting enough for project managers to want to do in their own shop, and (2) the relative efficiency of the mission group is hard to quantify since there are no competitive efforts to compare against. The main weakness of the mission-oriented organization is that, if the need for the mission disappears, the group is not prepared to perform effectively in other subject areas. Thus a Sort mission may write a set of general purpose sorts that are good enough to eliminate the need for further expenditures on sorting. After six to ten years writing sorts, the mission group is technically obsolescent with regard to all other software. They are hard to place on other jobs and, because of their relative seniority, they become an expensive overhead item. Historically, most mission managers have protected their group from total specialization by bringing in a number of small jobs from diverse areas.

As a project grows it begins to spin off functional groups as soon as a critical mass has been reached for each discipline. Eventually, the point is reached where the local labor market can no longer support the skill requirements of the growing project. The activity may now be so big that things like traffic congestion and parking become problems. More serious in such a large group—it is difficult for individual employees to identify with the project anymore. At this point *decentralization* to additional geographic locations is called for. No specific figures predict when this is necessary, but it appears that a single systems programming project probably should be less than 1,000 people, including support personnel. When there are several projects at one location, it is still advisable to have a population limit. Guidelines range from a ceiling of about 1,500 in rural areas to about 4,000 closer to large cities. (This represents the total size of a facility engaged in professional activity such as systems programming. Manufacturing, for instance, could have a higher ceiling.) Within these ceilings it is possible to stimulate the employees to do a better job because they have good working conditions and a real sense of belonging.

When the ceiling is reached, a new facility is established in a new labor market. Again, a critical mass—in this case quite a large one—is needed. A full cross-section of the old facility must be transported to the new facility in order to get it working as fast as possible. Once the new facility is operating it may take on any appropriate project/functional organization mix at the new location. The net result is that the various types of organization are freely mixed.

As indicated in Fig. 5.6, each type of organization emphasizes one objective that gives the organization certain advantages. The decentralized organization is included in the figure as a separate type, even though it is actually an outgrowth of the other types. It is labeled "location-oriented."

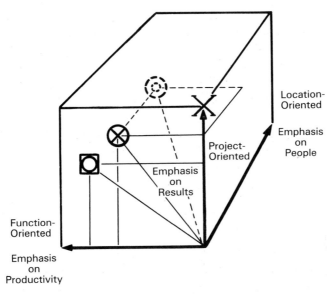

Fig. 5.6 Advantages of organizations.

Orientation	Emphasis	Advantages
Project	Results	Loyalty and esprit de corps
		Clean chain of command
		Good *control of resources*
		Design control
		Good interface with users
Function	Productivity	Quality
		Critical technical mass
		Good *allocation of resources*
		Technical leadership
Location	People	Good employee relations
		Availability of resources
		Manageable size

By combining the various types, a specific organization can be developed that has the best tradeoff among customer satisfaction, efficiency, and employee satisfaction. In geometric terms, no organization is pure; every organization lies somewhere within the cube defined by the three axes: project, function, and location. A pure project-oriented organization, such as the small team job represented by X in the figure, has the most freedom of action. The project manager can use the available resources without interfering with other groups. A larger project, indicated by ⊗, introducing some functional activities, falls in the plane of the PROJECT-FUNCTION axes. It loses some of the PROJECT advantages but gains some of the FUNCTION advantages. Obviously, there must now be some crossfunctional coordination and tradeoffs limiting the project manager's freedom. As the project size and the number of functional groups increase, $\square$, more PROJECT-oriented advantages slip away to the extent that the project focus is blurred. When that happens, employee commitment to the project objectives blurs as well, increasing the risk of project failure. In very large projects this risk is brought back under control by segmenting the job and providing better local management, $\bigcirc$.

PROJECT-oriented organizations are restricted in size but flexible when it comes to getting the job done. When the feasibility of a project-oriented approach has been exhausted, features of the FUNCTION and then the LOCATION axis are introduced. Each of these axes has its own management guidelines, orthogonal to all the others. This leads to potential communications blockage because, as indicated, project managers and functional managers just do not see eye to eye on what is important. Additional control is required to cope with these organizational interactions since they are inherently competitive rather than cooperative. But the controls are feasible. Managers must learn to negotiate to achieve the best results for their mutual boss. They must learn to compromise, to give a little, in order to gain their objective.

Junior managers are uncomfortable playing a negotiating role. Until they acquire some experience they find that they cannot give in on any controversial points. Since they are still learning how to manage their own shop their plans tend to be relatively rigid. They cannot absorb the major changes that might arise in negotiation. Higher-level managers learn through experience how to build flexible plans because they know it is necessary. They realize that if any party to a negotiation is rigid, an optimum arrangement cannot be reached. Either the negotiation is totally frustrated or the remaining parties to the conference accept changes in their areas that are extra costly or clumsy. The whole system can be distorted by the inability of one manager to compromise. In this sense the organization can be compared to a bridge. Some of the connections in the bridge are rigid and do not budge under any load. These linkages are like the first-level manager who concentrates on his or her own task and, although interaction occurs with other departments, is shielded from the effects of loads elsewhere in the structure. The same bridge contains some rotating or rolling connectors to absorb the stress of thermal expansion or impact loads. The flexible linkages act like higher-level managers who preserve the integrity of the structure by cooperating with other groups to reach a mutually satisfactory position. Consequently, even the complex matrix structure of Fig. 5.7, representative of some large projects, can succeed.

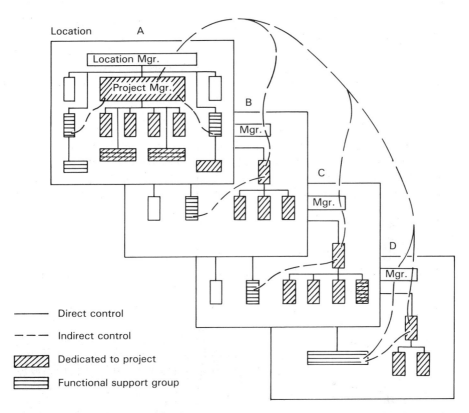

Fig. 5.7   Large project—Matrix structure.

5.2.2   Small Teams

The ideal development project organization is the self-sufficient small team. It consists of a manager, development professionals, and all the resources needed to do the job, including clerical support and computer service. The number of development professionals ranges from four to eight, and the total team size ranges from five to twelve. The characteristics that make small teams so desirable include:

- High productivity
- High quality
- Innovation
- Responsiveness

The members of the team, moreover, get great job satisfaction and enjoy what they are doing.

The reasons are obvious. In a small team, the sense of belonging to the group—as to a family—gives each team member an almost tangible feeling that the team product bears his or her handiwork. This feeling gets lost in the multilayered labyrinth of a large project. The small team product is better because the close-knit participants mutually share all the project information. No one has to make assumptions about component interactions; it is always easy to discuss such points directly with the involved programmers. The small number of people on the team permits the whole team to act as a unit, sharing project information en masse rather than passing data sequentially from one person to another. As a result, productivity is high. Misinformation is reduced as well, so quality is high. With these advantages, the team can afford to be flexible. New ideas can be tried out without great formality and without involving other departments. Likewise, user requests for product changes can usually be accepted without completely upsetting the project plan. All of these advantages are due to the fact that the small team is *manageable* because it is small and because it is a team.

When the group is too small, below the lower end of the range, it tends to behave more like several individuals than like a team. Furthermore, the jobs that can be done by two or three people are typically so small that the lifetime of such groups is too short to develop the interpersonal rapport that contributes to team performance. At the upper end of the range, a small team could consist of a first-level manager, eight programmers, one program librarian, and one secretary/administrator. The team could be using an on-line support system on its own computer or on a central service machine. If they have their own machine, the team members operate it themselves. In this case, the span of control of the FLM is broad enough to prevent him or her from being a working professional on the team. This is about as large a team as one FLM can handle without excessive risk. If more programmers are added, the FLM will be forced to break the team into a couple of groups and appoint a leader for each group in order to maintain control. At this point the organization ceases to be a "small team." (In one case, a team of exceptional senior programmers successfully operated as a small team in spite of having twelve programmers plus a working manager and secretary. The team was split between two cities with five programmers and a local working manager at each place. The team simulated a local environment by using a common, dedicated machine on which they had installed their own electronic mail capability. By learning how to communicate via online source code and messages, the programmers, each of whom had a well-defined component to build, were able to develop a complex, experimental, user-oriented operating system.)

The advantages of a small team are due to its size. Consequently, the advantages should apply even to teams consisting of poor programmers. In general, that is the case. All programmers, at all skill levels, appear to be more productive and less error prone when they work as members of small teams than otherwise. The small team reinforces their strengths and shields them from the consequences of complexity. (The only exception to this general rule is that some superior programmers perform best when working alone. Most programmers, however, work better as team members than as soloists. This suggests that the team not only reinforces their strengths but also provides some peer pressure that motivates the individual to do a good job.) It is impractical to assign a team to a task that can be done by one person. It is also impractical to expect a small team to do a job requiring hundreds of programmer-years. Where there is a choice to be made, however, the small team is always preferred. To give some examples:

- A task estimated at 1 KLOC—assign an individual rather than a group.

- A task estimated at 10 KLOC—assign a group of, say, three programmers rather than a team.

- A system estimated at 25 KLOC—assign a small team.

- A system estimated at 50 KLOC—assign a small team rather than a large team.

- A system larger than 100 KLOC—assign a large team.

Since productivity is sensitive to many factors, these examples cannot be taken as ground rules for any particular development shop. Nevertheless, because small team productivity can exceed large team productivity by a large amount, a small team can tackle quite large projects.

There are three types of small teams that differ in their operating methods. Type I is an ordinary FLM department with no other distinguishing features. It is advantageous but it is not as effective as the other two types. As for all small teams, a type I team is given an assignment—a program system development job—that is estimated to be within the capability of the small team over a reasonable period of time. For example, a project may be visualized as a 25 KLOC deliverable due in twelve to fifteen months. That could be a feasible assignment to a FLM who has eight programmers and a librarian/secretary. The FLM must organize the job, generate work assignments for the team members, and supervise the work. In a type I team there will normally be a mix of skills. The FLM will sit down with the more experienced programmers to lay out a technical plan, but all the team members will be kept informed on what is happening. Team discussions will be held often to talk about status, to agree on uniform methods, or to solve problems. Everyone can know enough about the whole job that no time is lost setting the scene during these discussions. Yet problems will occur. One common problem will be that the job cannot be broken up so everyone has a coherent task consistent with his or her ability. When this happens, the FLM must provide additional time for learning and for testing and interface management.

A type II small team (such as the team of senior programmers mentioned previously) consists of selected personnel acting as peers and using specialized team operating procedures. A type II small team gets better the longer it stays together. Everyone learns to understand and work with the others. Natural specialization occurs as one person shows talent for database work while another is particularly good with schedulers/supervisors. When a job comes in, the team as a whole studies it and decides how to attack it. Their normal mode of action is to reach decisions by consensus. There is an FLM who acts as one of the peers in most technical decisions. In the infrequent situation where the team cannot agree, the FLM will use his or her management authority to resolve the problem. A more important role of the FLM, at least in the eyes of the team, is to be the external interface buffering the team from outside distractions. The type II team tends to divide a job into roughly equal chunks, one for each team member. As a group, they are all aware of the entire project status at all times. In fact, they can practically treat their separate pieces of the project as though they were continuously integrated into a single system. (Some type II teams explicitly do this. They use an on-line development system that can link completed components at any time. Then, by doing each component top-down, a team member can contribute successively richer stubs to the current level of the integrated system.) A number of management considerations are implied by a type II team:

- The team members are selected so they are at comparable levels of capability in order to work together as peers.
- The team members are uniformly above average in capability.
- The team is part of a larger organization
- The team stays intact a long time working together on successive projects
- The tools used by the team may be more advanced than those used by the larger organization (because the team members have the capability to specify and use new tools and because the team is flexible enough to obtain and install a new tool without much lost time or effort).
- The team technical standards may be incompatible with those used by the larger organization (though not so as to affect the deliverable product).

In other words, a type II team becomes an elite group, isolated from the rest of the organization. This does not bother the team members. They have earned their position. They would rather stay with the team than move, even for a promotion. On the negative side, the knowhow of the type II team is not passed on to the rest of the organization.

A type III small team is a structured organization with differentiated skills and formalized tools and techniques. Type III is similar to type I in using a mix of skills, but it defines the work to be done in such a way as to maximize the effectiveness of the individual assigned to do it. Type III is similar to type II in using special tools and techniques to enhance productivity and quality; however, the tools and techniques are formalized and compatible with those of the home location. Type III differs from type II in using a structured top-down implementation rather than a peer system of parallel implementation. The best known version of a type III small team is the Chief Programmer Team referred to in Chapter 2 and described in more detail in Part 1. The technical team consists of a hierarchy with the Chief Programmer (CP) at the top; a Backup Programmer as an alter ego, counterfoil, and partner; supporting development programmers; and a program librarian. The CP receives the assignment and initiates the top-down design and implementation. At some point in this sequential process there will be tasks for the supporting programmers. Conceptually, a CP team acts like an individual, supported on request by specialists and kept on target by an associate who reviews progress and advises in technical areas. Here, the Chief Programmer is the technical leader both in terms of capability and in terms of responsibility. The CP may or may not be the FLM of the other team members. The CP can probably lead a team of five—the CP, a backup programmer, two programmers, and one librarian—and still do the critical design and implementation work assigned specifically to the CP. A team of eleven is probably too large. A practical maximum depends on many factors but is probably six or seven. Basic to CP operations is the use of all locally accepted IPT—as a minimum, structured programming, top-down implementation, inspections (or equivalent), and standard documentation. The formal requirement for IPT contributes to the productivity of a type III team compared to a type I team given the same team members. The CP structure of a type III team makes top-down implementation feasible. The CP finds the top, initiates the sequence of implementation, and controls the process. In a type I team, no one is responsible for this activity. In a peer-organized type II team, the emphasis on parallel development interferes with top-down implementation of the system (although it permits an individual team member to produce a chunk of the system top-down).

    In summary, a type I small team will outperform an equivalent number of people working as part of a large team or scattered among various ad hoc project groups. A type II small team will outperform a type I team by virtue of its uniformly good people who know how to work together. A type III team looks like a "superprogrammer" by virtue of its structure and tools that increase the productivity of each individual while retaining the advantages of a small team. Type III teams do not require selected highly skilled resources. An average type III team may not do better than a good type II team. There also appears to be a lower limit to the size of a type III team because the team leader carries a major portion of the development workload. The size of the system that can be built by a small team depends on team size and team productivity. It is possible to think in terms of a maximum size type II team handling a 50 KLOC job in a year. The largest type III team could handle a job 60 to 90 percent as large, depending on team history and team members' experience.

Mantei [23] analyzed the effect of programming team structures on programming tasks from a group dynamics viewpoint. She, too, found three types of teams, which she calls:

- Controlled Decentralized (CD)—similar to type I
- Democratic Decentralized (DD)—similar to type II and to Weinberg's "egoless programming team" [24]
- Controlled Centralized (CC)—similar to type III and to Mills/Baker's "chief programmer team" [25]

In her evaluation, a CD team could handle simple jobs of large size, short duration, high modularity, requiring high reliability. CD teams work best when the schedules are flexible. Team members need not be highly sociable. Mantei assumes CD teams should be good at large jobs requiring high reliability because there is a good balance between peer interaction and formal control. Experience suggests this is not the case, most likely because the implementation of CD teams has not achieved the right balance in practice. A good CD team will begin to behave like a type II team as its members learn to work with each other; interaction will improve and formal controls, while honored, will be low-key. In any case, a CD team is capable of outperforming an unstructured group. Mantei agrees that DD/type II teams are good at tackling difficult tasks but she would give them small jobs with long, lax schedules. She is probably right if the DD team is new and untried; however, an experienced type II team can handle more work than any of the other small team structures. Mantei does not have confidence in CC teams except when there is a strict job deadline. Her concern is based on the difficulty of finding chief programmers and on the potentially poor morale of the junior members of the team. Similar fears have inhibited the rate of acceptance of type III team structures. They are seldom used, but they perform well when the job scope fits the capability of the team, regardless of job duration or deadlines.

5.2.3   Large Teams

Clearly, if 25–50 KLOC is the largest size program system that can be produced by a small team, a larger job calls for a different organizational structure. The only alternative would be to redefine the large job so that its objectives can be met by one or more small program systems. *Individual conceptual ability* limits what one person can comprehend, *span of control* limits what one person can manage, and *complexity* results from exceeding these limits. Furthermore, complex activities are distinguished by the number of interfaces they have and the amount of communication across interfaces. From such concepts it is possible to use only three categories to describe all types of project organizations:

1. Individual—where one person can understand and do the entire job. In the data-processing industry, the so-called "end user" market segment has grown to serve individuals. The characteristic jobs in this segment are small application programs and problem-solving tasks.

2. Small team—where a group is required but the size of the group is within the span of control of one manager. Most of the remaining application programs and many special purpose systems, particularly those targeted at small computers, are done by small teams. In addition, more and more components of large systems are carefully designed to be isolated from the rest of the large system so a small team can do the work.

3. Large team—everything else; i.e., where the estimated workload can not be controlled by one FLM. Large applications and the bulk of systems programs fall in this category.

The significance of the three categories is that large teams are different in character from the others. Individuals concentrate on the problem solution and are not concerned with formal communications. Small teams emulate individuals because communications within the group are manageable and the problem is comprehensible to all team members. Large teams do not emulate individuals; they are clearly group activities. Large teams do not concentrate on the problem solution as much as they concentrate on managing the complexity of the project. Communications are not efficient in a large team even though formal procedures are adopted to improve communications. Individual team members, including managers and senior designers, do not understand the totality of the project. Consequently, the problem being addressed by the project team may be broken up in a way that omits features or introduces unwanted additions.

Formal procedures are used to control the work product, mainly by managing interactions at interfaces. All the formal procedures contribute to the complexity they are supposed to manage. First, they lead to an increase in the number of people on the team since the procedures represent real work and someone has to do it. Second, they increase the number of different skills to be managed since some of the extra people are clerks, some administrators, some accountants, and some specialists in various types of analysis. Third, they increase the project overhead since the extra people coordinate, monitor, and advise management but they do not produce code. These factors explain why the transition from a small team to a large team is abrupt. As soon as two FLMs are involved there is an increase in total team size that is disproportionately larger than the increase in the team's capacity for building programs. Compared to an individual who has no nonproductive support, a small team can have as much as half a person supporting each programmer (assuming a type I team of six with a non-working FLM and a clerk/secretary) but is more likely to have a very low nonproductive element. Table 1.6 showed how rapidly the nonproductive effort in a program project can grow. The simplest large team with two FLM departments, a Second Level Manager, and a secretary has four non-productive people. Assuming six programmers per FLM and one librarian for the project, there is one nonproductive person for every three produc-tive team members. Yet there are only twelve programmers compared to eight in the model of a maxi-type II small team. Note that the FLM in a large team is usually nonproductive because interface management takes so much time. A small team FLM is more often than not a productive pro-grammer. The largest figure in Table 1.6 is for a commercial general pur-pose operating system; there are eight people supporting each programmer. Some portion of the eight represent functional departments doing things such as documentation that are done by the programmers in a small team. Nevertheless, the amount of overhead due to system size is substantial.

Small teams emulate individuals by reaching consensus or by magnify-ing the productivity of a chief. In either case, a given situation has one re-sponse and everyone on the team has the same understanding of what that response is. Large teams try to achieve the same unity of action but cannot do as well. In any situation a large team will produce responses poorly understood by anyone outside the responding department. It is not possible to bring everyone up to the same level of understanding because, by defini-tion, the project is too big to be handled in its entirety by an individual or a small team. Thus where individuals and small teams proceed on the assump-tion that project knowledge is uniformly distributed, large teams must accept the fact that project knowledge is not the same in different groups. As noted in earlier chapters, the problem of incomplete and unequal distri-bution of project knowledge is dealt with through structure and procedures. Structure organizes the work to be done so that it can be mapped effectively on the resources available. In this way, at least, each individual can be given the project information relevant to his or her assigned task. Procedures ensure that the information gets to the right people at the right time in a usable form. Documentation standards, inspections, handover procedures, and project reviews serve this purpose among others.

Earlier, the team-of-teams organization was mentioned. The purpose of this structure is to bring more of the benefits of small teams into the large team environment. The merit of the approach is that it influences the project designers to create a clean structure. They are motivated to define sub-systems that are tightly bound and loosely coupled and that are the right size for small team implementation. When this is accomplished, each subsystem represents one team's task. Nevertheless, the fact that the subsystems are coupled even loosely makes the team-of-teams a "large team." All the exposures of a large team remain, although the team-of-teams reduces the risks. The size of a subsystem in this approach should be about half the size of a stand-alone small team project. That is, if you have a small team that can do a 50 KLOC *system* in twelve months you can expect the same team to do a 25 KLOC *subsystem* in twelve months. This very rough guideline reflects the cost of being part of a large team project. The key to the method is a good system design. Without that, "team-of-teams" is just empty nomenclature.

There will always be a lot of "ifs" regarding how good a large team can be. "If we understand the problem and if we have generated a reasonable design and if we have broken down the work assignments correctly and if we have set up the right information flow procedures and if our team members understand the information, then each individual will do a good job and the sum total will be the system we want." But for a large system, you never completely understand the problem—certainly not at the outset. Hence, your design is never exactly right. As a result, your work breakdown structure will not be exactly right for the real problem. So far, you can expect that each team member will be getting an incomplete and distorted picture of the system because what you have defined is only a partial representation of the system. As work proceeds, it will be evident that useful information is still falling through the crack because the means and media of communication are not perfect. Eventually, each team member has a different view of the project leading to the familiar characteristics of large teams: extensive management redirection and change activity.

5.2.4 Dynamic Organization Structure

Among the changes expected in a large team are changes in the project organization.[3] There are two reasons for this: (1) large teams start small and grow—the number of departments changes accordingly; and (2) the development life cycle moves through different types of activity, each of which has its own management emphasis. The organization charts in Figs. 5.3 through 5.5 are representative of the implementation stage of a project.

---

3. Smaller groups tend to have fixed populations throughout a project. It is convenient to allocate resources that way and, in the case of a type II small team, it is necessary to keep the team intact. The small groups adjust to the dynamics of the life cycle by modifying work assignments rather than by reorganizing.

Early in a project, there may be no development departments. The project manager will have only a project staff and a design group. The nucleus of the future development groups may be temporarily placed in the staff. Since the rate of actual personnel buildup is a function of recruiting, people may be on board before work is available. As they arrive they can be placed in their future development or functional departments. In some cases, it may be appropriate to create holding departments for the newcomers. While there, they will receive all the training and project indoctrination they need. On leaving, they will move into an implementation group with an assigned task.

Each department will be "normal" in the sense that it has a pyramid of job levels with more people at the lower levels than at the upper ones. Exceptions may occur in the large team when it is necessary to create a design team or a consulting function of uniformly high-level people. Overall, however, a large team is pyramidal. By contrast, a type II small team is flat—the members are roughly at the same level. A type III small team may be wasp-waisted, having high-level CP and backup programmer but low-level support—nothing in the middle. If the large team expects to operate as a team-of-teams using its pyramidal skill mix, the teams will either be type I or type III teams which have been forced into a pyramid shape. Type II is not practical because the project population cannot normally be subdivided into equally competent groups, each of which has been intact for a long time.

Top-down implementation builds a working framework for the system initially and then adds the detail. Many bottom-up implementations also produce a system driver initially so that code can be tested as soon as it is written. In either case, the first program development group will be more system/support-oriented and the last group will be more application-oriented. (Where the product is an operating system, the last groups to be formed probably do the error handling routines and the status reporting code.) In parallel, test development must get underway. The design group continues its work although it will gradually shift from designing new things to controlling the existing design. At some point, the design control function may disappear into the technical side of the project staff. The functional support departments remain stable throughout the project once they are established.

After delivery of the initial system, a project organization will be restructured to do a new job, to work on the next version of the delivered system, to maintain and upgrade the delivered system, or to maintain only. Or, the organization can be disbanded.

To do a new job, the dynamic cycle is repeated from the beginning. Since fewer people are needed at the start of a project it is usually necessary to reassign (or even lay off) people. Later, recruiting will be necessary to build a new team. Team continuity is lost and the average performance of the large team is no better on the second job than it was on the first job. When the next job is a new version of the delivered system, continuity can be maintained and capability can grow—at a cost. The cost is due to the idle time of people temporarily without work to do. They are retained in the team in anticipation of upcoming work. They are placed in holding departments and given training, analysis, report writing, or maintenance assignments until their next product development activity is defined. A multiversion project can absorb this cost without overpricing the product by judiciously overlapping system phases. Instead of letting the design department shrink into a staff control function during the implementation stage, the project manager can have the designers start work on the next version of the system while, in addition, controlling the current system design. By the time some implementation resources are available, there are new program specifications ready for them. Overlap cannot be complete because many Version 2 decisions depend on the outcome of Version 1; nevertheless, overlap can be sufficient to reduce the cost of idle time well below the cost of a layoff and rehiring program. Thus a management objective for a multiversion system is to maintain flat headcount (e.g., a constant population). The organization adopted for the late stages of Version 1 implementation (with design, development, test, and support all active) will stabilize through subsequent versions. Departments can remain intact, building some small team experience, as work assignments change with time.

To maintain and upgrade the delivered system, the large project team is reduced in size. Depending on the size and nature of the system, the maintenance and upgrade effort can be handled by one or more people. Given a large system that is expected to be upgraded by many functional enhancements (but not replaced by a new version), the maintenance and upgrade team may be organized as a miniature version of the system development team. In general it will not exceed one-third of the peak population of the development project. If the delivered system contains high-quality code, maintenance repairs will be few so the size of the post-delivery effort will be determined by the upgrade activity. Upgrade activity is controllable by arbitrarily limiting the resources available for upgrade and establishing stringent justification procedures for requested changes. Using such methods, maintenance and upgrade can be reduced to a workload suitable for a small team. In this case, the structure of the large team is not needed. The distinction between design, implement, and test may be retained, particularly in a type I team with a spectrum of senior and junior skills. However, if the function upgrades are small enough to assign to one person, it may preserve system quality and integrity to treat each change as an independent module. The implementer will design, build, and test the module. Second, if management decisions have eliminated upgrades, leaving only maintenance, one person can do the detective work necessary to find each fault and then fix it.

Since problems are reported at random, one team member will be as effective as any other in searching out the underlying fault. The nature of maintenance narrows the advantage of type II and III small teams over type I at this stage of the life cycle. Since type I teams are easy to assemble, they are often found in a maintenance role.

In an organization with many programs to service, the various teams, project groups, and individuals may be gathered into a functional organization. This move is most practical when the work is limited to maintenance; i.e., correcting faults. The functional manager is able to introduce tools and techniques specially suited to maintenance. Level headcount can be maintained as the declining maintenance requirements of an old system are balanced by the growing requirements of a new system. A functional maintenance department will be able to set up its own administrative group to interface with users. Such a group can improve responsiveness to user requests. It can screen problem reports for redundancy. It can track maintenance effectiveness and suggest ways to improve the process. It can also feed back maintenance history to the system development side of the house to emphasize cost trends related to program quality. In this way, the maintenance department can keep the project managers honest, preventing them from taking shortcuts at the expense of quality. Implicit in this description of what a maintenance department can accomplish is the assumption that the group, like any functional organization, has the right skills. Some companies create a maintenance department and then staff it with junior people. The result is poor maintenance, expensive maintenance, and ineffective control of maintenance activities.

A functional organization is not as useful when there is a significant upgrade content to the workload. The technical strength of the department relates to fixing code. The programmers do not know much about the applications performed by the code. Upgrades, i.e., functional enhancements, change the application and are best done by someone who knows the application. When the maintenance and upgrade team is drawn from the system development team, it is assumed that the people selected know what the delivered program does. That will not be true if the assignment is given to someone in the functional maintenance department who has been working on a completely different system for several years. The problem only arises when the maintenance and upgrade workload is too small to justify a project-oriented team. Early phases of a multiphase project take advantage of experience by assigning the maintenance and upgrade workload to a "module owner" in the development shop who has reason to know the purpose and functions of the program. The owner may be working on a related program or may simply have had past experience in the area. Upgrades handled by the owner should be consistent with the overall program design.

As the organization changes, management emphasis shifts from design to implementation, to integration and test, to maintenance and upgrade. Figure 2.4 plotted the amount of attention the project manager gives to key topics in each stage. The significant point was that the manager's attention must be shifted from system structure where interactions are important to unit implementation where people are important—then back to structure (for testing) and again to implementation (for maintenance). Consider the effects of each of the following project managers:

- Expert architect and designer
- Expert manager of programmers
- Expert general manager

The first will design a good system but he or she may be unable to get it built. The second will build a system but it may not be good. The third will produce an average version of a mediocre design. None will win an "E" for excellence. Three thoughts come to mind for improving the situation.

1. Find a project manager who is an expert in all areas.
2. Pick the expert general manager to maximize the possibility of completing the job but assign the others to head up the design (or design plus test) and development departments.
3. Pick the expert architect to get off to a good start but plan to replace him or her with the expert programming manager as the project enters the implementation stage.

One can play many variations on these themes. The essential point is that individuals are not equally good at all tasks. Some managers can do anything; most cannot. In a dynamic organization, the latter managers must either rely on their ability to assemble qualified subordinates or be replaced.

5.2.5 Administrative and Technical Staff

The word *staff* has not been defined precisely in this chapter. It has been used to refer to the entire population under a manager as well as to the subset of people reporting directing to the manager. The first group is the manager's "organization," the second group is the "management team." "Staff" is also used to refer to groups outside a manager's direct scope of control such as the functional organizations: Personnel, Finance, Plans and Controls, Supply and Logistics, Facilities, etc. When such specialists are within a project manager's direct scope of control they constitute the Project Staff—advising, counselling, and supporting the manager. Dale [4] distinguishes three ways a manager may use this staff. As a *personal staff,* the staff members typically look after the manager's well-being. In software projects, this type of staff is virtually unknown. It tends to be reserved to top executives in jobs where personal image carries a great deal of weight. Executive secretaries who often do many things of a personal nature for their boss are more appropriately classed as *specialized staff*. In this group are the people who do tasks that the manager cannot do personally. In software projects such tasks include clerical duties and technical activities regarding program design, support systems and other aids and tools, implementation techniques, etc. The specialists are expected to know the state-of-the-art at a detailed level. *General staff* plays more of a coordinating role. The general staff cuts across department lines to gather data and establish positions that summarize the recommended course of action for the manager to follow. A general staff may appear in the form of an "assistant to the manager" of a large software project.

The Project Staff includes both administrative and technical functions to the extent they are justified. Secretaries are classified as administrative staff but program librarians are not staff; they are part of the line development group. Therefore, some small teams will have an administrative staff (one secretary) but most will not. Small teams should not need a technical staff because the FLM is qualified to handle technical issues personally. As Newman [15] points out, a staff is desirable only when a manager's duties exceed his or her capacity to fulfill them because the manager (1) lacks time or energy, or (2) lacks specialized knowledge; and it is not feasible to delegate the duties to operating personnel because: (1) coordination across operating units is important, (2) a specialist can improve economy or effectiveness, or (3) the operating personnel are stretched to the extent of their time or ability. Having a staff increases department expenses and increases the span of control of the manager. It also increases the number of communication interfaces within the project; therefore, a staff is only justified when attempts to delegate would clearly fail.

Administrative staff is justified by the amount of administrative work to be done. It is so clear that trained secretaries and clerks are better than managers at typing, filing, making travel arrangements, maintaining project control records, etc., there is no need to explain why you want an administrative staff. You must, however, explain why you should have such a staff within the project rather than at a central facility. Three reasons exist. The most potent reason is that the workload in terms of pages/KLOC, or number of people to be supported, will keep one or more staff members busy full time. It is a potent reason because it promotes cost effectiveness. The other two reasons are: (1) security regulations that restrict who can handle project material, and (2) isolated location. Larger programming projects find they can justify an administrator (or business manager) on the staff to see that reports and contracts are executed properly and on time. The person will evaluate and summarize the reports for the project manager and fill in gaps by direct contact with the first-level managers. He or she will generally look out for the administrative health of the organization. A good administrator is knowledgeable about finance, personnel matters, facilities, contracts, etc. Such skills are hard to find in one person, so most good administrators are trained on the job.

A technical staff is justified by the organization structure and size. Since managers at the second level or higher manage managers, their technical strength should be in the field of management. They should know and understand programming in sufficient detail to control a project, but they should not get so involved in programming as to neglect their primary responsibilities. Programming is a broad subject with rapidly changing content and few simplifying laws or principles. FLMs can manage and, at the same time, participate in the technical work because their area of responsibility is small. HLMs cannot do the same thing. They must concentrate on managing. In a project organization with two or more levels of management, the project manager must therefore rely on a technical staff. Even though this conclusion is obvious, many HLMs fail to set up such a staff in the mistaken belief that they would lose the respect of their people if they showed any need for technical assistance. The right attitude should be: "I am responsible for building a program system to meet a specific requirement. I am going to make sure we deliver the best product in terms of content and quality built with the best methods consistent with our resources. To accomplish this I am going to draw on the best talent available and not rely on my own fallible technical knowledge." With this attitude, the project manager can proceed in various ways to make the best talent available at the appropriate time.

If the project is part of a larger programming house, technical experts outside the project may be available on demand. Certainly, a functional department that has been established to provide a service such as operating system advice and guidance will fit this pattern. In the absence of such functional departments (which are, in essence, the technical staff of the programming house as a whole), it may be possible to reach agreement with another project manager to borrow an expert from time to time. That would be a far less satisfactory arrangement since the expert may be tied up on his or her own project just when needed. Furthermore, the project manager would probably have to formalize the agreement in some sort of contract, perhaps involving payment for services rendered. A better arrangement would be to use people within the project manager's own organization. A *pseudo-staff* can be created by taking specialists who, due to past experience, have learned a topic particularly well, and ask them, in addition to their normal duties, to act as a technical staff. Specialists are quite effective when workload is moderate and the project is relatively simple. These conditions tend to apply to many medium-sized projects. Large projects or rush projects place heavy demands on every participant so part-time staff members tend to be ineffective. At this point, the project manager must start building a full-time technical staff. Initially, one person will be asked to handle all issues. Necessarily, the role will be that of a general staff. Not knowing everything, the staff person will continue to ask specialists in the line organizations for help, but the demands will be less of a burden for the line since, unlike the project manager, he or she can boil the questions down to very specific technical issues. Eventually, a very large project will form a technical staff of full-time specialists. Depending on the project size and subject matter, some sort of technical staff may be needed at each level of the organization except the lowest. Thus the project manager may have a full technical staff; at a lower level, there may be people acting as general staff to HLMs; still lower there may be pseudo-staffs.

Successful staff operation depends on a close and open relationship between the manager and his or her staff. The staff can relieve the manager of considerable work when: (1) they know what the manager wants, (2) they know the manager's objectives, and (3) the manager relies on their advice. A good relationship is built on two operating guidelines:

- Completed staff action—The staff does all the data gathering, analysis, coordination, and evaluation necessary to support a firm recommendation *before* presenting the recommendation to the manager. The "what if" questions have been answered. The manager merely has to decide whether to accept the recommendation.

- Staff consultation—The manager consults the staff prior to making any important decision.

By following these guidelines, a project manager can make the decisions that will result in delivering the best product built with the best methods.

5.3   DECISION MAKING

The dynamics of a system apply to a business or professional organization as well as they do to a product such as a computer program system; therefore, the effects of complex interactions can be expected to cause deviations from base plans. Management decisions are the mechanism for making changes to the plan that permit goals to be achieved and make the best use of resources in the process.

Effective organization facilitates management decision making. The organization structure provides a focal point for each type of decision. Normally, the focal point is a single manager; occasionally, the focal point is a management committee. In either case, decisive action is required if the goals of the organization are to be achieved.

A useful meaning of *decision* is to make up one's mind. For a given set of conditions, the decision process consists of analyzing the situation, designing alternative courses of action, and choosing a course of action [9]. Often, the choice redirects current activities. Sometimes it is simply a judgment that the present course of action should continue. The characteristics of a decision that make both of these situations possible are related to the dynamics of project management:

- A decision applies to a specified period of time, which may be quite long.

- At each *milestone,* defined as a point in time when a decision is required to maintain control of the activity, old decisions expire and new decisions must be made.

- The absence of an explicit decision at a milestone is an implicit decision to maintain the status quo.

- A "good" decision leads to a course of action that is directed toward an objective.

- A sequence of decisions is required to reach an objective.

The last characteristic summarizes the others. It implies that even a perfect manager must make more than one good decision to reach an objective. System dynamics cause the conditions that applied to his or her initial decision to change as time passes. Therefore, the manager has to make observations and measurements of the project status at periodic intervals to see whether the current course of action is appropriate. If it is, he or she lets it continue; otherwise, a new decision is made to fit the new conditions. Such a perfect manager can afford to space the project milestones quite widely.

No project manager is perfect. One may be very successful in the sense that, on average, one's decisions aim *at* objectives rather than away from them (Fig. 5.8a). As a result, no corrective action is required at several of the project milestones (diamonds). More often, one succeeds because he or she has placed milestones at appropriate points where out-of-line situations can be recognized and the project can be redirected to correct them (Fig. 5.8b). Each redirection is supposed to aim the project more accurately at the objective. Some decisions fail to accomplish this and actually cause a wider deviation from the desired path. Complete recovery from such a bad decision may be impossible. In this case, if the project is completed through a new, more tightly monitored plan (triangles in Fig. 5.8c) the results may be a near miss. The user will have to accept an alternate to the original objective. When the severe deviation is not caught in time (due to overconfidence leading to widely spaced milestones) or when panic sets in leading to further errors, the project will fail (Fig. 5.8d). Conceptually, the total length of each solid line in Fig. 5.8 represents project cost. Good decisions minimize cost. Bad decisions inflate cost, leading to project failure and overrunning the budget. Thus, if case b is normal, the good decisions of case a would save about 20 percent. The near miss would lead to a result but add about 25

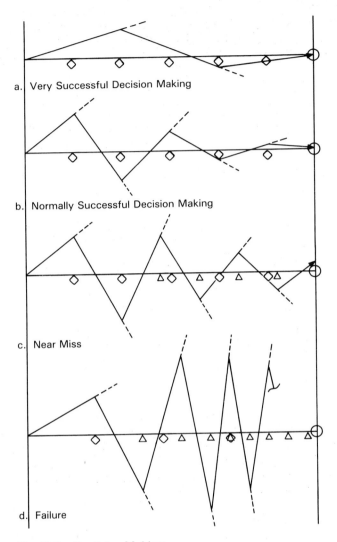

a. Very Successful Decision Making

b. Normally Successful Decision Making

c. Near Miss

d. Failure

Fig. 5.8   Decision Making.

percent to the expected cost of case b. Case d would more than double the normal cost and not even get the job done. These ratios are probably representative of real life.

5.3.1   Multiple Effects of Single Decisions

A specific decision consists of a judgment affecting one or more system elements. The fewer elements addressed by one decision, the easier the decision is to understand and implement. The scope of a decision cannot be easily

constrained, however. Since the elements of a system interact, every decision affects and is affected by every element to some degree. Unity of
command and structured design provide control over the propagation of effects; nevertheless, propagation will occur. In fact, hidden effects of decisions are often a major cause of system changes addressed in subsequent
decisions. Within the time available, a decision-maker should make every
reasonable effort to determine that all the factors affecting the decision
have been identified. Factors that have only a remote effect can be ignored.
Factors whose effect is unknown or indeterminate can be treated arbitrarily.
An early milestone can adjust for the errors that such procedures generate.
On the other hand, the factors treated in this manner should be noted and
carefully examined at subsequent checkpoints to get a better evaluation of
their importance.

In the last chapter, tradeoffs were discussed under the headings: system, hardware, software, function, tools, and techniques. Only at the system level was it possible to consider system-wide effects and, then, only in a
gross way. Yet, in any specific situation, a good manager must consider all
aspects of the multidimensional system. A convenient way to identify the
major dimensions of a system decision is to use a catchword. POSDCORB
was mentioned earlier as a mnemonic for management functions. Try
COMPUTE as the mnemonic to help a manager remember to check seven
key aspects of every decision. In science-fiction language, "test every decision to see if it COMPUTEs."

C—*commitments*. Examine the constraints imposed by existing commitments, internal and external.

O—*objectives*. Relate the decision alternatives to the objectives of the
project.

M—*method*. Consider how the decision relates to the implementation
methods, tools, and technology in use in the project.

P—*people*. Reestimate the resources to determine whether the budget
supports the decision. Evaluate *people* (quantity, and skill and
experience mix) and *resources used by people* (machine time,
spaces, money).

U—*user*. Coordinate proposed plans with the user to avoid conflicts.
Do the same for internal groups that use your output or support
your team.

T—*time*. Reestimate the schedule impact of the proposed decision.

E—*excellence*. Determine whether the decision will satisfy all quality
objectives and whether it will meet your internal standards of excellence.

What happens when these seven dimensions of a decision are applied to
a particular situation? Say that, in the project schedule of Fig. 2.18, Paul

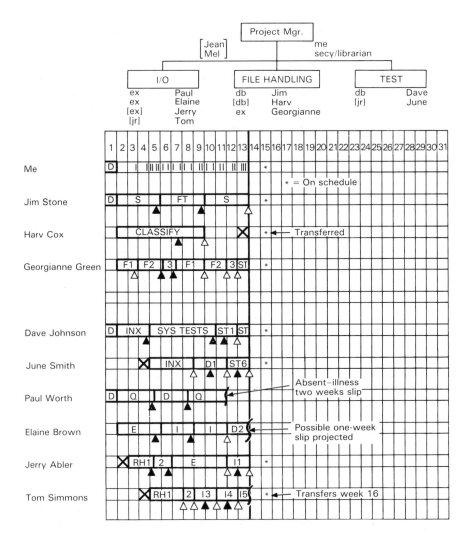

Fig. 5.9 Information retrieval—Work breakdown and bar chart schedule: Week 14.

Worth is home sick during weeks 12 and 13. Lucy Lee has to replan the rest of the schedule. Reviewing first her *commitments,* she sees no serious problem (Fig. 5.9). She had originally promised to deliver in thirty-four weeks to allow for contingencies in the twenty-nine-week schedule. If Worth picks up where he left off he will take two to three weeks longer than planned, finishing in week 31 or 32. How does Worth's absence affect the project *objectives*? Nominally, not at all because he will do what he had been expected to do. Both DISPLAY and QUERY were designed and inspected before his illness so no one else has been held up so far. Lee had selected a *method* based on top-down implementation in a structured high-level language. This helped because Worth's output so far is in a form someone could read if Worth's absence was lengthy. Worth was providing leadership for three *people.* Two are experienced and could carry on with minimal guidance from Lee. Furthermore, Elaine Brown could supervise the trainee, Tom Simmons, during this period since he was working on a component she designed. This extra effort may delay Brown up to a week. Luckily, June Smith, the trainee working in the Test Team, finished the display sub-sub-package she was doing under Worth's direction. He was the only one who could give her intelligent guidance. Lee herself had a strenuous two weeks what with inspections, normal management, and filling in for Worth. No people problems remain but there do appear to be some resource exposures. Whatever machine time Worth had planned to use in weeks 12 and 13 will now be scheduled later. There is a possibility that the time will not be available when he wants it. Lee will have to check this point out. She will also have to recheck expenditures-to-date and budget. Although she allowed thirty-four weeks for the job, she has been managing it as though it would be over in twenty-nine. She may find 13/29 of the budget spent instead of 13/34. If so, the projected slippage may cause an overrun.

The *user* has not expressed interest in how Lee gets the job done. He is aware of the internal twenty-nine-week target. It was mentioned in one of the early project reviews. Now, Lee will have to remind him of the formal thirty-four-week delivery commitment and explain why early delivery is unlikely. New schedules will have to be worked out with computer operations and publications managers as well. So far Lee has assumed that slack in the original plan is sufficient to absorb Worth's absence. To make sure the job will be completed on *time,* Lee has to recheck interactions and dependencies. The key dependency (see Fig. 2.14) is in the test of the I/O Package, event 38. It had been scheduled to begin in week 22. Worth has lost two weeks and had no slack. His absence will delay the test two weeks unless some of his assigned workload can be given to someone else. Elaine Brown is also on the critical path but she had one-and-a-half weeks slack before the start of testing. She agrees her slippage of up to a week can be absorbed.

With this much information, Lee sees three possible solutions to the schedule:

1. Slip two weeks without reassigning any tasks. Start testing in week 24.
2. Slip one week by assigning Worth's two-week task to write the system test, ST18, to Dave Johnson. Johnson has one week slack. That, plus the one week slip, will do the job. Tests will start in week 23.
3. Do not slip but sacrifice *excellence* by shortening tests from three weeks to two. Transfer ST18 to Dave Johnson as above. Start tests in week 23.

The first two approaches satisfy all constraints and objectives; however, they extend the schedule beyond the internal target of twenty-nine weeks. Alternative 3 sacrifices quality but holds down expense.

Lee decides to follow the second alternative. A decision is finally reached. It was made considering all the system implications and all the system participants. It definitely will move the project in the right direction.

5.3.2 "Uncertainty" Concept

In Chapter 4, a risk assessment procedure was discussed in connection with proposal evaluation. Strictly speaking, *risk* refers to situations where the probability distributions of alternative events are known. Risk can be contrasted with certainty [26]. Under conditions of *certainty,* the outcome of a decision is known and, given the same circumstances, it is repeatable. Under risk, the outcome of a decision depends on which combination of circumstances occurs. Only the probability distribution of each contributing factor is known. From this, the most probable or most likely outcome can be calculated. The probability distributions underlying this process are usually the result of data collection and analysis activities of a continuing nature. For instance, programmer productivity, pages of documentation per KLOC, average length of a design review per KLOC, etc., can be described for a given organization after several years of observation. In the software area, few organizations have such data. If they do, the database may be too small for statistical purposes. This leads to the process of decision under *uncertainty,* where the probability distribution of each factor is not known but is estimated from experience or by reference to conventional wisdom—the generally accepted guidelines within the software field. Decisions made under risk or uncertainty depend on identifying the factors that affect the project and assessing the effect of the factors individually and, where possible, jointly on the outcome of the project.

In a software project, decisions under certainty include such things as computer procurement, financial analysis, salary planning, and selection of on-line support systems. These examples all have known costs. The choice of various payment plans to lease or purchase a computer can be based on an analysis of the total payout (including interest gained or lost and the negative effect of tying up a large amount of money) for various periods of use. Each set of conditions yields one answer. Deciding when to approve salary increases without exceeding the salary budget may require a lot of arithmetic, but one solution can be found. Similarly, the relative cost of various on-line systems can be calculated once you have established the relative efficiency of each system in terms of programmer-hours per unit of work. Decision under certainty is not always easy. As these cases show, the decision may be mathematically complicated or it may involve unfamiliar formulas.

The hardest aspect, however, is establishing the utility of each possible outcome of the decision. It is a mistake to pick an on-line support system that costs $10 per programmer-hour if it uses $20 worth of batch time to convert results to the desired form and there is an alternative available that costs $20 per programmer-hour total. The cheaper on-line system will look even worse if it is functionally weak and uses more programmer time to complete the same amount of work. All the variables must be considered.

The preferred outcome of a decision has a value that may be defined in a variety of ways; the choice is dictated by the available data or by manager preference:

- The highest value in terms of revenue, profit, or other inflow
- The lowest cost in terms of expense, labor, or other outflow
- The highest rank in terms of subjectively weighted alternatives

In the choice of a computer financing plan, each alternative payout procedure produces a single life cost; the lowest cost is the best choice. Selection of the right mix of programmer support tools is more complicated. Uncertainty can be avoided by assuming that the value of each mode of programming is known. There remains the problem of determining how much of each type of support to include in the plan when total outlay is limited by the budget. Obviously, there are many ways to combine the options: so much batch, so much in-house on-line usage of time-sharing options A, B, C, . . . , so much on-line service obtained from a service bureau. A complete solution requires examining all possibilities to find the best. For even a few variables it is necessary to use methods requiring computer support: linear programming that treats the problem as an overspecified set of simultaneous linear equations, dynamic programming that converts the calculations to a step-by-step enumeration that causes the choice made at each step to be the optimum for all subsequent steps, branch-and-bound techniques that partition the problem into successively simpler segments [27]. Admittedly, most program project managers do not carry out these computations. They believe that the complete mathematical treatment is only justified in repetitive optimization tasks where good data exist. Production management of inventory levels, ordering quantities, machine scheduling, transportation, and warehousing justify the full treatment in their eyes [28]. Software development involves too many human factors to permit reliable quantification of utility in the eyes of these programming managers. In some cases they are right. Experience and frequent milestones can often achieve better results than computation. However, analytical methods are better than guesswork when they apply. Programming managers should take another look at their decisions. They will recognize that many of them, particularly those dealing with scheduling, resource utilization (people, facilities, storage space, etc.), and other aspects of plan preparation fit their own definition of decisions appropriate for analytical methods.

In the previous example of support tool selection, it was assumed that the costs and values of each approach were known precisely. Such an assumption is often unacceptable. When estimating KLOC per programmer-month, every manager knows there is no single figure that applies to each and every programmer. For any team there is some probability distribution that describes productivity. The actual productivity of an individual will lie within the distribution, most often near the mean. Since productivity is affected by the type of task, the programmer's experience, stress, personal factors, task constraints, and unknown factors, it is hard even to predict which side of the mean a particular assignment will fall on. It is nevertheless possible to say that there is an X percent probability that productivity will be at least Y KLOC. The probability that productivity will be worse is $1 - X$. Knowing both the probability and the utility of each course of action, it is possible to multiply them together to find the *expected utility* of each alternative. The alternative with the highest expected utility is the preferred choice since it provides the *maximum expected utility.*

In economics, "utility" is a quantity representing the usefulness of or the satisfaction received from a product or service. Much theoretical work is based on the concept of utility but, in practice, it is seldom possible to measure the absolute satisfaction one gets from each increase in a product or service. It is more realistic to make a subjective evaluation of alternatives in order to rank them as to the satisfaction they would provide. As is evident from the discussion of tradeoff analyses in the last chapter, you may judge several alternatives to be equally useful. In this case, you can be indifferent to the alternative selected as far as utility is concerned. The alternatives differ in other respects, though—cost, size, resources used, etc. You can select the best of the equals according to the objective you want to maximize/minimize. (The procedure is called *indifference analysis.*)

In what follows, the formal definitions of economics are not applied. *Utility* is simply a quantified value that may have been obtained either objectively or subjectively. Weighting methods are used to establish utility; the weights express a judgment as to the usefulness of an alternative with respect to some criterion. Weights can be dangerous because it is so easy to choose weights that confirm your prejudices. Nevertheless, weighting is a useful technique when the weights are selected either by the responsible manager—reflecting his or her personal opinion but backed by authority—or by negotiation—resulting in contractual acceptance of the weighting assumptions. Weights set by committee should be avoided. In the example, only elementary decision-making guidelines are given; yet they are more formal than methods commonly found in software projects.

5.3.2.1 Example

An example is given in Table 5.2. The array of data in Table 5.2a shows that there are three alternative project structures under consideration for a job. They differ in size. The smallest, a five-programmer team of experienced people, has a high average cost but a correspondingly high productivity under normal circumstances. The ten-programmer team is less productive but can finish the job earlier, as can the twenty-programmer team. The larger teams cost more but, as indicated in Table 5.2b, the project manager weights the value of early delivery twice as high as cost. There is a limit to the funds available so the manager gives cost and schedule equal value when the price exceeds 720. Using these data and assuming the job is normal, a decision under certainty can be made by finding which alternative has the maximum value. The procedure used to obtain subtable b was to assign the value 1 to the best schedule and the best cost. The other lower entries were ratios obtained by dividing the best value by the remaining values. "Utility" was taken to be the weighted sum of the row entries. (While there is no good rule for adding dissimilar things, it is advisable to be consistent in the treatment of weighted factors. Independent factors such as "schedule" and "cost" can be added. Dependent factors such as "number of simultaneous users" and "mean response time" can be multiplied.) Asterisks mark entries that are penalized by high cost to take a lower weight. From this exercise, a_2 gives the maximum utility. To arrive at this result, it was necessary to assume there was 100 percent probability that the normal figures would be achieved.

That assumption may be supported by history; in this case it is not. Subtable c shows that normal targets have been achieved 95 percent of the time by the small, experienced team but only 80 percent of the time by larger groups in this company. A set of data has been provided in subtable a for productivity in the abnormal cases. It shows code output dropping to half normal and schedule length doubling for the small team. Schedule length increases more than double for the larger teams whose internal communications decrease their relative efficiency. Using these additional data, it is possible to construct subtable d. The expected value in each row is the sum of the products of utility times probability for each state, s, that can occur:

$$\text{maximum expected utility} = \max_i \sum_j u_{ij} P(s_{ij})_m$$

The entries in the right-hand column, one for each row i, are the sum of the first utility, u_{i1}, times the first probability $P(s_{i1})$, and $u_{i2}P(s_{i2})$. The largest entry in the right-hand column is now a_1, the answer to be selected. The conclusion is that even though a_2 would be more valuable *if* it were to succeed, a_1 is a better choice because it is *more likely* to succeed; a_1 maximizes the expected utility objectives set by the manager.

TABLE 5.2. DECISION BASED ON UTILITY

Alternative	Programmers	Average cost	Normal KLOC per mo.	Schedule	Total cost	Low KLOC per mo.	Schedule	Total cost
a_1	5	10	.75	12	600	.375	24	1200
a_2	10	8	.50	9	720	.25	20	1600
a_3	20	7.5	.40	6	900	.20	15	2250

a. Alternatives—Input Data

Alternative	Schedule (Wt = 2)	Cost (Wt = 1)	Utility
a_1	0.5	1	2
→a_2	0.67	0.83	2.16
a_3	1*	0.67	1.67

b. Maximum Expected Utility Under Certainty

Alternative	Probability KLOC = normal	Probability KLOC = low
a_1	.95	.05
a_2	.80	.20
a_3	.80	.20

c. Uncertainty

Alternative	Schedule Wt = 2	Cost Wt = 1	Utility	Prob.	Schedule Wt = 2	Cost Wt = 1	Utility	Prob.	Expected value
→a_1	0.5	1	2	.95	0.25*	0.50	0.75	.05	1.94
a_2	0.67	0.83	2.16	.80	0.30*	0.38	0.68	.20	1.86
a_3	1*	0.67	1.67	.80	0.40*	0.27	0.67	.20	1.47

d. Maximum Expected Utility Under Uncertainty

*Wt = 1

5.3.2.2 Decision rules

The probabilities given in the example may not be known. If so, some work should be initiated to gather the necessary information to learn what the probabilities are. To save time it is advisable to structure the problem first. This process can be a significant aid in focusing the measurement effort when the important factors are easy to quantify. Such is the case in computer performance measurement where path lengths can be measured and where the probability of flow through a path is based on known decision elements [29]. Not only does this information show which paths carry the most traffic, thus dominating system behavior, but it also shows which factors, when changed, will have the greatest impact on system behavior. In many systems, these key factors are a small subset of all measurable factors. Concentrating on them reduces the analysis effort. The process is also useful for less precise situations [30]. As in the example, it is possible to know that team size affects productivity without knowing the magnitude of the effect. Nevertheless, the a priori knowledge can be used to structure the measurement and information gathering activity.

In the meantime, decisions must still be made. You can proceed by following one or more decision rules [26, 31, 32, 33].

■   Simplify—Look at the alternatives to see if you can discard any by inspection. In Table 5.2b no alternative is better than any other in all respects. However, in Table 5.2d, alternative a_3 is worse than both a_1 and a_2 if you compare the columns headed "Utility." It is bound to have a lower expected value. So you can ignore it and compare only a_1 and a_2. Note that this conclusion could be reached without knowing the probabilities.

■   Limit exposure—The *minimax* or *maximin* rules limit losses (in the case of the minimax) or gains. Applied to Table 5.2d, the *maximin* rule

$$\text{Max Min } u_{ij}$$
$$\quad i \quad\ j$$

says "find the minimum utility for each alternative, then pick the alternative with the largest value." The utilities u_{ij} are

a_1	2	0.75
a_2	2.16	0.68
a_3	1.67	0.67

$\text{Min } u_{ij}$ is
$\quad j$

→ a_1	0.75
a_2	0.68
a_3	0.67

$\underset{i \quad j}{\text{MaxMin }} u_{ij}$ is a_1—the same answer as before.

The interpretation of this rule is that, given utilities representing the relative value (gain) of each course of action, assume the worst and take the best of the pessimistic choices. Even if everything goes wrong, the project will have a value of 0.75 (instead of 0.68 or 0.67). On the other hand, if everything goes right, the project will be worth 2 (instead of 2.16). The maximin rule is a worst case rule that trades opportunity for protection of minimum objectives.

■   Take a risk—The worst case rule is unacceptable to an aggressive risk taker. The *Hurwicz criterion* balances pessimism and optimism by basing the decision rule on the manager's confidence. The *maximin* example represents a complete pessimist. In Table 5.2b, the assumption that all groups would perform at normal productivity rates follows the *maximax* rule of a complete optimist. The Hurwicz rule says "plot the choices, decide how confident you are that the maximum value can be achieved and select the corresponding alternative from the chart." If α is the confidence factor: $\alpha = 0$ is the maximin rule, $\alpha = 1$ is the maximax rule. Other values of α lead to the Hurwicz rule:

$$\underset{i}{\text{Max}}\left(\alpha \underset{j}{\text{Max}} u_{ij} + (1 - \alpha) \underset{j}{\text{Min}} u_{ij} \right)$$

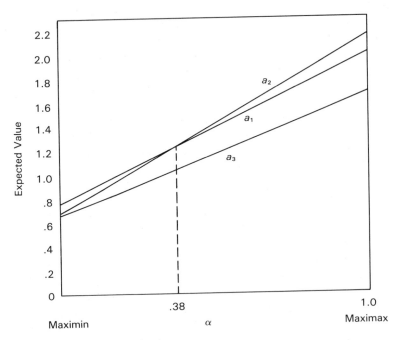

Fig. 5.10   Hurwicz criterion.

The data of Table 5.2 are plotted in Fig. 5.10. The chart shows, as expected, alternative a_3 is never a good choice. The preferred choice, when you are at least 38 percent confident the job at hand will be normal, is a_2. Thus if you take a 50–50 view about the job difficulty, pick a_2. If most jobs in your shop are "normal," pick a_2. Only if you lack confidence should you pick a_1. But, remember, you are making a judgment call. It is not based on any real information about probabilities. In fact, if the probabilities given in Table 5.2d are correct, a_1 is the best choice, and the Hurwicz criterion would have led an optimistic manager to the wrong conclusion.

■ Assume probabilities—The Hurwicz criterion does not conveniently allow for the case where one alternative has a better chance for success than the others. The use of assumed probabilities, therefore, may be safer than the confidence rule. The *Laplace criterion* is a starting point. It says "if probabilities are not known, assume each state is equally likely." The corresponding decision rule is

$$\underset{i}{\text{Max}} \frac{1}{n} \sum_{j=1}^{n} u_{ij}.$$

Average the utilities of each alternative and select the highest result. For the example

$$
\begin{array}{lll}
a_1 & 1/2(2 + 0.75) & = 1.375 \\
\to a_2 & 1/2(2.16 + 0.68) & = 1.420 \\
a_3 & 1/2(1.67 + 0.67) & = 1.170
\end{array}
$$

which selects a_2, the same result obtained by the Hurwicz rule with 50–50 choice. In most organizations rules of thumb permit less arbitrary assignment of probabilities. For instance, if standard estimating procedures are based on normal productivity and the estimates are achieved 75 percent of the time, a 75–25 allocation of probability in the example would make sense.

5.3.3 Use of History

The trivial example used in this section does not illustrate the contradictions that can arise among the decision rules. It is possible to design an example in which each rule gives a different answer. For example, Kline [in 26] presents a table containing five alternative actions, Table 5.3. Each action can result in one of four states but the likelihood of occurrence of any state is unknown. What is known is the utility of each state for each action. Given this data, the decision rules give (choice a_5 is dominated by a_2 and drops out):

TABLE 5.3. UTILITY ARRAY

	S_1	S_2	S_3	S_4
a_1	18	18	10	14
a_2	14	14	14	14
a_3	5	26	10	10
a_4	14	22	10	10
a_5	10	12	12	10

After J. M. English, ed., *Cost Effectiveness: The Economic Evaluation of Engineered Systems* (New York: John Wiley & Sons, 1968).

- Minimax   → a_2
- Maximax   → a_3
- Hurwicz   → a_2 when $0 \le \alpha \le 0.33$
            → a_4 $0.33 \le \alpha \le 0.56$
            → a_3 $0.56 \le \alpha$
- Laplace   → a_1

Such variability is dangerous unless the alternatives are so similar it makes no difference which is selected, but even in the simple programming example, it does make a difference. Therefore, the search for maximum expected utility should be backed up by as much relevant data as possible. Precision will vary from the Laplace condition where you assume no a priori information to the rule-of-thumb where you have a rough idea of "normalcy" to the complete probability distribution of a large history database. The ideal situation occurs when it is possible to say that the situation at hand is like known situations with known characteristics. Then it is not only possible to use realistic probabilities but also to raise confidence levels to approach a maximax result.

In the example, a very rough rule-of-thumb was used that segregated all jobs into those done at normal rates and those done at half-normal rates. A further segregation into small teams versus large teams led to the 95/5 and 80/20 probabilities. Suppose the job being estimated was known to have all the characteristics common to the "normal" class of jobs. It could then have a 100 percent chance of meeting normal objectives and the results of Table 5.2b would apply. Of course, you would need a detailed database, thoughtfully designed to identify job characteristics, in order to determine how well the current job matched the historically "normal" jobs. There is another way to approach the same question of improving the probability assessment by using additional information. Since each of the alternatives involves a team, presumably an existing team, you can ask the team manager for an assessment of how well the current job fits the pattern of normalcy for the group. Then, based on how good a predictor each manager is, you can refine the utility analysis.

Bayes' theorem is used to obtain the probability that normal rates apply, given the condition that the manager says they apply. The theorem can be written:

$$P(s_k|M) = \frac{P(M|s_k)\ P(s_k)}{\displaystyle\sum_{j=1}^{n} P(M|s_j)\ P(s_j)}$$

It gives the probability of one of n events, s_k, given that event M occurs. Applied to the estimating example, n is 2; s_1 would be the "normal" state; s_2 would be the "half-normal" state. M is the manager's assessment of whether the current job is normal. $P(s_1|M)$ is the probability of the current job being normal, given the manager's assessment. $P(s_1)$ is the probability that the job is normal, not considering the manager's assessment. $P(M|s_1)$ is the probability that, in the past, when the manager said a job was normal it turned out to be normal; $P(M|s_2)$ is the probability the manager's assessment is wrong; i.e., the manager says the job is normal but it is not. Ignoring alternative a_3, use the following data:

for a_1 $P(s_{11}) = 0.95$ $P(s_{12}) = 0.05$
           $P(M_1|s_{11}) = 0.90$ $P(M_1|s_{12}) = 0.10$

for a_2 $P(s_{21}) = 0.80$ $P(s_{22}) = 0.20$
           $P(M_2|s_{21}) = 0.75$ $P(M_2|s_{22}) = 0.25$

for a_1 $P(s_{11}|M_1) = \dfrac{0.90 \times 0.95}{(0.90 \times 0.95) + (0.10 \times 0.05)} = 0.99$

for a_2 $P(s_{21}|M_2) = \dfrac{0.75 \times 0.80}{(0.75 \times 0.80) + (0.25 \times 0.20)} = 0.92$

These improved estimates of probability are now used to replace those in Table 5.2d, giving

a_1 $2.00(0.99) + 0.75\ (0.01) = 1.99$
a_2 $2.16(0.92) + 00.68(0.08) = 1.99$

Now both alternatives are equally attractive; however, a_2 is the indicated choice since, with everything else equal, there is more upside potential with a_2.

5.3.4   Involvement of All Parties

The point has been made that system decisions must involve all system participants. Joint action is necessary to ensure that all relevant information is available and that all interactions are evaluated. Joint action is also necessary to ensure successful implementation of decisions.

When a decision changes a course of action, existing commitments may become invalid. New commitment agreements must be negotiated. Some obvious areas affected in a software project are people's assignments, machine schedules, delivery schedules, subcontracts, and baseline specifications. In each of these areas, the effects of the change can be felt outside the area controlled by the decision-maker. In those cases where the outside group provides a service, as does the computer facility, the decision-maker may be unable to negotiate a change in service. That calls for a new alternative plan. This is an acceptable state of affairs since the penalty for an inadequate initial decision is paid only by the decision-maker.

A special problem may occur with subcontractors whose contract does not provide for flexible changes in direction. A change calling for more subcontractor effort may not be feasible because the subcontractor cannot deliver the resources. A change calling for less may be meaningless because the contract guarantees a certain number of labor-hours. A change calling for a different piece of work may be beyond the subcontractor's ability to manage the technical requirements. For these reasons, many managers place a constraint on decisions such that at least one alternative exists that does not affect subcontractors. In organizations using formal management-by-objectives methods of appraising employees and where pay and promotion are strongly influenced by meeting objectives, the employee may behave like the subcontractor. Given a task the employee thinks he or she can do, the individual may resist a change that: (1) interferes with the good appraisal he expects on the original task, and (2) may be harder for him or her, leading to a poor appraisal on the new task.

In many cases, the outside group is not a service group but is a user of the products of the decision-maker. The user may be waiting for delivery of system elements that are prerequisites to his or her own work, or the user may be expecting people to be transferred to him or her when their work for the decision-maker is done, or the user may be expecting certain functions to be delivered as described in the specifications. Changes in these areas affect the user, causing delays and forcing a change of plans. Anticipating problems, the user will sometimes resist absorbing the effects of someone else's changes. He or she may even accuse the decision-maker of backing out of previous commitments in order to show the system manager who the culprit is. The proper protection against such tactics is to keep all the affected parties involved at all times. In that way they will understand the need for the change. They will recognize that their interests were considered, and they will become a party to the decision in the sense that they share some of the responsibility for making it succeed.

5.3.5 Restricting the Scope of Single Decisions

Self-imposed constraints on decisions protect the decision-maker against catastrophe. A truely bad decision leads to catastrophe for the system when it affects activities outside its own subsystem *and* when its undesirable effects are not noticed in time to take corrective action. Therefore, protecting the system against catastrophe involves: (1) restricting the scope of a decision insofar as possible to the subsystem or element controlled by the decision-maker, and (2) establishing frequent checkpoints and milestones to detect potential problems. Bad decisions are not eliminated by these guidelines, but the extent of the damage they produce is reduced. The project manager has better control and, when bad decisions are made, the source can be pin-pointed. The bulk of the corrective action must be taken by the manager who caused the problem. As a result, the project manager gets a reasonably clear view of each manager's ability—in terms of planning, decision-making, and controlling.

Within the decision-maker's area of responsibility, the same two guide-lines apply. The individual must protect his or her own portion of the system from catastrophe. Otherwise, the failure of a system element will eventually bring down the whole system. Frequent checkpoints of the whole will tell the project manager when one element is in trouble, but if it is really falling apart, the system is threatened—"all the King's horses and all the King's men couldn't put Humpty-Dumpty together again." Preventive measures, thus, have high priority.

A recommended way to implement the guidelines relies on *structure*. The manager at all times mentally carries models of the structure of the system, the element he or she owns, the project organization, the support functions and facilities, etc. Each of these models is a hierarchy of named units such as programs, people, procedures, machines, and so on. Some of the units can be broken down into smaller units but the manager has not found this necessary so far. The decision process starts by consciously selecting the one box in the model most affected by the problem (Fig. 5.11):

- Identify problem
- Set objectives for decision
- Decide
  1. Identify lowest level unit (in system model) for which a decision will satisfy objectives
  2. Identify other units affected by a change in the prime unit
  3. Lay out alternatives, coordinate with all parties, analyze alternatives, maximize expected utility
  4. Give preference to alternatives that isolate effects of decision even lower than the prime unit
  5. Make decision affecting prime unit
- Implement decision
  1. Trace effects of decision on other units
  2. Make decisions affecting other units under your control resulting from interactions with prime unit

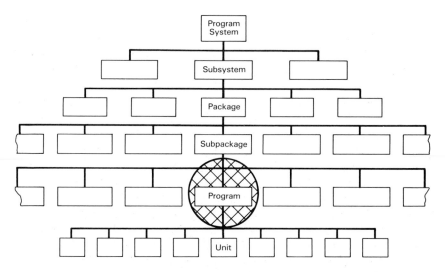

Fig. 5.11 Restricting decision to one-system element.

3. Coodinate with managers of other affected units so they make necessary decisions in their area
4. Establish plan for implementing decisions
   a. Lay out substructure of units under prime
   b. Lay out activities and/or resource utilization rates needed to implement decision in each unit
   c. Set checkpoints wherever an activity is due to be completed
   d. Set checkpoints to track resource utilization (expected time when ¼, ½, ¾ used up)
   e. Set milestones at unit completion and at checkpoints which, if missed, would require redirection of the plan
5. Track accomplishment and make conscious decision at milestones

Concentrating on *structure* helps show when a decision affects more than one system element. It also helps force the scope of a decision as low as possible in the system hierarchy, automatically restricting its scope further. Laying out the substructure of a unit affected by a decision yields more frequent opportunities for observing completion events; therefore, if the plan is not working, the manager will find out sooner. In Fig. 5.11, the prime unit is a program with obvious substructure. Even the lower-level units can be subdivided, though. Design, code and debug, and component testing are activities that are completed at points suitable for checkpoints. Inspections are events suitable for milestones. In other areas, an activity involving a new programmer may have substructure such as "familiarization," "practice assignment," etc. An analysis task may be broken into "interviews," "data consolidation," "draft requirements," "reviews and feedback," and "final requirements statement complete."

5.3.6 Conflicts and Tradeoffs

Assuming that utility and probability are known for each possible set of conditions in a decision oversimplifies real life. Often, the value of *A* is unknown. Only the preference for *A* over *B* is known and that can change as circumstances change. That leads to conflicts and tradeoffs.

In a tradeoff, the decision-maker searches for the most important, most valuable, most acceptable solution to a problem. "Most" implies that the alternatives can be listed in order of importance, value, etc. Thus the ranking of alternatives is fundamental to tradeoffs. "Rank" implies that a numerical preference can be assigned to each alternative. The number can range from a highly objective calculation of cost or performance parameters to a less objective estimate of relative merit based on a summation of weighted attributes to a completely subjective value based on management opinion. The interpretation of the ranked list depends on the objectivity and the accuracy of the values. Interestingly enough, it is easiest to interpret the ranks at extremes of the objectivity scale. That is, completely objective and completely subjective ranks are easy to handle. Anything in between is harder. "Most important" choices can be made using a *priority list*. "Most valuable" choices can use *weighted averages* representing the degree to which each alternative exhibits various attributes. "Most acceptable" choices may be based on sophisticated game theory or, as is more common, may be simple management judgments. The methods are not exclusive; for instance, priorities may be based on weighted averages. The methods all share two characteristics: the selected alternative must satisfy the objectives of the tradeoff, and cost must be evaluated in the decision process.

Prioritization is the best way to decide how to handle tough schedules. By prioritizing system requirements during the system analysis stage, it is possible to adapt to slipping schedules by stopping work on uncompleted requirements at the bottom of the priority list. This method has worked most effectively in the support of space flight. Many of the space missions have critical operational dates based on the relative positions of the Earth and a destination planet or satellite. Everyone on the project team knows the critical date and understands why it is so important. They can therefore accept a management decision that eliminates some mission capability in order to preserve the mission itself. Few other environments have such clear decision criteria. As a result, priority management is harder to sell and enforce outside the space flight environment.

In the most common case of prioritization, there is not enough project money to go around. The priority list represents the management decision regarding where the money will go. Only the items at the top of the list, above the budget cutoff line, are committed. Those items become the "in plan" items. Lower priority items are "out plan" or "below the line." That means they are identified as candidates for future action but no serious effort is expended on them. Some managers play a game with priority lists.

Knowing that a very simple tradeoff decision will be made, they try to force it to come out the way they would prefer: namely, to include all their items above the line. The trick they use is to invert the list. In every list, there is at least one item that is indispensable. By placing an indispensable item at the bottom of the priority list and giving some plausible explanation of why all items above it are prerequisites, the manager forces the "line" down. The hoped-for result is that resources will be diverted from some other part of the system to cover the manager's out-plan items. From the widespread existence of this tactic, you can conclude that the key to the budgetary tradeoff is a thorough, skeptical evaluation of the priorities proposed by contending parties.

The priority list represents an agreement as to the relative importance of many items. Although priorities can change, the status of the list at any given point in time provides a rigid, unequivocal basis for a decision. Furthermore, the priority list represents a current agreement as to the decision that will be made at some future date if certain conditions arise.

In the networking example of Chapter 4, the choice of approach was based on net revenue. A forecast was used to determine the relative profitability of the candidates. The analysis placed a value on the opportunity represented by a market of a given size. The costs of pursuing the opportunity were estimated and subtracted from the gross revenue to get a measure of relative value. In product planning, the relevant opportunity and cost are calculated over the entire projected life of the product. The cost of planning, developing, manufacturing, selling, supporting, and maintaining a product are estimated. The cost of the money used for these purposes is included since in many businesses debt service is a significant percent of expense. The cost of unproductive labor during recruiting and reassignment periods is also counted when it is too large to absorb as normal overhead. On the opportunity side, there is opportunity realized and, usually, some opportunity lost. A given product will win some portion of the market depending on its features and the date it is introduced. Delays in delivery result in lost opportunity and, assuming someone else gets that business, the rate of acceptance of your product will be reduced. Consequently, in value analyses it is necessary to analyze the risks and the advantages associated with a plan.

Prioritization freezes a decision rule at the beginning of the project. Value analysis also makes decisions at the beginning of a project which establish the decision criteria to be used throughout the project. Most other tradeoff decisions apply only "here and now" and are based on either: (1) management fiat, (2) a single "best" answer, or (3) a weighted average answer that is "best under the circumstances." In the case of deciding whether to build a banking system using the existing demand deposit software as a base, these three approaches would amount to:

■ Management fiat—"You will utilize the existing demand deposit software. Any exceptions from this directive require my approval." Management fiat need not be supported by explanation or justification. It operates through the authority of the decision-maker.

■ "Best" answer—"The planned system differs from the present system in seventy-three places, involving everything from minor modifications to existing code to complete redesign of I/O to handle teller terminals. Our initial estimate of the cost using the existing base is one million dollars. The comparable estimate if we start from scratch is six million dollars due to the large volume of code used in demand deposit accounting. Therefore, we will use the existing base." A ratio of 6:1 is enough to justify the "best" choice. A similar spread between the forecasts for type 2 and type 3 networking showed type 3 to be a better opportunity. However, since the inputs to the analysis have some degree of error, there is some uncertainty about the result. Barring mistakes, the results remain valid in spite of the errors in estimating. If the results show two alternatives are relatively close, say the difference between the results is less than the expected error in the estimates, you have not found a "best" answer.

■ "Best under the circumstances"—"The planned system differs from the present system in seventy-three places, involving everything from minor modifications to existing code to complete redesign of I/O to handle teller terminals. The cost of modifying the existing base is within 10 percent of the cost of starting from scratch according to our best estimates. We have examined several other attributes of the two approaches and weighted them as follows:

Reliability	10
Efficiency	8
Understandability	5
Modifiability	5
Testability	4
Human Engineering	4
Portability	1

We rated the acceptability of the approaches on a scale of 10 to get Table 5.4. This did not distinguish between the two approaches, so we examined the schedule and risk aspects of the situation. We determined that by sequencing the modification steps we could start using modified existing code in a single branch bank in eight months. As a result we could learn from experience how to improve the system utility without seriously affecting the schedule. The first deliverable of the brand-new system would not be available for at least eighteen months. At that time, its design would be pretty well frozen. We also noted that the estimates in our organization show that productivity is better on new code. Even though the new system was bigger,

TABLE 5.4. WEIGHTED ATTRIBUTES

Attribute	Wt.	Modify existing code		Build new system	
		Score	Value	Score	Value
Reliability	10	8	80	5	50
Efficiency	8	8	64	5	40
Understandability	5	5	25	8	40
Modifiability	5	5	25	8	40
Testability	4	5	20	8	32
Human Engineering	4	6	24	6	24
Portability	1	0	0	0	0
Total Value			238		226

the costs came out the same, because of the productivity rates used in the estimate. Actual costs for modifying code in our shop have been running 90 to 120 percent of the estimate. New code has been 90 to 150 percent of the estimate. If the worst case applies, the new code will cost 25 percent more. These final considerations led us to decide to modify the existing demand deposit system base." To reach this decision, a sequence of analyses was made. First, quality was tested to see if one approach was clearly more acceptable than the other. Then the schedule was examined on the basis that an early start was advantageous but not at the expense of quality. Finally, cost was reexamined in more detail to see if there were hidden risks that might weigh against a decision reached on more subjective grounds. If a utility value were placed on the schedule options, this case could be handled by formal methods.

A practical method of refining a ranked list when you cannot think of any additional discriminating factors is to poll other people. The initial criteria of a tradeoff tend to be narrowly drawn around a few key factors such as cost and performance. Whichever factors are selected, they tend to dominate the decision-maker's attention to the extent that he or she cannot see any other factors that would influence the decision. Associates and users will be able to think up plenty of additional factors. Of course, each person will identify the factors important to his or her own activities. The bias must somehow be eliminated before a reasonable ranking can be obtained. This is done by consensus-seeking. Have each person rank the consolidated list of factors. Items of system-wide benefit will generally be recognized by everyone and be ranked high in importance. Other items will be scattered through the list. A second round of review will show the consolidated results of the first round and ask each person for a new ranking; i.e., a new personal statement of the importance of each factor in the light of what other knowledgeable people think. The process then continues; however, a consensus will often develop as to which items are key. The decision-maker can then quantify the value of these items—if the reviewers have not already done so—and use the results to modify the previous tradeoff results.

The process of reaching a consensus in a subjective area can be as formal as you like. For small projects, it is usually sufficient to call a few people together for a single "brainstorming" or "planning" meeting. The meeting chairman sees that everyone understands the purpose of the meeting and that each gets to express his or her position. After everyone has stated a position, the leader summarizes the consolidated result. The leader then goes around the table again: "You all heard what the others had to say so you know how we arrived at this list. How do you think we should change the list to reflect the consensus opinion?" If a meeting is inconvenient, an analyst can be assigned to interview each contributor—once to get the biased view; subsequent times to seek consensus. In this case, the inputs must be very well documented by the analyst so each person can appreciate the merits of the views of other people with whom there is no direct contact. In very large projects, the process can be conducted by mail or via an on-line computer. Of course, without a human guide to explain what is going on, these approaches must be highly formalized. Consensus seeking, as described here, is a spin-off of the Delphi technique[4] which can be used for long-range technological forecasting [34]. Forecasting the distant future is about as subjective as you can get. Delphi techniques, with or without computer conferencing, draw on the opinions of many experts in a sequence of feedback cycles until the inputs converge on a more or less common forecast.

The time and resources required for consensus limit the applicability of the techniques so that most tradeoff decisions are made directly by the project management team who accept the risk that their decision may be wrong. Lack of consensus leads to conflict, which must be resolved by negotiation or, as a last resort, escalation to a higher level. It is always preferable to resolve conflicts at the lowest possible level—to save time, to preserve the working relationships between contending parties, and to obtain the decision from the people closest to the facts. Chase [35] recommends five principles of cooperation that improve chances for reaching agreement early:

1. Participation—Involve all affected parties in the decision process.

---

4. The Delphi technique preserves the anonymity of the forecaster. The results of each round are summarized in such a way as to eliminate clues as to who said what. Anonymity has the advantage that it reduces the effect of cliques and pressure groups. It also removes the fear of embarrassment that one's opinion may be widely different from the consensus. Obviously, a consensus-seeking *meeting* lacks anonymity. In a small group, a good discussion leader can achieve useful results anyhow.

2. Group energy—Emphasize group objectives in order to get everyone working on the global problem rather than some local optimization to suit each department.

3. Clearing communication lines—Remove obstacles to discussion by: (a) clarifying the subject, and (b) setting aside personal animosities and power plays.

4. Facts first—Complete the data gathering and analysis before jumping to a conclusion.

5. Feeling secure—Make everyone's role clear and aim for a decision that is equitable to everyone.

Managing along these lines lets each participant contribute to the group objectives without jeopardizing his or her own position.

5.3.7   Iterative Decision Making

Where ranks cannot be agreed to, system tradeoffs tend to be arbitrary. This is particularly true in new systems where uncertainty regarding market requirements makes it difficult to demonstrate that one function is clearly more valuable than another. Up to a point, a tradeoff decision can be postponed in the hope that additional information will be found to rank requirements. A method for controlling progress in this case is *incremental funding*. Work associated with each requirement is funded only up to a milestone at which time a decision must be made to continue (and release more funds) or stop work. To be effective, the work completed at the milestone must include enough analysis and design to yield trustworthy estimates of both the cost and the value of each time. This method applies when the budget will not cover all the requirements, yet is large enough to do all but one or two plus preliminary work on the rejected items. The milestones for the key items should cluster around a single date; otherwise, the decision will be uneconomically delayed until the last milestone is reached.

Tradeoff decisions are most visible and consequently most formalized in the early stages of a project. This is particularly evident in military systems where massive expenditures hang on a single decision. Defense projects are doubly difficult because they involve both the comparison of unfamiliar alternatives and the evaluation of the impact of possible enemy decisions on each alternative. In such an environment, game theory contributes to decisions that are a compromise between maximum benefit and minimum risk [26, 36]. In the early stages, tradeoff topics stress functional content of the project and cost. In the process of studying conflict management, Thamhain and Wilemon [37] found that as a project advances to the system design stage decisions continue to be affected by cost but the subject of most tradeoffs turns to project administration. This focus continues well into the implementation stage and then fades away. Additional topics rise in importance, some drawing substantial management attention throughout the project, others being of interest only until resolved. Drawing on Thamhain and Wilemon, Fig. 5.12 shows by the height of each line how much attention various conflicts demand at various stages of the project life cycle. Management of the conflicts results in tradeoffs. In addition to conflict management there is, of course, a requirement for the management of the substantive aspects of the project. As a very rough indication of the relative amount of attention given to conflicts vs. nonconflict situations, the chart includes the two elements, System Structure management and Unit Implementation management, shown in a different form in Fig. 2.4. Common management techniques for making decisions apply in all project stages but, as mentioned in earlier chapters, the changing focus of attention may make a manager with limited experience less effective in one stage than another.

In any case, decisions on a given subject improve as time passes and more information is generated about the subject. Explicit Bayesian computation is not essential to gain the benefit of the added inputs. Common sense is often enough [38]. The important thing is to use the information obtained after each step in an iterative decision process to make the next step more effective. In the operational decisions facing managers in programming projects, the availability of measurements and history data permits practical use of analytical decision-making methods, yet many managers do not use such methods and may even disdain them. There are both pragmatic and behavioral reasons for this attitude. The pragmatic reasons are based on known fallacies in the available methods. Kazanowski [in 26] identifies some of these fallacies:

- Sole-criterion—The assumption (made frequently by executives) that a decision can be based on one dominant factor; e.g., the assumption that only fuel consumption governs a buyer's choice of a car.

- Ratios—The belief that ratios (such as Performance/Price) are good criteria for selection, regardless of the magnitude; e.g., a computer system with P/P of 1.0 costing $10,000,000 is better than one with P/P = 0.2 costing $200,000 when the buyer has $300,000 to spend.

- Quantification—The assumption that all applicable factors can be quantified—and quantified with precision; e.g., safety, appearance, modifiability; furthermore, that all factors can be quantified in terms of dollar costs and benefits.

- Interrelationships—The belief that any set of "quantified" criteria can be related to each other, say in graph format, to create a "sole criterion"; e.g., computer arithmetic speed is stated in millions of instructions per second (MIPS), I/O is related to channel capacity which is related to MIPS, terminal response time is a function of I/O rates and can be stated in terms of MIPS, etc.; therefore, computer system performance can be completely characterized by the central processor MIPS.

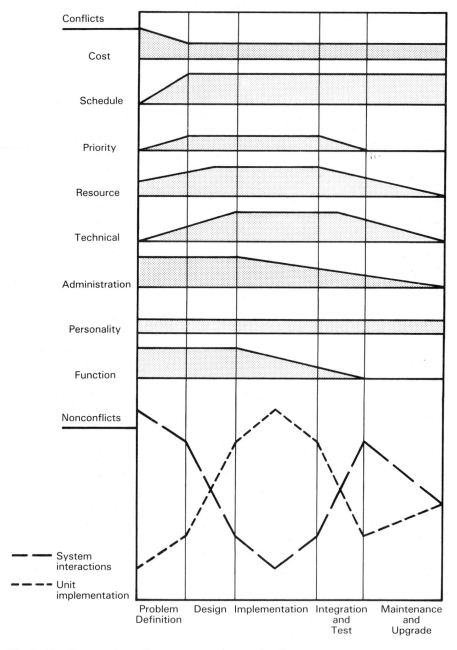

Fig. 5.12 Focus of conflict management tradeoffs.

- Weighting—The assumption that weights assigned to decision criteria are correct; e.g., the weights assigned are expected to be unbiased even though the person who selected the weights stands to gain from one particular solution. Are the weights to be added or multiplied? Are they ranks or do they reflect the magnitude of the criterion they represent? Are they based on facts or intuition? Are the weights a bona fide representation of the situation or are they conversion factors that yield a preordained result?

- Equations—The assumption that, because a model of a real-life situation can be expressed as a set of equations, the situation behaves like the equations. The same exposure occurs with algorithms in which mathematical symbols are used to represent both quantified and non-quantifiable criteria.

- Infallibility—The belief that your assumptions are always correct; e.g., you have guessed exactly the right probability of occurrence of some future event that has never happened before, you have selected the correct time period for amortizing capital costs, or you have accurately predicted future inflation rates.

- Simplification—The assumption that complexity can be ignored; e.g., you neglect spillover effects by assuming your activity is completely isolated; you make simplifying assumptions or define away problems hoping that decisions based on the simpler system will apply to the real system.

- Prescience—The belief that you know *the* answer; e.g., instead of deciding among alternatives your decision-making consists of justifying what you intended to do all along.

Part of the difficulty in dealing with these fallacies is that, at times, they are true. At such times, the manager who believed all along that ratios are good criteria or that weights should be added reinforces his fixed attitudes.

In behavioral terms, managers may avoid analytical methods because they do not understand them. The are afraid they will make a mistake. They may rely on junior professionals to do the analysis and, in the end, be embarrassed by their inability to follow the presentation. Worse, the analysts may intentionally mislead them in order to get more control of company affairs. A second cause of avoidance may be cultural. Many managers were trained in liberal arts. They feel uncomfortable with technologists and sometimes mistrust people who insist on quantifying everything. Third, managers convince themselves there is not enough time to do an analysis. Acting on this conviction, they decide not to invest in the data gathering and computer methods that would make fast analyses feasible. Their conviction is, consequently, a self-fulfilling prophecy.

Each of these three behavioral issues is rational since it is based on the individual's education and experience. Being rational, these attitudes can be changed when the manager recognizes that his or her decisions have become more complex and the success ratio has begun to slip. There remains one other type of behavioral problem that is usually not rational; namely, analytical methods are avoided because the manager thinks his or her intuitive judgment is superior.[5] Such a manager is unlikely to change habits. Like all gamblers, this individual will attribute successes to his or her superiority and failures to bad luck. He or she may remain successful for a long time—probably because so much information has been absorbed through experience that he or she can mentally but unconsciously analyze each situation. Yet the individual is always subject to gross error when a job outside his or her experience is underway. Like some of the great commercial speculators who built business empires by shrewd management of corporate finance only to see the empire collapse when interest rates rose, the intuitive manager of program systems can go down in flames when unfamiliar problems occur. The rational manager, on the other hand, can be equally daring and, forewarned of future problems by decision support methods, can avoid disaster. (Of course, the opposite is also true. Good judgment can avert a disaster that could be overlooked by formal methods.)

5.4 PERSONNEL

Programming teams blend the skills of managers and nonmanagers. Managers depend on their staff for advice on what to do. They depend on their operating personnel to carry out the actions. The techniques of leading a programming team to outstanding performance are similar to the techniques of "people management" in any organization. There is a large and constantly growing body of literature on people management and the subject as a whole is beyond the scope of this book. (Some already cited references [4, 5, 6, 8, 10, 11, 12, 15, 16, 21, 22, 40, 41, 42, 43] are useful but each year new books, including comprehensive texts become available and should be reviewed for current trends.)

---

5. Elstein [39] discusses a particular form of this attitude which he calls "clinical judgment." Psychological studies show that clinicians, typified by most physicians, disdain decision-making methods that depend on quantitative methods, formulas, tables, etc. They are convinced that the qualitative, informal methods used in clinical diagnosis are much better; in fact, dynamic, meaningful, deep, genuine, and sophisticated. Statistical methods to the clinician are artificial, static, pedantic, atomistic, and pseudoscientific. Statisticians hold diametrically opposite views. Interestingly, both groups make good judgments. The "statisticians" hold an edge in psychological tests; however, poor analysis or faulty data can lead to serious quantitative mistakes. Similarly, experience, good powers of observation, and sensitivity to interrelated factors can lead to correct qualitative judgments. As expected, Elstein recommends the use of both sets of methods.

Within the broad field, programming managers tend to have particular difficulty selecting and using staff members and specialists. Managers also have difficulty building up large teams from scratch. These topics are covered in the following sections. In addition, the question of how programmers in a team can be evaluated is addressed. Guidelines are provided for large teams where such issues are most likely to cause trouble, yet where they are most important to success.

5.4.1   Line vs. Staff

The operating personnel who produce the deliverable end product are called the *line;* their managers are *line managers*. Groups that contribute indirectly to project objectives are called *staff*. As Stewart [40] points out, however, the distinction between line and staff is not always clear. Applied research in programming techniques could be considered line activity in an R&D company but it might be a staff function in a software house. Further complicating the picture is the fact that all organizations are run as line departments by their manager even though they may be doing staff work for other departments. For these reasons, Stewart prefers to associate the line with accountability for results; "line tells, staff sells" reflects the authority that goes with accountability. Within a project, the line/staff distinction is usually explicit. The project manager is the top line manager. Reporting to the project manager are the project staff who advise, counsel, and support him or her. Also reporting to the project manager are the line managers who carry out his or her orders and direct the operating departments.

A relationship develops between line managers and project staff such that they complement each other. This occurs most successfully when the aides are "staff" types. Allowing for the fact that no individual ever fits the stereotype accepted as conventional wisdom, some observations can be made about line and staff characteristics that can help predict whether individuals will complement each other.

■ Line managers are concerned with *decision-making*. They do not want to develop all the detailed backup supporting a decision. They do not even want to see the backup data if they can avoid it.[6] Ideally, they want to be given a set of alternative courses of action based on completed staff action. The set should include the course of action recommended by the staff and sufficient summary information to show the consequences of each action. Management decision-making can be a selection process rather than an analysis process. In this manner, managers can handle a large number of complex decisions efficiently.

---

6. The staff members should have the backup data with them when they present their report. When the manager asks for detail, he or she is often probing for clues to the thoroughness and logic of the staff work. By showing the appropriate backup data, the staff establishes credibility for the recommendations.

■ The staff *advises* the line manager. Good advice is based on thorough knowledge, credibility, and completed staff action. Each of these attributes requires the staff aide to stay current on all activities related to the project. Reading will help the aide keep up with the state-of-the-art. It may help with the state-of-the-project, too. But the most effective way for a staff aide to build his or her knowledge and credibility is to talk directly to the people doing the work. Such contacts provide detailed data on status and plans. In addition, they show different points of view held up and down the organization and provide a forum for testing staff ideas.

■ There is a frequently held belief that people who seek and win line positions are decisive, optimistic, outgoing, intuitive, but technically shallow, whereas staff people are analytical, well-informed, pessimistic, deliberative, and probably introverted. What is more likely true is that a line manager likes people but prefers his or her contacts to be either decisive or purely social. The staff person is less likely to be gregarious, but is comfortable in small groups discussing technical subjects without necessarily reaching conclusions. The line manager is committed to accomplish a job. He or she looks for ways to turn potential solutions into real solutions. Potential solutions are seen as opportunities. In this respect, the line manager is an optimist. The staff member compares alternatives to select the best. One could say this individual selects the best of a bad lot because he or she looks for all the things that could go wrong to find the alternative that is least exposed. Like a pessimist, he or she finds it easier to recognize problems than to create opportunities.

■ Line managers often look for immediate results and expect immediate rewards. Staff members are more likely to take a long-term view. Knowing how much coordination and negotiation may be required to reach a consensus, staff members tend to be patient. They appreciate but do not expect rewards. In the view of a dedicated staff member, rewards should go to the accountable line manager who initiated a successful action.

■ At the risk of trivializing a difficult personnel selection task, the characteristics of line and staff candidates can be summarized:

1. Line manager
   a. decisive, perhaps opinionated
   b. deals with and through chain of command
   c. avoids detailed technical data collection and analysis
2. Staff member
   a. seeks out all sources of data
   b. solicits contradictory opinions, sees all sides of issue
   c. analyzes data to suggest and rank courses of action

Social scientists concerned with human motivation define various motives such as the need for *power* (having a strong impact on others), the need to *achieve* (doing a good job), and the need for *affiliation* (making friends or avoiding rejection). People motivated to be managers, executives, and entrepreneurs can be expected to have high scores in nPower—the *need* for power. They cause things to happen through the efforts of others. Top staff people should be high in nAchievement. They want to be the best at what they do. The power-seeker wants to stand out and be recognized. The high achiever is content in the knowledge that he or she has done well. Many others score higher in nAffiliation than the other motives. They tend to avoid competition and conflict, placing higher value on establishing and maintaining personal relationships [44]. While such labels oversimply the situation, they may suggest why conventional wisdom distinguishes between line/staff personalities. They also suggest that where personality differences exist, bridges must be built to achieve mutual understanding.

The quality of the advice provided by a staff member depends on completed staff action. Assuming that a complete job has been done, the impact the staff advice has on the project manager depends on:

- The manager's willingness to consult with the staff
- The ability of the staff member to communicate with the manager
  1. clarity
  2. simplicity
  3. relevance
  4. brevity
- The support provided by the rest of the management team

Clearly, a staff report will not influence a manager who refuses to study it. With the right sort of presentations the staff can convince the manager to pay attention. The burden is on the staff to learn how their manager thinks and how material should be presented to him or her.

The staff is only one source of advice available to managers. They also listen to the other people who report to them as well as to their superior, the user, and their associates. Staff advice holds the dominant position when it is based on completed staff action since, in that case, at least the views of the management team should already be reflected in the recommendations. The subordinate line managers may not all agree with the staff conclusions and they will speak up to present their case in opposition. The project manager will accept all the inputs and finally make a decision. The staff will have to win more often than it loses if it is to retain the manager's confidence.

While access to the project manager is essential to staff influence, access to the members of the operating and support departments is essential to completed staff action. A staff member has to be very careful how he or she establishes and uses contacts with individual team members. The staff member must let his or her sources know why certain data are needed and what will be done with the data. Improper use of an information source may close off that source for future use.

In a project, some data are global and are available to everyone, while other data are private to some restricted group within the project. The hierarchical modularity of the project encourages localization as a means of reducing the amount of communication between modules. Not all local data are the consequence of project/system structure, though. Some are private data that a manager wants to conceal or withhold. In this category are things such as unconfirmed rumors, partial or unproved results, and unfavorable data for which corrective action has already been initiated. Politically sensitive data are also private. For instance, one manager may be planning to steal a march on his or her peers by announcing an important accomplishment they are unaware of. A staff member should not interfere with normal line management by leaking such information to the project manager. Strict adherence to the rule of confidentiality means that all private data remain private until released by the owner. Only in the situation where a manager is violating project orders should the staff member blow the whistle. Even then, it is a good idea to explain the problem to the violator, giving the individual a chance to correct the situation on his or her own, before taking steps to protect the project.

Staff members who respect the rule of confidentiality find that they can talk freely with everyone in the project. They are welcome as supporters, not avoided as spies or hatchetmen. They can even step in when necessary to help a subgroup out of difficulty. The technical staff member who is asked to work directly on a problem takes direction from the line manager of the working group. For practical purposes, his or her staff role is suspended for the duration of the task assignment. Normally, of course, the staff members receive direction only from the project manager (or the Manager of the Staff if there is one). Lower-level managers do not have authority over the project staff. Staff members do not have line authority. The separation of line and staff is preserved when vacancies occur. A line management vacancy is temporarily filled either by the next higher level manager or by a manager reporting to the vacant position. The acting manager is replaced as soon as possible by a permanent appointee. A staff vacancy is temporarily filled by another staff member. Often it is left open until a qualified permanent replacement is found. If none is available, the position will be eliminated. From this comparision, you can see that line management positions are essential to the organization because the chain-of-command makes things happen. Staff positions are optional, depending on the availability of the right people who can make things happen more efficiently.

5.4.2 Specialists vs. Generalists

The advisory functions of a staff fall into two categories:

- Generalized—Coordination of multiple inputs to develop a single course of action
- Specialized—Use of detailed professional knowledge to improve plans, implementation, and quality

The generalist has broad knowledge and the ability to see the relationships among a number of activities. The specialist has deep knowledge in a particular area. As noted earlier, when a project manager first establishes a project staff, he or she brings in one generalized staff member. As the staff grows, a specialized technical staff is built to support and supplement the general staff. The individuals picked for the technical staff are the professionals who, through interest or experience, are so good in a subject that other people come to them for information and assistance. A very useful specialist in a programming project is the person who generated the operating system in the computer room. This person's background is the same as the line department programmers but special knowledge of the operating system leads people to seek him or her out. Similar specialists can cover DB/DC issues, specific hardware or software items, project management, installation management, development productivity, etc. The specialties have in common the fact that they are of interest to many people on the project, but they cover so many tools, techniques, and products that the average person can only skim the surface.

Specialists within a project hierarchy are measured in terms of their overall value to the project. Since it is uncommon for a line department to spend all its time in one technical aspect of development, specialists assigned to a department are not rated very highly by their FLM. An assignment to the project technical staff is better. From this position, the specialist can help all the FLMs and be evidently more valuable to the project. Best of all, the specialist can join a functional department built around the specialized subject area. In this group, each specialist is measured in terms of accomplishment relative to the state-of-the-art. Upward growth potential is virtually unrestricted. Now it may be appropriate to refer to the specialist as a consultant.

A consultant is an "expert" in a subject area. Many consultants are outstanding scientists or have an extensive educational background but it is not essential that all consultants be so qualified. Some of the best developed their capability through on-the-job experience. Consultants are called on for temporary assistance; they do not work full time for the people they assist. It is unlikely that they have a thorough understanding of the project they consult for, nor can they learn very much about it during the short term of the consulting assignment. Therefore, a project manager must be very careful in using consultants to ensure that their advice can be relied on. This is accomplished by:

- Identifying a specific problem to be solved
- Determining that the problem falls within the consultant's specialty
- Framing one or more specific questions to ask the consultant (the questions should permit objective answers)
- Engaging the consultant just long enough to answer the questions

The first two steps are the hardest. A problem that warrants the help of a consultant is usually outside the scope of knowledge of the project members. Their ability to recognize such a problem is severely limited. If they are clever enough to recognize that the problem is beyond their ability, they may still be unable to determine that it falls into some class of problems for which consultants can be found. No such difficulty exists with the OS specialist. The project members simply want to use the computer in a certain way and it is evident that they can only do the job if the OS provides certain functions. The OS expert can tell them if the installed version has those functions and, if not, whether they can be supplied by a special system generation. A more complex situation may occur in the design phase of a time-sharing system when a priority scheduling algorithm is required. The programmers may know the characteristics of the users of the system, but they may not know that these characteristics can be used to come up with a mathematical model of the service requests. They may not know that there are consultants who have studied many scheduling algorithms and can analyze a model of service requests to pick the best algorithm for that model. The likelihood that this situation will lead to a consulting agreement is slim.

Once the need for expert help is recognized and the existence of experts is determined, the rest of the process is simple. The reason for framing specific, objective questions is simply to save time and money. Bona fide consultants will do exactly what they are asked to do in order to earn their fee. If they are asked to answer questions they will do that to the best of their ability. If they are simply asked to visit the project and make recommendations for improvement, they will make the visit and deliver their report graciously and thoroughly, but they will have nothing to say; they can't. Consultants who merely observe an ongoing project will not see enough to trigger off meaningful recommendations. On the other hand, managers who are careful enough to phrase specific questions in the area of a consultant's specialty get full value for their money. Engaging a consultant only for limited periods reinforces the previous point. Consultants have maximum value when they can resolve a specific question. At other times, they are expensive burdens to the project since they have little to do, yet require the attention of the manager; they simply increase the system interactions without strengthening the system structure.

Of course, there are exceptions to the guidelines. It may be economically sound to keep a consultant on a retainer; i.e., pay a flat sum annually rather than a fee for every visit. The retainer does not require that the consultant join the project. Referring to an earlier example, a large organization may establish a centralized systems analysis department to do modeling and simulation for many projects. The cost of this department may be distributed either by dividing its annual cost proportionately among all potential users (a retainer) or by charging actual users for the service they get (a fee). In either case, the rates are high enough to cover the estimated idle time for the group during the year.

An exception to the rule that the consultant should only be asked to answer specific questions can be useful. There are times when a manager knows he or she is right but finds it impossible to convince the boss. By inviting a consultant to validate the conclusion, the manager can often use the consultant to "sell" his or her position to the boss. This is a peculiar way to achieve effective communications in the chain-of-command, but it remains a useful technique. Consultants can also be used to break deadlocks and to help achieve consensus.

Consultants are a valuable resource for specific short duration tasks. They provide:

- Expert knowledge of a special topic
- An unbiased point of view
- An independent review of the project status
- A validation of project decisions
- Inputs on the state-of-the-art
- Answers to specific questions

Managers who are not too proud or too stubborn to ask for help will take advantage of this type of resource to raise the quality of their product and to minimize the impact of unforeseen problems.

5.4.3 Recruiting

What kind of people does it take to carry out a proposed project plan? According to the proposal manager, it takes a mix of skills and job levels, which is a cross-section of the bidding organization. The project manager who is assigned a winning bid believes the job will require more people at higher-than-average levels of experience and income. The winner's financial manager would like to see cost reduced by using lower-than-average skills. In practice, the people actually assigned to the job will be those who are available. The project manager must recruit a mix of skills from the available resource pool, then organize to use the people effectively. The original proposal should have included an estimate of the availability of resources, but in the time between proposal submission and project initiation the availability situation may have changed. The situation may change again during the period of project growth. At each stage, the project manager will have to adjust his or her recruiting objectives to fit the situation.

The resource pool includes multiple sources, any one of which may be empty and any one of which may be shut off for business reasons. In a list of possible sources, the most desirable recruiting source is the one that best matches the proposed project requirements. It is usually the source most directly under the control of the project manager; for example, the group of key people named in the proposal who have been assigned to the project manager pending award of a contract for the project. In order of decreasing desirability, normal sources are:

- Key people—Individuals identified as critical to the project and who must be assigned to satisfy a contract requirement. These people are already in the company. The project manager knows them; they know the job characteristics; the user has confidence in them. Higher management must make them available to avoid contractual problems. This source is not common, however, since top management tries to avoid "key personnel" clauses in contracts.

- Type II small team—If a type II small team is available intact, its productivity makes it attractive. The project must either just fit the team, in which case recruiting is complete, or be large enough to provide a program subsystem task for the team. In practice, type II teams are in such demand they are seldom available when you want them. Existing type III small teams are equally attractive but it is less essential to preserve team integrity from one project to the next, so type III teams break up at the end of a job.

- Selected individuals in the company—In a high-priority project, the manager may be given the authority to take key people from other projects to form the nucleus of the new project. When all projects are equally important, this recruiting option will be shut off. In preference to such a disruptive levy (which usually represents inadequate preplanning in the proposal), the key people should be committed before the job is initiated.

- Individuals in the company who are between jobs—People between jobs are truly available and are looking forward to their next assignment. This is the normal source of people in a large organization. They will be enthusiastic and willing to work hard; on the other hand, they may have no applicable experience. In a large organization, this group should be a cross-section of the total population; therefore, it should be easy to build a hierarchical structure with the recruits. Periodically, though, the group will be biased toward one end of the seniority scale. If a large hiring program brought college graduates into the company (typically during the summer), their basic training will be over, say, six months later and the resource pool will be glutted with junior professionals in the first quarter of the following year. A senior surplus can also occur when a major project enters the maintenance and upgrade phase and releases half its people.

■ New hires, experienced—When hiring is permitted, experienced people are sought who, like key employees, can step right into the project and be productive. A premium price must be paid for this option. The new hires will demand a high salary to compensate for leaving the security of their last position. Raw recruiting costs will be high in terms of fees paid to personnel search firms, ads purchased, expenses paid for interviewees, and, of course, the management and personnel department time required to screen applicants. Costs accelerate in periods of competitive demand; i.e., when all software builders are growing at once. Considering that anywhere from 1 to 200 applications must be processed for each new hire, recruiting administration can be a great deal of work. If the job opening is not a bona fide career opportunity, there will be additional separation costs at the end of the project.

■ Task-oriented contract team—Software development firms try to limit their commitments so that the in-house population can do all the work. This is not always possible. In the data-processing department of user firms, it is even less feasible. They typically have two-thirds of the work force (in some cases, 90 percent) occupied with existing systems. Any new job requiring more than one-third of the in-house resource cannot be done, unless, of course, the firm uses new hires or contract support. Short of contracting out the entire job, it is feasible to subcontract a portion of the job. Fig. 5.13 shows that that contract option avoids a large increase in the permanent staff. Tasks suitable for a small team can be split off from the main project and put out for bid. Responsible bidders may be in-house departments with excess capacity or outside software vendors. In either case, the bidder will be unwilling to give up good people to work as individuals under your control. Likewise, the good people will not want to slide from job to job as free-lancers. On the other hand, the bidder will be willing to take on a meaningful, well-defined task for which he or she will set up a subproject. The work can be at the bidder's location or yours. You would have full control through a contract or contract-equivalent, through reviews, milestones, approval rights, etc. The task would then look like any other system component with two exceptions: it could cost more (because of intercompany communications and the bidder's profit) and it could involve cumbersome negotiations (because of the formality of the contract interface).[7]

---

7. Some large companies find that the total cost of jobs contracted to small software houses is less than the in-house estimate. This is due either to the lower overhead of the small company or to the fact that it is a center of excellence employing highly productive small teams. In the latter case, the software house tries to take only jobs within the capability of its teams.

■ Experienced contract personnel, on-site—Some service firms make people available to augment the staff of a client. Key people can be hired to work at the project manager's location under his or her direction for the duration of the project. Again, a premium is paid since the labor-hours fee includes the overhead and profit of the service firm. Loyalty and dedication to the project cannot be expected from the contract personnel.

■ New hires, inexperienced—Inexperienced new hires are often entering their first job after school. They may have had some computer-related training in school but they almost certainly cannot contribute productively to a project without some in-house training. Heavy dependence on inexperienced new hires will delay the project until the basic training is completed. At least six months' training can be expected. The delay will be less severe when the new hires are needed only to build up the organization during the program unit implementation stage.

■ Off-site contract personnel—A service firm or "body shop" that normally rents people by the hour may offer to do all or part of a project in its offices under managers it selects. This arrangement is usually unsatisfactory because your project manager has no direct control and the service firm can generally not carry out the project management responsibility.[8]

■ Inexperienced contract personnel—This source relieves the project manager of responsibility for finding jobs for people when the project ends. Unfortunately, inexperienced project personnel cannot do the job. They are sometimes below the standards you use for hiring and, as a result, may not be good enough even after your training program. This is a high-risk source.

A recruiting plan, part of the project plan, must be based on the best estimate of the resources that will be available in the future. The recruiting plan is updated in each stage of the life cycle, becoming a placement plan in the later stages. In the earliest draft of the recruiting plan, you decide what skill mix is needed and start to negotiate authority to fill your requirements from the most desirable source. First, you try to get permission to "earmark" selected individuals or small teams to join the project at various dates. Second, while you are studying the lists of names of people expected to be between jobs, you request permission to: (1) hire, and (2) subcontract.

---

8. The problem described here is that the service firm is a broker dealing in people. The firm is equipped for merchandising functions. It is not equipped to do programming project management and it is not experienced in the business areas of its clients. Therefore, its offer to staff an entire job relates to collecting a group of people rather than to meeting the project objectives. This situation is completely different from a proposal by an experienced software house to undertake project commitments. The software vendor commits to deliverables and takes the responsibility for managing the project. The body shop merely offers to deliver labor hours.

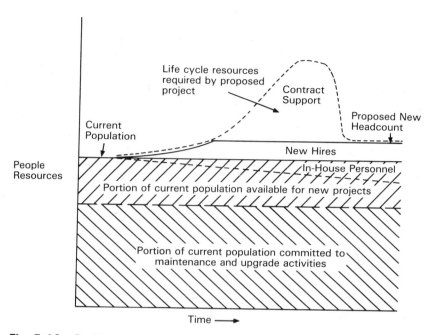

Fig. 5.13   Staff augmentation by hiring and subcontracting.

Each of the latter options has a long lead time so, even if your needs are eventually satisfied in house, you must initiate hiring and subcontracting procedures early if they are to be of much use. Part of the preparation involves writing very explicit descriptions of the jobs you want to fill or the tasks you are willing to subcontract. A good description is obviously necessary as a negotiating aid. When the actual hiring and contracting are handled by the personnel or contracts functional staff, the written descriptions become their working specifications.

As mentioned in Chapter 3, the recruiting plan should strive for a steady buildup rate. The number of people in a large project would overwhelm the managers if they all arrived at once. The project will be more manageable if people are introduced in small numbers. An exception to this rule obviously occurs when the people you want are available now en masse but will be dispersed to other projects next week. You should take the group now to meet your needs rather than risk project failure by underrunning the plan. The project work plan shows the work to be done each week or month. The recruiting plan shows how many people will be on board each week or month. The two plans will not always agree. *Workload* (WL) is based on productivity and can be expressed in fractional amounts of people-months; e.g., "program unit 3BAL will require 4.6 programmer-weeks," "during week 19, total workload is estimated to be 32.4 programmers."

Headcount (HC) is based on real people and should be expressed in whole numbers; e.g., "in week 19, there are 35 programmers on-board." If headcount runs consistently below workload, the project will slip unless productivity can be increased. A good recruiting plan will make headcount run parallel to or slightly ahead of workload (ignoring overtime). At times it will run a great deal ahead, as when you pick up an available group to avoid losing the resource. The cost of the excess, HC − WL, is a legitimate project cost and should be included in the budget estimates.

5.4.4 Indoctrination

New people join a project with little idea of what the project is about and what their role is to be. Even people who worked on the proposal or who have been members of similar projects are unsure exactly where they will fit in the new project. They should be told all they need to know as soon as possible after they arrive. A manager's briefing regarding the work assignment is essential but it is not sufficient. Total project understanding is a prerequisite to efficient execution of the plan. It is also the keystone of project esprit because an indoctrination program that presents the system overview provides the basis for system-wide teamwork. *Indoctrination* is probably a poor word to use here; it sounds like a forced conversion to a party line. But other words such as *familiarization, introduction,* or *project description* are inadequate. They do not convey the importance of getting each team member to understand his or her relationship to the project as a whole; nor do they convey the importance of each employee doing his or her best work within prescribed guidelines because the success of the project depends on it. The indoctrination program is more than an information session; it sells the team members on the need for teamwork and it even evangelizes regarding the value of the system to be built. This approach works when reinforced by the management team at regular department meetings. The results are seen in the high correlation between project success and "seeing the system as a whole." That is, in studies of the success or failure of projects, people on successful projects point out that they saw the system as a whole, they knew where their work fit, and they understood the objectives of the project. People associated with failed projects—failed by not meeting schedule or not staying within budget or not satisfying the customer—did not make similar statements. Furthermore, when asked questions that would show whether they held a system view, their answers showed they did not; at best, they held a subsystem view.

It can be taken for granted that it is not necessary to know all of the system details in order to have an overview of the system. Hence, the indoctrination program teaches structure and relationships rather than operating details. To be sure, the specific procedures adopted for internal communication are taught because they are relevant to everyone. In addition, the program teaches the reasons *why* the project is set up the way it is and why certain procedures have been adopted. To build up the feeling of team membership, each indoctrination session is scheduled so a reasonable number of people, preferably from different departments, can participate. Some old-timers join the session to share their experience. Through the questions and discussion, each person present gets a better understanding of the complexity of the project and the need for everyone to cooperate.

On a small team project, everyone attends the same session and, in the usual manner of a small team, everyone shares a common view of the project. A large project requires multiple sessions scheduled whenever enough new people are on board to justify a meeting. There are obvious drawbacks to this process. In Chapter 3, for example, the staff buildup for a large project, Table 3.3, added ten people between the second and fourth months of the project. Assume the ten people arrived one or two each week. A briefing session for all ten would mean someone would have been on board for two months without knowing much about the system. That person would probably have learned something in two months, though, and will be bored having to sit through the indoctrination. Later, forty-five people arrive in a two-month period. Here, there are more options for get-togethers; one session every two weeks would give a fair balance of timeliness versus critical mass. Timeliness can and should be even better, though. Project managers of large projects make every new team member aware of project objectives and the system viewpoint by handing them a written description as soon as they arrive. Their immediate manager discusses the system with them and, as would be done in any case, spells out the details of their individual work assignments. The newcomers still attend a group indoctrination session to gain the benefit of meeting other people and to smooth out any misinterpretations made by the first-level managers.

5.4.5   Evaluation

Managers constantly evaluate the quality and status of the activities they direct. The formal aspects of project evaluation, taking the form of reviews, inspections, and the like, were discussed in Chapter 3. This section deals with evaluating the performance of the project team members. A basic problem exists that interferes with simple measurement of individual accomplishment; that is, in a project each individual's performance is conditioned by the activities of other team members and by external forces. The individual does not have full control over his or her results; therefore, it may be unfair to use rigid evaluation criteria based on individual objectives. On the other hand, it may be of little value to evaluate individuals solely against project objectives. A compromise must be reached so that the evaluation methods measure against real, achievable objectives, that the measurements discriminate among individuals, and that the objectives motivate the individuals to do their best. A top-down approach that works from an overall evaluation of the project down to an evaluation of each subsystem, package, program, and unit will lead to a reasonable compromise. The program unit is what the individual is measured on (work unit or task for support people), but the measurement stays in a system context and provides a basis for rating the individual's contribution to the team. As with all evaluation methods, the results are highly subjective. Their value improves when evaluation is based on a continuing dialogue between manager and employee rather than on the single formal discussion when the evaluation is committed to paper to enter the employee's personnel folder.

5.4.5.1 Project evaluation

The three simple rules for project success are *completion:*

1. On schedule
2. Within budget
3. Happy customer

(By definition, a completed project meets its specification; otherwise it is incomplete and will fail on point 3.)

These rules were adopted by the author initially in a 1966 review of about twenty contracts completed or in progress at the IBM Federal Systems Division. The purpose of the review was to determine whether project management methods were significant to the success of these program development projects. If the answer was "yes," the Division would implement a programming project management course for all managers. If "no," the education effort would be directed toward programming techniques—languages, use of operating systems, database design, etc.—which were, at the time, considered the keys to project success. Naturally, a definition of "success" was needed in order to interpret the results of the review. Many definitions were suggested and discarded. Eventually, the definition was based on the three elements of time, money, and customer satisfaction. The first two were easily obtained from the project file and the accounting department. The third was even easier. The customer would tell you exactly what he or she thought of your performance. The customer's opinion is not necessarily justified, but it is certainly vocal.

In business terms all the review projects succeeded. All of them met (or were likely to meet) their contract terms and conditions. However, some of them renegotiated the contract along the way and perhaps were overrunning prior to the contract change. Rather than look solely at contract status, the reviewers looked at the management history of the project. Any project that failed one or more of the three criteria—in the judgment of the reviewers—was a "failure." The Division could and should do better. Thus, for the purpose of the study, every project was either a "success" or a "failure"; there was no middle ground.

Two sets of results came out of this brief study. The first result showed that small projects (FLM-led) succeeded, and large projects (HLM-led, larger than 150 people) failed according to the three criteria. This finding led to further study of how large projects differ from small team efforts. Chapters 1 and 5 deal with some of the consequences of this work. The second result was a list of factors that had the most effect, as far as the project manager was concerned, on the project. Actually, the factors represent the views of project managers and their management team after having been filtered by the review team. All the project managers claimed success. The review team had its own rating of each project. The factors emphasized by a project manager who was really a "success" by the rules of the study were taken as valid reasons for success. Overall, the results proved conclusively that in the Federal Systems Division, success depended on the effectiveness of project management more than anything else. The same conclusion is probably valid in all organizations.

Factors consistently identified as essential to success include:

- Project organization (structure, interface definition, job description)
- Seeing the whole job (system view)
- Control procedures (configuration management process)
- Higher management interest (effective chain-of-command)
- Contract relations (mutual understanding with customer)
- Working conditions (physical environment)[9]

All of these items are project management concerns rather than technical issues.

Factors that could lead to failure were also identified by the review team. The important ones were:

- Job difficulty
- Availability of hardware and/or software
- Availability of people in right skill mix

Job difficulty appeared to be the cause of failure in one project. On analysis it turned out that the failure occurred on a highly mathematical rocket tracking project. The team members could not cope with the mathematics. Similar projects had been done successfully in other parts of the Division. This particular project was badly staffed and failed for that reason. In-

---

9. The reviewers had some doubts about working conditions being so important. A follow-up, however, verified the original input. The Division had its own buildings where a certain standard of privacy, silence, and convenience was met. It also had many people in customers' buildings. One of these provided a large hangar-like room for over one hundred people. It was noisy, uncomfortable, and hard to get to. In this building, programmer productivity was approximately one-half the KLOC/month expected in Division facilities.

adequate staffing is a management problem; so is the failure to make hardware and software available at the right time. More accurately, project managers should develop plans that allow for flexibility. They should not let the project collapse because they planned on starting program checkout January 15 but the hardware slipped to February 15. The review team concluded that the negative factors would certainly affect your chances for success but that good planning would eliminate the negative factors in most cases. Good planning, of course, is a project management responsibility.

When the Division executive saw these results, his decision was obvious. He approved the project management course as the highest priority education program for his organization. The decision paid off. Within four years, success as defined above was the norm. (Once the projects were under control, attention turned to the next major area of concern—programmer productivity—and the same organization made major strides in the field of structured programming and IPT.)

5.4.5.2 Personnel evaluation

The evaluation of team and individual performance should be conditioned on the success or failure of the project. (Evaluations done while the project is in process are based on the management assessment of success or failure at completion.) If a project fails the time/money/customer satisfaction test, the team cannot have done an outstanding job. It is harder to say that no individual within the team was outstanding, particularly when some of the junior people may have had very limited objectives that they met perfectly. Therefore, project success or failure should have decreasing influence on the employee evaluations at lower levels of the project organization. The project manager is measured on project success. Subsystem managers are measured primarily on the success of their subsystem and secondarily on the success of the project. Lower-level managers are similarly measured on the success of their own assignment within the context of the next higher-level activity. Individuals with any kind of coordinating activity are also measured within the context of the next higher-level activity. Individuals with straightforward implementation responsibility for programs or service tasks are measured on their performance alone. (An exception to the last case would occur when a senior individual builds a unit or does a service task that has a critical system impact and the implementer knows it.) The rationale behind the dual evaluation criteria is that all system elements contribute to system success; therefore, system success is traceable back to the team members' performance. System failure is also due to team members' performance and they should be appraised accordingly.

In practice, only failure enters directly into an appraisal rating scheme. Assume that all employees are rated by their managers on a scale of 1 (outstanding) to 5 (unsatisfactory). A 1 performer on a successful project still gets rated 1. After all, the project plan was designed to be successful so there need be no prizes for carrying out the plan. A 1 performer on a failed project can be rated 2. In this case, although the individual may have handled the local aspects of his or her job in an outstanding way, something went wrong with the global aspects. A true 1 performer would have recognized the problem and, with the rest of the team, fixed it.

The goal of most employee appraisal systems is to evaluate the employee's performance on the job against the requirements of the job [45]. In the short term, the appraisal can help the employee improve performance either by improving work methods or by understanding the requirements better. In the longer term, the appraisal can affect the employee's salary, promotion, and career plan. Short-term counseling is based on the specific results achieved by the employee on an assigned scope of work. Long-term counseling also considers how well the employee compares to his or her peers. Three types of motivation make each employee strive for a good rating:

1. I want to get ahead—status, income, authority.
2. I enjoy my work more when I do it well—self-appraisal, self-control.
3. I want to get ahead of Lucille and Tom—competition.

There may be a negative motivation as well if the employee is afraid of a harsh manager. Ignoring that possibility, a manager can be expected to encourage the employee to do well. Normally, the manager supports the employee by:

- Setting clear objectives—Letting the employee know what is expected.
- Setting achievable objectives—Making it feasible for the employee to succeed, in an outstanding manner if possible.
- Measuring by objectives—Showing how much each objective will contribute to the final appraisal.

The principle of management by objectives (MBO) is that employees will work harder and more effectively when they have committed themselves to a set of objectives [46]; particularly when they have participated in defining the objectives. Since Drucker promoted the idea in 1954, more and more firms have started to implement MBO. The effect in some areas such as manufacturing and assembly has been very positive. In these areas, productivity can be measured in terms of X objects per hour or some similar quantitative measure. The worker can think of ways to increase X, say, by rearranging his or her work space or by stacking the objects differently or by simply moving faster. If the employee thinks it is worthwhile, he or she will commit to a higher rate and not only achieve it but quite often exceed it. Less success occurs with MBO in management and staff work or any intellectual activity where the work output is not countable. Objectives for these areas tend to be vague: "report on project status monthly," "determine hardware requirements and develop migration plan for next twelve months"; consequently, they are more subjective than objective. The employee may commit to do the task but does not know in advance what must be done to get an outstanding rating. Programmers and support groups fall somewhere between the two extremes. Programs are certainly countable. Unfortunately, an increase in KLOC/month is not necessarily an improvement. The output must meet quality objectives as well. The number of fixes applied by a maintenance team per month does not imply that a better team would have more errors to fix. An increase of CPU utilization in the computer room does not mean that more productive work was done. Care is required to make the MBO measurements realistic in a program development project. The goal is to state the objectives in terms of units of work that are definable, recognizable, and measurable; for example:

- For a programmer—assigned one or more program units:
  1. Output-related
     a. unit completion dates
     b. size objective
     c. compute resource used
     d. documentation pages
     e. errors/KLOC at inspections
     f. errors/KLOC post-release
     g. fix time/error, post-release
  2. Capability-related
     a. courses to attend
     b. tools and techniques to learn
     c. reports or technical papers to complete
- For a support team member—providing a service on demand:
  1. Output-related
     a. average response time per service request
     b. percent of responses less than X hours
     c. average queue length in backlog
     d. percent incomplete jobs
     e. percent rejected or incorrect jobs
     f. average cost per job
  2. Capability-related
     a. as for programmers

The suggestions illustrate the desirability of setting objectives that can be quantified even at the expense of some added data collection and paperwork. The objectives can either be pass/fail (meeting a date) or statistical (meeting an average service level). Results are carried forward where possible. Thus a typing pool may achieve this year's objective of 4 hours turnaround on correspondence typing. Next year, they may be challenged to accept a goal of 3 1/2 hours. MBO, given only one objective, puts all the employee's eggs in one basket. The employee has a better opportunity to succeed when given a fairly small number of objectives. A slip in one area can be offset by success elsewhere. Objectives are prioritized. A programming manager may tell a programmer that the highest priority, worth 60 percent of the appraisal score, is the objective associated with unit completion dates; lowest priority, worth 10 percent, goes to reports and technical papers. Objectives so low on the list that the employee will ignore them should be scratched out. An effort should be made to mix short-term and long-term objectives. People are very good at optimizing their performance to fit the measurement scheme. If the objectives are all short term, only short-term activities will get attention and the team may not be ready for tomorrow's challenges. When MBO includes long-term objectives, the measurement equation takes care of both today and tomorrow.

An important weakness of MBO as described here is that it assumes that objectives are set for individuals with no dependencies. The complexity of a program development process creates interrelationships at all levels that prevent the individual from acting entirely alone. An employee may say, "I could have met that objective if only John had done this and Mary had done that and the XYZ Company had met their delivery commitment and you had not sent me away to inspect Lou's program and . . . ." Moreover, the employee is probably right. The employee's manager can still evaluate the employee's work if all the dependencies fell in his or her department.[10] When external dependencies governed the performance difficulty, the manager is in no position to guess how well the employee might have done under different circumstances. He or she can evaluate the limited results actually produced by the employee. The effect is an upward bias. Eventually, there is so large a bias in the ratings that all employees appear equal and the appraisal system loses its value as a career and compensation guide.

The methods used to improve the evaluation procedure in complex projects consist of:

---

10. The manager would have a slightly different problem remaining. If the employee is right, various dependencies interfered with performance. All the dependencies were under the manager's control; therefore, the manager is responsibile for preventing the employee from getting a good appraisal rating. Most managers in this situation would choose to evaluate the employees as though he or she had successfully completed the job. This puts the onus of nonperformance on the managers and should lower their appraisal rating. In fact, this behavior simply contributes to a bias toward high ratings in the appraisal system.

- Modifying MBO to include the conditions under which the objective is to be measured. For example, "unit completion four work weeks after receipt of prerequisite units MBCAR and OSPRT."
- Setting department or team objectives over and above individual objectives. A programmer who is late due to team influences may still be appraised highly if the team is meeting its objectives.

An analogy can be drawn between objectives and sales incentive programs. A sales hierarchy of regional managers, branch managers, and sales personnel has two kinds of objectives: sales and product objectives. The salesperson accepts a productivity quota for annual net sales and then is free to meet that quota by selling one very high-priced item or any mix of other items. Since the company wants to sell everything it makes, an incentive is required to motivate the sales team to sell the mix most beneficial for the firm. Product objectives can be used to accomplish this. The salesperson's income is then the sum of a base salary plus the earnings due to making or exceeding the quota plus a bonus for meeting or exceeding the product objectives. By adjusting the value of each incentive, the company can expect the average salary of a salesperson to be generated by achieving 100 percent of each objective. Further, if some salesperson makes 150 percent of the sales objective but only 50 percent of the product objective, the net value to the company may be acceptable. To maintain the desired balance, however, a product objective is also given to the manager who uses his or her ability to plan and motivate to get the desired quality of sales from the sales team.

In a programming team, the productivity objective is set in terms of the directly measurable output of KLOC, program units, computer runs, etc. The quality objective can be set in terms of product quality, interface commitments, compliance with project procedures, economical mix of tools, etc. The productivity objectives are normally assigned to individuals. Quality objectives for directly measurable aspects of programs such as errors found are assigned to individuals. Certain observable style characteristics such as structured programming can be individual objectives. Broad measures such as modifiability or maintainability remain with managers as do all objectives related to group activities. If an appraisal rating of 3 meets requirements, then a programmer who meets all assigned objectives gets a 3. A programmer who meets all assigned objectives, exceeding some, may get a 2, and so on. More is expected of the manager. A manager whose people all meet productivity requirements and, in addition, meet the team quality objectives merits a 3.

The analogy to a sales incentive plan points out one additional feature of a good MBO system. Each individual has a small list of objectives. Four or five different types of objectives are manageable. More may confuse the individual.

5.5 SUMMARY

Program system development is a team activity; therefore, the structure and behavior of teams is a central interest of development managers. The wide literature of management and administration applies to programming teams; yet, in some ways, programming teams are unique.

Program development has had a short history with much fumbling and many trial-and-error approaches to project management. Only as the field matured have managers turned to more standard ways of doing things. Even so, program development is more difficult to manage than many of its sister activities such as hardware development or financial management. The extra difficulty is due to the "soft" characteristics of software. It is hard to define individual tasks that are independent of other team members' activities. It is hard to completely define individual tasks in the first place; there is always some degree of vagueness or ambiguity and there is certainly a likelihood of change. Therefore, management is highly dependent on good communications to make certain that the team members at least have a consistent view of what each individual is doing and how the team tasks relate to the project goals.

A heavy communications burden falls on first-level managers. FLMs supervise technical professionals and must give them direction and support in technical terms. At the same time, FLMs must communicate in management terms with other managers, including their boss. FLMs are expected to be technically competent in the subject of their area of responsibility so that they can participate in the technical decisions and, in some cases, do the technical work required. At the same time, they must carry out the normal duties of any manager: planning, organizing, staffing, directing, controlling, innovating, and representing. Since new FLMs were previously non-managers, they bring no on-the-job management experience to their job, yet they have a high probability of success, mainly due to the limited scope of their assignment.

Higher-level managers manage other managers. They tend to gradually lose their technical expertise as, say, programmers. They acquire new skills in the administrative aspects of management and, to be successful, they learn how to communicate and negotiate effectively. These skills are particularly important in team projects where strong managers compete with each other for limited resources. A strong chain of command is usually established to give all the managers in a project common goals and to resolve conflicts arising from competition.

The chain of command leads to the familiar tree-structured organization chart in which information flows freely but in which management orders follow the hierarchical structure of the tree. In very large projects, the tree is very tall and the high-level managers may make poor technical decisions without realizing it. To avoid such a situation, a matrix organization may be set up in which, typically, functional departments with a specific technical skill are given responsibilities that essentially cut across the project structure at various levels. Alone, the project may be technically unsound, or the functional specialists may take too narrow a view to build a well-integrated system. Together, in a matrix organization governed by a management system, the various groups can handle a major challenge.

Large teams are assembled out of necessity, seldom out of choice. Their size leads to too many problems. Yet there are many jobs that involve, or appear to involve, so much work that only a large team could complete it in a reasonable period of time. Small teams are, of course, preferable. There are three types of small teams that differ in their makeup and procedures. All three types are more productive than a large team of any type because they do not have the communications overhead of a large team. Type I, the least productive of the small teams, is simply a tree-structured organization under a FLM—a miniature large team. The group is the easiest to assemble and to reassign after the project is done. The most productive small team consists of an experienced group of talented peers who work well together. A type II group is a hard group to assemble; if one exists it is in great demand (it is not disbanded after each job). Almost as productive as the type II group—meaning that it can tackle many complete systems of the type found in commercial Information Systems departments—is the chief programmer team. The type III CPT substitutes standards and procedures for the years of teamwork that make a peer group effective. As a result, it can be assembled from available resources and can be disbanded after finishing the job.

Questions regarding team organization or resource allocation are typical of many questions requiring a management decision for which an arbitrary choice is not normally as good as a considered analysis. Managers depend on their staffs to do the completed staff work to obtain, organize, and study the data in the light of the project objectives in order to recommend a course of action. The data include not only facts and figures but also the positions taken by the management team. In other words, the staff should use all the information available in order to give the project manager the complete picture, unbiased by the staff's own preference for the outcome.

In a project of any size, the factors affecting each decision can be confusing, contradictory, and hard to quantify. The reliability of much of the data is poor since most software houses lack good history data and current measurements may be hard to interpret. Still, a manager must make a decision—even if it is to sit tight and not change the status quo. There are a variety of simple ways to reach a decision that depend on ranking quantified factors and combining them to maximize or minimize an objective. They force the manager to try to understand the data (in order to quantify it), to set priorities (in order to rank the factors), and to clarify objectives (in order to establish a basis for making a choice). A decision-making procedure does not prevent errors; particularly when the wrong factors are analyzed. To protect against errors, a manager depends on completed staff work and on his or her own knowledge of the project. The manager mentally checks each decision to be certain he or she has considered commitments, objectives, method, people, user, time, and excellence; and makes certain that all parties to the decision have been involved so that a technically sound decision is also a politically viable decision. Since all factors change in a dynamic system development process, a manager recognizes the need for periodic decisions, at appropriately spaced milestones, to adapt to changing conditions. Management decision-making, therefore, is an active, iterative task for a responsible manager working closely with line and staff associates.

In a small team, the close association of the team members leads to an informal but fully informed working relationship. Large teams lose this intimacy and maintain control by carefully defining each individual's scope of responsibility and by establishing formal communications links where they are required. A given individual has a very limited scope of responsibility, yet should know how his or her activity fits into the overall system. Since large teams may be recruited from sources with no previous experience in the subject area of the present job, they must quickly learn both their particular assignments and the "big picture." The success of large projects has been shown to depend on how well the team members understand their responsibility and their system role. It is natural to take these two points into consideration when evaluating employee performance.

EXERCISES AND DISCUSSION QUESTIONS

1. Managers and nonmanagers plan, control, innovate, and do other activities in common. What distinguishes the manager from the nonmanager?

2. Managers are either first-level (FLM), higher-level (HLM), or executive-level. How do the three classes differ? Why is it unnecessary to have more than three classifications?

3. Is a strong chain of command consistent with participative management?

4. You are a member of a large department that does all the system modeling and simulation for a software development firm. Your particular group is building a model of a new operating system, working very closely with the OS developer. Characterize the organization structure orientation and emphasis at each level.

5. You are the manager of eight people, including two who have been working with you for three years and six that joined when their last project ended. Your two associates have over five years of experience, as does one of the new people. Three others have three years of experience; two have only recently completed on-the-job training. Your assignment is about 30 KLOC in a subject your people have not handled before. What type of team would you use? How would you use the skills available?

6. How would you answer Exercise 5 if the 30 KLOC were a subsystem of a large system?

7. A study of internal sort performance* gives the relative performance of seven sort algorithms for various quantities of input. The input was either totally ordered or random. The random cases were either all different or contained duplicates. Table 5.5 lists the results. You run many sorts. Your records show that 25 percent of your sorts have $N = 100$ records blocked for internal sorting; there is a 50-percent probability that the blocks are in order from some previous operation. For 50 percent of your sorts $N = 1000$ and 10 percent are preordered. The remaining 25 percent of the sorts have $N = 5000$ with no likelihood of preordering. In all cases, half the sorts are expected to contain duplicate records.

    a. You want to minimize sort time. Which algorithm do you pick?

    b. You want to minimize sort time and conserve memory. Large record blocks occupy memory that could be devoted to other uses. Sort time is twice as important to you as memory usage. Which algorithm is best?

    c. Recent data show that your previous estimates of the likelihood of preordering have been correct only 75 percent of the time. Does this new information change your answers to questions (a) and (b)?

8. How do you use a specialist when you do not need his or her specialty? How do you evaluate the performance of a specialist who is not asked to apply his or her specialty?

9. Normally, a new FLM builds a type I small team by recruiting from available sources. Could he or she build a type II or type III team?

10. What types of information should a manager communicate to his or her people?

11. In a large organization where everyone is appraised and given an appraisal rating from 1 to 5 there should be a bell-shaped distribution of ratings—more 3s than 2s and 4s, etc.

    a. What does it mean if there are more 1s and 2s than lower ratings?

    b. What distribution of ratings is appropriate in a

        (1) type I team?

        (2) type II team?

        (3) type III team?

        (4) large team?

    c. If you inherit a group of twenty-five to thirty people, all of whom are rated average or worse, how would you organize?

---

*H. Lorin, *Sorting and Sort Systems* (Reading, Mass.: Addison-Wesley Publishing Co., 1975).

TABLE 5.5.   RELATIVE SORT SPEEDS

	N	Random	Ordered	Duplicated
Singleton[1]	100	1.0	0.7	1.0
(CACM 347)	1000	14.0	7.3	14.0
	5000	85.7	43.2	84.4
Quickersort[1]	100	1.3	0.8	1.3
(CACM 271)	1000	18.8	13.0	20.5
	5000	121.1	73.2	120.3
Treesort 3[2]	100	2.6	2.7	2.5
(CACM 245)	1000	34.3	37.9	36.3
	5000	220.8	230.8	220.7
Boothroyd/Shell[3]	100	2.0	1.0	1.8
(CACM 201)	1000	35.9	6.5	35.7
	5000	270.3	105.8	266.7
Hibbard/Shell[3]	100	2.2	1.3	2.5
(From CACM 6,	1000	42.3	20.8	36.3
May 1963)	5000	509.0	131.8	220.7
Stringsort[4]	100	4.7	2.7	4.7
(CACM 207)	1000	58.7	26.0	58.7
	5000	354.6	129.9	354.5
Shuttlesort[5]	100	7.0	0.3	6.7
(CACM 175)	1000	721.8	1.8	713.1
	5000	18,375.5	9.0	*

[1]Quicksort variant; [2]Tournament; [3]Shellsort variant; [4]Merge; [5]Sift; CACM *Communications of the ACM*; *Not collected.
From H. Lorin, *Sorting and Sort Systems* (Reading, Mass.: Addison-Wesley Publishing Co., 1975).

REFERENCES

1. Maher, J. J. *Proceedings of the Symposium on Managing the Development of Large Computer Program Systems.* Santa Monica, Calif.: System Development Corp., January 1963.

2. *The Management Process.* AFM 25-1. Washington D.C.: Department of the Air Force, September 1954.

3. Andrews, K. R. *The Concept of Corporate Strategy.* Homewood, Ill.: Dow Jones–Irwin, Inc., 1971.

4. Dale, E. *Management: Theory and Practice.* New York: McGraw-Hill, 1965.

5. Gulick, L., and Urwick, L. *Papers on the Science of Administration.* New York: Institute of Public Administration, 1937.

6. Shull, F. A., Jr. *Selected Readings in Management.* Homewood, Ill.: Richard D. Irwin, 1958. Also, Taylor, F. W. *Scientific Management.* New York: Harper and Bros., 1947. Also, Urwick, L. F. *The Elements of Administration.* New York: Harper and Bros., 1943. Also, Metcalf, H. C., and Urwick, L. *Dynamic Administration.* The Collected Papers of Mary Parker Follett. New York: Harper and Row, 1940. Also, Fayol, H. *General and Industrial Administration.* London: Sir Isaac Pitman and Son, Ltd., 1949.

7. Scott, B. W. *Long-Range Planning in American Industry.* New York: American Management Association, 1965.

8. Drucker, P. F. *Management: Tasks, Responsibilities, Practices.* New York: Harper and Row, 1974.

9. Simon, H. A. *The New Science of Management Decision.* New York: MacMillan, 1960. Also, Simon, H. A. *Administrative Behavior.* New York: MacMillan, 1957. Also, Simon, H. A., and March, J. G. *Organizations.* New York: John Wiley & Sons, 1958.

10. Metcalf, H. C., and Urwick, L. *Dynamic Administration.* The Collected Papers of Mary Parker Follett. New York: Harper and Row, 1940.

11. Scott, W. G. *Organization Theory: A Behavioral Analysis for Management.* Homewood, Ill.: Richard D. Irwin, 1967.

12. Roethlisberger, F. J., and Dickson, W. J. *Management and the Worker.* Cambridge, Mass.: Harvard University Press, 1956.

13. Suojanen, W. W. "The Span of Control—Fact or Fable" in *Selected Readings in Management.* Homewood, Ill.: Richard D. Irwin, 1958. Also, Urwick, L. F. "The Manager's Span of Control." *Harvard Business Review* 34, no. 3 (May–June 1956).

14. Sowa, J. F. *Conceptual Structures: Information Processing in Mind and Machine.* Reading, Mass.: Addison-Wesley, 1983.

15. Newman, W. H. *Administrative Action: The Techniques and Organization of Management.* Englewood Cliffs, N.J.: Prentice-Hall, 1963.

16. Fayol, H. *General and Industrial Administration.* London: Sir Isaac Pitman and Son, Ltd., 1949.

17. Badawy, M. K. "Organizational Designs for Scientists and Engineers: Some Research Findings and Their Implications for Managers." *IEEE Transactions on Engineering Management* EM-22, no. 4 (November 1975).

18. Urwick, L. F., and Brech, E. F. L. *The Hawthorne Investigations.* Vol. III: The Making of Scientific Management. London: Management Publications Trust, 1949. See also, Parsons, H. M. "What Happened at Hawthorne?" *Science* 183 (8 March 1974). Also, Roethlisberger, F. J., and Dickson, W. J. *Management and the Worker.* Cambridge, Mass.: Harvard University Press, 1956.

19. Seckler-Hudson, C. *Processes of Organization and Management.* Washington, D.C.: The American University Press, 1948.

20. Manley, T. R., and Dunne, E. J. "Project Managers Warning, Danger Ahead!" *National Defense* 60, no. 332 (September–October 1975).

21. Evans, P. B. "Multiple Hierarchies and Organizational Control." *Administrative Science Quarterly* 20, no. 2 (June 1975).

22. Davis, S. M., and Lawrence, P. *MATRIX.* New York: MacMillan, 1977. Also, Stallings, W. "A Matrix Management Approach to System Development." *Pathways to System Integrity.* Washington, D.C.: The Washington D.C. Chapter of the ACM, 1980.

23. Mantei, M. "The Effect of Programming Team Structures on Programming Tasks." *Communications of the ACM* 24, no. 3 (March 1981).

24. Weinberg, G. M. *The Psychology of Computer Programming.* New York: Van Nostrand Reinhold, 1971.

25. Baker, F. T. "Chief Programmer Team Management of Production." *IBM Systems Journal* 11, no. 1 (1972).

26. English, J. M., ed. *Cost Effectiveness: The Economic Evaluation of Engineered Systems.* New York: John Wiley & Sons, 1968.

27. Dantzig, G. B., and Veinott, A. F., eds. *Mathematics of the Decision Sciences.* Providence, R.I.: American Mathematics Society, 1968.

28. Bowman, E. H., and Fetter, R. B. *Analysis for Production Management.* Homewood, Ill.: Richard D. Irwin, 1957.

29. Lynch, W. C. "Structured Performance Evaluation" and "Load Variation, Scheduling and Measurement," in *Computing System Design.* Edited by B. Shaw. Proceedings of the Joint IBM University of Newcastle upon Tyne Seminar, Sept. 7–10, 1976. Newcastle upon Tyne, U.K.: University of Newcastle upon Tyne Computing Laboratory, 1977.

30. Rajala, D. W., and Sage, A. P. "Hierarchical Inference Structures in Decision Analysis." Proceedings of the IEEE Conference on Cybernetics & Society. New York: IEEE, Inc., 1976.

31. Kaufmann, A. *The Science of Decision-making.* New York: McGraw-Hill, 1968.

32. Raiffa, H. *Decision Analysis: Introducing Lectures on Choices Under Uncertainty.* Reading, Mass.: Addison-Wesley, 1968.

33. Howard, R. A. Special Issue on Decision Analysis. *IEEE Transactions on Systems Science and Cybernetics,* SSC–4, no. 3 (1968).

34. Linstone, H. A., and Turoff, M. *The Delphi Method: Techniques & Applications.* Reading, Mass.: Addison-Wesley, 1975.

35. Chase, S. *Roads to Agreement.* New York: Harper and Brothers, 1951.

36. Quade, E. S., and Boucher, W. I. *Systems Analysis and Policy Planning: Applications in Defense.* New York: American Elsevier Publishing Co, 1968

37. Thamhain, H. J., and Wilemon, D. L. "Diagnosing Conflict Determinants in Project Management." *IEEE Transactions on Engineering Management* EM-22, no. 1 (February 1975). Also, Thamhain, H. J., and Wilemon, D. L. "Conflict Management in Project Life Cycles." *Sloan Management Review* 16, no. 3 (Spring 1975).

38. Cyert, R. M. "Decision Making Under Uncertainty." Proceedings XX International Meeting. The Institute of Management Sciences. Jerusalem, Israel: Jerusalem Academic Press, 1975.

39. Elstein, A. S. "Clinical Judgement: Psychological Research and Medical Practice." *Science* 194 (12 November 1976).

40. Stewart, R. *The Reality of Organizations. A Guide for Managers and Students.* Garden City, N.Y.: Anchor Books, Doubleday & Co., 1972.

41. Gagne, R. M., ed. *Psychological Principles in System Development.* New York: Holt, Rinehart and Winston, 1962.

42. Herzberg, F. *Work and the Nature of Man.* Cleveland, Ohio: The World Publishing Co., 1966.

43. Likert, R. *The Human Organization: Its Management and Value.* New York: McGraw-Hill, 1967.

44. McClelland, D. C., and Steele, R. S. *Human Motivation: A Book of Readings.* Morristown, N.J.: General Learning Corp., 1973.

45. Scott, W. D.; Clothier, R. C.; and Spriegel, W. R. *Personnel Management: Principles, Practices, and Points of View.* New York: McGraw-Hill, 1949.

46. Beck, A. C., Jr., and Hillmar, E. D. *A Practical Approach to Organizational Development Through MBO—Selected Readings.* Reading, Mass.: Addison-Wesley, 1972.

6
Project Implementation

The result of project definition is a design requirements baseline. The baseline document is turned over to the design team to be converted into a series of increasingly detailed design specifications. These, in turn, will be handed to individual programmers who will develop the code as specified; then a test team will determine whether the finished code meets the specification. In parallel with each of these stages of implementation, plans for the subsequent stages are refined. Thus a test plan takes shape in the design stage and is improved during development. When the test stage starts, the test plan is fully detailed and adequately supported by a library of test cases. Naturally, the day-to-day expenses of the project increase during implementation as both programming and test groups add resources. It becomes critically important to keep the mushrooming activities on the right track. Frequent project reviews are used for this purpose.

In many application programming departments, individual tasks are prevalent. One person is given full responsibility for a program end product. He or she is analyst, designer, programmer, tester, and project manager all rolled in one. No handovers of formal documents between project stages are called for. If the product is poorly done it is because the responsible person is a poor implementer. The situation is quite different in a programming team in which no individual is completely independent. Since large applications and most systems programs are team efforts, such projects rely on formal procedures to control and enhance the activities of the semi-specialized team members.

6.1   DESIGN

The process of design is a process of discovery and resolution. Given a requirement, the designer offers a solution. In most cases, the solution is not obvious. There are alternatives to consider, obstacles to overcome, and optima to determine. As each problem is discovered, the designer must find (or invent) candidate solutions and then resolve the problem [1]. The capabilities implied by this process are:

- Knowledge of the subject
- Knowledge of the applicable technology
- Ability to structure and classify information
- Creativity to invent solutions
- Ability to make decisions

In addition, a designer should be fluent in his or her working language, oral and written.[1] Not surprisingly, good designers are rare.

To capitalize on the few good designers available, critical design activities are placed at the beginning of the project. At this point there are only a few key people involved in decisions. There is a minimum amount of confusion and the designers are not distracted by the administrative or supervisory tasks that are essential during development. The challenge, in this small team environment, is to produce a specification that is:

- Correct
- Clear and concise
- Complete
- Modular
- Responsive to the design requirements baseline
- Modifiable
- Suitable for high-quality development, maintenance, and upgrade
- Suitable for economical development, maintenance, and upgrade
- Consistent with applicable standards and control procedures
- Consistent with environmental factors during development and use

---

1. The working language should be the designer's native language. In the programming field, perhaps more than in other fields, English is used for implementation activities in some non-English-speaking countries. English source materials and development support tools coupled with limited translation facilities justify this approach.

6.1.1 Selecting Designers

While good designers are rare, rarer still are good designers who are equally adept at all aspects of design. Some designers are very good at finding novel and efficient algorithms to meet the baseline requirements but their designs are expensive to build and maintain. Other designers know how to hold down costs during development but their products are hard to modify. Some designers, conscious of the need for good project control, overspecify the standards and procedures to be followed. That may raise costs unnecessarily. Other designers emphasize technology rather than procedures; even to the extent of neglecting to study the operating environment of the end product. They may specify a design that can be built but not used. The strengths and weaknesses of designers are usually well-ingrained by experience. It is necessary, therefore, for the project manager to recognize the biases in the design team and give appropriate management guidance in order to obtain balanced results.

Many good designers, although they have some programming experience, are not good coders. If they are, they are candidates for Chief Programmer responsibilities or type II small team membership. Coding talent is not essential for designers; however, knowledge of what constitutes good code and which system structures or support techniques facilitate good code development should be part of a designer's store of subject matter knowledge. Designers should know the state-of-the-art in data processing and, more particularly, the hardware and software technologies available in the development organization. Overall, the best candidates for design activities are the individuals who have demonstrated their ability as designers in the past, who are interested in doing design, who are willing to accept design control, and, of course, who are available.

6.1.1.1 Demonstrated ability

The "best available" designers may be idle programmers assigned to the project so they can do some productive work. They may have no background in design above the level of a program unit. Faced with this admittedly unusual situation, a project manager can teach the "designers" the fundamentals of design in the context of the job to be done. On small- and medium-sized jobs, the project manager can do this personally. Temporarily, that project manager is the Acting Chief Designer. Or the project manager can borrow the talents of an experienced designer to teach two or three days of design fundamentals and, later, act as a design consultant. With inexperienced designers, frequent reviews early in the design stage are necessary in order to maximize the consultant's combined contribution to a good system design and on-the-job training of the designers. Reviews on a person-to-person basis twice a week for the first two weeks can be followed by group reviews once a week later.

A more normal situation would offer the project manager several candidates with design experience. The "best available" candidates in this group have a record of successful performance in projects relevant to the one at hand. Relative success can be estimated by looking up performance ratings. For candidates who have worked for the same company several years, appraisal ratings (formal or word-of-mouth from previous managers) are available. Peer evaluation is also useful in drawing an impression of the designer's capability. Designers have a lead role in a project since their work drives all subsequent work. Good designers quickly develop a reputation among other professionals. Bad designers develop a stigma for having caused problems within a project. A characteristic of good designs is that there is relatively little scrap and rework due to design modifications. Testing proceeds smoothly, too. People remember this. A little bit of discreet probing will turn up this type of information about candidates and their backgrounds. So much for other people's opinions. The project manager must now draw his or her own opinion about each candidate. In particular, each candidate should be interviewed to learn three things:

- Is the candidate articulate? A check on oral expression is needed to be sure the designers can be understood by the user, the project personnel, and the project manager. (Written expression was indirectly checked as an element of prior success; so were creativity, structured thinking, and decision-making [2]. These are not directly measurable characteristics.)

- Does the candidate want to be a designer? Motivation is always important. Lack of motivation is a warning that the candidate may realize that design is not his or her strongest skill.

- Will he or she accept project control? The candidate's attitude toward the controls in previous projects (or the freedom of action in small teams) indicates whether he or she will support or resist the controls adopted by the project manager. The most important controls to consider are change procedures and documentation standards.

The interviews plus the background search make up a subjective view of each candidate. The next step is to find out what each one knows that is relevant to the job.

Standards of performance for designers (as for programmers) do not exist because individuals vary so much. Rules-of-thumb deal only with aggregates and averages. A rule-of-thumb regarding design ability is that, given a job to design and apparently equal designer candidates, the candidate with the most recent, directly applicable experience is most likely to succeed. This is a good rule even though there is no way to define what makes two designers "equal" in the first place. It is a conservative rule because it places higher value on the benefits of related knowledge than it does on, say, the potential for a brilliant breakthrough. "Recent directly applicable" experience means at least one recent project dealing with similar subject matter, of similar size, using the same type of hardware and software in the development environment as well as in the operational end product environment. "Recent" also means that the designer has not yet forgotten the applicable project and that it was not so long ago that major changes in technology have occurred.

6.1.1.2 Applicable experience

One expects to find recent, directly applicable experience in a mission-oriented software shop. Here, by definition, the jobs are similar. Beyond this, a given designer may have acquired special skills in one area such as compilers, database management, data communications, operating systems or subsystems (schedulers, storage management), manufacturing applications, etc. The experience is directly applicable to a project in that single area; it is useful but less important in a project where that area is only one of many components. Experience with machines is directly applicable to identical system configurations. Several factors affect how far machine experience can be stretched:

- Language level—Where the standard development language is high level and performance is not critical, experience applies across all systems using comparable compilers.

- Memory size—People accustomed to large, virtual memories may have difficulty designing for small, real memories. Problems will show up in performance. Experience on small machines extends to large machines except for a lack of familiarity with the extra functions and a possible reluctance to use the extra power.

- Distributed function—Designers who have worked only with centralized systems may not understand how to distribute function and data in a system with a network of intelligent processors.

- Support software—Designers dependent on the support software and program libraries of one machine may not know how to create equivalent software for a machine that does not offer such support.

Where directly applicable experience is lacking, experience in a related area can be substituted. Areas are related both by subject and by complexity. Three complexity categories are sufficient:

- Difficult—many interactions with other system elements.
- Moderately difficult—some interactions.
- Easy—few or no interactions.

Experience at one level of complexity applies to jobs at lower levels. Single stand-alone programs fit the *easy* category, even when they use operating system services during execution. Most application programs fit this category since they are intentionally small and simple. They interact with the operating system or an access method or a larger application system through a well-defined application program interface. The majority of the easy application programs are tasks for one programmer rather than a team. *Moderately difficult* programs include many application systems, compilers, utilities, program generators, and other programs with multiple data interfaces and one or more control interfaces with other programs. They are usually team projects; project size depends mainly on the amount of code to be written. *Difficult* programs have many data and control interfaces. Operating systems, with their scheduling and supervisory subsystems, fall in the difficult category. The size of the team required for a difficult program depends on both complexity and the amount of code, i.e., a difficult program requires a larger team than a moderately difficult program with the same number of lines of code.

Some examples of related experience include:

■ Languages—Language experience is usually transferable across languages. Experience in COBOL compilers is more useful on a PL/I compiler project than on a real-time operating system project. COBOL compiler experience is also useful in developing an interpreter for an interactive language even though compilers and interpreters do not use identical techniques. Within subject area, complexity should be considered. Thus experience with a Fortran compiler is not necessarily applicable to a graphic language interpreter, which both generates executable code and constructs image databases. The latter activity complicates the problem.

■ DB/DC—Database management (DB) and data communications (DC) are so often complementary that designers can usually migrate between the areas. On the DB side, the database access method, which handles physical records, is difficult. The database manager, which handles inquiries and converts the user's view of a file to the physical view, is moderate to difficult depending on its generality. Certain aids such as a database dictionary tend to be moderately difficult, while others such as a database analyzer may be easy to program, even though the algorithms they implement are very hard to understand. On the DC side, the telecommunications access method, which forms and transmits messages, is difficult; the communications manager, which schedules transactions and initiates user programs, is moderate to difficult, depending on its generality; the user programs are easy.

■ OS components—The capabilities of an OS can be very loosely grouped into three types of programming activity. The most difficult activity deals with schedulers, supervisors, recovery, and other processes that are time-dependent and serve many other programs. Queues, interrupts, and priorities contribute to the complexity of these processes. The second activity, which probably accounts for the largest amount of OS code, deals with database management and analysis. The databases include catalogs of stored files, lists of resources and their current allocation, security protection data, job sequences, error messages, operator messages, program directories, and other lists required by the OS. The programs that are written in these areas can be very specialized but they must be very efficient. As a result, the programming activity tends to be difficult. The third activity deals with hardware-dependent processes, including error handling, diagnosis and maintenance, and special device support. The activity is not inherently difficult but it requires hardware knowledge that many programmers lack.

■ Applications—Experience in one type of business does not necessarily apply to another. Programmers, however, seem to make moves across industries with some success. The apparent reason for this is that experience in data-oriented design and knowledge of DB/DC are useful in a large number of problems in all types of business applications. Similarly, experienced scientific programmers can usually apply their knowledge of mathematical applications to diverse scientific subjects. Movement from business applications to scientific applications and vice versa is less successful because the experience covers too little of the work scope. It is less clear why systems programmers with large team experience in operating systems development are not interchangeable with applications programmers. In spite of the similarity of tools and techniques in both areas, the programmers seem to approach problems differently. The system programmer is process- and performance-oriented; the business applications programmer is data- and user-oriented. These distinctions may be sufficient to separate the two classes of programmers.

6.1.1.3 Management ability

What about management ability as a selection criterion for designers? There are two sides to this question. The first side relates to a designer who is also the project manager. The administrative, recruiting, and negotiating activities of a project manager do not mesh well with the concentration and mental activity of a designer. In a team project when ample resources are available there is enough nonoverlapping work to do to keep two people busy on a large job. Looking at that side of the question, you would not insist on management ability in a designer. On the other side, however, a designer's job requires a certain amount of leadership to sell the design and to get it developed properly. A designer need not be a manager to exercise personal

leadership but management ability may help a designer be a leader. Therefore, two guidelines to consider are:

1. Do not burden designers with project management responsibility (when
    you can afford it).
2. Select designers who are not only good designers and good communica-
    tors but who are capable of leading project members (and users) to
    accept the design.

In addition, there is a requirement in large projects for someone to manage
the design team. This person should be a designer. (The role is that of a
first-level manager in most cases; FLMs should be skilled in their subject
area.)

Designers, like experienced managers, are among the more senior
members of a project team. Since new managers are selected from this seniority group, designers often become candidates for project management
assignments. As mentioned in Chapter 3, there are three paths for designers
on a large project to follow after the design specification is complete. They
can be charged with design control responsibility; they can participate in
development and test activity as implementers; or they can move to another
project that needs designers. There is a fourth path; they can move to a non-
design task in another project or department. The best technical people tend
to stay in design. The designers with strong management interests move into
project development or other activities as managers, gradually losing their
credentials as designers.

6.1.2   Design Approach

Once the design team is selected, the project can proceed to respond to the
system requirements.

Designers start with the design requirements baseline. As explained in
Chapter 2, the project is usually constrained to a particular hardware configuration. Some constraints are implied rather than obvious. Such things
as company procedures, say covering allowable overtime or the number of
levels of approval required for a decision, can affect the length of time it
takes to do a given piece of work, forcing a change in the logical sequence of
design activity. Other constraints are simply not evident at the beginning of
the design stage. For example, an activity may depend on a piece of hardware having certain features; the hardware designer may omit one of the
features for technical or business reasons. The project team only learns this
after the hardware is delivered. Known constraints are respected in the
design. Unknown constraints are anticipated by consciously providing
enough flexibility in the design to absorb change.

The finished design is a specification document describing system modules that can be built by individuals (in the case of programs). Each of these modules preferably has a single function. The modules interact via their inputs and outputs. Designers are very much concerned with the form and content of the inputs and outputs. They are also concerned with functional content of each module but they leave the detailed design of the basic module to the programmer.

6.1.2.1 Architecture

The first steps in the design of a large system are often called *architecture*. Architecture describes the functions of the system and specifies the formats and protocols through which the functions interact. The architecture is an *external* description of the system because it shows how the system will appear to the user; it does not explain how the components work internally to provide the functions. In order for two functions to interact, the architecture specifies what messages must be exchanged across their interface. Message format is given. In addition, the sequence and timing of messages are given to control handshaking. These rules of precedence are called protocols. *Protocol* is used here in the sense of "ceremonial etiquette": formalities adopted to control exchanges between parties who may have different customs and languages and who may not even be on friendly terms.[2] Architectural protocols are fixed and permanent so all users can be aware of them in advance. A system architecture should last for the life of the system. Architects, therefore, try to create foundations that permit the system to change and grow over the years.

The architects of a multicomputer networking system, for example, recognize that such systems contain hosts and distributed processors, intermediate communications nodes, cluster controllers, and terminals among other things [3]. These are the building blocks of current single-host data processors. Networking requirements (see Table 4.4) call for information paths between applications on any pair of processors plus information paths from applications to terminals and between terminals. The architects establish message formats and protocols for data transmission to apply to each link in a path, even though some paths are not going to be offered initially. In particular, they specify the end user interface, keeping it as simple

---

2. As Gower points out in *Fowler's Modern English Usage* (London: Oxford University Press, 1965), this usage has replaced the prior meaning of "amendment or temporary change to a treaty." A still earlier meaning is "the first leaf glued on to a manuscript." Respectful of that definition, protocols remain today pretty sticky affairs.

as possible while giving the user full access to the system capabilities. (A vendor attempts to freeze the user interface as early as possible so it can be published and used for application development before the new software system is delivered.)

Considering the networking problem, an architect will think first about the primary function of networking: providing access to remote resources. The simplest way to do this is to permit the originator, A, to address the destination, B, by name. When A and B are part of the same component, there is a local table showing the actual address of B. In networking, A and B may be on different machines and neither knows the address of the other. So some sort of network control must be provided to supervise the addressing and the transmission. To keep A's task simple, the network control should respond to a set of commands that let A explain what network services are needed. For example, a reporting program, A, may send short reports to a database manager, B. B will notify A if the reports are late or incorrect. Therefore, A does not bother to request any transmission verification from the network services manager. In another case, C may be coordinating the operation of a manufacturing process, D. If the orders from C are not executed on time, they become invalid. In most cases, a retransmission would be successful. Therefore, C requests a time-stamped acknowledgment of receipt. E sends long reports of company financial data to a printer. The report segments must not only be delivered in sequence but they must be encrypted prior to transmission. The printer should run at full speed when possible. A single end-user interface should permit these services and others to be requested by an application or a terminal user.

The services must be carried out somewhere in the network. Some, such as breaking a long record into segments, can be done at the source. Some, such as generating an acknowledgment, occur at the destination. Others may occur at several points; for instance, priority routing could be done at any node. Most services lead to processing at both ends of a link as in the case of encryption and decryption. The reason A wants access to B is to exchange data in the form of a message. In a network with many addressable units, B's address is included in a transmission header attached to the message. The service requests that are to be executed at B or at intermediate nodes can be put in the header and sent along with the message. Still to be added are the routing codes that direct the message from node to node. The transmitted segment is now longer than the message and may interfere with performance requirements, so the header definition must be very carefully done. The rule of economy suggests that a variable-length header would be desirable so only necessary bits are transmitted. One place to save bits, hopefully increasing traffic capacity on slow links, is in the addressing portion of the header. Conceptually, the network consists of some nodes that form the basic networking paths plus some nodes that are end points at the

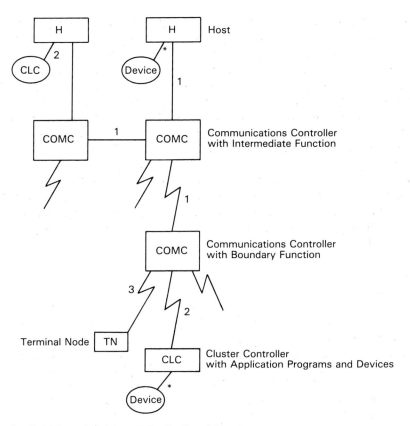

1 = Full Network Origin and Destination Addresses
2 = Local Area Abbreviated Origin and Destination Addresses
3 = Local Session Identifier
* = No Addressing

Fig. 6.1   Transmission addressing architecture.
R. J. Cypser, *Communications Architecture for Distributed Systems*
(Reading, Mass.: Addison-Wesley, 1978).

network boundary. Every node within the boundary has a network address; anything beyond the boundary, while it is known to the boundary node it is attached to, is unknown to the network. In Fig. 6.1, it is thus possible to show four different addressing situations:

1. Network hosts, intermediate nodes, and boundary nodes have network addresses, say 4 bytes. A message from one node to another carries 8 address bytes naming the destination and, for response and recovery purposes, the source.

2. Cluster controllers outside the boundary have local addresses, say 2 bytes, based on the number of logical units that can be attached to a boundary node. Messages from the boundary node to the cluster controller have 4 bytes of address data representing the 2-byte destination address and an abbreviated 2-byte version of the source address at the other end of the network path. The boundary node maintains the tables for converting the short form to a full network address.

3. Terminals may have multiple logical units such as a display and a keyboard, each addressable. In one byte it may be possible to address all the possible logical units, so one byte is used.

4. Devices which are the private property of an intelligent controller (or host) need no address header.

Two independent networks may use identical internal addresses. If the two networks are connected, the gateway node will have to generate unique end user addresses. This can be done by wrapping address headers in an envelope that shows which network is the source and which is the destination.

The thought sequence that leads to different header types is typical of the design activity. Given a requirement, the designer asks, "How would I do that if I had no constraints?" Then comes the practical question, "How can I do it within the constraints?" Architects deal mostly with the first question in order to preserve the generality of their solutions. By starting with the problem, the architect can visualize the fundamental processes in the system and build a conceptual structure that ties the processes together. Not only does the analysis of A's desire to communicate with B show what type of controls are required, but it shows at least one alternative for grouping system functions in various types of nodes. Further analysis suggests a way of looking at the system as a sequence of layers (Fig. 6.2) which accept the end user's message, interpret instructions regarding the message itself (character set, compression, formatting, editing), regulate the flow of data requests and responses, control transmission rates and route messages to the proper end user, select the path to the destination, and control the flow of data on the physical data link. The layered view[3] has the desirable property of modularity. If the architected interfaces between layers are well-defined, a layer can be replaced. The basic architecture conceals what happens within a layer. Parnas [6] has shown that this method of hiding information is particularly useful when the goal is to produce a broad family of pro-

---

3. Figures 6.1 and 6.2 and the accompanying descriptions are based on IBM System Network Architecture, SNA. For a complete description of SNA and the general topic of communications architecture for distributed systems see Cypser [4]. The relation of SNA to emerging international standards is discussed by Corr and Neal [5].

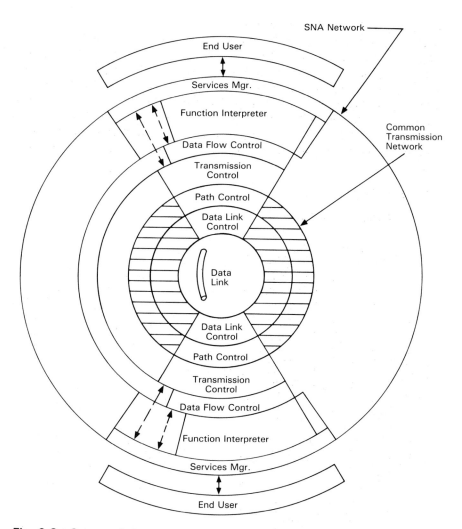

Fig. 6.2 Concentric layers in an SNA network.
R. J. Cypser, *Communications Architecture for Distributed Systems* (Reading, Mass.: Addison-Wesley, 1978).

grams. A good interface specification allows production of neighboring modules to proceed independently. Design decisions within a module can be postponed and, when made, can take many forms without disturbing the neighbors. The same SNA architecture then could work with different physical data links by changing Data Link Control. That gives the user a choice of communications systems where a choice exists. By replacing the whole Common Transmission Network, a choice of specialized communication carriers becomes possible.

Layered architectures permit but do not require layered implementation. In Fig. 6.2, the architected layers have interfaces separating the Data Link, Data Link Control, Path Control, Transmission Control, Data Flow Control (when present), Network Access Unit Services (which has an interface between its Function Interpreter and Services Manager segments), and the End User. If the system is built exactly this way, each layer will be identifiable and the system will be as modular as the architecture. Such a system would be highly adaptable, permitting free substitution of equivalent products of different vendors as long as they observe the interface protocols. Some vendors will prefer to hide some of the interfaces in a product which, if successful, may win them more revenue by giving them a large, undivided chunk of each subsystem procurement. Other vendors may create extra interfaces to invite complementary producers to build small products which, combined with the vendor's speciality, create an attractive business opportunity. As a general rule, designers should expose all architectural interfaces in their design. This gives maximum flexibility to the business decision-maker who will select the best interfaces to offer the user.

The architecture, as described, need not mention actual existing hardware; therefore, the designers retain their freedom of action. By defining abstract entities such as "nodes," an architect can describe how networking operates without specifying whether an Intermediate Node is a stand-alone box or simply a program running on a Host. The implementation is left to the designers. The architect is quite specific, though, in documenting the functions required (or permitted) in each defined entity, the interfaces between entities, and the protocols to be observed.

6.1.2.2 System design

Architectural entities are abstractions that must be mapped into physical components that can be built. System design proceeds to do the mapping. The activity consists of specifying the hardware units, programs, and supporting elements that satisfy the design requirements baseline within the given constraints. The designers are free to move within a space defined by analysts, business people, architects, and various other internal and external interested parties. Change control procedures protect the interested parties against unacceptable design proposals.

In the case of a vendor project to build a networking product Ⓝ, the requirements are very general. Business considerations may limit the requirements, at least initially, to those things that can be done on the vendor's hardware. This economy move may dictate where certain functions are implemented. For example, if the vendor makes a communication controller of limited storage capacity that is normally a slave to a host, the Ⓝ system design may have to divide intermediate node functions between the message handling processes that fit in the communications controller and all other processes (such as initialization of the node) which must go in the adjacent host. When it is appropriate to use existing facilities, it is often necessary to modify them in order to handle the new requirements. As an example, a single-host system network architecture may exist for the vendor's products. As such, there are no host-to-host transfers, no devices unknown to the host, and no destination for a terminal message other than an application in the host; consequently, this SNA does not need explicit addresses in its message headers, as are required in Ⓝ. No independent watchdog is required in this SNA to prevent conflicts among multiple hosts. These features and many others will have to be added to the single-host SNA to extend it to a networking SNA. The challenge is to make the extensions without disturbing the original. The designers will look for efficient ways to do this. Quite often they will not find a good answer and will, instead, propose replacing the current SNA with a new architecture more hospitable to Ⓝ. The change proposal should be reviewed by all affected parties including vendor departments that have a vested interest in the existing SNA. Assuming that consistency and compatibility for present customers outweigh the added value of Ⓝ, the business decision will be to retain the single-host SNA and try harder to extend it. The designers will go back to work and this time they will be ready to accept some loss of elegance and efficiency in their design. They may place a Ⓝ process alongside an existing process with a switch set to select one when a session is established. They may add conversion routines that accept old SNA messages and wrap them in Ⓝ headers. In any case, they will try to make the design transparent to the user; that is, old functions will look unchanged to the user, and new functions will look like additional features.

System design is a decomposition process in the sense that its purpose is to break high-level components into smaller units; yet, some of the smaller units may be predetermined by constraints in the requirements. These required modules are assigned to the appropriate high-level component. As decomposition proceeds, the high-level components suggested by the architecture are exploded into lower-level components following normal design guidelines for modularity, etc. As a result, the existing module that has been assigned to a component may not exactly match any of the newly specified pieces. To make the existing module fit, the designers can either modify it or modify the new modules that interface with it. They can also propose a change in the requirements to abandon the existing module and use a new one. The appropriate choice of action depends on the situation. A large, expensive module in wide use may be hard to modify without impacting the users; in this case, the new design should be adjusted. If the present users can be completely shielded from any change, the existing module should be modified to preserve the integrity of the new design. In either case, a very expensive or risky change may justify removing the constraint. Note that the situation arose because the design started out by searching for the best logical approach to the decomposition; it did not start out to find a solution that optimized the use of the existing module. Tying the design entirely to existing modules brings the system one step closer to obsolescence. So, when possible, generate a logical design and then adapt it to the constraints.

Designers are concerned not only with the technical aspects of "How will it work?" but they also ask "How will the work get done?" They plan experiments, models, and phases of implementation in order to validate new and risky sections of the design. For the vendor to whom Ⓝ is a new challenge, it is logical to test the basic protocols for message traffic among multiple hosts. A realistic test would process each expected type of traffic but need not cope with high volumes or unusual paths. The key thing is to see if messages can be transmitted successfully. A very simple physical hookup may be adequate. (The nodes could actually be simulated by virtual machines on a single real host.) The layout in Fig. 6.3 allows for messages to pass between A and B via link 1L2 or via path 1L3–2L3. Each terminal can also be reached by a direct link or an alternate route. Terminal T1, belonging to Host A, can be reached directly via a channel using old single-host SNA protocols. It can also be reached by Host B, with A's permission via 1L2 or 2L3–1L3 using the Ⓝ-extended SNA. Thus this simple layout supports some nontrivial tests:

- Session establishment, foreign host (session between T1 and application in Host B)
- Ⓝ transmission protocols, error detection, recovery
- Consistency of Ⓝ extensions and earlier SNA architecture
- Function of a stand-alone intermediate node (Node 3)
- Application-to-application communications
- Alternate paths
- Network address creation, table lookup, reinitialization after outage
- Network management of configuration and flow
- Operator interface

The software to support all these tests is extensive but it can represent the first phase of development on which subsequent phases will be built. The capabilities of the experimental layout are only a small subset of the user requirements. Nevertheless, they are the critical new things that have to be right in order for the rest of the system to function. Some early assessment of protocol design can be modeled interactively or even manually [7]; however, the thorough assessment implied by Fig. 6.3 requires actual current hardware and software. The design plan must take such things into account.

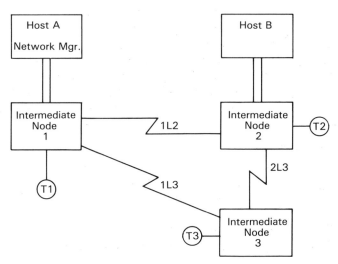

Fig. 6.3 Ⓝ design experiment.

At the high level of system design, decomposition decisions are largely intuitive. A designer is influenced by experience, by the current state-of-the-art, by specific project constraints, and by common sense. Nevertheless, the final decision to assign certain functions to a particular package may be arbitrary. Furthermore, it may not matter. Once the high-level decisions have been made, lower-level decisions are tuned to optimize the overall result. The effect can be seen in commercial software where two companies produce very different programs for similar requirements and both solutions are highly competitive.

In Fig. 6.4, the top-level flow diagram of a control system shows how some of the packaging decisions are made. The control system is supposed to adjust instruments, including TV and infra-red cameras, that are located in a satellite. The satellite surveys the land mass of the northern temperate zone, providing input for agricultural and mineralogical studies. Data are sensed, transmitted to earth, and forwarded to the control center. The control center edits and records the data in a history database for the use of scientists who access the file in a variety of ways. Meanwhile, the control center monitors the data to determine if the satellite has drifted or the instruments have gone out of focus. If so, the control center computer can issue corrective commands. A manual override is possible as well. The designers have identified nine high-level packages. Two of them are fairly obvious; the sensor input, 1.0, and the control output, 7.0, are unique packages because their implementation is physically isolated in the satellite. The history file, 4.0, is an interface with a separate, possibly undefined scientific

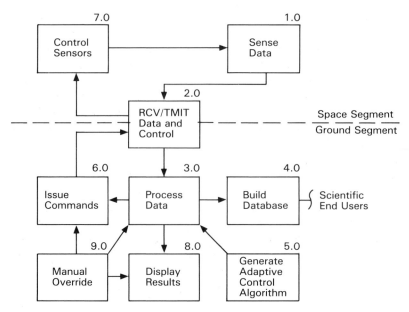

Fig. 6.4   Sensor control system packages.

analysis system. As a separate package, it may be easier to manage. Packages 2.0 and 6.0 are involved with communications facilities. The designers normally work with systems in which data processing and communications come under different management chains and where the facilities come from different vendors. Even if the system were totally owned by one group, as occurs in some military situations, the packages might be designed the same way because they handle I/O as distinct from processing. That would explain why the separate display package, 8.0, exists. The manual override is package 9.0. It requires a special console according to the requirements statement:

> R9.0   The sensor control system will include means for manually modifying an ongoing computation or a graphic display. Manual commands must be permitted to override computed commands to space-borne sensors. All manual inputs are to be collocated on a single Manual Input Console (MIC).

This requirement reflects the fact that human beings are far superior to computers in some aspects of evaluating visual images. Package 5.0 is a support package that provides the basic algorithms for monitoring inputs. The package is used prior to a mission but is occasionally used during real-time operations. That leaves the mainline process, 3.0.

Fig. 6.5 shows how additional information is developed when the design of the sensor control system is carried one level deeper. In Fig. 6.5a, it becomes clear that package 2.0 will be physically split into three parts: one in the satellite, one in the control center, and one in the earth station which connects the satellite communication link with terrestrial common carrier links. If the earth station is an existing public facility, the design of components 2.1 and 2.3 may be constrained in ways not anticipated by the analysts. The flow diagram also contains an interface between component 2.3 and package 4.0 which does not appear in Fig. 6.4 because, as a look at Fig. 6.5b shows, the designers decided to record all the raw data

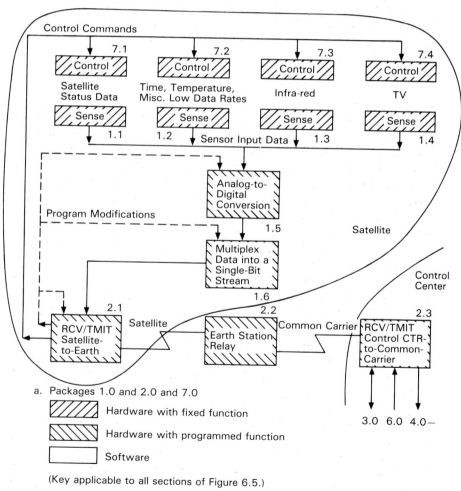

Fig. 6.5 Sensor control system decomposition.

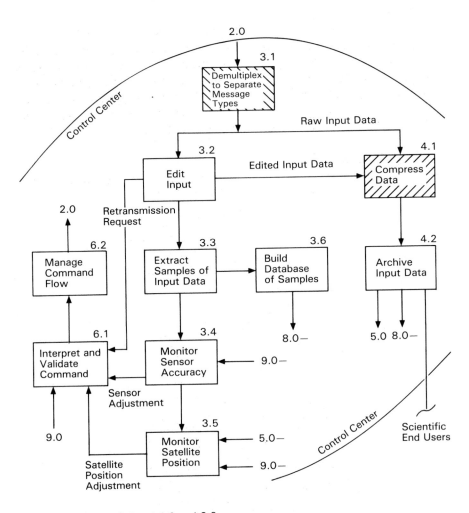

b. Packages 3.0 and 4.0 and 6.0

Fig. 6.5 Continued.

received from the satellite. In the satellite, everything is built into the hardware. The instruments are hard-wired but the conversion and communications devices are programmable. New algorithms can be implemented by transmitting new programs from the control center to the satellite where, following the dotted line, they can be fed to the programmable device. The analog-to-digital conversion shows that the sensors are analog and the communications are digital. Commands to the control devices, however, do not go through a digital-to-analog conversion. In other words, the system uses digitally controlled, analog sensors.

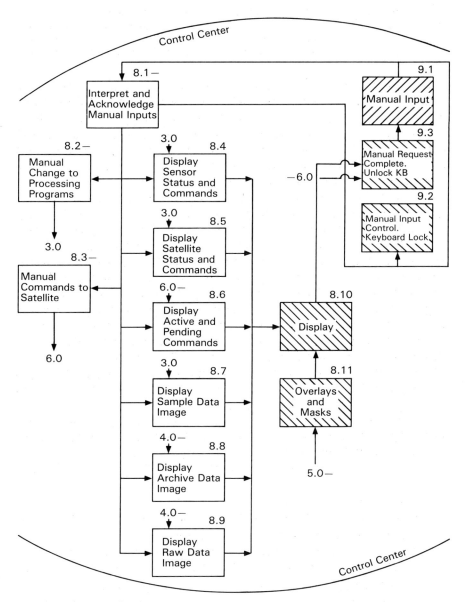

c. Packages 8.0 and 9.0

Fig. 6.5 Continued.

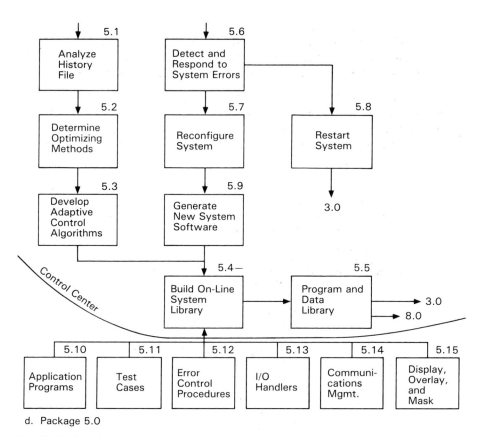

d. Package 5.0

Fig. 6.5 Continued.

Fig. 6.5b describes three more packages all of which are to be located in the control center. As a matter of fact, all the remaining operational packages will be installed in the control center. Only the activities that can be performed off-site, perhaps by subcontractors, are separate (Fig. 6.5d). As the architecture is clarified, more interactions show up that were not indicated in the highest-level flow diagram. Since the objective of the decomposition process is to specify clean modules with well-defined interfaces, all the loose ends that show up in each decomposition step should be investigated and tied down before proceeding to the next level of detail. Here is where the group characteristics of design activities are important. Since there are only a few designers working on the system architecture, they can work as a small team in which each has a global view of the system. They can also discuss and solve architecture problems by talking to each other. This is a mode of operation that becomes less practical as the project pro-

ceeds because the individual designers gradually build their detailed knowledge at the expense of global knowledge and, more important, the number
of people actively working on the design gets too big to communicate effectively in team mode. Information exchange shifts from a group discussion
where the group possesses all the system knowledge to person-to-person
conversations where the participants only know about a small piece of the
system personally and must rely on the system documentation for global
data.

In the sensor control system example, assume that there are four
designers engaged in the system design activity. As a group, they agreed that
the nine packages of Fig. 6.4 would best fit the requirements, the environment, and the development practices of their organization. Together, they
architected the basic external characteristics in order to obtain the user's
agreement that: (1) the system would fit the hardware constraints, (2) the
system operator and maintenance interfaces were appropriate, and (3) the
scientist's end-user interface was reasonable. Then, the group divided up
the work for the next stage of decomposition so that one person took packages 1.0, 2.0, and 7.0; another took 3.0, 4.0, 6.0; the third, 8.0 and 9.0; and
the fourth, 5.0. Each went away to work on the assigned packages with the
intent of meeting again as a group at least once a day. This is a typical
method of operation for a team: Generate ideas and assignments in a group
to take advantage of group communications, then carry out assignments
alone to take advantage of individual productivity.[4] The assignments also
explain how it is possible even at this high level of design to have
unanswered questions pop up in the results. For instance, the designer of
packages 3.0, 4.0, and 6.0 knows that all the sensor data and commands are
routed via package 2.0. The fact that they will be routed by subpackage 2.3
is not yet known. Likewise, the requirements show that packages 3.0 and
6.0 (as well as the display package, 8.0) can be affected by inputs from the
manual override package, 9.0. The designer of 3.0 and 6.0 allows for this by
deciding to feed the manual inputs directly to a subpackage that handles
sensor data, 3.4, and another that handles satellite status, 3.5. An override
input is also allowed on the command unit, 6.1. Each of these inputs is
wrong at the moment because the designer of packages 8.0 and 9.0 (Fig.
6.5c) decided to separate the assignment into a software-oriented piece and
a hardware-oriented piece. This led him to feed all manual inputs to the
software-oriented package, 8.0, where they would be interpreted, acknowl-

---

4. Task forces (Chapter 4) are not strictly classed as team efforts primarily because
they are not always able to make assignments that can be carried out by individual
task force members. As a result, they appear to waste a lot of time in inconclusive
group discussions. Their value is not in increasing individual output but in bringing
together diverse skills to increase overall understanding of a complex problem.

edged, formatted, and rerouted to the proper point. When the group meets to discuss progress, the designer of 3.0 and 6.0 will point out that she needs to know the form of input to expect from the manual input console. Her question will be answered by the designer of the manual input who will also explain how the data is routed. While talking about this interface, the group will probably also investigate whether the idea of using subpackage 8.1 as a master switch is desirable and, if it is, whether some functions previously assigned to other packages should be moved to package 8.0 or elsewhere.

Going back to Fig. 6.5b, the designer has specified a programmable controller to demultiplex, or separate, the messages in the incoming bit stream. This box, 3.1, is the mirror image of 1.6. The group will probably suggest reassigning that subpackage to the designer of 1.6. If so, it will probably be agreed that the package boundaries be changed so that both 1.6 and 3.1 fall in package 2.0 and are suitably renumbered. Processing has been divided into logical stages. Incoming data are edited for acceptability and to produce the desired record format. Certain unacceptable data must be retransmitted so subpackage 3.2 generates a retransmission request which it sends to the command package. (This routing is natural for the designer of 3.0 because she also owns 6.0. If editing had been assigned to package 2.0, that designer might have sent the retransmission request directly to 2.3 on the basis that the request is not a command but merely a transmission protocol. The architecture team should consider such alternatives since one may be preferable to another in terms of system performance or cost.) The second logical subpackage samples the data and builds a sample database that can be used by the display package to show approximately what the sensors see. The flow diagram shows an arrow from the database, 3.6 to package 8.0. But is this the link between packages 3.0 and 8.0 intended by Fig. 6.4? Obviously not, since package 8.0 also expects inputs from 3.4, which checks sensor accuracy and sends adjustment commands when a sensor goes out of limits, and 3.5, which checks satellite position and sends corrective commands when the attitude or drift are out of line. Package 3.0 needs more work on its interfaces. Package 4.0 is compact. Raw data streams as well as edited messages are to be compressed automatically by a hardware device and stored by a database management system. Anything in the archives can be displayed or referenced by scientists. In addition, the database provides the historical data for package 5.0 which calculates the parameters and provides the algorithms used to control system operation. According to the flow diagram, the results of package 5.0 only influence satellite position control. This may be a literal interpretation of the requirements but it hardly seems likely. The group is going to want to look into this some more to see if sampling rates and sensor limits should not also be reset on advice from package 5.0.

The design of packages 8.0 and 9.0 is straightforward, yet it highlights some points hidden in the system overview. The designer visualizes a manual end-user console that contains all the necessary input devices such as keyboards and light pens plus the output displays. He pictures the end user in the control center being in charge of system operations; the end user is the only source of display requests and an important source of system commands. The design gives the end user access to all data, including the current list of commands being issued by package 6.0. This interface is implied in the requirement that the operator be able to override system commands. Obviously, the operator must know what the system is doing in order to make a decision to override. The interface, though, is missing in Fig. 6.4, as is an interface to the database manager from which package 8.0 will draw image displays. From the flow diagram it appears that package 8.0 will accept data from the archives, the samples, and the processing/command modules which it will then set up in display format. Some further discussion is required to agree on what form the data should be in when it is supplied by 3.0, 4.0, or 6.0. At the moment, there is a chance of redundant display processing in the various packages. At least two more interfaces are missing in Fig. 6.4. One is a response from the command package to the end-user console reporting completion of a user command. The console is set up to prevent sequential inputs from interfering with each other. Each input device is locked when a command is entered and only unlocked when a completion code is received. The other missing interface is between package 8.0 and package 5.0. The display equipment not only has the ability to show pictures as viewed by a TV camera but it can also mix background overlays and masks with the displayed data. The mixing is done in the display hardware but the overlays and masks are held in a library file. Package 8.0 assumes the library is in package 5.0.

Package 5.0, Fig. 6.5d, does indeed have a program library function. The package has taken the form of a general support utility. The designer has been assigned the specific task of developing adaptive control algorithms and the general responsibility for anything that was overlooked in the architectural overview. The primary task led to modules that analyze the archives and produce mathematical and logical procedures to produce the best available control tactics for a given situation. The longer the system is used, the more effective the adaptive algorithms will get. The way this package works, the algorithms are generated periodically and stored. Whenever the processing modules need to initiate a control action, they search the file for the most appropriate entry under the circumstances. The designer, having decided on this approach, realized there was no place to store the algorithms. That led him to design a library support subpackage, 5.4 and 5.5, for the use of 5.3 and 3.0. His general responsibility for loose ends then led him to ask what other programs or files would be needed on-line by the operational system. All such support items, produced outside the control center, could be installed via his library support subpackage. Alternatively, they could be handled by the database manager of the archiving package. Further thought and group discussion, however, showed that the high-volume input streams and the behavior of scientific end users could make response times from the archives unpredictable. Therefore, the program library was kept as a separate unit. One of the data files in the library would be the system configuration table showing the names of active system elements and their true physical address. This table might change if a sensor, say, failed and was replaced by a device with a different identifier. But failure and reconfiguration have not been addressed at all so far. For that matter, routine error handling and system restart procedures have been overlooked. The Package 5.0 designer sketches these functions in his package but, as yet, does not know where the error information will come from and what it will mean. That is one more subject to take up with the whole design group.

So far, the expansion of the initial system overview has resulted in making the system structure more complex (Fig. 6.6a). An attempt to simplify it is agreed to (Fig. 6.6b). In this new view, the packages are redesigned but the subpackages are largely unchanged; they have simply moved around. The original package names that reflect the application requirements have evolved into more generic system functions. A major flow alteration makes the end-user package the main gateway to the user's console and also to the command package. That removes two ticklish interfaces with the command package, while recognizing the significance of the end-user's role. Now the architectural work begins to stabilize and the system design activity merges into package design.

A management decision is required before package design starts in earnest. The decision to proceed with package design is based on the results of a Preliminary Design Review (PDR).[5] Given the design requirements baseline and the system specification, the review team decides whether, from a technical point of view, the system design is complete and feasible. (The design should be responsive to the baseline, no more, no less. There is no reason to do more than was requested and there may be reasons to prevent the system from exceeding its requested capabilities. However, the user should expect quality and serviceability in the areas of security, performance, recovery operations, etc. Even in the absence of baseline requirements, the design should at least meet the norm for the developer's organization.) At the same time, a management review team decides whether the preliminary plans for the rest of the project are sound and affordable,

5. Project reviews, in general, are discussed in section 6.2.3.

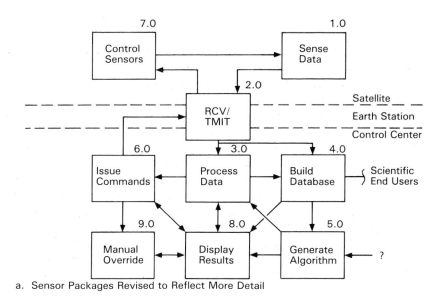

a. Sensor Packages Revised to Reflect More Detail

b. Sensor Packages Revised to Reflect Repackaging

Fig. 6.6   Sensor control system packages—Revised.

whether contract terms and conditions are being satisfied, and whether assumptions and dependencies in the plan for package design are realistic. If everything looks good at the PDR, the package design activity can be approved. Meanwhile, new people, having gone through indoctrination and training classes, will be assigned to the packages so far defined. They can learn the purpose of their package and think about how to design it. This preliminary study is one way, the most productive way in the project manager's opinion, to use the available people.

A PDR is not a one-hour meeting. For a large project it takes several days. Even so, the reviewers can only probe the most obvious issues. They concentrate on whether the system design:

- Satisfies the design requirements baseline
- Meets the organization's own standards
- Is correct
- Can be built with the resources available
- Will work when built
- Is compatible with the organization's own business objectives

A review of the revised sensor control system of Fig. 6.6b will show that there is a hole in the error handling and recovery portion of the design. The review team may not be concerned with the omission since the hole can be plugged during package design; however, the fact that the error and recovery capability is not fully designed will trigger the team to ask some questions: "Is it possible for an operator's override command to be ignored without the operator realizing it?" "Can an incorrect command cause the mission to fail?" The manual input/display console will also attract attention. It is a key element of the system both as a control point in the design and as the one real, physical piece of the system that the user will see. The console will raise such questions as: "Do we have the technical ability to build the console?" "What will be the effect on our future business opportunities if we supply or do not supply the console?" Looking at the database management package that serves scientific end users, the reviewers will want to know how many end users can be served at once without affecting the sensor control system. They will ask what response time requirement is established by the baseline for the scientists. If the answer is "None," they will ask what the designers expect the response time will be and evaluate the answer in terms of local standards or personal experience.

The outcome of the PDR is usually full or conditional approval to proceed with package design. Full approval implies that the review team is satisfied that the system design is acceptable and that all remaining issues can be resolved by the package designs. Conditional approval implies that some issues remain with the system design; they require further work that may change the system design but will not invalidate the bulk of the package design effort. Only rarely is the system design rejected. Occasions where this may occur tend to be due to surprises:

- A chemical compound data retrieval system was abandoned because it was based on a high-resolution display that, at the time, was beyond the state-of-the-art of cathode ray tube technology.

- An automated mapping application system design was unable to draw maps as well as the artists it was to displace. It was shelved awaiting new graphic techniques.

- An interactive planning tool patterned after a manual procedure actually took longer than the manual procedure. It had to be redesigned to make better use of the computer database.

- A system designed to inspect the accuracy of a national complex of air navigation aids contained an error in an estimate of the time required to do a critical calculation. When the error was corrected, it turned out that the proposed computer hardware would be too slow to do the calculation in real time; furthermore, data recording and data structuring decisions based on the characteristics of the selected computer were all wrong for the replacement computer configuration. The effects cascaded throughout the system design, resulting in a highly modified but successful approach.

The normal case where the system design is approved at the PDR justifies an early start on package design and explains why system design *merges* into package design rather than stopping abruptly.

6.1.2.3 Package design

In order to carry out the package design of the sensor control system, the system design team will break up. Each of the original designers will take one or more of the packages. Adding people as necessary, he or she will proceed to carry the package, as described in the system specification, to the next level of detail. Then individual programmers can pick up the unit specifications and build the programs. The considerations in assigning package design responsibility include:

- Assigning scopes of work that the package designers (or teams) can handle
- Maintaining continuity from system design
- Grouping tightly coupled packages together so one designer controls decisions affecting them
- Balancing workload so package designs are finished in the sequence required by the plan

Such considerations are not difficult for the system designers to handle while they are still together. Thus the group could probably agree that packages 8.0 and 9.0 should be handled by a single package design team since 8.0 essentially defines 9.0. The member of the group who handled system design for 8.0 and 9.0 is the logical candidate to head the package design.

The activity of package design is similar to system design with two exceptions:

1. Package design is often done by an individual, so the checks and balances inherent in a group may be absent.

2. Package design must be specific, whereas system design can often generalize.

Both of these exceptions permit design errors that are difficult to detect prior to system test. The type of error that occurs is due to design decisions that the designer believes are strictly local to the package but which, in fact, have global impact. A package designer working alone has no one to challenge such a decision. Also, if the decision is stated only in general terms, no one will recognize the potential error until its impact is felt. Walkthroughs and inspections catch many problems but, in this situation, they will often fail to bring the unstated decision to light because the reviewers have no clues to lead them to ask the right questions.

An example of such an elusive error situation can be found in the sensor control system. In package 9.0, each command from the manual input console causes the user's keyboard to lock until the command is executed and acknowledged. A command to the satellite will take a half second just to make the round trip. Complex commands or program overrides may take many seconds during which the user could be doing some useful work. The package designer may feel it is important to free up the console so the user can scan images or look at status reports. Therefore, the designer replaces the lock (scrapping units 9.2 and 9.3) with a procedure that warns the end user whenever he or she is about to override a pending command. The procedure could be an added feature of unit 8.6. Good documentation and thorough training could teach the user how to handle sequential commands; therefore, the designer assumes the procedure is an adequate and equivalent replacement for the lock. The error lies in the fact that the new design is discretionary, whereas the lock was a positive obstacle to user action. Given the lock, package 6.0 knew that each command received was valid. The new procedure permits the user to insert invalid commands, but no one tells the package 6.0 designer to look out for this since the package 8.0 designer does not expect the user to behave that way. The problem will not surface until some real user makes a mistake.

The rule, *maximize binding and minimize coupling,* implies that in a good design all decisions affecting actions within a module are truly local. As a practical matter, no decisions are guaranteed to be so restricted. At the package design level, coupling between packages is only partly defined because the system designers are only able to say how the system *should* work.

They do not yet know the details of how each package *will* work. It is at this level of design that the greatest risk of error exists.

In the previous example, a decision by the designer of packages 8.0 and 9.0 impacted package 6.0. What was thought to be a tightly bound decision turned out to be coupled in an unexpected way. A more predictable error of the same type can also be illustrated by the sensor control system. In package 3.0, input messages are edited and used to assess sensor accuracy. When necessary, commands are issued to adjust the sensors. The system implies that a sequence of messages from the satellite is received, without omissions, at the control center. To make this work, the satellite transmitter should be synchronized with the control center receiver; otherwise, message strings could be garbled or lost. If transmit and receive get out of synch, the tests in unit 3.4 should be suspended until synch is reacquired. Notice, however, that in the system design, there is a relay station, unit 2.2, between the satellite and the control center. It is possible for the satellite transmitter to be out of synch with the relay station while the relay is still in synch with the control center. It is thus possible for garbled messages to reach unit 3.4. This will trigger commands to adjust the sensors when, in fact, the sensors were accurate all along. The system could even work itself into a vicious circle where every attempt at correction leads to a further error.

This situation typifies a system problem caused by passing control information through a string of intermediate nodes. The solution is to minimize coupling; yet it is obvious that a system of any size must be modular and the modules must be coupled. Therefore, system integrity must be achieved through thoroughness and defensive procedures. Thoroughness implies design methods that evaluate all possible effects of a decision. The decision may meet a requirement but its side effects may violate a constraint or impact another part of the system. Defensive procedures imply inspections during design, test plans that exercise all aspects of coupling, simulation of the environment for realism, and similar activities intended to expose coupling problems. A suspicious attitude is helpful. When someone suggests a unit 5.6 consisting of a minicomputer to detect errors in the control center of Fig. 6.5, question the decision. Does this extra box generate signals that can be misinterpreted by the sensor control system? Will the sampling rate, dictated by the minicomputer's cycle time, catch the type of errors it is looking for? Can the minicomputer force a system reconfiguration when none is needed? Questions like these assume that a minicomputer implementation of unit 5.6 will work but that problems can occur elsewhere in the system when unit 5.6 does its job.

6.1.2.4 Systematic design

Package design and lower levels of design can use formal methods of decomposition with increasing benefit. The subject of the design gets more specific and the character of the implementation becomes clearer. By the end of package design, all the processes described in the system design should be allocated to hardware, software, or human processors. Global interfaces should be defined resulting in data formats and structures. Processes suitable for database or other general purpose software can be distinguished from those requiring special purpose programs. The project identification and numbering procedures should be established and in use, and the formal design practices and aids should be selected and understood by the team. The style of implementation adopted for package design can be carried all the way through program unit development. The design techniques should therefore be selected to fit in with the procedures and tools planned for general project use. Program design languages will apply to most projects. Techniques that rely on graphic representation will be less prevalent.

Program design language (PDL), as discussed in Chapter 2, should preferably be a subset of the high-order programming language to be used for implementation. Linger, Mills, and Witt [8] describe a process design language that was adopted as a standard by the IBM Federal Systems Division. The environment for FSD programs is not fixed; each customer can specify compatibility constraints, which often dictate the language to be used for programming. As a consequence, FSD creates a PDL subset for the major projects to retain the structured design advantages of PDL while working in the customer's language. The subset is not hard to specify and, in most cases, translators can be written to convert preexisting PDL to the project language subset with manual post-editing. A process design language is attractive because it is readable, understandable (when adequate comments are included), well-structured, and well-suited to on-line use. PDL is used with equal effect by designers on process-oriented or data-oriented tasks.

Semi-graphic methods are widely used in data-oriented design; less so in process-oriented work. Two well-known approaches are those of Jackson and Warnier [9]. Both of these techniques are distinguished by their simplicity. They are based on the principles of computer science but they are presented as straightforward step-by-step methods. Because they are easy to teach and easy to understand, they are widely used in application development shops. Both methods are effective and reliable. They have an excellent track record in data-oriented applications. Jackson specifies that program structure should mirror data structure. Warnier says it a little differently. "Programs, like data and results, are information files." In both cases, a program is a one-for-one mapping to a data structure. Design consists of finding that mapping.

Jackson starts the design process by drawing hierarchy charts of the inputs and output to the program. This is the graphical portion of the process. (The form of the chart corresponds to a context-free grammar but the designer need not know that [10].) The desired program is a series of steps that match the output to the input. In a sense, the Jackson method defines a string of simple programs, each of which takes an input data item and transforms it to an output data item—a sequential string system (see Fig. 1.3). Since most problems are not so simple, Jackson provides rules for reducing complex structures. The end product has a direct relationship between a program and a block in the data structure. As a result, it is relatively easy and economical to maintain a program when inputs or outputs change. The simple programs resulting from a design usually have a single function and are well structured, maximizing binding and minimizing coupling. Simplicity does not imply that the Jackson method breaks down on difficult jobs. On the contrary, it has certain advantages that make it attractive for system design in large problems.

The reduction process that leads to simple programs is called *inversion*. It is analogous to inversion of a database. In information retrieval, documents are often stored in sequence by catalog number. If you know the catalog number, you can go directly to the desired document; however, if you only know the key words describing the subject you are interested in, you would have to examine all documents to find the ones pertinent to your query. To help you in this situation, the database owner can provide an inverted index. The index is stored in sequence by key word and each index entry lists the catalog numbers of all documents related to the key word. Now you can not only locate documents on a given subject but you can combine key words in various ways to locate the answers to quite complicated queries. Inversion in the Jackson method produces programs which, like key words, refer to a single data item but apply to many instances of the data item. The programs can be combined in various ways to build a system [11]. Thus an on-line banking system will require programs to update customer account balances according to the nature of the customer's account (checking account/no interest/$500 minimum balance; NOW account/6 percent interest/$1000 minimum balance; certificate account/15 percent interest/$1000 minimum/withdrawal penalty; loan account/18 percent interest charged/fixed principal and term/late payment penalty). It is possible that one data structure fits all the different account types, although the programs differ. The outputs will also differ in report sequence and information content. When twenty tellers are actively processing customer deposits and withdrawals, there will be twenty program strings interleaved in the system but there will be less than twenty different programs active. Each string is a transaction-processing subsystem. By rearranging the programs and waiting until after the bank closes to start processing, the same programs can be used in a batch processing system.

Warnier starts with a hierarchy chart of the logical outputs. Then he structures the logical inputs, selecting the necessary data from one or more sources. Next, a list of logical sequences is prepared to produce the results from the inputs. The lists are usually presented semi-graphically with each level of the hierarchy grouped behind a bracket and the levels spread from left to right across the page. The graphic style limits what you can put on one page; however, a page of Warnier diagrams should correspond to a module in a well-structured program design (fifty lines). The only structures allowed are iteration and selection. Iteration (do process A once for each employee in the employee file) is controlled to make sure all elements are accounted for. Selection (do either process A or B) is controlled by use of truth tables to make sure all options are accounted for. The logical sequences have corresponding flow charts that are to be coded. Warnier controls the coding process by grouping all allowable instructions into six classes:

- Input (read) instructions
- Branch instructions
- Preparation of branch instructions
- Calculations and associated instructions
- Output instructions and associated housekeeping
- Subroutine calls

Taking one class at a time, he lists the blocks in the flow chart that require that type of instruction. All the reads are listed, followed by all the branching decisions, etc. After the six categories are listed, the lists are sorted to produce a program in execution sequence. This seemingly arbitrary approach has the pragmatic advantage of forcing the programmer to understand the logical sequence before getting wrapped up in the coding details. As a result, users report major reductions in debugging from twelve to fifteen tests per program unit to one or two tests [12]. Warnier's method extends to data-oriented system design and, as does Jackson's method, it interfaces with the languages and operating systems found in typical data processing centers.

6.1.2.5 Package design activities

A critical design review (CDR) is conducted when each package design is completed. Since the package design includes the specifications of program units to enter development, there is enough information available to list the tests necessary to verify the units when they are finished and to test the package at various stages of integration. During package design, the overall system integration and test plan is being written. It should incorporate the full set of tests from initial subpackage integration through all the planned regression tests up to the final integration and test of the release version of the full system [13]. Such a plan cannot be completed until the system implementation plan is available. The implementation, therefore, must also proceed in parallel with package design. The sequence of activities goes something like this:

1. Identify and order long lead time items (usually hardware) defined in system specification.

2. Lay out a tentative schedule of component availability; i.e., delivery dates for hardware, software, and supplies; availability dates for hardware, software, and supplies; availability dates of personnel and services—all estimated on the basis of system specifications.

3. In parallel:
   a. Start package designs either all at once or in a sequence determined by the date they are needed according to the tentative schedule.
   b. Start a test plan in a top-down manner by defining tests that demonstrate adequacy of the system assuming it meets its specification.
   c. Start refining the implementation plan by adjusting the tentative schedule to account for committed availability dates as the commitments are received.

4. Complete a package design CDR.

5. Modify the implementation plan to reflect the actual configuration of the package entering development. Adjust the plan to fit the package implementation proposal in with availability of services and support facilities.

6. Refine the test plan to reflect package interfaces in the package design specification; develop tests to verify that package function, performance, interfaces, and quality meet system requirements.
   a. Refer to the implementation plan for unit completion dates.
   b. Design tests suitable for first meaningful group of units.
   c. Define drivers, environment, and resources needed to run tests.
   d. Coordinate with the implementaion plan to find a date when tests can be run.
   e. Keying off previous test, define next larger subpackage to be tested.

7. Iterate until done.

One step depends on another. All the plans are constantly changing as actual results turn out to be different from estimates. The impact of changes is absorbed by schedule buffers built into the implementation plan. Three types of buffers are found, and usually all three appear in a single plan:

1. Task buffer—Assume that a task will miss its completion date by some amount (weeks or percent of schedule) and add some or all of the estimated variance to the schedule. (This approach is characteristic of activity nets and PERT processing.)

2. Project buffer—Assume that various factors, including planning oversights, will cause problems. Extend the project completion date by 20 to 30 percent of the raw schedule.

3. End date buffer—Assume that problems will be found in the finished product that require some rework or cleanup. Add a fixed amount of time, say three months on a twelve- to twenty-four-month job, to the schedule.

Buffers of the same type were included in the project proposal in order to come up with a reasonable forecast of job completion. The delivery date agreed on at the time is now a firm date, referenced in a contract or an in-house agreement. The buffers cannot be used to change the delivery date. They can only be used to indicate how much time is available for each task and where critical events occur. Knowing this, the project manager can try to arrange the implementation to relax the critical path. Tasks should be scheduled so high-risk activities do not affect each other. Resources for a high-risk task should be associated with resources for several low-risk tasks. If the risky one overruns and uses up its buffer plus part of the project buffer, the others may come in on time and release their buffers, restoring the project buffer pool.

6.1.3 Interface Management

A package designer will have a firm idea as to how the package should be assembled and tested, but the complexity of the system will usually prevent his or her original idea from being carried out. Schedule and resource clashes caused by contention and by missing or incompatible system elements force the implementation plan to be a compromise. The designers who, up to this point, have been well aware of interfaces among packages now begin to realize the importance of interfaces among team members, sequential events, support facilities, etc.

In the sensor control system, it is obvious that some functions depend on special hardware. The End-User Package 8.0 interfaces with a console, 9.0. Package 8.0 will not be fully tested until the console is delivered and attached successfully. Until that time, package 8.0 will have to interface with a simulated package 9.0. The simulator is not complicated; it is no more than a computer program running on the same machine as package 8.0. It intercepts messages addressed to package 9.0 and, after an appropriate delay, returns a response. Correct responses can be interleaved with selected error responses in a planned manner. In this case, the interface problem is easily contained because one person controls the sources of the problem and the mechanism for the solution.

Package 2.0 faces an identical problem in that units 2.1, 2.2, and 2.3 cannot actually talk to each other until they are implemented in hardware *and* all the communication links and the satellite are operating. The solution, again, is to simulate the missing elements. This time, however, there is no simple software solution. The requirement that the elements of the receive/transmit chain be synchronized means that the package 2.0 units must be tested with a simulator that can be precisely timed at the rate of the communications channel. Software simulation cannot always be controlled to such precise timing, particularly at the megabit data rates of satellite channels; therefore, a hardware device is called for. One must be designed and built (or procured) for this purpose. All tests of package 2.0 that depend on precision timing must be postponed until the device is installed and tested. Likewise, final tests of package 3.0 intended to show a certain response when package 2.0 loses synchronism must wait for initial tests of package 2.0. Unlike the first example, the package 2.0 designer may not control the solution mechanism. The hardware simulator may be supplied by another department or another company. Dependencies and interfaces not shown in Fig. 6.5 will have to be added to describe the actual situation.

6.1.3.1 Project file

Coordination of the many events in the implementation plan is further complicated as more and more people join the project and many activities are proceeding in parallel. Coordination and control occupy the bulk of the managers' time. If they are not careful, they will overlook things, even important things such as whether an activity actually meets its objectives. Some administrative tool is needed to help each manager concentrate on key issues without losing control of the details. For this purpose, a project file is useful.

A *project file* documents the system plans, designs, accomplishments, and outstanding problems. It is a reference that includes administrative instructions, standards and practices, and project procedures. As a development plan, the project file represents the growing product from inception to delivery. It is the master coordination and control document. Properly maintained (e.g., current and complete), the project file is a central database for all team members. Since most of them arrive after the early system decisions are frozen, the project file is their primary source for information about how their area of responsibility fits into the overall system.

When package design starts, the project file should already contain basic administrative, technical, and plan data describing the system and the way the project will be run. The structure of the file could be as shown in Fig. 6.7. Here, the hot items that require special management attention are isolated in a prominent way in Section I. Section II contains administrative and procedural material, including instructions on how to build and maintain the project file. It also describes support systems supplied to improve administration. The project file is not necessarily a single-volume book. It

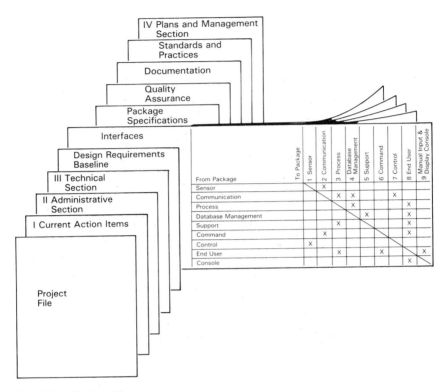

Fig. 6.7 Project file.

may very well be a combination of several volumes and several on-line databases. Section II will describe how to obtain a volume and how to use the on-line resource both to retrieve data and to change stored data.

Requirements and specifications for deliverable end items plus tests are in Section III. The design requirements baseline is included as a chart in which each end item is listed with identification number, name, change level, and responsible party. Changes not yet incorporated in the baseline are also listed with an indication of their status. Entries are indexed by their project identification number. As a result, pages are in hierarchical groupings with related items in the same general place. This is fine for retrieving an item but it is not much help in deciding what to retrieve. An interface section is used to solve the problem. It contains various cross-references such as a map of the system hierarchy, lists correlating specifications with the requirements they satisfy, and charts indicating which project elements interface with each other. A connection matrix for package interfaces is illustrated.

For each end item a detailed description is prepared and maintained throughout the project. At first, the description represents a requirement. Later it becomes an initial specification and then a final specification. By the end of the project, a software Section III contains the deliverable end item itself in the form of a program package. The detail covers everything from functional characteristics to quality objectives, documentation guidelines, and technical standards and practices. An outline of topics suitable for this system specification section is given in Table 6.1. The outline is expanded in Appendix A.

As a management tool, the technical section of the project file includes material describing the work in process as well as material that will be released to the end user. The work-in-process descriptions show the team members what is being built, how it works, the rationale for decisions, and the results of analytical studies and test runs. Standards and procedures instruct the whole team on the software engineering methods to be used and on similar technical procedures that are to be uniform throughout the project. In general, the project file should contain enough historical data to provide an audit trail and support recovery plans. In that way, if the latest technical decisions fail, the team can refer to the project file either to trace the decision process to see where they went wrong or to go back to a previous state of affairs that they knew to be right.

Additional interface information is found in Section IV. It contains plans, schedules, budgets, cost reports, and similar control information (Fig. 6.8). It also has management guidance for decision making, such as how priorities are set and what approvals are required before a decision can be implemented. These data provide the visibility needed for control. Progress against plans, project statistics, change activity, and approval procedures give the project managers a basis for anticipating and acting on problems. Thus a reported delay in Package X can be shown to affect Packages Y and Z by referring to the Section IV activity net. When a package designer makes a technical decision, such as removing the lock on package 9.0, he or she can look at the Interface Matrix in Section II of the project file to see that package 6.0 is affected, but the designer does not have to do anything about it. Management rules in Section IV should close that loophole by requiring the proposed change to be reviewed and concurred with by the affected parties.

The project file formalizes management and technical information flow within the project. It compensates for the fact that an individual team member has a restricted view of the overall project. Managers benefit because the project file organizes the project data so that management issues are highlighted and backup data are readily available. On very large projects, the management benefits are enhanced because key issues are easy to

TABLE 6.1. SYSTEM SPECIFICATION OUTLINE (See Appendix A)

1   General Information
  1.0   Summary
  1.1   Requirements and Specifications
  1.2   Responsibilities
  1.3   Reference Documents
  1.4   Document Control
2   Requirements Summary
  2.1   System Description
  2.2   Design Criteria
  2.3   Acceptance Criteria
3   Functional Characteristics
  3.1   Software End Items
  3.2   Hardware End Items
  3.3   Security
  3.4   Integrity
  3.5   Auditability
4   Performance
  4.1   Performance Statement
  4.2   Performance Management
5   Migration/Coexistence
  5.1   Conversion
  5.2   Use
6   Human Factors
  6.1   Physical Characteristics
  6.2   Task Characteristics
  6.3   Skill and Education of Users
  6.4   Experimentation
7   Rationale
  7.1   Architecture
  7.2   Design
  7.3   Alternatives
  7.4   Follow-on
8   Standards
9   Quality and RAS
  9.1   Implementation
  9.2   RAS Characteristics
  9.3   RAS Support Plan
10 Distribution of Program Packages
  10.1 Initial Release
  10.2 Modifications and Versions
  10.3 Publications
11 Evaluation

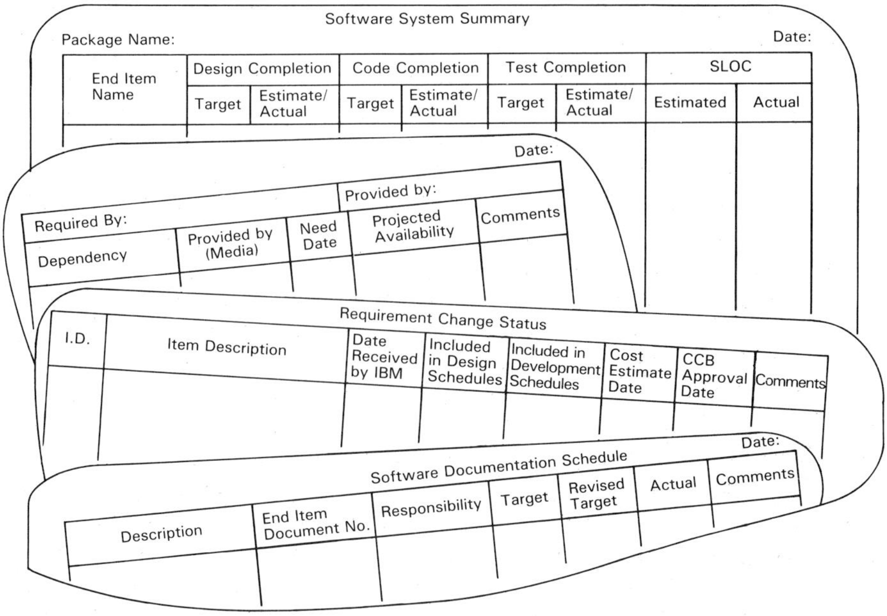

Fig. 6.8   Control visibility.

spot, often in time to avoid problems. In fact, the on-line portions of the project file lend themselves to automatic procedures for identifying interfaces and plan variances that will trigger management action.

6.1.3.2 Interface problems

Nominally, all interfaces are clearly and completely defined in the architecture and design documents. Actually, the interfaces are not all that clear or complete. They are merely as good as they can be given the environment and the fallibility of the project team. Therefore, it is perfectly normal for problems to arise between modules. The manager's challenge is to figure out whether a problem is real and to decide what to do about it. A real interface problem occurs when two modules are totally responsive to specs yet they do not interact properly. That type of problem can occur between people, too. It is caused by:

- Omissions—"Module A reads up to eight files and merges them into one data stream. Module B redistributes the data stream over eight files and returns to A. How do we get the process to stop?"

- Misunderstandings—"But, I say old chap, when I said the Gross Quantity could be a 'billion,' I meant a British billion: a million million. You left room only for a thousand million."

- Poor coordination—"Why are you blaming me for delivering my package late? I have been holding the completed package for a week waiting for you to come get it."

- Errors—"We aimed the rocket in degrees. The specifications should have called for radians. That must be why it crashed."

- Assumptions—"The vendor gave me a range of values for the time between receiving my command and executing it in the hardware. I assumed that I could issue the command anywhere in the range. Actually, it is the exact value for each and every piece of hardware that is important. I must personalize my program by serial number because the hardware has no resilience."

These are real problems because the system will not work as long as they remain. On the other hand, they are pretty easy to recognize. Better specifications and improved coordination/supervision should fix them at the price of time and money.

More troublesome interface problems occur when the interface seems right but the module builders do not want to abide by the interface specs. A common source of such problems is lax management. Instead of enforcing the system architecture from the beginning, the manager lets module builders go their own way. The first time the manager evaluates a module against the spec is at the CDR or later. Meanwhile, the module owner has prepared a strong argument to show that it would be difficult and expensive to change the module to fit the interface. The owner pressures the project manager to make an exception and allow the module to deviate from the spec. "After all," the argument goes, "you don't want to charge the user 30 percent more just because of some arbitrary rule for how many bytes are needed in a header." The weakness of this argument, of course, is that it would not have cost the user anything to get the right header if the module owner had followed the rules in the first place. Furthermore, the user may pay a bundle to get around the deviation when he or she migrates to the next "compatible" system.

The deviation results from letting one member of the project team protect his or her turf at the expense of the others. The process tends to be destructive because it suboptimizes the system and creates friction in the team. Firm and timely management supervision can minimize the need for deviations. Yet, similar interface problems can still occur due to poor estimates or inadequate performance. In these cases, one activity falls behind the plan and impacts all the activities with which it interacts. Firm and timely management is again needed, not to grant a deviation but to adjust the plan. It is usually possible to retain existing interfaces; however, handover dates will slip, additional scaffolding or simulators will be needed, and resources may have to be diverted from leading activities to the laggard. The leaders will be annoyed that they are being penalized to make a poor performer look good. The project manager must be particularly careful to explain to team members that they will benefit more from the success of the project than from the success of their component in a failed project.

One type of interface problem that has no obvious solution is due to poor understanding of the problem itself. People will agree that a problem exists and they will generally describe it in a uniform way, but they will be unable to characterize the problem objectively. As a result, it is never clear what has to be fixed. After fixes are applied, it may be difficult to get a consensus on whether the problem is gone or even whether the situation has improved or worsened. The subjective nature of the problem allows different, valid opinions about the status of the situation. A case in point relates to the voice quality in a communication system. When a computer-controlled digital voice network is attached to the conventional analog telephone system of a common carrier, the sound of the digitized voice is different from its analog counterpart.

In other words, if your office installs a digital local exchange and cuts over to the new service on Tuesday, the phone calls you make on Tuesday will sound different from those you made Monday. What has happened is that the original analog signal of about 4 megahertz is being converted by a computer program to a stream of bits, most likely 64,000 a second, representing the analog wave form. Theoretically, the digital version is equivalent to the analog. Your ear tells you they are different. Some people will say the new sound is better, some worse. You can adjust the digitizing algorithm, or you can tune the dynamic levels of the telephone lines, or you can add in background noise to simulate the faults of the analog system, but you can't get all listeners to agree that the result sounds good. This is a problem at the interface between the end user and the communications subsystem, yet all the modules and the interface specs are valid and the implementation of the system meets spec. The complaints are vague—"It sounds different and I don't like it"—and give you no clues as to how the specifications can be improved. There is even a possibility that the objectionable feature is the "difference." In time, even the complainers may come to like the new system; therefore, if you introduce an improvement after months of operations you will create a new "difference" and be faced with a renewed surge of dissatisfaction. Since there is no clear way to fix such a situation, the recommended approach is to try to identify all such subjective areas early in the design stage. For each area, conduct a series of tests with experimental subjects who can give you their reactions to various design alternatives. These human factors tests give you the opportunity to anticipate end-user attitudes and avoid surprises. They may even show you how to directly address subjective concerns in your design.

6.1.4 Modeling and Simulation

In order to conduct a human factors test, you must construct a model of the environments to be studied. The purpose of the studies is to evaluate alternatives and select a course of action. If the studies are done very early in the project, they are most cost-effective but they are least realistic. At early stages, prior to building any system components, your models are more like stage settings than like the ultimate system environment. Yet, if the studies are postponed until operational system components are available, the project will be so committed to a single design that no alternatives will be feasible. Furthermore, the budget late in a project is depleted and will support neither a major study effort nor a significant change in project direction. The most value is obtained from modeling and simulation when it is begun very early in the project and the models are kept in step with the developing system. Upgrading the study environment is usually much cheaper than building good models from scratch late in the project. This guideline applies to all modeling and simulation, not merely to human factors studies.

Since modeling and simulation are costly, they should be done for a specific purpose. Three common reasons for investing in studies are:

1. *Selection*—evaluating alternatives to reach a decision
2. *Validation*—testing a requirement or a conclusion to verify that assumptions are realistic and that the results obtained are desirable
3. *Understanding*—studying a subject to learn more about it

A simulation should be a controlled experiment with no extraneous activities. In this way, the experiment results should be directly interpretable; the simulation will also cost less.

6.1.4.1 Selection of alternatives

Selection implies that several analyzable alternatives have been suggested to satisfy a requirement and that one or two must be picked for further development. Also implied is a set of criteria for making the choice. As an example, a system has data flowing from a transmission link to a communications controller which is responsible for merging multiple data streams, synchronizing the data flow, encrypting and decrypting, and routing the data to the appropriate storage areas. Three proposed implementations have been drafted (Fig. 6.9). In one, all the functions are built into one box, the CC. The second proposal puts the multiplexing and synchronizing functions in one box, the MX, while everything else is in CCA. The third proposal separates out the crypto function so there are three boxes—MX, ED, CCB. None of the proposals omits anything; all three are functionally equivalent. It is not yet clear that all three work correctly. The criteria for selection must include proof that a proposal is technically sound and, in this example, that it is low in cost over the life of the system.

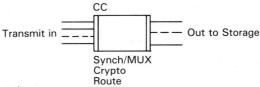

a. Cost Orientation

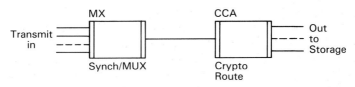

b. Function Orientation

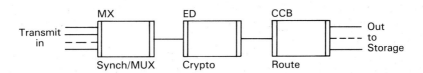

c. Modular Orientation

Fig. 6.9   System implementation selection.

Nothing has been built yet but each proposal gives a description of how the functions will be performed. The device count and program KLOC required for each named module are estimated. A model of each proposal can be structured from this input [14]. Data arriving from a transmission link can be represented by a program that generates data bits at the rate of the link. If the link is a 56kbps link, the model will require an algorithm that generates an output of "1" every $(17.857 + a)k$ microseconds. When $a = 0$ and $k = 1$, there will be 56,000 bits per real second. By setting k, the simulation can be run faster or slower than real time. If k is set to speed up the simulation, it may not be possible to simulate the 56kbps link with software. A hardware simulator might be required. The tolerance, a, is included in the model to represent the variability in real-world transmission links. The link specification will include a nominal value of $a = a_0$. The model should permit a to be much larger than a_0. During simulation, random values of $a \leq a_0$ will represent a normal link, and $a > a_0$ will represent link problems. The use of a wide range of values permits the simulator to compare the robustness of various proposed designs. Link protocols can be modeled to represent address headers and reference bits. With this information, a model of the synchronization component can be programmed. In the simplest sense, synchronization consists of recognizing reference bits at the start of a message, counting microseconds until subsequent bits should arrive, and counting bits until a complete message is received. The simulation, however, has to assume that bits do not arrive on time and maybe not at all. Oddball situations should be studied, such as what happens when a full message is received but there is no empty buffer to hold it. The crypto function also involves synchronization. It matches the bits in a message against a key which itself is modified during the process. When clear text is encoded, the initial value of the key is mapped onto the message. Later, when decoding the received message, the same key must be used in the same position. To do this, you must know where each message starts and you must know there are no missing bits in the message. Once the message is decrypted, it can be read to see what its disposition should be.

The selection process must find out if each proposal works and, if all do, it must rank them by life cycle cost. It is not necessary to model the internal workings of subcomponents. Crypto, for example, is described in terms of a standard algorithm. The implementation of the algorithm will be tested at a later stage of the project. That detail is not important to the selection; however, it is important to model and analyze all interfaces. It may be that proposal one has only one synchronization step in CC which is used for both flow control and crypto. CC cannot get out of synch between those two functions. The other two proposals have a physical interface between MX and the crypto function. They both introduce a new information transfer across a time-sensitive interface. Timing problems are more likely to occur there than in CC. From a cost standpoint, CC might be the cheapest to build. It has only one box and its buffers can be timeshared by all the functions from data link input to output storage. The MX/CCA proposal has two boxes (more hardware frames to buy) and must have buffers in both boxes. MX/ED/CCB again has more of everything with the associated likelihood that when MX is ready to hand something to ED (or ED to CCB) the receiver will be busy, aggravating the timing problems. While these assumptions *may* be true, it is not clear that they are true. Multiple simulation runs with varying inputs will build a set of test results which will show what will happen in each case. It may turn out that each proposal contains enough logic to adjust to all the peculiarities of the environment. Proposal number 3 may be the most costly to build because it contains the most hardware, yet, on a life cycle cost basis, it may be the most attractive because it is more modular. If only 20 percent of the users are expected to need crypto, only 20 percent need to install it in the MX/ED/CCB configuration. The other proposals either charge all users for crypto or include an expensive feature to permit crypto to be plugged in when needed. Likewise, maintenance costs may be lowest for the modular system because the design may permit one component to be serviced without disabling the entire system. The simulation can help evaluate the latter point by showing what will happen if two copies of each proposed system are installed and traffic is switched from the active side to the standby side allowing for switch delay and dropped bits.

In this example, three proposals were evaluated. Each met the same set of functional requirements for nominal values of environmental parameters. The development and construction costs of each proposal were easily calculated from estimates given for hardware and software. A selection based on this readily available data would have picked the CC proposal. Modeling and simulation were required to compare the proposals under extreme conditions of the environment, to trace the data flow across interfaces, and to see if system behavior would be acceptable under various maintenance policies. In order to concentrate on system issues, internal workings of components such as crypto were ignored. The resulting model was neither simple nor cheap. Many simulation runs would be required to test all the interesting environmental conditions, but the total cost compared to the cost of picking a poor solution would be small. Furthermore, the models used for this selection could be retained and used as the basis for other studies as the project proceeds.

6.1.4.2 Validating assumptions

In the process of selecting one of the three proposed implementations, the analysts *validated* each proposal. That is, they determined that specified inputs would produce the expected outputs if each functional element of the design acted the way its paper design said it should. The validation and, indeed, the selection involved measurement and prediction because the problem was time-sensitive.

Measurement in the example is a pseudo-process because the measurements are made on models rather than on operational modules. The results can be both useful and accurate if the modeler is careful. For each identified element of the model, an execution rate is determined. The rate can be expressed as a constant, as it might be for a program that always takes the same number of steps from start to finish. The value of the constant is estimated by the designer of that program or, if necessary, by the modeler. The estimate may be wrong, but the fact that the program execution time is invariant should be valid. If this element looks important, several simulation runs can be planned with different estimated values for the constant to see what effect it has. Some programs have several possible constant modes: k_1 cycles if branch 1 is taken; k_2 cycles otherwise. Here, an estimate must be made of the probability that the branch will occur. During simulation, when a token representing an input to this program arrives, the token is placed in a holding position for k_1 units of time for x percent of the occurrences and k_2 units of time for $(1 - x)$ percent of the occurrences. If enough is known about the program to say the distribution of its execution time follows some more complicated algorithm, the algorithm is invoked when the token arrives. The same simulation technique applies to generating events. Thus a digital communications line was simulated in the selection example by issuing a token representing a bit on the line every so many microseconds. After the first bit/token was released to the model of the synchronizer, the time on the simulated clock was marked. A delay was then calculated by selecting a value for a (assuming it varies according to a probabilistic distribution) and doing $(17.857 + a)k$. The delay added to the marked time gives the time for issuing the next bit/token. The process of issuing tokens is automated by the simulator program itself. The modeler deals in events, delays, execution times, routes, etc., and leaves all the timing calculations and token management to the support software. By requesting various reports, the modeler can have the support software measure the time it takes for a token to pass through the system, averaged over many trials. The best and worst times can be found. The distribution of the results can be plotted. Queuing data can be used to spot bottlenecks. Unsuspected behavior such as feedback and looping can be detected. Resource use can be observed as can the blocking effect of inadequate resources. All of this information is based on measuring the behavior of the model.

For a simple validation exercise, it may be sufficient to show that for a sample of data within the input data domain, all results were within the output range and were obtained within the allowed time (according to the simulator's clock). More often, it is necessary to predict what would happen if the environment does not match the specifications or if the model of the system is intentionally modified. *Prediction* is generally done by running multiple simulations of a measurable model. In the simplest case, a model of an existing system has been shown to behave like the real system with performance data within 5 to 10 percent of actual experience. The effect of a change to the operational system can be accurately predicted by studying the model. The element to be changed is replaced by a model of the proposed change and a number of simulations are run. The measurement obtained will depend on the accuracy of the estimates of the new element but they will be reliable enough for decision making. Such predictive simulation is widely used in managing the operations of real-time systems. In the Sensor Control System, an orbiting satellite can only be controlled when it is passing over an earth station. It may be in radio range from ten to twelve minutes. These minutes must be used carefully since a mistake may not be correctable for a full orbit. To protect the system, all the changes planned for a pass-over can be simulated first. If the controller plans to reorient the satellite to view a new area, the simulator can "execute" the commands and show the controller what the satellite will actually see in the new position. The simulation may show that the controller's command to view California actually points the sensors at Oregon. Both operator errors and system eccentricities can be caught by simulation. The same technique applies to control of very complex procedures. In a communications network where there may be thousands of terminals periodically interconnected, the impact of a network change may be too complicated for an operator to analyze. Simulation in this case validates a change by quickly and accurately doing a comprehensive network restructure incorporating logical tests of the new layout which show whether all desired links actually exist. Predictive simulation is also used for calibrating a process. Software vendors can develop useful marketing data about system performance by formulating a set of benchmark jobs. A series of runs can determine the mean running time of each benchmark. Run-to-run differences can be analyzed to learn how sensitive the model is to changes in each control variable. With this information, it is possible, in a sales situation, to compare a particular user's needs to the appropriate benchmark data.

   With capabilities for representation, measurement, and prediction, a project team can try out some of its design ideas by using models. In air traffic control, the system design assumes that human controllers will interact with the data-processing system according to well-developed procedures. To validate that the system would work under the assumed conditions, at least three levels of simulation are required. The first level, which can be run on one machine, faster than real-time, is used to verify that the data-processing subsystem has been put together correctly. It can also be used to establish a base of system performance data. The next level requires two machines. One represents the data-processing subsystem. The second represents the environment with human controllers. Synchronized and running faster than real time, the two machines process a script. The environment simulator generates air traffic. The data-processing machine processes the traffic as it is acquired through simulated radars. Output displays are prepared and passed back to the environment machine which simulates human operator delay and looks up the appropriate procedure to issue as the controller's command. This study shows that the procedures lead to the desired results and that there are no timing anomalies in the system design. (Note that the exercise can be performed on one processor with a virtual machine operating system.) The third level of simulation is structured to test the design against actual human behavior. In this case, the simulation runs in real-time—no speed up. There is a data-processing subsystem, a traffic generator, and a human controller subsystem with real people doing the controller's tasks. The test subjects need not be trained controllers since their role is simply to follow a script. Now when traffic is displayed, the "controller" looks at the script to see what action to take and acts. The simulation will show whether the design assumptions were right regarding controller response time. It will identify controller actions that are physically difficult or awkward. It will point out action sequences that can be done on time individually but that interact to upset an assumption. The simulation will also turn up procedures that are so poorly written that when the controllers follow the script their actions are wrong.

6.1.4.3 Understanding the system

Three levels of simulation validate the design but do not necessarily prove that the design is a good one. Certainly a group of housewives following a script does not prove that an air traffic control system is totally safe. A fourth level of simulation is needed to *understand* operationally realistic situations. At this level a real-time simulation is conducted with trained controllers. A wide variety of situations are generated in order to see whether the procedures are suitable, whether the controllers can follow the procedures under stress, and whether the system design accommodates the effects of controllers talking to each other and to pilots. The key to this type of simulation is that the human is an alternate source of system control. The system design takes this into account but assumes that the scope of human control is defined by standard operating procedures and training. This is an overly narrow assumption. The very reason the human is in the loop is to rely on human judgment and initiative to resolve problems the system designers cannot anticipate. Therefore, the design assumptions must allow for controller actions outside the SOP. To find out what the character, frequency, and outcome of such actions will be, operationally realistic simulations are run.[6] The results are studied to determine what controllers are able to do, what they choose to do, how successful their choices are, how unsuccessful choices can be avoided through new SOP or training, and how the system should be changed to raise its overall value.

Understanding improves with time. Early in a project, models are not very realistic except where they represent existing systems. Models get better if they are kept up-to-date with the project activity. If the purpose of model-

6. Models of program systems may occasionally interact with scale models of a physical environment; e.g., a sensor control system may be tested with a terrain model. DeLong [15] warns that scale models viewed by human subjects can lead to time distortion in a simulation. A subject of normal height in a full size environment can estimate time accurately. When viewing a scale model, the subject will estimate time according to the formula: $E = xT$ where T is the real elapsed time and x is the reciprocal of the linear scale of the model. With a $1/12$ scale model, five minutes will seem like sixty minutes to the observer. The observer's height is a factor—a child will estimate a smaller E than a full-sized adult.

ing and simulation is to understand the operational environment, a long-term commitment is therefore required. In a phased project, the commitment is justified by the fact that knowledge acquired in one phase can be applied to the next phase. In most operator-controlled systems there is the added justification that the final model can be converted into an operational training environment. New operators can be trained and current operator skills can be maintained by having them operate the model loaded with a script that presents them with problems to solve. The problems may represent situations that are so rare that they may never come up on the real system, but they are so critical that, if they occur, the controllers must know exactly how to react.

There are exceptions to the long-term commitment. Lots of small problems come up that should be understood. A process flow model of a proposed database manager interacting with a commercial operating system may help in the layout of disk file areas. The model could be written and simulated with APL. Prompts and help messages in an interactive system could be based on what you learn by having typical users react to various design options rigged up in a demonstration package. Here, the model can be as simple as a set of charts representing display screen formats.

6.1.4.4 Modeling "don'ts"

Modeling and simulation should not be used as:

- Routine exercises required to fill out the project file
- Demonstrations that well-known techniques will work
- Timing measurement tools in simple systems where timing can be estimated by observation or where timing is not important

Each of these "don'ts" can be violated for good reason. For example, in Phase 1 of a multiphase project, it may be a wise standard operating procedure to create a model of every system component in anticipation of using the models in later, more complex phases. Demonstration models are valueless if their purpose is to tell you what you already know. However, models can be justified in at least two demonstration situations. The first involves demonstration for sales purposes; the second involves operator training. In neither case is the project team trying to learn from the simulation. They have decided, though, that a demo model is the best aid for showing others how the system will perform. In the case of simulation as a measurement tool, some vendors find that even simple systems use up too many people-hours when a large number of timing and throughput analyses are required. They use a simulator as a productivity aid. It permits them to sell competitively by having each of many customers submit job specs and get back a detailed and precise estimate of how the job will run on the vendor's package.

Do not use just anyone as a test subject. Test subjects should be selected who can meet the requirements of the simulation run. If the only requirement is the ability to follow instructions, many people will qualify; some will not. The subject must be able to read and comprehend requests for a response or a control action. Consider the situation where the purpose of a software system is to support computer assisted instruction (CAI). The system design will depend heavily on the audience. Adults using CAI for self-teaching, remedial training, or vocational guidance can be expected to understand most displays and instructions written on a screen. The same is true of secondary school students, although an engineer may design messages that are misunderstood whereas a secondary school teacher should know how to get that message across. Grade school children may not even be able to read. Graphic messages may be required for them. In one experiment, pre-school children were used as test subjects only to learn that they lacked the strength to depress the keys on the input device. The right test subject is the person for whom the material under test was designed. Adults should not be used to study child behavior. Unskilled people should not be used in place of specialists where the quality of specialist support is of interest. Experienced programmers should not be used to simulate unskilled or casual users of an interactive programming system. The last case is the most common error in software human factors analysis. Rather than going out to find a typical user sample, the designer decides that "I can speed up the job by doing the experiments myself." The result is that the designer is satisfied but the system does not satisfy the intended user.

In summary, modeling and simulation can support measurements and predictions that help you make decisions. An early investment maintained throughout the project will provide quantitative data for comparing alternatives, for validating decisions, and for understanding the system. A good model is a simple but accurate representation of system interfaces and module behavior. The answers to specific questions are found by running several simulations to obtain a stable, repeatable characterization of system behavior. Economy is achieved by using simulation tools and by omitting unnecessary refinements. Realism is achieved by using real components where they exist and by having trained operational personnel participate in real-time simulations [16]. Economical realism is achieved by starting the modeling activity in the project definition stage and keeping it current throughout the project.

6.2 DEVELOPMENT

The focus of attention during design is on the system. Its structure and functions are developed on a unitary basis insofar as possible. Each new decision in considered in the light of the entire system. To accomplish this, the design team is kept small. Communication within the small team gives all team members the same system-level knowledge and everyone has a common view of the system. Inevitably, the focus shifts so that during development, management attention is mainly devoted to coordination and component evaluation. Once the project outgrows the intimacy of a small team, the individual team members will no longer have a common view of the system. At the least, their view will be colored by the characteristics and needs of the component they are working on. As they build and optimize their component, they gradually deviate from the original system. Project managers are responsible for controlling the behavior of the individual developers so that the end product is the desired system.

6.2.1   Transition from Design to Development

To preserve the original system, the project team documents it in the Project File. Then they use the Project File as the reference standard for development. It is a constantly changing reference, yet it is the only embodiment of the system that survives the transition from design to development. Managers who sat down with the design team and talked about the system as a whole, must now manage primarily from the information in the Project File and in periodic reports and reviews. Virtually all the input during the program development stage will relate to individual programs and to subpackages. Much of the development activity is not intended to be delivered to the user, yet it must be managed with the same care as deliverables. Managers must learn to analyze information in order to determine whether problems are confined to one program or affect larger system components. Problems in a single program, whether due to the implementation of the program or to faults in its support, can be directly addressed by the implementer. Problems in larger components suggest design errors and may require a reiteration of the top-down design. Since this is a time-consuming process, it is important to know that the problem is in the system and not in the support. Design control is exercised by the technical staff and the configuration control board throughout the project to recognize genuine system impacts and deal with them.

The plans and management section of the Project File supplements the technical section by showing when things happen and what resource, support, or interface dependencies affect the outcome. One possible format for this section of a Project File is given in Fig. 6.10.[7] The earliest version of the plan is a system level plan. In the illustration, it is broken into a development section, resource and financial sections, a support plan, and a performance plan. At the system level, the system structure from the Technical Section will be cross-indexed to the work breakdown structure and, if a

---

7. No single recommendation for Project File format is given in this book. While it is important to follow uniform procedures within a project and within an organization, it is not important that all projects or organizations follow the same procedure.

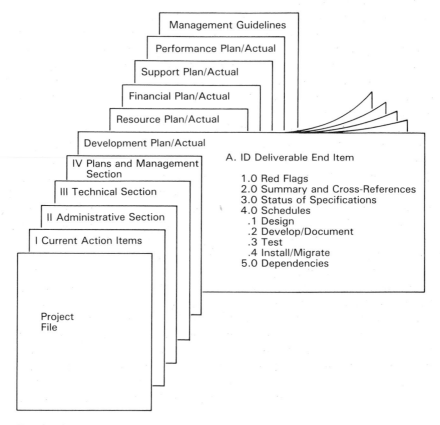

Management Guidelines

Performance Plan/Actual

Support Plan/Actual

Financial Plan/Actual

Resource Plan/Actual

Development Plan/Actual

IV Plans and Management
Section

III Technical Section

II Administrative Section

I Current Action Items

Project
File

A. ID Deliverable End Item

1.0 Red Flags
2.0 Summary and Cross-References
3.0 Status of Specifications
4.0 Schedules
  .1 Design
  .2 Develop/Document
  .3 Test
  .4 Install/Migrate
5.0 Dependencies

Fig. 6.10   Project file—Plans and management.

separate accounting work package numbering scheme is used, to the accounting breakdown. Schedule dependencies in the form of critical path analyses and precedence charts will be shown for all known components and activities. Resources in terms of people, machines, facilities, etc., will be quantified and scheduled as well as can be done at the system level. Budgets will be given with appropriate contingencies. The separate Support Plan and Performance Plan isolate the work to be done by groups outside the direct chain of command of the project manager. Once isolated, these plans can be the basis for negotiating with the supporting groups and getting their commitment to the plan.

The next level of detail expands Section IV by incorporating a set of plans for each deliverable end item or support activity. This should be an input from the manager responsible for the end item. The initial plan was prepared by the project manager and the small group of people working on design and planning. The end item plans should be prepared by the developer.

His or her submission says, "I gave due consideration to what you asked for; I accounted for all the requirements and constraints as I understand them; I applied the best ability of my team; now, here is what I intend to do." Even when that developer was one of the original designers, the detailed plan may impact the system design. In Fig. 6.10 a five-part development plan is outlined:

1.0 Red Flags—As the job proceeds, any item requiring attention from higher management or peer management is flagged by an entry in this section. Usually updated weekly, the manager's goal is to erase a flag as fast as possible by resolving the issue. (Each part of Section IV may have a similar red flag report; the more important items are tracked at the project level in Section I of the Project File.) When a red flag shows any type of problem with a peer group, it raises a suspicion that an interface design problem may exist.

2.0 Summary and Cross-References—This section describes the end item and points to other documents that relate to the end item. Each reference should be checked to make sure there are no new interfaces being created by this end item.

3.0 Status of Specifications—The current list of baseline specs plus changes (approved or pending) that are addressed by this end item may disclose redundancies and omissions when summed over the system.

4.0 Schedules—The schedules for an end item start out showing target dates based on the assumption that every event in the system plan occurs on time. Weekly updates will show actual activity completion dates moving around. Slippage suggests, first, that component implementation has slipped and corrective action should be taken by the developer. A second implication is that some external dependency prevented the developer from meeting a target. If so, the implication should be confirmed in 5.0. A third implication is that there is some technical obstacle. The obstacle should be reported by raising a red flag. In many cases, the obstacle can be traced to some peer group's failure to meet plan. Other cases turn out to be design errors or oversights which must be reprocessed through design control.

5.0 Dependencies—Since interaction is the name of the game at the system level, it follows that no end item developer is totally independent. A list of dependencies shows that both parties to an interaction recognize their mutual responsibilities. Dependencies in a plan are like brackets in a program—they occur in matching pairs. Failure to find the matching entry exposes a potential problem. Usually, the problem is due to poor coordination; occasionally, it represents a design flaw.

Everyone should have access to relevant information; yet it need not be equally open to all. The cost data, for example, may be restricted to authorized managers and accountants. For each partition of the file there ought to be both passive and active procedures for letting the authorized users get at what they need. Passive procedures consist of periodic updates that keep the file current. (Updates should stand out. Margin marks can be used to indicate the latest changes. All pages should be dated.) A quick review of the material related to one's area of responsibility will show if anything has been modified. Some people will not refer to the Project File as often as they should. Active procedures alert them that someone else is doing things they should be aware of. Passive use of the Project File gives the user a good understanding of his or her relation to the rest of the project. The active procedures ensure that the person does something about it.

Entries in the Project File are, in a sense, historical. They represent a decision, a change, a new piece of information describing status, content, or intent. Some balance must be struck between the amount of information in the file and the effectiveness of the file. The general rule is to include the minimum amount of information that conveys all the necessary *shared* knowledge of the project. Project managers draw out the required information by personal contact, scheduled reviews, and automated data collection as well as routine programmer reports. In a large project, the extent of the effort to manage internal communications is significant. Special work packages are set up to account for the activity as shown in a work breakdown of the Sensor Control System (Fig. 6.11). In this structure, work is assigned to departments. The deliverable sensor control system consists of the nine packages of Fig. 6.6b. These packages have been assigned to a development organization, SC3. Software packages have been separated from pure hardware, as in packages 4.0 and 9.0, where a subpackage has been delegated to the hardware side of the house. The development teams will use the services of a computer center, SC2A1, and a central laboratory, SC2A2. An independent organization, SC4, has been given responsibility for integrating the packages into a system, testing the system, and releasing a qualified system to the field. A training and installation group will help get the system into field operation. Field operations will continue indefinitely. The nucleus of the permanent operation will be formed by 2C2A4 and 2C4A.

The work breakdown structure covers dissimilar activities of varying duration in several organizations. Project management keeps it all sorted out. A correspondence between the work breakdown and accounting work packages is desirable since budget status affects system decisions and may throw light on the technical status of individual components. Headcount for the people who set up the data management system, the cost of managing system data, and the activities related to processing and interpreting the data are explicitly covered in the work breakdown, box SC1B1. Similarly, other project control activities are called out as work to be done.

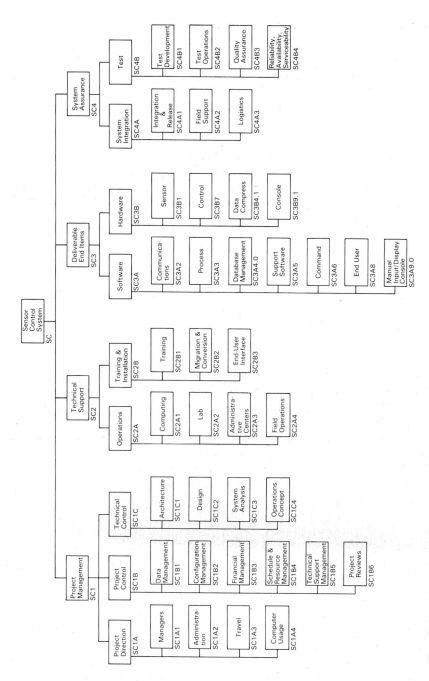

Fig. 6.11   Sensor control system—Work breakdown structure.

Treated this way, the control activities will be staffed, included in the budget, and assimilated in schedules. Lucy Lee, in the activity net example of Chapter 2, found out that she had to be explicit about project reviews in order to arrive at any believable estimate of project completion. Including such activities in the work breakdown structure is a good way to bring them to the attention of the project managers. The Sensor Control System work breakdown also illustrates the opportunity to use work packages to highlight sensitive or cross-organizational matters. SC1A3 covers travel; it gives the project manager direct control of the travel budget. Local travel control will be delegated to individual department managers, but long distance trips, to earth station sites for instance, will be approved by the project manager personally as a economy measure. Control over computer use has also been reserved, more to avoid contention than to save money. The shared computer resource must be carefully scheduled to permit program developers to get the service they need in spite of the fact that the facilities will be dedicated to hardware tests and system simulations for significant blocks of time.

Procedurally, all the work to be done has now been assigned. The next step is for the department managers to validate the assignments. The individuals or small teams will get very little detailed direction while they are doing their tasks. Therefore, the manager must be certain that they are starting out correctly.

- Double check the documents describing the assignment. Are they current? Do they agree with the Project File?
- Discuss the assignment. Does the implementer understand what is to be done?
- Discuss methodology. Is the implementer up to speed on the standards and practices adopted for the department? Will they be followed?
- Coordinate across interfaces. Are there any interface problems to be solved before implementation starts?
- Agree on the implementation plan. Obtain the implementer's commitment.

6.2.2   Control

At this point, there should be a mutual understanding between the implementer and the manager regarding work scope and work plan. Included in the understanding is a schedule of reviews whereby the manager will assess status and act to resolve problems in the task or in the project. Of course, management control should be anticipatory as well as reactive. It is better to prevent problems than to have to resolve them. Standards and practices are adopted for this purpose. When everyone follows uniform procedures, managers are confident that minor errors will be caught and fixed by each individual and that remaining problems will be easily recognized by reviewers.

6.2.2.1 Standards and practices

Large software organizations are finding that the value of one set of uniform procedures for the whole shop justifies a significant investment in training and procedure development [17]. The primary payoff is the ability to initiate a new project with minimum startup, cost, or delay. People are more flexible as well; they can join a project team at any point in the schedule and recognize familiar procedures. The trend in large organizations is to initially build a set of policies and procedures for managing the system life cycle at a high level; then they proceed to implement procedures at a more detailed level. The early policies are directed at team activities and cross-organizational coordination. The later policies cover the activities of individuals, concentrating on issues of quality, productivity, and communication. The organization usually has an existing body of corporate policies. Software policies can be merged into that structure. The result will be a smooth introduction of new guidelines in a familiar framework.

    TRW [18] took that approach by creating a category 3.4.0, of software development policies (Fig. 6.12) within their overall project management

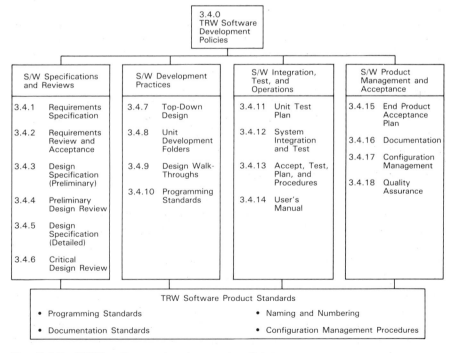

Fig. 6.12 TRW software development policies.
E. A. Goldberg, ''Applying Corporate Development Policies,'' *Software Development: Management.* The 71st Infotech State of the Art Conference, Maidenhead, England: Infotech, Ltd., 1980.

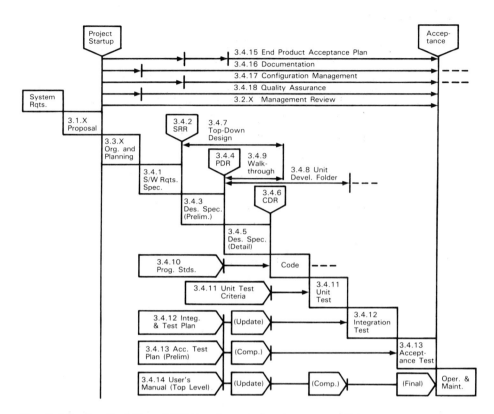

Fig. 6.13 Applicability of TRW software development policies.
E. A. Goldberg, "Applying Corporate Development Policies," *Software Development Management.* The 71st Infotech State of the Art Conference. Maidenhead, England: Infotech, Ltd., 1980.

series, 3.0. The policies are kept simple and specific, although very detailed product standards supplement the policies where appropriate. A glossary establishes a single definition of each stage of the life cycle as laid out by TRW, permitting the software development policies to be keyed to the life cycle. As shown in Fig. 6.13, each policy applies to a specified span of the project. At appropriate review points (as given in the 3.2.0 series of policies), the project manager can expect to see the benefits of the uniform procedures.

The Federal Systems Division of IBM has a similar method of managing software engineering. The approach is somewhat different because FSD has a long history of emphasis on the details of software design and development. Thus their policies governing individual implementation activities grew in parallel with policies for project management. A massive training program was conducted which taught a graduated sequence of courses (Fig. 6.14) based on the results of years of R&D and actual experience. All programmers and analysts completed the Systematic Programming Workshop. A selected subset went on to Systematic Design (SDW). A subset of those who were designers or architects took an Advanced Design course. Managers went from the SDW course to a Software Management Workshop [19]. They learned mathematically sound programming practices which, when mapped to the FSD version of the life cycle, provided a uniform policy for software development within the division. If you were to pick up three or four FSD proposals or development plans for software deliverables, they would all contain the same basic description of software engineering methodology and management, modified as necessary to satisfy the customer. As indicated in Table 6.2, the practices cover the technology of systematic programming plus the procedures for managing the technology. The practices (D-P) are augmented by standards (D-S) for specific languages or tools or formats. There are also a couple of guideline bulletins (D-B) where a uniform method is appropriate but there can be broad leeway in the way it is applied. A project manager may substitute a different design language for the PDL described in D-B3-7099 005 as long as it has the features required to support systematic programming.

In the case of PDL, the FSD bulletin gives a complete syntax for a process design language. The character of the technology practices ranges from broad concepts in areas of design to specific instructions in how to apply structured programming when using various high-order languages; from generalized procedures related to simulation to specific rules for using FSD automated cost accounting systems. The software design practices, Table 6.3, form a hierarchy in which the guidelines for individual programmers represent stepwise refinements on the broader practices for system level design [20]. In some cases, the practice is a combination tutorial and adviser. The FSD practice for Software Interface Specification Management, Fig. 6.15, reminds the reader to be thorough when specifying interfaces; then it draws a picture of what kinds of interfaces should be considered. What it does not do is set down firm rules for interface specification language or format or architecture. Decisions in these areas are left to the programmer. This example is typical of the structure of a practice. It also covers the management aspects of applying the practice. The second section describes the practice in more detail, sets requirements for applying the practice, and outlines the results expected from the practice. Additional sections can be added, as necessary, to explain difficult material, to justify nonobvious guidelines, or to give examples. The best practices are short, clear documents that are specific within their scope but leave complete freedom-of-action elsewhere. This is most easily achieved in practices that affect individuals' behavior and most difficult when organizational behavior is affected.

TABLE 6.2. SOFTWARE ENGINEERING PRACTICES—APPLICABILITY IN IBM FSD LIFE CYCLE

APPLICABILITY MATRIX

LIFE CYCLE ACTIVITY → WORK TO BE DONE (COST COMPONENT)

SOFTWARE ENGINEERING MANAGEMENT ↓ — FSD STANDARDS AND PRACTICES

FSD Standards and Practices	System Definition				Software Design					Software Development			Software System Test		System/Acceptance Test		Operational Support			General Support				
	Software Requirements Definition	Software System Description	Software Development Planning	Engineering Change Analysis	Functional Design	Program Design	Test Design	Software Tools	Design Evaluation	Module Development	Development Testing	Problem Analysis and Correction	Software System Test Procedures	Software Integration and Test	System Test Support	Acceptance Test Support	System Operation Support	Training	Site Deployment Support	Project Management	Configuration Management/Control	Software Cost Engineering	Quality Assurance	Administration Centers/Technical Pubs
Advanced Design	X	X																						
Systematic Design																								
D-P 3-7099 003 Modular Design		X			X	X	X		X				X											
D-P 3-7099 004 Data Design		X			X	X	X		X				X											
Systematic Programming																								
D-B 3-7099 005 Process Design Language (PDL)	X	X			X	X	X	X	X	X	X	X	X	X									X	
D-P 3-7099 800 Logical Expression	X	X			X	X			X	X		X												
D-P 3-7099 801 Program Expression					X	X	X	X	X	X		X												
D-P 3-7099 802 Program Design					X	X	X	X	X	X		X												
D-P 3-7099 803 Program Design Verification										X		X												

Category	Document	Title													
Code Management	D-P 3-7099 804	Programming Language	X	X				X	X					X	X
	D-P 3-7099 805	Coding Standards and Conventions	X	X				X	X					X	X
	D-P 3-7099 806	Computer Product Support Software	X		X	X			X						
	D-P 3-7099 807	Builds and Controls		X	X	X	X	X	X	X	X	X		X	X
	D-P 3-7099 808	Development Environment		X	X	X	X	X	X	X	X				X
	D-P 3-7016 004	Listing Commentary			X	X		X	X						
	D-P 3-7099 006	Simulation Software	X					X	X	X	X	X			
	D-P 3-7099 007	Processor Simulation Software						X			X				
	D-P 3-7099 008	Interface Simulation Software					X	X	X	X	X				
	D-P 3-7099 009	Environment Simulation Software					X	X	X	X	X				
Integration Engineering	D-P 3-7099 010	Computer System Simulation Software	X				X		X		X				
	D-P 3-7099 011	Application System Simulation Software	X					X	X		X	X			
	D-P 3-7099 811	Software Integration Methodology		X	X	X		X	X	X		X		X	
	D-P 3-7099 812	Incremental Software Development	X	X	X	X	X	X	X	X		X	X	X	X
	D-P 3-7099 813	Software Interface Specification Management	X	X	X	X	X	X	X	X	X	X		X	X
Top-Down Programming	D-B 3-7001 024	Coding in a Virtual Storage Computer			X	X	X		X	X					
	D-S 3-7010 991	Top-Down Programming Implementation	X	X	X	X	X	X	X	X		X			X

TABLE 6.2.   CONTINUED

APPLICABILITY MATRIX / LIFE CYCLE ACTIVITY	System Definition				Software Design					Software Development			Software System Test		System/Acceptance Test		Operational Support			General Support				
WORK TO BE DONE (COST COMPONENT) → FSD STANDARDS AND PRACTICES / SOFTWARE ENGINEERING MANAGEMENT	Software Requirements Definition	Software System Description	Software Development Planning	Engineering Change Analysis	Functional Design	Program Design	Test Design	Software Tools	Design Evaluation	Module Development	Development Testing	Problem Analysis and Correction	Software System Test Procedures	Software Integration and Test	System Test Support	Acceptance Test Support	System Operation Support	Training	Site Deployment Support	Project Management	Configuration Management/Control	Software Cost Engineering	Quality Assurance	Administration Centers/Technical Pubs
Structured Programming Language Requirements																								
D-S 3-9015 990 Structured Programming in FORTRAN										X														
D-S 3-9025 990 Structured Programming in COBOL										X														
D-S 3-9035 990 Structured Programming in PL/I										X														
D-S 3-9099 990 Structured Programming in JOVIAL J3										X														
D-S 3-9099 992 Structured Programming in CMS-2Y										X														

538

Category		1	2	3	4	5	6	7	8	9
Tools	D-S 0-4010 002 Software Support Tools	X		X	X	X	X	X		X
	D-S 3-7099 990 Programming Support Library System	X		X	X	X	X	X	X	X
Management	D-S 0-4010 001 Software Development Plan	X X		X	X	X	X		X	X
	D-P 3-7099 012 Design to Cost	X X		X					X	
	D-P 3-7099 013 Technical Reviews	X X		X	X				X	X
	D-P 3-7099 809 Software Cost Management	X X							X	
	D-P 3-7099 810 Software Program Management	X		X	X				X	X
	D-S 3-7099 991 Software Development Measurement	X					X		X	
	D-S 3-7099 992 Formal Inspections During Software Development	X X		X	X		X		X	X
Glossary	D-P 0-2004 008 Glossary, Software Engineering Practices	X X X X		X X X X	X X X X	X X	X X	X X X X	X X X X	X X X

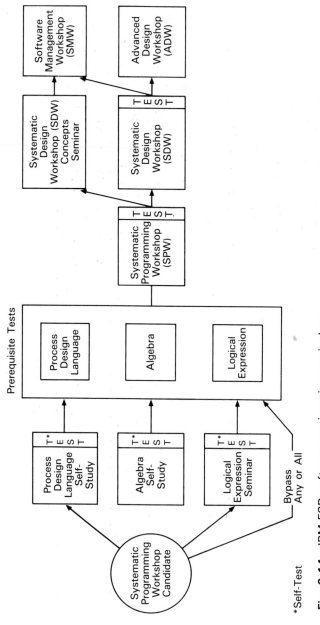

Fig. 6.14 IBM FSD software engineering curriculum.
D. O'Neill, "The Management of Software Engineering. Part II: Software Engineering Program." *IBM Systems Journal* 19, no. 4 (1980).

TABLE 6.3.   IBM FSD SOFTWARE DESIGN PRACTICES

Advanced design practices	
Software system specification	Defines a process based on state machines for creating a specification as the cornerstone documentation of a software system.
Real-time design	Defines a stagewise process for designing asynchronous software to achieve correct concurrent operation, with optimization to meet real-time processing requirements.

Systematic design practices	
Data design	Specifies the use of abstract data objects and operations in a high-level design framework.
Modular design	Defines techniques for designing synchronous software systems, based on state machines and design modules.

Systematic programming practices	
Logical expression	Prescribes mathematics-based techniques for precise expression and reasoning that apply to all phases of software development.
Program expression	Defines control, data, and program structures for recording program designs.
Program design	Specifies a process of stepwise refinement for recording structured program designs.
Program design verification	Prescribes function-theoretic techniques for proving the correctness of structured programs.

From R. C. Linger, "The Management of Software Engineering. Part III: Software Design Practices," *IBM Systems Journal* 19, no. 4 (1980).

Software Interface Specification Management	D-P 3-7099 813
	1978-07

Applicability: All Business Areas in FSD	*Manual: 33-09*

Introduction

1.1 SCOPE

This practice defines a minimum set of procedures for the specification and control of software/software, software/hardware, and software/person interfaces in a system development.

1.2 OBJECTIVE

The objective of this practice is to establish minimum procedures for the management of software interface specifications to support the phased integration methodology for system development. Through the use of this practice, software development shall be performed with increased reliability, manageability, productivity.

1.3 APPLICATION

This practice applies to any new FSD project, for which software implementation is a project element and explicit software interface specifications are required. Figure 1 suggests the potential interfaces required in systems, typical to the FSD business area. This practice requires specification and management of software interfaces when the following criteria apply:

- The interfacing elements are different in type, that is software, hardware, or people;
- The hardware and/or software controlling the interface are under concurrent development;
- The hardware and/or software controlling the interface shall be separately developed, where separation is either contractual, geographical or organizational in nature.

This practice identifies the minimum set of interfaces which require explicit specification and provides guidelines on the procedures required to manage the specifications. The formality with which the stated criteria shall be applied shall be dependent on contractual requirements, project organizational structure and the criticality of particular interfaces to the total system development effort.

1.4 AUTHORIZATION

This practice has been approved by the FSD Software Technology Steering Group and the FSD Standards Manager.

1.5 DEVIATION PROCEDURE

Approval to deviate from this practice must be obtained from the appropriate Business Area Software Executive Manager.

1.6 EFFECTIVE DATE

July 1978.

1.7 ORIGINATING AREA AND RESPONSIBILITY

This document is the joint responsibility of: 1) the appropriate Software Engineering and Technology Coordinator and 2) the Software Technology Steering Group.

1.8 PROPERTY STATEMENT

This document is the property of IBM. Its use is authorized only for proposal responses, contract performance, and internal software development work for IBM. All questions must be referred to the FSD Purchasing Office.

Fig. 6.15 IBM FSD Software Practice example.

Software Interface Specification Management	D-P 3-7099 813
	1978-07

| *Applicability: All Business Areas in FSD* | *Manual: 33-09* |

Practice

2.1 SOFTWARE INTERFACE DETERMINATION

Interface specification shall be accomplished as part of the software specification and design process. The software design process decomposes the system requirements into discrete functions, and organizes a set of hierarchically related modules to implement these functions. The identified and output requirements represent the potential set of interfaces for which explicit specification may be required.

The basis for selecting, from this total set, those interfaces for explicit specification is governed by the three criteria described in section 1.3.

The detailed data descriptions to be included in the interface specification are determined through a stepwise refinement process that is conducted as an integral part of the software design stepwise refinement.

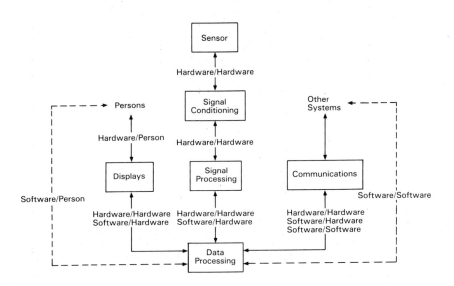

Fig. 6.15   Continued.

Cost management falls in the latter category. Efficiency usually demands centralized data-processing systems for cost accounting. Cost analysis requires aggregation across departments and transaction traces among departments. At some point, indirect costs must be allocated to individual departments or work packages to learn the true cost of an activity. The practice that describes all these requirements is often the bulkiest one in the project file. Instead of saying, "Design according to the following criteria . . . ," this practice says, "Let me explain all of the centralized systems used to track your time and expense. That will help you understand why you must fill out the forms and submit the reports listed in Section 2. It will also show the type of information available to you from the reporting system."

6.2.2.2 Project control management

Cost management is part of the project control exercised by the project manager. Schedule and support management are often expressed in terms of cost, and resource plans can be tracked directly to line items in a budget. Development and performance activities also have cost counterparts although expenditures do not necessarily represent technical progress. The project manager can take advantage of cost accounting by building a single cost-based project control management system. As long as the project manager is careful not to attribute false meaning to the cost data, he or she can benefit from the quantitative, consistent periodic reports and analyses inherent in such a database [21].

Fig. 6.16 assigns the project control management system (PCMS) to the financial portion of the project file since PCMS will be run as part of the organization's accounting processes. The requirements of the PCMS, however, involve everyone. Starting with the original work breakdown structure, accounting work packages are established; i.e., numbers are assigned to units of work so that all data regarding cost or time spent on the task are tagged with the same identifier. Each work package will be linked to the requirements and specifications it satisfies, to the system elements with which it interfaces, and to the departments responsible for and/or performing the work. The work directly applicable to a WP# is reported by the WP manager. Such things as heat, light, occupancy, and other indirect expenses are not under his or her control but these costs, project-wide, are known to the accounting department who can allocate them to each WP# by a standard formula. On a project-wide basis, schedules and budgets can be laid out by WP# and displayed by WP# or by date, or in an interface array, or by department. The project manager has considerable flexibility in manipulating the data once they are pulled together by the PCMS. Completeness is assured by enforcing requirements for input data and by insisting that all ex-

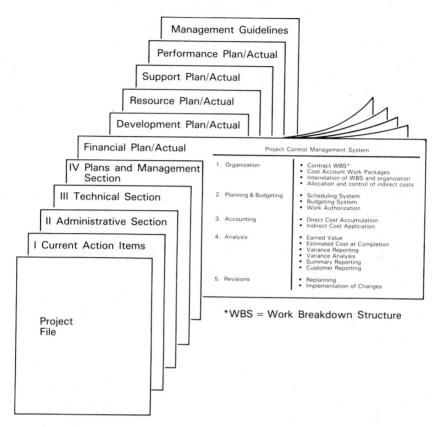

Fig. 6.16   Project file—Program Control Management System.

penses be charged against an authorized WP#. All the data in each report are current as of the closing date of the report. Monday reports may reflect data as of the close of business the previous Friday, meaning that virtually all the data due Friday were received in time for processing and missing data are indicated in a footnote. The single closing date makes all the data in the report consistent so that trends can be drawn, totals obtained, and variances spotted without confusing the manager and without having to double check the source. It is best to pick a closing day that every WP manager can meet even if the resulting reports are a little old when the project manager sees them. PCMS should be timely but not at the expense of reliability. Any problem that requires immediate action should be handled by personal contact rather than by routine reports in the first place.

A PCMS spans many of the data-processing programs found in a typical information systems department. One of the objectives of the PCMS is to integrate available data and combine the data with user inputs to provide better information for managers. One way to proceed is shown in Figs. 6.17 and 6.18. In this PCMS, patterned after FSD, the initial project plan is the source for the baseline budget, schedule, and list of authorized work packages. A direct budget system maintains the project plan. Allocable indirect costs are calculated by a separate overhead budget system that operates on a division level and applies to all projects. By defining work packages so they run from one checkpoint to the next (e.g., a program unit task can have three work packages: Design/Code/Unit Test), schedule and budget data can be keyed to each other. Budget data can be the source of checkpoint data for graphing schedule reports. As work proceeds, expenses are recorded in the form of time cards for individuals, accomplishments and change requests for work packages, purchase requests, and payments for goods and outside services. Weekly updates show actual costs for the week, the year to date, and the project from inception to date. Obligations already incurred through purchase commitments can be posted to current or future periods in the schedule. In the weekly update are the WP managers' estimates of status and effort to complete the task which can be processed by a forecasting procedure that updates the plan.

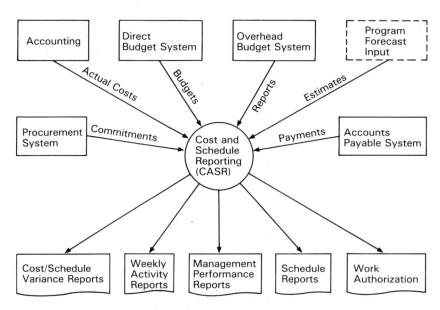

Fig. 6.17 Cost and schedule reporting.

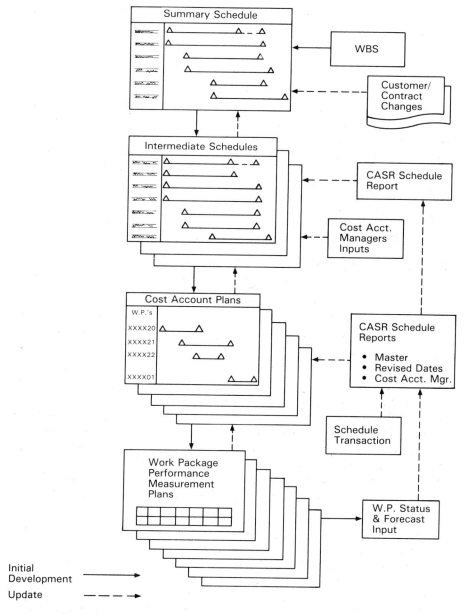

Fig. 6.18 Schedule development and maintenance.

CASR integrates all the source data and produces a set of reports. The cost/schedule variance compares actuals to plan. Graphic schedules are drawn and WP activity reports are run. Department data are pulled together from the various WPs and standard ratios are calculated as a gauge of manager performance. Comments and narrative are included as appropriate. A project summary is routed to the project manager. Based on the nature of the variances, the manager may choose to change the plan, updating the budget system, issuing the necessary new WP authorizations, and opening up new WP records in the accounting database. Various intermediate levels of reports are prepared for subsystem and package managers and detailed reports are sent to WP managers and department managers. Each person receiving a report has an opportunity and an obligation to submit change requests, revised estimates, and corrections. These are approved by the submitter's manager to preserve the integrity of the PCMS data. After review, the changes enter the weekly cycle where they are posted and analyzed to see how they affect the project as a whole. In the next set of reports, a new consistent view of the project is presented.

With CASR reports each manager in the project hierarchy can see how achievements compare to plans. At the WP level, a manager can see how much time each programmer charged to the job. This will show whether people are being diverted to low-priority tasks or whether absences are affecting the schedule. The cost data will show whether computer usage is tracking expectations or whether sloppy users are chewing up the computer budget too fast. At higher levels, the project manager can tell how many units have been completed and, from this, estimate how close to completion the project is. Weak departments can be identified by observing that their costs or schedule slippages are out of line with the plan and with the norm of other departments. Interactions can be studied to see if a problem in one area will propagate elsewhere. Changes to the plan can be made accordingly.

The fact remains that decisions based on CASR alone assume that cost and schedule data fully describe the project. They do not. Cost and schedule are readily obtained, easily manipulated, and easily understood. Variances in cost and schedule are almost always significant. Therefore, CASR is a valuable management tool as far as it goes. The missing facet of project control deals with work products. Content and quality of deliverable end units are critical aspects of project control; yet they are not covered adequately by CASR. In particular, CASR can report actuals exactly on plan when program development is a shambles. When a program is in real trouble, as indicated in Chapter 3, it is because the work done to date is not good. The money spent to produce it agrees with the planned cost to date so there is no dollar variance. There is a schedule variance, but until the manager realizes a new start is required, he or she will think the work is on schedule and the CASR output will accept the manager's evaluation. Project reviews of the work in process can avoid such situations. Thus a complete PCMS must augment the routine cost-based CASR with a schedule of project reviews involving careful evaluation of work practices and work products.

6.2.3 Project Reviews

In all development projects there is a great deal of uncertainty about how to proceed from the initial concept of the job through to final completion. It is the job of the management team to resolve these uncertainties by laying out a plan, monitoring progress, and taking corrective action as required. This is, of course, very difficult. To get a valid overview, the project manager must look at the interactions among all the individual tasks. No one person in the project can show the project manager what he or she needs to see regarding interactions. It is necessary to bring the key project participants together in concert. This can be accomplished by scheduling a review meeting at which the interacting parties talk to each other about the project. When they are all in the same room it is much easier to identify the need for coordination or uncover a hidden dependency. For this reason, every good manager holds periodic review meetings to establish communications among the various people on the project.

Reviews supplement other management and control techniques by providing a project overview that can be obtained no other way [22]. That is their primary purpose. In addition, reviews can determine whether:

- The project is adequately defined.
- Appropriate plans exist and are being followed.
- Plans, objectives, and budgets are mutually compatible.
- Organization, controls, and technical management are adequate.
- Appropriate skills and facilities are assigned.
- The technical work is acceptable.
- Responsibility for solving known problems has been clearly assigned.
- Adequate plans for terminating the project or obtaining follow-up work exist.
- Customer relations are good.
- The project is making the most effective contribution to the technical objectives of its parent organization.

More important, particularly where outside consultants are invited to join the review team, a review can be a valuable educational device. Each member of the project team, in preparing an explanation of his or her assigned area that will be clear to the outside reviewers, is forced to a fresh, deeper understanding of his or her job. This understanding is further improved when the team member applies the suggestions of the reviewers to his or her original plans. The very act of bringing the team together to coordinate interactions creates the opportunity to exchange information and experiences that can strengthen the project implementation.

Note that the list of benefits does not include "solving problems." It is unusual for a review team to know how to solve the problems it discovers. Occasionally, a reviewer will know the answer because he or she has seen the problem before. Most often, the problems are too complex to handle on the spot. Therefore, the role of the review team is to identify the problems, suggest solutions or sources of assistance, and recommend an action plan for reaching a solution. This procedure emphasizes one other point: The review team supports management; it does not replace it. A review team reports its findings and its recommendations to the project manager who is responsible for the action plan.

Oddly enough, some managers fail to take advantage of the review process to increase their chances for success. They get too wrapped up in day-to-day activities to stop for a review session, or they fall behind schedule and are afraid to stop for a review. Some lack confidence in their own ability and avoid exposing their project to the potential criticism of a review team. Of course, all of these managers are already in trouble and really need the help a good review provides.

6.2.3.1 Types of reviews

Most commonly, reviews are called to determine the status of the project and to confirm that everything is proceeding as planned. *Periodic reviews* can accomplish this if they are held regularly and often. In large projects, meetings every week are necessary for control. At the completion of a well-defined activity, it is a good idea to hold a more formal, more comprehensive review. The event completion or *milestone review* not only assesses current status but also predicts what will happen if the present plans are followed. The milestone is a decision point at which it is appropriate to modify future plans based on the results up to that point. In addition to the fact that milestones are a natural place to take stock, the milestone is a logical point to bring higher management up-to-date and to request help in those areas where the project manager lacks the resources or authority to act.

The scope of a review depends on the situation. Normally, it covers all aspects of the project since the review technique is most effective when dealing with the global aspects of the situation. Sometimes the project is too big to cover in one session. In this case, the global aspects of one subsystem may be covered in one session with other subsystems scheduled later. Then, in pyramid fashion, the partial results can be reviewed at a final sitting. Certain situations may require a detailed *technical review* to supplement the global look. A special case of the technical review is the *inspection* introduced in Chapter 2. Inspections (and the less-formal walkthroughs) are detailed examinations of program designs and code. The inspection procedure is rigorous, organized, and supervised by a trained individual. Its scope is very narrow, usually one work package. Its approach is entirely technical. That is, the inspection produces information about the program in process: its quality, structure, effectiveness, and only incidentally its cost and schedule.

Occasionally, the scope of a review may be narrowed down to a single question such as: "Is item *x* fully compliant with the terms and conditions of the contract?" Questions of this type should not arise if a conscientious program of periodic and milestone reviews has been followed, but no one is perfect and such questions do come up. They represent omissions or errors by the project manager which, when they reach the attention of higher management, cast doubt on the health of the project. If doubts persist, the higher manager may decide to call his or her own review of the situation. To distinguish this from a normal review, it is called an *audit*.

Periodic reviews. Managers of large projects typically schedule weekly meetings[8] to satisfy several objectives:

- Review project status by task.
- Review overall project interactions and dependencies.
- Obtain revised commitments.
- Identify outstanding problems.
- Assign responsibility for acting on problems.

These reviews are terse, informal meetings internal to the project. The discussion centers around the development plan which records the current task assignments. All participants say where their work stands and how they are responding to requirements placed on them by others. A common occurrence at these meetings is the report by someone that, because of problems

---

8. The frequency of periodic reviews should fit the situation. "Weekly" is used as an example.

with a certain task and because he or she has heard that a colleague is also slipping, the delivery date will be slipped on an item being produced for the colleague. Of course, the other person has been planning to recover lost time on the basis of getting the item on time. Now that they are in the same room and the issue is clearly identified—not just a set of rumors and presumptions—they can negotiate a solution.

When the meeting is over, everyone is at the same level of knowledge about the project. The atmosphere is relaxed and friendly but, nevertheless, there is great pressure on each member of the team to hold up his or her end of the project. Thus one purpose of the periodic review is to use and reinforce the power of group psychology. Commitments made to the group are much more meaningful than plans submitted through an impersonal written report system.

Milestone reviews.   Periodic reviews are an excellent and essential management tool for assessing current status but they are not the best tool for measuring risk. Occurring as they do at regular intervals, they are snapshots of the project in motion. Only by coincidence do they occur at the completion of a major activity. On the other hand, the results achieved in completing an activity can have important consequences on the work remaining to be done. Therefore, it is necessary to recognize the key checkpoints and re-evaluate the project on those dates. Checkpoints are chosen either because: (1) several tasks can be coordinated then, (2) a recommitment/redirection of the project plan is scheduled at that time, (3) higher management must intervene at that point to ensure further progress, or (4) the customer requires a review at that time. In the first case, any problems that arise can probably be contained within the project. In the other cases, higher management should be aware of and involved in the review.

The milestone review determines whether the tasks completed at the milestone satisfy the requirements of the phase just ended. The review also examines the results in the light of the system requirements to see if the plan for the upcoming phase should be modified. Such decisions are system-wide and call for an unbiased evaluation of the situation. For this reason, milestone reviews often involve outside reviewers who can take a detached view of the project and sometimes see things the project people missed.

A standard sequence of milestones can be specified by the PCMS. Experience has shown that cost and schedule are best managed when the reviews of Fig. 6.19 are conducted. They are described in Table 6.4 along with a number of technical reviews. All of the major milestone reviews cover financial as well as technical issues. Most of them are scheduled prior to a major commitment of effort that will only be authorized if the technical plan is sound.

TABLE 6.4. PROJECT MILESTONE AND TECHNICAL REVIEWS

Project stage	Review	Purpose	Timing	Entry criteria	Exit criteria	Technology criteria
Concept Formulation	Proposal Review	Evaluate technical and financial exposures.	Prior to project authorization.	Objectives, project plan, justification complete.	Approved plan, authority to proceed.	Adheres to organization standards, meets feasibility criteria.
Project Definition	System Requirements Review	Verify that work is going in right direction.	Midway in stage.	Initial project definition complete.	Project direction confirmed. Changes specified.	Adheres to systematic requirements guidelines. Responds to objectives in demonstrable manner.
	System Design Requirements Review	Establish system design requirements. Evaluate adequacy.	Completion of baseline.	Design Requirements Baseline complete.	Approved plan, baseline, management/control procedures; authority to implement.	Adheres to systematic requirements guidelines, responds to objectives, utilizes library/documentation tools.
	Proposal Review	Select implementer.	Prior to implementation.	RFP issued, responses received.	Selection decision; implementer's commitment.	Proposal traceable to design requirements. Selection adheres to risk evaluation guidelines.

TABLE 6.4. CONTINUED

Project stage	Review	Purpose	Timing	Entry criteria	Exit criteria	Technology criteria
Project Implementation (Design)	Software System Design Review	Technical review to verify compliance with requirements and adequacy of design.	Prior to PDR.	Software system architecture and design complete.	Software system design approved.	Adheres to software engineering practices for systematic design using design language. Requirements are traceable through to end product.
	Preliminary Design Review (PDR)	Evaluate system design for quality, completeness, feasibility, cost, and suitability.	Completion of system design.	Software system design specification complete and approved (technical). Project plan updated.	Authority to proceed to package design. Approved plan, including budget for computer resources.	Adheres to software engineering practices and management/control practices, including design-to-cost.
	Package Design Review	Technical review to verify consistency with system spec.	Completion of package design. (1 package at a time)	Top-down package design complete.	Authority to proceed to program design.	Adheres to software engineering practices and management/control practices.

Review	Purpose	Timing	Entry Criteria	Output	Adherence
Test Plan Review	Evaluate adequacy of integration and test plans.	Prior to completion of CDR.	System integration and test plan complete. All specs/rqmts tested in plan.	Approved test plan. Authority to implement test cases and test tools.	Adheres to software engineering practices for interface management, integration management, and testing. Utilizes standard tools.
Documentation Outline Review	Evaluate that proposed documents satisfy their objectives.	Prior to completion of CDR.	Document outlines complete.	Approved documentation plan.	Adheres to documentation guidelines, component documents map to deliverables, system documents cover interactions and system behavior.
Critical Design Review (CDR)	Evaluate package designs for quality, completeness, feasibility, cost, and suitability.	Completion of package design.	Completion of a package design. Alternatively, completion of all package designs.	Approved implementation plan, authority to proceed with programming.	Adheres to software engineering practices, management/control practices, systems analysis/performance guidelines.

555

TABLE 6.4. CONTINUED

Project stage	Review	Purpose	Timing	Entry criteria	Exit criteria	Technology criteria
Project Implementation (Development)	Design Inspection	Find and correct errors in program design, test spec.	Completion of a program design or test spec.	Completion of a program design or a test spec.	Inspection rework complete, authority to code.	Adheres to software engineering practices for software design, inspections.
	Code Inspection	Find and correct errors in code.	Prior to unit test.	Completion of unit coding.	Inspection rework complete, authority to test unit.	Adheres to software engineering practices for systematic programming, code management.
Project Implementation (Test)	Test Procedure Review	Evaluate test methods, materials, scenarios, controls against test plan.	Prior to package integration and test.	Completion of detailed test implementation plan.	Approved test implementation plan.	Adheres to software engineering practices for integration engineering, tools.
	Package Qualification	Determine that package meets spec.	Prior to package integration.	Completion of package components and basic test procedures.	Deficiencies fixed, code promoted from program development library to integration library.	Adheres to test procedures and software engineering practices for software integration methodology.

556

	Purpose	Timing	Completion	Output	Standards
Software System Qualification	Determine that system meets spec.	Prior to release.	Completion of package qualification and system test.	Deficiencies fixed, code promoted from integration library to master library.	Adheres to test procedures and software engineering practices for software integration methodology.
Product Configuration Inspection	Demonstrate satisfactory completion of product.	After system qualification.	Release of system to user, execution of acceptance tests, delivery of complete program package.	Customer acceptance.	Adheres to configuration management practices, software engineering management practices, contract terms and conditions.
Operation, Maintenance, and Upgrade / **Post-Installation Evaluation**	Evaluate adequacy of system in its operational environment.	After system stabilization (6–12 months after start of operation).	Migration complete, system in continuous use under normal conditions. System measurements available.	Evaluation report complete.	Adheres to system documentation.

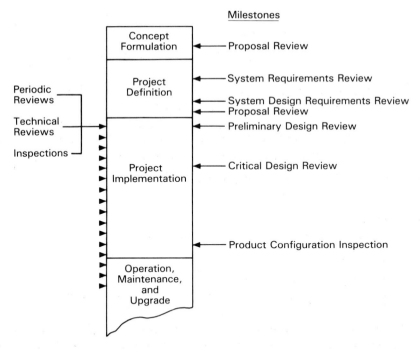

Fig. 6.19   Project reviews.

Technical reviews.   The list of reviews in Table 6.4 includes a number of technical reviews among the major milestones. In small- and medium-sized projects, technical reviews are wrapped into the appropriate milestone review. This becomes inefficient in a large project because the attendees are not all qualified to contribute to the technical discussion. Therefore, a separate meeting is set up ahead of time to go into technical details. The summary of this meeting is an input to the milestone review.

The technical review examines the statement of work and the specifications to be implemented. Obviously, the reviewers must be technically qualified to evaluate the project. There may be quite a few people involved so as to take a proposal apart in great detail in a short period of time. The idea is to bring in reviewers who are at least as well qualified as the project team (i.e., who could have been assigned the job instead of the project team) and have the project team justify its technical plans to the reviewers. The "two heads are better than one" theory says that this procedure will uncover loopholes and detect illogical designs. There will be a lot of "Why did you do it this way?" questions that help the project team discover inefficient or clumsy designs. "If I understand what you said, your design will be such-and-such" is the kind of reviewer response that causes the designers to re-examine how closely their designs conform to their intended objectives.

Audits. An audit is called when a project appears to be out of control. The project manager who loses control seldom recognizes it. That is why most audits originate outside the project. The audit team is made up of outside experts who are imposed on the project manager. They are given the authority to review anything they want to whether the project team wants to disclose it or not. This tends to make the audit a tense affair. Furthermore, if the audit confirms that the project is out of control, some of the project team may be blamed. They realize their exposure and tend to throw up a protective curtain which the audit team must then pull down.

Normally a review is the source of aid and encouragement for the project team. Audits can accomplish this, too, but more often they frighten the team. Audits can usurp the project manager's authority. This can alienate the project team and weaken the team's self-confidence. Alternatively, if the project is really in good shape, the audit may backfire and embarrass higher management. But audits may also save the project in trouble. Obviously it is more desirable to strengthen a project team by catching potential problems early through routine reviews than to resort to an audit.

A shirt manufacturer used an audit properly when he asked a consultant to determine why his data-processing center was unable to keep up with the demands of the business. The consultant found a conscientious but inexperienced dp manager, an overworked underpaid programmer, and a couple of untrained operators. Obvious recommendations made this group more effective. The prime finding of the audit, however, was that the dp center was not the source of the problem; top management was. By issuing vague instructions and by failing to allow time for dp analysis and programming, the company executives had made it impossible for the dp group to respond. This was an embarrassing report, but it led to corrective action.

A more difficult audit took place because a project manager had missed his original delivery date and his rescheduled date for a program. His boss wanted the auditor to determine when that program could actually be delivered. The question was concise and narrow; that is a good basis for an audit. The difficult aspect was that, if the project manager could not meet his own estimate delivery schedule, he could hardly meet someone else's estimate. This type of audit tends to have only two possible outcomes. Either the auditor agrees with the project manager on a most likely schedule or the auditor does his own independent estimate and gets assigned to replace the project manager to make it happen.

6.2.3.2 Setting up a review

Since the ultimate purpose of a review is to provide information for management decision, it is important that the review be called by the project manager. It is that person's authority that allows the review team to obtain the data that will lead to their conclusions. If a lower-level manager calls the review, the team may find that they have access only to that manager's department and cannot fully investigate the relations among departments. Closing the loop, the report of the review team should be delivered to the project manager. It is up to the project manager to disseminate the report as he or she sees fit.[9]

In *periodic* meetings the review is a direct information exchange because the project team *is* the review team. All team members have access to the development plan showing what has happened since the last meeting. *Milestone* reviews are best handled by a review team selected for its experience and lack of involvement in project details. Presentations to such a team include all the background needed to understand the current status.

The term *outside consultant* has been used to describe the unbiased reviewer. He or she should come from outside the area being reviewed and should have the experience and stature of a consultant respected by the project members. Such people are usually available within the organization to which the project belongs; i.e., "outside consultant" does not mean an expert hired from outside the company. In fact, most good review teams are made up of technical staff members and managers of projects similar to the one being reviewed. In selecting the review team, it is helpful to observe these guidelines:

1. Reviewers should be at least as senior and experienced as the reviewees. They should be competent in the subject area.

2. Reviewers should have no technical or political axes to grind.

3. Reviewers should be personable, articulate, and patient.

4. Reviewers must be tolerant and respectful of the reviewees even when the reviewees do a poor job.

The project manager should select the reviewers. Three or four are sufficient for any milestone review. One of them, designated chairperson of the review team, will run the review for the project manager and submit the report [23]. The project manager participates as a reviewee. Keeping the manager off the review team proper gives the reviewers more freedom to call a spade a spade.

The people present during the review include the review team, the key project managers,[10] and key people from the activity being reviewed. It is desirable to have few people present. On the other hand, the benefits of the review should touch as many people as possible. This tradeoff is usually resolved by inviting people to be present only when their activity is being dis-

---

9. Obviously, the project manager can tell the report writer to send copies to other people. The report writer should not personally decide who sees the report.

10. Key managers include the project manager, the managers reporting to him or her, and the chain of managers down to the manager of the activity being reviewed.

cussed. Key managers are present throughout the review and can answer questions or describe interactions as required. A recording secretary must take notes to help construct the final report. Typically, the secretary's job can be assigned to one of the reviewers. There is no need for a full transcription if the presentations have been well prepared.

Depending on the size of the activity being reviewed, a thorough review will take from a half-day to a week for presentations. (Longer review schedules are to be avoided since they interfere too much with project performance. Very large projects avoid long reviews by setting up multiple review teams each of which concentrates on one area or aspect of the project.)

The mechanics of the major milestone review call for a member of the project to coordinate affairs in the manner of a technical seminar. This individual is responsible for seeing that the project team is prepared to give a complete picture of its area properly supported with visual aids and documentation. He or she also must ensure that the review is conducted in a place and in a manner conductive to intensive work with few distractions.

The review team should be well-informed prior to the first presentation. This saves time and avoids embarrassing the reviewers. They get their information from documents supplied by the coordinator two to four weeks before the review meeting. Obvious documents for this purpose are the various baselines, plans, and overview narratives in the project file. It should not be necessary to create new documents for the benefit of the reviewers since, in principle, anything they will want to see will exist because it had equal value to the project personnel. The reviewers scan the documents rather than study them. They look for inconsistencies, contradictions, omissions, etc., with the main emphasis on interactions within the project. In addition, smart reviewers do a limited literature search to learn a few key concepts relevant to the subject matter of the project and to jot down the names of key people in the subject area. When the day of the review arrives, each reviewer is confident that he or she can understand the project team.

Several common types of sensitive issues arise. The reviewers should be briefed ahead of time so they can be appropriately tactful.

▪ Known problem areas—When a known problem exists, the people responsible have probably been getting a lot of management attention. They may be thin-skinned compared to other reviewees because they feel they are being singled out for criticism.

▪ Policy and private agreements—In some situations the reasons for taking a particular course of action have never been divulged to the members of the project team. They may be withheld to protect trade secrets or classified data. Sometimes they are withheld because they are distasteful. In any case, since the review team is there to help the project manager, reviewers may not divulge these reasons to the reviewees. They are, however, free to advise the project manager to do it.

■ Politics—Project development involves many parties with conflicting objectives. Managers try to control the contending parties to reach a mutual goal. The review team must be aware of the main areas of contention so that partisan politics are avoided.

■ Higher management involvement—When the project manager's superiors attend a review they will usually listen carefully and say little. The review team must avoid placing the higher managers in a position that requires them to make a statement. If they speak up, their comments can easily be mistaken for orders by the project members. This undercuts the project manager. Alternatively, the comments may expose the higher manager's ignorance of the project details and embarrass him or her unnecessarily.

■ Customer involvement—A general rule that usually works is that a well-informed customer is a more understanding customer. This rule suggests letting the customer attend selected reviews. Depending on the nature of the review, it may be a poor rule. Management control requires that all problems be solved at the lowest possible level; i.e., solve problems within the project before going to higher management and go to higher management before going outside the organization to the customer. Premature disclosure to the customer may weaken internal management control. It may also lead the customer to think the project is in trouble when, in fact, many avenues of solution remain open.

■ Secrecy—When the project is classified, the coordinator is responsible for checking the clearance level of the reviewers. He or she must also monitor the presentations to ensure that no security rules are violated.

All of these issues become magnified in an audit. It may be desirable to limit the attendance at an audit simply to minimize the effects of personal and political issues.

6.2.3.3 Conducting the review

Milestone reviews are intensive sessions that gain momentum as they go. When they are rolling, each reviewer's questions trigger relevant additional questions from others. This frequently leads to reviews that run through meal periods and on into the night.

About one-half the time is devoted to formal presentations by the project team—"formal" in the sense that they are scheduled, prepared talks supported by appropriate handouts. The purpose of the presentations is threefold:

■ Describe the project.

■ Display the project team's attitude.

■ Display, to some degree, the project team's knowledge and competence.

A checklist for a project milestone review is given in Appendix B. By covering the applicable points, the speakers fill in the sketchy picture of the project the review team brought to the meeting.

Project managers can get more for their money in the review process by seeing that their people are well prepared and know what to expect from the reviewers. Adequate preparation of talks by project personnel calls for rehearsals. The rehearsal has the added value of teaching the project team more about the project than they knew. In trying to put their best foot forward for the strangers in the review team, they uncover all sorts of useful information that had somehow never been mentioned before. Thus the preparation for the review serves the same function as the review itself: It provides information for management decisions that can improve the project and it fosters communication within the project.

Method of presentation.　Presentations should preferably be made by managers. They can bring their key technical people with them to field questions but they must show enough knowledge of their area to convince the reviewers that they can manage it. During and after each talk, the reviewers will ask questions. Most of their questions will be straightforward requests for clarification. Others will be intended to clarify a relationship or a thread of events that has been introduced by an earlier speaker. Good reviewers, realizing that their questions may be out of context to the current speaker, will try to explain the purpose of the inquiry. Occasionally, questions will be asked to unsettle the speaker. This happens when reviewers feel they are not getting the full story. The speaker who is in command of the situation can be selective in what he or she says. The reviewers recognize such behavior and seek to take command of the situation away from the speaker. Here is where the review team's homework pays off. By asking the speaker to relate his or her design or plan to such-and-such other project referred to in the literature, the reviewers either distract or unnerve the speaker. In the former case, the speaker has an answer but, in framing it, loses the initiative temporarily. In the latter case, the speaker has no answer and realizes that his or her ignorance will be exposed if the question is sidestepped. In either case, this technique causes the speaker to reveal data he or she intended to withhold. It is the only way the speaker can avoid looking unresponsive or uninformed. By careful questioning based on knowledge of other projects or knowledge of other parts of the project being reviewed, or based on feigned inability to understand the current project, a good review team can lead the speaker down any avenue it chooses. Consequently, a review can succeed even with reluctant reviewees [24].

Level of detail.　The coordinator should prepare a review schedule and agenda for all participants. Then, in the interests of maintaining schedule, the chairperson and the coordinator should cut off discussion of topics or levels of detail that are not of general interest or necessary to the review.

All reviewees should be prepared to discuss their area in the greatest detail. Their presentation, however, should be limited to a short background briefing and a thorough discussion of current issues. The reviewers will normally look for system-wide problems rather than for detailed implementation techniques.[11] Nevertheless, they will focus on details when necessary to study a significant component of the system or clarify how the system works or test the reviewee's credibility.

The review team's greatest value is its ability to relate the salient features of the project to similar situations in their experience. They do this by building a mental image of the project out of the data they review. If they see the project as a well-formed complete structure, they will give high marks to the project team. In this case, their main recommendation will be to proceed along the existing plan. Accepting the overall design, they will make detailed suggestions that address specific points that may be improved at the option of the project team. On the other hand, if they build an image of a structure with missing or incompatible components, they will restrict their recommendations to major issues of design, organization, plan, and even personnel. It would be pointless for them to comment on details of implementation when they believe the system itself is in trouble. The surest way to convince reviewers that the project is structurally weak is for the reviewees to show up with inadequate project documentation. The second best way to flunk out is for the speakers to describe their activities in a way that differs from the project documentation or that displays ignorance of what is going on in other areas. These are the symptoms of a project out of control. In the presence of such symptoms, everything a speaker says is taken with a grain of salt.

6.2.3.4 Completing the review

After listening to the prepared material and eliciting the data they want, the review team should withdraw for a closed-door caucus during which they summarize their conclusions and draft a report. This procedure ensures that the report is an independent view of the project rather than a rehash of the status reports already available to the project manager.

The key points on which there is a review team consensus are immediately discussed with the project manager. A written final report is prepared to give a comprehensive list of comments and suggestions to the project manager.

---

11. These comments apply to milestone reviews. A technical review specifically looks at details to the extent that time allows. The level of detail can be balanced against time available by deciding in advance where the critical design details are. Peercy [25] recommends a discipline for evaluating design based on questionnaires. The questions are derived from the quality characteristics selected at the start of the project. The discipline is most effective when several groups independently review the design and scores are compared.

Keeping in mind that the review is an aid to management, the written review report will go from the chairperson to the program manager. Reviewees should understand that they will not see it unless and until the project manager disseminates it. More important, the report will not go to the project manager's manager. This gives the project manager the opportunity to personally take corrective action before seeking help. (In audits, the report goes to the manager who called the audit.) Ultimately, the results of the review should be given to the project team. They need the feedback as a reward for the effort that went into the review. They also need the guidance and support provided by the reviewers; however, they should receive it from their chain of command.

A comprehensive review takes some time to digest. The report should be completed as fast as possible, although in many cases this may take several weeks. (Because of the time lag, it is not uncommon for the unedited draft to go to the project manager who then has a head start on high-priority items. Of course, salient points were also discussed with him at the review meeting.) In their report, the reviewers should:

- State the objective of the review
- State the conclusions
- State the recommendations
- Explain the basis for the conclusions and recommendations.

The conclusions and recommendations are prioritized so the manager can evaluate the review team's opinion of their urgency and the cost of rejecting them. The key items are summarized in a cover letter supplemented by the details in appendices. Care is taken to identify who is affected by each recommendation. The report may be sectionalized so each affected party can receive only appropriate pages. Several "don'ts" should be observed:

- No personalities are mentioned in the report. (If an individual is the source of a problem, the information can be passed on verbally.)
- No solutions are specifically designed. (The project team must solve the problem themselves; the report says what is wrong and describes the objectives to be satisfied by the solution—it may even give examples of a solution—but the decision as to how to handle the recommendation must be made by project management.)
- No impossible demands are made (such as adding a million-dollar task when there is clearly no more money available.)
- No claims to infallibility are made. (The review is recognized as one step in a constantly changing iterative process. The reviewers are only able to give their best judgment of the situation they reviewed: a subset of the system at one instant of time. Even if they are right, their recommendations will lose validity as time passes.)

The project manager sponsors reviews because he or she wants the advice of unbiased knowledgeable peers and also wants to use the review to bring the project team up to date and stimulate them through an information exchange. A smart project manager takes the review process seriously enough to lay out an implementation plan for the recommended actions. Every recommendation in the review report should be acted on even if the action is a rejection. The project manager should not allow review recommendations to become open items in the plan. He or she lets the team members know what was recommended and how it affects them, and he or she shows appreciation for their using the review as a vehicle for strengthening the project. For the future, the project manager plans to build the next major review on the foundation provided by earlier reviews. This will save time, particularly if the same review team will be available.

6.2.4   Programming Support Systems

Reviews have always been recognized as a means of controlling content and quality. Since the advent of on-line programming support systems, reviews have also been used to provide visibility. Most programming support systems capture data at the source and store it in machine-readable form where it is hidden from view until retrieved. Management control procedures have to take this fact into account; otherwise, decisions may be based on incomplete or misleading extracts from the database.

The objectives of programming support systems vary from organization to organization but usually include in some varying degree:

- Productivity improvement
- Quality improvement
- Project control
- Product control

Productivity is improved by speeding up individual tasks and by reducing the amount of work per task. Speed may be obtained by on-line entry, editing, and execution; by interactive compilation; by fast access to related materials; by time-sharing resources to reduce turnaround; etc. Quality is improved by the use of computerized analysis and test facilities; by the enforcement of formal procedures; by prompting; etc. Project control can be accomplished through automation of measurement and reporting procedures. Product control is obtained by building a single project library keyed to configuration accounting procedures. All of these objectives suggest the use of an on-line time-sharing system as the basis for support. Individual designers and programmers can work at terminals and take advantage of the productivity and quality features of the system. Managers and administrators can use terminals to access project information and analyze status. Test administrators can collect components from the library to construct a test environment, execute the tests, and obtain an analysis of errors all from a terminal. A project need not be large to take advantage of such support systems. At one time, only the largest computer vendors and software houses could afford a full-function development support environment. Given nationwide computer networks with standard architectures that let many types of terminals (including personal home computers) access resources anywhere in the system, support tools can be obtained by everyone.

Programming support systems reduce project visibility. Most of the information required for control resides in the system, but only prearranged reports come out of the system. A manager concerned about overall project status can combine the stored data in various ways, but the support system cannot be used to learn how the project team thinks things are going. A support system provides objective data only. Subjective opinions must be obtained by direct contact with the people. Reviews provide the contact opportunity. When the team assembles to talk about status, several other visibility concerns will emerge:

- Support systems reduce the personal contacts among team members so that each person knows less about the project than would be the case otherwise.

- Useful data, particularly forecasts of anticipated problems, may be missing from the database because team members do not realize anyone needs to see them.

- Incriminating data are not entered; therefore, potential problems may be concealed.

- Managers do not know when data entries are made so they may not act on a potential problem in a timely manner.

These concerns arise because an on-line system builds a link between the terminal user and the system database while, at the same time, it cuts links between people. All the team members talk to an abstract database and not to each other. What they say to the database is open to inspection by everyone, but it takes initiative on the part of the inspector. The support system gives few clues as to what to look for and when to look. Inspection is often inhibited as well by privacy measures. The support system contains protection mechanisms to prevent access to data that are not ready for others to share or that are intended only for authorized users. The best protection mechanism is to withhold data—keep data in the desk instead of the database. Team members who are in trouble and trying to get out before their manager sees what is wrong may use this protection method. The employee controls the information—at least one small piece of information—essential to project management. In this sense, programming support systems can invert the hierarchy of management control. Control is restored by extracting all the information about employee activities that can be obtained automatically by the support system. The manager must track these indicators to understand status.

In the manager-employee relationship, various types of data are exchanged:

- Work product: work in process, completed work releasable to others.
- Status reports: actual vs. plan, event completion
- Alarms: requests for assistance, missed targets
- Problems: interface problems, internal difficulties
- Control: direction, advice, coordination

An on-line DBMS gives both manager and employee a means of dealing with work product. A report generator can handle periodic status reports. The other data exchanges require special attention. DBMS and reporting functions assume that manager and employee both have a clear picture of what is in the database. Yet, the manager does not know that an event has occurred or that a problem report has been filed. The employee does not know when a new direction has been set by the manager. This information may appear in the next weekly report but, in a dynamic environment, action may be called for today. The support system can be designed to complete the information flow path by drawing the attention of appropriate users to action items. Passive methods are useful and easy to implement by placing the action items in an "electronic mailbox" which the user is invited to read at each log-on. Occasionally, active methods are justified—most often when system integrity or security is involved. In these cases, the user may be interrupted and directed to examine and acknowledge the action item. If there is no response within a specified time, a default rule is applied; e.g., if an unauthorized person tries to access a file, the security officer may be alerted and if he or she does nothing, the system can disconnect the snooper. The best active control is a manager who frequently scans the contents of the employees' working areas so that he or she knows what to expect when a unit of work is complete. Work in progress need not be interrupted; he or she can offer guidance at inspections or checkpoints.

In a project plan, dates on which occurrences are verified and decisions made are called checkpoints and milestones. The plan contains the minimum number of such points consistent with effective management control. In a completely manual system, the checkpoints are widely spaced and each point corresponds to a significant event. Between checkpoints there is continuous communication among team members and the work product is visible to all. On a daily basis, minor adjustments permit fine tuning of the

plan with no loss of control. A support system makes communication epi-
sodic: i.e., instead of continuous communication there is a periodic dump.
The effects of an adjustment may not be visible until the next dump. In this
situation, control is maintained by increasing the number of checkpoints.
The manual system has widely spaced checkpoints with frequent small corrections in the intervals and immediate feedback. An on-line system
achieves the same level of control by having closely spaced checkpoints with
relatively large adjustments at a checkpoint and few or none in the intervals;
feedback is obtained at the end of an interval. To minimize the amount of
control activity, exception reporting is recommended. Each event to be
monitored is characterized by some observable features such as the date to
be completed, the number of lines of code expected, successful execution of
selected tests, etc. Events that do not occur as expected are exceptions to be
reported at their checkpoint. Normal events do not generate a checkpoint
report but are included in the next periodic report.

6.2.4.1 Software facilities

A programming support system consists of facilities for preparing, filing,
executing, analyzing, and combining programs. To the extent that the
operating system provided with the development machine has these capabilities, the support system can use the OS. Figure 6.20 shows that facilities for
building libraries, for assembling or compiling programs, for linking
modules, and for general services such as sorting, dumping storage, or tracing program sequences are usually found in the OS. Time-shared access for

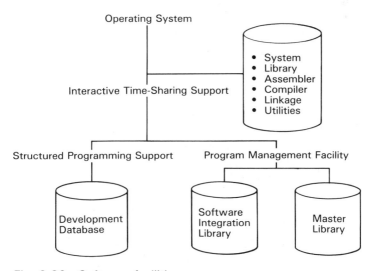

Fig. 6.20   Software facilities.

interactive programming is also provided by many operating systems, although it is not uncommon for the user to obtain a time-sharing system from another source [26]. The same is true of the structured programming support that contains facilities for:

- Editing
    1. data entry
    2. text manipulation
    3. structured formatting
    4. display layout
- User assistance
    1. dialog management (menus, prompting, synonyms)
    2. explanation (HELP command, on-line tutorial)
    3. skeleton management
- Command processing
    1. dataset allocation, movement
    2. job control
    3. working copy control (development copy on-line, hard copy)
- Interfacing with other facilities
- Analysis of work status and program characteristics

A certain amount of tailoring is appropriate for the structured programming facilities. They should incorporate local standards and should be personalized to the needs of the organization. When a user calls on a HELP routine because a message is unclear, the system will be most effective when it explains the message in terms applicable to the user's project. Skeleton programs and data descriptions can be provided in areas where several users will do similar tasks. The skeleton presents the unvarying part of the task; the user fills in the blanks. Other types of personalization often protect the integrity of the development database by setting bounds on what a user can do. The bounds can range from naming conventions to addressing restrictions and even task interruptions (to force inspections or manager reviews). Most personalization can be done by inserting project-specific data in an existing support system dataset or in a data dictionary. Sometimes it is necessary to modify support system code.

The program management facility is a DBMS tailored to hold the work in process. The functions of this facility include:

- Library maintenance (storage, retrieval, integrity, recovery)
- Control (authorization, accounting, reports)
- Version build

6.2.4.2 Library hierarchy

The library is a hierarchial structure (Fig. 6.21). Individual programmers submit debugged program units to the Level 1 development library. One copy of each program unit is retained at Level 1 where it is available for other programmers to use. If the unit is changed, the new copy displaces the old copy so only one is in circulation. The configuration control system should include procedures to ensure that everyone knows which copy is current. Programs in Level 1 will often be tested by the test team—not to repeat the debugging process but to verify that the functional and interface requirements have been met. Qualified program units can then be promoted to the next library level where they will be linked into strings in accordance with the test plan. Level 3 contains complete packages and Level 4 holds the

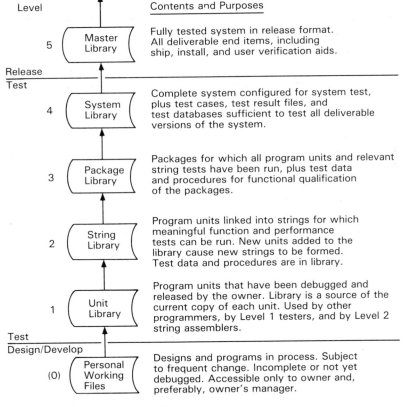

Fig. 6.21 Implementation library hierarchy.

entire system. Above Level 1, there can be multiple files in the library. The test plan will require different configurations of strings and packages for different tests. The same program unit can, therefore, appear in several test configurations simultaneously. In a similar manner, the release plan may permit several functionally different versions of the system to be in the field at the same time.

The library maintenance functions permit elements of one library to be manipulated and eventually promoted to a higher level. The control functions keep track of the contents of each level and govern access to the contents. Controls also monitor the conditions that qualify a program to advance up the hierarchy. The version build functions give the library users the ability to specify a desired configuration and have the support system collect, link, and initialize the necessary elements. When the system at Level 4 finally passes its tests and is ready for release, it is copied to the Master Library. The Master Library contains the deliverable end items. Each library level contains program code in source, object, and load module form. Test data and procedures, data recorded for analyses or status reporting, and configuration control data are also retained in the library levels. In this way, all the material needed for a given testing or release activity can be found in one place.

6.2.4.3 Software control

Promotion to a higher level of the library hierarchy is permitted only after an element has met predefined observable criteria associated with the test plan. The criteria must be clear and unambiguous so that both the current level manager and the next higher-level manager can agree that the criteria have been met. IBM's Federal Systems Division uses a standard system development library procedure in which promotion to a higher level is formalized. Each level of the library is the responsibility of the manager who uses it most—call this person the Level Owner. The element to be promoted—say a program or a package—belongs to the Element Owner. When the Element Owner believes the element at level n is qualified for promotion to level $n + 1$, he or she OFFERs it to the Level $n + 1$ Owner who may PROMOTE the element (i.e., accept it) or REJECT it. Rejection must be for cause and the Level $n + 1$ Owner must write a trouble report (TR) explaining the problem so the Element Owner can fix it. A rejected element remains in level n. Any element that was previously promoted can FAIL as the result of errors found in subsequent tests. Again, a trouble report will be written and the element may be pushed down a level. The Level n Owner has the option of retaining the element with an open TR; this will permit additional tests to run while the fix is prepared. If the element is returned to level

$n - 1$, though, it is disqualified for further use at level n or higher. After that element is fixed it must go through the OFFER process again.

Formal procedures also govern the flow of activity through the program management facility (PMF). As the main development and support tool for controlling the system software and documentation, the PMF contains the library hierarchy, the library update mechanism, and the procedures for controlling system generation and changes. It is impractical to allow anyone to change a library at will. Controls are required to maintain consistency in the databases. The usual form of control is based on periodic library updates at which all approved changes are made in a batch. The update process, called a *build,* accepts approved changes, verifies that they meet the requirements of an authorization database, and applies the changes to the old library to generate a new library. As in any file maintenance process, the old library and the current changes are retained for recovery purposes. PMF can be used to build as many different configurations as required for test and release. This is done by using a configuration database to specify which program units are to be included in a given build. Thus a new program unit can be inserted in an existing package for test purposes but omitted from the version of the package designated for release. A later release may include the added function. All the variations appear in the system integration and test plan; although each must be separately approved before it is built.

The PMF flow (Fig. 6.22) applies to the entire system life cycle. Initially, program units are built in response to design specifications and, when ready, are stored in the Level 1 library. During test and after release, errors are found and the trouble reports lead to program fixes. Change requests also occur over the life of the system as users learn how to make the system respond better to their changing needs. Change requests result in new design specifications. Whether a program unit is new or modified, it must sit in an update pool (a temporary holding area) until it is approved for the requested build or builds. Approval implies that the developer's manager agrees the unit is ready. The build coordinator and the configuration control board must also agree to process the unit in the next update run. The result of the update run is a new library dataset with appropriate on-line documentation and hard copy. Physical copies of each build may be distributed for test purposes and a copy of the updated system is set aside as a recovery vehicle.

A PMF is fundamentally a database management system containing computer programs. It can be extended to include other kinds of data, such as plans and schedules. Since the PMF already has control functions, it can be used with minor modifications to compare actual performance against plan. When a program unit enters the system or is promoted or released, the

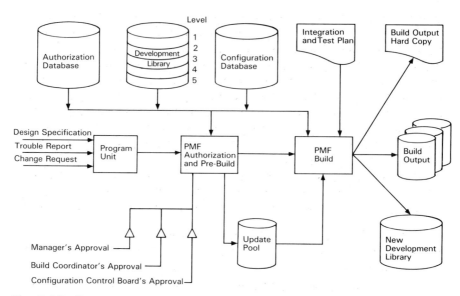

Fig. 6.22 Program management facility (PMF) control flow.

PMF can show whether the action occurred as planned. Variances can be reported and stored in a control database which can support several activities such as:

- Tracing the impact on other programs and alerting the affected people
- Estimating the schedule affect of the variance, particularly considering the impact on shared resources such as computer operations and publications support
- Analyzing trends in individual and group performance related to productivity and accumulated slippage

Similar control procedures can be applied typically to analysis of test results, measurement of program size and execution time, and assessment of compliance with standards. These are activities in which the normal functions of the PMF generate data which, with some effort, can be used to characterize the health of the project. Forecasts of future conditions based on the current status permit managers to change the plans as they see necessary.

The PMF process should continue from the design stage through operations and maintenance to termination because it:

- Establishes a controlled system for developing and releasing software
- Maintains a consistent set of documentation synchronized with each release configuration
- Provides a controlled method of introducing, evaluating, and incorporating program modifications in multiple, parallel releases
- Maintains the integrity and security of each release
- Increases visibility, efficiency, and accuracy through data control, progress tracking, and report generation provided by an automated library management and control system
- Supports multiple physical sites via telecommunications providing flexibility for developers and fast response for users and service personnel

Project managers who plan to obtain systems from subcontractors have to consider these benefits when they decide whether to constrain (at a cost) the subs to use the project PMF.

6.2.5 Performance Measurement and Prediction

Information about programmer performance can be generated automatically during the implementation stage of a project. The sort of information that can be obtained is:

- How long a programmer takes to design, code, and debug a program unit
- How many lines of source code are in a program unit
- How many lines of code have been changed or added to an existing program unit
- How many comment lines there are per executable source statement
- How many debug runs were required before a program unit was promoted to the Level 1 library

From this data, you can build a history of programmer productivity, program unit characteristics, and software engineering effectiveness [27]. On a spot check basis, you can compare individual performance to group norms. Assuming that program unit estimates were recorded in the early stages of the project, you can see which units are on target and which need help. As packages are built, additional information becomes accessible:

- How much virtual and real memory is required to run the program
- How many instructions on average are executed during normal operation (path length)

- Which instructions are never executed during tests
- Where I/O queues develop during execution and how the queues change under load
- How many bugs are detected during tests
- How many bugs per KLOC have been found in each module

6.2.5.1 Programmer performance

Measurements of programmer activity are useful only when there is an estimate against which to compare. As Pietrasanta said in 1968 [28]: "The problem of resource estimating of computer program system development is fundamentally qualitative rather than quantitative. We don't understand what has to be estimated well enough to make accurate estimates. Quantitative analyses of resources will augment our qualitative understanding of program system development, but such analyses will never substitute for this understanding." A useful approach to sizing a job is to get experienced people to estimate the gross requirements in the concept formulation and early design stages. Then, as unit design starts, ask the assigned programmers to estimate their tasks. The programmer responses are based on detailed analysis and carry the added value of commitments. When all the programmers' estimates are added up, they will fall short of the total project estimate. This is to be expected since the individual only knows about the program units he or she is assigned. Someone else has to add in the resources for management and support. The "someone" can be an experienced programmer or an administrative staff member who has been given guidelines for exploding the raw input.

In the 1950s and 1960s, it was quite common for the raw programming estimate to be adopted as an estimate of the project effort. Chapter 1 showed in Table 1.6 that actual project populations range from 1.5 to 4.5 times the number of programmers on the project. By overlooking this fact, many early projects were severely underestimated and project overruns were common. In the mid 1960s, project managers began to realize that major resource requirements were simply being omitted from their estimates. They started to correct the problem by adopting estimating guidelines that ranged from checklists to formulas. The approaches were meant to establish a ballpark estimate for the project workload that covered all applicable activities. While the guidelines were often quantitative, they were never good enough to invalidate Pietrasanta's statement. In the 1980s, program resource estimating remains qualitative, even though specific organizations have, through experience, developed some pretty good quantitative aids to estimating their customary jobs.

Experience remains the best basis for estimating. *Quantitative* methods are useful but not nearly as reliable as applicable experience. *Constraints* form the basis for an inverse form of estimating in which the estimate is known and the workload is adjusted to fit. A *Units of Work* method, common in business data-processing shops, is sometimes used for project estimating. Since the method is equivalent to a raw programmer's estimate, it is not applicable to systems.

■ Experience Method—This approach takes advantage of experience on a *similar* job. The new job must be clearly specified, at least down to the package level, so the estimator can compare the new system to one or more completed systems. Base data can come from the estimator's own experience or from other people, as long as genuinely similar projects are compared. If the two projects are alike in size and content, minor differences in algorithms or utility routines can be allowed for by adding a contingency factor to the total estimate. (In this method, the contingency should be less than 25 percent.) As in any method, it is wise to lay out the design in detail to permit the individuals who must implement the job to make their own estimates on their portion of the job. Their estimates will also be based on experience and should be more precise than the total estimate. In other words, two similar systems of 150,000 instructions each may be within 25 percent of one another in effort. Data-processing programs of 1,000 instructions each may appear in these systems. A specialist in that type of data processing should be able to estimate each specific task within 10 percent.

The major problem in the method is that it does not work on systems larger than the base used for comparison. System complexity grows as the square of the number of system elements; therefore, experience with a small system cannot account for all the things that will have to be done in a large system. Neither will the Experience Method apply to systems of totally different content. The Quantitative guideline is applicable in such cases.

■ Quantitative Method—The Quantitative Method is based on programmer productivity in terms of the number of deliverable program units produced per unit of time by an average programmer. The method is not precise; it is necessary to adjust the answer by large amounts. The estimator should never treat the answers as anything other than approximate representations of system size or resource requirements. The resource sizing equations in Chapters 1 and 3 are essentially models obtained from quantitative guidelines and tested against actual experience.

■ Constraint Method—This method is equivalent to taking an educated guess. Based on schedule, dollar, or headcount constraints, the manager simply agrees to do the job within the constraints. The decision is unrelated to the design complexity of the system. The merit of this approach is that it is often possible and, in some cases, beneficial for the user and the developer to reach mutual agreement on the constraints. Once agreed, they can proceed to define a set of specifications that can be achieved within the estimate. In cases in which either party does not understand the consequences of constraint estimating on product specifications, there is great risk of overrun. A given set of specifications will require a certain number of people-months to produce. If the people-months are not available, the specifications will have to be reduced in scope or the job will not get done. The Experience and Quantitative Methods assume the specifications are fixed and the people-months are estimated to satisfy the specification. The Constraint Method, if properly used, holds the people-months fixed and varies the specification to fit.

■ Units of Work Method—The history of small programming efforts, particularly in administrative and business data processing, shows far better estimating performance than large systems. This seems to be due to the use of a special case of the Constraint Method, which is called "Units of Work" for lack of a more descriptive name. In this method, each programming task is defined in such a way that it takes one programmer four to six weeks. Each task is designed, implemented, and tested independently of all other tasks. This approach eliminates the interactions that cause trouble in large systems but *programs written this way cannot normally be linked to form a large system.* (Guidelines for estimating individual program units are given in Part 1—The Individual Programmer.) A project estimate made by summing units of work will cover only the programming effort, omitting most management and support.

A specific quantitative estimating procedure was developed by this author to fit the history of large projects in IBM's Federal Systems Division from 1959 to 1969 [26]. The procedure found wide acceptance in other organizations, primarily because it was simple. The projects that contributed to the guidelines had not been carefully measured but general observations of staff growth and project organization were available. The life cycle chart that FSD used to represent their jobs had the form of Fig. 6.23. The scale of the life cycle resulted in the standard estimate that programming effort (crosshatched) represented 40 percent of the total project workload. Programming involved half the population from Package Design through Package Test. All the estimator had to do was estimate programmer workload and multiply by 2.5 to get the project workload. The estimator was told to sketch out the system in order to count the program units, then multiply the total number of units by the average number of instructions (basic assembly language (BAL) source statements plus data declarations) to get the number of instructions in the system. Dividing this figure by an appropriate productivity rate (Table 6.5) would give the total programmer-months required. To simplify the work there were only a few values in the

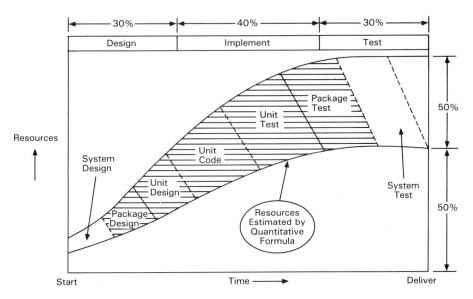

Fig. 6.23 Scope of quantitative estimate.
J. D. Aron, "Estimating Resources for Large Programming Systems," in *Software Engineering: Concepts and Techniques.* Edited by J. N. Buxton, P. Naur, and B. Randell. New York: Petrocelli/Charter, 1976.

table and interpolation was permitted. Increases in productivity due to learning were built in so that the right-hand column was more productive than the left-hand columns for "easy" and "medium" difficulty.

There is, of course, a hitch in this process. Everything depends on the instruction count in the system. This, in turn, is a function of the instructions in a program unit. But where does the latter figure come from? The author did not know at the time the work was published. He had used averages taken from a large sample. Nevertheless, the guidelines were useful. After several years, it became evident that the guidelines worked for several reasons. First, managers assign units of work to programmers in a consistent way. The size of a unit of work is based on the manager's conceptual ability, the presumed difficulty of the job, and the manager's evaluation of the programmer's ability. In a given group, assignments tend to result in programmer work loads of a fixed length. Managers accepted this and saw no inherent difficulty in estimating the size of the deliverable end product. Furthermore, in 1969, they agreed that an average program unit was 400 to 1,000 assembly-language instructions and it would take four- to six-programmer-weeks to be completed. The second reason the guidelines worked was that managers, after making an estimate, were willing to commit to it. The process built their confidence that the job could be done. If it was plausible, they would then proceed to make the estimate true.

TABLE 6.5. PROGRAMMER PRODUCTIVITY IN 1969

Duration / Difficulty	6–12 months	12–24 months	More than 24 months	
Row 1 — Easy	20	500	10,000	Very Few Interactions
Row 2 — Medium	10	250	5,000	Some Interactions
Row 3 — Hard	5	125	1,500	Many Interactions
Units	Instructions per Programmer-Day	Instructions per Programmer-Month	Instructions per Programmer-Year	

J. D. Aron "Estimating Resources for Large Programming Systems," in *Software Engineering: Concepts and Techniques*. Edited by J. N. Buxton, P. Naur, and B. Randell. New York: Petrocelli/Charter, 1976.

Table 6.5 shows that a 500 instruction program unit of medium diffi-culty would take two months. An easy program unit of the same size would take one month; a hard unit, four months. In practice, a manager would tend to make four- to six-week assignments. Holding the time period con-stant, the table implies that easy program units would be 500 to 750 instruc-tions; medium units would be 250 to 375 instructions; and hard units 125 to 200 instructions on the average in a large project. A project in which 70 per-cent of the programs were easy, 20 percent medium, and 10 percent hard would show a range of 410 to 620 instructions per program unit. This figure is consistent with the 400 to 1,000 range of consensus opinion. In 1969, most managers used 500 instructions per program unit as their rule-of-thumb.

The data from 1969 are too pessimistic for the 1980s. Improved pro-gramming techniques have at least doubled programmer productivity. Some people claim productivity rates of thousands of instructions per month, but these claims are usually associated with exceptional programmers, very easy jobs, or unreliable data. Productivity has improved but not dramatically. From 1960 to 1970, no change could be demonstrated. From 1970 to 1980, the factor of two seems to be validated by cost trends. Why isn't progress better? There have been various speculations about the reasons for the slow growth:

- Programming is an unstructured mental activity that is not accelerated by external aids and tools. This prevalent speculation seems to be refut-ed by the success of structured programming education and interactive support systems.

- Trainees are hired at a rate that holds the average capability of the pro-grammer population down. Perhaps; but there have been years when few new programmers were hired. Average capability should have risen in those years.

- Programmers do not learn improved methods. This has been widely true but will probably not be tolerated in the future.

- Programs are getting harder at the same rate that programmers get bet-ter. Programmers are given tasks that fit their capacity for work. They still produce the same number of units in a given time but each unit solves a harder problem and challenges a more powerful computer.

Table 6.6 is probably a realistic productivity model for the 1980s, assuming structured programming principles are applied. The entries in the table refer to the productivity of average programmers in terms of new assembly-language instructions plus data declarations written and delivered to the end user. Maintenance and update code modifies existing programs and involves more effort to make sure the unmodified code is not affected. Productivity for modified code is about half that for new code. There are two changes from Table 6.5 to Table 6.6. The entries are doubled and the productivity figures for easy and medium jobs in the six- to twelve-month category are slightly improved. The rationale for the latter change is that short jobs tend to be short because they are *relatively* easier to define and manage than long jobs. The workload should, therefore, be easier to carry out.

The quantitative estimating procedure assumes you know what you want to do. Some level of design is required in order to make the estimate. The degree of detail in the design depends on where you are in the life cycle and how much time you have to devote to the estimate. As a minimum, the system structure should be laid out in enough detail to support an estimate of the number of deliverable program units (PU). A first estimate is that the project will require *2.5 PU* people-months (for a single release end item) at one month per unit. After the first step of system design:

- Estimate difficulty of programs
- Estimate number of deliverable instructions
- Estimate duration of project
- Determine programmer-months
- Expand to project people-months
- Adjust result for unusual conditions

There is considerable flexibility in carrying out the process. When only a high-level design exists, units are estimated by the designers and all units are assumed to be the same size and difficulty. Later, each unit will be described in terms of instruction count and difficulty, as projected by a manager or as provided by the unit designer. Random errors in describing program units should cancel out when all the units are aggregated. Thus it is not essential to list all the units and calculate the programmer-months expended on each.

The total project estimate is

$$\text{Project people-months} = M \times \sum_{i=1}^{n} \left(\frac{\text{Deliverable instructions}}{\text{Productivity rate}} \right)_i$$

where M is a multiplier to expand programmer-months to project people-months. Programmer-months consist of the total project deliverable BAL instructions divided by an average productivity for the whole project ($i = 1$), or the sum of the easy/medium/hard workload ($i = 3$), or the sum of more detailed program units ($i > 3$). M depends on the nature of the project as shown in Table 1.6. If the instruction count is given in high-order language statements, the number of deliverable instructions will be about 1/4 of the size of equivalent BAL. The workload will only be about 1/2 as

TABLE 6.6. PROGRAMMER PRODUCTIVITY—NEW CODE

Difficulty	Duration 6–12 months	12–24 months	More than 24 months	
Row 1	Easy	50	1000	20,000	Very Few Interactions
Row 2	Medium	25	500	10,000	Some Interactions
Row 3	Hard	10	250	3,000	Many Interactions
Units	Instructions per Programmer-Day	Instructions per Programmer-Month	Instructions per Programmer-Year	

Note 1: Instructions consist of (BAL instructions + data declarations). If the number of deliverable instructions is given in terms of high-order language statements, table entries must be cut in half.
Note 2: Table entries apply to new code. Cut the entries in half to estimate modifications to existing code.

much; i.e., 100,000 BAL @ 500 LOC/month = 200 programmer months but 25,000 HOL = 100 programmer months. Therefore, when HOL is used in the numerator, productivity rates must be halved.

Since this method originated in FSD where large projects with three or more levels of management were the focus of attention, the assumption that $M = 2.5$ was applicable. Then a new group was spun off from FSD to work on commercial projects. These projects were small and the estimators, using $M = 2.5$, found they were overestimating the workload and losing competitive bids. The new environment produced data to show M should be as low as 1.5 in some cases. Several years passed before the relationships in Table 1.6 emerged. Now it is clear that project overhead is a function of project complexity. Complexity is related to size, which is related to structure and levels of management. The recommended value of M is 1.5 for jobs headed by a first-level manager; 2.0 for jobs headed by a SLM; and 2.5 for one-release jobs run by a TLM or higher. Multiple release projects such as a vendor OS have to extend their effort to support parallel and overlapping releases; the result is $M = 4.5$ for large multiple release jobs.

The productivity table assumes the use of average programmers organized in a normal pyramidal hierarchy. The formulas also assume an average development environment. No adjustment of the result is necessary unless the project deviates in an obvious way from the norm. Such an obvious deviation would be the assignment of all junior people with no experienced technical people to lead them. Another would be the requirement to use the first machine of a new line—one that has never been used before in an operational environment. The amount of adjustment appropriate is entirely subjective, since it represents the manager's confidence that he or she can overcome the effects of deviation. A typical range of adjustments is −25 percent to +100 percent, representing the fact that most managers assume any unusual situation represents a problem rather than an opportunity. Some deviations can double productivity by capitalizing on special skills in a small team. This improvement, however, may not be applicable to more than one or two projects within a large company.

Organizations with extensive historical data are able to identify some of the factors that affect their performance. The System Development Corporation spent several years in the 1960s to find a way to use these factors to predict project workload [30]. Starting with 104 variables in the programming process, they found 11 significant factors that seemed to predict project resource requirements. Unfortunately, the error of estimate was so large that the result was not acceptable from a business management viewpoint. A similar study by Walston and Felix, from 1975 to 1977 [31], had the advantage that the body of data came from one organization, the IBM Federal Systems Division. Sixty completed projects were described via a detailed reporting procedure covering 68 variables related to productivity, including delivered instructions and total people-months. A relation between these two factors was found for the completed projects.

$$E = 5.2L^{0.91} \text{ or approximately } E = 5L$$

where E is total people-months and L is KLOC delivered. As in SDC's work, the model has a large standard error: when $L = 100\,\text{KLOC}$, E is predicted to be 344 people-months plus or minus about 200 people-months. The approximation yields $E = 500$ people-months which is a conservative first guess. When the detailed database was run through regression analysis and 29 variables were selected as predictors, the error range was narrowed. To give each project manager the benefit of the history file, FSD built an interactive estimating aid. It accepts the manager's estimate of total workload along with a description of the project in terms of the predictor variables (Table 6.7). A regression is run to produce an estimate which not only gives the manager a cross-check on his or her own projection but also points out the variables that have the greatest leverage on the estimate. For example, variables 7–9 show the value of previous experience. Variable 17 shows that, in FSD top-down development projects, 321 deliverable source lines per programmer-month were produced, as opposed to 196 DSL/PM for old style programming. The project manager can act to change the value of these key variables to reduce project workload. The FSD estimating model is modified periodically to improve the results. Subsequent to the publication of [31] a revised model was based on 16 variables: 1, 2, 6, 7, 8, 12, 13, 17, 23, 24, 27, 28, 29 plus "KLOC delivered," "percent of effort at primary location," and "percent of code classified as fallback and recovery." In any case, the FSD model only applies to the FSD development environment. Halstead's "software science" [32] generalizes program measurement based on the number of operators and operands in the code. Although additional experience is needed with software science [33], it shows promise as a discipline for making choices while designing and coding a program. Boehm [34] developed a Constructive Cost Model, COCOMO, based on a study of 63 carefully screened projects from a spectrum of sources. For an average job with average attributes, Boehm's sample predicts

$$E = 3.2L^{1.05}.$$

(This is close to $E = 5.2L^{0.91}$ for programs of 10 KLOC to 100 KLOC. Boehm's predictor is lower for small programs and larger for very large programs.) Again, the predictor is less important than the attributes that contribute to the workload. Fourteen cost-driving attributes identified by

TABLE 6.7.   VARIABLES AFFECTING PRODUCTIVITY

Question or variable	Response group		
	Mean productivity (DSL/PM)		
1—Customer interface complexity	< Normal 500	Normal 295	> Normal 124
2—User participation in the definition of requirements	None 491	Some 267	Much 205
3—Customer originated program design changes	Few 297		Many 196
4—Customer experience with the application area of the project	None 318	Some 340	Much 206
5—Overall personnel experience and qualifications	Low 132	Average 257	High 410
6—Percentage of programmers doing development who participated in design of functional specifications	< 25% 153	25–50% 242	> 50% 391
7—Previous experience with operational computer	Minimal 146	Average 270	Extensive 312
8—Previous experience with programming languages	Minimal 122	Average 225	Extensive 385
9—Previous experience with application of similar or greater size and complexity	Minimal 146	Average 221	Extensive 410
10—Ratio of average staff size to duration (people/month)	< 0.5 305	0.5–0.9 310	> 0.9 173
11—Hardware under concurrent development	No 297		Yes 177
12—Development computer access, open under special request	0% 226	1–25% 274	> 25% 357
13—Development computer access, closed	0–10% 303	11–85% 251	> 85% 170
14—Classified security environment for computer and 25% of programs and data	No 289		Yes 156
15—Structured programming	0–33% 169	34–66% —	> 66% 301

C. E. Walston and C. P. Felix, "A Method of Programming Measurement and Estimation." *IBM Systems Journal* 16, no. 1 (1977).

TABLE 6.7.　CONTINUED

Question or variable	Response group		
	Mean productivity (DSL/PM)		
16—Design and code inspections	0–33% 220	34–66% 300	>66% 339
17—Top-down development	0–33% 196	34–66% 237	>66% 321
18—Chief programmer team usage	0–33% 219	34–66% —	>66% 408
19—Overall complexity of code developed	<Average 314		>Average 185
20—Complexity of application processing	<Average 349	Average 345	>Average 168
21—Complexity of program flow	<Average 289	Average 299	>Average 209
22—Overall constraints on program design	Minimal 293	Average 286	Severe 166
23—Program design constraints on main storage	Minimal 391	Average 277	Severe 193
24—Program design constraints on timing	Minimal 303	Average 317	Severe 171
25—Code for real-time or interactive operation, or executing under severe timing constraint	<10% 279	10–40% 337	>40% 203
26—Percentage of code for delivery	0–90% 159	91–99% 327	100% 265
27—Code classified as nonmathematical application and I/O formatting programs	0–33% 188	34–66% 311	>66% 267
28—Number of classes of items in the data base per 1,000 lines of code	0–15 334	16–80 243	>80 193
29—Number of pages of delivered documentation per 1,000 lines of delivered code	0–32 320	33–88 252	>88 195

Boehm can be ranked in order according to the potential gain in productivity an organization could get by improving its rating (according to guidelines spelled out by COCOMO):

1. Personnel/Team Capability
2. Product Complexity
3. Required Reliability
4. Timing Constraint
5. Applications Experience
6. Storage Constraint
7. Modern Programming Practices (IPT)
8. Software Tools
9. Virtual Machine Volatility
10. Virtual Machine Experience
11. Turnaround Time
12. Database Size
13. Schedule Constraint
14. Language Experience

As is often the case, the attributes with the greatest potential are the hardest to control and take the longest to change. Still, personnel development, IPT, and tools are very high on the list and provide a basis for management action. Boehm projects an opportunity for doubling organization productivity in three to four years and quintupling in six to eight years. The improvement (of about 20 percent per year compounded) is based on the assumption that all the attributes are independent. Thus, if $E = 3.2L^{1.05}$ when the tools and IPT ratings are both 1.0, $E = 0.8 \times 0.8 \times 3.2L^{1.05} = 2L^{1.05}$ after 20 percent improvements in those two attributes. It is very likely that the attributes are not independent and that the multiplier will be closer to 2.3 or 2.4. The rate of improvement will still be about 15 percent a year which is well worth a long-term commitment by management [35].

The initial estimate is the basis for evaluating individual programmers' estimates for the program units they will write. A unit that was classified as easy in the gross estimate should fit the norm for easy program units and, if the programmer's estimate is out of line, the manager should find out why. Nine times out of ten, the gross estimate was inaccurate and the programmer has the right estimate. In the tenth case, the programmer needs help. The responsible programmers' estimates go in the management database along with schedules and program unit characteristics. Trigger events are defined that report each instance of a program unit assembly and program execution. The trigger events can be recognized by analyzing the job control stream. At these points, physical information about the program unit can be collected—such as how many source lines are in the unit, how many are comments, etc. Date stamps permit the events to be related to schedules. From this type of data, information about each programmer's status and productivity can be deduced. The actual productivity for a single program unit is of little interest unless it is way out of line. In that case, the deviation is a trouble indicator but nothing more. The aggregate productivity for the productivity for the project is of interest because it shows whether the resource estimate for the project is still valid. Individual programmers will differ in productivity. Each programmer will vary from task to task. Rather than set targets for lines of code per day, managers track accomplishment in terms of scheduled events completed and task objectives satisfied. Programmer measurement is a gauge of the health of the project. It also helps in programmer career management. Direct supervision, comparing actual status with the programmer's committed plan for a unit of work, is still the best way to manage day-to-day performance.

During a project, predictions must be made about resources, schedules, and expenses. The most common way to predict is to say: "The current trend will continue unless I change something." If you have completed ten program units four weeks into a twenty-four-week development stage, but the plan calls for sixteen units, you are 37 1/2 percent behind schedule. If you do nothing to catch up, you can assume the twenty-four weeks will stretch at least to thirty-three weeks. A management decision to reassign programmers or borrow more people may recover the lost time, but a new estimate will be required. You will now have a new plan on which to base your next prediction. The actual "going rate" predicts the future outcome; if you do not like the prediction, you have to change the going rate. In dealing with programmer performance, you can speed up the rate by motivating the people, by extending the working hours, and by adding productivity tools. You can also change the workload.

6.2.5.2 System performance

Predictions must also be made about the behavior of the end items that are being developed. As an integral part of the design process, size and timing objectives are established. These objectives are constraints; therefore, program performance is normally estimated by a constraints method. Actual performance is determined when a unit is complete and can be run in an appropriate test environment. At any intermediate point, program performance must be predicted based on what is known at the time about path lengths, instruction mix, memory requirements, and quality.

These items and similar types of information are collected by observing and counting events. The instrumentation must be part of the project plan. Software data collection requires hooks in the code and tools for interrupting, recording, and reporting data. Hardware data collection requires interface design, tool design and procurement, etc. In either case, the instrumentation should not interfere with the operations that are being monitored. This can be done in software by running the live system in an artificial environment (a simulator). The simulator lets the live system run up to a point, stops it, records the system state, does whatever data collection is called for, restores the system state including the clock, and resumes execution. A simpler method relies on deterministic tools that interfere a precise known amount with the live system. The effect of the tool can then be subtracted from the data collected. In some systems there is not enough capacity to accommodate a desired software tool without distorting the live system behavior. The distortion has to be removed, either by giving up some of the desired data or by substituting a hardware monitor that is transparent to the live system.

The way to tell whether distortion is present is to examine system behavior with and without the tool. If a program is designed to use all the memory space it can get to speed up execution, it is predictable that a tool in memory will inhibit performance. This prediction is easy to verify. The live system is run without instrumentation and a stopwatch is used to measure elapsed time for a specific input load, given various memory allocations. A plot of several trials should show improvement in execution time as memory increases. Then the live system is run with the tool installed. The same memory allocations are made but now some of the space is used up by the tool. Each run with the tool should take longer than the corresponding run without it. Furthermore, the impact of the tool should be greater for small memory allocations because the tool, which is fixed in size, occupies proportionately more of a small memory (Fig. 6.24). If a series of runs under different conditions show that the tool impact is consistent, it can be calibrated. Measurement runs can then be adjusted to remove the tool impact; particularly if the affect is less than 5 to 10 percent of the measurement. If the tool impact is larger, you may mistake idiosyncrasies of the tool for problems in your program.

Program dimensions are relatively easy to measure. Static size can be obtained by counting source lines when the program enters a library. Object lines can be counted at assembly time or load time. Database size can be taken from job control commands or other references in program text. These measurements, however, are not going to reveal how the program runs. At best, they show whether the program system will fit within the real storage space. More interesting are measurements taken during execution. Each program unit has a natural working space but most of the time, the real space allowed for execution is less than what the unit would choose for itself. Two kinds of execution time measurements are needed to support predictions of performance. First, the path length and working space of the raw program should be obtained. This is done by allocating more than enough resources and running tests representative of the system load. Storage locations used by the raw program are recorded. Execution time is measured—job start to job end, average time per transaction or task in the input load, response time per transaction (which may be different from the time to process the transaction), and average time to execute each logical path or subprogram. Each test should invoke specific paths through the program—by design. Therefore, if the path length or, rather, the time required to execute all the segments of the path is known, the time to complete a transaction can be predicted. While measuring the path lengths, it is useful, when the tools are available, to note which instructions in the program are executed. Analysis of these data will give an average instruction time useful in forecasting the timing affect of program changes. It will also disclose code that was never executed. It might be unreachable dead code, or it might be a path overlooked by the test cases. The measurements taken so far characterize the raw program. As a rule, they represent the best performance that can be obtained from a program unit.

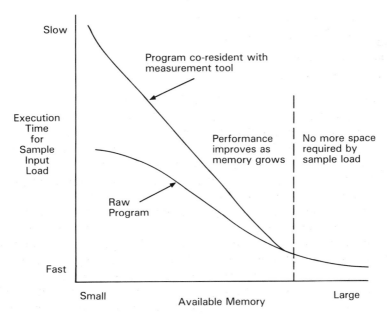

Fig. 6.24   Distortion due to measurement tool.

The second kind of execution time measurement examines a program unit embedded in its system environment. The environment may be simulated or real, depending on the maturity of the project. Now the program unit must share system resources with other modules. The same test cases will take longer to execute. Under the best circumstances, the execution time will be increased by the path length of the instructions that coordinate resource sharing. In addition, there will normally be a delay whenever the program unit requests a resource. Queues will build up in front of every shared resource. As a result, the system behavior of a program unit will be different from its behavior in an unconstrained environment. Measurements are needed to establish the average path length of coordinating elements and the queue lengths associated with various loads.

Analysis of system behavior often shows which features of a program have the most influence on performance. Knowing this, designers may decide to change some of the features. For example, Program A accepts a record from Program B and processes the record in 2,000 instructions average. Program B fetches records from disk, executing 10,000 instructions average. Programs like A generate record requests at an aggregate rate of 10 per second. The processor can execute one million instructions average per second. Data from the raw programs imply that $10(10,000 + 2,000) = 120,000$ instructions must be executed per second. When A and B are run together in a real environment, however, requests start to back up almost immediately. It turns out that B uses an operating system service to access the disk. The service takes 100,000 instructions per fetch—much of which is related to data integrity, disk access arm scheduling, and other coordination and management activities. Other very short OS services are called on to transfer control from A to B and back to A. The system environment measurements will be on the order of $10(10,000 + 2,000 + 100,000 + q_1 + q_2 + q_3 + q_4)$ where q_1 is the time A waits for B to be free in order to request a fetch; q_2 is B waiting for the OS service, q_3 is the OS service waiting for B (assuming the OS is smart enough to overlap all disk waiting time), and q_4 is B waiting for A to accept the fetched record. This is an oversimplified example (it ignores the path length for program switching services, among other things), but it is not extreme. Many database management systems operate exactly like this. A is an application written by the user shop. B is a subsystem written by the user shop or procured from a software house. The OS service is supplied by the computer vendor. The user can learn a great deal by measuring A and B but, to make predictions about the system, A and B must be measured in the OS environment.

System performance prediction is complicated by several factors. First, predictions are usually based on a mix of measured data and simulation results. Second, the number of system environment measurements that a project can afford is limited by cost and time; it is never possible to test all conceivable paths. Third, the characteristics of the workload are seldom known in detail; therefore, the frequency with which a particular path will be invoked is only an approximation. Likewise, the rate at which transactions arrive is an approximation. In a bank, for example, it is possible to sample the rate at which customers arrive at teller cages, but the sample will represent only a small portion of customer traffic. It will not necessarily represent the traffic after a new on-line banking system improves service. The normal way of handling this situation is to assume that future traffic will be some multiple of present traffic and that customer arrivals can be described as a Poisson process. The choice of a Poisson process facilitates calculation and, while it is not always applicable, it often fits system behavior. It has the property that the arrival rate does not vary with time:

- The number of customers arriving during any interval of time depends only on the length of the interval, not on when it starts.
- The number of arrivals in two nonoverlapping intervals are statistically independent.

When a number of statistically independent renewal processes merge, the resulting arrival process is approximately a Poisson process with an arrival rate equal to the sum of the arrival rates of the individual input streams. A bank teller receiving a customer does not know when the next customer will appear, but expects one to show up on the average t minutes after the first. The teller will enter a transaction through the on-line terminal sometime while serving a customer. On the average, t minutes later the teller will enter a transaction for the second customer. The distribution of customer arrivals around the mean, t, may be different from the distribution of transaction entries around t, but both are probably statistically independent renewal processes since they are based on the independent actions of individual customers. From the centralized host computer where all teller inputs are merged into one transaction stream, it will appear that traffic arrivals form a Poisson process; therefore, it is reasonably safe to assume they do.

Path lengths obtained by measurement or simulation describe the modules that could be involved in processing a postulated workload. System environment measurements show, for the test cases, which steps are actually invoked, how long they take, and how often they are called on by various types of transactions. A model can now be drawn up showing how a transaction enters the system, where it must wait for a shared resource, and the expected length of time it will occupy each resource. Different types of transactions take different paths and have different service times in each resource as determined by the measurement activities. Therefore, the queuing model can be calibrated for the expected mix of transactions making up the system workload. The model, if simple, can be mathematically analyzed;

complex models must be simulated. Interactive aids are available for defining queuing models and calculating resource utilization, throughput, and average response time. Simulations, of course, can be written in any suitable language. Systems such as GPSS or SIMSCRIPT simplify the effort. Lavenberg et al. [31] describe many techniques for computer performance modeling and simulation in their modeler's handbook. Spragins [32] takes note of the frequently poor data on which models are based and describes a number of approximate techniques for predicting performance. These include some unorthodox and, perhaps, mathematically unsound methods, but they tend to share two characteristics: They are easy to use on complex systems and they can be applied to situations that are not Poisson processes. Fortunately, most of these methods seem to be conservative; i.e., a prediction of execution time made with an approximate technique may be high—the finished product will run faster.

System performance predictions do not define a going rate. If a system takes 20 percent too long to process a job when the project is 50 percent complete, there is no reason to believe that the system will be 40 percent too slow on delivery. It may be at least 20 percent slow and, consequently, unacceptable unless something is done to speed up the job flow. The purpose of predicting performance is to compare expected results to requirements. When a prediction shows the system is too slow or too large, corrective action is required. The source of the problem should be isolated and the system design should be traced from that point back through the hierarchy to see where improvements are possible. Among the ways to improve speed are:

- Decoupling: eliminating dependencies that cause one piece of code to wait for another to complete
- Parallel dispatching: starting independent processes as soon as they arise if resources are available for allocation
- Fast path services: write specialized programs to handle I/O, program control, data access, etc., instead of using standard OS services
- Tuning: improve the code in a program unit
- Add resources: reduce queuing delays by having multiple disks and channels, more main memory, etc.

Storage utilization can be improved by using virtual memories, by tuning, and by separating code that must be resident from that which is only occasionally exercised. Unfortunately, all of these options may have a negative effect on performance. Corrective action through redesign must be an iterative activity. Predictions of the effect of each design change should make certain that each decision moves system performance in the right direction.

6.3 TEST

Tests are conducted to show that a product meets its specifications [38]. In team projects, the term *testing* is best used to refer to tests run by someone different from the product builder. The builder "debugs" a program unit and, when satisfied that it is correct, releases it to the system library for others to use. Once convinced that a piece of code is correct, no amount of additional effort will help the builder see a remaining error. The builder will also fail to recognize errors due to factors external to his or her assigned task. Consequently, the debugged programs in the system library may not be complete or correct and there is no assurance that they will interact properly. An independent tester will discover many, but not necessarily all, of the remaining errors when attempting to execute the programs in various combinations. The tester, of course, is looking for errors, whereas the builder is trying to demonstrate that the product is error-free. This difference in attitude permits the tester to recognize more errors than the builder. In addition, the tester has access to more information than the builder and can construct test cases that expose design errors affecting system interactions and ease-of-use as well as program unit defects.

The test plan is prepared in conjunction with design. As the system grows, the test plan evolves. Other quality assurance activities, such as design and code inspections, contribute information that can modify and improve the test plan or, at least, the test cases. Changes to the baseline must be reflected in the test plan, too. The tests themselves must be scheduled in such a way that the item to be tested, the test tools, the test cases and test data, and the computer on which the tests will run are all available at the same time. Furthermore, since tests can fail, the schedule must provide enough slack to permit faulty items to be repaired and retested without interfering with other planned activities.

6.3.1 Test Plan

A good test plan will provide a convincing demonstration that the system meets its specifications. In order to have a good test plan, you must leave enough time and money at the end of the project to handle the expected number of errors. Since you cannot predict which units will be affected by problems uncovered in testing, you hold everyone on board until package testing is finished. At this time, you can assume that individual units and packages are internally sound. Problems found in the next stage of testing are likely to be system structure issues. A smaller staff is able to respond to these since detailed knowledge of program units is not essential. In Chapter 3 (Table 3.2), a second-level project with 36 people in package test dropped to 18 people by the end of system test. A higher-level project had 250 people in package test and, again, half that at the completion of system test. The second-level project allocated 35 percent of the schedule and 38 percent of the effort to testing. The higher-level project allocated 42.5 percent of the schedule and 60 percent of the effort to testing. Other activities are included in these numbers but they nevertheless emphasize the large investment in testing. The disparity between the time devoted to test and the cost of the effort indicates that testing is a relatively inefficient activity. Everyone is available in case an error occurs in his or her area of responsibility but only a few people are actually engaged in fixing errors. The price paid for the idle staff is justified by the fact that a good test prior to final release is much cheaper than field repair of a faulty system.

A good test plan lists a number of tests, all of which must be completed for a reasonable judge to conclude that the system meets its specifications. A poor test plan lists a number of tests which, even if they were run completely, would not convince the judge. Poor test plans are written out of laziness or ignorance in some cases. More often, a poor test plan is the result of a budget squeeze. Testing comes at the end of the project and has to absorb the impact of all the overruns and slips that precede it. The type of problem that occurs can be illustrated with the second-level project in which there were to be thirty-six people on board for package testing starting in month 13 of an eighteen-month development effort. The people are recruited as planned, but a series of minor delays due to sickness, snow emergencies, and conflicts for machine time have caused a one-month slip in unit debugging. As long as the original budget holds, testing must now be squeezed into five months instead of six. The thirty-six people in month 13 did not do any package testing but they used up thirty-six people-months of the budget. The result, as shown in Table 6.8, is that the original plan to devote 38 percent of the project budget to the test stages must now be carried out with only 30 percent of the budget. The squeeze is magnified in many projects by the fact that the system itself has grown in size since the test resources were allocated; more tests will have to be run than were originally contemplated. The budget pressure may be relaxed if the quality of workmanship is higher than average. High quality reduces the amount of rework required. Unfortunately, the factors that cause the budget squeeze are frequently associated with low quality. The choices available to the project manager are to curtail testing to fit the budget—a poor plan—or to overrun the project plan in order to complete testing. The end user is best served by completing a good test plan. An overrun that results in a qualified deliverable product is generally cheaper than the cost and frustration associated with a delivered product full of errors. Testing in a controlled environment under the supervision of a project team that knows the product is far more effective and economical than the random problem reporting of end users.

TABLE 6.8. BUDGET SQUEEZE ON TESTING

Implementation effort

Month	Staff	Cumulative effort	Planned test	Actual test
12	35	290.5	———	———
				Lost
13	36	326.5		Effort
				———
14	36	362.5		
15	36	398.5	38%	
16	34	432.5		30%
17	26	458.5		
18	18	467.5	———	———
			Budget Limit	
(19)	(0)			

The contents of a test plan vary according to the complexity of the project. As a minimum, the plan should show what is to be tested, what is required to do the testing, and what criteria will be used to determine that testing has been successfully completed. One software project had the following test plan:

1.0 Introduction
   1.1 Brief description of the system to be tested
      1.1.1 System components
      1.1.2 Other components relevant to the tests
      1.1.3 General characteristics of the environment in which the system will be used
   1.2 Objectives of the test plan
      1.2.1 Types of tests—function, performance, documentation, stress
      1.2.2 Things that will not be tested as part of this plan—installation, readiness, unique user characteristics, etc.
   1.3 Method of Testing
      1.3.1 Integration and regression strategy
      1.3.2 Test case development, inspection, and verification
      1.3.3 Job stream and scenario control that isolates problems to a specific test case
      1.3.4 Problem reporting and resolution
      1.3.5 System test report
   1.4 Supporting Documents

2.0   Deliverables
  2.1   Test plan
  2.2   Test cases and inspection reports
  2.3   Test scenarios
  2.4   Report forms
  2.5   Operator procedures and training outline
  2.6   System test report
3.0   System Requirements
  3.1   Hardware
    3.1.1   Configuration required for developing test cases
    3.1.2   Configuration required for simulating test environments:
        host, terminals, communication links, load generator
    3.1.3   Configuration required for user acceptance tests
    3.1.4   Usage schedule: batch, interactive, dedicated
  3.2   Software
    3.2.1   Software system to be tested (in various configurations)
    3.2.2   Operating System
    3.2.3   Communications subsystems
    3.2.4   Network load simulation software
    3.2.5   Environment simulation software
    3.2.6   Measurement software
    3.2.7   Schedule for availability of each software system generation
4.0   Tests (for each type of test: function, performance, documentation,
    stress)
  4.1   Objectives
  4.2   Method
    4.2.1   List functions to be tested
    4.2.2   Select test cases for each regression level
  4.3   Configurations
  4.4   Entry Criteria
    4.4.1   Library release level of software to be tested
    4.4.2   Correspondence between test environment and user environ-
        ment (i.e., validate the use of simulation)
    4.4.3   Initial conditions of system variables
  4.5   Exit Criteria
    4.5.1   All functions exercised
    4.5.2   Test execution reviewed and verified: test duration, I/O vol-
        umes and rates, operator actions, correct outputs.
  4.6   Test Case Summary
    4.6.1   Brief description of each test case: objective, schedule
    4.6.2   Matrix showing which test cases apply to which functions
        (for each regression level)
    4.6.3   Operator scripts for each scenario
    4.6.4   Job stream makeup for batch inputs

As in most plans, it is impossible to fill in this outline at the beginning of the project. The plan is expanded as the project moves forward. Test objectives suggest a method of test implementation. Knowing what facilities are scheduled to be available at various points in time, the planner can lay out the sequence of tests to match the facilities. The initial set of test cases maps onto the system baseline specification; however, as the baseline changes, the details of the test case matrix change. Instructions on how to run the tests are added last, after scenarios and job streams have been designed. In a sense, the test plan is never finished because, during the test stage, problems arise which call for new or different test cases.

6.3.2   Test Objectives

A large program contains more possible execution paths than can be tested in a practical manner. A complete test would require that all possible inputs—legitimate and illegitimate—be studied for all possible program, machine, and environment states. Not only is a complete test too voluminous to consider, but the project team is probably unable to define a test plan that would be complete. There are too many variables, some of which were not even addressed in the system specification. An achievable test plan is, by necessity, a partial test of the system. The primary objective of the plan is to make the partial test convincing. A secondary objective is to limit the extent of the partial test so that testing is economical. The type of test plan that, at first glance, satisfies these objectives would have one test case for each function specified in the system design and each test case would be run once. Such a minimal approach is unacceptable. It is economical but not convincing. The single run of a test case ignores the effects of input variations. Only one set of system interactions is exercised by the test case, whereas you can be sure that the function it tests will invoke different interactions at different times. The plan also fails to convince because it limits the test cases to explicit functions. It fails to examine sequences and combinations of functions. It provides no information on performance (unless the specification has an explicit performance requirement). It is particularly weak because it does not probe the system to learn what can go wrong.

A couple of examples illustrate how a system can pass all the basic function tests and still fail as a system:

1. A security capability was added to an operating system to control end user access to programs and files. End users log on at a terminal, giving a security key as part of their identification. The design addressed the problem of typing mistakes by letting the end user make three attempts to log on correctly. If the user does not enter a correct key (i.e., one known to the system) in three tries, the system presumes an unauthorized person is trying to penetrate the security screen. The action taken at this point is to disable the end-user terminal and notify the Security Officer. The Security Officer, operating from any available terminal, can investigate and unblock the end-user terminal. Tests showed that the key recognition, authorization, retry, disabling, and notification functions all worked as specified for correct and incorrect keys. The system fails, however, whenever the Security Officer logs on incorrectly. In that case, no one can unblock the Security Officer's terminal.

2. A digital radio communications system for a local area has a central node that broadcasts periodic polling messages. Remote stations respond to the poll by sending a "ready-to-transmit" message. If more than one responds, the central node sends instructions telling each one when to start sending. Tested with three remote stations, everything worked fine. Calculations showed that up to twenty remote stations could be scheduled simultaneously. Then the system was installed for use by a company to dispatch maintenance engineers. While on a call, they key in questions for the central support staff to handle. The trial period went all right. As soon as the system was expanded for general use, problems appeared. When more than five remote stations called in at once, the central node stopped polling and the entire network had to be reinitialized. The test plan overlooked the effect of transmission errors. The central node could successfully schedule up to twenty remotes if and only if they responded without errors. In that case, the initial poll would elicit twenty "ready-to-transmit" responses; a schedule for twenty events would be issued; the twenty inputs would come in; and twenty acknowledgments would be issued. All this would take place before the next poll was required. Transmission errors disrupted this sequence. The central node would have to reject incorrect inputs and request retransmission from the responsible stations. As a result, there would be more than twenty events and they could not be accommodated within the original schedule. When the input schedule was extended, polling had to be suspended and could not be resynchronized without manual intervention.

The lesson here is that testing should look beyond the literal specification to consider implied and consequential behavior of the system.

The test plan specifies a list of test cases and a list of tests. Each test case serves a particular purpose and, where possible, only one purpose. The test case, combined with test inputs and files, is designed to yield predictable results; e.g., given a legitimate input and a valid database, it should produce a result within the range specified for the system. The result should be verifiable by manual means. The test case should also give predictable results when inputs outside the specified domain are supplied. The test runs are designed to exercise a controlled configuration of the system or some subset of the system. The objective of the numerous test runs is to evaluate the system with respect to the following points [39]:

1. Function
2. Performance
3. Structure
4. Usability
5. Quality

The baseline specification describes the functions to be performed by the system. It also gives performance specifications and may include explicit usability or quality requirements. Tests must be devised to show that each function is present and that it works properly. If there is a performance requirement, measurements must be taken to demonstrate that the requirement is met. Obviously, the measurements only apply to the situations represented by the test cases; therefore, the test plan must include cases that exercise the system realistically with respect to critical situations.

Regression testing, as discussed in an earlier chapter, is a consequence of the incremental nature of system integration. As program units are debugged, it becomes possible to assemble packages. The functions in a package can be tested independently of other packages; however, errors in later packages may cause changes in tested packages. Even if later packages are error-free, there may be package interactions that invalidate the test results of earlier runs. As a result, function and performance data obtained in the debugging and package testing stages should be treated as tentative. Only when the integrated system is tested can you be certain that its functions perform properly. System testing shows that a function that performs all right in isolation also performs properly in sequence with its specified predecessors and successors and is not fouled up by any other coexisting functions in the system.

A typical example of the difference between package testing and system testing occurs in most database management systems. Performance is specified in terms of the number of standard queries to a standard database that must be processed per minute. During top-down design and implementation, it is not practical to test processing time because there is no executable code. It is possible to test logic and data flow so that when the code is de-bugged and integrated into a query/response package, a query is processed as expected. Assume that the processing sequence consists of: (1) assigning a work space to the query, (2) analyzing the query, (3) forming a search re-quest, (4) calling on the retrieval function to fetch the requested data from the file, (5) processing the data, (6) formatting a response, and (7) placing the response in an output queue. Steps (2), (3), (5), and (6) are completely executed within the query/response package. Steps (1), (4), and (7) involve queues and services of other packages. Test of the query/response package in isolation can show how long it takes to execute the paths within the pack-age, but it cannot show how long it takes for the external functions to oper-ate. It will be necessary to run an integrated configuration under a variety of loads before you can adequately describe the expected number of queries per minute handled by the system.

The system specification is validated by *functional tests*. These tests re-quire many test runs. It would not be unreasonable to assume that they exer-cise all the code thoroughly. The fact is they do not. As Stucki reported [38], a program could pass all its functional tests and even be accepted for produc-tion when less than half its executable source statements had actually been tested. In the example he quoted, only 45 percent of the source statements, only 35 percent of the branches, and 37 percent of the subroutine calls were tested. What about the rest? Is it necessary? Would it work if it had been test-ed? Can it cause problems? If you drive down Main Street observing all the traffic rules, you can still be demolished by a speeder running a red light at an intersection. In Stucki's example, the tests showed that a safe driver could navigate Main Street. They didn't say whether there were any speeders car-eening around the side streets. *Structural tests* examine the side streets. Structural, or path, tests show that what has been built has been put together right. Combined with functional tests, the structural tests raise your confi-dence that the system will be acceptable under all circumstances. When struc-tural tests are finished, you should have executed 100 percent of executable code, branches, and calls. There may be unreachable segments of code, but at the end of path testing you should be able to explain why they are there.

Usability, except where it is specified to meet a performance require-ment, is usually tested informally. The test team is the first group to work with the integrated system. They are the first people to learn whether the de-liverable system is easy or hard to use. Their negative comments should be reported as "trouble" to be resolved. In the absence of a usability specifica-tion, it is not necessary to fix the so-called trouble. The project team, however, has a view regarding how the system is to be used. This view is based on the design and the original purpose of the system. It is also based on the normal guidelines for usability accepted within the developer's organization. If the trouble will prevent the system from meeting the project team's own standards, it should be corrected (with due concern for the cost and schedule implications of the repair).

Quality cannot be tested in the usual sense. For one thing, no one is quite sure what "quality" is. If, as many people would agree, quality refers to the probability that the system will work correctly at all times and under all allowed conditions, no test will suffice. Tests tell you something about the present; they do not forecast. Tests locate errors; they do not prove the absence of errors. If you want to test software to determine its mean time to failure (MTF), you will be unsuccessful. The corresponding question is handled for hardware by running life tests on machines and components and calculating the probability that any critical system element will fail. Alternatively, one can say that a machine "has 10,000 hours MTF on the average" if a large number of those machines were produced and field experience has been monitored to support the figure. Software cannot be treated the same way because it is not important to know the life of the components (namely, the instructions); it is only important to know that the right instructions will be invoked at the right time. Error-free software should never fail. If the error-free software has been installed wrong by an operator who entered incorrect initial values, the software may give the wrong results. The same thing can happen if invalid data is fed to a valid program. Common sense suggests that mistakes like these are not related to software quality. On the other hand, errors found in the software are a possible indicator of quality. Interest in this area has led to a variety of efforts to count errors in the package and system test stages in order to predict the number of errors in a delivered system [40].

The rationale for accumulating error statistics is that there is a relationship between the number of errors found prior to system release and those reported after release. The relationship depends on the way the developer works and on the nature of the post-release reporting. Large organizations with many programs can acquire enough data to influence their planning. Even in large organizations, the data may be of limited value unless it applies to programs that are distributed to a large number of users. When the conditions are right, an organization will be able to plot the rate at which errors are found by testing; later they will know the number of unique new errors found by all the users. On a system by system basis, it is then possible to say that when a system is coded it contains N errors per KLOC. Of these N errors/KLOC:

- a were removed during testing.
- b were discovered by users (and subsequently removed).
- $N - (a + b)$ remain.

The system originally delivered to users contained $X = N - a$ errors/ KLOC. X is unknown, but you can assume that $X \cong b$; in other words, the users find all the errors; certainly, they find all the ones that affect system performance.

If your database is large and stable, you can predict X if you know a; you can measure a during the test stages. By increasing a, you can theoretically make $X = 0$. This corresponds to the impossibly expensive case of testing every possible path under all possible conditions. If $X \cong b$, you can consider increasing a just enough to reduce b to an economical level. In practice, the number of unique errors found by users of a widely distributed program is a very small fraction of the number of trouble reports submitted to the maintenance group. Out of one hundred trouble reports, there may be only one or two new errors. The rest of the reports are duplicates, misunderstandings, or documentation errors. In this environment, reducing b may save a lot of maintenance expense [41]. If there is only one user, you may choose to let X rise. The user will report the bulk of the significant errors in the first few months after installing the system. After that, error reports just trickle in. For many months $X \gg b$ and, again, your maintenance expense can be held down. Organizations who have this type of data try to select an objective for X that is appropriate for the product, the user, and the business case. X might be set at 6 errors/KLOC over the life of a general-purpose system. That is, a 100 KLOC system will contain 600 unique errors when it is released to the field. To achieve 6 errors/KLOC with the available technology may require a test budget of $400,000. Continuing improvements in software engineering tools and techniques may permit the organization to establish a five-year plan to reduce X to 3 errors/KLOC for the same class of product while holding the line on test costs.

Software is capable of surviving many kinds of failures; therefore, the likelihood that the system will fail is a function of its recovery mechanisms [42]. Defensive coding can prevent errors produced at one point in a program from propagating any further. Reasonableness checks and alarms can alert the program to conditions that could lead to failure, permitting the system to remove the dangerous conditions before proceeding. The program may have been written to anticipate the problem, in which case it can correct the situation and continue running. Otherwise, it may be necessary to curtail operations, reinitialize, saving the status of key parameters, and resume operations with a warm start. Some problems result in a cold start in which current status information is wiped out, and the system must back up to a recovery point. Quality tests determine that recovery mechanisms are present and that they work. By timing the recovery procedures, the test team can estimate the availability of a system given an estimate of the frequency of system outages. The latter estimate is a judgment based on observation of system behavior during the test period.

6.3.3   Levels of Testing

Testing proceeds through several stages from debugging to package testing to system integration and testing, to the Product Configuration Inspection (PCI), to Acceptance Testing [43]. Each stage concentrates on a different aspect of the system, but the stages may overlap a great deal. All stages may use a common library of test cases; therefore, the same test may be run in several stages. To prevent the test effort from growing out of control, the test plan is structured. Tests appropriate at the debugging stage are not repeated at higher levels. This guideline permits the scope of testing to grow at each successive stage without necessarily increasing the resources required.

As summarized in Table 6.9, functional tests occur at all levels. Debugging is concerned with the function of a program unit. Are the equations right? What is the execution time? Have the boundary conditions been handled correctly? Package testing looks at the functions of a package which involves stringing units together as required by the test cases. User commands and communications interfaces are checked out at the package level. String testing of packages occurs at the system level where the functional tests are often built around a mission profile. The mission profile describes the system environment, the conditions of use, and the job to be accomplished by the system. Test runs against the profile are the basis for performance measurements. They also expose system limitations, usability problems, undefined interfaces, and other issues that may have serious effects on the system readiness.

Structural tests are run at the lower levels of the testing hierarchy. The best time to achieve 100 percent coverage of executable statements is during debugging. The author of a program unit is the best qualified person to determine how to set up a test that will exercise a particular path in the code. The debugging stage is also the most economical time to do path testing. The number of possible paths through a program unit may be say, 2^6. Ten such units have 10×2^6 paths, but the package they constitute could have 2^{60} paths. By exhaustively testing the unit, you need only examine its internal paths again when some functional test invokes the unit.

Debugging is done by unit programmers while higher-level testing is done by test teams who will want to know the extent of path testing during debugging. Record-keeping can often be a byproduct of debugging. The test environment can include mechanisms for flagging executed code and for tracing branches and calls. After execution, a report can be prepared showing the coverage for that run. A cumulative report will show the coverage achieved by the debugging process. Some analysis by the unit programmer is recommended because the object code may have been changed between runs. The test environment is usually not sophisticated enough to recognize this. Therefore, a string of code tested in run 1 but replaced prior to run 3

TABLE 6.9. LEVELS OF TESTING

Test characteristic	Level of testing				
	Unit	Package	System	PCI	Acceptance
Objectives	Execution time Unit interfaces Function Equations Procedures Boundary conditions Logic paths Every instruction executed	Package interfaces Intra-, Inter- Function Operation String test User commands	System interfaces Mission profile Limitations Performance Timing User response	Function Operation Accountability Performance Measurement Accountability Other specifications Operation Accountability	Function Operation Acceptability Performance Measurement Acceptability Usability Operation Documentation Acceptability
Responsibility	Unit programmer	Independent tester	Independent tester	Verification and validation group	End user
Test cases—Source	Structure of program Unit specification	Package specifications	System baseline specifications	All structure doc. All specifications	Requirements doc. End user doc.
CPU	Real or simulated	Real or simulated	Real or simulated	Real	Real
Test data	Real or simulated	Real or simulated	Real or simulated	Real plus simulated	Real
Application environment	Simulated	Simulated	Simulated	Simulated	Real (if available) or simulated

must be executed in run 3 or later to be counted in the coverage report. If 100 percent coverage is reported, the test team will be inclined to suspect that subsequent troubles are due to system interactions; whereas, if only 30 percent was achieved, they might study program unit implementation before blaming system design for the trouble.

Package testing examines assembled units to see whether they interact properly and whether the assemblage carries out the function of the package. As a secondary objective, package testing is intended to expose problems as early as possible. The secondary objective calls for several levels of packaging testing. Rather than wait for the "Protocol Conversion Package" consisting of a reader, a protocol converter, a protocol table builder, and thirty separate I/O terminal device processors, the plan will provide tests for:

- Package flow—As soon as the reader, formatter, and one device processor are available, determine whether a command to the package will invoke these units as required. A dummy table can be used by the protocol converter.

- Package function I—When the table builder is ready, test it with the reader, protocol converter, and as many of the device processors that are complete. Include fixes to date.

- Package function II—With all the device processors done, test the complete package. Include all fixes to date. Test all the processors and verify that the contents of the tables are correct.

- Limits test—When the package includes fixes from previous tests, see how it behaves under stress. Overload it by increasing the input rate and by invoking various combinations, sequences, or repetitions of device processor calls. Put invalid data in the tables and observe the effect. Insert errors in the commands that invoke the package or in the responses the package expects from other parts of the system.

This is just an example of how a package test can be structured, but it illustrates several points.

- Units within a package should be scheduled for completion in a sequence that fits the test plan.

- Early package tests exercise interfaces between units; later tests look at interfaces among packages.

- Early test runs show that the package function is carried out correctly. Consequently, early tests can use dummy data but later tests should have realistic databases.

- Systems do not operate in ideal environments; therefore, tests should provide information about package behavior in non-ideal circumstances.

- Errors found at one level should be corrected at that level. (Compromises may have to be made on this point in order to maintain library control.)

System integration and testing proceeds in steps like package testing. At this level, an initial assumption is made that all the packages are correct; therefore, it is only necessary to verify that the packages interact properly when the system is carrying out its mission. As noted earlier, this is the first opportunity to obtain meaningful performance data on system behavior. It is also the first time that users will be involved. Problems will appear at every human interface because the users will do things that were never anticipated in the design. Limitations of the system will have to be addressed. Following the general rule that all specified functions should be present and all other functions should be excluded (or adequately isolated), limitations will fall into two categories: things the system should do but cannot, and things the system should not do but does. Frequently, the system will not meet its timing specifications. In operator-controlled systems, performance failures are often due to the operator's inability to act on time, either because the action is too difficult or because the system was sluggish in responding to user requests. Some things the system should not do are the result of:

- Oversights: A U.S. pilot flying from Salt Lake City to Reno wants to view a map of the ground below at 40° latitude/115° longitude. (The pilot omits *North* and *West* since all U.S. points are north of the equator and west of Greenwich.) The computer, programmed for worldwide coordinates, displays a map for 40°N/115°E. Thus, instead of seeing the Nevada map, the pilot is looking at Beijing (Peking). The computer should have been programmed to ask for more data if there were any chance of misinterpreting the pilot's input.

- Naiveté: Assuming that users submit jobs at random with a normal distribution of storage requirements, an operating system used a simple FIFO queue to process service requests. It took the users less than two weeks to analyze the effect of this strategy on response time. They then started to bias the system in their individual favor. By logging on early in the morning, asking for large disk allocations, and submitting a sequence of canned requests, a user could win a position at the top of the priority list and keep it all day without submitting any more work. If the intent of the OS design was to provide fair service to all users, the design should have been subjected to misuse to see that it was robust under all conditions.

■ Awkward design: A telecommunications system keeps an error log in a file that is periodically dumped to an archive. If the system has an outage, the cause of the outage is often explained by the last few error reports. Maintenance personnel can examine these on-line. To make sure there is always room to add error reports to the log, the system notifies an operator when the file is 85 percent full. The operator can then issue the dump command. In practice, this system failed because the operators had so many other things to do, they ignored the 85-percent warning. The logs filled up and current errors were not recorded. Naturally, that is when a hardware failure would occur. The maintenance people would search for diagnostic clues in the log but would not find any recent entries. Whatever caused the failure would remain in the system. In this case, the system should not have depended on manual initiation of the dump procedure. The 85-percent alert should have been given and the dump should have proceeded automatically unless the operator intervened to stop it. Alternatively, the log could be designed to wrap around so that old messages are sacrificed to make room for current data.

An objective of system testing is to expose problems such as these. The project manager must decide whether to fix each problem prior to release. The options are:

■   Delay release of the system until the fix is integrated and tested.

■   Release the system without fixing the problem but document the restrictions that will make the system acceptable despite the known problem.

The first option is appropriate when the problem interfaces with system effectiveness. The second option is more common. The documentation shows the user how to make the system perform properly. In most cases, the user will be unaware of the existence of the problem. That gives the project manager two more options for followup activity:

■   Fix the problem as part of a subsequent release.
   1. If the fix repairs a deficiency, it is included in a maintenance release.
   2. If the fix removes a restriction, it may be released as maintenance or sold as a system enhancement.

■   Do nothing.

The severity of the problem, coupled with the cost of the fix, dictates which of these options is appropriate. Questions of quality and cost are involved that affect the user. For these reasons, the user (and, where applicable, the buyer) should be consulted before the final decision is made.

Successful completion of system test means that the system is ready to release. A deliverable package is put together and handed over to the user with a report on the system test results. The careful user, at this point, insists on two more tests: Product Configuration Inspection (PCI) and Acceptance Test. The PCI is an inspection to determine that all the deliverables are in the package and that the system works in the user's facility. The user knows that the system was fully tested, but the tests were conducted by the project manager's team at the team's facility, maybe on simulated equipment, using canned data. PCI gives the user an opportunity to independently account for all the deliverables and observe them working on the real target equipment with real data in addition to canned tests. In a contract, the PCI proves to the buyer that the vendor has done the requested job. Since the emphasis in the PCI is on accountability, the buyer may take a "show me" attitude, letting the vendor run the tests while the buyer observes. The PCI can be combined with Acceptance Test, in which case the user should conduct the tests while the vendor observes and assists.

The emphasis during Acceptance Test in on "How *well* does the system work?" and "Does the system do my job?" For this type of test, a simulated environment is undesirable. The system should be installed and operated for a period of time in a live environment. The loads may be a subset of the total workload for the application but they should be realistic. Actual end users and real data should use the system under normal operating conditions, if at all possible. The desired outcome of Acceptance Test in a contract situation is acceptance of the delivery, relieving the vendor of further responsibility. If the contract is satisfied, but the user does not find the system acceptable, any rework would represent a new scope of work calling for a contract amendment. Final delivery is not the time to learn that the system you bought does not meet your requirements. A phased implementation plan avoids such surprises.

6.3.4   Test Group Organization

Each level of testing involves a different set of people. Unit test is done by unit programmers as part of their development responsibility. Package and system testing are done by test teams usually drawn from the development organization. PCI and acceptance testing are run by independent test teams. A separate quality assurance group may exist to monitor the adequacy of the test activities. At each level, the point of view is slightly different. The lowest level (development test) concentrates on structure and accuracy. The middle levels (integration test) concentrate on function and performance. The highest levels (verification and validation) emphasize accountability and acceptability.

The organization dynamics of testing depend on project size. In a large project, a test and evaluation department will be established at the beginning. This group develops the detailed test plan and builds the test case library to be used for package testing and subsequent tests. The group also sets up and maintains a status file that records what has been tested and what the results were. As packages become available, test teams are drawn from this department to run package tests. Problems identified in the tests will be turned over to the unit programmers who are standing by for this purpose. After the first stage of package testing, the unit programmers can be drafted into the test organization since few subsequent errors will be directly traced to a single unit. As the test group grows, it will evolve into three or four subgroups. The largest subgroup conducts tests. The others are responsible for building test configurations, for maintaining these reports and tracking problem disposition, and for writing additional test cases when necessary.

Smaller projects cannot afford so much parallel activity. As a result, package testing has to wait until enough unit programmers complete their assignments to constitute a test team. Sometimes test cases can be prepared in parallel with deliverable units, sometimes not. In either case, the project manager has to trade off the thoroughness of testing against the time required to write the desired number of test cases. System integration in a small project is a byproduct of library management. One person is responsible for master library control but everyone may be authorized to extract items from the library to build test packages. "Public documentation" shows what is being tested, what is being changed, and who is doing the work. Being public, the documentation gives the same story to each person who refers to it. Tests will not be wasted because they are run on obsolete versions of the base system.

Development testing is done by the developer because familiarity with the code improves the efficiency of testing. Peer reviews and inspections support the developer. As the system is integrated, test teams concerned with system structure, library status, and test procedures are formed. Their motivation parallels that of the developer; namely, they want to use the testing process to improve the system. Organizationally, they usually report to the project manager (directly or via a strong dotted line) because their function is to help get the product out the door. Verification and validation are quite different. The PCI and acceptance testing are concerned with compliance and qualification. They are part of a handover procedure involving contracts, payments, and shifts of responsibility. After the handover, the development stage is finished and the operations and maintenance stage begins. It is important to both parties that the PCI and acceptance tests be fair. Neutral test teams belonging to neither the project manager nor the buyer/user would be appropriate (yet only the largest organizations maintain permanent quality assurance groups for this purpose). Typical projects negotiate a compromise approach. Initially the developer and acceptor agree on the basis for the PCI. This involves identifying the specifications to be verified and listing the tests to be run. They also agree on what constitutes an acceptable environment and a successful result for each test on the list. With this checklist, it is possible for a nontechnical observer from the accepting organization to see that each test is truely and fairly run. Under the circumstances, anyone could run the tests. The developer's test team is best qualified; let them do it. In this manner, the buyer/user controls the verification and validation procedures but uses the project manager's people to carry out the work. The same approach could be used for acceptance testing but it would not make much sense. User personnel are going to operate the system. The system should be acceptable to them. User personnel should control and carry out the acceptance tests. The project manager can help by providing technical support, guidance, and training, but that is all.

It is difficult to build much test expertise in any but the largest organizations. The unit programmers who rotate through the test group at the end of a project have no special training or experience as testers. The few experts who move from project to project rely on test plans and procedures to achieve the quality control demanded by the organization. Then, to verify that the plans and procedures are followed, a quality assurance group examines all the projects periodically. This can be done at periodic reviews by managers but, in large organizations, quality assurance is the responsibility of a permanent organization. It monitors the implementation of procedures, standards and practices, organizational guidelines, and contract requirements. The group looks at:

- Quality management
- Adherence to standards, practices, and guidelines imposed by a contract or by the organization
- Configuration accounting procedures
- Document inspection procedures
- Test plans and controls
- Library control
- Reporting procedures
- Procurement quality assurance
- Compliance with government regulations
- Deliverable package verification

If the quality assurance reviews turn up discrepancies, they are corrected fast so that, at the end of the project, it is safe to say, "Our procedures are sound and we carried them out properly."

6.3.5   Test Case Development

The quality of testing depends on the quality of the test cases. As in any investigation, you have to ask the right questions to get the right answers. At every stage of a software project, questions are selected to show that the work to date is consistent with the specifications, that it is complete, necessary, and correct. Test cases are designed to provide the answers to the questions. Howden [44] points out that test cases are required throughout the life cycle and, in general, are designed to meet the same objectives at any stage of the life cycle. Cho [45] recommends that a specification of the input domain be incorporated in the project file as a vehicle for life-cycle continuity. The specification, SIAD (Symbolic Input Attribute Decomposition), is a form of decision table. It supports objectives such as:

- Each conceptually different function requires separate tests.
- Each abstract class of data requires separate tests.
- The unique properties of each data class should be tested.
- The boundaries and special values of each data class should be tested.
- Data and control flow paths should be traced to show they exist and lead to the right conclusion.
- Invariants should be tested to see that they do not change.
- Values that are set or referenced should be tested to see that they get set and are used.
- Data structures should be tested to see that the structure is preserved and that all entries are reachable.
- Error detection routines and alarms should be tested to see that they work in the presence of errors and abnormal conditions.
- Intermediate results are tested to show that assertions applicable at each point are valid.
- Messages are tested to see that they evoke the expected response.

A banking system that processes teller transactions may distinguish inputs less than twenty characters long from all others. The system provides a fast path for the short transaction on the assumption it came from a customer who is in a hurry. In this system, a deposit carries transaction code "1"; withdrawals of cash are "2"; withdrawal by cashier's check "3"; etc. There are twenty codes in all. Each is a different function and must be tested. On the other hand, the routine that examines the transaction code and branches to the appropriate process need not be tested twenty times. It suffices to show that the routine can recognize any code from 01–20 and branch accordingly *and* that it can recognize codes of 00, 21 or higher, or alphameric codes and signal an error. The class of transaction codes (01–20) has homogeneous attributes; if one member of the class works correctly, any member should work correctly. The class of numeric values that are not transaction codes (00, 21–99) has the same attributes but fails a limits test. The class of alphameric values fails the numeric attribute test. By defining the abstract data classes, the number of discrete values that must be represented by test cases is reduced. Furthermore, the definitions give enough information about the date class to permit you to design a generator whose output is known to be in (or not in) the class.

A teller transaction, type 1, should cause the customer's account balance to increase by the amount of the deposit. The transaction router sends the transaction to a deposit process where it either gets the fast path treatment or the normal treatment. Normal treatment posts the balance immediately. The fast path queues the deposit amount but tells the customer it has been posted. Obviously, the system should be tested to see that: (1) the entries in the fast path queue are eventually posted to the customer accounts, and (2) there is no sequence of transactions that can erase, modify, or duplicate entries in the queue. The customer's master record is identified by an invariant customer number. When the demand deposit application is running, this number should not change; otherwise, money could disappear or fall into the wrong hands. Tests should verify that the customer number has not changed and, moreover, that there is no path in the code that would change it. The opposite type of test backtracks to verify that when a variable is set its value actually changes to the correct new value.

When the customer opens a new tax-free investment account, it is represented as a branch of a tree structure. The root is the customer name record. The first level of branches separate bank accounts from loan accounts, real estate data, and credit history. The second level under bank accounts separates the various types of checking and savings accounts. The new account is entered here logically, but physically it may be stored on a separate disk due to overflow. Tests should show that: (1) any record at any level can be accessed regardless of physical location, and (2) only authorized accesses succeed. It is also a good idea to remove the second disk and see if the system raises an appropriate alarm when it seeks the customer's new account. Intermediate results of the logical-to-physical mapping of the database should show that the desired record is located on a disk listed in the system configuration table. If there is no such entry in the table, an operator message should be issued that causes the operator either to mount a disk or report that there is no such disk.

A test case can consist of a simple item of data or it can grow to a full-blown scenario. A program that routes transactions can be tested by feeding it one record of appropriate size in which all fields are blank except the transaction code. A more thorough test would involve a string of records with various entries in the transaction code field to test all features of that class of data. It may be necessary to schedule the arrival of each record to test the ability of the routing program to clear its buffers and reinitialize its status in time to accept the next record. If the program notifies an operator when it recognizes an illegal transaction code, an operator must be on hand to see the notice, interpret it, and reset the program status so processing can continue. As this example expands, it becomes evident that even a simple test case can become very involved. What with documenting the test case itself, plus preparing associated files and writing programs to be used in running the test, it is not unusual for the volume of work done in writing test cases to equal the amount done in writing the deliverable end products being tested. Each test case becomes a document containing:

- Identification (within the project numbering scheme)
- Objectives
  1. Purpose of the test
  2. Rationale for running such a test
  3. Scope of test (what program, what function, what path is tested)
- Environment
  1. Hardware/software configuration required to run the test
  2. Drivers, exercisers, simulators required for support
  3. People needed to run test (test team, user proxies)
- Test Conditions
  1. Sequence diagram (where does this test fit in the development and test plan with respect to prerequisites and subsequent activities)
  2. Timing (is the test run in real-time, simulated time, with manual control, or remote batch mode)
  3. Resource utilization estimates
  4. Recording and data reduction requirements (what is to be collected—how much, how often—and what tools are to be used; how the data will be processed for further analysis)
- Test Description
  1. Test case input (specific values and formats)
     a. system initialization data
     b. data inserted during the test (volume and arrival rate)
  2. Test case data files (specific values, file structure, placement of values or dummy data)
  3. Step-by-step description of test execution
  4. Outputs expected
  5. Action to take in special situations
  6. Completion criteria
- References

Bank withdrawal transactions could be tested initially in batch mode to verify logic. Later, withdrawals entered through terminals would have to be checked with real teller terminals or cash dispensers operated in real-time by people acting as tellers or users. In each case, a set of supporting programs would be required to:

- Generate a customer account file.

- Generate withdrawals for different customers.

- Copy the record actually accessed by the withdrawal transaction before and after processing.

- Analyze the data collected to verify that the new balances are correct and that the customer identifiers are unchanged.

- Analyze the error log to verify that illegal customer names and over-drawn accounts were properly reported.

- Scan the unused portions of the database to see that they are un-changed.

The supporting programs become part of the test case; although they may be incorporated by reference when they are common to several tests.

Test cases can be written in parallel with program implementation for all tests related to baseline specifications. Test cases related to path testing and change specifications are written after the implementation has proceeded far enough to provide the information needed to start. Still later, during the test stage, static analysis reports will show that parts of the deliverable system have not been covered by any test in the library. At this point, new test cases are designed specifically to reach into the untouched areas and exercise the code. A backtracking technique is used to find a path from the target area back to the program entry point. Looking at Fig. 6.25, where the heavy lines represent portions of a program covered by tests already run, two paths remain untested. In this example, the test cases relate to withdrawals from a bank account. The withdrawal must have a transaction code of 2, 3, or 4. Inputs with these codes can be intermingled with other types of transactions to test all the branches of "ROUTE Transaction." Inputs with code 2 or 3 must also have a customer number, an amount, and, optionally, a mode of delivery. Varying the values of these fields covers branches 2 and 3 of "ROUTE Withdrawal." Code 4 requests that the funds withdrawn from the customer's account be transferred to another account. The transfers can end up in the same bank, even in another account belonging to the same customer, or the funds can go to an account in another bank.

A simple way to test transfers would be to initialize a test database so that the records represent a nearly complete sequence of customer numbers, all with the same account balance. This set-up makes it easy to scan an out-

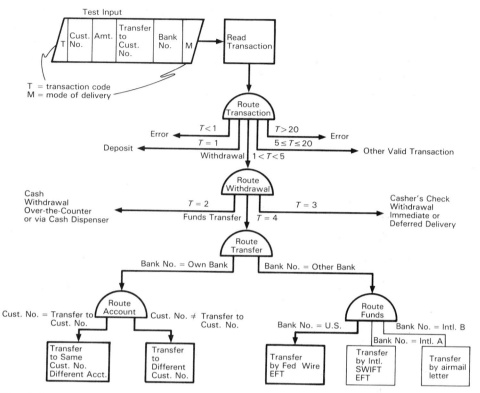

Fig. 6.25 Path testing—Backtracking.

put listing to see if the withdrawals took place and if the arithmetic was done correctly. Since the sequence has some customer numbers missing, the file supports tests on illegal or incorrect inputs. Any entry in the Bank Number field different from the processor's own bank tests the ability of the system to ship funds elsewhere, but this latter test is limited to the use of the Fed Wire electronic funds transfer (EFT) facilities of the Federal Reserve System in the United States. Static analysis of path coverage will disclose this limitation. An examination of the omitted paths shows that a Bank Number different from "Own Bank" and outside the United States is required. So far, the data needed to run the tests have been limited to the dummy customer account database and a constant identifying "Own Bank." Backtracking leads to a requirement for another database containing a list of Bank Numbers, flagged to show: (1) whether they are United States or foreign, and (2) whether they are members of the SWIFT international EFT network. Now by inserting additional test cases with appropriate Bank Number values in the test case input·stream, you can reach all paths.

6.3.6   Testing

The writeup for each test case includes a set of step-by-step instructions for the test team. This is important because the test team usually has no prior experience with the program being tested, or with the test case, or even with the process of testing. By following the instructions in the test case, the operators can run it correctly, in most cases. [12] To help with reports, the test cases will call for specific results to be printed and for dumps to be taken under certain conditions. The operators will also be asked to write down their observations. The printouts are hard data that are the best source of help when a problem arises, but they are voluminous. The operator's comments are soft data that is often vague, perhaps wrong, and generally lacking in detail, but it may be the best clue to the cause of a problem. Therefore, a test report should always include both the tester's comments and the test printouts. The quality of the tester's comments can often be improved by training and drills. It is of little use to read on a trouble report: "The machine stopped." The tester should have been taught to record the available status indicators when the machine stops. Through drill, the tester can learn to record manual operations and timestamp significant events as they occur and before recovery actions erase the failure symptoms.

An observant tester will report symptoms that an automatic recording instrument may be unable to sense. Automatic recorders are pretty much limited to an awareness of their immediate environment. Furthermore, when the recorder is given false information, it may accept it as true. The test operator can see the entire test environment, not just the subset being measured. If the test is being run in a simulated environment, the tester can tell whether the simulator has been set up properly and whether the necessary real resources are available. In a situation where an input workload is simulated by a separate computer, the operator will recognize when the input generator is saturated. A programmed performance monitor, in the same situation, may imply that the input rate leveled off because the program under test was overloaded. The monitor, after all, is unaware of the existence of the input generator. When real terminals are used, the tester can see garbage printed out and conclude that the print element on the terminal is not the one indicated in the log-on procedure; automatic recorders will accept the log-on as a valid description of the physical terminal. Of course, the tester can also be fooled. When a copy of a system program carries the wrong label on its container, the tester will believe the label. When errors occur, the tester will normally assume they are due to program faults

---

12. The system test library is very large. It would be cumbersome to handle; therefore, a test folder is made up for each test run. The folder is tailored to the run so the test team need not search through unrelated material for instructions or explanations.

rather than to an incorrect test setup. This is a case where automatic procedures can be used to avoid testing problems. In other words, the test team and the test tools complement each other.

6.3.6.1 Test scheduling

Testing consumes a great deal of computer time and people's time. Effective use of this time calls for careful scheduling. Tests at many levels of the test plan can run on the same day. A particular version of the system has to be generated for each test; therefore, many different versions may have to be put together each day. The integration group does this, working a day or more ahead when they can. Using the system library and the development support system, they can interactively assemble the components of a version which can be dispatched to an overnight batch process to be linked and initialized. Then, each version can be loaded into the host processor. Testing can proceed if the required hardware, software, and human resources are on hand and available for the expected duration of the test.

A schedule that resolves the constraints implied by these conditions is very difficult to plan. A similar problem exists in the management of satellite launch and control operations. There are only a few launch pads and there are a limited number of tracking stations spotted around the world. A launch pad must be reserved for a week or more for each satellite launch. After the launch, the satellite will pass over various tracking stations. The stations must be reserved for a short time in each orbit to track the satellite and send up commands. As more satellites are orbitted, the requests for resources conflict as several satellites pass over the same station at the same time. Eventually a computer program is needed to find feasible schedules. Program projects seldom use scheduling optimization programs; instead, they trade scheduling ease for testing efficiency. Each test implies that a particular configuration of hardware, software, and people will be reserved for a definite period. Several tests that use the same resources may occur on the same day. In some cases, they can share the resources and run simultaneously. Otherwise, they must run separately; one after the other, if possible. Sequential use of the same resources minimizes overhead. The same program version can be retained in the host, and configuration setup can be kept simple. A conflict arises when the second test is the responsibility of a different test team. You do not want to make the first test team stand around doing nothing while the second team uses the facility. You should try to schedule tests in such a way that one test team handles all the tests related to a given version and facility configuration. One way to do this is to assign all the tests at a given level to one team. This solution is applicable to the latter levels of package test and subsequent tests. Unit testing and early package testing are less demanding of resources and can usually be run in shared resources; particularly in a virtual machine host large enough to support several test teams operating in parallel. Still, the test stage of a project will involve idle time and inefficient resource usage due to schedule conflicts.

6.3.6.2 Test sequencing

Tests are expected to fail. The whole point of the testing exercise is to find problems so they can be fixed before the product is released. Failure causes regression. A package that appeared to be ready to release yesterday may not be ready today. Prior to the first release of a product, the implementation library contains all the system components in various stages of readiness. When a test reveals a problem, the test report is routed to the people who can fix the problem. When the component is fixed and retested successfully, it can be promoted. Eventually, all components will reach level 4 (Fig. 6.21) where they can be integrated into a system ready for release. On release, the system moves to level 5, the master library. When the first release is placed in use, the phased implementation plan is moving Release 2 up the levels of the implementation library. Release 3 is not far behind.

Now a new issue arises. Every version of the system contains errors which, when found, lead to a potential change. There will be functional deficiencies, too. Some of the problems will be important enough to justify changes to Release 1. The others will be assigned to Release 2 or later releases. In the meantime, the work in progress on Release 2 is going through levels of testing, exposing the need for changes in Release 2 and subsequent releases. What should be done first? Considering only the relation between Release 1 and Release 2, there are several alternatives for the Release 2 development group including:

- Fix errors found in Release 2; defer action on changes originating in Release 1 until Release 2 is complete.
- Change Release 2 to fix errors found in Release 1; defer testing Release 2 until a new baseline is established; then test and fix the final Release 2.
- Make changes as they are approved regardless of their source; update test plan to match the changing Release 2 baseline.

The first alternative is the easiest for the development group to control. It restricts their attention to what they know. Errors in Release 2 code will probably be fixed fastest and most reliably under this alternative. However, the impact of deferring Release 1 changes may lead to costly and difficult modifications after Release 2 has reached the level 4 system library. The second alternative disrupts the Release 2 development plan. It forces developers to drop what they are doing and refocus on parts of the system they may be unfamiliar with. On the other hand, a Release 1 change made promptly may save a lot of wasted effort. The third alternative is the hardest to control. Changes are made as they arise and there is no opportunity to get an overview of the impact of one change on another or of the set of changes on the system architecture, yet this can be the cheapest alternative if the system does not collapse. Control is important enough to make the first alternative more attractive than the others. (It corresponds with the general guideline that fixes should be made at the level where the problem was found.) An even better solution is to make essential repairs directly on Release 1 and defer other Release 1 changes to Release 3. This procedure gives each phase a sound baseline at the start and reduces turmoil in the middle of the phase. Restated as a guideline: Submit all trouble reports, regardless of source, to the configuration control group for evaluation; changes required to permit Release N to function should be made as temporary fixes (implemented as patches if necessary) to Release N; changes that significantly change system architecture are made in Release $N + 1$ for economy; all other changes are assigned to Release $N + 2$ or later releases based on their urgency and economic value; permanent fixes replacing Release N patches will appear in Release $N + 2$.

Many users have adopted a migration strategy based on a similar procedure. A mature installation can make minor changes to its system programs at any time, but a major change, such as installing a new release of the operating system, can only be made once or twice a year. It takes six to twelve months for the new system to settle down and provide the stability so important to normal operations. The phase plan for major operating systems produces a new release about every six months. Therefore, a user with Release N can expect to approach but not achieve stable operation before Release $N + 1$ is offered. Further, there is reason to expect that problems encountered in Release N will not have been fixed in Release $N + 1$. Release $N + 2$ is the better migration vehicle for the user. The "skip-release" schedule has benefits for both the developer and the user.

The integration and test environment is built up in a sequence that provides the appropriate support at each level of testing. Small application systems being added to the inventory of programs in a corporate Information Systems Department can often be tested in the normal job stream of the data-processing center. Test time has to be scheduled well in advance, but few facility changes will be required. At the other extreme, a real-time system of large size needs a specially tailored environment that eventually is dedicated to the new application. An example will illustrate the sequence of events for a system designed to manage a series of satellite missions. Some of the satellites gather military intelligence data; for these, a *security control* system is required. Approved missions are scheduled as part of the *planning and management* process. All satellites in orbit send telemetry data to a single *tracking* system. A *command* package lets the controllers in the tracking center issue instructions to modify any of the satellite mission profiles. The system has a lifetime of ten years. As it ages, maintenance will be required. To prevent physical repairs from interrupting missions, the *maintenance* system is coordinated with mission control. All these functions are interactive.

Initially, the development team can use the existing computer facility support to build an implementation library that can be accessed from display terminals. A specialized display manager may be required to establish the vocabulary and formats common to the project development (Fig. 6.26). The development team produces a new real-time operating system and a set of application packages that will run on the real-time OS. As these packages are assembled, however, the real-time OS is incomplete so the applications are tested using the facility OS. The facility OS is both a gateway to the functions available so far in the real-time OS and a source of other functions needed by the applications (Fig. 6.27). Each package can be tested by itself with this capability. Data flow paths among packages require a more complete static testing environment (Fig. 6.28). The real-time OS must be able to establish the interfaces necessary for the path traces. Part of the interface will be supplied by the interactive subsystem which is the command input and display output processor for the system. The interactive subsystem must be available at a basic level of capability; however, tests in the static environment do not require that timing dependencies and performance features be present. Now that the testing environment supports data flow through several packages at a time, manual methods of collecting data about the tests are impractical. Tools for measuring behavior and collecting statistics are built in to the environment as are utilities for taking dumps and setting up special runs. The full-blown environment suitable for dynamic system testing (Fig. 6.29) incorporates all the features of the deliverable product. The application packages, which have been growing over time, are now complete except for regression changes. Additional packages, such as security management and maintenance, have been finished so that now all the features of the system can be tested against an operational scenario.

Environment Support

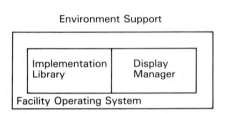

Fig. 6.26   Satellite mission management—Initial internal environment.

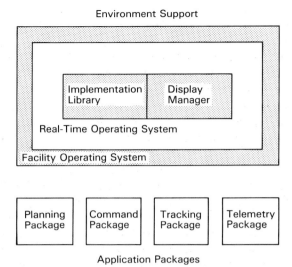

Fig. 6.27 Satellite mission management—Early package testing environment.

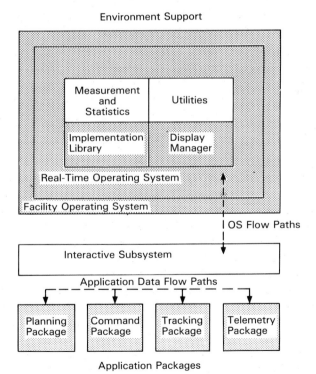

Fig. 6.28 Satellite mission management—Static testing environment.

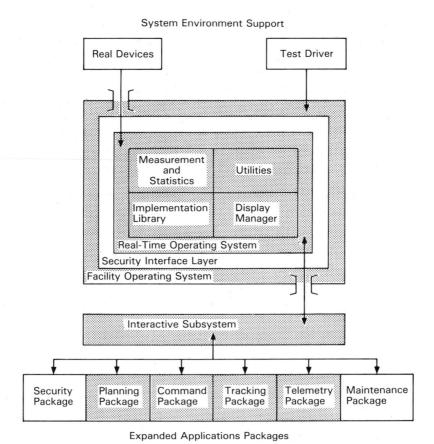

System Environment Support

Real Devices

Test Driver

Measurement and Statistics

Utilities

Implementation Library

Display Manager

Real-Time Operating System

Security Interface Layer

Facility Operating System

Interactive Subsystem

| Security Package | Planning Package | Command Package | Tracking Package | Telemetry Package | Maintenance Package |

Expanded Applications Packages

Fig. 6.29 Satellite mission management—Dynamic system testing environment.

Real-time paths exist among the applications end users—controllers at display terminals—and the real-time OS. This is accomplished by using the facility OS to get started and then creating a gateway through the facility OS, permitting the end users to communicate directly with the real-time OS. The gateway can be closed for simulation runs. When open, the gateway can be merely a path through the facility OS to a virtual machine running the real-time OS. Or the gateway can be a true direct connection achieved by rolling out the facility OS and rolling in the real-time OS. The total environment can be dedicated to the system under test in the latter case. Real devices can be attached to the dynamic environment (assuming compatibility with the host interfaces). Loads can be generated by a test driver, which may be running on an attached machine. Finally, the system security layer can be added. No commands or data will cross the layer without authorization. Dynamic security testing is usually deferred because of this feature. Tests that would otherwise succeed can abort because the dummy data that are adequate for a test may not pass the security check.

6.3.6.3 Test results

A test has a limited set of outcomes:

1. An attempt to run the test fails at the start.
2. The test runs but does not complete and cannot be restarted.
3. The test runs but stops on error and runs to completion after being reset.
4. The test runs to completion but gives the wrong result.
5. The test runs to successful completion.

If every test ran to successful completion on the first attempt, you could plot a straight line to predict when testing would be finished according to when attempts are scheduled (Fig. 6.30a). Normal testing experience shows that early attempts fail. Retries eventually succeed. A plot of number of test cases that have been attempted versus the number that have succeeded normally looks like Fig. 6.30b. While only a small percentage of the early tests succeed, the test process overcomes the early problems and the rate of success accelerates. Departures from the normal pattern, such as Fig. 6.30c, indicate that serious problems exist either in the system or in the test process. Such a poor test picture should lead the project manager to consider falling back to an earlier stage of development to redo the work.

Fig. 6.30b shows a project in which all the test cases succeed; however, the plot does not indicate how long it takes to complete the test plan. If the plot has the shape of Fig. 6.30b but the time allocated for testing is exhausted, it may be appropriate to terminate the testing activity. The cost of further testing may not be justified. The criteria for deciding what to do include the following:

- All tests have been attempted.
- Some 95 percent or more of the planned tests have succeeded.
- The unsuccessful tests have been analyzed to determine:
    1. the severity of the problem represented by the presumed error
    2. the probable cost of completing the test

If testing is stopped and the system is released, remaining errors will be shipped to the user [41]. Quality assurance dictates that you know enough about the system to protect the user against severe problems. Therefore, you should at least have observed all the planned tests. If any of the outstanding problems could be severe, they should be addressed prior to release. There are two ways to do this: (1) fix the problem and complete the test, and (2) restrict the released system to work around the problem. The first approach extends the current test stage. The second approach defers the problem to a later release and, in the meantime, changes the baseline function of the current release.

When a test cannot be run at all, there is a strong suspicion that something is wrong with the test case or the test environment. When the test runs but produces a wrong answer, it is very likely that the program being tested has an error in it. Other problems run the gamut from machine errors to operator mistakes. In order to narrow down the investigation of a problem, the trouble report should cover all the symptoms. The standard test report should contain a complete configuration description at the start of the test and, if anything changed, at the end of the test. Physical machine units should be identified since some errors that look like program logic errors can actually be caused by machine malfunctions. Systems that have interfaces with the public communications network are prone to errors caused by misidentified lines and lines whose actual specifications are different from

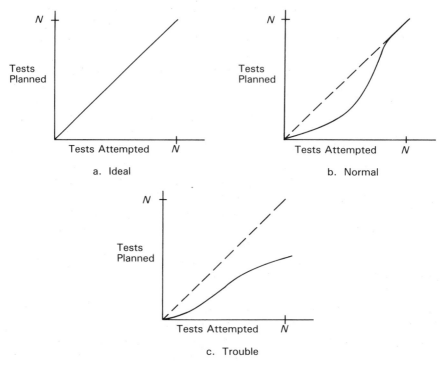

Fig. 6.30   Testing progress.

the nominal values in the common carrier's manuals. Many software components are designed to identify themselves on initiation; a message is displayed to the operator. The test report should show that such software components were correctly verified. As stated earlier, the report should be a record of the steps followed by the test team; system status on termination is also put in the record along with the team's opinion as to what went wrong. (The same format applies to trouble reports after release.)

With this type of report, trouble diagnosis consists of, first, matching the reported conditions against the conditions specified for the test (or for the operational environment, after release). An incorrect setup directs the diagnostician to problems in the environment or the procedures. A correct setup directs attention to the test target or the test case. As in all software maintenance activities, there is no guarantee that the symptoms point to the real problem. The symptoms represent the state of the system at some point after the problem occurred. There may be one and only one path that could produce the recorded status. Most cases are not so obvious. A study of the symptoms will usually permit the fix team to identify at least one potential source of error. They can then fix it. The fix will probably prevent a recurrence of the same symptoms, yet it may not have eliminated the original error. Both before and after release, the fallability of diagnosis and repair leads to regression. In extreme cases, repairs can increase the number of errors in a program. To avoid such a situation, you should manage maintenance activities with the same development process and discipline you used in the original implementation.

6.3.7 Document Review

The point has been made several times that software exists only in its documentation. Verification and validation procedures are based on this premise. *Verification* is a review of documents to see that a product corresponds with its specifications. *Validation* is a test to see that a product does what it should. It goes without saying that the validated product is the same product described by the documents that were verified. This is not always the case. Project managers intend to maintain consistent documentation but their intentions are sometimes undermined by writing or reproduction schedules [46]. By the time the documents are printed and distributed to the verification team, the product has changed. On-line documentation aids go a long way toward solving this problem. Project reviews expose problems of lagging documentation but it takes management action to adjust project schedules to permit documentation to catch up.

Documents are written to be read. They should contain the right information in a readable style. Reviewers should put themselves in the role of an end user and critique the quality of the document as well as the content.

Structured programming guidelines address readability when they recommend program size limits, "paragraph" indentation, comment density, etc. A programmer who follows the guidelines produces a program that reads like a book. Similar guidelines apply to other system documents. Design and test documents, for example, should give the user an overview of the system and then, in hierarchical fashion, branch to descriptions of subsystem and lower level topics. Individual program unit or test case descriptions can be located quickly by a reader due to the structure of the document. In this way, new readers can use the document as effectively as experienced readers who know module names and relationships. A design manual that contains program unit writeups in sequence by identifying code name, but which gives no information about the system interactions, data flow, or applications is a poor tool for maintenance activities. When a problem occurs, the diagnosis will probably identify a suspect unit. The programmer assigned to fix the problem will go to the master library for a copy of the unit and will look in the design manual to see what other units or data blocks are affected by the action of the unit. Since the manual does not treat the unit in a system context, the programmer will be forced to assume that a change to the unit will only affect immediate neighbors. A fix prepared on this assumption may work but it may generate serious problems elsewhere in the system.[13]

Document identification is important in the verification review. As a system progresses through several releases, it is possible to design the modules so that back-level code is fully compatible with all subsequent versions of the system. The cost of this design option is high; few project managers choose it. Normally, all the components of Release N must be at the Nth level. To simplify verification, it is desirable to present a wholly consistent set of documents to the reviewer. Components from Release N-1 that are used without modification in Release N are copied and relabelled as N-level components as the system is built.

The document review that takes place at PCI should verify that all the required deliverable end items are present; that the end items in the release package are the ones described by the documentation; that all deliverables are at the correct level; and that the obligations undertaken by the project developer/vendor have been carried out. When the buyer/user is satisfied, the system can be released for use.

---

13. Many operating systems are designed so that OS code cannot be modified during execution. In this case it is possible, with an automated scanner/editor, to search the master library to find all modules that use or are used by any unit.

6.4 SUMMARY

The project implementation stage starts with a requirement and ends with a released product. Success in this stage is highly dependent on the ability of the project manager to control the activities of many people in spite of a changing baseline. It helps considerably to have good people on the project team; particularly in the design stage since the quality of the design will determine how good the end product *can* be. The rest of the implementation effort determines how good the end product *will* be; but it can be no better than its architecture and design allow.

Architecture and design proceed from the top down. This is the natural way to expand a generalized statement of requirements into a detailed specification of work to be done. Top-down design produces a tree structure which, as it grows, permits more people to join the team in order to work on the branches. As soon as this happens, communication gaps are created which must be bridged by formal procedures. A project file is a bridge. It collects all the relevant information about the project in one accessible document (or computer database) and makes it possible for everyone on the project team to have a common level of knowledge. The file is supplemented by meetings, reviews, system analyses, and other activities to promote the common level of knowledge to a common level of understanding. Standards are introduced to achieve a common level of quality and productivity. The result is that the project team, consisting of a mix of new and experienced people, behaves as though it were uniformly experienced.

Productivity is improved by increasing the useful output per unit of effort. Tools and techniques that offer a mechanical advantage are productivity aids. Higher-order languages fall in this category as do utility programs and prepackaged code. They share the characteristic that each statement written by the programmer is automatically expanded to more than one operation in the deliverable code. Other types of tools and techniques are used in maintaining project control.

Two important categories are decision support aids and programming support systems. Decision support aids include analytic tools such as modeling and simulation. These tools help the project team understand the probable outcome of a decision. The best alternative can then be selected from a set of possible decisions. The same tools can be used to construct simulated environments which are indispensable when it comes to testing and measuring the developing system. Project reviews are also a form of decision support tool. Timely reviews expose potential problems early, permitting the project manager to redirect the project plan before a lot of effort is wasted. Programming support systems also avoid wasted effort. They organize the project data so that it is easy to capture changes, track status, and manage multiple versions of the system. All three categories of tools and techniques, those that: (1) multiply the effort of team members, (2) support decisions that keep the project on track, and (3) control the product, are productivity aids.

Reviews play an important role in quality assurance. Quality is an intangible characteristic of a program. It is described in terms of error rates which can only be determined after the program is written. The best way to obtain quality during the implementation of a program is to have the work in progress reviewed by good people. As a result of reviews and inspections, a program should be logically sound. It should conform to its specifications and it should be properly coded. In practice, programs that pass all the inspections will still contain some errors, mainly those due to unspecified requirements. The test process is intended to find the majority of these errors. Even an elaborate test will not guarantee that all errors have been fixed prior to release. Management decisions, trading cost and time against customer impact, are made to determine when to stop testing. The general rule is that testing stops after a convincing demonstration that the system satisfies its specifications and contains no apparent errors that interfere with its effective use. The system can then be released.

EXERCISES AND DISCUSSION QUESTIONS

1. You are the manager of a project to build the software required by a planned teaching laboratory in a university. Students and faculty will use the lab to learn how to construct effective courses for computer-assisted instruction (CAI). They will also perform education research. In the process, they will conduct courses in the lab with students of appropriate age as experimental subjects. Custom-built terminals holding a limited amount of course material are to be used in CAI. The university computer, normally programmed in PASCAL, will be the host machine. An objective of your project is to minimize the host workload by supporting as much lab work as possible in the terminals.

A "course" is a set of "frames" that display information and/or ask questions. The primary sequence of frames teaches a specific amount of information and tests the student's understanding and retention of the course material. Depending on the situation, the sequence of frames can be altered to backtrack or diverge in order to help the student.

The lab must contain at least:

- A library of courses
- A student activity monitor
- A means of evaluating course effectiveness (content and presentation)
- A means of constructing and modifying courses
- A means of modifying frames

   a. You decide three designers are required for the project. There are eight candidates. Select three and explain your selection.
>   1) John—8 years experience as a small team member. Excellent reputation as a database designer for accounting applications. COBOL, PL/1. No management experience. No large project experience.
>   2) Mary—5 years experience; currently managing a group doing a communication subsystem for an operating system (machine language). Previously worked on interactive I/O processing programs.
>   3) Lewis—11 years experience as a programming instructor, teaching OS/370, PL/1, structured programming to new and experienced programmers.
>   4) Joan—8 years experience in large projects. Last 3 years in design group which has been working on the interactive support features of the university host operating system. No management experience. PASCAL, APL.
>   5) Reed—4 years experience (including 2 as a graduate student) doing research with the Professor of Education. PASCAL, APL. Speciality: course construction.
>   6) Laura—recent graduate in psychology with emphasis on the human factors of information transfer in interactive environments. PASCAL.
>   7) Kenny—10 years experience as a programmer (machine language, APL); most recently engaged (5 years) in designing and implementing conversational dialogue support for business applications.
>   8) Helen—10 years experience in education research, primarily concerned with test procedures and test validation. Has programmed her own data analysis in PASCAL.

   b. Will you ask the three designers to work together on all requirements or will you divide the work according to each designer's specialty?

   c. Which, if any, of the designer's will manage the design group? If not any of them, who?

   d. What documents will the designers produce?

2. In the project of Exercise 1, assume the course library is in the host. Describe "a means of modifying frames" to improve student response. (Improved student response consists of: (a) higher probability of correct initial response to questions about a frame, and (b) shorter total time for successful completion of a course.) Consider the data required to show an improvement. Allocate modification functions between the host and the terminal. Distinguish between tentative modifications and permanent changes to the library.

3. Referring again to Exercise 1, the student activity monitor contains the following sequence control:

Display a frame of information.
>   Hold for 10 seconds or until student requests NEXT.

Display questions about the frame.
>   Prompt student to answer questions.

If no answer, prompt again. Exit to error routine.

If correct answer:
    Acknowledge.
    Move to next frame in sequence.
If incorrect answer:
    Show student an error message.
    Display supplementary information.
    Return to questions.
If still incorrect:
    Display second supplementary information.
    Return to questions.
If still incorrect:
    Go back three frames and repeat lesson.

Would you accept this control sequence at the preliminary design review? If not, what are the deficiencies?

4. The laboratory of Exercise 1 contains a specially-built terminal for which your team must write programs. The terminal is being built for the first time and will be delivered prior to your scheduled package tests.

    a. What do you need to work with prior to delivery of an actual terminal?
    b. How will you determine that your designs for interactions, dialogues, and frames are suitable for students and researchers?
    c. Suppose the delivered terminal is different from what you expect; how can you protect the work already done?

5. Your project is in the development stage. The design provides hooks in many places to attach measurement programs. The measurements are to be accumulated and analyzed to produce characteristic parameters. Thus, in the CAI laboratory, measurements are made of reading time, response time, correct answers, etc., for each frame of each course. When averaged over time and correlated with student age and experience, the measurements can be used to set the sequence controls governing how long a frame is displayed or how to branch after an incorrect wrong answer. As you enter the package test stage, team members start complaining because the sequence controls are slowing down the tests. This is caused by the fact that raw measurements are being placed in the parameter list with no prior analysis. The analysis activity is not scheduled to be completed for several weeks. What should you do?

    a. Rush the analysis task to completion to get realistic parameters.
    b. Make up a list of parameters that look reasonable and insert it in the software for everyone to use.
    c. Change the initialization component to permit each user to insert a private parameter list.
    d. Continue to run with unrealistic parameters.
    How will your action affect the Project File?

6. A project review is scheduled to take place in five days. Your critical path activity is running a week or two behind schedule. Should you postpone the review so the activity can be completed and the review can be properly prepared?

7. A system is planned to have 800 program units. Of these, 150 are judged to be hard, 200 medium, and 450 easy. The system is required in 18 months.

a. Estimate the number of people-years required if all the code is new.

b. Assume that a good portion of existing code can be carried over with modifications so that there are 100 new hard units, 100 new medium units, and 200 new easy units, plus 5,000 lines of code (LOC) to be modified in hard units, 5,000 LOC in medium units, and 12,500 LOC in easy units. What would your estimate of people-years be?

c. Compare to $E = 5.2L^{0.91}$ where L is the number of lines of code in thousands (KLOC).

d. The number of program units is a rough estimate made by the designers. It will be refined later by the programmers. At this stage, do you want the estimate of people-years to err on the high side or the low side?

8. Your implementation of CAI results in a highly flexible program in the CAI terminal. Using 60 percent of the terminal memory, you can handle all the required controls and record-keeping. The remaining 40 percent is allocated to course material. An initial analysis of courses shows that different subjects will place different loads on the host:

a. All courses, regardless of subject, have a basic load each time they are used:
   1) Administrative data exchange averaging 20 transactions of 100 bytes each with 20 byte responses from host
   2) Initialization to load course material; 20 byte log-on followed by 10,000 byte load from host

b. In addition, each subject has N file search requests per session to fetch data that exceeds initial course capacity:
   1) Math: $N = 5$ average, each fetch is 100 bytes.
   2) Psychology: $N = 25$ @1,000 bytes
   3) Geography: $N = 100$ @4,000 bytes
   4) Physics: $N = 100$ @20 bytes

The laboratory design should ultimately support hundreds of CAI terminals. Describe the tests you would run to find out how many terminals can be supported when you know the mix of courses simultaneously in operation.

9. When testing the CAI control program, is it necessary to have a real course running on the terminal?

10. Math courses employ short exercises. The scope of branching is limited. Psychology uses much more complex pedagogy with deep branching and repetitive reinforcement. Should your CAI system have a simple Release 1 for Math courses to be followed by a more general Release 2? Or would it be wiser to design initially for complex courses?

REFERENCES

1. Freeman, P. "The Nature of Design." in *Tutorial on Software Design Techniques.* Edited by P. Freeman and A. I. Wasserman. Long Beach, Calif.: IEEE Computer Society, 1980.

2. Thomas, J. C., and Carroll, J. M. "Human Factors in Communication." *IBM Systems Journal* 20, no. 2 (1981).

3. Tanenbaum, A. S. *Computer Networks.* Englewood Cliffs, N.J.: Prentice-Hall, 1981.

4. Cypser, R. J. *Communications Architecture for Distributed Systems.* Reading, Mass.: Addison-Wesley, 1978.

5. Corr, F. P., and Neal, D. H. "SNA and Emerging International Standards." *IBM Systems Journal* 18, no. 2 (1979).

6. Parnas, D. L. "On the Design and Development of Program Families." *IEEE Transactions on Software Engineering* SE-2 (March 1976).

7. Green, P. E., Jr. *Computer Network Architectures and Protocols.* New York: Plenum Press, 1980.

8. Linger, R. C.; Mills, H. D.; and B. I. Witt, *Structured Programming: Theory and Practice.* Reading, Mass.: Addison-Wesley, 1979.

9. Jackson, M. A. *Principles of Program Design.* London and New York: Academic Press, 1975. Also, Warnier, J. D. *Logical Construction of Programs.* Leiden, Netherlands: H. F. Stenfurt Kroese, B.V., 1974, and New York: Van Nostrand-Reinhold, 1976. Also, Orr, K. T. *Structured Systems Development.* New York: Yourdon Press, 1977.

10. McGowan, C. L., and Kelly, J. R. "A Review of Decomposition and Design Methodologies." *Structured Design.* Infotech State of the Art Conference. 18–20 October 1976. Maidenhead, England: Infotech International, Ltd., 1976.

11. Ratcliff, K. "Data Structure and Structured Design." *Structured Design.* Infotech State of the Art Conference, 18–20 October 1976. Maidenhead, England: Infotech International, Ltd., 1976.

12. Dambrine, M. "A Data Structured Approach to Data Processing." *Structured Design.* Infotech State of the Art Conference, 18–20 October 1976. Maidenhead, England: Infotech International, Ltd., 1976.

13. Dyer, M. "The Management of Software Engineering. Part IV: Software Development Practices." *IBM Systems Journal* 19, no. 4 (1980).

14. Kobayashi, H. *Modeling and Analysis: An Introduction to System Performance Evaluation Methodology.* Reading, Mass.: Addison-Wesley, 1978.

15. DeLong, A. J. "Phenomenological Space-Time: Toward an Experimental Reality." *Science* 213, no. 7 (August 1981).

16. Hirsch, R. S. "Procedures of the Human Factors Center at San Jose." *IBM Systems Journal* 20, no. 2 (1981).

17. Mills, H. D. "The Management of Software Engineering. Part I: Principles of Software Engineering." *IBM Systems Journal* 19, no. 4 (1980).

18. Goldberg, E. A. "Applying Corporate Development Policies." *Software Development: Management.* The 71st Infotech State of the Art Conference. Maidenhead, England: Infotech, Ltd., 1980.

19. O'Neill, D. "The Management of Software Engineering. Part II: Software Engineering Program." *IBM Systems Journal* 19, no. 4 (1980).

20. Linger, R.C. "The Management of Software Engineering. Part III: Software Design Practices." *IBM Systems Journal* 19, no. 4 (1980).

21. Quinnan, R. E. "The Management of Software Engineering. Part V: Software Engineering Management Practices." *IBM Systems Journal* 19, no. 4 (1980).

22. *Managing the Application Development Process: Project Reviews.* Independent Study Program SR20–7297. Poughkeepsie, N.Y.: IBM Corporation, 1979.

23. Jay, A. "How to Run a Meeting." *Harvard Business Review* 54, no. 2 (March–April 1976).

24. Haire, M. *Psychology in Management.* New York: McGraw-Hill, 1956.

25. Peercy, D. E. "A Software maintainability Evaluation Methodology." *IEEE Transactions on Software Engineering* SE–17, no. 4 (July 1981). Also, Boehm, B. W.; Brown, J. R.; Kaspar, H.; Lipow, M.; MacLeod, G. J.; and Merritt, M. J. *Characteristics of Software Quality.* Amsterdam and New York: North-Holland Publishing, 1978.

26. Scowen, R. S. "A Survey of Some Text Editors." *Software—Practice and Experience* 11, no. 9 (September 1981).

27. Perlis, A.; Sayward, F.; and Shaw, M. *Software Metrics: An Analysis and Evaluation.* Cambridge, Mass.: The MIT Press, 1981.

28. Pietrasanta, A. M. "Resource Analysis of Computer Program System Development," in *On the Management of Computer Programming.* Edited by G. F. Weinwurm. Princeton, N.J.: Auerbach Publishers, 1970.

29. Aron, J. D. "Estimating Resources for Large Programming Systems," in *Software Engineering: Concepts and Techniques.* Edited by J. N. Buxton, P. Naur, and B. Randell. New York: Petrocelli/Charter, 1976.

30. Weinwurm, G. F., ed. *On the Management of Computer Programming.* Princeton, N.J.: Auerbach Publishers, 1970.

31. Walston, C. E., and Felix, C. P. "A Method of Programming Measurement and Estimation." *IBM Systems Journal* 16, no. 1 (1977).

32. Halstead, M. H. *Elements of Software Science.* New York: Elsevier North-Holland, Inc., 1977.

33. Christensen, K.; Fitsos, G. P.; and Smith, C. P. "A Perspective on Software Science." *IBM Systems Journal* 20, no. 4 (1981).

34. Boehm, B. W. *Software Engineering Economics.* Englewood Cliffs, N.J.: Prentice-Hall, 1981.

35. Mohanty, S. N. "Software Cost Estimation: Present and Future." *Software—Practice and Experience* 11, no. 2 (February 1981). Also, Roach, M. G. "A Comparison of Cost Estimation Techniques for Software Development Projects." *Pathways to System Integrity.* Washington, D.C.: The Washington D.C. Chapter of the ACM, 1980.

36. Lavenberg, S. S.; Sauer, C. H.; MacNair, E. A.; Markowitz, H. M.; Shedler, G. S.; and Welch, P. D. *Modeler's Handbook.* New York: Academic Press, 1981.

37. Spragins, J. "Approximate Techniques for Modeling the Performance of Complex Systems." *Computer Languages* 4 (1979).

38. Miller, E. F., and Howden, W. E. *Tutorial: Software Testing and Validation Techniques.* Long Beach, Calif.: IEEE Computer Society, 1981. Also, Walker, M. G. *Managing Software Reliability.* New York: North-Holland, Inc., 1981.

39. Howden, W. E. "Functional Program Testing." *IEEE Transactions on Software Engineering* SE-6, no. 2 (March 1980).

40. Mohanty, S. N. "Models and Measurements for Quality Assessment of Software." *ACM Computing Surveys* 11, no. 3 (September 1979). Also, Littlewood, B. "Theories of Software Reliability: How Good Are They and How Can They Be Improved?" *IEEE Transactions on Software Engineering* SE-6, no. 5 (September 1980).

41. Okumoto, K., and Goel, A. L. "Optimum Release Time for Software Systems." *Proceedings: COMPSAC 79.* Long Beach, Calif.: IEEE Computer Society, 1979.

42. Anderson, T., and Randell, B. *Computing Systems Reliability.* Cambridge, England, and New York: Cambridge University Press, 1979. Also, Glass, R. L. *Software Reliability Guidebook.* Englewood Cliffs, N.J.: Prentice-Hall, 1979.

43. Myers, G. J. *The Art of Software Testing.* New York: John Wiley & Sons, 1979.

44. Howden, W. E. "Life-Cycle Software Validation." *Computer* 15, no. 2 (February 1982). Also, Chandrasekaran, B. "Special Collection on Program Testing." *IEEE Transactions on Software Engineering* SE-6, no. 3 (May 1980).

45. Cho, C. K. *An Introduction to Software Quality Control.* New York: John Wiley & Sons, 1980.

46. Vardaman, G. T.; Halterman, C. C.; and Vardaman, P. B. *Cutting Communications Costs and Increasing Impacts.* New York: John Wiley & Sons, 1970.

7
Conclusion

The culmination of the implementation stage is the release of a useful end product. Team projects are seldom single-release programs because their very size dictates a phased implementation. When the initial release goes into operation it will contain some errors of unknown severity. It may have restrictions and work-arounds for deficiencies that were not fixed in the test stage. Almost certainly, the user will find better ways to use the capabilities of the system; new requirements will come out of these discoveries. Minor problems can be corrected by a maintenance release but major repairs and functional updates justify a complete new release of the system. Both the maintenance release and the new release go through the same disciplined development cycle, as explained in earlier chapters. The maintenance release, however, is controlled to a narrow objective: Fix the known problems and integrate the fixes into the system but avoid other changes. The new release provides an opportunity for design revisions, new components, performance improvements, and any other economically justified changes that will improve the usability, utility, or marketability of the system.

7.1 RELEASE PACKAGE

The release package is the physical embodiment of the end product. It contains a copy of the master library, usually delivered on disk or tape, with the necessary routine to load it on the user's system. In a phased plan, the utility that loads the master copy can be extended to support later releases. Knowing that later releases will incorporate some components of earlier releases, the load utility can be given the capability to selectively replace and add modules. Only the new modules need be shipped in the updated release. An index to the contents of each release is a standard part of the package. It contains enough information for the loader to determine how to assemble the new release at the right change level. This type of loader can even be designed to overlay individual lines of code to modify the current release. Patches of this type are undesirable because they are hard to control; nevertheless, a patch may be the best temporary fix to an urgent problem. (At all times, back levels of the system should be retained for recovery purposes.) The selective loader saves the user hours of system generation time. The vendor uses fewer disks and disk preparation time. When the system is distributed to many users, the savings can be substantial.

All the system documentation due on delivery is also included in the release package. The mode of delivery can vary from hard copy to microfiche to machine-readable media. All modes must be readily reproducible as hard copy for all the people who need the documents. An on-line system may have its documentation (except maintenance data) in storage, accessible by terminal. Even self-teaching courses can be handled that way if they are done well. More typically, system documentation is delivered in hard copy in small quantities sufficient for the user's system programmers, service people, and instructors. They can make additional copies as necessary. General-purpose programs with many users can justify printed and bound manuals for much of their documentation. No matter which approach is taken, the documentation should be updated at the same time as the system. On-line documentation is treated just like system code; it can be updated by the same loader. Small quantity hard copy is usually kept in a ring binder so it can be updated by replacing pages. In this case, the same degree of control is required as for program changes and patches. (Each page bears a date and revision number; the table of contents is updated to show what pages are current every time there is a change.) Printed manuals present a special problem: The turn-around time for printing may not mesh with the phase plan. Consequently, the information in the new manual may not precisely describe the program in the release package. The importance of consistency between the program and its documentation outweighs the advantages (to the user) of printed manuals. Manuals describing how the system appears to the user can be printed to save production costs. The information in these manuals is relatively stable from release to release. Manuals describing how the system works in detail change with every release and should be printed only if timely delivery can be assured.

The vendor of a general-purpose system announces the capabilities of a new release in a brochure that contains enough information so a user could order the system. A sample of such an announcement is shown in Fig. 7.1. (It describes a prepackaged collection of programs offered in 1980 by the IBM Corporation. The programs form an Installation Productivity Option (IPO) designed to reduce vendor and user effort associated with new releases of the VSE operating system. The IPO is generated by the vendor using a selective loader to assemble the set of components requested by each user. The announcement, therefore, describes a system release similar to Release 1 of any product.) In this sample are all the elements of an announcement that should accompany any release, general-purpose or not. The sample does not include training materials or maintenance data. The vendor sells these as components of separate services. They would be appropriate components of a release to an in-house or contract buyer.

The annotations accompanying the announcement text of Fig. 7.1 show that the release includes both identification data and explanatory data. All the components of the release are identified; in this case by name, number, release level (REL LVL), and registration number. (The registration number corresponds to a subscription, permitting each user to receive follow-up materials automatically.) Other identification data cover the minimum and recommended configurations of hardware and software needed to run the system for various applications. Part numbers are also given to identify the mode of delivery of machine-readable components. The explanatory data tell the user what the system is for, how to order it and receive continuing service, what components are in the package, and which are optional. The user is told how to put together a system with special characteristics. Instructions are included for starting up the system and verifying that the machine-readable materials are correct. Document lists are included showing which items will be useful and how to obtain them if they are not in the package. Finally, operating instructions are given (although none are shown in Fig. 7.1) explaining how to use the system. If there are restrictions on use or known anomalies between the code and its documentation, these are listed. One or more copies of the package are delivered to the buyer according to how many are required to install the system on all user host machines. The master copy, of course, is retained in the vendor/developer's library.

7.2   POST-RELEASE ACTIVITIES

After release, the system is in the Operations, Maintenance, and Upgrade stage. The user is responsible for this stage. The development project manager will have turned attention to the next phase of the project or to a different project, yet the user will often want the advice or assistance of the project team. (In a contract environment, post-release support costs money. If the user has no budget for this type of activity, the project manager will be forced to turn down requests for help. An exception to this rule occurs when the project manager prices the original development project in such a way as to build up an escrow account to be used for post-release effort.)

VSE System Installation Productivity
Option/Extended (VSE System IPO/E)
Release 2.1
——————— *program name*

5750-AAA	DB/DC
5750-AAB	DC

——————— *identification number*

The VSE System IPO/E is designed to reduce the time
and skill level of customer personnel required
to install DOS/VSE and selected licensed programs. —— *description of purpose*
The VSE System IPO/E includes pre-generated   *and applicability*
systems control and licensed programs, with a level of
preapplied service ready to use in a specific operating
environment.

VSE System IPO/E Release 2.1 will be especially
attractive to:

- Users planning their first installation of DOS/VSE on
  an IBM 4300 Processor.

- Existing DOS/VS System IPO users migrating to VSE.

- VSE users installing CICS/VS Release 1.5.

- VSE users installing ACF/VTAME, or ACF/VTAM and
  ACF/NCP/VS Release 2.1.

- Existing VSE System IPO/E Release 1 or Release 2
  users who wish to upgrade their System IPO/E base
  or add a System IPO/E component program product
  to their Release 2 System IPO/E. (See VSE System
  IPO/E Environments section for component program
  product release levels.)

Planned availability: March 1981 ——————— *release date*

Service level, VSE System IPO/E: The VSE System —— *level of currency*
IPO/E Release 2.1 will be available with PUT 8008
preapplied.

Program update tapes (PUT): The most recent PUT will —— *method of handling*
be provided with the initial VSE System IPO/E order. The   *changes subsequent*
customer should contact the support center prior to   *to current level*
installing any portion of this PUT. The service contained
on the PUT may be optionally applied. After the
installation of the individual components of the VSE
System IPO/E, the customer will continue to receive the —— *follow-up via*
periodic distribution of customized PUTs based upon the   *registered profile*
customer's then current profile of licensed programs.

Fig. 7.1 Announcement of a release package.

VSE System IPO/E environments

A series of environments based on the VSE System
IPO/E will be available to support the IBM 4300   ——— processor types
Processors and comparable S/370 systems.

- The VSE System IPO/E provides through component
  products, support for commercial interactive   ——— application types
  applications in both stand-alone and remote
  configurations.

Operating environments

The following chart summarizes the minimum hardware
configurations for VSE System IPO/E environments: ——— operating configuration
(Additional requirements may exist for hardware systems   (minimum)
service.)

Processors	IBM S/370, IBM 3031, IBM 4331 and IBM 4341 supported by DOS/VSE that meet the minimum processor storage requirements described below.
Terminals	One 3277 Model 2 or one 3278 Model 2 (locally attached)
Printer	One printer supported by the operating system
Tape	One tape drive supported by the operating system
Reader	One card image device required for hardware systems service

VSE System IPO/E Environments

Processor Storage: 1.OMB

DASD: 3310*   5
       3330*   5
       3340*   5
       3350   3
       3370**   3

**Indicates number of actuators

Fig. 7.1   Continued.

Detailed information on VSE System IPO/E hardware —— *where to look for additional detail about configurations*
requirements will be provided in an updated version of
the VSE System IPO/E Planning Guide (GC20-1875).

The minimum DASD recommendations will accommodate
base product installation and service application. Users —— *limitations of minimum configuration*
of optional features should assess the applicability of
these minimums to their environment. The customer is
responsible for installing configurations sufficient to
permit use of the products selected.

VSE System IPO/E content

The VSE System IPO/E is comprised of: ——————— *description of package contents*

- Pre-generated, component-synchronized systems with
  a level of preapplied service that have been designed
  for operation in specific environments.

- Structured problem reporting system based on
  VSE/IPCS to assist in APAR generation and problem
  management.

- Interactive Productivity Facility

  - Interactive procedures and/or documentation that
    simplify the installation of VSE System IPO/E
    licensed program features and the servicing of
    DOS/VSE systems, utilizing the MSHP/PUT
    process.

  - Full-screen prompts and aids that reduce the
    potential for user errors in installing, servicing and
    using the system.

  - On-line information in the form of explain facilities
    and a first use tutorial to increase or refresh
    knowledge of System IPO/E.

  - User oriented procedures that provide system
    guidance and direction.

Each VSE System IPO/E consists of a preconfigured —— *options available for selecting subsets of announced capabilities*
base and a series of optional features.

Fig. 7.1 Continued.

The base is an integrated set of software components, pre-generated, preallocated with a level of preapplied service and configured to a specific operating environment.

Other components are available as optional features. These optional features are assumed present when ——— *assurance that base system is coordinated with features* generation parameters are selected. Base and optional components contain synchronized service assuming coexistence of the optional features.

Detailed base and optional features content of the VSE System IPO/E are:

Program Name	Number	REL LVL
Base Content		
DOS/VSE SCP	5745-030	2
VSE/Advanced functions	5746-XE8	2
VSE/IPCS	5746-SA1	2
VSE/ICCF	5746-TS1	2
VSE/POWER	5746-XE3	2
VSE/VSAM	5746-AM2	2
Interactive Productivity Facility	5748-MS1	3
CICS/VS	5746-XX3	1.5
DL/I DOS/VS	5746-XX1	1.5ICR2
ACF/VTAM*	5746-RC3	2
+ VTAM SCP	5747-CF1	2
ACF/VTAME*	5746-RC7	1
+ VTAM SCP	5747-CG2	1
BTAM-ES*	5746-RC5	1
+ BTAM SCP	5747-CG1	1

*A telecommunication access method is required in the base.—— *options available to suit telecommunications interface*
–VSE DC and DB/DC users should select one of the three.

Fig. 7.1 Continued.

Features

VSE/Fast Copy**	5746-AM4	1
DATA DICTIONARY	5746-XXC	3
DMS/CICS/VS-DOS	5746-XC4	2
DMS/APP. GEN. FEATURE	5746-XC4	2
VSE/POWER/RJE	5746-XE3	2
VSE/DITTO	5746-UT3	1
DOS/VS COBOL	5746-CB1	2.5
RPG II	5746-RG1	3
PL/I OPT./LIB.	5736-PL3	5.1
PL/I OPT.	5736-PL1	5.1
PL/I RES. LIB.	5736-LM4	5.1
PL/I TRANS. LIB.	5736-LM5	5.1
SORT/MERGE II	5746-SM2	3
EP/VS	5747-AG1	3
VSE/ACCESS CONTROL-	5746-XE7	1
LOGGING and REPORTING		
ACF/NCP/VS	5735-XX1	2.1
+SSP for		
ACF/NCP/VS	5735-XX3	2.1
+NCP/SSP SCP	5747-CH1	2.1
+EP Feature 6004	5747-CH1	2.1
ELIAS-I	5746-XXV	1

**The VSE/Fast Copy optional feature is used to support the Inter-
active Productivity Facility tailoring, service, and feature install —— *prerequisites*
tasks. Either the VSE/Fast Copy licensed program or its equivalent
is required to perform backup/restore functions.

Documentation support for the following ———— *where to look for*
products will be provided. This support consists of *information on products*
instructions in the VSE System IPO/E Planning Guide. *related but outside*
The instructions will indicate the steps necessary to *the scope of this*
install the product on the VSE System IPO/E. Example *release*
jobstreams will be provided in SAMPLIB and referenced
in the installation steps.

VSE/PT	5796-PLQ 1.1
CICS/VS PA II	5798-CFP 1.4
VSE RJE Workstation	5746-RC9 2

Fig. 7.1 Continued.

If these products are to be installed, they must be ordered independently of the VSE System IPO/E Release 2.1.

Data security: Customers using System IPO/E can use ——— *specification of related program that customer is responsible for* the security facilities provided by VSE/ICCF in the VSE System IPO/E. The customer is responsible for the selection, implementation and adequacy of these facilities.

VSE System IPO/E Installation Testing

Prior to availability, the VSE System IPO/E base and ——— *how the user can verify that the release package is complete and operable* optional feature programs are installed in the VSE System IPO/E Operating Environment. This installation is performed using the Interactive Productivity Facility licensed program and the instructions provided in the VSE System IPO/E Program Directory and Planning Guide. Where available, the Installation Verification Procedures (IVPs) or applicable test programs are executed using the pregenerated systems supplied with the System IPO/E.

Ordering information: For VM/VSE System IPO/E - DB/DC.— *how to order a copy of the release package*

Type: 5750. Model: AAE. Scheduling: Normal.

Basic material

Documentation: Memo to users, VM/ VSE System IPO/E Planning — *applicable documents* Guide, VM/VSE System IPO/E Program Directory and Interactive Productivity Facility VM/VSE Feature User's Guide.

Machine readable material: A base set of software products and — *package components supplied on disk or tape* separately orderable software product features.

To order, specify 5750-AAE and select the feature number of the desired base which will include all base products. Additionally, if you are ordering VSE/ ICCF, specify the appropriate 59XX feature code instead of 50xx feature code to receive the proper VM/VSE base tapes. Users ordering VSE/ICCF must be registered for that product.

Fig. 7.1 Continued.

	Distribution Medium Feature Number (M Tape)	
	9/1600	9/6250
VM/VSE DB/DC base	9002	9003

ID of package for ordering purposes

	Special System IPO/E Registration Feature Number	
Prerequisite program	9/1600	9/6250
VM/370 (Note 1)		
5749-010	9002	9003
VM/Basic Systems Extension		
5748-XX8	9403	9404
Display Editing System		
5796-PJP	9403	9404
VM/IPCS Extension		
5748-SA1	9403	9404
DOS/VSE		
5745-030 (Note 2)	9403	9404
VSE/Advanced Functions		
5746-XEB	9403	9404
VSE/IPCS		
5746-SA1	9403	9404
VSE/ POWER		
5746-XE3	9403	9404
VSE/VSAM (Note 14)		
5746-AM2	9407	9408
Interactive Productivity Facility		
5748-MS1	9405	9406
CICS/VS		
5746-XX3	9403	9404
DL/I DOS/VS		
5746-XX1	9403	9404

ID of prerequisite programs which are shipped automatically with the ordered system

DASD Type Without ICCF		
3330	5024	5025
	5026	5027
	5028	5029
	5030	5031

ordering codes to identify the type of disk to be used

Fig. 7.1   Continued.

			9403	9404
FORTRAN (Mod II) Lib. 5734-LM3	6334	6335	9403	9404
FORTRAN Int. Debug 5734-FO5	6336	6337	9403	9404
VSE/VSAM (Note 13) 5746-AM2	6348	6349	9405	9406
VM/IFS 5748-XXC	6350	6351	9403	9404
Directory Maintenance 5748-XE4	6352	6353	9403	9404

Notes: ——————— *list of ordering guidelines plus system restrictions and special instructions affecting this release*

1. When ordering VM/370 (5749-010) for the first time via System IPO/E, a customer should be registered as a user of record of VM/370.

2. VSE/Advanced Functions integrated with 5745-030.

3. The indicated program requires VSE/ICCF for the generation of its input data.

4. Users who order both the CMS version (6310/6311) and the DOS CICS version (6222/6223) of IIS must specify 9405 (9/1600) or 9406 (9/6250) when registering for 5748-XX6.

5. Users who order both versions of RPGII, feature numbers 6226/6227 and 6322/6323 must, when registering, specify 9405 (9/1600) or 9406 (9/6250) to receive proper service.

The chart that starts on the next page lists all programs contained —— *list of documents and machine-readable materials associated with individual components of the release*
within the VM/VSE System IPO/E.

Key to the chart

• Product Name

Name of the base or optional feature product and SLSS identification number (SLSS ID). When subscribing under SLSS, all SCP and licensed publications are available under an assigned SLSS identifier (Note: SCP specifications must be ordered directly from Mechanicsburg). A special SLSS ID, as indicated under each program name, has been assigned to obtain profiled documentation for VM/VSE System IPO/E Release 2.

• Product Number

Program product or system control programming number.

• Basic material

Fig. 7.1   Continued.

One copy of each document listed in this area, indicated with an asterisk (*), will be supplied automatically with the machine readable material when the product is ordered from PID. This will include memo, program directory, specifications, and source code tape, when required for maintenance.

Product Name	Product No.	Basic Material Title	Additional Copies Form Number	Price/Copy	Feature Number	Licensed Documentation (Order by Feature Number)	Additional Copies Feature Number	Form Number	Price/Copy	Readable Material 9/1600	9/6250
VSE/FASTCOPY (SLSS ID 7799-DAF)	5746-AH4	Specifications	*GT33-6080	N/C							
		General Information	GT33-6081	.60	7450	Fiche	8215	LTC7-0469	3.00	7429	7431
		Installation Reference	*GT33-6082	1.50	7440	Logic	8214	LT73-9090	5.40		
DOS/VS COBOL COMPILER & LIBRARY (SLSS ID 7799-DAC)	5746-CB1	DOS Full ANS COBOL	*GT28-6394	14.00							
		VM/370 CMS User's Guide (COBOL)	ST28-6469	6.60	8207	Fiche (First copy not free)	8207	LTC7-5050	52.00	7429	7431
		Programmer's Guide	*GT28-6478	9.20	7440	Logic	8205	LT68-6423	40.00		
		Installation Reference Manual	*ST28-6479	3.60	7440	Logic	8206	LT68-6424	13.00		
		Specifications	*GT28-6487	N/C							
ACF/VTAM (SLSS ID 7799-DBV)	5746-RC3	Programming Reference	8T27-0449	34.00	7440	Logic Overview	8216	LT78-3021	14.00	7429	7431
		Specifications	*GT27-0460	N/C	7441	Logic VOL 1	8217	LT78-3022	39.00		
		General Information: Intro	GT27-0462	1.50	7442	Logic VOL 2	8218	LT78-3024	28.00		
		General Information: Concepts	GT27-0463	5.20	7443	Data Areas	8219	LT78-3026	45.00		
		Installation Manual	*ST27-0464	8.40	7450	Assembly Listings	8221	LTB1-0408	112.00		
		PreInstallation Planning	*ST27-0465	13.50	7444	Control Panel Overview	8220	LT00-0641	1.30		
		Operations Manual	*ST27-0466	7.40							
		Messages & Codes	*ST27-0467	14.50							
		Reference Summary	ST00-0640	7.20							
		Diagnostic Techniques	ST78-3020	60.00							
BTAME-ES (SLSS ID 7799-DBB)	5746-RC5	Specifications	*GT38-0291	N/C							
		General Information	GT38-0292	1.00	7450	Assembly Listings	8223	LTB1-0407	2.80	7429	7431
		Programming Reference	ST38-0293	22.00	7440	Logic	8222	LT77-8030	39.00		
		Installation	*ST38-0294	1.90							
		Messages	*ST38-0295	1.50							
ACF/VTAME (SLSS ID 7799-DBE)	5746-RC7	Specifications	*GT27-0437	N/C							
		General Information: Intro	GT27-0438	1.40	7450	Assembly Listings	8227	LTB1-0458	126.00	7429	7431
		Installation	*ST27-0439	9.60	7440	Logic Overview	8224	LT78-3013	17.00		
		Pre-Installation	*ST27-0441	5.80	7441	Logic Basic	8225	LT78-3014	69.00		
		Programming	ST27-0442	29.00	7442	Diagnostic Data Areas	8226	LT78-3016	55.00		
		Operation	*ST27-0443	9.20							
		Messages & Codes	*ST27-0444	10.50							
		General Information: Concepts	GT27-0451	4.40							
		Reference Summary	ST00-0642	5.60							
		Diagnostic Techniques	*ST78-3012	11.50							
		...al Information	GT40-2199	1.40							
		...s Reference Manual	*ST40-2205	8.20	NONE		NONE	NONE		NONE	
			*ST40-2206	9.60							
			*GT40-4557	N/C							
VM/IPCS EXTENSIONS (SLSS ID 7799-TAD)	5748-SA1	Specifications									
		Users Guide									
		General Information									
VM/DIRECTORY MAINTENANCE (SLSS ID 7799-TDD)	5748-XE4	Specifications	*GT20-1...								
		Installation & Sys Administrator's Guide	*ST20-1840	12.3						NONE	
		Guide for General Users	ST20-1839	6.80							
RSCS NET-WORKING (SLSS ID 7799-TCR)	5748-XP1	Specifications	*GT44-5003	N/C	7450	Microfiche	8138	LTC0-9006	4.40	NONE	
		Program Ref and Operations	*ST44-5005	14.00							
		Licensed Documentation Feature Number									
		Logic Manual	8139	LT64-5203	18.50						
DMS/CMS (SLSS ID 7799 TAD)	5748-XXB	Specifications	*GT24-5200	N/C	7440	Logic Manual	8140	LT64-5206	7.40	7429	7431
		General Information	GT24-5197	.70	7450	Source Listings Microfiche	8141	LTC0-9008	4.40		
		Guide and Reference	ST24-5198	5.20							
VM/IFS (SLSS ID 7799-TC1)	5748-XXC	Specifications	*GT24-5199	N/C	7440	Logic Manual	8142	LT84-5205	7.40	7429	7431
		General Information	GT24-5195	.80	7450	Source ListingsFiche	8143	LTC0-9009	5.00		
		Guide & Reference	ST24-5196	6.60							
VS BASIC (SLSS ID 7799-TAB)	5748-XX1	Basic TSO Introduction	*ST28-8300	9.20	7440	Logic Manual	8144	LT68-6422	13.50	7429	7431
		Basic CMS Introduction	*ST28-8310	7.40	7450	Source Listings Microfiche	8145	LTC7-5051	226.00		
		Basic Language Reference	*ST28-8303	4.80							
		TSO Terminal Users Guide	*ST28-8304	5.00							
		TSO Reference Summary	*ST00-0626	.50							
		CMS Terminal Users Guide	*ST28-8306	6.80							
		CMS Reference Summary	*ST00-0621	.70							
		Programmers Guide	*ST28-8308	6.60							
		Installation Reference	*ST28-8309	9.20							
		Specifications	*GT28-8311	N/C							
		VSPC Ref. Summary	*ST00-0628	.90							
		VSPC Terminal Users Guide	*SQ40-9060	9.00							
		General Information	GT28-8302	.70							
IIS (SLSS ID 7799-TA1)	5748-XX6	Administrators Guide	*SQ40-1896	11.00		Licensed Documentation (Order by Feature Number)				NONE	
		Course Authoring Guide	*SQ40-1897	22.00	7440	Logic Manual	8146	LT60-2285	14.50		
		Specifications	*GQ40-4535	N/C	7451	Source Listings fiche	8147	LT80-2380	17.00		
		CMS Operator's Guide	*ST40-1898	4.40	7452	CICS Assembly Listings fiche	8163	LT80-2409	15.50		
		CICS Operator's Guide	*ST40-1904	6.80							
INTERACTIVE INSTRUCTIONAL SYSTEM (SLSS ID 7799-TA1)	5748-XX6	Administrator's Guide	*ST40-1896	11.00	7451	CMS Listings	8147	LT80-2380	17.00	NONE	
		Authoring Guide	*ST40-1897	22.00	7452	CICS Assembly Listings	8163	LT80-2409	15.50		
		Specifications	*GT40-4535	N/C	7440	Logic	8146	LT60-2285	14.50		
		CICS Operator's Guide	*ST40-1904	6.80							
		CMS Operators Guide	*ST40-1898	4.40							

Fig. 7.1 Continued.

The O&M stage consists of Migration, Operation, Post-Install Evaluation, Maintenance and Upgrade, and Termination. These activities were discussed in Chapter 3. Maintenance and Upgrade was also covered in other chapters since the activity is so closely related to development. Maintenance fixes errors in a released system but the fixes have to be integrated (and regression tested) in the next/next-plus-one release. Upgrades generate new functions that have to be added to some future release. Both activities are managed like any other development. The same type of discipline and control is applied, although design control may actually be harder for post-release changes. The original design is done in top-down fashion so that system interactions are exposed at all times. Post-release changes are done bottom-up in the sense that the change request usually refers to a function residing in a single module. The programmer assigned to that change request determines whether it affects the system design by starting with the module and backtracking through the system specification to find potential interactions. He or she may not find them all. When maintenance is performed by user personnel who played no part in the original design backtracking is exactly like searching a labyrinth. The programmer has no idea where to look next. The project team that built the system, if still in existence, can help at this point.

Advice from the developer *may* also be useful in the migration and operation areas. *May* is used here since many developers never learn what users do with systems. The environment in which systems programs are used is a mystery to the developers [1]. The developer can explain how to use the system in general terms but the answer may not fit the user's needs. The user should treat the project team as consultants; that is, questions should be phrased precisely and narrowly. Do not ask, "How should I migrate my Demand Deposit database to the new system?" Ask, "For a file of 100K records of 40 bytes each in which 80 percent of the transactions affect 20 percent of the records, how should I store the file to minimize average access time on your system? I have six disk drives available and I will be doing the following other work on the machine: .....In addition, I am currently using the database on system X, where it is arranged as follows: ....."

Six to twelve months after installation, the user should verify that the system meets the original requirements. Since the acceptance test, people have changed their behavior by using the capabilities of the system. Does their new method of operation change the requirements? Is the user still satisfied with the system? If not, should the user improve training and operating procedures to make the system satisfactory? Should the user ask for upgrades to the system? Has the operation changed so much that the user will need an entirely different system? If so, when, considering the cost and the effect the change will have on ongoing operations? Questions such as these are part of a post-install evaluation, which has two purposes:

1. Determine that the installed system meets its original objectives.
2. Determine the adequacy of the system in light of current objectives.

The first evaluation measures achievement; the second plans for growth.

7.3 SUMMARY

The program development process is a controlled method of building complex systems [2]. A *system* is a structured aggregate of elements that satisfies a set of functional and performance objectives. The systems of concern in this book have been computer programs with particular emphasis on large programs. Complexity is a function of the number of elements in a system; therefore, large program systems are inherently complex. Considering that the elements of a program development project include people, machines, and programs, large software projects are very complex indeed. One of the functions of project management is to reduce, or at least compensate for, the complexity of a system. Complexity can be reduced in the design stage by minimizing coupling among system elements. If you cannot actually eliminate an element, you can limit its contribution to system complexity by isolating it as much as possible from other elements. Complexity that cannot be reduced must be managed.

Various project management procedures exist that give the project manager the ability to control all the activities and resources under his or her direction [2, 3]. These procedures do not give the project manager control of the numerous external influences of buyers, users, and other interested parties, but they do establish a basis for planning and implementing the system within a control framework that flags problems and permits corrective action. Within this stable framework, it is practical to standardize the tools and techniques used throughout the project. Development and test tools have reached a sophisticated level of technology. Analysis and design tools are coming along, yet at a slower pace. The cost of using a suitable tool kit can rise to uneconomic heights, but some of the best tools and techniques—such as higher-order languages, structured programming, and other improved programming techniques (IPT)—are low in cost and easy to use. Any project, regardless of size, is advised to use them.

Status control is also automated in large projects. Work breakdown structures, configuration identifications, configuration accounting, and activity schedules can all be tied together in a coordinated data-processing application. These data relate to who is working on various tasks, what the deliverable end items are, and when they will be delivered. Financial accounting can be tied into the same database so that budget status can be tracked with an eye on technical progress. A little analysis will then show whether the project is on plan or not. The plan lays out work to be done in a sequential manner. Program development projects all follow the same overall sequence of activities—the system development *life cycle.* The life cycle consists of a concept formulation stage, project definition, project implementation (design, development, and test), operation, maintenance and upgrade, and termination. These stages overlap on a large project; i.e., development of some components can start before design of others is complete. Because they overlap, work completed in one stage may have to be done over due to new information generated in another stage. The life cycle contains many iterative subcycles. To keep everything under control, the project manager creates a *baseline* specification and ensures that all changes are added to the baseline before they are added to the system. A configuration control board (or individual) reviews all proposed changes to assess whether they should be incorporated in the baseline. By evaluating and selectively adopting proposed changes, the project team can keep a lid on system growth and simultaneously keep the system from getting more complex. System dynamics theory shows that program systems all grow as maintenance repairs are made and as new requirements are satisfied. For instance, modern distributed systems use a common operating system (OS) but, sooner or later, each separate processor in the network will tailor the OS slightly to adapt it to local needs [4]. The result is more program growth. Accompanying this growth is an increase in entropy, reflected in structural degradation of the system. A well-structured system will become poorly structured if it grows without limit. Rules of thumb exist for determining when a system is approaching a point at which it should be restructured before further functions are added.

A model of the life cycle can be constructed that plots resource requirements against time. In the model, direct programming resources can be distinguished from indirect support and management resources. The shape of the life-cycle curve is predictable for an organization with knowledge of its historical performance. Therefore, the life-cycle model can be used to plan recruiting objectives, estimate monthly expenses, estimate computer time requirements, and allocate headcount to various departments in a project. An organization with extensive history data can refine the life-cycle approach to reflect the benefits of IPT, obtaining more precise estimates. Another use of the life-cycle model is as a basis for scheduling services from functional support groups such as the computer center or the printing/reproduction shop. As the project proceeds, it will often deviate from the plan. Typically, expenses will be on target but technical progress will have fallen behind. The life-cycle model helps determine how to revise the project plan under these circumstances. You can decide to keep to the original end date, or you can stay within the budget, or you can change the system specifications. The life cycle will suggest different plan adjustments in each case.

Tradeoffs like these are prevalent in program development. Original plans are always optimistic and reality catches up with them in time. As a result, the project manager must live with constraints that often conflict with each other. In order to manage under these circumstances, the project manager has to carefully define the problem to be addressed. When it appears that there is no direct solution to the problem that conforms to the constraints, the manager looks for alternative courses of action. Each alternative is supported with applicable data and with an analysis of what it will cost. The most attractive alternative can then be selected by any one of several decision rules. At the very early stages of a project, system requirements must be established. Requirements usually start out as a wish list containing everything imaginable—too much to afford. Tradeoffs start right at that point and continue throughout the project.

The user's requirements list is reduced, first, by the budget limitations imposed on the user's organization and, second, by technical limitations on development. As a consequence, the developer's proposal for doing the job will offer a less attractive deal than the user sought. When several developers are willing to compete to do the job, the user has the opportunity to request proposals from them all. Each proposal will be a sales pitch. It will combine the vendor's best offer with a list of reasons why the vendor is the best choice to do the job. The vendor who has put together the best offer in terms of price, performance, functional capability, schedule, and quality should win the job. A contract will be developed (formally for an outside vendor, informally for an in-house development department) and the vendor will be obligated to do what was proposed. This implies that the vendor was prepared, when the proposal was written, to commit to stand behind the offer. The sales pitch must be backed up with the ability and the intent to perform under a binding contract.

The development team starts out small and grows rapidly. A strong plan and a project control mechanism should be put in place at the start so that the project does not grow out of hand. The control mechanisms that are most effective are built around a tree-structured hierarchy, just like the program system. In fact, the program structure can often be mapped directly onto the organization chart. The advantage of the hierarchical structure is that it maximizes binding and minimizes coupling. Each departmental unit in such an organization can do most of its work without interacting with other units. When communication with another unit is required, standardized procedures ensure that the responsibilities of the two units are clear and that their managers are aware of the agreements reached and actions initiated. In this way, if two groups agree to change, say, a program unit completion date but, unknown to them, other units depend on the program unit, the project controls will alert the managers to the need for further coordination. The controls conform to the hierarchical structure and take into account that people in the working departments know a lot about one leaf of the tree but not much about the tree. Managers higher up know a lot about the tree but would be overwhelmed with data if they tried to learn the details of every leaf in their set of branches. Appropriate filters are applied to communications within a project to give the people at each level what they need.

Communications are related to complexity. In a small team, everyone can know what everyone else knows about the system. The team members accomplish this by talking to each other easily and informally. As a group, larger teams cannot gather around a table every morning and share the knowledge of all team members. In large teams, communications are formalized. If every individual had to tell every other individual what is going on in his or her area, communications would take so much time no productive work would get done. The formal procedures rely on directed communications where one individual passes information to a few others who need to know (as deduced from the project plan and system design). Other information is placed in a public file where everyone has access to it. Large teams are relatively inefficient because of the communications problem; therefore, project managers try very hard to carry out their projects with small teams. An ordinary small team can only do a small job. Special small teams can do much more with the same number of people. In a peer group, the higher productivity is achieved by virtue of the experience of a close-knit group. In a chief programmer team, the productivity is the result of IPT and structured work assignment. "Large" jobs cannot be done with small teams but project managers can try to make a large team behave like a small team. They use IPT to standardize production methods and they further refine the hierarchical organization structure to reduce coupling—permitting the small teams within the large project to operate more independently of one another.

Just as project planning is critical to project management, a good design is critical to project implementation. Design is an intellectual process that is done well by some people. The best of these are the ones to select for a project. The document produced by the designers is the baseline specification to be used and updated throughout the project. It is a basic part of the project file and, as such, is the reference for all subsequent project stages. Individual programmers work to specifications prepared by package designers. Test teams verify that programs submitted to the implementation library satisfy the specifications prepared during the design stage. Maintenance and upgrade teams refer to the same database to determine how to change the released product without impacting the integrity of the system [5]. Because a good design is so important, it is examined with a fine-tooth comb in design inspections—the first of many reviews.

Project reviews are conducted throughout the schedule. The cost of a change to the project plan or to a specific piece of work grows as time passes. Again, complexity is the culprit. During the design stage, there are only a few people on the project. Even if they all stopped work to concentrate on making a change in the design, the cost would be small. At the test stage, there are so many people and so many activities affected, the cost of making a change, however trivial, is large. Project reviews are meant to catch problems early to prevent them from coming up later. Both technical reviews and project status reviews contribute to the objective. The comprehensive tests run during the test stage also serve the same purpose by removing errors that would otherwise be found by the user. Post-release errors not only inconvenience the user; they cost even more to fix than pre-release problems. The tests serve another purpose, too. They are the basis for agreement between the developer and the user that the end items are indeed ready for release and acceptable to the user.

7.4 CONCLUDING REMARKS

Project management is a difficult challenge. Program system development is a particularly difficult challenge. Nevertheless, program project management has advanced to the stage where it is now reasonable to expect projects to succeed. In the 1960s, that was not the case; users expected to get what they wanted on the second or third try. As the programming field matured, it became more like other engineering fields. Discipline became acceptable and teamwork became respectable. Above all, people began to recognize the need to get the project off on the right foot. Good planning and design at the start of the project are essential [6]. A second key lesson from history is that project management and control are more important to success than technical accomplishment. The best design cannot be implemented when the project is in disarray.

A few other points to remember were selected by Martin Belsky [7] from his extensive experience as project manager of several very large systems. If you want to succeed in program system development:

- Identify, quantify, and manage all the major goals for your project and your organization.
- Staff with (only) good people.
- Organize by project as opposed to function.
- Structure your organization to allow first-line managers to provide technical and control leadership.
- Evaluate the product requirements.
- Establish system acceptance criteria and lay out the system test plan early—even before design.
- Avoid the myths of design—follow logical steps and evaluate the design as you proceed.

- Freeze the baseline early; stonewall new requirements; simplify; reduce function.
- Manage to every checkpoint.
- Test your product from the user's point of view.
- Fix and evolve what you have, as opposed to starting over.

These guidelines establish a plan and define a controlled process. Control is maintained throughout the project. The end result will be on time, within budget, and it will satisfy the user.

REFERENCES

1. Withington, F. G. *The Environment for Systems Programs.* Reading, Mass.: Addison-Wesley, 1978.

2. Tausworthe, R. C. *Standardized Development of Computer Software.* Englewood Cliffs, N.J.: Prentice Hall, 1979.

3. McClure, C. L. *Managing Software Development and Maintenance.* New York: Van Nostrand Reinhold, 1981.

4. Ebert, R.; Lügger, J.; and Goecke, L. *Practice in Software Adaption and Maintenance.* Amsterdam and New York: North-Holland Publishing, 1980.

5. Swanson, E. B. "The Dimensions of Maintenance." *Proceedings 2nd International Conference on Software Engineering.* New York: IEEE, Inc., 1976.

6. Thayer, R. H.; Pyster, A. B.; and Wood, R. C. "Major Issues in Software Engineering Project Management." *IEEE Transactions on Software Engineering* SE-7, no. 4 (July 1981).

7. Belsky, M. A. "The Technology of System Management." *Proceedings: COMPSAC 79.* Long Beach, Calif.: IEEE Computer Society, 1979.

Appendix A:
System Specification

A format is presented here that can serve as an outline for a program system or package specification. The user should include only the topics that apply to the project at hand. The amount of detail increases as design proceeds from the system to the package level. Detail also increases as the project moves forward. The same outline used during project definition for recording requirements (R) can be used in expanded form for the Initial Programming Specification (I) produced in the design stage and the Final Programming Specification (F) submitted to the integration and test phase of the development stage. A recommended usage for each line item is indicated in the columns R, I, and F.

		R	I	F
1	GENERAL INFORMATION			
1.0	SUMMARY			
	The summary should give an overview of the system; it should describe the management and technical approach; and it should explain how to use the System Specification.	X	X	X
1.1	REQUIREMENTS AND SPECIFICATIONS			
1.1.1	*Requirements*—Requirements statements should be sufficient to convey the needs to be met. They are written to allow the developer maximum technical freedom. They are updated as necessary during the project life cycle. The system design requirements review is the basis for entering the implementation stage.	X		

	R	I	F
		X	

1.1.2   *Initial Specifications*—In response to the requirements, the initial specifications are sufficient to evaluate the adequacy of the proposed deliverables. They provide an understanding of how the requirements will be met. The design stage concludes with critical design reviews of the initial specifications.

1.1.3   *Final Specifications*—As an outgrowth of the initial specifications, the final specifications describe the deliverable end items entering the test stage. They contain: **X**

- Function definition sufficient to allow approvers and reviewers to determine what can and cannot be accomplished with the finished programs/systems.

- System structure (architecture) information sufficient to allow approvers and reviewers to determine how the new function will interact with all other hardware and software functions.

- Packaging information sufficient to allow approvers and reviewers to determine marketability, installability, performance, and serviceability.

1.2   RESPONSIBILITIES

Perform = *P*   Approve = *A*   Review = *R*

	User	Developer	System Architect	Support Developer	Field Support
Requirements	P	A*	A*	R	R
Specifications**	A	P	A	R	R
Cost Estimates**	A	P		A	A

1.3   REFERENCE DOCUMENTS

1.3.1	*Corporate Standards, Practices, Guidelines*	X X X
1.3.2	*Reference Manuals, Background Papers, Bibliography*	X X X
1.3.3	*Working Papers*	X X

---

*Internal requirements should conform to the common architecture and implementation standards of the organization; customer requirements will be reviewed by architects and developers acting in an advisory role.

**Manufacturer and Distributor approvals are required when end items are to be delivered in quantity.

	R	I	F
1.4 DOCUMENT CONTROL			
1.4.1 *Status* (list of currently valid pages)	X	X	X
1.4.2 *Procedures and Responsibility for Document Control*	X	X	X
1.4.3 *Review and Update Schedule*	X	X	X

2 REQUIREMENTS SUMMARY

2.1 SYSTEM DESCRIPTION X X X

State the purpose of the system; describe the operational environment and the functions to be performed; describe the human factors. If there is an existing system, explain its deficiencies. Indicate the user's migration strategy and list existing features to be retained in the new system. Identify any boundaries and constraints: technical, financial, etc. Summarize the economic justification for the system.

2.2 DESIGN CRITERIA X X X

List the requirements that affect design; e.g., user-specified programming language, host machine, compatibility with existing database. Describe existing databases, support program interfaces, and communications facilities. Give performance goals and operating cost requirements.

2.3 ACCEPTANCE CRITERIA X X X

Describe the conditions agreed to by the user for determining that the delivered end items are acceptable. Give the date for initial user operation of the delivered system.

3 FUNCTIONAL CHARACTERISTICS

Functional characteristics, in combination with performance and configuration specifications, conversion information, and support information, describe the system or product to the user. In the Initial Specification, the functions are only detailed enough to show how the requirements will be satisfied. The Final Programming Specifications completely describe the externals of the support. They are source material for customer and service information.

	R	I	F

For completeness, consider the following checklist:

System Generation (Sysgen)	Dynamic Configuration Change
Initial Program Load (IPL)	Checkpoint/Restart Recovery
Compile/Linkedit	Operator Communication
Execute Time	Dump/Maintenance Log
Open/Close/End of Volume	Trace/Debug Tuning
Abnormal End (Abend)	Accounting
Initiation/Termination	Monitoring & Recording
Cancel	Unattended Operation
Noninterruptible Operation	Configuration Verification

3.1   SOFTWARE END ITEMS
A separate specification is required for each end item.

3.1.1   *Description*—Describe what the program does. Give   X X
an overview of how it operates not only from the
point of view of the developer but also from that of
the user.

If there was a counterpart in a previous release,
describe the changes in this release and enumerate
the differences point by point.

List the functions performed and, for each function, list the input, processing performed, and
output.

3.1.2   *Invocation*—Describe how the program is used or   X X
invoked. Identify the macros and/or commands and
their principal parameters and defaults.

3.1.3   *Interactions with User*—Describe the interactions   X X
between the functions and the user. Consider both
immediate (on-line) and deferred (off-line) situations
in which the purpose of the program depends on a
user activity.

3.1.4   *Error Handling*—Describe and explain how the func-   X
tions respond to errors of implementation, errors of
use, and abnormal terminations. List the modules
that detect the errors. List the diagnostic programs
to be provided.

	R	I	F

3.1.5   *Messages*—Describe the messages generated and the system/user action and response. List the modules and conditions that cause the issuance of messages.   F: X

3.1.6   *Size*—Estimate the total number of source statements, excluding comments. For maintenance or update releases, give the number of new and changed source statements.   I: X F: X

3.1.7   *Interfaces*—Summarize the interfaces. Reference the prime sources; that is, the project file interface section and appropriate manuals.   I: X F: X

3.1.8   *Program Structure*—Describe the program to relate its various elements to each other and to the overall system. All significant data paths and interfaces should be shown. This section should grow from initial system specifications to final package and unit specifications. The structure includes control blocks, processes, databases, and manual procedures described by: I: X F: X

- Narrative description of the program, its purpose, logical organization, and plans for achieving its objectives.
- Storage maps and table descriptions/layouts.
- Diagrams to show how the tables, control blocks, and storage areas will be used to achieve objectives.
- Flowcharts, HIPOs, and other appropriate techniques that describe the program logic at several levels of detail, each level leading into a lower level of detail.

3.1.9   *Hardware Considerations*—Describe the hardware type, size, and configuration on which the system will run. Indicate which hardware components still under development are in the critical path. Consider: R: X I: X F: X

- CPUs
- Primary and auxiliary storage used by the system (In the Final Specifications, describe resident main storage requirements in detail. Describe the effect of options if parts of the system are optional.)

	R	I	F

- Primary and auxiliary storage available to the user (Recommend minimum storage capacity for typical classes of application.)
- Channels
- Control units
- I/O devices
- Nongraphic consoles
- Graphic devices
- Communications devices (links, switches, channel extenders)

3.1.10 *Software Considerations*—Describe the programs— type, size, application, and version—on which this system depends, including diagnostics and exercisers.   X X X

3.2   HARDWARE END ITEMS
A separate specification is required for each end item.

3.2.1 *Purpose and Description*   X X

- Product classification (type, model, feature, accessory)
- Capacity ranges (speed, format, size, etc.)
- Compatibility with appropriate architecture
- Programming support
- RAS highlights (Reliability, Availability, Serviceability)
- Customer and Service Information highlights

3.2.2 *Logical Design*   X X

- Basic data flow
- Data flow unit descriptions (e.g., registers, special circuits, new/unique components, etc.)
- Addressing level, restrictions, etc.
- Operational/functional characteristics
- Type and location of error detection/correction capabilities; error accumulation and recording facilities
- Detailed machine-level functions

3.2.3 *Programming Considerations*   X X X
- Instruction/command definitions
- Priority levels and priority handling
- Restrictions

	R	I	F

- Error indications and device condition after error
- Error-recovery procedures
- Condition of device after reset
- Program-related reliability features
- Error recording procedures

3.2.4 *Timing*   X X
- Instruction/command execution timings
- Data-transfer rates
- Device timings
- Timing variations (on-line vs. off-line, etc.)
- Line-control considerations

3.2.5 *Features*   X X

- Operator/programmer controls, indicators, procedures
- Control panel description
- Measurement tools and recorders
- Emergency power off
- Attachable units
- Ancillary products, supplies, I/O media
- Options, models, field installable features, compatibility

3.2.6 *Physical and Environmental Specifications*   X X X

- Physical
  - weights and floor loading
  - dimensions
  - service clearance (gate swings, cable cutouts, etc.)
- Electrical
  - input power
  - AC and DC loads
  - power sequencing
  - external cables and cords
- Environment (see standards documents)
  - ambient conditions
  - electromagnetic compatibility
  - vibration and shock
  - acoustic level
  - safety
  - Environmental Impact Assessment
  - temperature control (air conditioning/water cooling)

	R	I	F

- Packaging
  - replaceable units, repair/replacement philosophy
  - adjustments permitted
  - layout of components, assembly procedures
  - visual identification

3.2.7 *RAS*   X X

- Preventive maintenance schedule
- Spare parts
- Tools and test equipment, service aids, convenience outlets, test points

3.2.8 *Installation/Upgrade/Replacement*   X X

- Physical planning
- Parallel operation, shared components
- Cutover, automatic switchover
- Verification procedures

3.3 SECURITY   X X X

Describe the facilities/features provided to control access to resources. Include how:

- Personal identification is established, verified, and used to control access.
- Data are protected from unauthorized disclosure, modification, or destruction.
- Resource access is audited (e.g., by logging).
- Physical security is provided.
- Maintenance service is supported while user security measures are enforced.

The following information should be clearly understood:

- Effect on the user. What does the user have to do, and what are the controls placed on the user? What happens to other users when one user violates security?
- Effect on the hardware and software environment. Does this product override, displace, interface to, extend, or depend on features provided by other hardware or software products?
- Effect on the installation management. What new or extended controls are provided to installation management to improve control of user access to resources? What installation management procedures or security measures are being recommended or depended upon?

	R	I	F
		X	X

3.4   INTEGRITY

Describe the privileges required by a program to
show what other programs and databases it is
authorized to access or modify. Indicate how the
system controls authorized activities and detects
unauthorized activities. Show how the privileges of
the program affect the user, the environment, and
the installation management.

3.5   AUDITABILITY   X   X

Describe the features of the system that will make it
easier for an auditor to ensure that:

- Access and change to resources are adequately
  detected, controlled, and recorded.
- Data processing results are complete and accurate.

4   PERFORMANCE

4.1   PERFORMANCE STATEMENTS   X   X   X

Performance should be stated for each system component in terms of the basic operating times and
resources used by the basic operations. Enough data
should be supplied to allow the user to estimate the
time required to do a job. For example, a computer
could be described in terms of instruction cycle times
but the user may find it easier to work with a single
average instruction time based on a job mix and an
operating system typical of the user environment. A
program is best described in terms of the instruction
path length and storage required to process a typical transaction or in terms of the elapsed time and
storage required to process a typical batch job
stream.

**4.1.1   *Performance Specification*—The performance of   X   X
each component should be described in terms of the
quantity of resources consumed/required to execute
a representative set of specific paths through the
component.**

- The maximum elapsed time
- The path length (number of instructions executed)
- The number of instructions executed under a lock
- The number of bytes referenced and changed
- The storage occupied (virtual, real, fixed)

	R	I	F

The developer should identify those resources whose usage is variable and sensitive to the choice of path through the component.

4.1.2   *Verifiability*—All performance statements should be verifiable by measurement, with the technology required for the measurement known at the time the component is complete.   X (F)

4.1.3   *Completeness*—A performance statement should apply to stand-alone component performance and to component performance when used in the system. In addition, the statement should describe the impact, if any, on system performance when the component is present but not used.   X (F)

4.1.4   *Environment*—Performance statements should define (and include the effect of) the particular operating systems and hardware configurations for which the estimates apply. Where possible, guidelines should be given for translating the stated estimates to different environments.   X   X   X

4.2   PERFORMANCE MANAGEMENT   X   X   X
In order to determine the performance of a component or system and in order to tune the performance a particular configuration under various conditions of use, a management plan is required. It should provide for collecting performance data from existing components, for projecting performance of components being developed, and for simulating system performance with the use of a model. Simulation runs should represent various system environments and various applications. The results of simulation predict the effects of different environments and uses of the system. The results should also be used to identify the sensitivity of system performance to changes in each controllable parameter. Tuning guidelines should be provided to the user.

5   MIGRATION/COEXISTENCE   X   X   X
To support orderly transition from an existing system to a new system, a migration plan is required. Stable operations should be assured by making each step in the migration easy to install and easy to remove. Restoration of the preexisting system should be fast and simple in case of installation or cutover

R   I   F

problems. Migration steps should be spaced widely enough to permit one step to stabilize before the next occurs. Each step should improve the functional capability of the system. A user may simultaneously operate several versions of the system; incompatibilities among versions should be listed. Function restrictions due to migration steps should be identified.

5.1   CONVERSION   X X

Identify conversion techniques that are required; for example, operation in a compatibility mode, emulation, simulation, recompilation, revision of catalog procedures, or conversion of user data and programs. Identify tradeoffs between conversion techniques and additional design/development.

5.2   USE   X

Give examples to show how to use the nonobvious details of the system; e.g., if the performance of an interactive system depends on the priority assigned to it in a multiprogrammed environment, explain the requirement and show the effect of low priority on user response time. If an interactive system permits users to update the master database, recommend a procedure that prevents an update transaction from interfering with query responses to other users. The purpose of this section is to demonstrate the adequacy of the deliverables and to supply source material for user information documents.

6   <u>HUMAN FACTORS</u>   X X X

Describe each group of end users and the tasks they will perform with respect to the system. Include the skills they have and the training they will need. Indicate what measurable or testable criteria will be used during the qualification period. Categorize end-user activities to distinguish casual users from dedicated users and to relate activities to the migration steps in the system life cycle.

6.1   PHYSICAL CHARACTERISTICS (for operators,   X X

users of interactive programs). Examples:

6.1.1   *Vision*—Discrimination among similar characters on a display, color recognition, ability to see displays from normal working position

	R	I	F

6.1.2   *Motor Performance*—speed of response, placement of keys to be hit simultaneously

6.2   TASK CHARACTERISTICS   X X X

- Description of task: existing method, proposed method.
- Work schedules, or length of time to perform a specific task.
- Any ancillary tasks the user will be expected to perform. (Examples may be problem determination and recovery procedures.)
- Constraints imposed by law, custom, union contract, languages, etc., on the amount or kind of work a user can do.
- User productivity requirements such as the expected amount of work to be done on each task in a given period of time, accuracy level required, and the system response time required.
- Any motivational measures, including pay, used by employers to maintain or improve productivity levels.

6.3   SKILL AND EDUCATION OF USERS   X X X

- Training/education required for employment in the job users are doing. Descriptions or copies of any tests required by an employer and the score necessary for employment should be included, if possible.
- Skills or training acquired from previous jobs or other programs.
- Training/education programs to further prepare users for their jobs. Any on-the-job training or instruction should be included. Entry level skills or performance, duration of training programs, and level of skill or performance following training should also be described.
- Self-instructional, prompting, error checking or other user aids that should be incorporated into the program.
- The information users will need in documentary form and how it will be used.

6.4   EXPERIMENTATION   X X
Measure system usability and acceptability (e.g., time to learn how to use the system, obstacles to learning, effectiveness of displays, messages, user aids).

		R	I	F
7	RATIONALE			
7.1	ARCHITECTURE		X	X

Include the necessary details of the protocols, formats, codes, commands and responses, etc., that are defined by (or, in their absence, take the place of) the applicable subsystem architectures. Briefly list and reference the applicable architecture documents, by number, level, date, title, etc. Where options are permitted, include the specific options or subsets to be implemented in detail.

For communications products define, in addition to the above:

- The structure required for records that will be interchanged among dissimilar nodes.
- The link controls and headers used.
- The network control, session control, and data flow control functions supported and used by the product.

7.2 DESIGN   X

Outline the approach, algorithms, and tradeoffs used in the design. Give an overview of the logic used.

7.3 ALTERNATIVES   X

Identify the alternatives considered but not used in the final design.

7.4 FOLLOW-ON   X

Identify functions that are not performed and that are candidates for follow-on development. Describe why these functions are desirable. Indicate what allowance has been made for these potential future additions.

8 STANDARDS   X X X

Include a list of applicable standards and approved deviations.

9 QUALITY AND RAS   X X X

Describe the quality requirements and the procedures used to produce the requested level of quality, reliability, availability, and serviceability. Where experience permits, quantify the guidelines for defects per KLOC to be detected at each inspection stage and project the number of defects expected to be found by users during operation (a basis for service cost planning).

	R	I	F

9.1   IMPLEMENTATION $\underline{\text{R}} \ \underline{\text{I}} \ \underline{\text{F}}$ / X X X

- Specify the implementation language. Where more than one is specified, justify the diversity and explain how the multiple languages and their associated support tools are related.
- State any implementation requirements such as development and test technologies.
- Briefly describe the plans for defect discovery and removal through high- and low-level design inspections, code inspections, and test plan and test case inspections.
- Briefly describe the plans intended to verify that the functions supported by the programming entity are tested, that the specified compatibility level is achieved, and that the performance specifications are met.
- State special considerations required for a successful implementation of these plans. A comprehensive test plan is required as a separate document.

9.2   RAS CHARACTERISTICS   X X X

- Give the criteria governing RAS design; e.g., cost   X
  objectives for maintenance, availability measures and goals for uninterrupted operation, allowable repair time, and allowable design and development response time for fixing problems in various priority classes.
- Give guidelines for maximum operational loads,   X X
  minimum storage for various levels of performance, storage reserved for program fixes, checkpoint/restart support, and other design parameters aimed at improving RAS.
- Specify the RAS elements of the design such as: X X
  - automatic error detection
  - automatic error isolation
  - error recording
  - error recovery
  - problem determination capabilities through facilities and documentation:
    Monitoring/tracing (hardware/software)
    Data reduction/status analysis
    Status display
    Procedures

R I F

– error isolation capabilities through diagnostic
tools
  Dumps
  Traces
  Error data analysis programs
– reconfiguration capabilities available to user
and/or support personnel
– RAS dependencies on other products/software
– health and safety

9.3   RAS SUPPORT PLAN   X X
Outline a support plan consistent with the RAS characteristics of the system. Since support responsibility
may be assigned entirely or in part to the developer,
or the user, or a third party, give enough information to permit the support group, wherever it resides,
to prepare a detailed support plan.

- Overall support plan
  – total support structure
  – description of responsibilities and working inter-
    faces for each unique group of support personnel
- User involvement
  – system setup, system generation
  – problem determination
  – reporting
  – knowledge required
- Support organization
  – support group hierarchy from field site to
    central maintenance or development facility,
  – knowledge required at each hierarchical level
- Documentation
- Tools and aids
- Emergency procedures
- Normal problem fix procedures
- Control procedures
  – program/engineering level control
  – compatibility with applications, systems soft-
    ware, data dictionary
  – network level control

10   DISTRIBUTION OF PROGRAM PACKAGES   X X X
Explicitly describe what will be shipped.

10.1   INITIAL RELEASE

	R	I	F

10.2   MODIFICATIONS AND VERSIONS
- Projected number and timing
- Turn-around time
- Change control support system

10.3   PUBLICATIONS

- Documents to be produced
  - purpose and use
  - form and audience
  - release date and distribution
  - relation to education courses
- Glossary of terms to be used. Maintain consistency with the data dictionary, with prior releases, and with general use in the operating environment

11   <u>EVALUATION</u>   X   X

Describe the post-release procedure for determining how well the system satisfies the requirements:

- Function
- Performance
- Cost
- RAS
- Growth potential and any other objectives that can only be evaluated after an extended period of observation and measurement

Appendix B:
Project Review Checklist

The following outline, modified as appropriate for local use, can be helpful to reviewers and reviewees. It should be handed out well before a scheduled review so reviewees can use it as a guide in preparing presentation material. It should be on hand at the review as an aid to complete coverage of relevant points. The outline applies to general project management reviews. It is not an outline for formal inspections, nor financial audits, nor any similar specialized functional review. This outline covers all functional areas on the assumption that more detailed reviews are being conducted regularly.

I. What Is a Review for?
   A. Purpose of Project Review
      1. Determine if adequate definition exists of the problems to be solved.
      2. Determine if appropriate plans, checkpoints, and budgets have been established and are being adhered to.
      3. Determine if plans, objectives, and budget are mutually compatible.
      4. Determine if organization, controls, and technical management are adequate.
      5. Determine if appropriate skills and facilities are assigned.
      6. Determine if adequate marketing plans exist for securing follow-on and related business.
      7. Determine if customer relations are good and if organization for handling customer contacts is adequate.
      8. Determine if the project is making maximum contribution to the technological objectives of the organization to which it belongs.

9. Recommend corrective actions to problem areas.
10. Establish follow-up procedure to corrective actions.
B. Function of Project Review
  1. Assess actual status of the project relative to planned status and commitments.
     a. Technical approach
     b. Variance from plan
     c. Future plan of action
  2. Assess documentation, management reports, and related information.
     a. Determine if this information exists, is used, is of value, can be improved, etc.
     b. Evaluate the project review procedures
     c. Evaluate standards and administrative procedures
  3. Interchange useful information.
     a. Exchange techniques with other projects
     b. Inform development team members of project status
     c. Identify sources for assistance on special topics
  4. Identify and resolve problems.
     a. Technical
     b. Management
     c. Financial
     d. Resources
     e. Personnel
     f. Contractual
     g. Customer
     h. Marketing
  5. Review project management.
     a. Assignment of responsibilities
     b. Organization
     c. How managers spend their time
     d. Plans for project followup and growth in related areas
  6. Report to project manager (or manager who called the review).
     a. State review objectives, conclusions, and key recommendations in a brief cover letter
     b. Explain conclusions in detail with specific examples of data influencing key conclusions
     c. Explain methodology of the review if any unusual methods were used
     d. State recommendations in priority order, showing who is responsible for action in each case
     e. Give examples of results expected if recommendations are adopted

II. Project Review Preparation by Project Manager
   A. General Information
      1. General program description.
      2. Contract Number(s) or internal project identification.
      3. Contract or Project Title.
      4. Buyer, user, or sponsor.
      5. Period of performance.
         a. Approved and funded
         b. Planned through completion of project
      6. Definitization status of contract.
      7. Type of contract.
      8. Potential.
         a. Follow-on, new business
         b. Relationship to other programs or areas of business
   B. Management Information
      1. Program status.
         a. Deliverable end items
            (1) What the end items are
            (2) End items already delivered
            (3) End items to be delivered
            (4) Project performance to date
         b. Budgets and actuals
            (1) Project performance to date
            (2) Budget to complete
            (3) Estimate of complete
            (4) Reasons for variance
            (5) Recovery plan
            (6) Fee/profit in percent and dollars
            (7) Tangible/Intangible benefits vs. total cost
         c. People
            (1) Assigned
            (2) On requisition
            (3) Staffing schedule
         d. Skill requirements—skill mix, current and planned
         e. Facilities and equipment
            (1) Own/customer furnished
            (2) Adequacy of service, location, available hours
            (3) Special requirements, actual and anticipated
            (4) Computer usage forecasts versus actuals
         f. Relations with other departments and subcontractors
            (1) Current work breakdown
            (2) Relationships among participants
            (3) Project requirements—actual and anticipated
            (4) Performance: quality, schedule, cost

2. Special problems—areas that might require assistance from higher management levels.
   a. Technical
   b. Management
   c. Financial
   d. Resources
   e. Personnel
   f. Contractual
   g. Customer
   h. Marketing
   i. Other
3. Program controls—review the various methods of internal controls employed.
   a. Operational program plans
   b. Program status reports
   c. Marketing plans
   d. Project control and management system, including reviews and inspections.
   e. Financial summaries
   f. Project file
   g. Development and test plan
   h. Change control
   i. Other
4. Customer-imposed controls—review various customer control requirements.
   a. Schedule
   b. Financial
   c. Technical
   d. Other
5. Responsibility—Project organization chart showing areas of responsibility and customer/contractor relationships.
C. Technical Information
   1. Description of program.
      a. Technical objectives
         (1) Purpose of the job
         (2) Operational characteristics
         (3) Specifications
      b. Character of end items—what the end items are—analysis, programs, training courses, hardware, system integration, etc.
      c. Technical approach
         (1) Utilization and application of existing techniques and technology
         (2) Application of skills
         (3) Technical plan

    d. Key technical problems
        (1) Define
        (2) Requirements to solve
        (3) Status
    e. Future of program area—application of technical
        developments to other project/business areas
2. Technological value.
    a. Personnel experience
        (1) What does project/organization gain
        (2) Application to other areas
    b. Degree of technical advancement
        (1) Little or no advancement
        (2) Advance the state-of-the-art
        (3) Breakthrough
    c. Application of techniques
        (1) Application to other current or future programs
        (2) Application to other business areas
        (3) Plan for applying to other areas
    d. Utilization of techniques developed elsewhere—ensure
        optimum utilization
    e. Technical papers, patent disclosures
        (1) What was published on this project
        (2) Should anything be published—who may authorize
           release
        (3) Benefits to be derived
    f. Computer programs
        (1) Deliverable end items
           (a) Ownership
           (b) Maintenance plan
           (c) Follow-on versions
           (d) Responsibilities
        (2) Support programs
           (a) Ownership
           (b) Maintenance plan
           (c) Follow-on versions
           (d) Responsibilities
        (3) Are there any programs of interest outside the proj-
           ect (as products, as the basis for different projects)
        (4) Are the programs suitably designed and documented
           for general use or are they specialized to fit this proj-
           ect
        (5) Should any special programs be generalized
3. Technical performance.
    a. Specifications and approach
        (1) Design requirements baseline

        (a) External—for users
        (b) Internal—for implementers
    (3) Technical standards—design language, implementation language, structured programming, etc.
  b. Plans
    (1) Development plan
    (2) Test plan
    (3) Documentation plan
    (4) Conversion and maintenance plan
    (5) Resource plan
  c. Schedules and estimates
  d. Interactions
    (1) Activity network
    (2) Work breakdown structure, modularity
    (3) Program interfaces
    (4) Data and control flow
  e. System analysis and evaluation
    (1) Predictive models
    (2) Measurement tools
    (3) Quality assurance
    (4) Test results
    (5) User acceptance
    (6) Evaluation of installed system
        (a) Suitability
        (b) Usability
        (c) Effectiveness
        (d) Cost
        (e) Comparison with original objectives
  f. Productivity
    (1) Measures of productivity
    (2) Tools for increasing productivity
    (3) Productivity objectives

Index